Evidence-Based Practice in Infant and Early Childhood Psychology

Evidence-Based Practice in Infant and Early Childhood Psychology

Edited by

Barbara A. Mowder
Florence Rubinson
Anastasia E. Yasik

WILEY

John Wiley & Sons, Inc.

Library of Congress Cataloging-in-Publication Data:

Mowder, Barbara A.
  Evidence-based practice in infant and early childhood psychology / Barbara A. Mowder, Florence Rubinson, Anastasia E. Yasik.
    p. cm.
  Includes index.
  ISBN 978-0-470-39526-4 (cloth)
  1. Infant psychology. 2. Child psychology. I. Rubinson, Florence. II. Yasik, Anastasia E.
III. Title.
  BF719 .M692009
  155.42'2—dc22   2008051538

Printed in the United States of America

10 9 8 7 6 5 4 3 2 1

Contents

Preface

T HIS BOOK, *Evidence-Based Practice in Infant and Early Childhood Psychology*, represents the first comprehensive presentation of evidence-based practice in infant and early childhood psychology. To appreciate the relevance of this text, some historical notes might prove useful. Widerstrom, Mowder, and Sandall (1991) published the first practice-oriented book on at-risk newborns and infants and those with disabilities. That book, *At-risk and Handicapped Newborns and Infants: Development, Assessment, and Intervention*, integrated a variety of professional perspectives (e.g., early childhood education, early childhood special education, nursing, occupational therapy, psychology) with implications for assessment and intervention.

The Widerstrom et al. (1991) book was based on prior journal publications (e.g., Mowder, Widerstrom, & Sandall, 1989) establishing the need for multidisciplinary services for young children and their families. Indeed, prior to that book, Widerstrom and Mowder, while teaching at University of Colorado at Denver (UCD), secured the first federally funded grants (1986–1989) integrating early childhood education, early childhood special education, nursing, and school psychology training. Thus, for the first time, the needs of young children and their families were broadly articulated in terms of suggested infant and early childhood practice and training.

Subsequent to the Widerstrom et al. (1991) book and integrated training at UCD, a few additional books related to meeting the needs of young children and their families were written (e.g., Widerstrom, Mowder, & Sandall, 1997), including a book exclusively devoted to early childhood personnel preparation (Bricker & Widerstrom, 1996). Collectively, these books and related publications helped establish the relevance of psychology, especially school psychology (Mowder, 1996), in early childhood practice. Subsequently, Foley and Mowder (2000) argued for and outlined doctoral level training for school psychologists working with infants, young children, and their families and Foley and Hochman (2006) produced a book exclusively focused on mental health issues with infants and young children, entitled *Mental Health in Early Intervention: Achieving Unity in Principles and Practice.*

In contrast to the previous infant and early childhood books, *Evidence-Based Practice in Infant and Early Childhood Psychology* takes a distinct position of embracing science as the foundation of practice, integrating contemporary research, and offering evidence-based practice implications. To be sure, some areas of early childhood practice possess a more comprehensive evidence-base than other areas. Regardless, this book represents contemporary knowledge regarding infant and early childhood psychology (in many chapters the term *early childhood* is used to refer to both developmental time periods), presented in conjunction with multicultural and diversity issues, training implications, and ethical concerns. These themes are woven through each of the chapters, written primarily by professionals with considerable research and practice experience and expertise. The range of experience blends to provide a comprehensive presentation of early childhood practice.

A few words on terminology will assist the reader. First, this book is designed for professionals in training or currently working with infants, toddlers, and young children. As such, authors refer to professionals using various terms including *clinician*, *practitioner*, and *psychologist*. These variations are not meant to confuse, but rather they reflect authors' preferences and perspectives. Similarly, throughout the chapters authors use terms such as *infants*, *young children*, and *youngsters*. Unless otherwise specified, these terms refer to young children generally between birth and early elementary school age.

The coeditors would like to recognize individuals who assisted in the completion of this work. Barbara Mowder and Anastasia Yasik appreciate the varied contributions from the Pace University Psychology Department graduate students, faculty, and staff. Florence Rubinson particularly notes the contributions of Dana Freed, Erika Levavi, Amy Sandigorsky, Marissa Schneider, and Issac Silberstein. The coeditors also extend heartfelt appreciation to the many authors contributing to this book; their expertise, attention to detail, and prompt response to comments helped in making this book exceptional.

Barbara A. Mowder
Florence Rubinson
Anastasia E. Yasik

REFERENCES

Bricker, D., & Widerstrom, A. H. (1996). *Preparing personnel to work with infants, young children, and their families*. Baltimore: Brookes.

Foley, G., & Mowder, B. A. (2000). Training doctoral level school psychologists to work with infants, young children, and their families: Helping students to think and practice. *Zero to Three*, 20(6), 23–25.

Foley, G. M., & Hochman, J. D. (2006). *Mental health in early intervention: Achieving unity in principles and practice*. Baltimore: Brookes.

Mowder, B. A. (1996). Multidisciplinary training in school psychology early intervention services. In D. Bricker and A. Widerstrom (Eds.), *Preparing personnel to work with infants, young children, and their families*. Baltimore: Brookes.

Mowder, B. A., Widerstrom, A. H., & Sandall, S. (1989). New role: School psychologists serving at-risk and handicapped infants, toddlers, and their families. *Professional School Psychology*, 4, 159–171.

Widerstrom, A. H., Mowder, B. A., & Sandall, S. (1997). *Infant development and risk: An introduction*. Baltimore: Brookes.

Widerstrom, A. H., Mowder, B. A., & Sandall, S. (1991). *Newborns and infants at risk: A multidisciplinary approach to assessment and intervention*. Englewood Cliffs, NJ: Prentice Hall.

Contributors

Vincent C. Alfonso, PhD
Fordham University

Carol Sober Alpern, PhD
Pace University

Laura M. Anderson, PhD
East Carolina University

Melissa A. Bray, PhD
University of Connecticut

Rahil Briggs, PsyD
Albert Einstein College of Medicine

Amanda Boutot, PhD
Texas State University

Susan Chinitz, PsyD
Albert Einstein College
   of Medicine

Gerard Costa, PhD
YCS Infant and Preschool
   Mental Health

Mary DeBey, PhD
Brooklyn College of the City
   University of New York

Jacqueline DeGroat, PsyD
Pace University

Athena A. Drewes, PsyD
The Astor Home for Children

Greta L. Doctoroff, PhD
Yeshiva University

Nancy Jo Evangelista, PhD
Alfred University

Madeline Fernández, PsyD
Pace University

Dawn Flanagan, PhD
St. John's University

Roy Grant, MA
Children's Health Center

Sarah E. Grigerick, MA
University of Connecticut

Michelle Guttman, PsyD
Pace University

Virginia Smith Harvey, PhD
University of Massachusetts–Boston

Thomas J. Kehle, PhD
University of Connecticut

Robyn Kuraski, MS
St. John's University

Gayle L. Macklem, MA
University of Massachusetts–Boston

Paul McCabe, PhD
Brooklyn College of the City
    University of New York

Barbara A. Mowder, PhD
Pace University

Molly L. Nozyce, PhD
Albert Einstein College of Medicine

LeAdelle Phelps, PhD
University of Buffalo, State
    University of New York

Margaret B. Pulsifer, PhD
Harvard Medical School

Florence Rubinson, PhD
Brooklyn College of the City
    University of New York

Renee Shamah, BA
Pace University

Janet Cohen Sherman, PhD
Harvard Medical School

K. Mark Sossin, PhD
Pace University

Mark D. Terjesen, PhD
St. Johns University

Rachelle Theise, BA
Yeshiva University

Susan Vig, Ed M, PhD
Albert Einstein College of Medicine

Deborah Walder, PhD
Brooklyn College and Graduate
    Center of the City University of
    New York

Molly Romer Witten, PhD
Erikson Institute

Anastasia E. Yasik, PhD
Pace University

Michele Zaccario, PhD
Pace University

Dianne Zager, PhD
Pace University

PART I

FOUNDATIONS OF PRACTICE

CHAPTER 1

Infant and Early Childhood Psychology

NANCY J. EVANGELISTA

P ROVIDING PSYCHOLOGICAL SERVICES to infants, toddlers, and young children is complex, demanding a wide-ranging and integrative set of knowledge and skills. The *early childhood psychologist* (throughout this chapter, the term is meant to include infant and early childhood practice) draws from knowledge bases recognized as essential to the professional practice of psychology (Commission on Accreditation, 2007). These bases include, for instance, biological, cognitive, affective and social aspects of behavior, human development, individual differences, developmental psychopathology, and social–cultural impacts on family and society. In addition, early childhood work requires a deep and fluent knowledge of child development, developmental disabilities, and family functioning. Those who work on a daily basis with very young children utilize a flexible and creative repertoire of applied skills in assessment and intervention (e.g., engaging in play such as hide-and-seek, building block towers, coaching mothers in interactive reading). Early childhood psychologists usually are experts in preschool curriculum as well as the informal curriculum of home and family caregiving; more specifically, they apply evidence-based practice to support the efforts of parents, caregivers, and teachers in assuring the best possible outcomes for infants and young children.

Who are early childhood psychologists? What is distinctive and unique about working with very young children? What type of training and experiences best prepare psychologists for early childhood practice? What evidence is available to guide the selection of assessment, consultation, and intervention approaches and help train and support parents and teachers in applying best practices? Addressing these inquiries is the focus and purpose of this text dedicated to the practice of early childhood psychology; this chapter provides an overview of the issues that frame our work.

AN INTEGRATIVE SPECIALIZATION WITHIN APPLIED PSYCHOLOGY

The divisional structure of the American Psychological Association (APA) was established to recognize unique areas of practice and research. There is one current division dedicated to child psychology (i.e., Division 53: Clinical Child and Adolescent Psychology) but no subspecialty of infant and early childhood psychology. Instead, psychologists working with children and families are served by the three major *applied practice divisions* of clinical, counseling, and school psychology, and the *additional practice divisions* devoted to intellectual and developmental disabilities, family psychology, and pediatric psychology. Other divisions represent *research and policy efforts* addressing children's issues, such as developmental and educational psychology, community psychology, and child and family policy. (See Table 1.1 for a listing of relevant divisions.) These multiple focus areas are representative of the integrative nature of early childhood work, encompassing knowledge bases, skill sets, and policy across various aspects of psychology research and practice. The significant array of divisions that touch on psychological practice with infants, toddlers, and young children also illustrates the difficulty in identifying early childhood psychologists as distinct, since the nature of the work also cuts across practice areas.

A subspecialty of psychological practice with young children was presented in Barnett's (1986) review of training and practice needs of school psychologists working within preschool settings. Barnett's article was published just as the Education for All Handicapped Children Act was amended

Table 1.1

Divisions of the American Psychological Association Relevant to Early Childhood Psychology

Division	Title
7	Developmental Psychology
12	Clinical Psychology
15	Educational Psychology
16	School Psychology
17	Society of Counseling Psychology
27	Community Psychology
33	Intellectual and Developmental Disabilities
37	Society for Child and Family Research and Policy
43	Family Psychology
53	Clinical Child and Adolescent Psychology
54	Pediatric Psychology

as P.L. 99-457, in 1986, mandating free and appropriate special education services for students with disabilities be extended downward to preschool (ages 3–5), with incentives for states to also serve infants and toddlers with disabilities. The passage of P.L. 99-457 spurred a movement to train, or retrain, school psychologists to perform assessments and design interventions within preschool special education and infant and toddler early intervention programs (McLinden & Prasse, 1991). Refinements of a practice label, such as "applied developmental psychologist" or "developmental school psychologist," were offered by Bagnato and Neisworth (1991) to underline the heavy influences of developmental principles and ecological perspectives to this practice specialty.

Within the early intervention arena, a broader role of infant and preschooler mental health specialist gained recognition. Weatherston (2000) describes infant mental health specialists as ascribing to a set of core beliefs and clinical strategies, rather than belonging to a particular discipline. She notes that practitioners who utilize relationship-based approaches to working with families with young children are infant mental health specialists, including, for instance, early childhood educators, nurses, psychiatrists, physical and occupational therapists, and social workers as well as psychologists.

Practice Settings

Early childhood psychologists are employed in a diversity of settings, including preschool special education and infant early intervention programs (Bagnato & Neisworth, 1991; Barnett, 1986; Widerstrom, Mowder, & Willis, 1989). The psychologist's contributions to preschool special education and early intervention programs continue to be highlighted through research on roles and collaborative efforts (Rubinson, Sweeny, Mowder, & Sossin, 2003) and by policy and position statements offered by organizations such as the National Association of School Psychologists (NASP, 2003). Additional service settings may include child trauma centers, foster care agencies, and Head Start, as well as hospitals, medical clinics, and social services.

One consistent theme of early childhood services is mental health consultation (Donahue, Falk, & Provet, 2000). Indeed, early research (e.g., Piotrkowski, Collins, Knitzer, & Robinson, 1994) documented mental health consultation as a high priority for Head Start programs. Currently, Federal Head Start regulations (U.S. Office of Health & Human Services, 2007) require each program to have a mental health professional available, providing consultation regarding child behavior and mental health, promoting health and wellness, and assisting in securing services for children with disabilities or atypical behaviors. These mental health professionals could be psychologists, as well as social workers, counselors, or other behavioral specialists.

Donahue and colleagues (2000) offer an interesting historical reflection on involvement by psychologists as Head Start mental health consultants. Subsequent to the documented need for early childhood mental health consultation, the APA called on members to volunteer their services to Head Start programs. Many practitioners responded, but few had the requisite knowledge and training in early childhood issues and appropriate consultative practices. Thus, this early practice initiative essentially failed to meet the needs of children, families, and staff in Head Start programs. A sense of urgency followed the sobering recognition that specific skills are necessary for working in early childhood settings. In other words, many psychologists attempted to utilize skills in working with older children (e.g., elementary school aged, adolescents) as well as adults and apply those psychological services to young children and their families.

The early, and continuing, need for psychological services is clearly illustrated by the unsettling preschool expulsion statistics. Using data drawn from the most recent National Prekindergarten Study, Gilliam (2008) found that 10% of prekindergarten teachers reported making at least one dismissal within a 12-month period. The resulting rate of expulsion (i.e., 6.7 per 1,000) is more than three times greater than the rate for students enrolled in kindergarten through 12th grade. The majority of expulsions were due to challenging behavior, which Gilliam (2005; 2008) believes can be addressed effectively through mental health consultation.

As health care has expanded to encompass a wide range of mental health services, the role of the psychologist in heath care settings has also expanded (Brown, 2004). Traditionally, applied developmental psychologists offered diagnostic services for young children with intellectual or developmental disabilities (e.g., mental retardation, autism spectrum disorders) or in providing follow-up services and supports for medically fragile children (e.g., premature infants) (Minde, 2000; Thurman, Gottwald, Cornwell, & Korteland, 1997). Currently, psychologists play a pivotal role in family interviewing (Seligman, 2000), conducting observations of children and parent–child interactions (Benham, 2000; Brassard & Boehm, 2007), and administering developmental assessment measures (Brassard & Boehm, 2007; Finello, 2005; Gilliam & Mayes, 2000). Kaplan-Sanoff, Lerner, and Bernard (2000) articulate a model for utilizing developmental specialists within pediatric care settings to help assess developmental progress and provide assistance to parents in managing behavioral concerns. The developmental specialist role might be filled by a number of professionals with training in development, family systems, and assessment, such as psychologists but also including nurses, social workers, and other mental health professionals.

Finally, services for children who have experienced significant trauma (e.g., exposure to violence, placement in foster care due to abuse or neglect) rely heavily on the contributions of psychologists and other mental health professionals specializing in early childhood (Banerjee & Castro, 2005; Donahue et al., 2000; Gimpel & Holland, 2003; Scheeringa & Gaensbauer, 2000). These children and families, seen in settings such as clinics, therapeutic nurseries, or specialized early intervention programs, receive developmentally appropriate mental health interventions. Few other psychological service areas or practice settings involve such a high degree of skill integration, knowledge, and collaboration involving physical and mental health assessment of young children, intervention within family systems, and the design of comprehensive family-based treatment services.

Although early childhood psychologists may be employed in many settings (e.g., agencies, community programs, hospitals, medical offices, schools), the actual delivery of services often occurs within young children's natural settings (e.g., child care, home, preschool classroom) rather than psychologists' private offices. Harden and Lythcott (2005) even use the term *kitchen therapy* to convey the intimacy and flexibility needed to meet the needs of young children and their families.

ESTIMATING THE NUMBER OF EARLY CHILDHOOD PSYCHOLOGISTS

Estimating how many psychologists specialize in early childhood services is difficult. This challenge is partially due to the diverse nature of settings in which early childhood psychologists might be employed as well as the lack of standard reporting of personnel data across settings. However, statistics are available for personnel working within the infant, toddler, and preschool special education programs.

Data collected during the fall of 2001 for the Individuals with Disabilities Education Act (IDEA) Report to Congress counted 1,691 psychologists providing services to infants, toddlers, and their families (U.S. Department of Education, 2004). Similar statistics for psychologists working within the preschool special education programs are not reported in the IDEA Reports to Congress, as these preschool specialists are folded into the data for total numbers of psychologists (29,628) serving children ages 3–21 in special education programs (U.S. Department of Education, 2005). However, a 2003 survey of school psychologists in New York State (Rubinson et al., 2003) did reveal that approximately 26% of the respondents are involved at some level with early childhood services; apparently, this proportion is consistent with prior reports in the literature. By employing a 25% estimate to the 2005 IDEA count of psychologists, possibly 7,500 psychologists are serving young children with special education needs.

As of 2007, Head Start operated 18,875 program centers, each of which required a mental health consultant (Administration for Children and

Families, 2007). Since there are various professionals (e.g., psychologists, social workers) filling these mental health roles, the specific number of Head Start psychologists is unclear. Further, statistical reports on the numbers of psychologists working in settings such as community agencies, foster care, or medial settings are not readily available. Thus, a quantitative portrait of early childhood psychologists is far from complete or finished.

Unique Aspects of Practice

Although working with infants, toddlers, and young children in any setting requires core foundation knowledge, early childhood practice typically is founded on unique values and skills. For example, values such as (1) appreciation of principles of development to guide programs; (2) recognition of the primacy of parents and family relationships; (3) provision of culturally congruent and respectful services; (4) utilization of collaborative, team-based models; and (5) reliance on evidence-based approaches to design and evaluate interventions permeate the early intervention and infant mental health literature (Bagnato & Neisworth, 1991; Foley & Mowder, 2000; Thurman et al., 1997; Weatherston, 2005) and are the foundation for policy and position statements influencing early childhood practice (Division for Early Childhood [DEC], 2007; NASP, 2003). A deep appreciation of these foundation values leads to models for service delivery that respect the needs of young children and their families, within their cultural context, involving collaboration within and among early childhood providers.

DISTINCTIVE DEVELOPMENTALLY APPROPRIATE PRACTICE

The daily routines, learning opportunities, and systems to promote health and well-being for young children are designed in concert with contemporary understanding of child development and learning. The National Association for the Education of Young Children (NAEYC) has promulgated a set of guidelines for early childhood programs (Bredekamp & Copple, 1997) that articulate developmentally appropriate practice standards for curriculum design and delivery, assessment, and family involvement which respect the developmental stages, learning styles, and relationship needs of infants, toddlers, and preschool-age children. An extension of those standards for educating children with disabilities, issued by the DEC (2007) of the Council for Exceptional Children (CEC), offers additional guidance in designing learning environments, assessments, and program evaluations that recognize individual differences within a developmentally appropriate framework. For the early childhood psychologist, developmentally appropriate practices might involve conducting assessments utilizing play with toys, respecting children's need for naps and snacks, and keeping parents in close proximity. Developmentally appropriate practices also guide consultation; for example, recommendations regarding the selection of early literacy activities and measures for monitoring the progress of at-risk learners might be addressed.

EARLY CHILDHOOD PSYCHOLOGY INVOLVES WORKING WITH FAMILIES

The primacy of the family in young children's lives is one of the core values encompassing all work with infants, toddlers, and preschoolers. Contributors to early childhood services have approached the topic of family influence and interventions from a variety of theoretical frameworks, including, for instance, family systems theory (Cornwall & Korteland, 1997; Seligman & Darling, 2007), parent–child interactions and family dynamics (Mowder, 1997b; Sameroff, 2004), family needs and resources (Erickson & Kurz-Riemer, 1999; Trivette, Dunst, & Deal, 1997), and developmental impacts of family variables (Crockenberg & Leerkes, 2000). Cornwall and Korteland, borrowing from family therapy literature, describe the "family as a system and context for early intervention" (1997, p. 93). At a practical level, this means that families are present at, participate in, and may be the subjects of assessment; their priorities and goals for services for their children are significant; and interventions are designed to incorporate and/or target parents and/or the family. Within early childhood intervention, the term *family-centered services* is often used to describe a strengths-based approach wherein families are viewed as partners and collaborators in problem solving to produce positive outcomes for their children (Brown & Conroy, 1997; Seligman & Darling, 2007).

EFFECTIVE SERVICES BUILD ON CULTURAL AND SYSTEM CONTEXTS

Appreciating the family context requires sensitivity to families' cultural milieu, which includes factors such as language, ethnic heritage and tradition, neighborhood, and ways of thinking about and behaving toward children. One of the first steps toward professionals' cultural sensitivity is self-examination of one's own cultural experiences and beliefs. Self-examination usually leads to an appreciation of the impact of culture on families, spurring consequent practice modifications (Brassard & Boehm, 2007; Erickson & Kurz-Riemer, 1999).

For example, a thorough understanding of how linguistic and cultural diversity affect the assessment of young learners is a critical competency for early childhood psychologists. The process of self-examination is highlighted in Brassard and Boehm's (2007) frank analysis of myths about language and cognitive skill acquisition in young non-native English-language learners. Such myths include beliefs that English language learning is endangered by use of another language while bilingualism interferes with cognitive development, and misperceptions that conversational skills represent English language mastery, or that expected differences in acquisition of English for second-language learners (e.g., word-finding problems or articulation difficulty) are signs of communication disorders. Brassard and Boehm also offer research-based guidelines for screening and assessment of culturally and linguistically diverse preschoolers, including, for instance, a decision-making tree for examining primary language proficiency and need for further communication or cognitive assessment, and guidelines for selecting and training interpreters and paraprofessionals.

Working from research bases drawn from cultural beliefs about the nature of children and child-rearing practices, Iglesias and Quinn (1997) weave cultural perspectives into guidelines for competent service provision within early intervention programs. For example, cultural groups have different belief systems about the degree to which infants are viewed as willful or innocent, or to which extended families share responsibility for raising young children. Awareness of cultural perspectives on child development and behavior should then lead to culturally appropriate early intervention practices, such as involving extended family in treatment sessions or setting goals for child behaviors that are congruent with family expectations for infant development.

EARLY CHILDHOOD SERVICES PROVIDED BY TEAMS

Using a multidisciplinary approach for assessment of children with disabilities is a cornerstone of special education law, as the original special education law, P.L. 94–142 (1975), and subsequent revisions continue requiring that eligibility for services is based on a multifaceted, multidisciplinary evaluation. Models for effective assessment in early childhood intervention programs have evolved beyond multidisciplinary approaches to interdisciplinary and transdisciplinary models (McLean & Crais, 2004). For example, members of a multidisciplinary team each offer a specific area of expertise, but do not necessarily work together to provide integrated services. Unfortunately, this model may lead to duplication of efforts (e.g., gathering background information), leading to service fragmentation and/or omission of some service components; medical services are often based on a multidisciplinary model. In contrast, the interdisciplinary team offers individual assessments and interventions, but meets together to share information and plan programs (e.g., the Individualized Education Plan [IEP] team model for special education services). The highest level of team integration is afforded by the transdisciplinary model, where members jointly plan and conduct assessments, offering services that are targeted to improve child functioning across several domains. Parents are considered part of the transdisciplinary team and, therefore, are integrated in planning, delivering, and evaluating services.

For transdisciplinary teams to work effectively, McLean and Crais (2000) suggest a number of guidelines. For example, they emphasize learning about team members' disciplines as well as supporting team members by integrating their professional expertise through role "release" and sharing service delivery tasks. Not surprisingly, this model requires a significant level of communication and trust among team members. The transdisciplinary model is consistent with Weatherston's (2005) reflections on infant mental health practice. She notes that relationship-based approaches involve the parent–child relationship as well as relationships among many individuals, such as practitioners, family members, and supervisors.

EVIDENCE-BASED PRACTICE GUIDES SERVICE DELIVERY

The call for evidence guiding psychological services is not new, and is based on a long tradition of psychotherapy research informing practice (e.g., Garfield & Bergin, 1978). In fact, volumes (e.g., Jacobson, Foxx, & Mulick, 2005) have been written to help practitioners differentiate evidence-based treatments for individuals with developmental disabilities (e.g., autism) from fads and gimmicks. Nonetheless, emphasis on evidence-based interventions was accelerated by the passage of federal initiatives (e.g., No Child Left Behind [NCLB], 2002) to improve educational outcomes. The requirement that instructional choices are based on scientific evidence, helped encourage a growing body of intervention research. For early childhood psychologists, these options included, for example, family-based interventions (Kumpfer & Alvarado, 2003), family-school intervention partnerships (Bates, 2005), and mental health prevention programs (Beckwith, 2000; Durlak & Wells, 1997). In fact, practitioners now learn about effective practices from many sources, such as journals devoted to evidence-based outcomes (e.g., *Early Childhood Services: An Interdisciplinary Journal of Effectiveness*), databases (e.g., the *National Registry of Evidence-Based Programs and Practices* [www.nrepp.samhsa.gov]), the *What Works Clearinghouse* (www.whatworks.ed.gov) maintained by the U.S. Department of Education's Institute of Education Sciences, and the Florida Center for Reading Research (www.fcrr.org), which has reviews of prekindergarten literacy programs.

The growing database of effective programs for young children ultimately aids the selection of specific programs and interventions. Interventions, however, need to be tailored specifically for infants and young children and appropriate for local schools and agencies. Beyond selection and implementation, program evaluation and accountability is essential for developmentally appropriate practice (DEC, 2007). Gilliam and Leiter's (2003) article on designing early childhood program evaluations provides a valuable road map. For example, they recommend that programs build a logic model to map how each service component is connected to program goals, and to identify both proximal (short-term and direct) and distal (long-term and less direct) outcomes desired as a result of program efforts. The components of a program evaluation may focus on implementation (also called process study or formative evaluation), attainment of targeted outcomes, or more scientifically rigorous investigations that link outcomes directly to program components (e.g., through use of control or comparison groups). Thus, programs can complete the circle of evidence-based practice, by starting with program design based on selection of the most effective interventions available to fit program goals and cultural contexts, moving to monitoring of implementation processes, then assessing attainment of desired outcomes, and finally closing the loop by making modifications of program goals, interventions, or processes based on evaluation data.

RECOMMENDATIONS FOR TRAINING

As infant and early childhood psychology has grown, there have been increasing calls for training incorporating early childhood values, knowledge, and skills. As early as the 1970s, leaders in infant mental health services (e.g., Selma Fraiberg), formulated guidelines for professional training. The major components of such training, as described by Weatherston (2005), included (1) building a knowledge base in infant development; (2) developing skills for practice in observation, assessment, and interventions; (3) processing experiences with teachers and mentors; and (4) working on individual practice issues through reflective supervision.

Shortly after the preschool and infant early intervention special education laws were passed, McLinden and Prasse (1991) articulated the need for training of preservice school psychologists to prepare for roles with very young children, while advising that established professionals retool some of their skills and approaches to better serve young children. McLinden and Prasse addressed differences in training and practice for skill sets associated with early childhood assessment and intervention, family supports, and case management and team collaboration. Foley and Mowder (2000) offered perspectives on the distinctive processes for learning essential skills for practice with infants, young children, and families. In particular, they highlight how observations and practicum experiences help trainees internalize transactional views of child development, as well as understand relationships between families and early childhood practitioners. Although the training they describe is somewhat specific to school psychology, Foley and Mowder recognize that hybrid programs in clinical–school psychology may also provide the platform for early childhood skills.

In addressing retraining, Mowder, Goliger, Sossin, and Rubinson (2003) surveyed school psychologists across New York State (NYS) regarding their early childhood roles and training needs. Of the 812 surveys completed, 27% indicated they worked with the infant, toddler, or preschool population. The most frequently endorsed training needs were approaches to intervention (83%), followed by assessment skills (80%), diagnosis of disabilities (66%), and pharmacology issues with young children (64%). Although the least frequently endorsed topics were collaboration with other early childhood professionals and multicultural issues, they nonetheless were identified as needed by one-third of the early childhood psychologists responding to this survey. Workshop formats were the most commonly preferred format, followed by graduate courses; an institute format was less popular, but still endorsed by over 30% of the early childhood respondents.

An extension of this survey reached 1,019 licensed doctoral psychologists in NYS (Gallagher, Mowder, Sossin, & Rubinson, 2006). In terms of percentages, fewer licensed psychologists (i.e., 19%) provide services to young children and their families compared to school psychologists. Of licensed psychologists indicating early childhood practice, the highest percentage (47%) were clinical psychologists, followed by school psychologists (19%), with the percentages of other licensed respondents (e.g., counseling, developmental, educational psychology) accounting for a combined total of approximately 15%. According to the respondents, the primary pathway to infant and early childhood knowledge and skills was gained through reading and on-the-job experiences. The ranking of training needs was similar to school psychologists, with information about assessment, interventions, and pharmacology among the highest continuing education priorities, and workshop formats preferred.

The continuing education priority topics revealed by the surveys of both NYS school psychologists (Mowder et al., 2003) and licensed doctoral psychologists (Gallagher et al., 2006) lend themselves to the workshop formats both groups preferred. However, such formats appear unlikely suited to the particular demands of either reflective practice and supervision articulated by Weatherston (2005) or building relationships with families (Foley & Mowder, 2000; Zeanah, Larrieu, & Zeanah, 2000). In fact, these two elements of early childhood practice are highlighted in Delahooke's (2005) reflections on retraining to work with infants and young children. For example, she combined postgraduate coursework with over 200 hours of continuing education; however, the opportunity for reflective supervision, gained as a member of a multidisciplinary clinical services team, was the most helpful in fully appreciating the integrative nature of the work and the primacy of familial relationships.

Moving away from the discipline of psychology, Zeanah et al. (2000) offer training guidelines for infant mental health specialists. They outline a comprehensive curriculum, including (1) knowledge of infant development, developmental psychopathology, infant mental health and developmental disorders; (2) applied skills in assessment, intervention, and prevention skills; and (3) professional skills related to relationships with clients (families), interdisciplinary collaboration, and legal and ethical issues. Zeanah et al. promote this training for all professionals in the infant mental health field, encompassing child welfare officials (e.g., child protection workers, judges), child care providers (e.g., day care center directors), medical professionals (e.g., psychiatrists, nurses, pediatricians, nutritionists), educators (preschool teachers), special education personnel (e.g., child development specialists, physical, occupational, and speech therapists) as well as traditional mental health professionals (e.g., counselors, psychiatrists, psychologists, social workers). Recently, a group of early childhood professionals developed the California Infant/Preschool/Family Training Guidelines (Finello & Poulsen, 2005), which recommend a tiered program of training with a higher level of preparation for infant mental health professionals (e.g., psychologists, child development specialists, social workers) and core early childhood skills and competencies for service providers in other disciplines (e.g., day care providers, physical therapists).

MODELS FOR CONCEPTUALIZING INFANT AND EARLY CHILDHOOD ISSUES

Early childhood psychologists draw on various models for conceptualizing, organizing, and delivering services. Some of the models with the greatest influence on early childhood psychology practice include the (1) medical model; (2) mental health model; (3) development, disability, and psychopathology models; (4) learning theory and behavior change models; and (5) early educational models for typical as well as those children with disabilities. These models rely on the rich history of psychology, education, and applied mental health practice, and are woven together into distinctive ways of thinking, relating, and assisting others that characterize the specialty practice area of infant and early childhood psychology.

MEDICAL MODEL

The linear processes of diagnosing, prescribing treatment, and suggesting prognoses and outcome form the essence of the medical model. This model

presumes that behaviors deviating from the norm are due to internal processes specific to the individual, and thus remedies are directed toward the
individual patient (Reynolds, Gutkin, Elliott, & Witt, 1984). For example,
applied to psychological practice, regularly scheduled, office-based, individual therapy appointments would be an intervention consistent with an
identified individual relationship difficulty.

The medical model has multiple implications for service delivery. For
example, insurance-driven funding requires that services are identified as
specific to an individual, consistent with a diagnosis, and billable as a coded
event. Although these assumptions may work in medical settings, numerous
difficulties emerge when applied to other settings (e.g., day care centers,
schools) and when psychological services may target groups of children,
changes in teachers' behavior, and/or alterations in the learning environment
(Reynolds et al., 1984). The linear medical model typically places physicians
in the role of the healing expert and the recipients of services in an illness role
(e.g., the term patient); one result is that families' role in healing may be
minimized or the family may be viewed as the causative agent of the child's
difficulty (Cornwall & Korteland, 1997). In addition, the medical model tends
to exclude the influence of prior experience and fails to recognize the
malleability of many disorders (Sroufe, 1997).

Despite a poor fit, the traditional medical model tends to be a powerful
force within early childhood services. One reason is that psychologists
providing services to young children and their families may be employed
in hospital-based or pediatric practice settings. Further, early childhood
psychologists working in clinics, preschools, and early intervention programs
likely serve children with a variety of biologically-based developmental
disorders (e.g., Down syndrome, Fragile X, prematurity, neuromotor impairments). Thus, knowledge of how these disorders affect the development of
young children is a core competency for early childhood psychologists
(Nickel & Widerstrom, 1997).

Associated to some extent with the medical model, the public health
view of service delivery offers a somewhat better fit with early childhood
services. The public health model targets change at systems rather than the
individual level, where goals tend to be the prevention of adverse outcomes
rather than treatment of disease or pathology (Strein, Hoagwood, & Cohn,
2003). Strein et al. point out the advantages of a public health perspective in
designing and delivering mental health prevention programs (e.g., bullying
prevention, school violence) in schools. Some advantages include a focus on
positive behaviors and health (as opposed to a focus on problem behavior
and disease model), building connections between community agencies,
schools, and health care providers, and applying scientific principles to
evaluate impacts and evaluate program efforts. One example of public

health service delivery with particular relevance to early childhood is the home visiting program for infants and toddlers, which has its roots in the public health nursing service model. Home-based public nursing programs have a long tradition of offering preventive services, such as developmental guidance and support to mothers, especially high-risk groups (e.g., teen mothers, low-income parents) (Barnard, 1997; Olds, Henderson, Kitzman, Eckenrode, Cole, & Tatelbaum, 1999). One specific advantage of public health home-based early intervention or prevention programs is that they provide services in the child's home consistent with the family, neighborhood, and cultural context.

MENTAL HEALTH MODELS

Mainstream mental health models draw from many elements of the medical model in conceptualizing pathology and the delivery of services. Current thinking about mental disorder is epitomized by the *Diagnostic and Statistical Manual*, 4th edition, Text Revision (DSM-IV-TR), developed by the American Psychiatric Association (2000). The DSM-IV-TR is a catalog of mental disorders that somewhat parallels the International Classification of Diseases (ICD-10) system utilized by medical professionals for disease diagnoses (World Health Organization, 1992). The DSM-IV-TR operationalizes the first step, diagnosing the mental disorder, in terms of mental processes. In contrast to the ICD-10, the DSM-IV-TR multiaxial system attempts a more contextual view of mental disorder; for example, two of the five axes encourage clinicians to consider additional interactions of other conditions and environmental factors. That is, Axis III, General Medical Conditions, recognizes physiological conditions that may be responsible for, or exacerbate, mental symptoms and Axis IV, Psychosocial and Environmental Problems, is designed to raise awareness of stressful circumstances or life events that may create or exacerbate mental disorders, as well as recognize secondary psychosocial problems resulting from patterns of maladaptive behavior due to a mental disorder. In the end, using the multiaxial DSM-IV-TR system theoretically creates a more transactional view of mental disorders than relying solely on an Axis I (Clinical Disorders) or Axis II (Personality Disorders and Mental Retardation) diagnosis to describe functioning and plan treatments.

To be sure, the DSM-IV-TR focuses primarily on cataloging of adult disorders. Although the current system begins with mental disorders of childhood, specific criteria to adapt other diagnoses are quite variable. That is, many issues arise in utilizing the DSM-IV-TR with very young children, such as the lack of developmentally sensitive mental health constructs and parameters, and the failure of the system to address the impact of parent and family functioning (Jensen & Hoagwood, 1997; Mayes, 1999). Nonetheless, discussions of many mental health disorders, even in young children, follow the DSM-IV-TR parameters for conceptualization and expression (Brassard & Boehm, 2007; Poulsen, 2005).

In response to these and other concerns, the Zero to Three: National Center for Clinical Infant Programs (Zero to Three, 1994) published an alternative framework for considering mental health disorders in very young children. This system, the *Diagnostic Classification of Mental Health and Developmental Disorders of Infancy and Early Childhood, Revised (DC:0-3R)* (Zero to Three, 2005) incorporates key DSM aspects (e.g., multiaxial system) while modifying or replacing some diagnoses with more developmentally appropriate formulations. One of the most substantive changes is the replacement of mental retardation and personality disorders from Axis II with a scale considering the quality of the child and caregiver's relationship. Table 1.2 provides a comparison of the DC:0-3R axes with those of the DSM-IV-TR, while Table 1.3

Table 1.2

Comparison of Multi-Axial Mental Health Diagnostic Systems

Axis	DC:0-3R	DSM-IV-TR
Axis I	Clinical Disorders	Clinical Disorders and Other Conditions
	Primary mental health diagnoses specific to infants and young children	Principal diagnoses and problems that are the focus of treatment (V codes)
Axis II	Relationship Classification	Personality Disorders and Mental Retardation
	Identifies difficulties in relationships between child and caregiver	
Axis III	Medical and Developmental Disorders and Conditions	General Medical Conditions
	Includes physical, mental health, and/or developmental diagnoses	Includes any significant physical disorders and medical conditions
Axis IV	Psychosocial Stressors	Psychosocial and Other Environmental Problems
	Considers stressors influencing emotional functioning in infancy and early childhood	Considers problems affecting the diagnosis, treatment, and prognosis of mental disorders
Axis V	Emotional and Social Functioning	Global Assessment of Functioning
	Rating of the young child's expression of affects, cognitions, and interactions	Rating of overall psychological, social, and occupational functioning.

Table 1.3

Comparison of Axis I & Axis II Mental Health Disorders Relevant to Early Childhood

DC: 0-3 Axis I Disorders		DSM-IV-TR Axis I Disorders	
100	Posttraumatic Stress Disorder	309.81	Post-traumatic Stress Disorder
		303.8	Acute Stress Disorder
150	Deprivation/Maltreatment Disorder	995.54	Physical Abuse of Child
		995.53	Sexual Abuse of Child
		995.52	Neglect of Child
200	Disorders of Affect		
210	Prolonged Bereavement/Grief Reaction	V62.82	Bereavement
220	Anxiety Disorders of Infancy and Early Childhood		
221	Separation Anxiety Disorder	309.21	Separation Anxiety Disorder
222	Specific Phobia	300.29	Specific Phobia
223	Social Anxiety Disorder	300.23	Social Phobia
224	Generalized Anxiety Disorder	300.02	Generalized Anxiety Disorder
225	Anxiety Disorder Not Otherwise Specified (NOS)	300.00	Anxiety Disorder Not Otherwise Specified (NOS)
		313.23	Selective Mutism
230	Depression of Infancy and Early Childhood	296.xx	Major Depressive Disorder
231	Type 1: Major Depressive	300.4	Dysthymic Disorder
		311	Depressive Disorder NOS
232	Type 2: Depressive Disorder NOS	296.xx	Bipolar Disorder
240	Mixed Disorder of Emotional Expressiveness		
300	Adjustment Disorder	309.xx	Adjustment Disorder
400	Regulatory Disorders of Sensory Processing		No parallel DSM category
410	Hypersensitive		
411	Type A: Fearful/Cautious		
412	Type B: Negative Defiant		
420	Hyposensitive/Underresponsive		
430	Sensory Seeking/Impulsive		
500	Sleep Behavior Disorder		
510	Sleep Onset Disorder (Protodyssomnia)	307.42	Primary Insomnia
520	Night Walking Disorder (Protodyssomnia)	307.47	Nightmare Disorder
		307.46	Sleep Terror Disorder

DC: 0-3 Axis I Disorders		DSM-IV-TR Axis I Disorders	
		307.46	Sleepwalking Disorder
		307.46	Parasomnia Not Otherwise Specified
600	Feeding Behavior Disorder		
601	Feeding Disorder of State Regulation	307.53	Rumination Disorder
602	Feeding Disorder of Caregiver–Infant Reciprocity	307.59	Feeding Disorder of Infancy or Early Childhood
603	Infantile Anorexia	307.1	Anorexia Nervosa
604	Sensory Food Aversions		
605	Feeding Disorder Associated with Concurrent Medical Condition	307.52	Pica
606	Feeding Disorder Associated with Insults to the Gastrointestinal Tract		
700	Disorders of Relating and Communicating		Pervasive Developmental Disorders
		299.00	Autistic Disorder
		299.80	Asperger's Disorders
		299.80	Rett's Disorder
		299.10	Childhood Disintegrative Disorder
710	Multisystem Developmental Disorder (for ages 2 and under)	299.80	Pervasive Developmental Disorder – NOS
800	Other DMS-IV or ICD-10 Disorders	314.xx	Attention Deficit Hyperactivity Disorder
		312.81	Conduct Disorder: Childhood Onset
		313.81	Oppositional Defiant Disorder
		312.0	Disruptive behavior Disorder: NOS
Axis II: Relationship Classification			
	Parent-Infant Relationship Global Assessment Scale	V61.20	Parent-Child Relational Problem
	Relationship Problems Checklist – Quality Features	313.89	Reactive Attachment Disorder of Infancy or Early Childhood
	Overinvolved		
	Underinvolved	V61.21	Neglect of Child
	Anxious/Tense		
	Angry/Hostile		
	Verbally Abusive		
	Physically Abusive	V61.21	Physical Abuse of Child
	Sexually Abusive	V61.21	Sexual Abuse of Child

compares the primary DC:0-3R and DSM-IV-TR diagnoses for young children.

A recent review of the limited evidence-base supporting the original DC:0-3R diagnostic system (Zero to Three, 1994) reveals concerns regarding symptom specificity, validity of some diagnoses, and the relationship with established DSM-IV-TR diagnoses (Evangelista & McLellan, 2004). In addition, Rosenblum (2004) notes that the original DC:0-3 system is strikingly similar to the DSM-IV-TR, employing a categorical system leading to the dichotomous decision of presence or absence of a disorder. Based on these and other concerns, the DC:0-3R clarifies symptom descriptions and refines diagnostic criteria to reflect recent research on etiology and progression of major mental health disorders (e.g., attachment disorders, depression, feeding disorders, oppositional defiant disorder) in young children (Sturner, Albus, Thomas, & Howard, 2007; Task Force on Research Diagnostic Criteria: Infancy and Preschool, 2003). Until research demonstrates the reliability and validity of the DC:0-3R, however, this alternative diagnostic system may be most valuable in conceptualizing childhood expression of mental health and relationship disorders, rather than providing a uniform set of mental health diagnoses for young children (Brassard & Boehm, 2007; Evangelista & McLellan, 2004).

In contrast to the medical model, with pathology assigned solely to the identified patient, the infant mental health model considers young children's functioning as part of relationships (e.g., parent-child). Sameroff (2004), for example, maintains that the parent-infant relationship is often the real patient. The recognition of relationship importance in understanding infant mental health is clearly exemplified by the inclusion of a relationship scale on the DC:0-3R's Axis II. In addition, Weatherston (2005) summarizes infant mental health practice core beliefs, including recognition that (1) all development occurs within the interactive relationship between caregiver and child; (2) these relationships can be windows of change and growth for families; (3) early experiences affect development across the life span; and (4) therapeutic work with infants and their parents can change the nature of relationships, and thus the course of development for the child. Infant mental health practice, therefore, is thus a transactional process, as the interactive relationship allows a platform for interventions targeting infants, parents, and/or their relationships (Emde, Everhart, & Wise, 2004; Gilkerson & Stott, 2000; Sameroff, 2004; Sameroff & Fiese, 2000).

Proponents of the infant mental health model from many fields (e.g., early education, nursing, psychiatry, psychology, special education) joined forces in 1977 to establish the *Zero to Three: National Center for Infants, Toddlers, and Families*, an interdisciplinary organization formed to promote healthy development of young children by supporting and strengthening families and those who work with them. Zero to Three developed the DC:0-3R diagnostic framework, and together with other organizations (e.g., the Michigan Association for Infant Mental Health), and other researchers, has defined infant mental health as a unique specialty area.

The infant mental health model's emphasis on transactional processes has had considerable influence on the practice of infant and early childhood psychology. For example, assessment practices incorporate transactional relationships between caregivers and children at every step (Brassard & Boehm, 2007; Finello, 2005, Greenspan & Wieder, 2006), even directly assessing the parent-child relationship (Brassard & Boehm, 2007; Comfort, Gordon, & Unger, 2006). From this model, interventions target caregivers, parents, and children in improving relationships through, for example, dyadic therapy (Donahue et al., 2000; Maltese, 2005), child–parent psychotherapy (Lieberman, 2004), and interaction guidance (McDonough, 2004). The evidence-base for these relationship-based approaches continues to build, especially for treatment of attachment disorders (Pryor & Glaser, 2006).

One very specific manifestation of the mental health model is developmental, individual-difference, relationship-based (DIR) model (Greenspan & Wieder, 2006); DIR is based on transactional principles and aims to improve children's cognitive, communicative, motor, and social-emotional functioning and development through engaging parents in meaningful interactions and activities. DIR is designed for infants, toddlers, and preschoolers with a variety of developmental delays or disabilities, as well as young children and parents whose interaction patterns suggest risk for mental health disorder. DIR is mostly known, however, as an approach for treatment of autism (Wieder, Greenspan, & Kalmanson, 2008), despite the disappointing lack of DIR research validation (Metz, Mulick, & Butter, 2005).

DEVELOPMENTAL AND PSYCHOPATHOLOGY MODELS

Early childhood psychologists necessarily are knowledgeable about developmental disabilities (e.g., autism, chromosomal disorders, pervasive developmental disabilities, sensory impairments) frequently encountered in infant, preschool, and other early childhood settings (Batshaw, Pellegrino, & Roizen, 2007). Atypical development may also be linked to exposure to biological risks, such as prematurity or prenatal substance exposure, to environmental risk factors, such as poverty or domestic violence, or relationship risks, such as insecure or disrupted attachments, abuse and neglect, or parental mental disorder.

Developmental psychopathology models, in contrast to developmental models, bring together many factors accounting for pathways to young children's typical development and mental health, as well as, conversely, atypical development and related disorder(s). Although the transactional model for infant mental health is based on contributions of the child and the parent in their developing relationship, the developmental psychopathology framework is rather more comprehensive in scope, accounting for multiple risk factors as well as the role of experience. Sroufe (1997) has been a major contributor to theory of developmental psychopathology, explaining the inseparability of children from their context of development:

> Behavioral and emotional disturbance is viewed as a developmental construction, reflecting a succession of adaptations that evolve over time in accord with the same principles that govern normal development. Just as personality or the emergence of competence involves a progressive, dynamic unfolding in which prior adaptation interacts with current circumstances in an ongoing way, so, too, does maladaptation or disorder (Sroufe, 1997, p. 252).

This dynamic perspective has major implications for thinking about the progressive nature of social, emotional, behavioral, and developmental disorders, and for conceptualizing how and when to intervene. Sroufe (1997) summarizes these implications: (1) disorder unfolds as progressive deviation over time, largely due to repeated failures of adaptation; (2) multiple pathways can give rise to similar outcomes, depending on the unique interplay of individual differences and experiences; (3) different outcomes can result from similar pathways, as progressive experiences change the course of development; (4) change is possible at many points in development, which leaves openings for intervention; and (5) prior adaptation, or maladaptation, works to constrain change.

From this perspective, the iterative process of experience and adaptation causes changes in neurodevelopmental capacity, perhaps mediating the potential for change. For instance, Blair's (2002) comprehensive review of the factors needed for school readiness (e.g., attention, self-regulation, social competence) trace research explaining the interplay between experiences and their impact on use-dependent neural structures in the frontal cortex; thus, he helps delineate and explain the interplay between nature and nurture. The concepts of risk and resilience are also accounted for by the developmental psychopathology model, as each successive experience either elevates the potency of risk as negative patterns become ingrained or mediate risk by introducing new opportunities for positive adaptation (Cicchetti & Sroufe, 2000).

A substantive body of research supports developmental psychopathology's theoretical framework. Rutter and Sroufe (2000) discuss longitudinal studies in which key risk factors and experiences, which affect outcomes at different points in time, have been identified for a number of infant and early childhood disorders (e.g., attachment disorders, attention deficit hyperactivity disorder, depressive disorders). Further, they discuss how the developmental psychopathology perspective may be applied specifically to understanding the progression of autism, pointing to intervention windows of opportunity.

In addition, the environmental and cultural context of the family is another potent variable in development and developmental psychopathology. Although often perceived as less direct in terms of influence, their impact on conceptualizing, developing, and delivering services is profound. Sroufe (1997) provides a helpful illustration in his discussion of longitudinal pathways to attention deficit hyperactivity disorder (ADHD) in young children. For example, exposure to environmental toxins (e.g., lead) is linked to family income and neighborhood, and may lead to central nervous dysfunction, which manifests as ADHD. Eradicating lead levels is therefore an intervention to improve health within a home or a targeted community. Yet Sroufe's longitudinal studies of children show that as early as six months of age, the single best predictor of eventual ADHD is the mother's marital status, with single motherhood putting a child at risk. By the preschool years changes in the caregiver's support system became the most potent predictor, with stable caregiver relationships and supports reducing risk and instability compounding it. Sroufe's illustration does not address specific linguistic or ethnic differences, but research on cultural values and traditions (Diller, 2007) recognizes that many cultural groups have strong traditions of extended family support for single parents. Therefore, familiarity with the cultural context for a young parent—illustrated here as the supports provided by partners, extended family, and neighborhood linkages—is a key to conceptualizing and delivering child- and family-focused interventions. Indeed, cultural factors influence psychological services at program, community, state, and national levels.

Psychologists working with vulnerable populations of very young children, therefore, may draw upon typical and atypical child development, research, and developmental psychopathology models. Fundamentally, comprehensive developmental knowledge is critical in order to intervene with children, their caregivers and parents, and their respective relationships.

Table 1.4 provides an overview of some of the major research bases, as associated with Sameroff's (2004) transactional model, within an environmental and cultural context. Space does not permit a thorough examination of each variable within this overview, but a number of these issues are covered in depth in subsequent chapters of this volume, such as childhood difficulties and disabilities (e.g., autistic spectrum disorders, health impairments,

Table 1.4
Knowledge Bases Relevant to Early Childhood Psychology Practice

Child-Based Variables	Parent/Caregiver Variables	Relationship Variables	Cultural/ Environmental Context
Growth and Development	Family Composition	Parent-Child Attachment	Dominant Language in Home
Developmental Disabilities	Parental Education	Parenting Style and Skills	Cultural Traditions
Genetic Disorders	Family Income Level	Abuse of Child	Cultural Beliefs about Children
Prematurity	Parental Employment	Neglect of Child	Neighborhood Safety/Trauma
Sensory Impairments	Parental Disability	Changes in Caregiver	Community Resources
Health Problems	Parental Mental Health	Domestic Violence in Home	Intervention Programs
Prenatal Substance Exposure			Childcare or Preschool Programs
Temperament			
Mental Health Disorders			

pervasive developmental disorders), caregiver variables (e.g., parent assessment and intervention), family functioning (e.g., family assessment and intervention), and contextual variables (e.g., trauma and crises).

BEHAVIORAL MODELS

The impact of behavioral learning theories on applied practice has been profound, as many evidence-based treatment approaches are based on this model. Early in the development of psychology, Watson, Thorndike, and Skinner challenged notions of internal processes and the impact of parent–child relationships, instead reducing learning and development to the forces of conditioned associations, reinforced patterns of behavior, and punishing events (Hergenhahn, 2005). Principles of behaviorism (e.g., defining and recording observable behavior) are basic to applied psychology practitioners (e.g., clinical, counseling, and school psychologists).

These reductionistic approaches have been expanded to include the role of cognition and perceptions in behavioral expression, espoused by both cognitive-behavioral (e.g., Aaron Beck) as well as social learning theorists (e.g., Albert Bandura) (Goodwin, 1999). Indeed, applied psychology can credit the combined efforts of behavioral, cognitive–behavioral, and social learning theories for the many evidence-based treatment approaches for various mental disorders (e.g., anxiety, depression, phobias) as well as behavioral difficulties (e.g., aggression, social withdrawal) (Goodwin, 1999). In addition, operant conditioning principles form the core of approaches termed *behavior analysis* or *modification*, often first-line evidence-based interventions to improve behavioral functioning (Handen & Gilchrist, 2006). Indeed, several professional organizations have been formed to advance the use of behavioral approaches in treatment (e.g., APA Division 25: Experimental Analysis of Behavior, Association for Behavioral Analysis International (ABAI)); early childhood psychologists no doubt are counted among their members.

Behavioral treatment approaches represent important tools for psychologists working in early childhood. Intervention guides designed for preschool educators (Dunlap, 1997; Essa, 2003; Lerner, Lowenthal, & Egan, 2003), parents (Clark, 1996), and psychologists working in early childhood settings (Barnett, Bell & Carey, 1999; Donahue et al., 2000; Gimpel & Holland, 2003; Knoff, Stollar, Johnson & Chenneville, 1999) mostly are based on behavioral principles for improving personal and social functioning. These resources draw upon well-researched, effective behavioral techniques (e.g., defining observable behaviors, establishing reinforcements and related schedules of reinforcement, observing behavior to determine baseline and measure progress toward goals, targeting behaviors for change) to build, strengthen, and/ or reduce targeted behaviors.

Specific behavioral approaches have been institutionalized (e.g., the 1997 and 2004 revisions of the IDEA) to address challenging, dangerous, and/or disruptive behaviors. In fact, behavioral intervention plans for children with disabilities are often addressed in their individualized education programs (IEPs). Further, the basis for such plans usually is derived from a functional behavior assessment (FBA), considering both antecedent factors that may trigger as well as behavioral consequences that may maintain or increase specific behavior(s). By using the antecedent–behavior–consequence (ABC) paradigm, psychologists typically determine the function of the behavior (e.g., needs met through maladaptive behavior) and then develop alternative approaches to meet children's needs, reduce reliance on problem behaviors, and/or increase adaptive behavior (Knoster & McCurdy, 2002). Applications specifically for preschool students provide a practical and useful tool for designing interventions to address challenging behaviors (Boyajian, DuPaul, Handler, Eckert, & McGoey, 2001; McEvoy, Neilson, & Reichle, 2004).

Finally, behaviorally-based interventions have been extraordinarily influential as treatment approaches for young children with autism spectrum disorders. The spotlight on applied behavioral analysis (ABA), as a treatment for autism, was spurred by research demonstrating that 47% of a group of young autistic children receiving intensive ABA treatment were determined to no longer need special education services upon kindergarten entry, and, further, 42% maintained this improvement through age 11 (McEachin, Smith, & Lovaas, 1993). Metz et al. (2005) maintain that the 47% improvement statistic is "arguably the most impressive claim ever made for a psychological intervention" (p. 256). Numerous additional longitudinal and ABA replication studies for autism (also known as discrete trial training), failed to produce such encouraging outcomes (Shea, 2005). At the same time, Gresham, Beebe-Frankenberger, and MacMillan (1999) recognize that research standards for gauging treatment effects (e.g., random assignment) have yet to be fulfilled in ABA research with autistic children. Nonetheless, behavioral approaches consistently facilitate meaningful improvements in young children with autism spectrum disorders (Newsom & Hovanitz, 2006).

EARLY EDUCATION AND EARLY CHILDHOOD SPECIAL EDUCATION MODELS

Most early education models subscribe to the *developmentally appropriate practice (DAP)* standards promulgated by the NAEYC (Bredekamp & Copple, 1997) which have already been mentioned as an influential force driving the values and philosophy of many daycare and early education programs. The DAP model stresses that learning activities are designed based on the age and developmental needs of the young child, yet need to be individually matched for each child, based on the teacher's ongoing observations and assessments of the child's learning. Child-centered activities provide opportunities for active learning through choices and engagement with toys, playmates, and teachers. The DAP principles are incorporated into Head Start regulations (U.S. Office of Health and Human Services, 2007) and modified for young children with disabilities to offer more targeted instruction in skill deficit areas (Bricker, Pretti-Frontczak, & McComas, 1998).

The active learning component of DAP was drawn from the *cognitive/constructivist* model for learning, based on Piagetian principles (Lerner et al., 2003). In this model, for example, children interact with developmentally appropriate toys and learning materials, developing critical thinking skills by engaging in problem solving. DAP represents a significant departure from behavioral models, ascribing to a *behavioral curriculum*, characterized by a set sequence of learning objectives, direct teaching of desired skills, and teacher-directed instruction (Lerner et al.). In contrast, DAP approaches provide activities and instruction developmentally appropriate for each child's stage of development.

The influence of relationships, as discussed in infant mental health models, often are echoed in the DAP *psychosocial curriculum*; this curriculum gives priority to the development of healthy relationships with teachers and peers through the preschool experience. Lerner et al. (2003) trace the psychosocial curriculum model found in some preschool and nursery programs to Erickson's work on drive theories. Not surprisingly, DIR models (Greenspan & Wieder, 2006) share many of the psychosocial curriculum core values.

DAP, well established in preschool programs, is also often used as the educational model in early intervention programs for younger children. For example, center-based programs usually maintain a classroom-like setting, where infants and toddlers have access to an array of stimulating toys and opportunities for interactions with others. In fact, the DAP guidelines (Bredekamp & Copple, 1997) and the guidelines for developmentally appropriate practice for young children with disabilities (DEC, 2007) address services for infants and toddlers as well as for preschool children. Mowder (1997a) and Karabinos (1997) note that center-based programs for young children with disabilities, sometimes known as infant stimulation programs, typically integrate parents in teaching sessions with their youngsters. In addition, individual or group sessions with physical, occupational, and/or speech therapists may also be scheduled during family visits to early intervention centers (Lerner et al., 2005).

Family-based child care is the most common child care arrangement for young children, with 26% of children ages 5 and under cared for by relatives, and another 15% cared for in the homes of nonrelative providers (Kreader, Ferguson, & Lawrence, 2005). The goals of family day care are provision of safe, supervised care in a setting that promotes development; children with disabilities are often served in such settings where specialists intervene directly with the child and provide consultation to the child care provider (Golbeck & Harlan 1997). In contrast, home-visiting programs may have goals to support the development of children, to teach or support parents, or multigenerational goals to enhance the functioning of both children and parents (Klass, 1996). Recent research on the effectiveness of home visiting (Peterson, Luze, Eshbaugh, Jeon, & Kantz, 2007) has identified facilitation of parent–child relationships as an infrequent, but potent ingredient in this model. Thus, early childhood psychologists will need to be familiar with home visiting practices and the integration of relationship-focused therapeutic approaches. In addition, the home interventionist may face challenging situations, ranging from derailment of treatment sessions by other more pressing events in the home, to witnessing impaired functioning of family members (Klass, 1996; Peterson, Bair, & Sullivan, 2004). The provision of reflective supervision and mental health consultation services to home visitors is a consistent theme in recommendations to enhance the outcomes from this service model (Klass, 1996; Peterson et al., 2004; Peterson et al., 2007).

EARLY LITERACY MODELS

Acquisition of literacy skills traditionally is seen as part of school readiness. Decades of research regarding foundational literacy skills have sharpened the focus on literacy skills acquisition within preschool settings (Hojnoski & Missall, 2006). For example, the federally funded Early Reading First program requires participating preschool programs to provide instruction in oral language and vocabulary development, phonological awareness, alphabetic knowledge, and print awareness (U.S. Department of Education, 2007). These literacy components have been incorporated into curriculum regulations for preschool programs such as Head Start (U.S. Office of Health and Human Services, 2007), the Even Start Family Literacy Program (U.S. Department of Education, 2003), and publicly operated prekindergarten programs (e.g., New York State Education Department, 2008).

Furthermore, the Response to Intervention (RTI) movement shifts priorities away from identification and remediation of learning problems, to prevention of problems through (1) use of evidenced-based curriculum and teaching practices; (2) universal screening of children to identify those with skill deficits; (3) group adaptations and individually tailored interventions for at-risk learners; (4) ongoing monitoring of progress; and (5) sequentially more intensive individual interventions for children who fail to respond to lesser levels of interventions (Bradley, Danielson, & Doolittle, 2005; Fuchs & Fuchs, 2006; Marston, 2005). Although VanDerHeyden and Snyder (2006) compare RTI with preschool education models (e.g., DAP), McCabe (2006) has gone ahead, articulating the skill sets needed by early childhood educators to implement RTI models. The pressure for early childhood education settings, including the home, to provide the experiential basis for literacy success also expands organizational consultation and systems roles for early childhood psychologists. One primary function would include providing support needed to prepare young learners for school success.

SUMMARY OF MODELS

This brief review of models for early childhood practice illustrates the diversity of theoretical perspectives psychologists draw upon. Consideration of early childhood practice roles (e.g., assessors, behavioral and program consultants, parent and child therapists, program evaluators, systems change agents) in a range of settings (e.g., clinics, homes, hospitals, schools) leads to a fuller appreciation of the specialized nature of work with infants, toddlers, pre-schoolers, and their families and teachers. For example, the early childhood psychologist may consult with teachers in a preschool program to integrate literacy skills instruction within an educational curriculum model based on developmentally appropriate practice. Or a psychologist might use knowledge of developmental psychopathology and training in infant mental health to provide home-based dyadic therapy to improve the parent–child relationship for a toddler with behavioral outbursts. An alternative role might be to design an assessment and treatment program, including program evaluation, for a clinic that serves young children with autism spectrum disorders. These examples illustrate how the knowledge bases and intervention models inform early childhood practice in psychologists in various settings and roles.

SCOPE OF PRACTICE FOR INFANT AND EARLY CHILDHOOD PSYCHOLOGY

Defining a scope of practice helps professionals articulate their field of expertise and identify some of the unique aspects of their work. In addition, describing practice opens the door to continued discussion of practice requirements for training and supervision and refinements to professional identity. An articulated scope of practice is in many ways the sign of a mature field that has forged agreement regarding the nature of the discipline, the role of practitioner, benefits to clients or consumers, the training and skills needed for practice, and ethical standards. The gradual process of defining a scope of practice is not only drawn from applied research, but also serves as a springboard for the next generation of research to continue to provide evidence to support practice. Thus, establishment of a scope of practice is an important next step for approaching these goals of shared sense of identity, defined roles, professional training expectations, and establishment of an active research agenda for early childhood psychologists.

The field of early childhood psychology benefited from past position papers distinguishing practice with infants and young children from that with older children and adolescents. Early examples include the 1998 joint position paper of the School Psychology Educator's Council of New York State (SPECNYS) and the New York Association of School Psychologists (NYASP) (Lidz, Alfonso, Mowder, Ross, Rubinson, & Thies, 1998), as well as several position papers adopted by the NASP, especially the statements on psychologists' roles in early childhood care and education (2002), early childhood assessment (2005), and early intervention services (2003). These position statements have moved early childhood psychology closer to defined unique roles and the knowledge and skills necessary for practice.

Confounding the development of a scope of practice is that infant mental health includes a wide range of professionals (e.g., counselors, psychologist, psychiatrists), as does the field of early childhood special education (e.g., early childhood educators, early childhood special educators). This sharing of roles across professional domains is not unique to early childhood practice, as cooperation to some extent characterizes the broader state of mental health professions, where the disciplines (e.g., counseling or social work) overlap in their provision of some types of services offered and skills used to deliver them. Yet the various functions (e.g., assessor, therapist, consultant, program evaluator, systems change agent) and knowledge bases (e.g., child development, curriculum, literacy, psychopathology, developmental disorders, family functioning, cultural diversity) of the psychologist in early childhood settings exceed the parameters of infant mental health and underline the need for a unique scope of practice. The field of clinical child psychology has produced numerous distinguished researchers and practitioners in infant and early childhood psychology, but has not taken a lead role in identifying concurrent infant and early childhood practice. Perhaps school psychologists have led the way based on a closer match between early childhood psychology's roles and practice settings and those experienced by contemporary school psychologists, which include curriculum knowledge and systems consultation, in addition to more traditional assessment, classification of disability, and treatment roles (Bagnato, 2006).

A WORKING DEFINITION OF INFANT AND EARLY CHILDHOOD PRACTICE

A scope of practice for early childhood psychology is necessarily founded upon the pivotal values which influence the field: assimilation of developmental principles and knowledge into every level of service, working closely with families as partners, understanding and respect for cultural and ethnic diversity, provision of integrated, team-based services, and use of research and evidence-based evaluation processes to guide programs and services. The preceding pages have outlined these values, as well as knowledge bases and models for conceptualizing issues for infants, toddlers, and young children. The scope of practice that follows has been drawn from these determinants of early childhood psychology.

GOALS FOR PRACTICE

Early childhood psychologists engage in practice activities that enhance the growth and development of infants, toddlers, and young children; prevent or minimize disability, disorder, or other difficulties in learning, socialization, and adaptive functioning; expand the knowledge and skills of caregivers of young children; and support personnel and programs serving young children and their families.

ELEMENTS OF PRACTICE

Early childhood psychologists utilize skills and approaches that define the practice of psychology, including psychological testing, counseling, and psychotherapy; diagnosis and treatment of mental health, cognitive, or behavioral disorder; use of accepted classification systems; and consultation and collaboration with other professionals and service providers. In applying these general skills and approaches to support healthy functioning and optimal development of infants, toddlers, and young children, the scope of early childhood psychology practice consists of:

- Assessment, using naturalistic and systematic observations of young children, families, and settings; culturally and developmentally appropriate screening, curriculum-based, play-based, and standardized measures of child skills and behaviors; and multidisciplinary, family-systems and ecological approaches, that relate to learning, development, adjustment, and adaptation of individuals or groups of young children.
- Development and implementation of evidence-based therapeutic interventions to improve cognitive, behavioral, social, and adaptive function of young children; to increase positive parenting skills and knowledge of caregivers; and to enhance the relationship between infants, toddlers, and young children and their parents.
- Consultation with parents and families of young children, with teachers and child care providers, and with representatives of schools, agencies, or organizations serving young children and their families, to support learning and positive adaptation and to reduce or prevent the development of learning, behavioral, or adjustment problems in young children.
- Design, implementation, and evaluation of learning and child care environments, child and family intervention programs, and service systems that enhance growth, prevent disorders and disabilities, and promote adjustment and positive outcomes for young children and their families.
- Provision of leadership and advocacy to ensure that all young children have access to comprehensive, high-quality educational and child care programs that are culturally sensitive, family centered, and developmentally appropriate.

CONCERNS AND CHALLENGES FOR EARLY CHILDHOOD PSYCHOLOGISTS

This chapter has introduced broad themes that frame the role and practice of the early childhood psychologist. Yet a number of barriers exist that curtail the potential contributions of psychologists to support infants, toddlers, and preschool children. Some of these barriers have been erected by policy decisions and public priorities which restrict young children's access to essential services, while other concerns arise when considering applications of mental health work with culturally diverse families in various service settings. Finally, the lack of a cohesive identity, along with other practice issues, presents a set of ethical challenges for early childhood psychologists.

CHILDREN'S ACCESS TO SERVICES

First and foremost, American families do not have universal access to quality early childhood services. Kreader et al.'s (2005) analysis of the Early Childhood Longitudinal Study (ECLS) highlights patterns of child care usage that vary significantly according to income. Low-income working mothers are more likely to have relatives look after their infants and toddlers than to use fee-based services. Higher-income mothers have more options available and a greater percentage of select center-based or family-based child care. Children in the care of relatives are largely in unregulated settings, where critical components of quality care (e.g., developmentally focused activities and curriculum, problem-solving opportunities, stable caregiver–infant relationships), may vary substantially. Lack of access to quality child care means young, poor children often have limited access to the psychological supports that can optimize child care experiences.

In addition to limited access to quality day care, numerous American families do not have universal access to quality medical services. Statistics provided by the National Coalition on Health Care (2008) reveal that 8.7 million children in the United States were uninsured in 2006, totaling 11.7% of child population. This was an increase of nearly 610,000 children compared to the number of uninsured children in 2005. Families who cannot afford medical insurance usually have low-wage jobs and likely associated stressors, such as worries about access to child care, finances, and medical issues. Families in such circumstances are unlikely to receive psychological services to assist with behavioral challenges posed by their young children or difficulties regarding parent–child relationships. Furthermore, the current lack of parity of mental health services with physical health services, a factor of our insurance-driven medical system, restricts access to psychological supports for young families, even those who have insurance benefits.

Educational programs are in a similar state of fragmentation and variable access. Young children with developmental delays, or with conditions likely resulting in disability, are entitled to services under the IDEA. Yet for children who grow up amid risk factors such as poverty, limited parenting skills, and exposure to violence, educational program options are also far from comprehensive. Fortunately, Head Start continues to fill a vital niche as the only federally funded preschool program available for low-income preschool-age children. But program availability is dependent on congressional funding, and thus the capacity of Head Start to serve needy children varies from year to year (Hamm, 2006). While state-funded prekindergarten programs continue to grow, they are far from universal (Barnett, Hustedt, Friedman, Boyd, & Ainsworth, 2007), and, when available, they often differ in goals, level of service, and eligibility requirements (Bagnato, 2006). The vagaries of funding persist despite compelling longitudinal evidence documenting the cost-effectiveness of quality preschool and day care as prevention programs. Cost savings are recouped since participants in these early interventions require fewer expenditures than matched controls on later interventions such as special education, incarceration, and public welfare benefits (Barnett, 1993; Heckman, Grunewald, & Reynolds, 2006). Heckman and colleagues reached the conclusion that early education and intervention is an economic development strategy with payoffs that eclipse more widely accepted community endeavors, such as building office towers or sports stadiums.

CONTEXTUAL AND CULTURALLY SENSITIVE FAMILY PRACTICE

Even within programs available for young children, there are many conflicts and controversies regarding the role of the psychologist. For example, what does it mean for a mental health professional to be family centered within an educational services context? What type of family assessment is appropriate, culturally sensitive, and ethical? Psychologists often are called on to perform assessments of young children to determine eligibility for services for infants and toddlers with developmental delays or disabilities. Early on, Mahoney, Spiker, and Boyce (1996) cautioned against incorporating relational procedures into routine developmental assessment practice. They felt the lack of strong normative data for interactional measures could lead to erroneous and potentially damaging interpretations, a view echoed by Brassard and Boehm (2007) in their recent review of family assessment measures.

Further, relational assessment and intervention may violate the parent–professional partnership in family-centered services that are ultimately targeted toward the child. Such shifts in focus regarding the identified client may be congruent with a family therapy approach but need to be negotiated carefully within educational, familial, and other contexts (Brassard & Boehm, 2007; Mahoney et al., 1996). The evolution of roles by psychologists is perhaps a response to the lack of a full array of mental health services available to support families with young children. Nonetheless, this is but one example of how carefully psychologists must work within the mission of their program model and, of course, the constraints of their professional expertise and training.

A related concern is that the assessment tools available to early childhood psychologists, especially those developed for family assessment, may not provide sufficient options for use in working with children from culturally and linguistically different backgrounds. Although many standardized developmental and cognitive assessment measures for infants, toddlers, and preschoolers are now available for non-English (primarily Spanish-speaking) populations, techniques for family assessment have lagged behind other assessment areas. The risk of using procedures with limited reliability and validity is further exaggerated when applied to families from diverse cultural backgrounds, as child-rearing beliefs and interactional patterns may not match the practices of the majority normative population. Thus, mindfulness that evidence-based interventions may not have included children or families from diverse language or cultural backgrounds in their research studies raises caution for practitioners.

ETHICAL ISSUES

Early childhood work is characterized by collaborations among different professionals and agencies and, to some extent, overlap between roles. This diffuse practice environment can lead to ethical issues resulting from differing agency policies, unclear roles, and lack of professional boundaries. One specific concern is that families who are involved with early childhood services may be working with professionals from a variety of different agencies (e.g., day care provider, child protective worker, psychologist working through the early intervention program), which may have different sets of ethical standards. For example, a family member providing child care will not typically follow a specified code of confidentiality, while the child protective worker will follow a strict code. In the absence of a formal procedure to share essential information, professionals could possibly breech confidentiality when discussing a family's needs, or, conversely, policies protecting unauthorized disclosures could be perceived as barriers preventing a beneficial working relationship across agencies. Psychologists need to follow established ethical standards for respecting the confidentiality of private information, yet need to work with other agencies and with parents to develop procedures that allow for joint planning when a collaborative approach will benefit the child.

Another concern arising from the diversity of early childhood professionals working together, especially when aspects of practice have some degree of overlap, is that roles may become blurred. This dilemma could arise, for example, if a speech therapist working with a toddler with an expressive language delay targets turn-taking in games as a therapy goal, and the psychologist arrives at the same goal for developing relationship skills. One or the other professional might view this as encroaching on professional turf, leading to concerns over who should focus on this skill. Special education services address these concerns through participation in joint planning through development of the Individualized Family Service Plan (IFSP) for infants and toddlers with disabilities, and the Individualized Education Plan (IEP) (U.S. Department of Education, 2004) for preschoolers with disabilities, but services provided by other types of organizations may not allot joint planning time for professionals.

The issue of role clarity may become muddied when working with families, especially in the home-visiting context. When exposed to the many needs of families, as Klass (1996) has described during home visits, the mental health practitioner may be tempted to work on issues that are, at best, peripheral to the child's needs, or the worst case, which exceed the boundaries of professional training and competence. For example, exposure to arguing between parents may lead a well-intentioned professional to attempt to help mediate the situation by providing martial therapy. Unless the psychologist has specific training and expertise with this treatment, and the family has specifically assented to provision of this additional therapy, exceeding the bounds of expertise is clearly a violation of ethical standards (APA, 2002). Training and supervised experiences working with families, as well as ongoing supervision, are needed to help practitioners to handle such situations appropriately.

FORMING A COHESIVE IDENTITY

This chapter has reviewed the diversity of training backgrounds, roles and employment settings, and theoretical perspectives that, for the most part, represent the foundation for psychological practice with infants and young children. Although role diversity is positive with regard to maintaining practice opportunities, the lack of specificity may at the same time highlight policy problems and weak social structures to care for our youngest children. As Bagnato (2006) succinctly states, "No field of early childhood exists, let alone a system" (p. 616). The corollary is that infant and early childhood practice may struggle, while comprehensive early childhood care, education, and services emerge.

In the meantime, psychologists committed to serving young children and their families can leverage their expertise and skills to form a cohesive professional identity and offer meaningful and valuable services. For example, the founding of the *Journal of Early Childhood and Infant Psychology* in 2005 established a forum for sharing research findings, theoretical perspectives, and policy discussion for psychologists working with young children in various settings. Participation in interdisciplinary organizations dedicated to improving the lives of young children (e.g., Zero to Three) continues to raise the profile of psychologists in working with young children and their families.

Adoption of training guidelines and standards for practice ultimately should ensure that psychologists who aspire to touch the lives of young children are prepared with the knowledge and skills necessary to be effective and valued. Indeed, training standards may spark expansion of opportunities for early childhood specializations within clinical practice and inspire research on issues related to the scope of psychological practice with young children. Increased research, along with cultural and diversity sensitivity and careful attention to ethical issues and potential conflicts, ultimately enhance practice. To be sure, advocacy at local, state, and national levels (e.g., social and fiscal priorities) is necessary to address the various needs of young children (e.g., behavioral, emotional, learning). By attuning ourselves to each of these issues, early childhood psychology should not only strengthen and reaffirm their professional identity but, more importantly, strengthen psychological contributions to the growth and development of young children and their families.

REFERENCES

Administration for Children and Families. (2007, February). Head Start Program [Fact sheet]. Retrieved from www.acf.hhs.gov/programs/ohs/about/fy2007.html.

American Psychiatric Association (2000). *Diagnostic and statistical manual of mental disorders* (4th ed., text revision). Washington, DC: Author.

American Psychological Association (2002). *Ethical principles of psychologists and code of conduct*. Washington, DC: Author.

Bagnato, S. J. (2006). Of helping and measuring for early childhood intervention: Reflections on issues and school psychology's role. *School Psychology Review, 35,* 615–620.

Bagnato, S. J., & Neisworth, J. T. (1991). *Assessment for early intervention: Best practices for professionals*. New York: Guilford Press.

Banerjee, L., & Castro, L. E. (2005). Intensive day treatment for very young traumatized children in residential care. In K. M. Finello (Ed.), *The handbook of training and practice in infant and preschool mental health* (pp. 233–255). San Francisco: Jossey-Bass.

Barnard, K. E. (1997). Influencing parent-child interactions for children at risk. In M. J. Guralnick (Ed.), *The effectiveness of early intervention* (pp. 249–268). Baltimore: Brookes.

Barnett, D. W. (1986). School psychology in preschool settings: A review of training and practice issues. *Professional Psychology: Research and Practice, 17,* 58–64.

Barnett, D. W., Bell, S. H., & Carey, K. T. (1999). *Designing preschool interventions: A practitioner's guide*. New York: Guilford Press.

Barnett, W. S. (1993). Benefit–cost analysis of preschool education: Findings from a 25-year follow-up. *American Journal of Orthopsychiatry, 63,* 500–508.

Barnett, W. S., Hustedt, J. T., Friedman, A. H., Boyd, J. S., & Ainsworth, P. (2007). *The state of preschool 2007: State preschool yearbook*. National Institute for Early Education Research (www.nieer.org).

Bates, S. L. (2005). Evidence-based family-school interventions with preschool children. *School Psychology Quarterly, 20*, 352–370.

Batshaw, M. L., Pellegrino, L., & Roizen, N. J., (2007). *Children with disabilities* (6th ed). Baltimore: Brookes.

Beckwith, L. (2000). Prevention science and prevention programs. In C. H. Zeanah, Jr. (Ed.), *Handbook of infant mental health* (2nd ed., pp. 439–456). New York: Guilford Press.

Benham, A. L. (2000). The observation and assessment of young children including use of the Infant–Toddler Mental Status Exam. In C. H. Zeanah, Jr. (Ed.), *Handbook of infant mental health* (2nd ed., pp. 249–266). New York: The Guilford Press.

Blair, C. (2002). School readiness: Integrating cognition and emotion in a neuro-biological conceptualization of children's functioning at school entry. *American Psychologist, 57*, 111–127.

Boyajian, A. E., DuPaul, G. J., Handler, M. W., Eckert, T. L., & McGoey, K. E. (2001). The use of classroom-based brief functional analyses with preschoolers at risk for attention deficit hyperactivity disorder. *School Psychology Review, 30*, 278–293.

Bradley, R., Danielson, L., & Doolittle, J. (2005). Response to intervention. *Journal of Learning Disabilities, 38*, 485–486.

Brassard, M. R., & Boehm, A. E. (2007). *Preschool assessment: Principles and practices.* New York: Guilford Press.

Bredekamp, S., & Copple, C. (1997) *Developmentally appropriate practice in early childhood programs.* Washington, DC: National Association for the Education of Young Children.

Bricker, D., Pretti-Frontczak, K., & McComas, N. (1998). *An activity-based approach to early intervention* (2nd ed.). Baltimore: Brookes.

Brown, R. T. (2004). Introduction: Changes in the provision of health care to children and adolescents. In R. T. Brown (Ed.), *Handbook of pediatric psychology in school settings* (pp. 1–20). Mahwah, NJ: Erlbaum.

Brown, W., & Conroy, M. (1997). The interrelationship of context in early intervention. In S. K. Thurman, J. R. Cornwell, & S. R. Gottwald (Eds.), *Contexts of early intervention: Systems and settings* (pp. 229–240). Baltimore: Brookes.

Cicchetti, D., & Sroufe, L. A. (2000). The past as prologue to the future: The times, they've been a-changin. *Development and Psychopathology, 12*, 255–264.

Clark, L. (1996). SOS help for parents: A practical guide for handling common everyday behavior problems. Bowling Green, KY: Parents Press.

Comfort, M., Gordon, P. R., & Unger, D. G. (2006, May). The Keys to Interactive Parenting Scale: A window into many facets of parenting. *Zero to Three, 26*(5), 37–44.

Commission on Accreditation. (2007). *Guidelines and principles for accreditation of programs in professional psychology.* Washington, DC: American Psychological Association.

Cornwall, J. R., & Korteland, C. (1997). The family as a system and a context for early intervention. In S. K. Thurman, J. R. Cornwell, & S. R. Gottwald (Eds.), *Contexts of early intervention: Systems and settings* (pp. 93–109). Baltimore: Brookes.

Crockenberg, S., & Leerkes, E. (2000). *Infant social and emotional development in family context*. In C. H. Zeanah, Jr. (Ed.), *Handbook of infant mental health* (2nd ed., pp. 60–90). New York: Guilford Press.

Delahooke, M. M. (2005). Retraining clinicians to work with birth to five-year-olds: A perspective from the field. In K. M. Finello (Ed.), *The handbook of training and practice in infant and preschool mental health* (pp. 162–180). San Francisco: Jossey-Bass.

Diller, J. (2007). *Cultural diversity: A primer for human services* (3rd ed.). Belmont, CA: Thomson Brooks/Cole.

Division for Early Childhood (2007). *Promoting positive outcomes for children with disabilities: Recommendations for curriculum, assessment, and program evaluation.* Missoula, MT: Author.

Donahue, P. J., Falk, B., & Provet, A. G. (2000). *Mental health consultation in early childhood*. Baltimore: Brookes.

Dunlap, L. L. (1997). Behavior management. In L. L. Dunlap (Ed.), *An introduction to early childhood special education* (pp. 276–299). Boston: Allyn & Bacon.

Durlak, J. A., & Wells, A. M. (1997). Primary prevention mental health programs for children and adolescents: A meta-analytic review. *American Journal of Community Psychology, 25*, 115–152.

Emde, R. N., Everhart, K. D., & Wise, B. K. (2004). Therapeutic relationships in infant mental health and the concept of leverage. In A. J. Sameroff, S. C. McDonough, & K. L. Rosenblum (Eds.), *Treating parent–infant relationship problems: Strategies for intervention* (pp. 267–292). New York: Guilford Press.

Erickson, M. F., & Kurz-Riemer, K. (1999). *Infants, toddlers, and families: A framework for support and intervention*. New York: Guilford Press.

Essa, E. (2003). *A practical guide to solving preschool behavior problems* (5th ed.). Clifton Park, NY: Delmar Learning.

Evangelista, N., & McLellan, M. J. (2004). The Zero to Three diagnostic system: A framework for considering emotional and behavioral problems in young children. *School Psychology Review, 33*, 159–173.

Finello, K. M. (2005). Training in assessment of birth to five-year-olds. In K. M. Finello (Ed.), *The handbook of training and practice in infant and preschool mental health* (pp. 51–70). San Francisco: Jossey-Bass.

Finello, K. M., & Poulsen, M. K. (2005). Developing standards for training in infant and preschool mental health. In K. M. Finello (Ed.), *The handbook of training and practice in infant and preschool mental health* (pp. 307–325). San Francisco: Jossey-Bass.

Foley, G. M., & Mowder, B. A. (2000, June/July). Training doctoral-level school psychologists to work with infants, young children and their families. *Zero to Three, 20*(6), 23–25.

Fuchs, D., & Fuchs, L. S. (2006). Introduction to response to intervention: What, why, and how valid is it? *Reading Research Quarterly, 41*, 93–99.

Gallagher, S. F., Mowder, B. A., Sossin, K. M., & Rubinson, F. (2006). Continuing education interests of licensed New York State psychologists serving the zero to five-year-old population. *Journal of Early Childhood and Infant Psychology, 2,* 201–220.

Garfield, S. L., & Bergin, A. E. (1978). *Handbook of psychotherapy and behavior change: An empirical analysis* (2nd ed.). New York: Wiley.

Gilkerson, L., & Stott, F. (2000). Parent–child relationships in early intervention with infants and toddlers with disabilities and their families. In C. H. Zeanah, Jr. (Ed.), *Handbook of infant mental health* (2nd ed.) (pp. 457–471). New York: Guilford Press.

Gilliam, W. S. (2005, May). Prekindergarteners left behind: Expulsion rates in state prekindergarten programs (Policy Brief Series No. 3). New York: Foundation for Child Development.

Gilliam, W. S. (2008, January). Implementing policies to reduce the likelihood of preschool expulsion. New York: Foundation for Child Development.

Gilliam, W. S., & Leiter V. (2003, July). Evaluating early childhood programs: Improving quality and informing policy. *Zero to Three, 23,* 6–13.

Gilliam, W. S., & Mayes, L. C. (2000). Development assessment of infants and toddlers. In C. H. Zeanah, Jr. (Ed.), *Handbook of infant mental health* (2nd ed., pp. 236–248). New York: Guilford Press.

Gimpel, G. A., & Holland, M. L. (2003). Emotional and behavioral problems of young children: Effective interventions in the preschool and kindergarten years. New York: Guilford Press.

Golbeck, S. L., & Harlan, S. (1997). Family child care. In S. K. Thurman, J. R. Cornwell, & S. R. Gottwald (Eds.), *Contexts of early intervention: Systems and settings* (pp. 165–189). Baltimore: Brookes.

Goodwin, C. J. (1999). *A history of modern psychology.* New York: Wiley.

Greenspan, S. I., & Wieder, S. (2006). Infant and early childhood mental health: A comprehensive developmental approach to assessment and intervention. Arlington, VA: American Psychiatric Publishing.

Gresham, F. M., Beebe-Frankenberger, M. E., & MacMillan, D. L. (1999). A selective review of treatments for children with autism: Description and methodological considerations. *School Psychology Review, 28,* 559–575.

Hamm, K. (2006, August). More than meets the eye: Head Start programs, participants, families, and staff in 2005. Washington, DC: Center for Law and Social Policy.

Handen, B. L., & Gilchrist, R. H. (2006). Mental retardation. In E. J. Mash & R. A. Barkley (Eds.), *Treatment of childhood disorders* (3rd ed.) (pp. 411–454). New York: Guilford Press.

Harden, B. J., & Lythcott, M. (2005). Kitchen therapy and beyond: Mental health services for young children in alternative settings. In K. M. Finello (Ed.), *The handbook of training and practice in infant and preschool mental health* (pp. 256–286). San Francisco: Jossey-Bass.

Heckman, J., Grunewald, R., & Reynolds, A. (2006, July). The dollars and cents of investing early: Cost–benefit analysis in early care and education. *Zero to Three, 26* (6), 10–17.

Hergenhahn, B. R. (2005). *An introduction to the history of psychology* (5th ed.). Belmont, CA: Thomson Wadsworth.

Hojnoski, R. L., & Missall, K. N. (2006). Addressing school readiness: Expanding school psychology in early education. *School Psychology Review, 35*, 602–614.

Iglesias, A., & Quinn, R. (1997). Culture as a context for early intervention. In S. K. Thurman, J. R. Cornwell, & S. R. Gottwald (Eds.). *Contexts of early intervention: Systems and settings* (pp. 55–72). Baltimore: Brookes.

Individuals with Disabilities Education Act, Amendments of 1997. Retrieved June 10, 2008, from www.ed.gov/offices/OSERS/Policy/IDEA/regs.html

Individuals with Disabilities Education Act, Amendments of 2004. Retrieved June 10, 2008, from www.ed.gov/offices/OSERS/Policy/IDEA/regs.html

Jacobson, J. W., Foxx, R. M., & Mulick, J. A. (2005). Controversial therapies for developmental disabilities: Fad, fashion, and science in professional practice. Mahwah, NJ: Erlbaum.

Jensen, P. S., & Hoagwood, K. (1997). The book of names: DSM-IV in context. *Development and Psychopathology, 9*, 231–249.

Kaplan-Sanoff, M., Lerner, C., & Bernard, A. (2000, October/November). New roles for developmental specialists in pediatric primary care. *Zero to Three, 21*(2), 17–23.

Karabinos, R. (1997). Early intervention centers. In S. K. Thurman, J. R. Cornwell, & S. R. Gottwald (Eds.), *Contexts of early intervention: Systems and settings* (pp. 201–214). Baltimore: Brookes.

Klass, C. S. (1996). Home visiting: Promoting healthy parent and child development. Baltimore: Brookes.

Knoff, H. M., Stollar, S. A., Johnson, J. J., & Chenneville, T. A. (1999). Assessment of social–emotional functioning and adaptive behavior. In E. V. Nuttall, I. Romero, & J. Kalesnik (Eds.), *Assessing and screening preschoolers: Psychological and educational dimensions* (pp. 126–160). Boston: Allyn & Bacon.

Knoster, T. P., & McCurdy, B. (2002). Best practices in functional behavioral assessment for designing individualized student programs. In A. Thomas & J. Grimes (Eds.), *Best practices in school psychology IV* (pp. 1007–1028). Bethesda, MD: National Association of School Psychologists.

Kreader, J. L., Ferguson, D., & Lawrence, S. (2005, August). Infant and toddler child care arrangements. *Research-to-Policy Connections (1)*. Retrieved June 12, 2008, from www.childcareresearch.org/SendPdf?resourceId=6871.

Kumpfer, K. L., & Alvarado, R. (2003). Family-strengthening approaches for the prevention of youth behavior problems. *American Psychologist, 58*, 457–465.

Lerner, J. W., Lowenthal, B., & Egan, R. W. (2003). *Preschool children with special needs: Children at risk and children with disabilities* (2nd ed.). Boston: Pearson Education.

Lidz, C. S., Alfonso, V. C., Mowder, B., Ross, R., Rubinson, F., & Thies, L. (1998). *School psychology services in early childhood settings: A position paper*. School Psychology Educators' Council of New York State (SPECNYS) and New York Association of School Psychologists (NYASP).

Lieberman, A. F. (2004). Child–parent psychotherapy: A relationship-based approach to the treatment of mental health disorders in infancy and early childhood. In A. J. Sameroff, S. C. McDonough, & K. L. Rosenblum (Eds.), *Treating parent–infant relationship problems: Strategies for intervention* (pp. 97–122). New York: Guilford Press.

Mahoney, G., Spiker, D., & Boyce, G. (1996). Clinical assessments of parent-child interaction: Are professionals ready to implement this practice? *Topics in Early Childhood Special Education, 16*, 26–50.

Maltese, J. (2005). Dyadic therapy with very young children and their primary caregivers. In K. M. Finello (Ed.), *The handbook of training and practice in infant and preschool mental health* (pp. 93–113). San Francisco: Jossey-Bass.

Marston, D. (2005). Tiers of intervention in responsiveness to intervention: Prevention outcomes and learning disabilities identification patterns. *Journal of Learning Disabilities, 38*, 539–544.

Mayes, L. C. (1999). Addressing mental health needs of infants and young children. *Comprehensive Psychiatric Assessment of Young Children, 8*, 209–224.

McCabe, P. (2006). Responsiveness to intervention (RTI) in early childhood: Challenges and practical guidelines. *Journal of Early Childhood and Infant Psychology, 2*, 157–180.

McDonough, S. C. (2004). Interaction guidance: Promoting and nurturing the caregiving relationship. In A. J. Sameroff, S. C. McDonough, & K. L. Rosenblum (Eds.). *Treating parent–infant relationship problems* (pp. 79–96). New York: Guilford Press.

McEachin, J. J., Smith, T., & Lovaas, O. I. (1993). Long-term outcome for children with autism who received early intensive behavioral treatment. *American Journal on Mental Retardation, 97*, 359–372.

McEvoy, M. A., Neilson, S., & Reichle, J. (2004). Functional behavioral assessment in early education settings. In M. McLean, M. Wolery, & D. B. Bailey Jr. (Eds.), *Assessing infants and preschoolers with special needs* (3rd ed., pp. 236–261). Upper Saddle River, NJ: Pearson Education.

McLean, M., & Crais, E. R. (2004). Procedural considerations in assessing infants and preschoolers with disabilities. In M. McLean, M. Wolery, & D. B. Bailey Jr. (Eds.), *Assessing infants and preschoolers with special needs* (3rd ed., pp. 45–70). Upper Saddle River, NJ: Pearson Education.

McLinden, S. E., & Prasse, D. P. (1991). Providing services to infants and toddlers under PL 99-457: Training needs of school psychologists. *School Psychology Review, 20*, 37–48.

Metz, B., Mulick, J. A., & Butter, E. M. (2005). Autism: A late 20th century fad magnet. In J. W. Jacobson, R. M. Foxx, & J. A. Mulick (Eds), *Controversial therapies for developmental disabilities: Fad, fashion, and science in professional practice* (pp. 237–263). Mahwah, NJ: Erlbaum.

Minde, K. (2000). Prematurity and serious medical conditions in infancy: Implications for development, behavior, and intervention. In C. H. Zeanah, Jr. (Ed.), *Handbook of infant mental health* (2nd ed., pp. 176–194). New York: Guilford Press.

Mowder, B. A. (1997a). Early intervention program models. In A. H. Widerstrom, B. A. Mowder, & S. R. Sandall (Eds.), *Infant development and risk: An introduction* (2nd ed., pp. 289–314). Baltimore: Brookes.

Mowder, B. A. (1997b). Family dynamics. In A. H. Widerstrom, B. A. Mowder, & S. R. Sandall (Eds.), *Infant development and risk: An introduction* (2nd ed., pp. 125–154). Baltimore: Paul H. Brookes.

Mowder, B. A., Goliger, I., Sossin, K. M., & Rubinson, F. (2003). Continuing education interests and needs of New York State early childhood school psychologists. *The School Psychologist, 57*, 130–139.

National Association of School Psychologists (2002, March). *NASP position statement on early childhood care and education.* Bethesda, MD: Author.

National Association of School Psychologists (2003, April). *NASP position statement on early intervention services.* Bethesda, MD: Author.

National Association of School Psychologists (2005, July). *NASP position statement on early childhood assessment.* Bethesda, MD: Author.

National Coalition on Health Care. (2008). *Facts on health insurance coverage.* Retrieved June 1, 2008 from www.nchc.org/facts/coverage.shtml.

New York State Education Department (2008, January). Regulations of the Commissioner of Education, Subpart 151–1: Universal prekindergarten programs. Albany, NY: Author.

Newsom, C., & Hovanitz, C. A. (2006). Autism spectrum disorders. In E. J. Mash & R. A. Barkley (Eds.), *Treatment of childhood disorders* (3rd ed., pp. 455–511). New York: Guilford Press.

Nickel, R. E., & Widerstrom, A. H. (1997). Developmental disorders in infancy. In A. H. Widerstrom, B. A. Mowder, & S. R. Sandall (Eds.), *Infant development and risk: An introduction* (2nd ed., pp. 89–124). Baltimore: Brookes.

Olds, D. L., Henderson, C. R., Kitzman, H. J., Eckenrode, J. J., Cole, R. E., & Tatelbaum, R. C. (1999, Spring/Summer). Prenatal and infancy home visitation by nurses: Recent findings. *The Future of Children 9*(1), 44–65.

Peterson, C. A., Luze, G. J., Eshbaugh, E. M., Jeon, H., & Kantz, K. R. (2007). Enhancing parent–child interactions through home visiting: Promising practice or unfulfilled promise? *Journal of Early Intervention, 2*, 119–140.

Peterson, S., Bair, K. & Sullivan, A. (2004, July). Emotional well-being and mental health services: Lessons learned by Early Head Start Region VIII programs. *Zero to Three, 24*(6), 47–53.

Piotrkowski, C. S., Collins, R. C., Knitzer, J., & Robinson, R. (1994). Strengthening mental health services in Head Start: A challenge for the 1990s. *American Psychologist, 49*, 133–139.

Poulsen, M. K. (2005). Diagnosis of mental health in young children. In K. M. Finello (Ed.), *The handbook of training and practice in infant and preschool mental health* (pp. 71–92). San Francisco: Jossey-Bass.

Pryor, V., & Glaser, D. (2006). *Understanding attachment and attachment disorders: Theory, evidence, and practice.* London: Kingsley.

Reynolds, C. R., Gutkin, T. B., Elliott, S. N., & Witt, J. C. (1984). *School psychology: Essentials of theory and practice.* New York: Wiley.

Rosenblum, K. L. (2004). Defining infant mental health: A developmental relational perspective on assessment and diagnosis. In A. J. Sameroff, S. C. McDonough, & K. L. Rosenblum (Eds.), *Treating parent–infant relationship problems: Strategies for intervention* (pp. 43–78). New York: Guilford Press.

Rubinson, F., Sweeny, K. A., Mowder, B. A., & Sossin, K. M. (2003). Collaborative practices of New York State early childhood school psychologists. *The School Psychologist*, *57*, 74–85.

Rutter, M., & Sroufe, L. A. (2000). Developmental psychopathology: Concepts and challenges. *Development and Psychopathology*, *12*, 265–296.

Sameroff, A. J. (2004). Ports of entry and the dynamics of mother-infant interventions. In A. J. Sameroff, S. C. McDonough, & K. L. Rosenblum (Eds.), *Treating parent–infant relationship problems: Strategies for intervention* (pp. 3–28). New York: Guilford Press.

Sameroff, A. J., & Fiese, B. H. (2000). Models of development and developmental risk. In C. H. Zeanah, Jr. (Ed.), *Handbook of infant mental health* (2nd ed., pp. 3–19). New York: Guilford Press.

Scheeringa, M. S., & Gaensbauer, T. J. (2000). Posttraumatic stress disorder. In C. H. Zeanah, Jr. (Ed.), *Handbook of infant mental health* (2nd ed., pp. 369–381). New York: Guilford Press.

Seligman, S. (2000). Clinical interviews with families of infants. In C. H. Zeanah, Jr. (Ed.), *Handbook of infant mental health* (2nd ed., pp. 211–221). New York: Guilford Press.

Seligman, S., & Darling, R. B. (2007). *Ordinary families, special children* (3rd ed). New York: Guilford Press.

Shea, V. (2005, Winter). A perspective on the research literature related to early intensive behavioral intervention (Lovaas) for young children with autism. *Communication Disorders Quarterly*, *26*(2), 102–111.

Sheeringa, M. S. & Gaensbauer, T. J. (2000). Posttraumatic stress disorder. In C. H. Zeanah, Jr. (Ed.), *Handbook of infant mental health* (2nd ed.) (pp. 369–381). New York, NY: The Guildford Press.

Sroufe, L. A. (1997). Psychopathology as an outcome of development. *Development and psychopathology*, *9*, 251–268.

Strein, W., Hoagwood, K., & Cohn, A. (2003). School psychology: A public health perspective I. Prevention, populations, and, systems change. *Journal of School Psychology*, *41*, 23–38.

Sturner, R., Albus, K., Thomas, J., & Howard, B. (2007). A proposed adaptation of DC:0-3R for primary care, developmental research, and prevention of mental disorders. *Infant Mental Health Journal*, *28*, 1–11.

Task Force on Research Diagnostic Criteria: Infancy and Preschool (2003). Research diagnostic criteria for infants and preschool children: The process and empirical support. *Journal of the American Academy of Child and Adolescent Psychiatry*, *42*, 1504–1512.

Thurman, S. K., Gottwald, S. R., Cornwell, J. R., & Korteland, C. (1997). Neonatal intensive care units. In S. K. Thurman, J. R. Cornwell, & S. R. Gottwald (Eds.), *Contexts of early intervention: Systems and settings* (pp. 113–138). Baltimore: Brookes.

Trivette, C. M., Dunst, C. J., & Deal, A. G. (1997). Resource-based approach to early intervention. In S. K. Thurman, J. R. Cornwell, & S. R. Gottwald (Eds.), *Contexts of early intervention: Systems and settings* (pp. 73–92). Baltimore, MD: Brookes.

U.S. Department of Education (2003, September). Guidance for the William F. Goodling Even Start Family Literacy Programs (Part B, subpart 3 of Title I of the Elementary & Secondary Education Act). Washington, DC: Author.

U.S. Department of Education (2004). 26th annual report to Congress on the implementation of the Individuals with Disabilities Education Act. Washington, DC: Author.

U.S. Department of Education. (2005). 27th annual report to Congress on the implementation of the Individuals with Disabilities Education Act. Washington, DC: Author.

U.S. Department of Education (2007, January). Guidance for the Early Reading First Program (Subpart B, Part B, Title I of the Elementary and Secondary Education Act). Washington, DC: Author.

U.S. Office of Health and Human Services. (2007). *Head Start Program performance standards and other regulations (45 CFR Parts 1301–1311).* Retrieved from www.acf.hhs.gov/programs/ohs/legislation/index.html.

VanDerHeyden, A. M., & Snyder, P. (2006). Integrating frameworks from early childhood intervention and school psychology to accelerate growth for all young children. *School Psychology Review, 35,* 519–534.

Weatherston, D. J. (2000, October/November). The infant mental health specialist. *Zero to Three, 21*(2), 3–10.

Weatherston, D. J. (2005). Returning the treasure to babies: An introduction to infant mental health service and training. In K. M. Finello (Ed.), *The handbook of training and practice in infant and preschool mental health* (pp. 3–30). San Francisco: Jossey-Bass.

Widerstrom, A. H., Mowder, B. A., & Willis, W. G. (1989). The school psychologist's role in the early childhood special education program. *Journal of Early Intervention, 13,* 239–248.

Wieder, S., Greenspan, S., & Kalmonson, B. (2008, March). Autism assessment and intervention: The developmental individual-difference, relationship-based, DIR/Floortime model. *Zero to Three, 28*(4), 31–37.

World Health Organization (1992). *The ICD-10 Classification of mental and behavioural disorders: Clinical descriptions and diagnostic guidelines.* Retrieved June 9, 2008, from www.who.int/classifications/icd/en/bluebook.pdf.

Zeanah, P. D., Larrieu, J. A., & Zeanah, Jr., C. H. (2000). Training in infant mental health. In C. H. Zeanah, Jr. (Ed.), *Handbook of infant mental health* (2nd ed., pp. 548–558). New York: Guilford Press.

Zero to Three (1994). *Diagnostic classification of mental health and developmental disorders of infancy and early childhood (DC:0-3).* Arlington, VA: National Center for Clinical Infant Programs.

Zero to Three (2005). *Diagnostic classification of mental health and developmental disorders of infancy and early childhood: Revised edition (DC:0-3R).* Washington, DC: Zero to Three Press.

CHAPTER 2

Professionals Working in Infant and Early Childhood Psychology

SUSAN VIG

Professionals work with infants, young children, and their families to achieve the goals incorporated in the following definition:

> Early childhood intervention consists of multidisciplinary services provided to children from birth to 5 years of age to promote child health and well-being, enhance emerging competencies, minimize developmental delays, remediate existing or emerging disabilities, prevent functional deterioration, and promote adaptive parenting and overall family functioning. These goals are accomplished by providing individualized developmental, educational, and therapeutic services for children in conjunction with mutually planned support for their families. (Shonkoff & Meisels, 2000, pp. xvii–xviii)

Accomplishing these goals requires the expertise of professionals representing many different disciplines and service systems. This chapter explores some of the ways in which early intervention (EI) and other early childhood professionals work together, using theory as well as current research, to provide evidence-based services.

Traditionally, early childhood services were available for infants and young children with established disabilities or at significant biological risk for disabilities. The services tended to be developmental in nature, provided directly to children by clinicians and educators, often occurring in educational environments (Ginsberg & Hochman, 2006). Legislation over the past two decades expanded the scope of early childhood services to include families as both team members and service recipients. The broadened child and family perspective created a need for professionals to consider environmental factors (e.g., psychosocial risk), family stressors (e.g., financial, social–emotional), and mental health issues in planning and implementing services (Ginsberg &

Hochman; Guralnick, 2001, 2004, 2005a). So far, there has been no general agreement about how to accomplish this goal or, indeed, if all these issues should be addressed. The broadened perspective, however, opens an important avenue for psychologists to provide services to children and families who experience psychosocial stressors.

Despite the increased scope of early childhood service provision, there have been increasing calls for accountability and evidence-based practice. Although the accountability demands are clear, many professionally accepted early intervention and early childhood practices lack evidence-based support (Rapport, McWilliam, & Smith, 2004). The Division for Early Childhood (DEC) of the Council for Exceptional Children (CEC) incorporated an evidence-based approach in the development of DEC Recommended Practices (Sandall, Hemmeter, Smith, & McLean, 2005). Recommended practice was based on literature reviews, expert opinion, priorities identified by nine national stakeholder focus groups, and field validation through widely distributed questionnaires. (See Smith, McLean, Sandall, Snyder, and Ramsey (2005) for further description of the process.)

Despite the multifaceted efforts, some of the recommended practices are not currently supported by research (Rapport et al., 2004). Based on a review of the 19 practices comprising the interdisciplinary models, Rapport et al. find research or partial support for only 7. Some of the practices lacking full support are relatively common recommendations, including, for instance, that all team members participate in the individualized education program/individualized family service plans (IEP/IFSP) process, team members use a transdisciplinary model to plan and deliver services, and teams should provide services in natural environments (e.g., home settings). The disparity between common and evidence-based practice suggests that many professional services for young children and their families have yet to be validated. One barrier to conducting program efficacy research is the ethical issue of incorporating a control group of individuals receiving no services into common research paradigms (Warfield & Hauser-Cram, 2005).

The current need for research regarding early childhood practice suggests an additional potential avenue of involvement for psychologists, who usually are well trained in conducting and interpreting research. Indeed, their research expertise and involvement could be tapped in various settings (e.g., university-agency program partnerships, interagency collaborations), utilizing a variety of methods (e.g., case studies, longitudinal investigations), to examine multifaceted practice outcomes (e.g., child development, educational progress, family functioning, service delivery quality).

SERVICE PROVIDERS

Early EI legislation identified 10 professional disciplines to provide early childhood services (i.e., audiology, medicine, nursing, nutrition, occupational therapy, physical therapy, psychology, social work, special education, speech–language pathology). In addition, because children and families often have complex needs, additional professionals representing other service systems frequently become involved. For instance, attorneys and judges, child welfare and protective services professionals, and substance abuse professionals, among many others, provide invaluable contributions. Therefore, multidisciplinary teams usually draw on the discipline-specific expertise of their members, as well as consultants, in conceptualizing, planning, and implementing services for children and families.

The 10 professional disciplines most commonly involved in early childhood service delivery may be grouped, for discussion purposes, a variety of ways. For the purpose of this chapter, the disciplines are described in terms of clinical (i.e., audiology, nutrition, occupational therapy, physical therapy, psychology, social work), educational (i.e., early childhood special education), and medical (i.e., nursing, medical) services. Although the presentation implies no priority or hierarchy, the focus is decidedly on psychological services. Parenthetically, clinical and medical services tend to predominate with infants and toddlers, and clinical and educational services with young children.

CLINICAL PROFESSIONALS

Even within the clinical arena, professionals may be categorized, somewhat arbitrarily, into those focused predominantly on children's biologically or physiologically-based needs (i.e., audiology, nutrition, occupational therapy, physical therapy, speech–language pathology) and those addressing children's and families' social–emotional functioning (i.e., psychologists, social workers). Although all of the clinical professionals rely on developmental knowledge and an appreciation of children's familial context, each has a somewhat unique role in assisting young children and their families.

Audiologists, for example, identify hearing irregularities that can affect attentional, language, and speech skills. Often, they may recommend interventions such as hearing aids and classroom adaptations. For example, FM (frequency modulation) systems are listening systems used in large areas such as classrooms (DEC Recommended Practices and Examples: Technology Applications, 2005; James, 2007). The FM system uses a wireless microphone and loudspeakers mounted on walls or ceilings to amplify a teacher's voice above the level of background classroom noise. Audiologists work with other professionals on aural habilitation (e.g., enhancing perception of speech sounds in children with hearing impairments) and cochlear implant projects (Niparko, Marlowe, Bervinchak, & Ceh, 2007). Nutritionists, with expertise in diet and feeding-related behavior, provide services to infants and young children often by working with families. They often provide recommendations for nutrition-related concerns (e.g., failure to thrive, obesity, or limited food preferences of young children with autism spectrum disorders).

Occupational therapists address sensory and motor impairments that interfere with children's functional skills of daily living (e.g., helping a child to tolerate different kinds of clothing textures, developing the fine motor control needed to button clothing or hold a pencil). Physical therapists, usually implementing services prescribed by physicians, mainly address young children's motor needs (e.g., sitting, walking). Often working together, occupational and physical therapists address needs for adaptive equipment (e.g., adaptive walker, motorized wheelchair, optical pointer attached to a child's head to indicate picture choices) and assistive devices (e.g., modified handles on eating utensils, switches to activate toys). In contrast to professionals addressing issues such as hearing, nutrition, and motor skills, speech–language pathologists have expertise in communication (e.g., nonverbal, preverbal, verbal), speech, and feeding issues. They frequently address these needs by providing alternative and augmentative communication devices (e.g., communication boards, picture cards, computerized picture to voice communication devices) for children with speaking difficulties. Each of these five professional practice areas require a graduate degree as well as supervised internship or practicum experiences to qualify for certification and licensure.

The two clinical professionals specifically trained in social–emotional development and functioning are psychologists and social workers. In addition to training in areas such as child development, measurement and research, psychosocial stressors, and psychotherapeutic interventions, psychologists receive extensive training in adaptive behavior, cognitive, and social–emotional assessment. Indeed, psychologists (i.e., clinical, counseling, school) are the only professionals trained to administer standardized intelligence tests identifying children's cognitive status (e.g., intellectual disabilities, mental retardation). In most states, licensed psychologists must complete a doctoral program that includes a supervised internship and dissertation or comparable field project. School psychologists are trained at both doctoral and nondoctoral levels. Nondoctoral school psychologists, with an advanced 60-graduate-credit-hour degree, often practice in school settings but do not provide EI services. Social workers in the early childhood field, like psychologists, have expertise in child development, psychosocial stressors affecting development, and psychotherapeutic interventions. In particular, social workers often assist families in accessing community resources (e.g., financial assistance, housing, nutrition) and provide therapeutic interventions (e.g., counseling services). A 60-graduate-credit-hour master's degree and supervised internship usually are required for independent social work practice.

Education Professionals

Early childhood education professionals often include early education teachers, early childhood special education teachers, and paraprofessionals. States usually require a bachelor's or master's degree and supervised student teaching experience for teacher certification. Paraprofessionals usually have a high school diploma, although many also complete a 2-year associate's degree. As noted by Musick and Stott (2000), paraprofessionals usually are hired from their community, often providing a helpful link among intervention programs, neighborhood, and the community. The DEC provides an extensive list of competencies for early childhood special educators (DEC Recommended Practices and Examples: Personnel Preparation, 2005; Miller & Stayton, 2005). For example, some of the areas of competence include advocacy, development and implementation of intervention plans, informal assessment, interagency coordination, and team planning.

Medical Professionals

Medical professionals (e.g., family practice physicians, nurses and nurse practitioners, pediatricians) address health issues essential to young children's well-being. Beyond the more typical developmental monitoring and anticipatory guidance, Dworkin (2000) identifies a number of medical practices beneficial to young children with suspected or identified developmental problems. Indeed, Dworkin describes practices more common in Denmark and the United Kingdom than the United States, including, for example, home visiting, office-based literacy programs (e.g., volunteers reading to children in waiting rooms and providing books to families), and parent-held child health records. Thus, Dworkin describes a model of well-child care in which groups of families gather for information and discussion prior to children's individual appointments.

The more typical approach is for medical professionals to provide health-related information and services to families. Bailey and Powell (2005), for example, note more than 750 genetic disorders associated with mental retardation and other disabilities. By providing information regarding research findings, such as those documenting a genetic explanation for developmental problems, families may be assisted in understanding and planning for child and family needs. In fact, recent research findings documenting genetic explanations for developmental problems find families increasingly requesting genetic information from medical professionals.

ETHICAL ISSUES FOR SERVICE PROVIDERS

There are numerous ethical issues facing providers of infant, early childhood, and family services. Many issues tend to be of a general nature and relate to most early childhood providers, almost regardless of individual specialty areas; others are specific to a specialty area and refer to field-specific ethical codes or guidelines. The issues of a more general nature include, for example, the experimental nature of much of early therapeutic care, pain and suffering associated with surgical and other medical procedures, and treatment costs (e.g., meeting the extensive medical needs of very-low-birthweight [VLBW] infants) (Harrison, 1997). Often, these and many other ethical issues are addressed in training programs, field training sites, and ethical codes developed by field-specific professional organizations. However, the guidelines and codes do not always cover areas relevant to early intervention, such as working with other adults through consultation (Wesley & Buysse, 2006). In other cases, guidelines and codes may conflict with legislative mandates and recommended professional practice. For example, areas of concern may include confidentiality, boundaries of competence, scope of practice, and sharing professional roles with others (e.g., "role release" associated with the transdisciplinary model of team practice).

Psychologists, in particular, adhere to a rigorous and comprehensive code of ethics entitled the *Ethical Principles of Psychologists and Code of Conduct* (American Psychological Association, 2002). However, several of the American Psychological Association's (APA's) ethical principles conflict with EI practices; for example, Principle 2.01 (Boundaries of Competence) states that psychologists provide services, teach, and conduct research within their boundaries of competence. Essentially, this suggests psychologists should not exchange roles with (e.g., transdisciplinary practice) or perform activities not associated with their area of competence and training. In addition, Principle 4.05 specifies that confidential information can be disclosed, without consent, only in certain specific circumstances (e.g., child abuse). For example, psychologists work with families and may have sensitive knowledge regarding parental issues (e.g., mental illness, substance abuse); ethically, psychologists should not share this kind of information with other team members without parental informed consent. Thus, ethical issues present challenges for psychologists, creating potential barriers impeding team functioning and interagency collaboration and cooperation. Undoubtedly, ethical challenges will grow as early childhood practice, as advocated by many experts (Chazan-Cohen, Stark, Mann, & Fitzgerald, 2007; Foley & Hochman, 2006a, 2006b; Kalmanson & Seligman, 2006; Katzive, 2006: Weston, 2005), increasingly incorporates mental health perspectives and addresses the wide range of environmental risk difficulties.

SERVICE SETTINGS

Traditionally, infants and children under 3 years of age receive publicly funded EI services in their homes, sometimes supplemented by periodic center-based activities. For example, according to the National Early Intervention Longitudinal (NEIL) study, approximately 76% of infants and toddlers receive services in their homes (Spiker, Hebbeler, & Mallik, 2005). Preschool children (i.e., 3–5 years of age) with disabilities, however, usually receive services in group settings (e.g., special education classrooms). In some cases, services for both age groups are provided in settings such as agency facilities, clinics, hospitals, and specialized developmental centers.

The 2004 Individuals with Disabilities Education Improvement Act (IDEIA) reauthorization specifies that children receive services in natural environments (e.g., settings with children without disabilities) whenever possible. Natural environments may include settings such as day care, Early Head Start and Head Start programs, homes, and public and private child care and preschools.

Parents often, but not always, prefer homes as service settings, particularly for the birth to 3-year age group. Guess, Baker, and Miller (2006) examined this issue, finding that over 70% of parents preferred home-based services prior to the formal identification of their child's disability. Indeed, far fewer parents indicated a preference for services provided in hospitals or clinic settings. Spagnola and Fiese (2007) also note that by providing home-based services, practitioners can encourage and, with parental consent, embed interventions within family routines. If interventions become part of family routines, many opportunities for family practice and generalization are created.

Despite potential benefits, the home may not be the preferred service setting for all families. Because many work outside the home, parents may not be available to receive and work with providers (Warfield & Hauser-Cram, 2005). Further, some families may prefer the support of and interaction with other parents, often available in center-based programs (Hanft & Pilkington, 2000). Additionally, some cultural groups may be uncomfortable about the perceived or real intrusion and the somewhat forced intimacy characterizing many home-based services (Hanson, 2004). Based on a review of Early Head Start research, Knitzer (2007) concludes that programs combining center-based experiences, family supports, and home visiting likely are best for low-income parents with infants and toddlers. This combination seems to bring together the assets (e.g., peer support) associated with each individual approach.

For children aged 3–5 years, natural environments are usually group, inclusive settings bringing together children with and without disabilities.

Investigating blended classrooms, including Head Start and some early childhood special education programs, Rosenkoetter (2005) documents teachers' beliefs that children with disabilities meet IEP goals more quickly in blended classrooms than through specialized services. The teachers attribute the superiority of blended classrooms to expanded opportunities for children with disabilities to communicate with nondisabled peers.

Despite teacher beliefs about the superiority of inclusive settings, the behavior problems of children with disabilities can present significant challenges (Etscheidt, 2006). For example, Spiker et al. (2005) describe some reasons why children with disabilities may be difficult social partners. They may be less apt to initiate social exchanges, less predictable in their social interactions, and less responsive to social cues than children without disabilities. Further, they may have trouble regulating arousal and attention and exhibit atypical behaviors. Based on a review of earlier empirical literature on inclusion, Odom (2000) concludes that children with disabilities engage in social interaction with peers less often in inclusive than in specialized classrooms. In addition, children with disabilities are at high risk for peer rejection and less preferred as playmates in inclusive classrooms.

Some barriers to successful inclusion include difficulty complying with Americans with Disabilities (ADA) mandates, funding issues, and inadequate staff training. Odom (2000) finds that in some programs, special education teachers are not allowed to work with typical children because their salaries are paid through special education and not general education funds. Further, Sweet (2008) discusses the implications of ADA concepts of discrimination, reasonable modifications, and undue burden for inclusive child care. For example, a center cannot refuse to admit a child over age 3 who is not toilet trained or refuse to make reasonable modifications (e.g., cutting food into small pieces for a child with a swallowing disorder), even though these accommodations are not offered to other children. However, if the cost is prohibitive, a center is not required to provide or hire a full-time personal care worker for a child with a disability.

TEAM MODELS

Services for infants and young children, for the most part, tend to be both multidisciplinary in nature and, at least to some extent, coordinated. Team models for implementing services often vary in degree of collaboration and shared sense of purpose. Teams are not always successful in their efforts to serve children and families, since there are barriers to effective team functioning (e.g., inadequate funding, lack of administrative support, personnel shortages). Even when teams function well, there usually are needs for discipline-specific services. The following discussion illustrates some of the ways practitioners work together in providing services to children and their families; the three models discussed are presented according to relative level of integrated team functioning. The least integrated model is the multi-disciplinary, followed by the interdisciplinary, and, finally, transdisciplinary team model.

MULTIDISCIPLINARY TEAM MODEL

Within the multidisciplinary model, professionals from various disciplines provide services almost as private practitioners or through contract agencies and vendor systems, with fee-for-services as the principal funding mechanism. There may be little or no contact among professionals providing services to the same children and families. Thus, services tend to be relatively discrete and distinct, and often families are in the position of coordinating the various services (Woodruff & Shelton, 2006). Criticisms of the multidisciplinary model abound (e.g., lack of service coordination, inadequate supervision of providers) (Ginsberg & Hochman, 2006).

INTERDISCIPLINARY TEAM MODEL

The interdisciplinary team model involves a greater degree of collaboration than the multidisciplinary model. Members of interdisciplinary teams serve children and families by retaining discipline-specific perspectives and skills, but work together with team members representing other disciplines. McWilliam (2005), for example, describes some ways interdisciplinary services are delivered (e.g., consultation with families and/or other professional service providers, direct work with children in home or community-based settings, individual or group activities in classrooms, individual or group pullout in preschools). Within an interdisciplinary model, contacts with discipline-specific professionals may be formal (e.g., scheduled team meetings) or informal. During the formal meetings, team members often collectively identify or diagnose children's developmental difficulties, working together to conceptualize, develop, and implement intervention plans.

There is a range of potential barriers to effective interdisciplinary team functioning (e.g., administrative support, financial resources, mutual professional respect, time). For instance, funding often is not provided for interdisciplinary team meetings, and time for meetings, therefore, becomes a scarce resource (Ginsberg & Hochman, 2006: Kruger & Lifter, 2005; Woodruff & Shelton, 2006). Similarly, there typically is a lack of support (e.g., funding, time) for staff training (Kruger & Lifter; Woodruff & Shelton). As a consequence of these issues, one DEC Recommended Practice point suggests that indirect service time should be scheduled and considered part of professionals' workdays (DEC Recommended Practices: Interdisciplinary Models, 2005). Finally, among many difficulties, interdisciplinary teams do not function well if team members lack respect for the expertise of other disciplines or become involved in turf disputes (Horn & Jones, 2005). Due to many issues, therefore, interdisciplinary teams face many challenges to effective functioning.

TRANSDISCIPLINARY TEAM MODEL

The transdisciplinary model represents the greatest degree of collaboration, not only among professionals, but also between professionals and families. Thus, transdisciplinary teams include family members and a diverse array of professionals; this model is more commonly practiced with infants and young children from birth to 3 years than for preschool children aged 3–5 years.

One key feature of the transdisciplinary model is role release. Role release refers to a specific professional practitioner's role (e.g., occupational therapist, psychologist), which is "released" to a professional from another discipline. For example, a speech–language pathologist may work on positioning an infant for feeding (a role more commonly undertaken by an occupational therapist). Or a nutritionist, who is part of a transdisciplinary feeding team, may work on desensitizing a child's mouth area to permit introduction of a spoon (a role more traditionally assumed by a speech–language pathologist or occupational therapist). Another typical feature of the transdisciplinary model is an arena assessment, during which professionals and family members simultaneously work together to assess a child.

Several advantages of the transdisciplinary model are evident. The model provides services when there are personnel shortages (Harbin, McWilliam, & Gallagher, 2000), and avoids duplication of services (Horn & Jones, 2005). An additional advantage is that family members share full decision-making responsibilities, helping to ensure that their priorities are addressed (DEC Recommended Practices: Family-Based Practices, 2005).

Although there are advantages with trandisciplinary models, there also are challenges and difficulties. For example, Kruger and Lifter (2005) describe confusion about roles and responsibilities, suggesting that a pair of team members might share responsibilities to reduce potential confusion. Further, psychologists may not be able to function as team members in role release models without violating their code of ethics (Hochman, Katzive, Hillowe, Rothbaum, d'Emery, & Foley, 2006). In addition, a fee-for-service funding environment may not provide adequate payment for transdisciplinary services (Ginsberg & Hochman, 2006; Woodruff & Shelton, 2006).

Consistent with some of the challenges associated with interdisciplinary models, there also may be a lack of administrative support and/or funding for indirect services such as team meetings, supervision, and training (Ginsberg & Hochman, 2006). Importantly, many families, including those from other cultures, may not have the time or comfort level to engage in partnerships with professionals or function as team members (Ginsberg & Hochman, 2006). Unfortunately, traditional transdisciplinary models assume that families have adequate child development knowledge, interest in being active team members, and resources to participate. Because many children and families experience environmental and psychosocial risk factors (Guralnick, 2004), and some parents themselves have developmental disabilities (Feldman, 2004), the transdisciplinary model is not necessarily optimal.

CONSULTATION

Professionals, representing diverse early childhood–related disciplines, often provide indirect services through consultation. In part due to personnel shortages, therapists sometimes serve as consultants to other professionals, rather than providing services directly (Harbin, McWilliam, & Gallagher, 2000). Consultation may involve developmental or mental health perspectives, and, regardless of theoretical orientation, requires significant sensitivity. Horn and Jones (2005) point out that consultation is apt to be unidirectional, implying an unequal status or power within the consulting relationship. The inequality can lead to practices inconsistent with shared decision-making among early childhood professionals and the parents served.

Emphasizing the need for evidence-based practice, Wesley and Buysse (2006) describe several ethical issues relevant to consultation. At the outset, consultants need substantial knowledge regarding both content (e.g., children's needs, program evaluation) and process (e.g., supporting consultees). Issues of confidentiality, power relationships, and professional boundaries represent significant issues to consider. For example, informed consent means that, once consultation parameters are explained, the consultee agrees or chooses not to participate and, in addition, may sever the consultation relationship at any time. Similarly, the consultee has the right to accept or reject the consultant's suggestions.

Because of the high rates of school expulsion among preschoolers, a survey of Head Start directors, staff, and consultants regarding the efficacy of mental health consultation, was conducted (Green, Everhart, Gordon, & Garcia Getman, 2006). Information from 655 respondents reveals that consultation frequency and quality of consultation relationships (e.g., between consultant and Head Start staff) are associated with consultation efficacy and improved child outcomes. Dependent variables included increasing children's positive behaviors, reducing children's externalizing behaviors, and increasing staff well-being. Better outcomes occur when mental health specialists integrate consultation into the daily activities of the center and are not perceived as outside experts. These findings have particular relevance for psychologists who, by virtue of background and training, often provide mental health consultation services.

SERVICE PROVISION AND COORDINATION

PROVIDING SERVICES FOR CHILDREN

Target Population and Needed Services The target population for early childhood services includes infants and young children with established (i.e., formally assessed and identified) disabilities and those at risk for disabilities. Children with disabilities certainly are eligible for appropriate services, and for the most part there is general agreement that those at risk (e.g., due to biological or environmental difficulties) also should receive publicly funded, developmental services. Biological risk includes a variety of relatively well established issues (e.g., low birth weight, prematurity, presence of a syndrome commonly associated with disabilities), and usually there is little question that services should be provided. Environmental risk (e.g., abuse or neglect, lack of social support, parental mental illness, parenting difficulties, poverty) (Guralnick, 2004; Sameroff & Fiese, 2000), however, is fraught with controversy.

One concern about providing services to children at environmental risk is the sheer number of children who may be included. For example, data from the NEIL study, summarized by Spiker et al. (2005), suggest that many children with developmental disabilities, including those already receiving services, are also exposed to environmental risk. Indeed, the EI population experiences environmental risk at higher rates than the general population (Warfield & Hauser-Cram, 2005). Children in foster care are a particularly vulnerable group, with their multiple, complex service needs (Vig, Chinitz, & Shulman, 2005). Aware of these many issues, Guralnick (2005b) points out that few communities have systems to identify children at risk, much less provide relevant services.

There are social and financial implications concurrent with the numbers of children potentially at risk environmentally. Meisels and Shonkoff (2000), for example, suggest significant financial consequences of identifying children at risk and increasing the size of the service population. The issue includes not only service provision, but also prevention. Focusing on prevention, however, presents its own set of difficulties; Knitzer (2007), for instance, notes that, "Federal dollars flow after serious problems have occurred, rather than being allocated for prevention" (p. 239). In the end, at-risk children and families often need mental health as well as other developmental services. During the coming years, struggles in identifying service needs, as well as securing funding, will likely increase.

Identification of Children's Developmental Difficulties The first and most important step toward addressing children's potential needs is accurate identification of developmental issues. Vig and Kaminer (2003) describe some of the ways in which the interdisciplinary evaluation process itself can become an intervention (e.g., confirming suspected developmental problems, providing diagnostic clarification and education for parents, serving as a context for observation). Regardless of additional potential benefits, evaluations are fundamental to the identification of potential difficulties and development of appropriate services.

Identification of children's developmental problems inevitably includes formal assessment. Most states employ eligibility criteria based entirely or at least in part on standardized test scores, particularly for children 3–5 years of age. Although nearly uniformly the practice, there is a good deal of controversy about the usefulness of standardized tests within the early childhood professional community. Neisworth and Bagnato (2005), for example, criticize the use of "tabletop testing with tiny toys" (p. 46). To some extent addressing this issue, the DEC Recommended Practices suggest, in addition to the use of norm-referenced scales, developmental observations, criterion or curriculum-based interviews, and informed clinical opinion (DEC Recommended Practices and Examples: Assessment, 2005). Regardless of the criticism of one form of assessment or another, most disciplinary evaluations (e.g., educational, psychological) utilize multiple approaches and sources of information to identify children's developmental needs.

Documentation of children's development typically involves assessment of cognitive, physical, speech and language, self-help, and psychosocial areas. Psychologists, due to their training and expertise in assessment, often are uniquely prepared and qualified to provide cognitive assessment and administer standardized intelligence tests. Regardless of their assessment expertise, psychologists often are challenged to find developmentally appropriate instruments (Vig & Sanders, 2007a, 2007b); in fact, differing opinions about the suitability of intelligence tests for young children, as well as use of labels such as intellectual disability and mental retardation for young children, can compromise team functioning.

Assessment also includes mental health issues, particularly parent–child attachment, that may affect children's development and functioning. In discussing an integrated model of early intervention and infant mental health, Foley and Hochman (2006b) suggest each early childhood professional address parent–child relationships, in addition to identifying children's specific service needs (e.g., cognitive, language, motor). However, not all professionals are equally attuned to parent–child relationship issues. The need for professional familiarity with mental health issues points to another potential consulting role for psychologists. Indeed, psychologists may share their expertise in parent–child relationships and working with other early childhood professionals (e.g., occupational therapists, physicians, speech–language pathologists), ultimately improving services for children and their families.

Conceptualization and Implementation of Services Early childhood professional teams use varying degrees of collaboration as they develop, plan, and provide services for children and their families. To address some children's developmental needs, expertise not available within the early childhood team is required, necessitating referrals to external providers and service systems. As a result, in terms of making recommendations and referrals, early childhood professionals need familiarity with the range of evidence-based practice. In order to evaluate the efficacy of intervention alternatives, and avoid controversial fads and ineffective treatments, knowledge regarding research methodology and data-based outcome analysis is also essential.

Psychologists with substantial training in research and data-based problem solving are well suited to evaluate the efficacy of intervention approaches and services. Further, they help families as well as other professionals sort through available treatment options, identifying those likely to be helpful as well as those potentially ineffective or even harmful. Their expertise also helps determine evaluation plans to assess and help establish when and whether treatments are helpful.

PROVIDING SERVICES FOR FAMILIES

Family Adaptation to a Child's Disability Although having a child with a disability may create extra stress for families, most adapt well without the assistance of professionals (Barnett, Clements, Kaplan-Estrin, & Fialka, 2003). Others, however, experience challenges and face significant difficulties. Orsmond (2005) finds, compared to parents of children with typical development, parents of children with disabilities experience greater stress and social isolation, and often feel less competent as parents. The stress is likely due to children's behavior problems, rather than the disability or concurrent developmental delays.

Barnett et al. (2006) conducted a longitudinal study of adaptation in families having a child with a congenital disorder. Results suggest better adaptation for families of children with correctable conditions (e.g., cleft palate, physical disfigurement) than for neurological conditions not amenable to correction (e.g., cerebral palsy, spina bifida). Further, the severity of the disorder was less significant in terms of family functioning than was the disorder's correctability. Indeed, there were high rates of anxiety, depression, maternal stress, and poor attachment for the families of children with neurological conditions.

Based on earlier longitudinal research, Foley (2006) describes stages of a loss–grief cycle for parents of children with a disability. Cumulative losses (e.g., the dissonance between the desired child and the real child) theoretically result in several stages of grief (i.e., disequilibrium, acknowledgment, recovery, maintenance). The grief issues potentially influence family functioning, and families may benefit from psychological services addressing their challenges. More specifically, Foley recommends that psychologists discern what having a child with a disability means for the parent. The parent is then helped to develop a new "personal mythology" (belief system) that includes the child and to reconstruct an inner representation of the child based on the child's actual, rather than hoped-for, attributes. Foley notes that grief may re-emerge at times of transition.

Parent–Professional Collaboration   Members of early childhood teams establish parent–professional collaborations, partnerships, and/or relationships in implementing intervention goals. A number of models for family-centered practice, for example, have been described. In terms of general parent–professional collaboration, Turnbull, Turbiville, and Turnbull (2000) propose four models. The parent counseling/psychotherapy model assumes that having a child with a disability creates family stress or psychopathology that can be addressed through a psychotherapeutic approach. The parent-training model takes a different perspective, providing training that enables parents to teach their child. The family-centered model focuses on improving family well-being in order to optimize child outcomes; in this model, family strengths and choices are emphasized. The collective empowerment model expands the family-centered model focus to include access to resources and community participation. Collectively, these models suggest the range of collaboration that may occur between professionals and the families they serve.

Dunst (2002), based on a review of quantitative and qualitative research, identifies four models of parent professional collaboration (i.e., professionally centered, family allied, family focused, family centered). Not unlike the Turnbull et al. (2000) depiction, each of these models highlights varying relational and participatory components. The relational component includes clinical skills and attitudes about parenting capacities, and the participatory component involves practices that are flexible, provide opportunities for family choice, and are responsive to family priorities. According to Dunst (2002), early childhood team practices are less family-centered than is generally believed. Consistent with this point of view, Fialka (2005) observes that professionals often are more eager to form partnerships than parents. For example, parents may be uncomfortable expressing emotion or crying in front of a professional, a relative stranger with whom they are expected to have an instant closeness. If the professional fails to appreciate or understand that relationships gradually develop over time, parents may be reluctant to engage in or even return for further services.

Family Assessment Family assessment is apt to be more challenging than young children's assessment. Sources of challenge include, for instance, family ambivalence or discomfort about being assessed, stressors affecting the family, and parent characteristics potentially negatively influencing family functioning and child development. Early childhood professionals necessarily exercise both sensitivity and caution in conducting family assessments, setting appropriate limits on the scope of their explorations. Along this vein, Orsmond (2005) emphasizes, "A family typically enters an early intervention program because of concerns about their child's development, not because of difficulty within the family." Keeping these issues in mind, if handled with care, the family assessment process can assist in building the family–professional working alliance (Kalmanson & Seligman, 2006).

Most family assessments focus on the child and the family's experience parenting that child. Kelly, Booth-LaForce, and Spieker (2005) suggest some areas to explore with families (e.g., concerns about the child, description of the child, the child's typical day, the parent–child relationship, social support systems). These experts caution that challenges affecting parenting should be addressed in initial assessment only if parents bring up the issues and want to discuss them.

Based on family needs survey research, Bailey and Powell (2005) describe several appropriate areas to explore with families (e.g., handling children's behavior; needs for information regarding the child's condition, resources, and social supports). In contrast, families tend to find questions about marital interactions and parenting stress intrusive; indeed, professionals themselves find information of this sort to be of little use in providing services. More generally, the mere wording of questions may be significant in eliciting responses and communicating collaborative intent. For example, Bailey and Powell state that the wording of their research survey format was changed from "I need help" to "Would you like to discuss this topic with a staff person from our program?" (p. 162).

In conducting family assessments, sensitivity to cultural and diversity attitudes and practices is essential. Psychologists and other professionals should develop an understanding of differing cultural perspectives on child-rearing practices, roles of various family members, ideas about disability and its causes, attitudes toward intervention, and family health practices. Lynch's (2004) guidelines for home visitors suggest useful topics to explore with families representing other cultures: identification of family decision-making processes, beliefs about feeding, responses to child disobedience or night wakening, and the degree to which families wish to be directly involved in intervention. A lack of cultural sensitivity in family assessment may lead to intervention goals that are contrary to cultural beliefs and practices.

An important family assessment emphasis is the identification of family strengths (e.g., educational background, family functioning, extended family support). The recognition of strengths not only provides a more comprehensive assessment of children within their family context, but also highlights, for instance, avenues and capabilities that may be built upon in developing intervention options. For example, a parent with artistic talent may wish to explore ways that art materials may be used to help a child develop fine motor skills and finger dexterity. Members of a supportive extended family may be encouraged to help a child develop social skills at family get-togethers.

When environmental risk, related to issues such as psychosocial stressors or mental health issues, arises, early childhood teams have several assessment options. They may identify the team member(s) with appropriate background to address the family's issues; if an appropriate professional is not available within the team, an outside referral may be necessary.

Ultimately, family assessment involves numerous activities, such as the administration of formal instruments, interviews, and observation information. Kelly et al. (2005) and Krauss (2000) describe a number of useful family assessment instruments (e.g., Family Needs Survey, Family Information Preference Inventory, Family Support Scale). In the end, assessment of families with infants and toddlers is usually less formal than with families of relatively older youngsters. In actuality, family assessment is more of an ongoing process than a static activity; children's and families' needs change over time, necessitating adjustments in functioning, perspectives, and relationships with professional service providers.

Transition Planning Once children are identified as having a disability or being at risk, professional services usually represent ongoing processes. Often, part of the service provision process involves preparing children and their families for transitions (e.g., early intervention to preschool, early childhood special education to elementary school). Although legal mandates for early intervention require the development of transition plans, the process does not always proceed smoothly. Guralnick (2001) and Hanson (2005) point out that transitions may disrupt, among many things, established routines and relationships between parents and providers. In fact, new reminders of the child's disability and anxiety about the child's future may emerge.

Hanson (2005) suggests that transitions would occur more smoothly if the originating professional(s) provides information to the receiving professional(s), helps children acquire appropriate skills needed in the new setting, and makes arrangements for visits to the new environment(s). In addition, receiving professionals could exchange information and help arrange pre- and posttransition visits. To aid in the transition, Hanson (2005) suggests that families bring children's art, photographs, and family videos to planning meetings.

Information and Supports Many families want specific information about their child's condition. Research conducted in medical settings indicates parents' preference for timely information regarding their child's disability and their dissatisfaction with professionals' uneasiness about sharing comprehensive developmental information (Abrams & Goodman, 1998; Quine & Rutter, 1994). The common use of specific diagnostic labels (e.g., mental retardation) often leads families to various pertinent information resources (e.g., advocacy and support groups, Internet resources, professional literature) (Vig & Sanders, 2007a). For example, many families use the Internet as a source of information and support, especially in rural areas, and particularly those whose children have low-incidence conditions (Zaidman-Zait & Jamieson, 2007).

Although many informational resources are available, the quality of the material is quite variable. Zaidman-Zait and Jamieson (2007) caution that there is no review or approval of Internet content, and, in addition, information may be presented at a reading level too challenging for some families. Early childhood providers have an important role in pointing families toward reliable sources of information and support. Indeed, Zaidman-Zait and Jamieson suggest that professionals develop web sites designed specifically for and accessed by the families they serve.

Beyond information, families of young children with disabilities also benefit from a variety of community resources (e.g., adult education, financial support such as supplemental security insurance [SSI] for children with disabilities, library resources, respite services, transportation). Early childhood professionals' knowledge about, as well as access to, community resources may be invaluable to parents.

Finally, parent support groups also provide an important resource. Some parents value opportunities to meet with other parents of children with disabilities, while others do not. Parent groups often incorporate an educational focus as well as provide emotional support. Harbin et al. (2000) express concern that traditional support groups may be perceived as too therapeutic by many families. Instead, they observe that informal contact (e.g., picnics, other informal social activities) may offer support in a more preferred format.

Parent–Professional Consultation   In addition to providing direct services for children, many early childhood professionals offer consultation to parents about enhancing children's development. As consultants, professionals respect family preferences and cultural beliefs, minimizing any perceived power differential (Sandall, McLean, Santos, & Smith, 2005). Hanft and Pilkington (2000) offer some practical advice, especially for home-based consultation. For example, they caution not routinely bringing special toys or equipment into the home to model intervention approaches. One issue is that the materials will not be available to the family when the consultant leaves, likely reducing the probability that modeled interventions will be practiced and generalized.

Mental Health Services   Developmental services (e.g., early childhood special education, occupational therapy, physical therapy, speech–language therapy) usually do not target parent–child relationship issues. These relationship and other mental health issues typically involve infant mental health services and, not infrequently, dyadic psychotherapy. These services generally are provided in mental health facilities, often necessitating specific referrals to mental health professionals. Mental health practitioners provide early relationship assessment and support, clarifying and addressing issues (e.g., parent's childhood experiences of being parented) affecting the developing relationship between parent and child (Weston, 2005). Because many young children with disabilities also experience environmental risk (e.g., difficulties in parent–child interaction), early childhood providers usually are sufficiently familiar with infant mental health issues to make appropriate referrals.

Early childhood mental health issues are so significant that service delivery models integrating mental health are being proposed (Kalmanson & Seligman, 2006; Shahmoon-Shanok, Henderson, Grellong, & Foley, 2006). These models, for the most part, emphasize capitalizing on family strengths; they also suggest collaborative training of mental health and developmental specialists, cross-disciplinary supervision, and transdisciplinary team functioning. Although comprehensive and undoubtedly superior to current practice, there are numerous implementation barriers (e.g., high-risk parent–child interactions, inadequate funding mechanisms, narrow eligibility criteria) (Baggett, Warlen, Hamilton, Roberts, & Staker, 2007; Foley & Hochman, 2006a; Ginsberg & Hochman, 2006).

SERVICE COORDINATION

Initial EI legislation, pertaining to the birth-to-age-3 group, mandated service coordination for each family receiving services. The legislative intent was to avoid or minimize service fragmentation and enhance service coordination (e.g., assisting families in identifying service providers, coordinating and monitoring service delivery, coordinating interdisciplinary evaluations, helping develop transition plans, informing families of advocacy services, participating in IFSP development) (Bruder et al., 2005).

In theory, service coordinators may be involved with children and families at all stages of service provision (e.g., assessment, referral to professional service providers). In practice, however, few states practice a model in which a service coordinator is designated at the time of referral (Bruder, 2005). In fact, most service coordinators become involved well after the assessment has been completed, often at the time of IFSP development (Bruder, 2005).

Service coordination models include varying degrees of independence between the service coordinator and the agency providing services. Recently, Dunst and Bruder (2006) studied the relationship among three different service models and nine service coordination practices. Within the dedicated model (also known as the dedicated and independent model), the service coordinator role is strictly dedicated to service coordination. In this model, the service coordination agency operates independently from the agency providing the services. Within the intra-agency model (also known as the dedicated but not independent model), the service coordinator role also is dedicated solely to service coordination, but the coordinator works for the same agency providing the services. In the blended model, the service coordinator provides both service coordination and early childhood services.

Based on 299 completed surveys, from 46 states, the dedicated and independent model is associated with fewer service coordination practices and less contact with children and families than the intra-agency or blended models (Dunst & Bruder, 2006). Further, Bruder et al. (2005), surveying service coordination practices in each of 57 states and territories, find that 27% of respondents report using a dedicated model in which there was one person solely responsible for service coordination. Complicating the picture, variability in models apparently occurs in 47% of states and territories. Of note, the majority of states did not require training for service coordinators.

Bruder et al. (2005) also examined service coordination outcomes, conducting a series of studies to identify stakeholder (e.g., administrators, child care providers, program coordinators and providers, physicians) desired outcomes. Following complex data reduction and validation processes, prioritized outcomes include family self-sufficiency, family familiarity with community resources, family quality of life, enhanced child development, successful transitions, and effective services. Clearly, family services emerge as a leading set of priorities.

Along with priorities, there are a number of identified barriers (e.g., lack of credentialing for service coordinators, difficulties with quality control) to effective service coordination (Bruder & Dunst, 2006). For example, McWilliam (2006) suggests that some coordinators are intimidated by service providers, who often have strong academic credentials. Consequently, service coordinators may recommend unnecessary services, unwittingly misleading families into thinking more service provision is better than less. Service coordinators, although mandated by law to know about legislative regulations, child development, and community resources, often lack appropriate and/or desirable training (Bruder & Dunst; Ginsberg & Hochman, 2006; McWilliam). Coordinator caseloads are apt to be too large (Ginsberg & Hochman), sometimes due to inadequate funding. In fact, some states limit the number of contacts service coordinators are allowed with families (Dunst & Bruder, 2006), even restricting attendance at team meetings (Bruder, 2005). In the end, despite extensive research identifying service coordination best practice, implementation efforts often fall short.

CROSS-SYSTEMS COLLABORATION

Even though early intervention legislation mandates collaboration among providers as well as systems, this often serves as a goal and does not necessarily represent reality. However, there are some model programs demonstrating how collaboration may be achieved. One such program involves collaboration among 60 community agencies in a low-income Kansas county (Baggett et al., 2007). Collectively, the agencies address child and family needs in areas such as child care, developmental disabilities, domestic violence, education and job readiness, housing, mental health, public health, and substance abuse evaluation and treatment. The collaboration, initiated by an Early Head Start program, focuses on issues such as child find, referral, and screening activities. Interagency agreements established formalized partnerships for 12 of the agencies, targeting eligibility requirements, identification of risk domains, and selection of screening measures and procedures. Systems evaluation documented family satisfaction, which, in turn, furthered program growth.

A research partnership between university and child care systems also has been described (Walker, Harjusola-Webb, Small, Bigelow, & Kirk, 2005). Within this partnership, teachers and researchers work collaboratively as a team, with parents involved in evaluating intervention practices. For example, teachers helped define research questions and design the intervention strategies studied. Researchers inquired about teachers' preferences regarding meeting times as well as the compatibility of intervention strategies with planned classroom activities. The investigators emphasize benefits associated with partnerships (e.g., ecologically valid research), which differ from traditional top-down approaches where research activities are imposed on and not generated by teachers.

PERSONNEL PREPARATION AND TRAINING

Initial EI legislation mandated all EI personnel meet the highest entry-level standards; to accomplish this mandate, individual states implemented comprehensive systems of personnel development. Despite these efforts, training continues to be an unmet need and personnel shortages persist. Miller and Stayton (2005) comment that personnel preparation is influenced more by policy, legislation, and philosophy than by empirical data. They find that evidence-based practice in personnel preparation remains more of a goal rather than a reality.

A number of experts have investigated the adequacy of training for early childhood professionals. For example, Gallagher, Mowder, Sossin, and Rubinson (2006) conducted a survey of licensed psychologists in New York State; 194 respondents providing early childhood services offered information about their training. Fewer than half report completing a specialized graduate course in early childhood development, assessment, intervention, or diversity. Indeed, over 60% report acquiring background in these areas through on-the-job experience.

Further, Early and Winton (2001) completed a nationally representative survey of chairpersons and directors of early childhood teacher preparation programs. Only 60% of 4-year programs preparing teachers to work with children from birth to age 4 require a course in working with children with disabilities. In addition, only 60% of the programs require a course on infants and toddlers, and 63% practicum experiences with infants and toddlers. Bruder and Dunst (2005) surveyed university faculty, investigating the extent to which students in early childhood special education, occupational therapy, physical therapy, speech–language pathology, and multidisciplinary programs receive training in five EI practices (i.e., family-centered practice, IFSPs, natural environments, service coordination, teaming). Physical therapists apparently have the least training in these practices; no discipline provides adequate training in service coordination.

Inadequate early childhood training most likely is due to a number of factors. There is a shortage of faculty with specific expertise in early childhood (Early & Winton, 2001; Klein & Gilkerson, 2000), emphasis on children under age 4 is more apt to occur in 2-year than in 4-year teacher training programs, and credits do not necessarily transfer from 2-year to 4-year programs (Early & Winton, 2001). Further, training in infant mental health may not be available in graduate training programs, with availability more likely on postgraduate or postprofessional levels (Weston, 2005). Many universities providing clinical training do not necessarily offer teacher training, so inter-disciplinary training often is not available (Klein & Gilkerson, 2000).

Efforts to address the need for well-trained early childhood personnel are occurring; for example, a Web-based interdisciplinary, preservice, evidence-based practice was described by Lifter, Kruger, Okun, Tabol, Poklop, & Shishmanian (2005). The program, which offers an inter-disciplinary curriculum, includes faculty from five university departments (i.e., education/special education, nursing, physical therapy, school coun-seling/psychology, speech–language pathology). Participants were students from discipline-specific master's degree programs and field personnel seeking to be credentialed by the state. Empirical investigation of program efficacy, through field force analysis and faculty survey, indicates the importance of the university's organizational structure as well as strong ideas as forces facilitating change.

CULTURAL AND DIVERSITY COMPETENCE

Cultural (e.g., ethnic background) and diversity (e.g., religious, sexual orien-tation) competence is essential for early childhood professionals. One useful checklist for promoting cultural sensitivity, with an emphasis on early childhood settings, is available through the National Association of School Psychologists (NASP) web site (www.nasponline.org/resources). The con-tent, relevant to psychologists as well as other professionals, includes issues such as using appropriate foods during assessments and displaying materials reflecting children's cultural backgrounds.

Cultural competence is important when selecting settings for service provision and formulating intervention goals (Odom, 2000; Ostrosky & Lee, 2005). In introducing the DEC Recommended Practices, Sandall and Smith (2005) outline four principal, desirable, early childhood outcomes (i.e., enhanced family functioning, improved social competence, independence, problem solving). Setting aside the first outcome (i.e., enhanced family functioning), the remaining three outcomes seemingly reflect Western cultural values. For example, Japanese and American beliefs about attach-ment appear to vary considerably (Rothbaum, Weisz, Pott, Miyake, & Morelli, 2000), and a study of Korean and American mother–child inter-action (McCollum, Ree, & Chen, 2000) suggests that prioritizing autonomy and encouraging parents to be teachers are not necessarily values in Asian cultures. Thus, cultural sensitivity and competence are imperative when working with families.

Within a linguistically and culturally diverse society, families embrace differing beliefs about, for instance, child development, developmental dif-ferences and their possible causes, interactions with professionals and expectations associated with intervention, and parenting practices (American Academy of Pediatrics, 2007; Hanson, 2004; Lynch & Hanson, 2004). Further, cultural groups may vary considerably in their ideas about which family member(s) should address professionals' questions (Hanson). Early childhood professionals are not expected to exhibit familiarity with all cultural beliefs and practices, but are usually comfortable inquiring about family beliefs and incorporating those beliefs into service provision.

Sometimes, when working with families representing specific cultural/ linguistic groups, interpreters (for oral material) or translators (for written material) are necessary. Ohtake, Santos, and Fowler (2005) provide useful guidelines for working in these circumstances. For example, interpreters are cautioned to remain neutral and not change, distort, interject, or maximize/ minimize information. This is especially challenging when the interpreter belongs to the same cultural/linguistic group as the family as well as when the information likely will cause distress for the family. Ohtake et al. stress the importance of establishing partnerships with interpreters and considering them integral members of teams.

SUMMARY

There are numerous, significant issues related to the team provision of early childhood services for at risk children and those with disabilities, and their families. Each team professional member has field specific training and skills, and, hopefully, ultimately embraces the contributions of all professionals and family members in conceptualizing, planning, and implementing assessment, consultation, intervention, and prevention services. To the extent early childhood teams rely on evidence-based practice, their services address children's and families' needs, benefiting them as well as society as a whole. At the same time, evidence-based practice implies strong professional training, including knowledge and practice skills, provided within an ethical framework. In the end, to the extent that all these requirements for team functioning are met in the context of cultural and diversity competence and sensitivity, early childhood services provide an invaluable contribution to young children and their families.

REFERENCES

Abrams, E. Z., & Goodman, J. F. (1998). Diagnosing developmental problems in children: Parents and professionals negotiate bad news. *Journal of Pediatric Psychology, 23,* 87–98.

American Academy of Pediatrics. (2007). *Bright futures: Prevention and health promotion for infants, children, adolescents, and their families.* Elk Grove, IL: Author.

American Psychological Association. (2002). *Ethical principles of psychologists and code of conduct*. Washington, DC: Author.

Baggett, K. M., Warlen, L., Hamilton, J. L., Roberts, J. L., & Staker, M. (2007). Screening infant mental health indicators: An Early Head Start initiative. *Infants and Young Children, 20*, 300–310.

Bailey, D. B., & Powell, T. (2005). Assessing the information needs of families in early intervention. In M. J. Guralnick (Ed.). *The developmental systems approach to early intervention* (pp. 151–183). Baltimore: Brookes.

Barnett, D., Clements, M., Kaplan-Estrin, M., & Fialka, J. (2003). Building new dreams: Supporting parents' adaptations to their child with special needs. *Infants and Young Children, 16*, 184–200.

Barnett, D., Clements, M., Kaplan-Estrin, M., McCaskill, J. W., Hunt, Butler, C. M., et al. (2006). Maternal resolution of child diagnosis: Stability and relations with child attachment across the toddler to preschooler transition. *Journal of Family Psychology, 20*, 100–107.

Bruder, M. B. (2005). Service coordination and integration in a developmental systems approach to early intervention. In M. J. Guralnick (Ed.), *The developmental systems approach to early intervention* (pp. 29–58). Baltimore: Brookes.

Bruder, M. B., & Dunst, C. J. (2005). Personnel preparation in recommended early intervention practices: Degree of emphasis across disciplines. *Topics in Early Childhood Special Education, 25*, 25–33.

Bruder, M. B., & Dunst, C. J. (2006). Advancing the agenda of service coordination. *Journal of Early Intervention, 28*, 175–177.

Bruder, M. B., Harbin, G. L., Whitbread, K., Conn-Powers, M., Roberts, R., Dunst, C. J., et al. (2005). Establishing outcomes for service coordination: A step toward evidence-based practice. *Topics in Early Childhood Special Education, 25*, 177–188.

Chazan-Cohen, R., Stark, D. R., Mann, T. L., & Fitzgerald, M. E. (2007). Early Head Start and infant mental health. *Infant Mental Health Journal, 28*, 99–105.

DEC Recommended Practices and Examples: Assessment. (2005). In S. Sandall, M. L. Hemmeter, B. J. Smith, & M. E. McLean (Eds.). *DEC recommended practices* (pp. 51–69). Missoula, MT: Division for Early Childhood.

DEC Recommended Practices and Examples: Family-Based Practices. (2005). In S. Sandall, M. L. Hemmeter, B. J. Smith, & M. E. McLean (Eds.), *DEC recommended practices* (pp. 113–126). Missoula, MT: Division for Early Childhood.

DEC Recommended Practices and Examples: Interdisciplinary Models. (2005). In S. Sandall, M. L. Hemmeter, B. J. Smith, & M. E. McLean (Eds.), *DEC recommended practices* (132–146). Missoula, MT: Division for Early Childhood.

DEC Recommended Practices and Examples: Personnel Preparation (2005). In S. Sandall, M. L. Hemmeter, B. J. Smith, & M. E. McLean (Eds.), *DEC recommended practices* (pp. 195–210). Missoula, MT: Division for Early Childhood.

DEC Recommended Practices and Examples: Technology Applications. (2005). In S. Sandall, M. L. Hemmeter, B. J. Smith, & M. E. McLean (Eds.). *DEC recommended practices* (pp. 151–162). Missoula, MT: Division for Early Childhood.

Dunst, C. (2002). Family-centered practice: Birth through high school. *Journal of Special Education, 36*, 139–147.

70   FOUNDATIONS OF PRACTICE

Dunst, C. J., & Bruder, M. B. (2006). Early intervention service coordination models and service coordinator practices. *Journal of Early Intervention, 28*, 155–165.

Dworkin, P. H. (2000). Preventive health care and anticipatory guidance. In J. P. Shonkoff & S. J. Meisels (Eds.), *Handbook of early childhood intervention* (3rd ed., pp. 327–338). New York: Cambridge University Press.

Early, D. M., & Winton, P. J. (2001). Preparing the workforce: Early childhood teacher preparation at 2- and 4-year institutions of higher learning. *Early Childhood Research Quarterly, 16*, 285–306.

Etscheidt, S. (2006). Least restrictive and natural environments for young children with disabilities: A legal analysis of issues. *Topics in Early Childhood Special Education, 26*, 167–178.

Feldman, M. A. (2004). Self-directed learning of child-care skills by parents with disabilities. *Infants and Young Children, 17*, 17–31.

Fialka, J. (2005). The dance of partnership: Why do my feet hurt? *Young Exceptional Children Monograph Series No. 6: Interdisciplinary Teams*, 1–10.

Foley, G. M. (2006). The loss–grief cycle: Coming to terms with the birth of a child with a disability. In G. M. Foley & J. D. Hochman (Eds.), *Mental health in early intervention* (pp. 226–243). Baltimore: Brookes.

Foley, G. M., & Hochman, J. D. (2006a). *Mental health in early intervention*. Baltimore: Brookes.

Foley, G. M., & Hochman, J. D. (2006b). Moving toward an integrated model of infant mental health and early intervention. In G. M. Foley & J. D. Hochman (Eds.), *Mental health in early intervention* (pp. 3–32). Baltimore: Brookes.

Gallagher, S. F., Mowder, B. A., Sossin, K. M., & Rubinson, R. (2006). Continuing education interests of licensed New York State psychologists serving the zero to five-year-old population. *Journal of Early Childhood and Infant Psychology, 2*, 201–220.

Ginsberg, S., & Hochman, J. D. (2006). Policy, implementation, and leadership. In G. M. Foley & J. D. Hochman (Eds.), *Mental health in early intervention* (pp. 297–311). Baltimore: Brookes.

Green, B. L., Everhart, M., Gordon, L., & Garcia Getman, M. (2006). Characteristics of effective mental health consultation in early childhood settings: Multilevel analysis of a national survey. *Topics in Early Childhood Special Education, 26*, 142–152.

Guess, P. E., Baker, D., & Miller, T. (2006). Early intervention services: Family preferences in identifying natural environments. *Journal of Early Childhood and Infant Psychology, 2*, 63–77.

Guralnick, M. J. (2001). A developmental systems model for early intervention. *Infants and Young Children, 14*, 1–18.

Guralnick, M. J. (2004). Effectiveness of early intervention for vulnerable children: A developmental perspective. In M. A. Feldman (Ed.), *Early intervention: The essential readings* (pp. 9–50). Malden, MA: Blackwell.

Guralnick, J. J. (2005a). An overview of the developmental systems model for early intervention. In M. J. Guralnick (Ed.), *The developmental systems approach to early intervention* (pp. 3–28). Baltimore: Brookes.

Guralnick, M. J. (2005b). Inclusion as a core principle in the early intervention system. In M. J. Guralnick (Ed.), *The developmental systems approach to early intervention* (pp. 59–69). Baltimore: Brookes.

Hanft, B. E., & Pilkington, K. O. (2000). Therapy in natural environments: The means or end goal for early intervention? *Infants and Young Children, 12*, 1–13.

Hanson, M. J. (2004). Ethnic, cultural, and language diversity in service settings. In E. W. Lynch and M. J. Hanson (Eds.), *Developing cross-cultural competence: A guide for working with children and their families* (3rd ed., pp. 3–18). Baltimore: Brookes.

Hanson, M. J. (2005). Ensuring effective transitions in early intervention. In M. J. Guralnick (Ed.), *The developmental systems approach to early intervention* (pp. 373–398). Baltimore: Brookes.

Harbin, G. L., McWilliam, R. A., & Gallagher, J. J. (2000). Services for young children with disabilities and their families. In J. P. Shonkoff & S. J. Meisels (Eds.), *Handbook of early intervention* (2nd ed., pp. 387–415). New York: Cambridge University Press.

Harrison, H. (1997). Ethical issues in family-centered neonatal care. In A. H. Widerstrom, B. A. Mowder, & S. R. Sandall, *Infant development and risk* (2nd ed). Baltimore: Brookes.

Hochman, J. D., Katzive, M. C., Hillowe, B. V., Rothbaum, P. A., d'Emery, C., & Foley, G. M. (2006). Implementation of a coordinated system of early intervention and infant mental health. In G. M. Foley & J. D. Hochman (Eds.), *Mental health in early intervention* (pp. 325–341). Baltimore: Brookes.

Horn, E. & Jones, H. (2005). Collaboration and teaming in early intervention and early childhood special education. *Young Exceptional Children Monograph Series No. 6: Interdisciplinary Teams* (pp. 11–20).

James, K. S. (2007). Amplification options. In S. Schwartz (Ed.), *Choices in deafness: A parents guide to communication options* (3rd ed., pp. 99–103). Bethesda, MD: Woodbine House.

Kalmanson, L. B., & Seligman, S. (2006). Process in an integrated model of infant mental health and early intervention practice. In G. M. Foley & J. D. Hochman (Eds.), *Mental health in early intervention* (pp. 245–265).

Katzive, M. C. (2006). Procedural safeguards and professional standards: How the statute that created early intervention has shaped service delivery. In G. M. Foley & J. D. Hochman (Eds.), *Mental health in early intervention* (pp. 313–323). Baltimore: Brookes.

Kelly, J. F., Booth-LaForce, C., & Spieker, S. J. (2005). Assessing family characteristics relevant to early intervention. In M. J. Guralnick (Ed.). *The developmental systems approach to early intervention* (pp. 235–265). Baltimore: Brookes.

Klein, N. K., & Gilkerson, L. (2000). Personnel preparation for early childhood intervention programs. In J. P. Shonkoff & S. J. Meisels (Eds.), *Handbook of early childhood intervention* (2nd ed., pp. 454–483). New York: Cambridge University Press.

Knitzer, J. (2007). Putting knowledge into policy: Toward an infant-toddler policy agenda. *Infant Mental Health Journal, 28*, 237–245.

Krauss, M. W. (2000). Family assessment within early intervention programs. In J. P. Shonkoff & S. J. Meisels (Eds.), *Handbook of early childhood intervention* (2nd ed., pp. 290–308). New York: Cambridge University Press.

Kruger, L., & Lifter, K. (2005). From service teams to learning teams: A reconceptualization of teamwork. *Young Exceptional Children Monograph Series No. 6: Interdisciplinary Teams*, 83–98.

Lifter, K., Kruger, L., Okun, B., Tabol, C., Poklop, L., & Shishmanian, E. (2005). Transformation to a Web-based preservice training program: A case study. *Topics in Early Childhood Special Education*, 25, 15–24.

Lynch, E. W. (2004). Developing cross-cultural competence. In E. W. Lynch & M. J. Hanson (Eds.), *Developing cross-cultural competence: A guide for working with children and their families* (3rd ed., pp. 41–77). Baltimore: Brookes.

Lynch, E. W., & Hanson, M. J. (Eds.), (2004). *Developing cross-cultural competence: A guide for working with children and their families* (3rd ed.). Baltimore: Brookes.

McCollum, J. A., Ree, Y., & Chen, Y. J. (2000). Interpreting parent–infant interactions: Cross-cultural lessons. *Infants and Young Children*, 12, 22–33.

McWilliam, R. A. (2005). DEC recommended practices: Interdisciplinary models. In S. Sandall, M. L. Hemmeter, B. J. Smith, & M. E. McLean (Eds.), *DEC recommended practices* (pp. 127–131).

McWilliam, R. A. (2006). What happened to service coordination? *Journal of Early Intervention*, 28, 166–168.

Meisels, S. M., & Shonkoff, J. P. (2000). Early childhood intervention: A continuing evolution. In J. P. Shonkoff & S. J. Meisels (Eds.), *Handbook of early childhood intervention* (2nd ed., pp. 3–31).

Miller, P. S., & Stayton, V. D. (2005). DEC recommended practices: Personnel preparation. In S. Sandall, M. L. Hemmeter, B. J. Smith, & M. E. McLean (Eds.), *DEC recommended practices* (pp. 189–194). Missoula, MT: Division for Early Childhood.

Musick, J., & Stott, F. (2000). Paraprofessionals revisited and reconsidered. In J. P. Shonkoff & S. J. Meisels (Eds.), *Handbook of early childhood intervention* (2nd ed., pp. 439–453). New York: Cambridge University Press.

National Association of School Psychologists: NASP Resources. (n.d.) Promoting cultural diversity and cultural competency: Self-assessment checklist for personnel providing services and supports to children and their families. www.nasponline.org/resources.

Neisworth, J. T., & Bagnato, S. J. (2005). DEC recommended practices: Assessment. In S. Sandall, M. L. Hemmeter, B. J. Smith, & M. E. McLean (Eds.), *DEC recommended practices* (pp. 45–50). Missoula, MT: Division for Early Childhood.

Niparko, J., Marlowe, A., Bervinchak, D., & Ceh, K. (2007). The cochlear implant. In S. Schwartz (Ed.), *Choices in deafness: A parents guide to communication options* (3rd ed., pp. 105–120). Bethesda, MD: Woodbine House.

Odom, S. L. (2000). Preschool inclusion: What we know and where we go from here? *Topics in Early Childhood Special Education*, 20, 20–27.

Ohtake, Y., Santos, R. M., & Fowler, S. A. (2005). It's a three-way conversation: Families, service providers, and interpreters working together. *Young Exceptional Children Monograph Series No. 6: Interdisciplinary Teams*, 33–43.

Orsmond, G. I. (2005). Assessing interpersonal and family distress and threats to confident parenting in the context of early intervention. In M. J. Guralnick (Ed.), *The developmental systems approach to early intervention* (pp. 285–213). Baltimore: Brookes.

Ostrosky, M. M., & Lee, H. (2005). Developing culturally and linguistically responsive teams for early intervention. *Young Exceptional Children Monographs Series No. 6: Interdisciplinary Teams*, 21–31.

Quine, L., & Rutter, D. R. (1994). First diagnosis of severe mental and physical disability: A study of doctor–parent communication. *Journal of Child Psychology and Psychiatry, 35*, 1273–1287.

Rapport, M. J. K., McWilliam, R. A., & Smith, B. J. (2004). Practices across disciplines in early intervention: The research base. *Infants and Young Children, 17*, 32–44.

Rosenkoetter, S. E. (2005). Together we can: Suggestions from the pioneers of multiple early childhood programs. *Young Exceptional Children Monograph Series No. 6: Interdisciplinary Teams*, 45–58.

Rothbaum, F., Weisz, J., Pott, M., Miyake, K., & Morelli, G. (2000). Attachment and culture: Security in the United States and Japan. *American Psychologist, 55*, 1093–1104.

Sameroff, A. J., & Fiese, B. H. (2000). Transactional regulation: The developmental ecology of early intervention. In J. P. Shonkoff & S. J. Meisels (Eds), *Handbook of early childhood intervention* (2nd ed., pp. 135–159). New York: Cambridge University Press.

Sandall, S., Hemmeter, M. L., Smith, B. J., & McLean, M. E. (Eds.). (2005). *DEC recommended practices*. Missoula, MT: Division for Early Childhood.

Sandall, S., McLean, M. E., Santos, R. M., & Smith, B. J. (2005). DEC's recommended practices: The context for change. In S. Sandall, M.L. Hemmeter, B. J. Smith, & M.E. McLean (Eds.). *DEC recommended practices* (pp. 19–26). Missoula, MT: Division for Early Childhood.

Sandall, S., & Smith, B. J. (2005). An introduction to the DEC recommended practices. In S. Sandall, M. L. Hemmeter, B. J. Smith, & M. E. McLean (Eds.), *DEC recommended practices* (pp. 11–18). Missoula, MT: Division for Early Childhood.

Shahmoon-Shanok, R., Henderson, D., Grellong, B., & Foley, G. M. (2006). Preparation for practice in an integrated model. In G. M. Foley & J. D. Hochman (Eds.), *Mental health in early intervention* (pp. 383–422). Baltimore: Brookes.

Shonkoff, J. P., & Meisels, S. J. (2000). Preface. In J. P. Shonkoff & S. J. Meisels (Eds.), *Handbook of early childhood intervention* (2nd ed., pp. xvii–xviii) New York: Cambridge University Press.

Smith, P. J., McLean, M. E., Sandall, S., Snyder, P., & Ramsey, A. B. (2005). DEC recommended practices: The procedures and evidence base used to establish them. In S. Sandall, M. L. Hemmeter, B. J. Smith, & M. E. McLean (Eds.), *DEC recommended practices* (pp. 27–39). Missoula, MT: Division for Early Childhood.

Spagnola, M. & Fiese, B. H. (2007). Family routines and rituals: A context for development in the lives of young children. *Infants and Young Children, 20*, 284–299.

Spiker, D., Hebbeler, K., & Mallik, S. (2005). Developing and implementing early intervention programs for children with established disabilities. In M. J. Guralnick (Ed.), *The developmental systems approach to early intervention* (pp. 305–349).

Sweet, M. (2008). *A thinking guide to inclusive childcare.* Madison, WI: Disability Rights Wisconsin. http://www.disabilityrights.org

Turnbull, A. P., Turbiville, V., & Turnbull, H. R. (2000). Evolution of family–professional partnerships: Collective empowerment as the model for the early twenty-first century. In J. P. Shonkoff & S. J. Meisels (Eds.), *Handbook of early childhood intervention* (2nd ed., pp. 630–650). New York: Cambridge University Press.

Vig, S., Chinitz, S., & Shulman, L. (2005). Young children in foster care: Multiple vulnerabilities and complex service needs. *Infants and Young Children, 18*, 147–160.

Vig, S., & Kaminer, R. (2003). Comprehensive interdisciplinary evaluation as intervention for young children. *Infants and Young Children, 16*, 342–353.

Vig, S., & Sanders, M. (2007a). Assessment of mental retardation. In M. Brassard & A. Boehm. *Preschool assessment: Principles and practices* (pp. 420–446). New York: Guilford Press.

Vig, S., & Sanders, M. (2007b). Cognitive assessment. In M. Brassard & A. Boehm. *Preschool assessment: Principles and practices* (pp. 382–419). New York: Guilford Press.

Walker, D., Harjusola-Webb, S. M., Small, C. J., Bigelow, K. M., & Kirk, S. M. (2005). Forming research partnerships to promote communication of infants and young children in child care. *Young Exceptional Children Monograph Series No. 6: Interdisciplinary Teams*, 69–81.

Warfield, M. E., & Hauser-Cram, P. (2005). Monitoring and evaluation of early intervention programs. In M. J. Guralnick (Ed.), *The developmental systems approach to early intervention* (pp. 351–371). Baltimore: Brookes.

Wesley, P. W., & Buysse, V. (2006). Ethics and evidence in consultation. *Topics in Early Childhood Special Education, 26*, 131–141.

Weston, D. R. (2005). Training in infant mental health: Educating the reflective practitioner. *Infants and Young Children, 18*, 337–348.

Woodruff, G., & Shelton, T. L. (2006). The transdisciplinary approach to early intervention. In G. M. Foley & J. D. Hochman (Eds.), *Mental health in early intervention* (pp. 81–110). Baltimore: Brookes.

Zaidman-Zait, A., & Jamieson, J. R. (2007). Providing Web-based support for families of infants and young children with established disabilities. *Infants and Young Children, 20*, 11–25.

CHAPTER 3

Multicultural Evidence-Based Practice in Early Childhood

MADELINE FERNÁNDEZ

T HE UNITED STATES' strong immigration tradition and diverse cultural representation can be traced back to the colonial period. Religious freedom was one of the cultural dimensions that motivated western Europeans to sacrifice leaving their homeland and risk their lives for the opportunity to live in a society that afforded the promise of increased tolerance. Although tolerance was cultivated among the settlers who came from different countries of western Europe and whose living practices reflected a range of distinctive cultural patterns, this tolerance was not unilaterally extended to all groups as demonstrated by the experience of the Native American Indians. Although the immigration tradition in the United States has remained fairly consistent, varying factors (e.g., religious, economic, political) have been the primary catalyst for the immigration experience of different groups. The perception and process of integration of immigrant groups in the United States has also fluctuated significantly over time. With the influx of immigrants from divergent ethnic, religious, and language backgrounds from non–western European countries, questions of how different cultures are regarded and included have resurfaced. Attempts to address these cultural differences within the existing U.S. society have been reflected in the various paradigms that have evolved over the years (e.g., acculturation, assimilation, cultural pluralism, melting pot). These paradigms have represented a shift from an "Anglo Conformity Model" to an increased recognition of the value of ethnic identity (Bridges, 2004).

With globalization, the immigrant experience and resulting pluralistic society that was primarily identified within the United States is now a more common experience in many other countries as well. Societies continue to grapple with how to integrate groups from multiple cultural backgrounds. As practitioners, in particular, have been engaged in identifying how to best address the educational and mental health needs of individuals from diverse groups, there has been a growing impetus toward the systematic implementation of more sensitive approaches. The scope of the present discussion will first focus on a brief overview of bi/multiculturalism and bi/multilingualism as they have evolved in the United States, followed by multicultural practice issues in early childhood.

MULTICULTURAL THEORY

While considered by some as an approach, multiculturalism is perceived by others as a "general theory complementing other scientific theories to explain human behavior" (Pedersen, 1991, p. 6), representing a fourth perspective along with the psychodynamic, behavioral, and humanistic theories (Ponterotto & Casas, 1991). As a theory, multiculturalism attempts to establish a conceptual framework that incorporates the diversity of a pluralistic society while identifying mutually shared perspectives by emphasizing both culture-specific and culture-general characteristics. Characteristics of culture can serve to differentiate, as well as unite. Whereas the melting pot perspective emphasized culture-general characteristics that are shared across cultures while disregarding culture-specific characteristics, multicultural theory seeks to balance universalism, the underlying tenet of the melting pot premise, with relativism, which considers the culturally learned perspectives that are unique to each culture (Bridges, 2004; Pedersen, 1991).

The definition of culture becomes a critical component in multicultural theory. A broad definition of culture seeks to consider social system variables such as ethnographics, demographics (e.g., disability, education, gender, race, sexual orientation) and status affiliation, with the intent of preparing practitioners to deal with the complex differences among ourselves and the individuals whom we serve in a complicated social context. Diversity is often used to encompass these comprehensive cultural aspects that comprise individuals' multiple identities (American Psychological Association [APA], 2003). Knowledge about and familiarity with the interplay of individuals' multiple identities is crucial in providing effective mental health services.

Multicultural theory sparks debate as to whether the definition of *culture* that embraces diversity is too broad and so inclusive that it can become meaningless, rendering cultural differences as the equivalent of individual differences. There are inherent dangers in the adoption of a definition of *culture* that is either too broad or narrow (Pedersen, 1991). The APA (2003) distinguishes between multiculturalism and diversity and adopted a narrow multicultural definition in its multicultural guidelines by including "interactions between individuals from minority ethnic and racial groups in the United States and the dominant European–American culture" (p. 378). They further specified these ethnic and racial groups to include "individuals of Asian and Pacific Islander, sub-Saharan Black African, Latino/Hispanic, and Native American/American Indian descent" (APA, p. 378). While the focus of the present discussion will mostly adhere to the narrow definition of multiculturalism, many of the aspects discussed are relevant with diverse populations.

Psychologists' attempts to address the needs of individuals from diverse linguistic and cultural populations have led to an increased emphasis in promoting psychological practice from a multicultural perspective. The APA's (2003) multicultural guidelines call attention to psychologists' need to modify the "you/they" perspective when incorporating multicultural issues in our practice to a "we" perspective that recognizes that no one is "culture free." This paradigm shift reflects a critical stance in advocating that every individual practitioner must carefully reflect on how his/her own cultural lens interfaces with the individuals and groups whom they serve. The APA multicultural guidelines underscore that psychologists must first and foremost be aware of and knowledgeable about their own cultural perspectives as an initial step toward having an appreciation for and an understanding of how assessment, intervention, and research are impacted by these cultural references. Consequentially, the inherent cultural perspectives of psychological theories that are utilized should also be evaluated.

Bi/Multiculturalism

While the linguistic and cultural facets of an individual are intertwined, for the purposes of this discussion, these will be presented separately from an early childhood perspective. Both the terms *young child/ren* and *early childhood* will be used to refer to the developmental period from infancy to preschool age (0–5 years).

A multicultural framework requires examination of the individual's background from a deeper perspective. Beyond identifying the demographics of ethnicity and race, multiculturalism entails a comprehensive consideration of how these and related factors (e.g., oppression, prejudice) potentially impact the individual's functioning. Furthermore, multiculturalism in early childhood necessitates the evaluation of these factors and their impact on the child, as well as the parents and caregivers. The provision of psychological services to young children goes hand in hand with the provision of services to their parents and caregivers. A psychologist operating from a multicultural perspective becomes familiar with what the potentially relevant cultural factors might be for a particular young child and the family and how best to obtain the information related to those factors within their cultural framework.

One important dimension in multiculturalism to consider is the worldview of the young child's family. Knowledge of the child's and the family's worldview provides the psychologist with a framework that can facilitate the gathering of information about the child, increase sensitivity with regard to how and what pertinent questions to ask, and provide appropriate expectations about how responses might be given by the child and family. Familiarity with the child's and family's worldview diminishes the potential for judgments to infiltrate the interactions.

A related but distinctive aspect that is incorporated in multiculturalism, that is particularly applicable to early childhood, is knowledge about the family structure. Awareness of the range of family system structures and the patterns of responsibility associated with each structure among different cultural groups assists in identifying who the central figures are in the child's life. Such knowledge enables practitioners to more readily recognize the differences rather than deficiencies, as well as utilize the strengths of young children and their families from diverse cultural backgrounds. Combined with information about the worldview, an understanding of the family structure provides insights about the patterns of behavior exhibited by young children and the values families place on certain ways of fostering developmental milestones (Villarruel, Imig, & Kostelnik, 1995). Gender role definitions and interactions are also relevant cultural characteristics that may be embedded within the family structural patterns.

With the surge of early intervention and special education preschool services in the United States in the past two decades as a result of federal legislation (Short, Simeonsson, & Huntington, 1990), increased attention has been focused on young children's negotiation of more than one cultural framework or ethnic identity. How young children navigate between multiple cultures may be similar in some aspects to that of older children and adults. However, from a developmental standpoint, a marked difference in early childhood is that very young children have not yet fully established an identity within a particular cultural framework. The literature on ethnic identity formation in early childhood is limited, but preliminary findings suggest that young children's school identity and that of their home environment are not only different, but are also maintained separate with potential negative effects in the development of home–school partnerships (Rich & Davis, 2007). Within the context of ethnic identity, areas that have also been identified in early childhood include the significant role of multiculturalism in social and emotional development (Javier, 2007; Oades-Sese, 2006), as well as the development of self-concept (Fernández, 2006). Despite the importance of ethnic identity, social and emotional development, and self-concept in early childhood, these issues are in the beginning phases of being explored and insufficient, evidence-based measures are available to assess these areas in early childhood.

Acculturation, a measure of the degree to which aspects within an individual's particular culture interface with the cultural aspects of the mainstream culture, is a key aspect in multicultural discussions. The range of options along the continuum of language choice is one example of how individuals may vary in how they acculturate to the mainstream culture in one particular domain (e.g., speaking only one's native language, speaking either one's native language or the language of the mainstream culture depending on the context, or speaking only the language of the mainstream culture). The current understanding of acculturation is that it is a multidimensional construct with many domains, including language use/preference, social affiliation, daily living habits, cultural traditions, communication style, cultural identity/cultural pride, perceived prejudice/discrimination, generational status, family socialization, political, work, economic, social, religion and cultural values. (Chun, Organista, & Marín, 2003; Navas et al., 2005). Others have identified distinct acculturation strategies (i.e., assimilation, integration, separation, or marginalization) (Berry, 1997). From an early childhood stance, in most instances, the young child's family's level of adaptation to the changes resulting from their contact with the U.S. culture is a critical factor (Lieber, Chin, Kazuo, & Mink, 2001). Awareness of a young child's family's acculturation strategy and acculturation level in specific domains provides vital information with regard to the degree to which the child and the child's family may be experiencing stressors that impact level of functioning.

Varying levels of acculturation have been related to increased depressive symptomology (Canabal & Quiles, 1995), increased risk for psychiatric disorders and substance abuse (Ortega, Rosenheck, Alegría, & Desai, 2000), increased family conflict and affective difficulties in both parents and children, maladaptive behaviors and psychopathology in children (Lavretsky, Meland, & Plotkin, 1997), and adverse effects on standardized measures of intelligence (Flanagan & Ortiz, 2001). Inconsistent findings have been reported regarding the relationship of the level of acculturation or acculturation strategy to mental health and cognitive performance. Contradictory findings may be attributed to the evolving conceptualization of acculturation and the range of scales that have been utilized to correspond to the changes in how acculturation is measured (e.g., unidimensional, bidirectional). Data is emerging on acculturation and young children (Aguera Verderosa, 2008) and holds the promise of a valuable, evidenced-based construct.

Bi/Multilingualism

Psychologists have long demonstrated an interest in individuals who possess linguistic diversity. Early writings (Hakuta & McLaughlin, 1996) on bilingualism attempted to understand how the ability to speak two or more languages affected the organization of information and how this ultimately impacted cognitive performance, as well as social-emotional functioning. These areas have been and continue to be the focus of a vast array of the bilingual research and literature in psychological journals. However, the bulk of the early research was based on a deficit model that sought to investigate how cultural differences that were not representative of the dominant, western European culture contributed to certain disadvantages, particularly in the cognitive domains. Regrettably, many of the studies that reported deficits of bi/multilingual children on cognitive measures did so without regard to the normative deficiencies and the inherent biases of the instruments used, as well as without consideration of other variables that might have contributed to their findings.

During the initial phase of bilingual research in the United States, individuals who spoke two or more languages were theorized to develop and maintain separate brain systems corresponding to each language (Cummins, 1996), thus giving rise to and support for the notion that a second language *interfered* with an individual's, particularly a child's, capacity to learn and effectively utilize acquired skills (Gupta, 2000). Bi/multilingualism was strongly discouraged and parents were "advised" and sometimes admonished about the adverse consequences of exposure to more than one language for young children. With the emergence of research that incorporated better methodology and a broader or perhaps alternate perspective, during the next stage of bilingual research, findings contradicted the "deficit model." This second stage of bilingual research might be characterized as the "defense of bilingualism" phase. Findings during this period pointed to the flaws of prior research and demonstrated that children who were exposed to more than one language were not necessarily at a disadvantage. Particularly on cognitive domains where much of the focus was directed, it was demonstrated that bi/multilinguals performed at comparable levels to their monolingual peers when equally matched on relevant variables (Cummins, 1996).

Various constructs that attempted to capture the developmental and contextual aspects of bi/multilingual acquisition were proposed. Different types of bi/multilinguals were identified, such as coordinate and compound bilinguals, and distinctions between additive and subtractive bilingualism were made (Lambert, 1997). Subsequently, two types of childhood bilingualism were recognized, simultaneous (bilingual first language acquisition) and sequential (Genesee & Nicoladis, 2007). As categories of bilingual individuals were refined, an improved understanding of whether and how bi/multilingual individuals merged or differentiated their skills and experiences based on the language of contact was achieved. Research that systematically identified the multiple, inherent variables when working with bi/multilingual individuals was generated. Some of the primary variables that researchers began to consider were age and context of language acquisition. Up until this point, most of the research on bi/multilingualism had centered on school-aged children and adults.

A parallel shift from a deficit perspective to a more neutral one was also evident in the legislative and, subsequently, educational fields with regard to language acquisition, particularly second language acquisition. During what can be characterized as the deficit stage, children who entered schools and did not speak English were identified as *Limited English Proficient* (LEP; Bilingual Education Act, 1968). As the field became more sensitive to linguistic diversity, the terms *culturally and linguistically diverse* (CLD) and *English language learner* (ELL) were utilized to identify these children in an effort to acknowledge the experiences and skills that they already possessed, as well as to more accurately identify and reflect the skills that are being addressed from an instructional standpoint (Ortiz, 1992; Wiese & Garcia, 2001).

Another example of how a deficit model was applied to children who were bilingual is evident in how code-switching was initially perceived. Code-switching refers to bilingual individuals' ability to shift languages in mid-sentence or midconversation. Initially, the use of code switching was assumed to reflect bilingual individuals' language deficits (since they were thought to be unable to maintain one language when speaking). However, with later research, code-switching was found to reflect individuals' higher language skills, as it requires knowledge of the syntactical and phonological rules of both languages. The present view of code-switching is that of a normal pattern of interaction among bilinguals (Milroy & Muysken, 1998).

These shifts away from a deficit view of bi/multilingualism are particularly relevant in early childhood. With very young children, it is often the case that they have not yet developed or are in the very early stages of developing a diverse linguistic identity or competence. Typically, during early childhood, young children are exposed to their parents' language. In the United States, when parents speak one language in the home that is not English, many of these young children are not bilingual upon their entry into preschool; rather, they are monolingual in a language other than English. In early childhood, ELL may represent a more apt label for young children who, although they may be on their way to becoming, are not yet linguistically diverse due to their limited exposure to influences outside of their home environment. However, these children may still be considered culturally diverse, as even at their young age, they often have already begun to navigate between two or more cultures. Even once these children are exposed to English, they may be linguistically diverse for only a brief period. Particularly in early childhood, once introduced to English in school settings, many young children abandon their first language. In fact, one quarter of children who have access to interactions in two languages do not become bilingual (Pearson, 2007). There is another cohort of young children for whom CLD is the most suitable categorization. These young children are being raised in homes where two or more languages are used by the caregivers who may be from different cultural backgrounds as well. Yet another group of young children who are placed in foster care sometimes find themselves in homes where the caretakers' language and culture are different from what they had been exposed to in their biological home. Clearly, a wide continuum of cultural and linguistic patterns exists in early childhood (Genesee & Nicoladis, 2007). Each of these cultural and linguistic patterns may require variations in approaches with regard to how assessment and intervention are conducted (Souto-Manning, 2006).

Advances in the understanding of second language acquisition from the psycholinguistic, neurolinguistic, and educational fields, combined with psychological findings, have shed light on the functional organization of the multilingual brain, as well as how and when children exposed to two or more languages during early childhood are able to manage their languages and transfer knowledge learned from one language to the other (Proverbio, Adorni, & Zani, 2007). Young children have been reported to be able to identify language choice and initiate switching between languages by 2.5 years of age (Comeau, Genesee, & Mendelson, 2007). Findings such as these have dispelled the earlier "two brain" theory of bi/multilingualism, at least within the research community (Fernandez, Boccaccini, & Noland, 2007). The identification of critical second language acquisition factors was instrumental in highlighting the importance of the developmental and contextual under-standing of bi/multilingualism. This helped pave the way toward the current multidimensional theory of bi/multilingualism. With these more recent conceptualizations, bi/multilingual research may be entering a third stage, reflecting a "positive/assertive approach" whereby rather than disparaging or defending linguistically diverse individuals, nonjudgmental acceptance along with recognition of the benefits of bi/multilingualism and the specific advantageous skills that are developed as a result are being identified (Bialystok, 2007; Morton & Harper, 2007).

MULTICULTURAL PRACTICE IN EARLY CHILDHOOD

As mentioned previously, much of the impetus for the implementation of more culturally and linguistically sensitive and appropriate approaches in the United States has come from federal laws that have sought to address the needs of children who require special education services. As attempts to differentiate children with true learning difficulties from those who are culturally or linguistically diverse within the special education systems in the United States, more explicit criteria have been included in subsequent revisions of these federal mandates with regard to assessment and intervention strategies. In the last several years, the No Child Left Behind (NCLB, 2002) legislation has been a driving force in the utilization of effective, empirically-based practices (Conroy, Dunlap, Clarke, & Alter, 2005). Much work is needed in the identification and implementation of minimum standards that incorporate best multicultural practice. Despite the progress that has been made in encompassing a developmental perspective for individuals who are ELL and/or CLD, there are significant gaps in the current psychological literature, empirical findings, and professional guidelines with regard to the identification of methodology for how to best address assessment and intervention with young bi/multicultural and bi/multilingual children. Utilizing the framework of current multicultural and multilingual theories discussed earlier, what follows is an attempt to discuss assessment and intervention from an early childhood and evidenced-based perspective.

MULTICULTURAL ASSESSMENT IN EARLY CHILDHOOD

Early childhood psychologists are quite aware of the inherent difficulties that are encountered when assessing very young monolingual children (see Chapters 4 and 5). For early childhood psychologists who work with young children who are ELL and/or CLD, the challenges are compounded. The complexities faced in conducting unbiased assessments of young children who are ELL and/or CLD are not unique to early childhood and exist when assessing older children, as well as adults who are bi/multilingual (Rhodes, Ochoa, & Ortiz, 2005). A primary issue centers on the availability of psychologists who are trained and qualified to conduct assessments with young children who are ELL and/or CLD. There is a vital need for the establishment of uniform qualifications for psychologists who conduct assessments of young children who are ELL and/or CLD in the United States. To date, only two states, California and New York (National Association of School Psychologists, n.d.) have minimum standards (i.e., language proficiency, as well as training in working with ELL and CLD populations) that must be met by school psychologists who identify themselves as bi/multilingual. Interestingly enough, these minimum standards are required only of bi/multilingual psychologists working in school settings and not of licensed psychologists working in nonschool settings in those states. New York has also developed a cascade approach (Office of Vocational and Educational Services for Children with Disabilities, 2002) that identifies a continuum of qualified personnel that may conduct CLD assessments when appropriately credentialed psychologists are not available in the target language/culture. Given the anticipated need for increased numbers of psychologists who have received training on the assessment needs of bi/multilingual children in early childhood, the development of uniform, minimum qualifications required to conduct bi/multilingual assessments is paramount (Achenbach, 2005).

In addition to the identification of who is qualified, the "how" of appropriate ELL and CLD assessment of young children is another major obstacle encountered. There is also a lack of standard methodological approaches for use in the assessment process of young children who are ELL and/or CLD (Thordardottir, Rothenberg, Rivard, & Naves, 2006). That is, there is considerable variability in the process of determining when and how a child's diversity in language and culture should be incorporated. The term *bi/ multilingual assessment* can have a range of interpretations, depending on an individual's frame of reference. As Rhodes et al. (2005) point out, there is a significant difference between assessing a child bi/multilingually and assessing a bi/multilingual child, with many variations along the continuum. Issues with regard to how one determines which language to use before one even begins interacting with the young child and the child's parent(s)/caretaker(s) have been discussed at length. These discussions consistently extol the advantages of communicating with the child and parent(s)/caretaker(s) in the language(s) in which they are most fluent and/or comfortable. Even once the language(s) to be utilized for the assessment is identified, no clear standards exist to guide the selection of which language(s) should be used at particular junctures of the assessment.

In addition to considering language choice, multiculturally competent assessment calls for the integration of cultural factors (e.g., acculturation, cultural identity, family structure, attitudes toward mental health interventions/psychological assessment) in both the approach and process of the entire assessment interaction. The development of a cultural formulation can guide how this is achieved (Ecklund & Johnson, 2007). It is worth noting that practitioners should be knowledgeable about their own, as well as the child's and family's, cultural framework prior to the initial contact (APA, 2003).

A third critical aspect in the assessment of young children who are ELL and/ or CLD is the limited development of appropriate evaluation instruments. Despite guidelines (National Association for the Education of Young Children [NAEYC], 2005) advocating the use of alternate assessment approaches with very young children, the criteria for the qualification of specialized educational services (e.g., gifted programs, special education programs) often require some form of standardized scores (Shaunessy, Karnes, & Cobb, 2004). Many of the instruments available are merely translations of the English items, suggesting an implicit, albeit erroneous assumption of psychometric equivalency along with cultural and linguistic appropriateness (Achenbach, 2005; Fernandez et al., 2007). Cultural differences in the manner in which psychological problems are manifested, the models used to understand these problems, and the development of standardized assessment tools or assessment paradigms that incorporate these elements are in the early stages of research and development (Achenbach). The scarce availability of adequately standardized assessment instruments, particularly for use in early childhood (Fernández & Zaccario, 2007), often place psychologists working with young children who are ELL and/or CLD in a true quandary in which they find themselves making educational, as well as diagnostic decisions and recommendations based on experience and judgment rather than standard methodology (Bridges, 2004). Achenbach has stated that "until assessment instruments, diagnostic criteria, and taxonomic constructs are tested and supported in multiple cultures, we will not know whether they are valid for children in general or only for children in a single culture" (2005, p. 545).

This cursory review of some of the critical gaps that currently exist in the assessment of young children who are ELL and/or CLD can lead to only one conclusion. There is a fundamental lack of evidence-based, bi/multicultural assessment in early childhood and there is vast room for improvement. In some respects, this is not surprising given that some in the psychological field believe that evidence-based assessment in child assessment in general is limited (Achenbach, 2005). While the multidimensionality of young children who are ELL and/or CLD is recognized (Thordardottir et al., 2006) as one of the major reasons why there has been a reluctance to establish uniform procedures for assessment practices, there is a growing call among psychologists who work with this population to move beyond general guidelines and toward the establishment of minimum standards. Presently, individual psychologists working with young children who are ELL and/or CLD, by default, are designated with the task of individually integrating the approaches proposed by the emerging ELL and CLD assessment models with those proposed in the field of early childhood and developing their own standards for the particular population that they serve. Some ELL and CLD assessment models that begin to address the current gaps have been proposed (Flanagan & Ortiz, 2001; Gopaul-McNicol, & Brice-Baker, 1998; Rhodes et al., 2005). The establishment of minimum standards in the methods utilized for assessments of young children who are ELL and/or CLD should be developed and guided by strategies or models that are supported by data.

MULTICULTURAL INTERVENTION IN EARLY CHILDHOOD

As in the case with multicultural assessment, much of the literature that addresses multicultural interventions remains predominantly descriptive and theoretical (Bridges, 2004). The APA (2003) multicultural guidelines also refrained from providing prescriptive techniques to be utilized when working with racial/ethnic groups and identified multicultural interventions as an area to be further developed.

Attempts to identify ethnicity-specific interventions have been met with considerable debate. In part, some of the difficulty lies in the complexity of characterizing any cultural group without promoting stereotypes and a narrowness in approach. In addition, some question the viability of implementing approaches that have no or insufficient supporting data and at times, contradictory research findings (Achenbach, 2005; McIntyre, 2007, as cited in Kauffman, Conroy, Gardner, & Oswald, 2008). In a review of the literature on cultural differences and behavior principles, Kauffman et al. found no evidence for interventions based on cultural markers, such as ethnicity, gender, and religion, to be more successful. However, they acknowledged that the lack of evidence in the literature does not deny the possibility that different cultural groups may respond differently to behavior principles. In fact, Kauffman et al. highlight the lack of sufficient cultural information about participants in studies published in the leading behavioral journals that prevents the analysis of cultural differences. An inadequate representation of members of ethnic/racial groups is also noted in studies of evidence-based treatments (Whaley & Davis, 2007). Research findings on interventions applied with diverse ethnic groups and that clearly identify cultural characteristics are needed.

The multicultural dimensions highlighted previously should be incorporated as a first step in any intervention services provided to young children and their families. The use of acculturation measures, whether by interview, observation, or questionnaire (Rhodes et al., 2005), should help guide the extent to which and/or the manner in which intervention services are adapted for young children and their families.

An area that has received much attention in the literature is the use of code or language switching during interactions when working with individuals who are bi/multilingual. The findings regarding which language to use and whether to switch languages have been inconsistent, perhaps related in part, to the heterogeneity of the bi/multilingual population. The finding reported earlier about the facility of children, as young as 2.5 years of age, to switch between languages, suggests that this is an area in need of more research (Comeau et al., 2007; Kohnert, Yim, Nett, Duran, & Duran, 2005).

From an educational perspective, there seems to be adequate, evidence-based support for the instructional intervention of young children in their first language along with English (Fillmore, 1991; Makin, 1996). However, political and economic factors seem to thwart the generalized implementation of these findings (Wiese & Garcia, 2001).

ETHICAL AND TRAINING IMPLICATIONS

As a profession that is committed to developing knowledge and practice that enhances our understanding of ourselves and others (APA, 1992), training in multicultural assessment and practice should be a standard requirement for all psychologists, whether they are monolingual or bi/multilingual. Such training should go beyond an introductory multicultural sensitivity and awareness course and should include comprehensive knowledge about CLD methods and second language acquisition factors. As early childhood psychologists, we should be well versed in the critical steps toward providing services to young children whose backgrounds are different from our own, whether or not we speak their language (Achenbach, 2005).

Ethically, psychologists are required to utilize valid assessment measures with all populations. This includes young children and their families who are ethnically diverse and who are bi/multilingual. As a profession, we should strongly and more vocally pressure publishers of psychological assessments to invest in the development of adequate instruments that represent appropriate norms for young children who are bi/multilingual and bi/multicultural. In addition, with adequate training, monolingual and bi/multilingual psychologists will be able to address the cultural and linguistic needs of young children and be better equipped to address the overrepresentation of ELL and CLD young children in special education.

Multicultural practice in early childhood also calls for training in working with families and other collaterals. Skills in obtaining assessment data from multiple informants who have a different cultural perspective and who may be coping with acculturation stressors are vital toward providing adequate intervention services.

In order to implement multicultural, evidence-based practice well, improved multicultural evidence-based assessment is critical (Achenbach, 2005). A consistent thread noted in this review of multicultural, psychological services with young children and their families is the lack of adequate data to guide development and implementation of standardized approaches in assessment.

REFERENCES

Achenbach, T. M. (2005). Advancing assessment of children and adolescents: Commentary on evidence-based assessment of child and adolescent disorders. *Journal of Clinical Child and Adolescent Psychology, 34*, 541–547.

Aguera Verderosa, F. (2008). Examining the effects of language and culture on the Differential Ability Scales with bilingual preschoolers. *Dissertation Abstracts International: Section B: The Sciences and Engineering, 68*(10-B), 6990.

American Psychological Association. (1992). Ethical principles and code of conduct. *American Psychologist, 48*, 1597–1611.

American Psychological Association. (2003). Guidelines on multicultural education, training, research, practice, and organizational change for psychologists. *American Psychologist, 58*, 377–402.

Berry, J. W. (1997). Immigration, acculturation, and adaptation. *Applied Psychology: An International Review, 46*, 5–68.

Bialystok, E. (2007). Cognitive effects of bilingualism: How linguistic experience leads to cognitive change. *International Journal of Bilingual Education and Bilingualism, 10*, 210–223.

Bilingual Education Act. (1968). PL9O-247, 81 Stat 816.

Bridges, S. J. (2004). Multicultural issues in augmentative and alternative communication and language: Research to practice. *Topics in Language Disorders, 24*, 62–75.

Canabal, M. E., & Quiles, J. A. (1995). Acculturation and socioeconomic factors as determinants of depression among Puerto Ricans in the United States. *Journal of Social Behavior and Personality, 23*, 235–248.

Chun, P. C., Organista, P. B., & Marín, G. (2003). *Acculturation: Advances in theory, measurement, and applied research.* Washington, DC: American Psychological Association.

Comeau, L., Genesee, F., & Mendelson, M. (2007). Bilingual children's repairs of breakdowns in communication. *Journal of Child Language, 34*, 159–174.

Conroy, M. A., Dunlap, G., Clarke, S., & Alter, P. J. (2005). A descriptive analysis of positive behavioral intervention research with young children with challenging behavior. *Topics in Early Childhood Special Education, 25*, 156–166.

Cummins, J. (1996). *Negotiating Identities: Education for empowerment in a diverse society.* Ontario, CA: California Association for Bilingual Education.

Ecklund, K., & Johnson, W. B. (2007). Toward cultural competence in child intake assessments. *Professional Psychology: Research and Practice, 38*, 356–362.

Fernandez, K., Boccaccini, M. T., & Noland, R. M. (2007). Professionally responsible test selection for Spanish-speaking clients: A four-step approach for identifying and selecting translated tests. *Professional Psychology: Research and Practice, 38*, 363–374.

Fernández, M. (2006). Bilingual preschoolers: Implications for the development of identity and self-concept. *Journal of Early Childhood and Infant Psychology, 2*, 5–16.

Fernández, M., & Zaccario, M. (2007). Bayley III: A preliminary overview. *Journal of Early Childhood and Infant Psychology, 3*, 223–233.

Fillmore, L. W. (1991). When learning a second language means losing the first. *Early Childhood Research Quarterly, 6*, 323–347.

Flanagan, D. P., & Ortiz, S. O. (2001). *Essentials of cross-battery assessment.* Hoboken, NJ: Wiley.

Genesee, F., & Nicoladis, E. (2007). Bilingual first language acquisition. In E. Hoff & M. Shatz (Eds.), *Blackwell handbook of language development* (pp. 324–342). MA: Blackwell.

Gopaul-McNicol, S., & Brice-Baker, J. (1998). *Cross-cultural practice: Assessment, treatment, and training.* New York: Wiley.

Gupta, A. F. (2000). Bilingualism in the cosmopolis. *International Journal of the Sociology of Language, 143*, 107–119.

Hakuta, K., & McLaughlin, B. (1996). Bilingualism and second language learning: Seven tensions that define the research. In D. Berliner & R. Calfee (Eds.), *Handbook of educational psychology* (pp. 603–621). New York: Macmillan Library Reference.

Javier, R. A. (2007). *The bilingual mind: Thinking, feeling and speaking in two languages.* New York: Springer Science & Business Media.

Kauffman, J. M., Conroy, M., Gardner, R., III, & Oswald, D. (2008). Cultural sensitivity in the application of behavior principles to education. *Education and Treatment of Children, 31,* 239–262.

Kohnert, K., Yim, D., Nett, K., Duran, P. F., & Duran, L. (2005). Intervention with linguistically diverse preschool children: A focus on developing home languages(s). *Language, Speech and Hearing Services in Schools, 36,* 251–263.

Lambert, W. E. (1997). The effects of bilingualism on the individual: Cognitive and sociocultural consequences. In P. Hornby (Ed.), *Bilingualism: Psychological, social and educational implications* (pp. 15–27). Washington, DC: Georgetown University Press.

Lavretsky, E., Meland, D., & Plotkin, D. (1997). Children from the former Soviet Union. In G. Johnson-Powell, J. Yamamoto, G. E. Wyatt, & W. Arroyo (Eds.), *Transcultural child development: Psychological assessment and treatment* (pp. 328–346). New York: Wiley.

Lieber, E., Chin, D., Kazuo, N., & Mink, I. T. (2001). Holding on and letting go: Identity and acculturation among Chinese immigrants. *Cultural Diversity & Ethnic Minority Psychology, 7*(3), 247–261.

Makin, L. (1996). Bilingualism in early childhood education. What do we know? What do we do? *Learning Languages, 1,* 24–27.

McIntyre, T. (2007). Are behaviorist interventions inappropriate for culturally different youngsters with learning and behavior disorders? http://maxweber.hunter.cuny.edu/pub/eres/EDSPC715jMCINTYRE/CBehModR.html Retrieved June 7, 2008.

Milroy, L., & Muysken, P. (Eds.). (1998). *One speaker, two languages: Cross-disciplinary perspectives on code-switching.* New York: Cambridge University Press.

Morton, J. B., & Harper, S. N. (2007). What did Simon say? Revisiting the bilingual advantage. *Developmental Science, 10,* 719–726.

National Association for the Education of Young Children (NAEYC). (2005). *Screening and assessment of young English-language learners: Supplement to the NAEYC position statement on early childhood curriculum, assessment, and program evaluation.* Washington, DC: Author.

National Association of School Psychologists. (n.d.). *Cultural competence FAQs.* Retrieved June 7, 2008, from www.nasponline.org/resources/culturalcompetence/faq.aspx.

Navas, M., García, M., Sánchez, J., Rojas, A., Pumares, P., & Fernández, J. (2005). Relative Acculturation Extended Model (RAEM): New contributions with regard to the study of acculturation. *International Journal of Intercultural Relations, 29,* 21–37.

No Child Left Behind Act of 2001. (2002). Pub. L. No. 107–110, 115 Stat. 1425.

Oades-Sese, G. V. (2006). The relationship among child resilient attributes, acculturation, bilingualism and social competence of Hispanic American preschool children. *Dissertation Abstracts International: Section B: The Sciences and Engineering, 67* (6-B), 3484.

Office of Vocational and Educational Services for Children with Disabilities of the New York State Education Department. (2002). *Key Issues in Bilingual Special*

Education Work Paper #5: Qualified Special Education Personnel. Retrieved June 5, 2008, from www.vesid.nysed.gov/lsn/bilingual/trainingmodules05rr.pdf.

Ortega, A., Rosenheck, R., Alegría, M., & Desai, R. (2000). Acculturation and the lifetime risk of psychiatric and substance abuse disorders among Hispanics. *Journal of Nervous and Mental Disease, 188,* 728–735.

Ortiz, A. (1992). Assessing appropriate and inappropriate referral systems for LEP special education students. In Office of Bilingual Education and Minority Languages Affairs (Ed.), *Focus on Evaluation and Measurement: Proceedings of the National Research Symposium on Limited English Proficient Student Issues, 1.* Retrieved September 7, 2008, from www.ncela.gwu.edu/pubs/symposia/second/vol1/assessing.html.

Pearson, B. Z. (2007). Social factors in childhood bilingualism in the United States. *Applied Psycholinguistics, 28,* 399–410.

Pedersen, P. B. (1991). Multiculturalism as a generic approach to counseling. *Journal of Counseling & Development, 70,* 6–12.

Ponterotto, J. G., & Casas, J. M. (1991). *Handbook of racial/ethnic minority counseling research.* Springfield, IL: Charles C. Thomas.

Proverbio, A. M., Adorni, R., & Zani, A. (2007). The organization of multiple languages in polyglots: Interference or independence? *Journal of Neurolinguistics, 20,* 25–49.

Rhodes, R. L., Ochoa, S. H., & Ortiz, S. O. (2005). *Assessing culturally and linguistically diverse students: A practical guide.* New York: Guilford Press.

Rich, S., & Davis, L. (2007). Insights into the strategic ways in which two bilingual children in the early years seek to negotiate the competing demands on their identity in their home and school worlds. *International Journal of Early Years Education, 15,* 35–47.

Shaunessy, E., Karnes, F., & Cobb, Y. (2004). Assessing culturally diverse potentially gifted students with nonverbal measures of intelligence. *School Psychologist, 58,* 99–102.

Short, R. J., Simeonsson, R. J., & Huntington, G. S. (1990). Early intervention: Implications of Public Law 99-457 for professional child psychology. *Professional Psychology: Research and Practice, 21,* 88–93.

Souto-Manning, M. (2006). Families learn together: Reconceptualizing linguistic diversity as a resource. *Early Childhood Education Journal, 33,* 443–446.

Thordardottir, E., Rothenberg, A., Rivard, M., & Naves, R. (2006). Bilingual assessment: Can overall proficiency be estimated from separate measurement of two languages? *Journal of Multilingual Communication Disorders, 4,* 1–21.

Villarruel, F. A., Imig, D. R., & Kostelnik, M. J. (1995). Diverse familias. In E. Garcia & B. McLaughlin (Eds.), *Meeting the challenges of linguistic and cultural diversity in early childhood education* (pp. 103–124). New York: Teachers College Press.

Whaley, A. L., & Davis, K. E. (2007). Cultural competence and evidence-based practice in mental health services: A complementary perspective. *American Psychologist, 62,* 563–574.

Wiese, A., & Garcia, E. (2001). The Bilingual Education Act: Language minority students and U.S. federal education policy. *International Journal of Bilingual Education and Bilingualism, 4,* 229–249.

PART II

EVIDENCE-BASED INFANT
AND EARLY CHILDHOOD
PRACTICE: ASSESSMENT
AND INTERVENTION

CHAPTER 4

Assessment of Infants and Toddlers

MICHELE ZACCARIO,
K. MARK SOSSIN, and
JACQUELINE DEGROAT

T HE ASSESSMENT OF infants and toddlers is *particularly* challenging due to the breadth of skills that need to be considered, the compliance and motivational issues that hallmark the evaluation of such a young population, and the selection of appropriate tests and measures. An evaluating psychologist needs to be well versed in developmental milestones; typical versus atypical development; cognitive, language, play, and motor skills acquisition; and infant mental health issues, attachment, and social-emotional development (Greenspan & Wieder, 2006). Vulnerable populations need to be understood, such as preterm infants and children with acquired or developmental disabilities, as well as medical, environmental, cultural, and socioeconomic contributing factors (Fernandez & Zaccario, 2007; Individuals with Disabilities Education Improvement Act, 1990, 1997, 2004; Lichtenberger, 2005; Lollock, 2001; National Association for the Education of Young Children [NAEYC], 2005; Ross & Lawson, 1997). Any one of the aforementioned points can alone constitute a chapter or book, and thus an in-depth analysis of each is beyond the scope of this particular discussion. Instead, this chapter will focus on providing an overview of infant and toddler assessment by delineating what constitutes a thorough psychological evaluation along with the appropriate and relevant evidence-based techniques, practices, and evaluation tools.

THE IMPORTANCE OF COLLABORATION

An integrated developmental model of infant and toddler assessment (Meisels & Atkins-Burnett, 2000) involves multiple sources of information and has as its cornerstone the child's relationship and interactions with his or her most trusted caregivers. There is respect for and utilization of standardized and validated measurement tools, but also an emphasis on the uniqueness and multidimensionality of factors that each child and parent-child relationship brings to the fore. This necessitates a clinical perspective and a set of observations that capture the complex neurodevelopmental and relational worlds within which the infant or toddler is growing up. The importance of professional-practice reliance on clinical judgment in early childhood assessment has been highlighted by Bagnato and Simeonsson (2007). In addition, Neisworth and Bagnato (2004; Bagnato & Neisworth, 1994) have strenuously expressed concerns that overreliance on conventional, norm-referenced tests and decontextualized practices risk the mismeasurement of young exceptional children, and hence may impede their opportunities. They have articulated eight standards captured by *authentic assessment* methods: utility, acceptability, authenticity, equity, sensitivity, convergence, congruence, and collaboration; and emphasize that assessment of young children requires close collaboration with parents (Brink, 2002) as well as with interdisciplinary colleagues.

CHILD AND FAMILY HISTORY

A thorough infant and toddler assessment often begins with an in-depth caregiver interview and history (Benoit, Zeanah, Parker, Nicholson, & Coolbear, 1997). Ideally, this history should take place with each parent or primary caregiver present, and with ample time allotted for thorough coverage of pertinent information. Most often, these interviews last a couple to several hours, but there are some interview formats, like those conducted by and advocated for by Stanley Greenspan and colleagues (Greenspan & Wieder, 2006), that take place over a period of 6–7 weeks, and are extensive before ever meeting the infant. Generally, interviews are typically broad in scope and detailed in nature, but should always remain respectful of parental agenda and primary concerns. At its culmination, the caregiver interview will yield information regarding family composition and dynamics; parental history; sibling history (if applicable); conception, prenatal, birth, and postnatal history; the child's medical and developmental histories; and the child's social-emotional history.

Regarding family history and dynamics, it is often useful to begin with a genogram (McGoldrick, Gerson, & Petry, 2008) mapping two to three generations of maternal and fraternal family members. If a genogram is not conducted, then birth order, relevant diagnostic issues, and important biological and experiential incidents should be obtained regarding the parents' and (if possible) the grandparents' generations. Parental developmental, medical, psychiatric, academic, social, and work histories are ascertained, including any significant milestones or notable difficulties. Finally, current family structure, including siblings, birth order, and parental roles, are determined. Interviewing regarding family dynamics may also reveal further information about the parental relationship, the degree of involvement of each caregiver with the infant, and level of satisfaction within the family situation.

Pre-pregnancy history should be respectfully gleaned, including: conception planning and achievement of pregnancy, pregnancy course, potential stressors and complications, potential exposure to toxins and tetragenic substances, and length of pregnancy. Birth, perinatal, and postnatal histories need to be documented, including length of labor and mode of delivery, perinatal complications, Apgar scores, postnatal complications, length of hospital stay for mother and infant, and condition of mother and infant at discharge.

Before concluding the interview process, the clinician must turn attention to the child's personal history, including developmental milestones to date, adaptive skills, feeding and sleeping histories, infant attachment and bonding, participation in play groups/day care/nursery school, socialization skills, disposition, and temperament. Other relevant information, including significant historical events (moves, losses, etc.) may also be ascertained. Additionally, parent(s) and caregiver(s) should be given the opportunity to add additional information that they feel might be pertinent.

By the end of the interview process, an examiner will ideally have enough relevant biographical, historical, developmental, and familial data to write a thorough background information section in a report. Time, budget, or other constraints may preclude ascertaining all the aforementioned data, so priority should be given to the most pertinent information and the priorities of the parents.

FORMULATING BEHAVIORAL OBSERVATIONS

Careful behavioral observations in both the clinical and naturalistic (home) environment are essential components of the infant/toddler assessment process. Opportunities to informally observe the infant and toddler in caregiver dyads and triads, with siblings and/or peers, and during different times of day and circumstances can provide invaluable information about the child's developmental trajectory, social abilities, temperament, bonding, and play skills. During these informal observations, evaluators take note of the child's mood and affect, emotional regulation, social interest and reciprocity, ability to calm and soothe, fluidity of movement, expressive and receptive language skills, joint attention, and ability to tolerate transitions.

During more formal aspects of the assessment process, thoughtful observations are made with regard to praxis, gross motor abilities, handedness (if applicable), motivation and interest in test items, problem-solving skills, visual scanning skills, and attention and concentration skills. In addition, it is once again important to note mood and affect, modulation of emotion, ability to tolerate transitions, social interest, and joint attention skills. A child's ability to follow directives, to express verbally or nonverbally under demand conditions, and to tolerate separation from primary caregivers is also highly relevant.

Observations of both the formal and informal aspects of the evaluation process assist an examiner with formation of general and specific impressions of the infant or toddler, inform treatment recommendations, and provide valuable information for a culminating report and the parental feedback process.

VIDEO CODING IN THE CONTEXT OF EVALUATING SOCIAL–EMOTIONAL AND INTERACTIVE FUNCTIONING

For the purposes of close observational coding of behavioral nuances, bearing on the child, the parent, and the dyad, research-born measures have become useful for the clinician sufficiently trained in the methodology applied. Hence, clinical evaluation of an infant or toddler may include video analysis of the child while he or she is relating to a caregiver. Qualitative aspects of the parent-child relationship have been taped using the Parent-Child Early Relational Assessment (PCERA; Clark, 1985; Thomas & Clark, 1998), allowing the clinician to organize and scale many features, including the child's style of being with the parent and vice versa, as well as the overall affective tone of the dyad. As with other video-coding methods, use of the PCERA involves training and the attainment of reliability. A total of 65 items are distributed across 29 parents, 27 infant, and 8 dyadic items, and each is scored on a 5-point Likert scale in terms of frequency, duration, and intensity. In clinical applications, it is not necessary to use all items. In a research application, Kivijarvi, Räihä, Kaljonen, Tamminen, and Piha (2005) exemplify the utilization of a select group of PCERA items by operationalizing "Maternal Sensitive Behavior" in the aggregate of seven specific variables.

Similarly, the Emotional Availability (EA) Scales (Biringen, 2000; Biringen et al., 2005) offer a clinically relevant way to denote reciprocal emotional signaling between child and parent/caregiver, tapping such crucial and attachment-related variables as parental sensitivity, intrusiveness, structuring, and ability to regulate negative emotions, as well as the child's responsiveness and pleasure when interacting with the parent/caregiver. By linking EA results to different children's clinical presentations (between 6 weeks and 3 years, 10 months), the EA Scales have been shown to have direct relevance to the clinical assessment process and for the determination of dyadic risk status (Wiefel et al., 2005), providing information pertaining to treatment recommendations as well as providing a powerful tool for family feedback.

In addition, the Functional Emotional Assessment Scale (FEAS; Greenspan, DeGangi, & Wieder, 2001) also offers the clinician a way of observing and profiling the infant/toddler in the context of relating to a parent and or caregiver, and has been normed from 7 months to 4 years of age. The FEAS was specifically designed for young children experiencing problems in self-regulation, attachment, communication, attention, and behavioral control. Framed by Greenspan's developmental framework of the six levels of emotional development, the FEAS incorporates distinct child and caregiver scales. The FEAS can be usefully incorporated into assessment of young children deemed at risk for autism spectrum disorders, as can the Autism Diagnostic Observation Schedule (ADOS; Lord et al., 2000), Autism Diagnostic Interview-Revised (ADI-R; Lord, Rutter, & Le Couteur, 1994), Social Responsivity Scale (SRS; Constantino et al., 2003) and other measures reviewed in Chapter 17 (this volume).

The importance of nonverbal behavior in infancy and in parent–infant interaction has been frequently demonstrated (Beebe, 2006; Trevarthen, 2005). Toward this end, systems for the assessment of facial expressions and communicative behaviors has been enhanced through the development of the Baby Facial Action Coding System (Baby FACS; Oster, 2005), a biologically informed and highly detail oriented anatomically-based coding system. Stepping from research to clinical applications, informed coding of affect-, attention- and regulatory-relevant facial expressions, especially in interactive context, can generate useful ideas regarding the child's affective repertoire and specific reactivity. Furthermore, training in and application of Laban-rooted developmentally sensitive movement coding systems (e.g., Tortora, 2006) also informs the clinician regarding elements of affect, temperament, learning styles, states of comfort and discomfort, and relational dispositions, as reflected in the original work of Kestenberg (Kestenberg & Buelte, 1977) and in further work pertaining to the Kestenberg Movement Profile (KMP; Kestenberg-Amighi, Loman, Lewis, & Sossin, 1999; Sossin, 2002). Extending research to practice, the KMP can also be applied in assessment of interactional features, such as denoting concordance, discordance, and stress transmission (Sossin & Birklein, 2006).

DEVELOPMENTAL EVALUATION

A thorough infant and toddler assessment will necessarily also include an evaluation of developmental milestones and progression: namely, cognition, social-emotional skills (to be discussed more thoroughly in the next section and in Chapter 13), speech and language, gross and fine motor skills, and adaptive skills. Often, a psychologist's developmental evaluation distinctly surveys cognition and social-emotional development while more generally assessing motor and speech and language skills. Follow-up evaluations performed by speech and language therapists, occupational therapists, and physical therapists tend to be more in-depth evaluations of a specific domain of skills. Typically, at its culmination, a developmental evaluation is thorough enough to vividly and aptly describe a child's developmental processes, to detect areas of strength and difficulty, and to justify any needs for further assessment. Thus, knowledge of early childhood, developmental milestones, and appropriate training in assessment tools is essential before such an undertaking can commence.

There are many infant and toddler developmental assessment instruments that are available to a clinician and potentially appropriate for an adequate survey of skills. Some devices are broadband in scope, surveying many different skills, and some are narrow, surveying only language (e.g., Preschool Language Scale [PLS-4], Zimmerman, Steiner, & Pond, 2002) or motor skills (e.g., Movement Assessment of Infants [MAI], Chandler, Skillen, & Swanson, 1980; Peabody Developmental Motor Scale [PDMS-2], Folio & Fewell, 2000) for example. Some are standardized, meaning that they have been developed utilizing extensive normative samples (e.g., Battelle Developmental Inventory-Second Edition [Battelle-II], Newborg, 2004; Bayley Scales of Infant and Toddler Development, Third Edition [Bayley-III], Bayley, 2006; Mullen Scales of Early Learning [MSEL], Mullen, 1995), and some are criterion- or curriculum-referenced (Hawaii Early Learning Profile Scales, HELP-2, Parks, 1997). Some are designed to be screening devices only (e.g., Brigance Screens II, Brigance, 1985; Denver-II, Frankenburg, Dodds, & Archer, 1990), while still others are designed to be comprehensive batteries (e.g., Battelle-II, Bayley-III, MSEL).

In the past several years, practice standards have moved toward the utilization of empirically derived, norm-referenced testing such as the Battelle-II (Newborg, 2004), Bayley-III (Bayley, 2006), and MSEL (Mullen, 1995). Governmentally funded programs, such as Early Intervention (Ginsberg & Hochman, 2006), have increasingly moved toward suggesting and even mandating the elimination of criterion-referenced checklists, screeners, and narrow-band tests, in favor of these comprehensive and normative batteries, and such devices have always been the standard for infant developmental research and publications. However, clinicians may still choose checklists and criterion-referenced tests for qualitative information on developmental milestone achievement. Whichever device or devices are chosen, ultimately both quantitative and qualitative information is necessary for an adequate understanding of development. The clinician is challenged to balance the benefits of a well-normed instrument with the richness of parental report and attribution measures, alongside appropriate use of criterion measures, while still exercising expert observational skills and clinical judgment. The importance of ecological validity, thorough knowledge of early development, and cultural sensitivity in such appraisal cannot be underestimated. Cultural factors have been shown to remarkably bear upon infant appraisal. The neurobehavioral repertoires of Chinese and Japanese neonates, for example, assessed using the Brazelton Neonatal Behavioral Assessment Scale were shown to differ such that Japanese newborns habituated more readily to stimuli and were less irritable than newborns in the Chinese sample (Loo, Ohqui, Zhu, Howard, & Chen, 2005). Feldman and Shafiq (2007) found culture-specific effects of risk and protective factors, as culture moderated the effects of ecological risk differently in Israeli-Jewish and Palestinian infants.

Brown and Barrera (1999) expand the concept of *cultural competence*, a requisite proficiency of the clinician performing early childhood assessments. Specifically, they describe the importance of a multilensed approach in promoting the perception of *lines of difference* as well as lines of common concern, of *third space* thinking to respect dissimilar values, and they introduce the term *skilled dialogue* that is reciprocal, respectful, and responsive. As the target of assessment has shifted from the infant solely to the infant-in-family and community context, the true appreciation of cultural and family manners and values becomes pivotal in successful early childhood evaluation.

Once appropriate tests and measures have been chosen within the realm of developmental cognition, it is important for the clinician to glean information regarding alertness, attention, problem-solving capabilities, reasoning, comprehension of directions, visual reception and scanning, and concept formation (Bremner, 2001). For example, it is important to access early major cognitive milestones such as visual tracking abilities, object permanence, the understanding of cause and effect relationships, and the understanding of size and spatial relationships. Qualitatively, it is essential for the clinician to note not only whether the cognitive milestone was successfully achieved, but the manner in which it was attempted and executed. Precociously mastered skills, emerging skills, skill approximations, and even the young child's reaction to challenge and failure are important pieces of the puzzle to ascertain.

In the speech and language arena, both expressive and receptive skills should be investigated, both during the infant's engagement in the formal assessment process, and via incidental observations of spontaneous utterances or conversations. The developmental progression of expressive language is important for a clinician to understand and assess; specifically, crying and cooing; the utterance of open vowel sounds, transitional sounds (e.g., *agoo*, the *raspberry*, single consonants); early vowel–consonant blending, babbling, and prattling; nonverbal communication; the formation of word approximation and first words; labeling skills; single and multiword communication; sentence formation, use of structure, grammar, and syntax; and reciprocal conversational skills (Shipley & McAfee, 1998).

Receptively, noteworthy milestones include: the presence of a startle response; the ability to localize a sound; the ability to attend to voices; differentiation of voices; the understanding of simple verbal input—such as the word *no* or one's own name; the development of a receptive single-word vocabulary; the understanding of simple verbal directives, one-step commands, and multilevel commands; the understanding of sentence structure, grammar, and syntax; and discerning complex conversational skills (Shipley & McAfee, 1998). As in cognition, qualitative information is pertinent and relevant, such as the ease with which a child communicates, his/her quality of speech, fluency, volume, prosody, frustration tolerance, eye contact, and social reciprocity, to name just a few examples. Cultural considerations need to be considered during language evaluations, and provisions need to be made for non-English speakers and children exposed to multiple languages (Chavda et al., 2003).

In the motor arena, it is important to assess fine motor skills: specifically, reflexes, midline skills, grasp and praxis, visual-motor skills, as well as handedness and graphomotor skills when applicable (Case-Smith & Bigsby, 2001; Parks, 1997). In the gross motor arena, one needs to consider comfort in supine and prone positions; the ability to roll from tummy to back and vice versa; getting up on hands and knees; crawling; pulling to stand; cruising; first steps; walking; climbing stairs, nonalternating and alternating; walking a straight line; walking backward; and running, jumping, hopping, and skipping, among other milestones (Case-Smith & Bigsby; Parks). Again, qualitative observations of the child's comfort level, mode and ease of execution, risk taking behaviors, and frustration tolerance are also relevant.

An evaluation of adaptive, also known as self-help, skills is also an essential part of a developmental assessment, and can be ascertained as part of a comprehensive battery or via an additional instrument. For example, the HELP-2 (Parks, 1997) has a self-help section as part of its developmental checklist, and the Bayley-III now has the Adaptive Behavior Assessment System (ABAS; Harrison & Oakland, 2003; Richardson & Burns, 2005) embedded within its comprehensive system. Alternatively, the Vineland Adaptive Behavior Scales, 2nd edition (Sparrow, Cicchetti, & Balla, 2005), is often given to the parent in interview or self-report format, and can be added as a separate instrument to an assessment battery. Whatever format is chosen, an examiner should assess directly and indirectly an infant and toddler's adaptive abilities. Additionally, some adaptive scales (e.g., ABAS) also screen sensory sensitivities, play skills, and emotional regulation. Specifically, these skills include: activities of daily living (e.g., eating, feeding, toileting); functional communication; social skills; community and home living skills.

Feeding and sleeping behavior are particularly important adaptive skills for a clinician to ascertain, as they are essential for the maintenance of a child's health and well-being. In addition, problems in these domains often signify underlying medical issues and can be disruptive to the child-parent relationship. Specifically, information regarding familial sleeping arrangements, the child's ability to sleep through the night, napping behavior, self-soothing and pacifying, are all important pieces of data with regard to sleep hygiene. However, familial priorities and cultural considerations also need to be gleaned and respected by the clinician, particularly with regard to parental-child co-bedding versus sleeping in separate beds and rooms (Mao, Burnham, Goodlin-Jones, Gaylor, & Anders, 2004).

Similarly, feeding milestones should also be ascertained bearing familial and cultural factors in mind. Generally, infants and toddlers are expected to transition comfortably from liquid feeding to soft solids to finger foods, and later harder solids (Parks, 1997). However, there are a variety of contributory factors that also need to be considered, including allergies, physiological anomalies, and family food preferences, to name a few. In particular, information regarding whether an infant is breast or formula fed needs to be gleaned in a sensitive manner, as the decision to pick one over the other is often more emotionally charged than a checklist would indicate. Family pressures, hospital protocols, financial considerations, and maternal and child health and physiology may all be factors contributing to the decision to nurse, bottle feed, or both.

In summary, a thorough infant and toddler evaluation should always include a comprehensive developmental assessment, after careful consideration of the most suitable assessment device(s) and practices. Cognitive development, speech and language functioning, motor skills, and adaptive skills should be examined via a combination of careful behavioral observations, formal assessment via standardized instruments, and caregiver report(s). At the conclusion of this evaluation an examiner should have enough information to discuss a child's developmental trajectory, to contextualize this development within a familial and cultural framework, to make recommendations for follow-up and/or intervention, and to provide a specialist or treating therapist with continued assessment needs.

SOCIAL–EMOTIONAL ASSESSMENT

The special nature of mindfulness demanded of the early childhood clinician peering into the mind of the developing child as well as into the state of the child-caregiver dyad is exemplified in the early case reports of such original contributors as Selma Fraiberg and Sally Provence (e.g., Ferholt & Provence, 1976; Fraiberg, Adelson, & Shapiro, 1975). Emerging in these early works was a focus on emotional sharing between baby and caregiver, and on the concept of intergenerational transmission. Technically, a growing appreciation of the importance of home visits, videotape analyses, and parent–clinician co-observations surfaced, in addition to the rise of various means of interpreting the significance of subtle nonverbal behaviors. Early work in the field of infant mental health captured the essential nature of close observation alongside an informed model of development in providing meaningful assessments that enlighten therapeutic intervention. The baby was no longer looked at in a compartmentalized way, separate from the interactive parent–child system.

One can pave a historical pathway from such informed observation to recent advents of video feedback (Beebe, 2003), video microanalysis therapy (VMT; Downing, 2006), and in the mentalization-based approach of the Minding the Baby program (Slade et al., 2005). Such models, though primarily interventional, incorporate assessment of features that in turn become the focus of change. A further example is the Clinician-Assisted Videofeedback Exposure Session (CAVES), which incorporates research, assessment, and intervention components, and which allows for parent–clinician conjoint viewing of distinct videotaped excerpts, with the goal of gauging, and then enhancing parental reflective function (Schechter et al., 2006).

Such methods build on infant research demonstrating that the very young infant is contingency expectant, and that the early capacity to extract contingency from emotional interaction leads the infant to anticipate interactivity and agency (Gergely & Watson, 1999; Hains & Muir, 1996; Tremblay, Brun, & Nadel, 2005). The attribution of intentionality to others builds on the infant's expectations of contingency. Hence, there is a notable risk factor affecting infants of depressed mothers, as the capacity to expect suffers from noncontingent exchanges, and early withdrawal replaces agency, which becomes underdeveloped (Field et al., 1988).

Clinical attentiveness to nonverbal and qualitative features of social engagement during formalized assessment procedures, supplemented by thoughtful observational home visits and/or family free-play sessions, along with thorough-going history gathering, have come to be deemed necessary steps for the clinician to offer an accurate diagnosis and useful treatment planning, as exemplified in case reports by Lieberman (1997), Shahmoon-Shanok (1997), and others writing in the *Zero to Three Diagnostic Classifications (DC:0-3) Casebook* (Lieberman, Wieder, & Fenichel, 1997). Notably, Black (1997) articulates, through a case example, how integrative the clinician's perspective must be to consider the neuropsychological, behavioral, social–emotional, and relational features together, and how important differential diagnosis can be. Comprehensive assessment, incorporating meaningful appraisal of social–emotional functioning, necessitates an ecological perspective and a solid grounding in neurotypical development as well as early childhood diagnostics (Finello, 2005). It is anchored in depthful and ongoing training (Gallagher, Mowder, Sossin, & Rubinson, 2006) and in an understanding of relational and reflective processes in provision of services and in supervision (Gilkerson & Ritzier, 2005; Shahmoon-Shanok, 2006), while guided by a respect for multidisciplinary skill sets (Weatherston, 2005; Woodruff & Shelton, 2006).

An emergent scale for the assessment of infant social behavior is the Alarme Distress de Bebe Scale (ADBB; Guedeney & Fermanian, 2001). This scale originated in France, but has been utilized in several other countries. Designed for use in the context of routine medical examinations as a screener, the scale could also be incorporated into an infant developmental evaluation. The ADBB requires the trained practioner to engage the infant in social behavior by talking, touching, and smiling, rating (from 0 to 4, with 0 being optimal) across eight items: facial expression, eye contact, general level of activity, self-stimulation gestures, vocalizations, briskness of response to stimulation, relationship to the observer, and attractiveness to the observer. In addition to finding a link between an infant's withdrawn social behavior and the mother's report of negative mood states since the birth of the child (not the mother's current mood state), Matthey, Guedeney, Starakis, and Barnett (2005) detailed further information about the scale's psychometric properties and factor structure.

Furthermore, a rich research-anchored and theory-evolving literature has emerged providing a deep well of facts, concepts, and constructs from which the infant mental health clinician draws. Many notable infant observers paved the path that is still evolving, in which the complexity of the baby's mind and early relationships have been increasingly understood. Beebe (2005), Brazelton (Brazelton & Cramer, 1990), Emde (1991), Greenspan (2007), Kestenberg (1975), Sander (1988), Stern (1995), Trevarthen (Trevarthen & Aitken, 2001) and Tronick (2007) exemplify those who have provided rich insights, theoretical models, and clinical derivations bearing on self-regulation, dyadic- and co-regulation, affect-regulation, mutuality, reciprocity, matching/mismatching, infant agency, the roles of body experience and movement, rhythmicity, intersubjectivity, temporality, and meaning-making, each of which adds to the clinician's ever-enlarging frame of reference. Fonagy and Target (2003) offer a model of mentalization, and of an associated *reflective function* that underscores how a developmental capacity to experience mental states as representations evolves over the first few years in relation to qualities of caregiving, affect mirroring, and perceived contingencies in addition to innate individual differences. The clinician is reminded to attend to the child's early development of metacognition and pretend play as progressions that offer important information about how the young child processes experience.

Attachment theory highlights predictive formulations in which individuals with secure internal working models of relationships expect and behave in ways that foster open, supportive, and trusting interactions, whereas individuals with insecure working models are more likely to expect and behave in ways that manifest mistrust (Ainsworth, 1979; Bowlby, 1988). The Strange Situation has proven remarkably robust in predicting later outcomes. The disorganized toddler, for instance, appearing to lack a coherent attachment strategy (as in *freezing/stilling*) and seeming confused as to goal and intention, is especially at risk for early, and later, psychopathology (Fonagy & Target, 2003; Lyons-Ruth & Jacobvitz, 1999; Solomon & George, 1999). Measures of attachment security have extended beyond the original constraints of the Strange Situation; they have been employed as research tools, and some have evolved into clinical use as well. Measures based on laboratory observations, home observations (as in the Q-sort of Waters, Hamilton, & Weinfeld, 1995), and symbolic representations, including doll play, are reviewed by Solomon and George. Some clinical consultations have begun to incorporate the Adult Attachment Interview (AAI; Hesse, 1999; Main, Kaplan, & Cassidy, 1985), which is a semistructured protocol that taps an individual's most salient early attachment experiences and their perceived effects. In the nature of adult discourse, what is classified is not the nature of the attachment of the adult, but rather the person's overall state of mind regarding attachment. Notably, the parent's state of mind corresponds to the child's experience of attachment. A parent classified as dismissing loses coherence in narrative and predicts an avoidant infant in strange-situation reunion behavior. Knowing a parent's state of mind regarding attachment processes, may bear as much, or more, predictive power regarding the later mental health of the baby than anything one might derive directly from the child's response to test stimuli.

DIAGNOSTIC ASSESSMENT OF INFANT MENTAL HEALTH

Addressing the well-known deficiencies in *Diagnostic and Statistical Manual of Mental Disorders*, 4th edition, Text Revision (DSM-IV-TR; APA, 2000) regarding the diagnosis of young children, as well as the need for a shared nomenclature in clinical description and a reference point for research, two multiaxial frameworks for early childhood diagnosis have emerged, specifically the *DC:0-3R* (Zero to Three, 2005) and the *Diagnostic Manual for Infancy and Early Childhood* (ICDL-DMIC; ICDL, 2005). Both frameworks are developmentally-informed, multidisciplinary in origin and influence, and both take the quality and nature of relationships into account. Both appreciate biological/constitutional, environmental, and cultural differences in developmental progressions, and the manner in which caregiver–child relationships can, to degrees, moderate outcomes in light of vulnerabilities. Infant and early childhood mental health diagnoses are indeed possible, always against the backdrop of the potential for change given maturational and environmental factors (Lieberman, Barnard, & Wieder, 2004).

The frameworks differ. The DC:0-3R presents a five-axis system, in which Axis I pertains to Clinical Disorders, Axis II pertains to Relationship Classification, Axis III pertains to Medical and Developmental Disorders and Conditions, Axis IV pertains to Psychosocial Stressors, and Axis V pertains to Emotional and Social Functioning. Hence, the DC:0-3R system closely parallels the DSM-IV-TR in style, notably substituting a relationship classification for DSM's Axis II personality disorders. The DSM's Axis V global assessment of functioning (GAF) is replaced by DC:0-3R's to rate capacities for emotional and social functioning. Six such capacities are noted, paralleling those levels of functioning formulated by Greenspan, (2007; Greenspan & Wieder, 2006): (1) attention and regulation, (2) forming relationships or mutual engagement, (3) intentional two-way communication, (4) complex gestures and problem solving, (5) use of symbols to express thoughts and feelings, and (6) connecting symbols logically and abstract thinking.

The ICDL-DMIC, an eight-axis system, is organized differently, and is anchored even more deeply in the Developmental, Individual-Difference, Relationship-Based (DIR) model: Axis I pertains to Primary Diagnosis, which may be: Interactive Disorder, Regulatory-Sensory Processing Disorder, Neurodevelopmental Disorder of Relating and Communicating, Language Disorder, or Learning Challenge. Interactive Disorders (of which 16 are identified) are "characterized by the way a child perceives and experiences his emotional world and/or by a particular maladaptive child-caregiver interaction pattern" (ICDL-DMIC, 2005, p. 31). Notably, one of the ICDL-DMIC Axis I Interactive Disorders is Mood Dysregulation–Bipolar Patterns, exemplifying the developmental pathway model, and the multiple foci upon different areas of development kept in mind by the diagnosing clinician. An " . . . over-responsivity to sound, touch, or both coexists with a craving for sensory stimulation, particularly movement . . . they become agitated, aggressive, and impulsive" (ICDL-DMIC, 2005, p. 48). This pattern is combined with a caregiver–child interactive pattern in which coregulation of reciprocal affective exchanges is lacking, and in addition, the fifth and sixth functional emotional levels of development have not been mastered. Furthermore, ICDL-DMIC Axis II pertains to Functional, Emotional, Developmental Capacities; Axis III pertains to Regulatory–Sensory Processing Capacities; Axis IV pertains to Language Capacities; Axis V pertains to Visuospatial Capacities; Axis VI pertains to Child–Caregiver and Family Patterns; Axis VII pertains to Stress; and Axis VIII pertains to Other Medical and Neurological Diagnoses.

The DC:0-3R (Zero to Three, 2005) text offers guidelines for a full evaluation, noting that a "minimum of three to five sessions of 45 or more minutes each" is required, and though it specifies the importance of direct observation, it does not specify how information is gleaned regarding language, cognition, and affective expression. It does specify "assessment of sensory reactivity and processing, motor tone, and motor-planning capacities" (DC:0-3R, 2005, p. 8), areas that have become increasingly attended to in the training of pediatric occupational therapists, but have sometimes been underattended to in the training of child psychologists. Disorders of affect, reflected by depressed mood, anxiety/fear, and anger, are noted to be more widespread than had been appreciated.

The clinician must be able to observe and classify such characteristics as: (1) depressed/irritable mood or anhedonia, as would be necessary in the identification of depression in infancy and early childhood; (2) excessive distress, as would be necessary in the identification of anxiety disorder (differentiating excessive anxiety from anxious temperament characteristics); and (3) sensory hyperreactivity and sensory hyporeactivity to auditory, visual, olfactory, taste, tactile, vestibular, and proprioceptive stimuli, as would be necessary in diagnosing regulation disorders of sensory processing. In doing so, the clinician with appropriate training could employ the Infant/Toddler Sensory Profile (ITSP; Dunn, 2002), a judgment-based caregiver questionnaire, which taps the caregiver's perception of the frequency of behaviors that, via standardization and section scores, are indicative of difficulties with sensory processing and performance. The ITSP has 36 items for children from birth to 6 months and 48 items for children 7–36 months. Typical performance is distinguished from probable differences and definite differences across such dimensions as sensation seeking, sensory sensitivity and sensation avoiding, in addition to comparing functioning in specific sensory modalities.

The clinician is challenged to be developmentally aware and sensitive so as to be able to differentiate diagnostically significant oppositional behavior, defiance, and a preference for repetition, as well as impairment in the ability to engage in an emotional and social relationship with the caregiver, from behaviors that may be perceived by others as such, but nonetheless fall in the typical, subclinical range. In other words, the clinician must have remarkably well honed observational and referential skills, developed over a substantial period of observation of both typical and atypical infants, toddlers, and preschoolers. Can the clinician determine when relatedness is too unconnected (i.e., when social reciprocity is not developmentally appropriate), when affect is too flat, when exploration is too limited, play is too restricted, when an infant is reacting to trauma, or when motor planning (and/or the underlying body schema) is poor? Training and exposure issues are critical in equipping the clinician to differentiate typical from atypical functioning in social and emotional spheres.

Regulatory disorders pertain when difficulties with sensory and information processing hinder developmental attainments and disrupt interpersonal functioning. Parents/caregivers vary widely in tolerance for and ability to accommodate to hypersensivity or hyposensivity, so there is not a 1:1 correspondence between child behavioral levels or styles and parent-child interactive problems. There is a notable but variable correspondence between regulatory difficulties with motor, attentional, tactile, visual, auditory and other processing factors and the child's capacity to regulate emotions and relationships. Regulatory difficulties often underlie reported sleep and feeding difficulties, emotional volatility/low frustration tolerance, and self-stimulatory behaviors (Cesari et al., 2003; ICDL, 2005; Zero to Three, 2005).

Measurement of social-emotional development in early childhood is distinct from such evaluations at later ages. With babies, one is more reliant on direct observation and parent report. A useful clinical assessment in early childhood needs to strike a balance with regard to structured and unstructured assessment procedures, as systematic information about a number of infant mental health domains is invaluable, but so is clinical attentiveness to qualities of behavior and interaction, and to parental emotions and perspectives derivable from interview narratives and their stylistic qualities. Attributional measures of social-emotional development, and/or social-emotional problems in young children serve important purposes. Usually, the parent or primary caregiver is the informant, so that in addition to using the measure as an identifier of risk, the consulting clinician has a direct parent/caregiver report of the child's behavior, which forms a basis for further communication about the child and about the parent's/caregiver's perceptions.

An example is the set of Ages & Stages Questionnaires (ASQ; Squires, Bricker, & Twombly, 2002; 2004), deemed especially suitable as a first-level screening program utilizing 19 questionnaires distinguished by brief age intervals between 4 and 60 months of age across communication, gross-motor, fine-motor, problem-solving, and personal–social sections. The personal–social domain incorporates six questions per age related to age-expected social and/or independent functioning, and the parent notes whether the behavior is present, occurs sometimes, or is not yet evident. Specifically, the ASQ: Social–Emotional (SE) asks 30 questions for each age interval (e.g., at 30 months asking the caregiver if the child checks to make sure the caregiver is near when exploring new places) on a 3-point scale of "most of the time," "sometimes," or "rarely/never." The social-emotional areas screened are self-regulation, compliance, communication, adaptive functioning, autonomy, affect, and interaction with people. Demonstrating good reliability and validity, and normed on a sample of more than 3,000 children, the ASQ:SE qualifies as a useful screener and monitoring system (Squires et al., 2004), and has been incorporated into Early Head Start, Head Start, preschool settings, and pediatric practices. A comparable screener is the Brigance Screens-II, covering ages birth to 90 months across the Brigance Infant and Toddler Screen for children 0–23 months, the Early Preschool Screen for children 24–32 months, and the Preschool Screen for children 33–56 months (Brigance, 1985).

The Bayley-III has incorporated the Social–Emotional Scale, also filled out by the parent/caregiver, which is developed and interpreted in line with Greenspan's Social-Emotional Growth Chart (cf., Greenspan et al., 2001). Other developmental screening tools surveying several aspects of developmental progression that tap less specific aspects of young children's emotional development, and derive from parent/caregiver attributions include: the Child Development Inventory (CDI) for Assessing Toddlers and Preschoolers (Doig, Macias, Saylor, Craver, & Ingram, 1999), applicable for children aged 15 months to 6 years; the Brigance Parent-Child Interactions Scale (Brigance, 1985) applicable for children aged 0–30 months; the Eyberg Child Behavior Inventory (ECBI; Eyberg, 1999) applicable for children aged 24 months to 16 years; the Parents' Evaluation of Developmental Status (PEDS) and the associated PEDS: Developmental Milestones (PEDS:DM; Glascoe, 2003) applicable for children between birth and 8 years. The PEDS measures were especially developed with pediatricians in mind and have been shown to detect the presence of behavioral and emotional problems (Glascoe). Additional curriculum-based instruments that incorporate social-emotional appraisal tools are the Assessment, Evaluation, and Programming System for Infants and Children (AEPS; Pretti-Frontczak & Bricker, 2001, 2004), the Brigance Diagnostic Inventory of Early Development–Revised (Brigance, 1991), the HELP (Parks, 1997), the Early Learning Accomplishment Profiles (E-LAP; Glover, Preminger, & Stanford, 1995), and the Transdisciplinary Play-Based Assessment and Transdisciplinary Play-Based Intervention–2nd edition (TBPA2 & TPBI2; Lindner, 2008). Please refer to the compendium of tests in the Appendix.

A comparison of some screening tools used for the early identification of social and emotional problems in children birth to 3 years old was presented by Squires (2000), who underscored the importance of early identification of social and emotional problems because of their stability over time without early intervention. Support was demonstrated for the ASQ:SE and for the Infant/Toddler Symptom Checklist (ITSCL; DeGangi, Poisson, Sickel, & Wiener, 1999).

A more in-depth questionnaire regarding children ages 1–3 years is the Infant-Toddler Social and Emotional Assessment (ITSEA; Carter, Little, Briggs-Gowan, & Kogan, 1999). A brief version (i.e., BITSEA) is also available which offers information more in line with a screening instrument. The ITSEA itself focuses on social-emotional problems and social competency, identifying symptoms and symptom clusters. It has been demonstrated to be sensitive to multiple dimensions of infant behavior. Subscales include aggression/defiance, peer aggression, activity, impulsivity, and internalizing as well as externalizing symptoms. Carter et al. report that maternal ITSEA ratings of infant problem behaviors and competencies were associated not just with maternal ratings of infant temperament, but also with infant attachment status, attachment behaviors, emotional negative reactivity, regulation following stress, and task mastery. Validity of the BITSEA has been documented by Briggs-Gowan, Carter, Irwin, Wachtel, and Cicchetti (2004), demonstrating correspondence to Child Behavior Checklist for ages 1.5-5 years (CBCL/1.5–5) scores and concurrent problem ratings and observed competencies, along with high test-retest and interrater reliabilities.

The empirically-based assessment paradigm of the Achenbach System of Empirically-Based Assessment (ASEBA) includes the preschool forms: The CBCL/1.5-5 and the Caregiver-Teacher Report Form (C-TRF; Rescorla, 2005). These forms are downward counterparts of the other frequently employed ASEBA measures. Both scales yield scores on normed empirically-based syndrome scales, DSM-oriented scales, and Internalizing, Externalizing, and Total problems aggregate scales. Notably, the CBCL/1.5-5 also incorporates the Language Development Survey (LDS; Rescorla & Alley, 2001), which has been demonstrated to show reliability, validity, and clinical utility as a screener in identifying expressive language delay in toddlers. Use of norms is especially important given the proclivity of girls to attain larger vocabularies than boys at 2 years of age. Children on the CBCL/1.5-5 can be categorized, using the scales, in normal, borderline, or clinical ranges.

In the prospective study of developmental psychopathology following babies from birth reported by Skovgaard et al. (2007), the utility of some of the measures described here is evident, as the Bayley-II, CBCL/1.5-5, ITSCL, Parent–Infant Relationship Global Assessment (PIR-GAS), PCERA and DC: 0-3 diagnostic classification system were incorporated into the study. Results underscore the need of professionals to identify at-risk infants and toddlers as early as possible, as employment of ICD-10 or DC:0-3 diagnoses found that 16-18% of infants ($N = 211$ in a general population) met diagnostic criteria for a disorder by 1.5 years of age. In fact, 7.1% met criteria for DC:0-3 Regulatory Disorder and 8.5% met criteria for a relationship disturbance. Comparable findings were reported by Keren, Feldman, and Tyrano (2001). Such prevalence highlights the use of early-identification tools in identifying children in need of more thorough clinical evaluations. The Keren et al. findings further demonstrate the correspondence between clinically referred infants and difficulties in the domains of parental sensitivity, support, structuring of the interaction, home envioronment, dyadic mutuality, and quality of interactive exchanges, stressing the need to assess the distressed infant in multisituational and family contexts using a multiaxial approach.

PLAY EVALUATION

Observation of play in the first two years of life provides a window into the rapid development of infant capacities in nearly every area of functioning: cognitive, social/emotional, communication, and motor. To understand play assessment as a vital complement to evaluation with more traditional instruments and methods, the clinician must examine the role of play in the very young child's life.

In the first year of life, the typically developing infant exercises his/her growing motor and sensory skills to reach, explore, and manipulate the environment. The infant responds to all that is seen, heard, and touched. Soon after birth the infant can visually track a moving object; at 4 months will turn his/her head to look for the source of a sound. When the infant can grasp and hold objects at 4-5 months of age, a whole new world of exploration is open: The infant can bang, throw, and mouth objects. The infant perceives weight and texture. He or she experiences the effect of their body on the environment in a new way. Later, at 8-9 months, the infant is able to share a response to objects with others, for example, looking back and forth between an interesting toy and a mother's face. This *joint attention* is an important component of later social interaction. The infant's experimentation with movement, sensations, and the qualities of objects through physical play was called by Piaget (1962) "sensorimotor practice play," an apt description of the preparation for more complex activities. Play in the first year can require the integration of skills in many areas: sensory acuity, motor coordination, cognitive intent and attention, and social interest.

Early building blocks of play skills lead to the emergence of functional and representational play in the second year. A 12-month-old may show recognition of the "purpose" of objects by throwing a ball, but shaking a rattle. The infant will show further awareness of object functions by placing a toy spoon into a bowl, or holding a toy phone to his/her own ear. Responses to objects are motivated not only by physical attributes but by what they mean to the infant or toddler. Now one witnesses the true transformation in the toddler's thinking and response to their world. At the same time that toddlers begin to use words to represent important objects and needs, they represent their environment and their experiences in play. With realistic and familiar props, the toddler re-enacts eating and sleeping, riding in the car and talking on the phone. The toddler reaches out through words and gestures to include important others in play. The child pretends to feed mother; while requesting an interesting toy he or she sees. As the toddler's ability to mentally manipulate thoughts and experiences increases, he or she will engage in pretend scenes and these will incorporate sequential ideas. The toddler will represent activities in play that both are and are not, from his/her experience (e.g., mommy cooking or daddy reading; Westby, 2000).

A child's natural attraction to those objects and activities that are interesting and enjoyable–that is, to play—has an enormous impact on continuing development. Achievements and deficits in any functional area will be expressed through play. Visually impaired toddlers have been observed to engage in less functional play with toys and less reciprocal communication which is linked to early visual cues, leading to limitations in preschool peer interaction (Sacks, Kekelis, & Gaylord-Ross, 1992). Delays in the development of pretend play have been related to hearing impairment (Meadow-Orleans, Spencer, & Koester, 2004) and autism spectrum disorders (Jarrold, 2003), as well as external factors such as low socioeconomic status (Farran & Son-Yarbrough, 2001). In contrast, significantly advanced pretend play as toddlers, facilitated by maternal support and *scaffolding*, has been associated with higher preschool IQ scores (Morelock, Brown, & Morrissey, 2003).

Regardless of developmental status, a child at play is in an optimal state to demonstrate developmental skills. As evaluators, we ask ourselves, "At the child's best, what is the level of highest comfort, attention, and interest?" In this way, assessment through play differs from traditional evaluation in that it is spontaneous and child-driven rather than structured and item-driven. Given the broad range of information to be gained from observing play, it is not surprising that instruments for the assessment of infant play vary widely in design. They may take the form of behavioral checklists, structured observations or parent questionnaires, and may take a broad approach or focus on more specific skills. Choice of instrument should be determined by specific referral questions and information already obtained through structured testing.

The Westby Developmental Play Scale (Westby, 2000) examines play in early development beginning at the age of 8 months, when the infant begins to demonstrate differentiated responses to toys as well as means-end and social behavior with toys. Used from infancy to age 5, the Westby scale follows the increasing complexity of play as it reflects *presymbolic* object use and attempts to communicate during and through play, and later capacities for symbolic representation and role taking. Using a checklist of play and language behaviors arranged by age, the evaluator notes behaviors the child spontaneously demonstrates, as well as those the child can actively join in and those he or she can only imitate. This allows the evaluator to estimate the child's age level in play and language skills. A playroom with a recommended set of toys is necessary for this instrument; the need for professional experience in the field of speech/language or child development is implied.

The Symbolic Play Test (SPT; Lowe & Costello, 1988) and the Test of Pretend Play (ToPP; Lewis & Boucher, 1998) can both be administered to children 12 months of age and older, and are based on the child's use of prescribed sets of toys. The SPT, despite its title, focuses almost exclusively on concept formation and functional play capacities, scoring the child's ability to use various sets of toys (e.g., doll, bedding, toy bed) according to their function. In contrast, the ToPP assesses play behaviors that reflect demonstration of symbolic capacities, such as substituting one object for another object or person, attributing an imagined property to an object or person, or making reference to an absent object, person, or substance.

Parent questionnaires pertaining to overall infant/toddler behavior and development typically include inquiry into aspects of play. Measures of adaptive functioning, mentioned earlier, such as the *Vineland Scales of Adaptive Behavior*, 2nd edition (Sparrow et al., 2005) and the *Adaptive Behavior Assessment System*, 2nd edition (Harrison & Oakland, 2003), ask parents to rate the frequency with which an infant demonstrates fundamental social/play skills such as engagement in simple interactive games like *peekaboo*, or a toddler's ability to interact in play with peers. Standard scores are derived in comparison to age peers, and these instruments can be administered and interpreted without extensive training. While there are obvious limitations to the depth of understanding provided by questionnaire responses, parents' perceptions of infants' developmental status obtained through written screening instruments have proven to be generally reliable and valid (Rydz, Shevell, Majnemer, & Oskoui, 2005).

Several available measures utilize a structured observation of specific aspects of infant–parent play. The PCERA (Clark, 1985) and the Parent-Child Interaction Play Assessment (Smith, 2000) were designed as measures of broader qualities of parent-child interaction related to the child's cognitive and social-emotional development. Both use videotaped observations of interaction between parent and child in activities that include structured and unstructured play, both with a prescribed set of toys, and both employ quantitative scaling of parent, child, and dyadic qualities. As Casby (2007) notes, play develops following four major ordinal levels: sensorimotor-exploratory, relational-nonfunctional, functional-conventional, and symbolic. As play becomes symbolic, it also becomes decontextualized and decentered. The young child develops a capacity to represent actions outside of current time/space (decontextualization) and to move actions away from oneself (decentering). Imagination grows, as does the capacity for pretense, and Casby suggests that the agent, the instrument, and the scheme all become integral components of symbolic play. Moreover, Casby outlines developmental steps in play development from 2 to 4 months to 30 months, manifested in a developmentally-based, criterion-referenced protocol for the assessment of play in infants, toddlers, and young children. Casby also introduces a *naturalistic-interactive* play context for examiner and young child in which the examiner may model and encourage, and thus appraise the utility of scaffolding for the child.

SUMMARY

At the conclusion of a thorough infant and toddler evaluation, a clinician will have ample data regarding: (1) child and familial history; (2) how the child presents during both the assessment process and in his or her naturalistic environment; (3) developmental milestones, including cognition, speech and language, motor skills, and adaptive skills; (4) social-emotional functioning; and (5) play skills. Interview, parent-attribution scales, direct observation and engagement (in some cases, incorporating more detailed codings from videotape), and administration of standardized measures each contribute to a thoroughgoing appraisal. Engaging the parents and caregivers in collaborative roles is essential.

A fair and appropriate evaluation needs to also be mindful of cultural norms, the needs of special populations, and any environmental and or medical factors that may have interfered with or precluded the attainment of reliable and interpretable data. For example, children from non-English speaking or bilingual households should be tested by trained bilingual evaluators utilizing tests and measures that have been translated into their language and/or standardized on appropriate populations (Fernandez & Zaccario, 2007; Lollock, 2001; NAEYC, 2005). Likewise, children diagnosed with developmental disabilities, those who are born prematurely, and/or those who have been diagnosed with genetic or other medically-based conditions, may require special testing accommodations and or may only be properly assessed with certain devices normed on their special populations (Individuals with Disabilities Education Improvement Act, 1990, 1997, 2004; Lichtenberger, 2005; Ross & Lawson, 1997). Any concerns regarding appropriateness of testing, reliability and validity of results, and testing accommodations needs to be clearly indicated by a clinician in both the final test report and in feedback sessions with the family or other professional personnel. A thoughtful clinician is mindful of assessing both areas of developmental strength and of concern, of providing caregivers with useful recommendations and follow-up, with providing as accurate and thorough an assessment as possible, and with informing parents of findings in a respectful and clinically sensitive manner. Appropriate clinical training, knowledge of development during early childhood, the skillful use of clinical judgment, sufficient attention to child-caregiver relationships, the use of appropriate tests and measures, ample time for completion of the assessment, and a proper evaluation of the validity and reliability of results is essential for the attainment of a comprehensive and meaningful infant or toddler evaluation.

REFERENCES

Ainsworth, M. D. (1979). Infant-mother attachment. *American Psychologist, 34,* 932–927.

American Psychiatric Association. (2000). *Diagnostic and statistical manual of mental disorders, text revision* (4th ed.). Washington, DC: Author.

Bagnato, S. J., & Neisworth, J. T. (1994). A national study of the social and treatment "invalidity" of intelligence testing for early intervention. *School Psychology Quarterly, 9,* 81–102.

Bagnato, S. J., & Simeonsson, R. J. (2007). *Authentic assessment for early childhood intervention: Best practices.* New York: Guilford Press.

Bayley, N. (2006). *Bayley scales of infant and toddler development* (3rd ed.). San Antonio, TX: Harcourt Assessment.

Beebe, B. (2003). Brief mother-infant treatment: Psychoanalytically informed video-feedback. *Infant Mental Health Journal, 24*(1), 24–52.

Beebe, B. (2005). Mother-infant research informs mother-infant treatment. *Psychoanalytic Study of the Child, 60,* 7–46.

Beebe, B. (2006). Co-constructing mother-infant distress in face-to-face interactions: Contributions of microanalysis. [Special Issue: The use of video in infant observation]. *Infant Observation, 9,* 151–164.

Benoit, D., Zeanah, C. H., Parker, K. C. H., Nicholson, E., & Coolbear, J. (1997). A working model of the interview: Infant clinical status related to maternal perceptions. *Infant Mental Health Journal, 18,* 76–91.

Biringen, Z. (2000). Emotional availability: Conceptualization and research findings. *American Journal of Orthopsychiatry, 70,* 104–114.

Biringen, Z., Damon, J., Grigg, W., Mone, J., Pipp-Siegel, S., Skillern, S, et al. (2005). Emotional availability: Differential predictions to infant attachment and kindergarten adjustment based on observation time and context. *Infant Mental Health Journal, 26*(4), 295–308.

Black, L. M. (1997). Regulatory disorders: Type I: Hypersensitive. In A. Lieberman, S. Wieder, & E. Fenichel (Eds.), *The DC: 0–3 casebook* (pp. 195–218). Washington, DC: Zero to Three.

Bowlby, J. (1988). *A secure base: Parent-child attachment and healthy human development.* New York: Basic Books.

Brazelton, T. B., & Cramer, B. G. (1990). *The earliest relationships: Parents, infants, and the drama of early attachment.* Reading, MA: Addison Wesley Longman.

Bremner, J. G. (2001). Cognitive development: Knowledge of the physical world. In J. G. Bremner & A. Fogel (Eds.), *Blackwell handbook of infant development* (pp. 99–139). Hoboken, NJ: Blackwell Publishing.

Brigance, A. N. (1985). *Brigance Screens II.* North Billerica, MA: Curriculum Associates.

Brigance, A. N. (1991). *Brigance Diagnostic Inventory of Early Development-Revised.* North Billerica, MA: Curriculum Associates.

Briggs-Gowan, M. J., Carter, A. S., Irwin, J. R., Wachtel, K. I., & Cicchetti, D. V. (2004). The Brief Infant-Toddler Social and Emotional Assessment: Screening for social-emotional problems and delays in competence. *Journal of Pediatric Psychology, 29*(2), 143–155.

Brink, M. B. (2002). Involving parents in early childhood assessment: Perspectives from an early intervention instructor. *Early Childhood Education Journal, 29,* 251–257.

Brown, W., & Barrera, I. (1999). Enduring problems in assessment: The persistent challenges of cultural dynamics and family issues. *Infants and Young Children, 12,* 34–42.

Carter, A. S., Little, C., Briggs-Gowan, M. J., & Kogan, N. (1999). The Infant-Toddler Social and Emotional Assessment (ITSEA): Comparing parent ratings to laboratory observations of task mastery, emotion regulation, coping behaviors, and attachment status. *Infant Mental Health Journal, 20*(4), 375–392.

Casby, M. W. (2007). Developmental assessment of play: Model for early intervention. *Communication Disorders Quarterly, 24,* 175–183.

Case-Smith, J., & Bigsby, R. (2001) Motor assessment. In L. T. Singer & P. S. Zeskind (Eds.), *Biobehavioral assessment of the infant* (pp. 423–442). New York: Guilford Press.

Cesari, A., Maestro, S., Cavallaro, C., Chilosi, A., Pecini, C., Pfanner, L., & Muratori, F. (2003). Diagnostic boundaries between regulatory and multisystem developmental disorders: A clinical study. *Infant Mental Health Journal, 24,* 365–377.

Chandler, L. S., Skillen, A., & Swanson, N. W. (1980). *Movement assessment of infants* (MAI). Rolling Bay, WA: Infant Movement Research.

Chavda, U., Kao, R., Soldatou, A., Gardner, A., Knudson, P., Su, H., et al. (2003). Important issues in the care and evaluation of bilingual/multilingual children. *International Pediatrics, 18,* 8–13.

Clark, R. (1985). *The Parent-Child Early Relational Assessment. Instrument and manual.* Madison, WI: Department of Psychiatry, University of Wisconsin Medical School.

Constantino, J. N., Davis, S. A., Todd, R. D., Schindler, M. K., Gross, M., et al. (2003). Validation of a brief quantitative measure of autistic traits: Comparison of the Social Responsivity Scale with the Autism Diagnostic Interview-Revised. *Journal of Autism and Developmental Disorders, 33*(4), 427–433.

DeGangi, G. A., Poisson, S., Sickel, R. Z., & Wiener, A. S. (1999). *Infant/Toddler Symptom Checklist: A screening tool for parents.* San Antonio, TX: Psychological Corporation.

Doig, K. B., Macias, M. M., Saylor, C. F., Craver, J. R., & Ingram, P. E. (1999). The Child Development Inventory: A developmental outcome measure for follow-up of the high-risk infant. *Journal of Pediatrics, 135,* 358–362.

Downing, G. (2006, July). *WAIMH conference lecture.* Presentation at Congress of World Association of Infant Mental Health, Paris, France.

Dunn, W. (2002). *Infant/Toddler Sensory Profile: Users manual.* San Antonio, TX: Psychological Corporation.

Emde, R. N. (1991). Beyond dual drive theory. *PsycCritiques, 36,* 328–329.

Eyberg, S. (1999). *Eyberg Child Behavior Inventory & Sutter-Eyberg Student Behavior Inventory.* Odessa, FL: Psychological Asssessment Resources.

Farran, D. C., & Son-Yarbrough, W. (2001). Title I funded preschools as a developmental context for children's play and verbal behaviors. *Early Childhood Research Quarterly, 16,* 245–262.

Feldman, R., & Shafiq, M. (2007). The role of culture in moderating the links between early ecological risk and young children's adaptation. *Development and Psychopathology, 19,* 1–21.

Ferholt, J., & Provence, S. (1976). Diagnosis and treatment of an infant with psychophysiological vomiting. *Psychoanalytic Study of the Child, 31,* 439–459.

Fernández, M., & Zaccario, M. (2007) Bayley III: A preliminary overview. *Journal of Early Childhood and Infant Psychology, 3,* 223–233.

Field, T., Healy, B., Goldstein, S., Perry, S., Bendell, D., Schanberg, S., et al. (1988). Infants of depressed mothers show "depressed" behavior even with nondepressed adults. *Child Development, 59,* 1569–1579.

Finello, K. M. (2005). Training in assessment of birth to five-year-olds. In K. M. Finello (Ed.), *The handbook of training and practice in infant and preschool mental health* (pp. 51–70). San Francisco: Jossey-Bass.

Folio, M. R., & Fewell, R. R. (2000). *Peabody Developmental Motor Scale (PDMS)* (2nd ed., *Gross Motor*). San Antonio, TX: Harcourt Assessment, Inc.

Fonagy, P., & Target, M. (2003). Evolution of the interpersonal interpretive function: Clues for preventive intervention in early childhood. In S. W. Coates, J. L. Rosenthal, & D. S. Schechter (Eds.), *September 11: Trauma and human bonds* (pp. 99–113). New York: Analytic Press/Taylor & Francis Group.

Fraiberg, S., Adelson, E., & Shapiro, V. (1975). Ghosts in the nursery: A psychoanalytic approach to the problems of impaired infant-mother relationships. *Journal of the American Academy of Child Psychiatry, 14,* 387–421.

Frankenburg, N., Dodds, J., & Archer, P. (1990). *Denver-II: Technical Manual.* Denver, CO: Denver Developmental Materials.

Gallagher, R., Mowder, B., Sossin, M., & Rubinson, F. (2006). Continuing education interests of licensed New York State psychologists serving the zero to five-year-old population. *Journal of Early Childhood and Infant Psychology, 2,* 201–220.

Gergely, G., & Watson, J. S. (1999). Early socio-emotional development: Contingency perception and the social-biofeedback model. In P. Rochat (Ed.), *Early social cognition: Understanding others in the first months of life* (pp. 101–136). Mahwah, NJ: Erlbaum.

Gilkerson, L., & Ritzier, T. T. (2005). The role of reflective process in infusing relationship-based practice into an early intervention system. In K. M. Finello (Ed.), *The handbook of training and practice in infant and preschool mental health* (pp. 427–452). San Francisco: Jossey-Bass.

Ginsberg, S., & Hochman, J. D. (2006). Policy, implementation, and leadership: Making an integrated model of mental health and early intervention practice an operational reality. In G. M. Foley & J. D. Hochman (Eds.), *Mental health in early intervention: Achieving unity in principles and practice* (pp. 297–312). Baltimore: Brookes.

Glascoe, F. P. (2003). Parents' evaluation of developmental status: How well do parents' concerns identify children with behavioral and emotional problems? *Clinical Pediatrics, 42,* 133–138.

Glover, M. E., Preminger, J. L., & Stanford, A. R. (1995). *The Early Learning Accomplishment Profile for Young Children: Birth to 36 months.* Chapel Hill, NC: Chapel Hill Training-Outreach Project.

Greenspan, S. (2007). Levels of infant–caregiver interactions and the DIR model: Implications for the development of signal affects, the regulation of mood and behavior, the formation of a sense of self, the creation of internal representation, and the construction of defenses and character structure. *Journal of Infant, Child and Adolescent Psychotherapy, 6*(3), 174–210.

Greenspan, S. I., DeGangi, G., & Wieder, S. (2001). *The Functional Emotional Assessment Scale (FEAS) for infancy and early childhood: Clinical and research applications.* Bethesda, MD: Interdisciplinary Council on Developmental and Learning Disorders.

Greenspan, S. I., & Wieder, S. (2006). *Infant and early childhood mental health: A comprehensive developmental approach to assessment and intervention.* Washington, DC: American Psychiatric Association.

Guedeney, A., & Fermanian, J. (2001). A validity and reliability study of assessment and screening for sustained withdrawal reaction in infancy: The Alarm Distress Baby Scale. *Infant Mental Health Journal, 22,* 559–575.

Hains, S. M. J., & Muir, D. (1996). Effects of stimulus contingency in infant–adult interactions. *Infant Behavior and Development, 19,* 49–61.

Harrison, P. L., & Oakland, T. (2003). *Adaptive Behavior Assessment System* (2nd ed.). San Antonio, TX: Psychological Corporation.

Hesse, E. (1999). The Adult Attachment Interview: Historical and current perspectives. In J. Cassidy & P. R. Shaver (Eds.), *Handbook of attachment: Theory, research, and clinical applications* (pp. 395–433). New York: Guilford Press.

Individuals with Disabilities Education Act of 1990, Public Law 101-476. *U.S. Statutes at Large* (1990).

Individuals with Disabilities Education Act of 1997, Public Law 105-17 (IDEA Reauthorized), *U.S. Statutes at Large* (1997).

Individuals with Disabilities Education Improvement Act of 2004, Public Law 108-446 (IDEA Reauthorized). *U.S. Statutes at Large 118* (2004), 2647.

Interdisciplinary Council on Developmental and Learning Disorders (2005). *Diagnostic manual for infancy and early childhood (ICDL-DMIC).* Bethesda, MD: Interdisciplinary Council on Developmental and Learning Disorders.

Jarrold, C. (2003). A review of research into pretend play in autism. *Autism, 7*(4), 379–390.

Keren, M., Feldman, R., & Tyrano, S. (2001). Diagnoses and interactive patterns of infants referred to a community-based infant mental health clinic. *Journal of the American Academy of Child and Adolescent Psychiatry, 40,* 27–35.

Kestenberg, J. S. (1975). *Children and parents.* New York: Jason Aronson.

Kestenberg, J. S., & Buelte, A. (1977). Prevention, infant therapy and the treatment of adults 1. Towards understanding mutuality. 2. Mutual holding and holding oneself up. *International Journal of Psychoanalytic Psychotherapy, 6*, 339–396.

Kestenberg-Amighi, J., Loman, S., Lewis, P., & Sossin, K. M. (1999). *The meaning of movement: Developmental and clinical perspectives of the Kestenberg Movement Profile.* Amsterdam: Gordon & Breach Publishers.

Kivijärvi, M., Räihä, H., Kaljonen, A., Tamminen, T., & Piha, J. (2005). Infant temperament and maternal sensitivity behavior in the first year of life. *Scandinavian Journal of Psychology, 46*, 421–428.

Lewis, V., & Boucher, J. (1998). *Test of pretend play.* Oxford: Pearson Assessment.

Lichtenberger, E. O. (2005). General measures of cognition for the preschool child. *Mental Retardation and Developmental Disabilities Research Reviews, 11*, 197–208.

Lieberman, A. (1997). Mood disorder: Prolonged bereavement/grief reaction. In A. Lieberman, S. Wieder, & E. Fenichel (Eds.), *The DC:0-3 casebook* (pp. 61–68). Washington, DC: Zero to Three.

Lieberman, A. F., Barnard, K. E., & Wieder, S. (2004). Diagnosing infants, toddlers, and preschoolers: The Zero to Three Diagnostic Classification of early mental health disorders. In R. DelCarmen-Wiggins & A. Carter (Eds.), *Handbook of infant, toddler and preschool mental health assessment* (pp. 141–160). New York: Oxford.

Lieberman, A. F., Wieder, S., & Fenichel, E. (Eds.) (1997). *The DC:0-3 casebook: A guide to the use of 0 to 3's diagnostic classification of mental health and developmental disorders of infancy and early childhood in assessment and treatment planning.* Washington, DC: Zero to Three.

Lindner, T. (2008). *Transdisciplinary Play-Based Assessment 2 (TPBA-2) and Transdisciplinary Play-based Intervention 2 (TPBI-2).* Baltimore, MD: Brookes.

Lollock, L. (2001). *The foreign population born in the United States: March 2000.* Current Population Reports P20–534, U.S. Census Bureau, Washington, D.C.

Loo, K. K., Ohqui, S., Zhu, H., Howard, J., & Chen, L. (2005). Cross-cultural comparison of the neurobehavioral characteristics of Chinese and Japanese neonates. *Pediatrics International, 47*, 446–451.

Lord, C., Risi, S., Lambrecht, L., Cook, E. H., Leventhal, B. L., DiLavore, P. C., et al. (2000). The Autism Diagnostic Observation Schedule—Generic: A standard measure of social and communication deficits associated with the spectrum of autism. *Journal of Autism and Developmental Disorders, 30*(3), 205–223.

Lord, C., Rutter, M., & Le Couteur, A. (1994). Autism Diagnostic Interview–Revised: A revised version of a diagnostic interview for caregivers of individuals with possible pervasive developmental disorders. *Journal of Autism and Developmental Disorders, 24*(5), 659–685.

Lowe, M., & Costello, A. J. (1988). *Symbolic Play Test* (2nd ed.). Windsor, Berkshire, UK: NFER-Nelson.

Lyons-Ruth, K., & Jacobvitz, D. (1999). Attachment disorganization unresolved loss, relational violence, and lapses in behavioral and attentional strategies. In J. Cassidy & P. R. Shaver (Eds.), *Handbook of attachment: Theory, research and clinical applications* (pp. 520–545). New York: Guilford Press.

Main, M., Kaplan, N., & Cassidy, J. (1985). Security in infancy, childhood, and adulthood: A move to the level of representation. *Monographs of the Society for Research in Child Development, 50,* 66–104.

Mao, A., Burnham, M., Goodlin-Jones, B. L., Gaylor, E. E., & Anders, T. F. (2004). A comparison of the sleep–wake patterns of cosleeping and solitary-sleeping infants. *Child Psychiatry and Human Development, 35*(2), 95–105.

Matthey, S., Guedeney, A., Starakis, N., & Barnett, B. (2005). Assessing the social behavior of infants: Use of the ADBB scale and relationship to mother's mood. *Infant Mental Health Journal, 28*(5), 442–458.

McGoldrick, M., Gerson, R., & Petry, S. (2008). *Genograms: Assessment and intervention* (3rd ed.). New York: Norton.

Meadow-Orleans, K. P., Spencer, E., & Koester, L. S. (2004). *The world of deaf infants: A longitudinal study.* New York: Oxford University Press.

Meisels, S. J., & Atkins-Burnett, S. (2000). The elements of early childhood assessment. In J. P. Shonkoff & S. J. Meisels (Eds.), *Handbook of early childhood intervention* (2nd ed., pp. 231–257). New York: Cambridge University Press.

Morelock, M. J., Brown, P. M., & Morrissey, A. (2003). Pretend play and maternal scaffolding: Comparisons of toddlers with advanced development, typical development, and hearing impairment. *Roeper Review, 26*(1), 41–51.

Mullen, E. M. (1995). *The Mullen Scales of Early Learning* (AGS Ed.). Circle Pines, MN: American Guidance Services.

National Association for the Education of Young Children (NAEYC) (2005). *Screening and assessment of young English-language learners: Supplement to the NAEYC position statement on early childhood curriculum, assessment, and program evaluation.* Washington, DC: Author.

Neisworth, J. T., & Bagnato, S. J. (2004). The mismeasure of young children: The authentic assessment alternative. *Infants & Young Children, 17*(3), 198–212.

Newborg, J. (2004). *Battelle Developmental Inventory* (2nd ed.). Chicago: Riverside Publishing.

Oster, H. (2005). The repertoire of infant facial expressions: An ontogenetic perspective. In J. Nadel & D. Muir (Eds.), *Emotional development: Recent research advances* (pp. 261–292). New York: Oxford University Press.

Parks, S. (1995). *Inside HELP: Administration and reference manual* (2nd ed.). Palo Alto, CA: VORT.

Piaget, J. (1962). *Play, dreams, and imitation in childhood.* New York: Norton.

Pretti-Frontczak, K., & Bricker, D. (2001). Use of embedding strategy during daily activities by early childhood education and early childhood special education teachers. *Infant-Toddler Intervention, 11,* 111–128.

Pretti-Frontczak, K., & Bricker, D. (2004). *An activity-based approach to early intervention* (3rd ed.) Baltimore: Brookes.

Rescorla, L. A. (2005). Assessment of young children using the Achenbach System of Empirically Based Assessment (ASEBA). *Mental Retardation and Developmental Disabilities Research Reviews, 11,* 226–237.

Rescorla, L., & Alley, A. (2001). Validation of the Language Development Survey (LDS): A parent report tool for identifying language delay in toddlers. *Journal of Speech, Language, and Hearing Research, 44,* 434–445.

Richardson, R. D., & Burns, M. K. (2005). Adaptive Behavior Assessment System (2nd ed. by Harrison, P. L., & Oakland, T. (2002). San Antonio, TX: Psychological Corporation. *Assessment for Effective Intervention, 30,* 51–54.

Ross, G., & Lawson, K. (1997). Using the Bayley–II: Unresolved issues in assessing the development of prematurely born children. *Journal of Developmental & Behavioral Pediatrics, 18*(2), 109–111.

Rydz, D., Shevell, M. I., Majnemer, A., & Oskoui, M. (2005). Developmental screening. *Journal of Child Neurology, 20*(1), 4–21.

Sacks, S. Z., Kekelis, L. S., & Gaylord-Ross, R. J. (1992). *The development of social skills by blind and visually impaired students.* New York: AFB Press.

Sander, L. W. (1988). The event-structure of regulation in the neonate–caregiver system as a biological background for early organization of psychic structure. *Progress in Self-Psychology, 3,* 64–77.

Schechter, D. S., Myers, M. M., Brunelli, S. A., Coates, S. W., Zeanah, C. H., Davies, M., Grienenberger, J. F., et al. (2006). Traumatized mothers can change their minds about their toddlers: Understanding how a novel use of video feedback supports positive change of maternal attributions. *Infant Mental Health Journal, 27,* 429–427.

Shahmoon-Shanok, R. (1997). Multisystem developmental disorder, pattern B. In A. Lieberman, S. Wieder, & E. Fenichel (Eds.), *The DC:0-3 casebook* (pp. 335–358). Washington, DC: Zero to Three.

Shahmoon-Shanok, R. (2006). Reflective supervision for an integrated model: What, why, and how? In G. M. Foley & J. D. Hochman (Eds.), *Mental health in early intervention: Achieving unity in principles and practice* (pp. 343–381). Baltimore: Brookes.

Shipley, K. G., & McAfee, J. M. (1998). *Assessment in speech–language pathology: A resource manual* (2nd ed.). San Diego: Singular Publishing Group.

Skovgaard, A. M., Houmann, T., Christiansen, E., Landorph, S., Jorgensen, T., Olsen, E. M., et al. (2007). The prevalence of mental health problems in children 1½ years of age—the Copenhagen Child Cohort 2000. *Journal of Child Psychology and Psychiatry, 48,* 62–70.

Slade, A., Sadler, L., De Dios-Kenn, C., Webb, D., Currier-Ezepchich, J., & Mayes, L. (2005). Minding the baby: A reflective parenting program. *The Psychoanalytic Study of the Child, 60,* 74–100.

Smith, D. (2000). Parent-child interactive play assessment. In K. Gitlin-Weiner, A. Sandgrund & C. Schaefer (Eds.), *Play diagnosis and assessment* (2nd ed., pp. 340–370). New York: Wiley.

Solomon, J., & George, C. (Eds.). (1999). *Attachment disorganization.* New York: Guilford Press.

Sossin, K. M. (2002). Interactive movement patterns as ports of entry in infant–parent psychotherapy. *Journal of Infant, Child, and Adolescent Psychotherapy, 2,* 97–131.

Sossin, K. M., & Birklein, S. B. (2006). Nonverbal transmission of stress between parent and young child: Considerations and psychotherapeutic implications of a study of affective movement patterns. *Journal of Infant, Child, and Adolescent Psychotherapy, 5,* 46–69.

Sparrow, S. S., Cicchetti, D. V., & Balla, D. A. (2005). *Vineland Adaptive Behavior Scales* (2nd ed.). Bloomington, MN: Pearson Assessments.

Squires, J. K. (2000). Identifying social/emotional and behavioral problems in infants and toddlers. *Infant-Toddler Intervention, 10*(2), 107–119.

Squires, J. K., Bricker, D., & Twombly, E. (2002). *The ASQ:SE user's guide: For the Ages & Stages Questionnaires: Social-emotional.* Baltimore: Brookes.

Squires, J. K., Bricker, D., & Twombly, E. (2004). Parent-completed screening for social emotional problems in young children: The effects of risk/disability status and gender on performance. *Infant Mental Health Journal, 25,* 62–73.

Stern, D. (1995). *The motherhood constellation.* New York: Basic Books.

Thomas, J. M., & Clark, R. (1998). Disruptive behavior in the very young child: Diagnostic Classification: 0-3 guides identification of risk factors and relational interventions. *Infant Mental Health Journal, 19,* 229–244.

Tortora, S. (2006). *The dancing dialogue: Using the communicative power of movement with young children.* Baltimore: Brookes.

Tremblay, H., Brun, P., & Nadel, J. (2005). Emotion sharing and emotion knowledge: Typical and impaired development. In J. Nadel & D. Muir (Eds.), *Emotional development: Recent research advances* (pp. 341–363). New York: Oxford University Press.

Trevarthen, C. (2005). First things first: Infants make good use of the sympathetic rhythm of imitation, without reason or language. *Journal of Child Psychotherapy, 31*(1), 91–113.

Trevarthen, C., & Aitken, K. J. (2001). Infant intersubjectivity: Research, theory and clinical applications. *Journal of Child Psychology and Psychiatry, 42,* 3–48.

Tronick, E. (2007). *The neurobehavioral and social–emotional development of infants and children.* New York: Norton.

Waters, E., Hamilton, C. E., & Weinfeld, N. S. (1995). The stability of attachment security from infancy to adolescence and early adulthood: General introduction. *Child Development, 71,* 678–683.

Weatherston, D. (2005). An interdisciplinary training model: The Wayne State University Graduate Certificate Program in infant mental health. In K. M. Finello (Ed.), *Handbook of training and practice in infant and preschool mental health* (pp. 326–342). San Francisco: Jossey-Bass.

Westby, C. (2000). A scale for assessing children's play. In K. Gitlin-Weiner, A. Sandgrund, & C. Schaefer (Eds.), *Play diagnosis and assessment* (2nd ed., pp. 15–57). New York: Wiley.

Wiefel, A., Wollenbweber, S., Oepen, G., Lenz, K., Lehmkuhl, U., & Biringen, Z. (2005). Emotional availability in infant psychiatry. *Infant Mental Health Journal, 26,* 392–304.

Woodruff, G., & Shelton, T. L. (2006). The transdisciplinary approach to early intervention. In G. Foley & J. D. Hochman (Eds.), *Mental health in early intervention: Achieving unity in principles and practice* (pp. 81–110). Baltimore: Brookes.

Zero to Three (2005). *Diagnostic classification of mental health and developmental disorders of infancy and early childhood, Revised* (DC:0–3R). Washington, DC: Author.

Zimmerman, I. L., Steiner, V. G., & Pond, R. E. (2002) *Preschool Language Scale* (4th ed.). San Antonio, TX: Pearson Education.

APPENDIX A

Overview of Selected Instruments

Test	Age Ranges	Areas of Assessment	Publisher
Adaptive Behavior Assessment System (ABAS-II)	Parent/Primary Caregiver Form: Ages 0–5 Teacher/Day care Provider Form: Ages 2–5 years	Assesses adaptive skills; including conceptual, social, and practical skills.	Western Psychological Services
Autism Diagnostic Interview–Revised (ADI-R)	Children and adults with mental age above 2.0 years	Communication and language, social interaction, and restricted, repetitive behaviors.	Western Psychological Services
Autism Diagnostic Observation Schedule–Generic (ADOS-G)	Toddlers to Adults	Communication, social interaction, and play.	Western Psychological Services
Ages & Stages Questionnaires (ASQ), A Parent-Completed, Child-Monitoring System, 2nd ed.	4–60 months	Communication, gross motor, fine motor, problem solving, and personal–social	Brookes
Alberta Infant Motor Scale (AIMS)	Birth–18 months	Motor development	Saunders
Assessment, Evaluation and Programming system for Infants and Children, 2nd ed. (AEPS-II)	Birth–6 years	Fine motor, gross motor, cognitive, adaptive, social-communication, and social	Brookes
Batelle Developmental Inventory (BDI)	Birth–8 years	Screening form identifies children at risk for developmental handicaps. Full-scale form identifies young children's developmental strengths and weaknesses.	DLM Teaching Resources
Bayley Scales of Infant and Toddler Development, 3rd ed. (Bayley-III)	1–42 months	Assesses developmental domains of cognition, language, social-	Pearson Education

		emotional, motor, and adaptive behavior.	
Bayley-III Screening Test	1–42 months	Screens for cognitive, language, and motor development delays	Pearson Education
Brigance Infant and Toddler Screen	Infant: Birth–11 months Toddler: 12–23 months	Fine motor skills, receptive and expressive language, gross motor skills, self-help skills, and social-emotional skills.	Curriculum Associates
Child Behavior Checklist (CBCL)	$1\frac{1}{2}$–5 years	Assesses behavioral problems and social competencies of children as reported by parents	Thomas M. Achenbach, Research Center for Children, Youth, & Families
Child Development Inventory (CDI) for Assessing Toddlers and Preschoolers	15 months–6 years	The developmental scales measure social, self-help, gross motor, fine motor, expressive language, language comprehension, letters, numbers, and general development	Behavior Science Systems
Denver Developmental Screening Test, 2nd ed. (DDST-II)	1 month–6 years old	Screens for possible developmental problems. Fine motor adaptive, gross motor, personal–social, and language skills are assessed	Denver Developmental Materials
Developmental Activities Screening Inventory (DASI-II)	Birth–60 months	Provides early detection of developmental difficulties in infants	ProEd
Developmental Profile II (DPII)	Birth–9 years	Assesses physical, self-help, social, academic, and communication development	Western Psychological Services
Differential Abilities Scale (DAS)	2 years, 6 months–5 years, 11 months. (To age 7 for children with delays.) 2–16 years	Assesses verbal, reasoning, perceptual, and memory abilities Conduct problems	Psychological Corporation

(Continued)

(Continued)

Test	Age Ranges	Areas of Assessment	Publisher
Eyberg Child Behavior Inventory			Psychological Assessment Resources
Fagan Test of Infant Intelligence	6–12 months	Assesses cognitive potential and identifies children with cognitive deficits	Infantest Corporation
The Functional Emotional Assessment Scale (FEAS)	6 age specific versions (i.e., 7–9 mos., 10–12 mos., 13–18 mos., 19–24 mos., 25–35 mos., & 36–48 mos.)	Observes and assesses a child's emotional and social functioning	Pearson Education
Greenspan–Leiberman Observation System for Assessment of Caregiver–Infant Interaction during Semi-Structured Play (GLOS–Revised)	2–30 months	Assesses social-emotional behaviors. Defines observable and measurable indicator behaviors and characterizes clinical aspects of the mother/caregiver–infant interaction process.	S. Greenspan, A. Lieberman, and S. Poisson/Sue Poisson, 1990
Hawaii Early Learning Profile (HELP)	Birth–36 months	Cognition, expressive-language, gross motor, fine motor, social-emotional, self-help	VORT
Infant/Toddler Sensory Profile	Birth–36 months	Examine patterns in children who may be at risk or have specific disabilities; measures sensation seeking, sensory sensitivity, sensation avoiding	Pearson Education
Infant–Toddler Social-Emotional Assessment (ITSEA)	12–36 months	Analysis of emerging social-emotional development and intervention guidance	Pearson Education
Movement Assessment of Infants (MAI)	Birth–12 months (can be used to assess children over 12 months functioning below that age level)	Measures tone, primitive reflexes, automatic reactions, and volitional movement.	Infant Movement Research

Mullen Scales of Early Learning	Birth–68 months	Measures cognitive functioning; including visual, linguistic, and motor domains; distinguishes between receptive and expressive processing	Pearson Education; American Guidance Service
Neonatal Behavioral Assessment Scale, 2nd ed. (NBAS-II)	Neonates (37–44 weeks gestational age)	Assesses newborn behavioral repertoire; habituation, orientation, motor processes, range of state, regulation of state, autonomic stability, and reflexes are assessed	Lippincott
Nursing Child Assessment Satellite Training Instrument (NCAST)	6–36 months and their caregivers	For child: Clarity of cues and responsiveness to parent For parents: Sensitivity to cues, response to child's distress, social-emotional growth fostering, and cognitive growth fostering	NCAST
Parent–Child Early Relational Assessment (PCERA)	4–12 months and their parents	Measures the quality of parent–child relationships	Department of Psychiatry, University of Wisconsin Medical School
Parenting Stress Index (PSI), 3rd ed.	Parents of children 3 months–10 years	PSI screens for stress in the parent child relationship; identifies dysfunctional parenting; and predicts the potential for parental behavior problems and child adjustment difficulties within the family system Child domain: Distractibility/ hyperactivity,	Western Psychological Services

(Continued)

(Continued)

Test	Age Ranges	Areas of Assessment	Publisher
		adaptability, reinforces parent, demandingness, mood, acceptability Parent domain: competence, social isolation, attachment to child, health, role restriction, depression, spouse.	
Peabody Developmental Motor Scales (PDMS)	Birth–6 years, 9 months	Evaluates gross and fine motor development	DLM Teaching Resources
Preschool Language Scale–3 (PLS-4)	Birth–6 years, 11 months	Measures receptive and expressive language; identifies and describes maturational lags; assists in planning language interventions	Psychological Corporation
Receptive–Expressive Emergent Language Scale (REEL-2)	Birth–3 years	Identifies young children who may have specific language handicaps requiring early intervention	ProEd.
The Rossetti Infant–Toddler Language Scale	Birth–36 months	Assesses preverbal and verbal aspects of young children's communication and interaction	L. Rossetti/ Lingua Systems
Social Responsiveness Scale	4–18 years	Distinguishes autism spectrum conditions from other child psychiatric conditions by identifying presence and extent of autistic social impairment	Western Psychological Services
Symbolic Play Scale	9–36 months	Assesses cognitive, play, and language development problems	C. Westby

System to Plan Early Childhood Services (SPECS)	2–6 years	Assists teams to organize informed judgments in order to make decisions for children with disabilities or at risk for disability; to plan and evaluate interventions. Communication, sensorimotor, physical, self-regulation, cognition, and self-social development are rated	American Guidance Service
Test of Early Language Development, 3rd ed. (TELD-3)	2–7 years	Identifies children who are experiencing language delays or difficulties and may be candidates for early intervention	Pearson Education
Transdisiplinary Play-Based Assessment & Transdisciplinary Play-Based Intervention, 2nd ed.	Infancy–6 years	Cognitive, social-emotional, communication and language, and sensorimotor development	Brookes
Vineland Adaptive Behavior Scales	Birth–18 years, 11 months; also low-functioning adults	Assesses adaptive behavior in communication, daily living skills, socialization, and motor skills	American Guidance Service

CHAPTER 5

Assessment of Preschool Children

VINCENT C. ALFONSO
and DAWN P. FLANAGAN

CCORDING TO KELLEY and Surbeck (2007) the assessment of young
children may seem to be a relatively new activity for educational
and psychological professionals, but preschool assessment "issues,
practices, and techniques have links to practices that began in Europe and
America roughly 200 years ago" (p. 3). Nevertheless, preschool assessment
gained its greatest momentum after the passage of several federal public laws
including, most recently, the Individuals with Disabilities Education Act
(IDEA) of 2004, which requires states to provide a free and appropriate public
education for all individuals with educationally handicapping conditions
between birth and 21 years of age.

In addition to early influences and recent legislation on the assessment of
young children, research on children with developmental disabilities,
including children with autism spectrum disorders, has played a significant
role in the emphasis on and popularity of preschool assessment. Moreover,
because research has demonstrated that early intervention services are
effective in ameliorating current, and inhibiting future, psychoeducational
difficulties in young children (Campbell & Ramey, 1994; Casto &
Mastropieri, 1986; Guralnick, 1997; Price, Cowen, Lorion, & Ramos-McKay,
1988; Ramey & Ramey, 1998), preschool assessment will continue to provide
valuable information to families, professionals, community members, and
others who nurture and teach young children.

The purposes of preschool assessment include screening, diagnosis,
individual program planning and monitoring, and program evaluation
(Nagle, 2007). This chapter focuses on assessment instruments that are
used for screening and diagnostic purposes. In particular, this chapter
provides a framework for evaluating the adequacy of the technical characteristics of norm-referenced instruments for preschoolers in five
domains of assessment.

129

DOMAINS OF ASSESSMENT

The major domains of young children's functioning and thus assessment are cognitive, language, behavioral and social-emotional functioning, adaptive behavior, and motor skills (Bracken & Nagle, 2007). Although we recognize that other domains such as play and physical development are also important in understanding young children, there are few norm-referenced instruments available to assess these domains (see Chapters 4 and 10, also see Gitlin-Weiner, Sandgrund, & Schaefer, 2000, for a comprehensive review of play diagnosis and assessment). Therefore, we focus on the five areas that are typically measured with norm-referenced instruments and that are most critical for screening for developmental delay and making diagnostic and educational placement decisions.

COGNITION

The assessment of cognitive functioning in young children usually includes the evaluation of abilities and processes such as vocabulary development, reasoning, visual processing, auditory processing, memory, and the preacademic skills necessary for the acquisition and development of reading, writing, and math skills. Today's cognitive tests are far more sophisticated than they were a decade ago. For example, most current cognitive tests are grounded in contemporary psychometric theory, particularly the Cattell-Horn-Carroll (CHC) theory (Flanagan, Ortiz, Alfonso, & Dynda, 2008). As such, these tests have stronger construct validity than their predecessors. In addition, because current cognitive tests are based on well-defined and validated theories, their corresponding interpretive approaches are more reliable and valid than those that were based on logical categorizations of tests (e.g., Kaufman, 1979; Sattler, 1988). Furthermore, the growing body of outcomes research that demonstrates the relationships between theoretical cognitive constructs and academic skills assists in both tailoring assessments to referral concerns and making predictions about performance (see Flanagan, Ortiz, & Alfonso, 2007).

In addition to outcomes research, there have been a number of neuroimaging studies that highlight the effectiveness of early intervention for children with cognitive processing deficits (e.g., Fletcher, Lyon, Fuchs, & Barnes, 2007). For example, recent neuroimaging research demonstrated that phonological processing deficits in young children can be trained, through appropriate instruction and interventions, resulting in age appropriate phonological skills and later reading skills (McCloskey, 2007). Overall, recent advances in test development and research in cognitive assessment suggest that current cognitive tests will likely be more effective and therefore yield data that are more informative for the purposes of diagnosing developmental delay, mental retardation, and giftedness (Daniel, 1997; Flanagan et al., 2008; Keith, 1994; Neisser et al., 1996).

LANGUAGE

"Language refers to the communication code that is used for representing the information and ideas to be shared" (Wyatt & Seymour, 1999, p. 218). Broadly speaking, the assessment of language functioning most often includes receptive and expressive language skills. However, many researchers and practitioners agree that there are several linguistic subsystems that must be mastered by children in order to "know a language" (Nelson & Warner, 2007, p. 363). These subsystems include phonology, morphology, syntax, semantics, and pragmatics (Allen, 1989; Nelson & Warner). Evaluation of these subsystems is critical given the number of developmental language disorders that can be diagnosed in preschool children (e.g., Allen; Paul, 1995). Thus, the importance of having technically adequate language instruments is clear (McCauley & Swisher, 1984; Oades-Sese & Alfonso, 2003, 2008; Plante & Vance, 1994; Wyatt & Seymour, 1999).

BEHAVIORAL AND SOCIAL-EMOTIONAL FUNCTIONING

The assessment of behavioral and social-emotional functioning typically involves evaluating how young children interact with peers, adults, and the environment in general. More specifically, assessment in this domain explores the extent to which children demonstrate problem behaviors such as hitting and throwing objects, and prosocial behaviors, such as demonstrating concern for others and sharing toys with peers. It is important to measure this domain of functioning because atypical development may involve anxiety and mood disorders (e.g., depression), attachment disorders (e.g., reactive attachment disorder), pervasive developmental disorders (e.g., autism), and attention-deficit/hyperactivity disorder (Campbell & James, 2007; Knoff, Stollar, Johnson, & Chenneville, 1999).

Knoff et al. (1999) add that it is critical to assess this domain in the preschool years "because many of these affective and skill-related areas form a foundation that guides and influences children's later functioning in home, school, and community domains" (p. 126). Thus, comprehensive evaluation of young children's behavioral and social-emotional functioning is essential because obtained data inform decisions regarding intervention goals and methods (Campbell & James, 2007). One of the most commonly used methods of assessing this domain of functioning in young children is norm-referenced behavior rating scales (e.g., Achenbach & Rescorla, 2000; Conners, 2008; Martin, 1988; Reynolds & Kamphaus, 2004).

ADAPTIVE BEHAVIOR

Adaptive behavior functioning has been defined as an individual's personal and social sufficiency or independent and autonomous functioning (Sparrow, Cicchetti, & Balla, 2005). Essentially, adaptive behavior develops as an individual ages and is an important domain of functioning to assess in young children especially those suspected of having severe intellectual impairments or other developmental disabilities (e.g., autism). Adaptive behavior and cognitive functioning are often assessed concurrently to inform decisions about mental retardation (American Association on Mental Retardation, 2002; Harrison & Raineri, 2007; Jacobson & Mulick, 1996). Typical areas of adaptive behavior functioning that are assessed via interviews or rating scales include communication, daily living skills, socialization, and motor skills (Harrison & Oakland, 2003; Sparrow et al., 2005).

MOTOR

The assessment of motor development in young children is important because it "is a universally recognized means for assessing the overall rate and level of development of the child during the early months and years after birth" (Williams & Monsma, 2007). In addition, the motor system is a medium through which other developmental domains such as cognitive, language, and socio-emotional interact with the environment (Dunn, 1999).

There are two broad categories of motor skills, namely, fine and gross motor. Fine motor skills typically involve the use of hands and fingers, and sometimes the interaction of the visual system with these small muscle masses (i.e., visual-motor integration). The assessment of fine motor skills which is usually conducted by an occupational therapist includes items such as reaching for objects, placing beads or blocks in a cup, scribbling, and prewriting tasks (Bayley, 2006). Gross motor skills involve the use of the large muscle masses of the body such as legs, arms, and trunk (Williams & Monsma, 2007). When assessing the gross motor skills of young children, a physical therapist will usually evaluate how a child walks, runs, jumps, skips, and moves within his/her environment (Bayley).

A comprehensive assessment of a child across all five domains mentioned here requires the expertise of a number of individuals. Furthermore, each of the five domains of functioning should be assessed through one or more methods and sources of assessment.

METHODS AND SOURCES OF ASSESSMENT

A variety of methods of preschool assessment exist, including the use of observations and interviews, as well as norm-referenced, curriculum-based, play-based, dynamic, and ecological assessment. We firmly believe that each of these methods has a place in the assessment of preschoolers and that a multimethod, multisource, and multisetting approach is the best one to take when trying to determine a young child's strengths and weaknesses in each domain of functioning (e.g., Knoff et al., 1999; Merrell, 2003). For example, family members (e.g., parents and siblings), school personnel (e.g., teachers), professionals (e.g., occupational and physical therapists), and community members often provide information that is invaluable in understanding the thoughts, feelings, and behaviors of young children. When assessment of young children does not include at least some of these individuals in the evaluation process, it is likely that the potential for misdiagnosis will increase.

Space limitations preclude a discussion of the procedures involved in each assessment method as well as their advantages and disadvantages in the evaluation of young children. Therefore, in this chapter we focus on norm-referenced assessment via the use of tests, rating scales, and standardized interviews usually administered by a psychologist or other trained assessment professional (e.g., speech-language pathologist) for the following reasons. First, these instruments tend to have the strongest psychometric properties of all methods of assessment. Second, they are used by most practitioners and clinicians to assist in screening, diagnostic, placement, and treatment decisions. Third, they are time and cost-efficient, and have a long and rich research history (Kelley & Surbeck, 2007).

NORM-REFERENCED ASSESSMENT OF PRESCHOOL CHILDREN

Over the past two decades, the adequacy of the technical characteristics of preschool instruments has been investigated by a number of independent researchers (e.g., Alfonso & Flanagan, 1999; Bracken, 1987; Bracken, Keith, & Walker, 1998; Bradley-Johnson, 2001; Evans & Bradley-Johnson, 1988; Flanagan & Alfonso, 1995; Oades-Sese & Alfonso, 2003, 2008). According to Nagle (2000), reliable and valid assessment of preschoolers is difficult due to a number of factors including rapid and uneven development in a number of domains of functioning (e.g., cognitive) and behavioral issues typical of young children (e.g., short attention span, low frustration tolerance). These factors can adversely affect the accuracy, stability, and predictive validity of the developmental level and cognitive capabilities of young children (Bracken & Walker, 1997). Bracken et al. (1998) noted that instruments intended for use with preschool-age children, especially for children under 4 years of age, presented significant technical inadequacies. While there has been a demand for improved technical adequacy of tests intended for preschool populations, there is a lack of agreed-upon criteria for evaluating many technical characteristics of tests (e.g., standardization characteristics, such as match of demographics to the U.S. population, length of test-retest intervals, range of age divisions in norms tables).

There have, however, been several attempts to establish and apply such criteria to instruments intended for young children. In 1987, Bracken presented criteria for evaluating the psychometric quality of 10 instruments intended for preschool-age children. Specifically, Bracken reported criteria for adequate median subtest reliabilities, total test internal consistency reliability coefficients, total test stability coefficients, subtest floors, total test floors, and subtest item gradients. Almost a decade later, Flanagan and Alfonso (1995) applied similar criteria in their evaluation of intelligence tests for preschoolers. In their review, each of five tests was evaluated according to size of the test's normative sample, recency of the normative data, match of the demographic characteristics of the normative group to the U.S. population, total test internal consistency reliability, test-retest reliability, subtest floors, subtest item gradient violations, and validity evidence found in both test manuals and as well as external sources (e.g., journals, book chapters).

More recently, Bradley-Johnson (2001) used many of Bracken's (1987) criteria to evaluate cognitive tests intended for infants and toddlers from birth to 2 years. Other reviews that included specific criteria for evaluating the technical adequacy of tests for preschoolers were conducted for language scales (e.g., Bracken & Pecyna-Rhyner, 1991; Oades-Sese & Alfonso, 2003, 2008), behavioral and social-emotional rating scales (e.g., Bracken et al., 1998; Campbell & James, 2007; Floyd & Bose, 2003), and adaptive behavior rating scales (e.g., Evans & Bradley-Johnson, 1988; Shands et al., 2008). Table 5.1 summarizes the most salient criteria used by the abovementioned researchers to review the adequacy of the technical characteristics of norm-referenced instruments for preschoolers. This table also includes references to sources that provided comprehensive descriptions and qualitative reviews of preschool instruments.

Although the importance of closely examining the adequacy of the technical characteristics of instruments intended for preschoolers is clear, the information provided in Table 5.1 demonstrates that not only does variability in criteria exist, but many investigators did not use any criteria in their evaluation of the instruments they reviewed. In an attempt to move toward a uniform set of criteria for evaluating adequacy of the technical characteristics of instruments for preschoolers, the next section provides a detailed description of technical characteristics as well as corresponding criteria and evaluative classifications that we believe are the most appropriate to incorporate in any review of preschool assessment instruments. By establishing and applying criteria for evaluating the adequacy of preschool instrumentation, practitioners who are formally trained in assessing young children can make informed decisions regarding test selection and draw appropriate conclusions from test results.

Table 5.1

Sources that Include Comprehensive Descriptions and Reviews of and Criteria for Evaluating Norm-Referenced Instruments for Preschoolers

Source	Assessment Domain(s)	Norm-Referenced Test Characteristics						
		Standardization	Reliability	Norm Table Age Division	Test Floors	Item Gradients	Validity
Bracken (1987)	Various including cognitive, language, and general development	Not addressed	Median subtest internal consistency ≥0.80; total test internal consistency ≥0.90; total test stability ≥0.90	Not addressed	Average subtest floor ≥ 2 standard deviations below the mean; total test floor ≥ 2 standard deviations below the mean	Each test item is equivalent to no more than one-third standard deviation	Presence or absence of validity evidence in test manual only, but no evaluation of the evidence
Flanagan & Alfonso (1995); Alfonso & Flanagan (1999)	Cognitive	Evaluated the size of the normative group, recency of the normative data, and number of demographic variables (see Table 5.2 for specific criteria)	Evaluated total test internal consistency and test-retest as well as test-retest sample characteristics (see Table 5.2 for specific criteria)	Norm tables between 1-2 months evaluated as *Good*; 3-4 months evaluated as *Adequate*; >4 months evaluated as *Inadequate* (see Table 5.2)	Similar to Bracken (1987) (see Table 5.2 for application of specific criteria)	Same as Bracken (1987) (see Table 5.2 for application of specific criteria)	Presence or absence of content, criterion-related, and construct validity evidence and authors' evaluation of the evidence (see Table 5.2 for specific criteria)

(Continued)

135

Table 5.1
(Continued)

		Norm-Referenced Test Characteristics					
Source	Assessment Domain(s)	Standardization	Reliability	Norm Table Age Division	Test Floors	Item Gradients	Validity
Bracken & Walker (1997)	Cognitive	Not addressed	Same as Bracken (1987)	Suggested 1-2 month intervals, but no evaluation according to this criterion	Same as Bracken (1987)	Same as Bracken (1987)	Not addressed
Bradley-Johnson (2001)	Cognitive	Described but no evaluation according to specific criteria	Same as Bracken (1987)	Not addressed	Same as Bracken (1987)	Same as Bracken (1987)	Author's evaluation of content, construct, and criterion validity evidence
Lidz (2003)	Cognitive	Same as Alfonso & Flanagan (1999)	Same as Alfonso & Flanagan (1999)	Recommended Alfonso & Flanagan (1999), but no evaluation according to specific criteria	Not addressed	Recommended Bracken (1987), but no evaluation according to specific criteria	Same as Alfonso & Flanagan (1999)
Saye (2003)	Cognitive	Described but no evaluation according to specific criteria	Same as Bracken (1987)	Recommended Bracken (2000), but no evaluation according to specific criteria	Recommended Bracken (1987), but no evaluation according to specific criteria	Recommended Bracken (1987), but no evaluation according to specific criteria	Author's evaluation of select validity evidence

Reference	Domain	Col 1	Col 2	Col 3	Col 4	Col 5	Col 6
Ford & Dahinten (2005)	Cognitive	Not addressed	Described but no evaluation according to specific criteria	Not addressed	Described but no evaluation according to specific criteria	Described but no evaluation according to specific criteria	Described but no evaluation of the evidence
Kamphaus (2005)	Cognitive	Described but no evaluation according to specific criteria	Described but no evaluation according to specific criteria	Not addressed	Not addressed	Not addressed	Author's evaluation of select validity evidence
Bradley-Johnson & Johnson (2007)	Cognitive	Described but no evaluation according to specific criteria	Same as Salvia & Ysseldyke (2004)	Described but no evaluation according to specific criteria	Same as Bracken (1987)	Same as Bracken (1987)	Author's evaluation of content, construct, and criterion validity evidence
Vig & Sanders (2007)	Cognitive	Described but no evaluation according to specific criteria	Described but no evaluation according to specific criteria	Not addressed	Not addressed	Not addressed	Described but no evaluation of the evidence
McCauley & Swisher (1984)	Language	Same as: APA (1974); Salvia & Ysseldyke (1981); Weiner & Hoock (1973)	Same as Salvia & Ysseldyke (1981)	Not addressed	Not addressed	Not addressed	Presence or absence of validity evidence in test manual only, but no evaluation of the evidence
Bracken & Pecyna-Rhyner (1991)	Language	Described but no evaluation according to specific criteria	Same as Bracken (1987)	Not addressed	Same as Bracken (1987)	Same as Bracken (1987)	Same as Bracken (1987)

(*Continued*)

137

Table 5.1
(Continued)

Source	Assessment Domain(s)	Norm-Referenced Test Characteristics					
		Standardization	Reliability	Norm Table Age Division	Test Floors	Item Gradients	Validity
Plante & Vance (1994)	Language	Same as: APA (1974); Salvia & Ysseldyke (1981); Weiner & Hoock (1973)	Same as Salvia & Ysseldyke (1981)	Not addressed	Not addressed	Not addressed	Same as McCauley & Swisher (1984)
Wyatt & Seymour (1999)	Language	Described but no evaluation according to specific criteria	Not addressed	Not addressed	Not addressed	Not addressed	Not addressed
Dockrell (2001)	Language	Total sample size reported, but no evaluation according to specific criteria	Presence or absence of reliability evidence in test manual, but no evaluation of the evidence	Not addressed	Not addressed	Not addressed	Presence or absence of validity evidence in test manual only, but no evaluation of the evidence
Brassard & Boehm (2007)	Language	Described but no evaluation according to specific criteria	Described but no evaluation according to specific criteria	Not addressed	Not addressed	Not addressed	Described but no evaluation of the evidence
Nelson & Warner (2007)	Language	Not addressed	Not addressed	Not addressed	Not addressed	Not addressed	Not addressed

Oades-Sese & Alfonso (2003, 2008)	Language	Described but no evaluation according to specific criteria	Same as Flanagan & Alfonso (1995)	Described but no evaluation according to specific criteria	Same as Bracken (1987)	Same as Bracken (1987)	Same as: Flanagan & Alfonso (1995); AERA, APA, & NCME (1999)
Martin (1988)	Behavior and Social-Emotional	Described but no evaluation according to specific criteria	Described but no evaluation according to specific criteria	Not addressed	Not addressed	Not addressed	Author's evaluation of select validity evidence
Wilson & Bullock (1989)	Behavior and Social-Emotional	Described but no evaluation according to specific criteria	Internal consistency reliability described; test-retest and interrater reliability as per Anastasi (1982)	Not addressed	Not addressed	Not addressed	Presence or absence of validity evidence including content, criterion-related, and construct and authors' evaluation of the evidence
Bracken, Keith, & Walker (1998)	Behavior and Social-Emotional	Described but no evaluation according to specific criteria	Same as Bracken (1987)	Not addressed	Same as Bracken (1987)	Same as Bracken (1987)	Same as Bracken (1987)
Knoff, Stollar, Johnson, & Chenneville (1999)	Behavior and Social-Emotional and Adaptive Behavior	Described but no evaluation according to specific criteria	Described but no evaluation according to specific criteria	Not addressed	Not addressed	Not addressed	Described but no evaluation of the evidence
Kamphaus & Frick (2005)	Behavior and Social-Emotional	Described but no evaluation according to specific criteria	Described but no evaluation according to specific criteria	Not addressed	Not addressed	Not addressed	Described but no evaluation of the evidence

(*Continued*)

139

Table 5.1
(Continued)

Source	Assessment Domain(s)	Norm-Referenced Test Characteristics					
		Standardization	Reliability	Norm Table Age Division	Test Floors	Item Gradients	Validity
Floyd & Bose (2003)	Behavior and Social-Emotional	Same as Flanagan & Alfonso (1995)	Same as Bracken (1987)	Not addressed	Same as Bracken (1987)	Same as Bracken (1987)	Same as: Flanagan & Alfonso (1995); AERA, APA, & NCME (1999)
Lidz (2003)	Behavior and Social-Emotional and Adaptive Behavior	Described but no evaluation according to specific criteria	Described but no evaluation according to specific criteria	Not addressed	Not addressed	Not addressed	Described but no evaluation of the evidence
Merrell (2003)	Behavior and Social-Emotional	Described but no evaluation according to specific criteria	Described but no evaluation according to specific criteria	Not addressed	Not addressed	Not addressed	Author's evaluation of select validity evidence
Brassard & Boehm (2007)	Behavior and Social-Emotional and Adaptive Behavior	Described but no evaluation according to specific criteria	Described but no evaluation according to specific criteria	Not addressed	Not addressed	Not addressed	Described but no evaluation of the evidence
Campbell & James (2007)	Behavior and Social-Emotional	Not addressed	Described but no evaluation according to specific criteria	Not addressed	Not addressed	Not addressed	Not addressed

Evans & Bradley-Johnson (1988)	Adaptive Behavior	Same as Salvia & Ysseldyke (1981)	Same as Aiken (1985)	Not addressed	Not addressed	Not addressed	Authors' evaluation of select validity evidence
Shands et al. (2008)	Adaptive Behavior	Described but no evaluation according to specific criteria	Same as Bracken (1987)	Not addressed	Same as Bracken (1987)	Same as Bracken (1987)	Same as Flanagan & Alfonso (1995)
Dunn (1999)	Motor	Not addressed	Not addressed	Not addressed	Not addressed	Not addressed	Not addressed
Williams & Monsma (2007)	Motor	Described but no evaluation according to specific criteria	Not addressed	Not addressed	Not addressed	Not addressed	Not addressed
Emmons & Alfonso (2005)	Various (screening)	Described but no evaluation according to specific criteria	Same as Flanagan & Alfonso (1995)	Not addressed	Not addressed	Not addressed	Same as Flanagan & Alfonso (1995)
Brassard & Boehm (2007)	Various (screening)	Described but no evaluation according to specific criteria	Described but no evaluation according to specific criteria	Not addressed	Not addressed	Not addressed	Described but no evaluation of the evidence

Note: Although many reviews are included in this table, the list is not exhaustive. Instead, we included only recent or the most often cited journal articles and book chapters that addressed the quality of norm-referenced tests for preschoolers in the following domains: cognitive, language, behavioral and social emotional functioning, adaptive behavior, and motor skills.

TECHNICAL CHARACTERISTICS OF NORM-REFERENCED INSTRUMENTS

STANDARDIZATION

According to Urbina (2004) one meaning of *standardization* concerns the use of standards for evaluating test results. These standards are typically referred to as norms that are obtained from a group of individuals known as the normative or standardization sample. Evaluation of the demographics and characteristics of the norm sample in comparison to the demographics and characteristics of the population provides an indication of the success of the sampling procedure.

When there is correspondence along the various descriptive indices between the sample and the population, it can be inferred that representation is adequate. Accurate representation is not, however, the only measure of norm sample adequacy. Beyond simple demographic matching lie issues related to sampling methods and psychometric procedures for deriving norms that also play a significant role in determining the overall quality of a given standardization group. Typically, the adequacy of the standardization sample of any given instrument can be effectively gauged through an examination of the size of the normative group, recency of the normative data (as reflected by the date when data were collected), average number of individuals per age or grade interval included in the standardization sample, size of the age blocks used in the norm tables across the entire age range of the test, and number and types of variables included in the norming plan (Flanagan & Alfonso, 1995; Flanagan, Ortiz, Alfonso, & Mascolo, 2002, 2006; Hammill, Brown, & Bryant, 1992).

The adequacy of the *size of the normative group* is dependent on the adequacy of its component parts. Although it is true that the larger the sample size the more likely it is to be a better estimate of performance of the population as a whole, it is important to note that size alone is an insufficient indicator of norm sample adequacy. A carefully constructed small sample may, in fact, provide a closer match or correspondence with the population than a larger sample that is collected with less care or attention. Thus, evaluation of a standardization sample's component parts provides additional important indicators regarding the appropriateness of the overall sample size. In general, it is reasonable to assume that when the component characteristics of a standardization sample are adequate, the size of the normative sample is probably large enough to ensure stable values that are representative of the population under consideration (Anastasi & Urbina, 1997).

Review and evaluation of the *average number of participants at each age and or grade interval* in the normative sample provides important information about the generalizability of the sample. For instance, suppose that a particular battery was normed on 6,000 individuals aged 2–85 years. Relative to the size of most norm groups, 6,000 is quite large and therefore would appear to represent adequately the true performance of the general population of individuals from 2 to 85 years of age. However, suppose that a careful examination of the number of individuals included at every 1-year age interval revealed that only 50 individuals comprised the "3 years, 0 months, to 3 years, 11 months" interval, whereas all other 1-year age intervals include 200 individuals. The small number of 3-year-olds in this example suggests that this test does not adequately represent all 3-year-olds to whom this test might be given. In order to ensure that norms at a particular age (e.g., age 3) may be generalized to all individuals of that same age in the general population, practitioners should ensure that the average number of participants at the age level corresponding to the age of the individual being tested is adequate.

Evaluation of the *recency* of the normative data for instruments is also important because up-to-date normative comparisons must be made to ensure accurate interpretation of an individual's obtained score. For example, the use of outdated norms (i.e., more than 10 years) may lead to overestimates of young children's functioning. In the vast majority of cases, normative information for any given instrument is gathered typically within 2–3 years of the instrument's date of publication. However, not all normative data are as recent as might be implied by the publication date of the instrument. Therefore, careful reading of an instrument's technical manual is important.

The *age divisions of norm tables* are also important, particularly for very young children. An age division or block in a norm table contains the data from a selected age range of the normative sample against which an individual's performance is compared. Age blocks can range from 1-month intervals to 1-, 5-, or even 10-year intervals. Although it is possible, and even desirable, to provide norms for every specific age (e.g., 3 years, 1 month; 3 years, 2 months; etc.), the dramatic increase in the number of individuals needed to develop such norms makes this task impractical. Therefore, authors and publishers of preschool instruments generally attempt to ensure that the age divisions are small enough to yield valid estimates of an individual's functioning relative to similar, but not necessarily identical, same-aged peers in the general population. Norms for ages or grades that were not sampled directly are derived by interpolation. Naturally, age blocks at the youngest age range (e.g., 2-5 years) of the test should typically be quite small (e.g., 1-month intervals) due to the rapid rate of growth along the ability dimensions measured by the instrument. Conversely, age divisions at the upper end of the test's age range (e.g., 75–95 years) may be rather large (e.g., 5-year age blocks) due to slower and less variable growth rates of older individuals along the ability dimensions measured by the test.

Also important to understanding the overall adequacy of a test's standardization is the match of the demographic characteristics of the normative group to the U.S. population. According to the *Standards for Educational and Psychological Testing*, the demographic characteristics of a standardization sample are important variables that play a role in the test selection process. Specifically, "selecting a test with demographically appropriate normative groups relevant for the [individual] being tested is important to the generalizability of the inferences that the [practitioner] seeks to make" (American Educational Research Association [AERA], American Psychological Association [APA], National Council on Measurement in Education [NCME], 1999, p. 120). Therefore, the variables included in the norming plan provide information about the representativeness of the norm sample, or how well the characteristics of the norm sample reflect the characteristics of the general population.

Evaluation of the variables included in the norming plan, and hence the representativeness of the norm sample relative to the general population, is particularly important because "the validity of norm-referenced interpretations depends in part on the appropriateness of the reference group to which test scores are compared" (AERA et al., 1999, p. 51). Therefore, the standardization sample on which the norms of an instrument are based should be appropriately representative of the individuals on whom the instrument will be used. Appropriate representation is achieved primarily through consideration of both the *number* and *type* of variables included in the norming plan.

Typically, test developers look to establish as much correspondence between their norm sample and the general population on the basis of stratification of a wide variety of characteristics that typically include gender, race, ethnicity, socioeconomic status (SES), geographic region, and residence location. The greater the stratification of a norm sample on the basis of these and other variables, assuming that a close correspondence with the true proportion of these variables in the general population was achieved, the more likely the norm sample provides a reliable and accurate estimate of the performance of the population as a whole. For example, SES may be represented by a single variable, such as parental income. But, more frequently, it is represented by a combination of subcategories in addition to parental income, such as occupation and educational attainment. Going to such lengths to represent SES, for example, is important because this variable has been found to be a strong predictor of a number of outcomes, including overall cognitive ability and academic achievement (Collier, 1992; Gould, 1981; Neisser et al., 1996; Thomas & Collier, 1997).

Because it is impractical to achieve an exact match between the standardization sample and the U.S. population characteristics through a purely random sampling method, weighting procedures have become routine (see McGrew, Werder, & Woodcock, 1991). In general, tests that have relatively large standardization samples (e.g., 2,000 participants or greater) and that possess adequate component characteristics will likely have norm groups that closely match the general population characteristics. This will not, of course, be true in every case; therefore, practitioners should pay close attention to the number and type of demographic variables included in the norming plan.

Table 5.2 lists the criteria and evaluative classifications for judging the standardization sample characteristics of norm-referenced instruments. Four aspects of a test's standardization sample (i.e., size of normative group, recency of normative data, age divisions of norm tables, and match of demographic characteristics to U.S. population) were described here and are presented in Table 5.2. This table also shows that each of these four aspects of a standardization sample can be judged to be *Good*, *Adequate*, or *Inadequate*. It is incumbent on test users to determine whether the criteria listed in Table 5.2 have been met. The evaluative classifications are intended to assist test users in understanding the quality of each test characteristic.

RELIABILITY

Reliability refers to "the consistency of scores obtained by the same persons when they are reexamined with the same test on different occasions, or with different sets of equivalent items, or under other variable examining conditions" (Anastasi & Urbina, 1997, p. 84). The reliability of a scale affects practitioners' interpretations of the test results because it guides decisions regarding the range of scores (i.e., standard error of measurement) likely to occur as the result of factors that are not directly relevant to actual ability or performance (e.g., measurement error, chance). Test reliability, in its broadest sense, indicates the extent to which individual differences can be attributed to true differences in the characteristics under investigation or to error or chance (Anastasi & Urbina). The degree of confidence a practitioner can place in the precision of a test score is related directly to the estimated reliability of the test score. Unreliable test scores can result in misdiagnosis and inappropriate placement and treatment decisions. This potential problem can be significantly reduced by selecting tests that have good reliability and thus less error associated with their scores or by combining individual test scores into composite scores. In the latter case, measurement of similar or highly related abilities provides information that converges toward true performance, thereby increasing reliability. For in-depth treatment of reliability concepts, the reader is referred to Anastasi and Urbina, AERA and associates (1999), Crocker and Algina (1986), Lord and Novick (1968), Nunnally (1978), and Salvia and Ysseldyke (1981).

As shown in Table 5.2, the reliability of preschool instruments can be characterized as *Good* (coefficients of 0.90 and above), *Adequate* (coefficients of

Table 5.2

Criteria for Evaluating the Adequacy of the Technical Characteristics of Preschool
Assessment Instruments

Technical Characteristic	Criteria	Evaluative Classification
Standardization[a]		
Size of normative group and number of participants at each age/grade interval	200 persons per each 1-year interval and at least 2,000 persons overall	Good
	100 persons per each 1-year interval and at least 1,000 persons overall	Adequate
	Neither criterion above is met	Inadequate
Recency of normative data	Collected in 1999 or later	Good
	Collected between 1989 and 1998	Adequate
	Collected in 1989 or earlier	Inadequate
Age divisions of norm tables	1–2 months	Good
	3–4 months	Adequate
	>4 months	Inadequate
Match of the demographic characteristics of the normative group to the U.S. population (e.g., gender, race) with SES included	Normative group represents the U.S. population on five or more important demographic variables	Good
	Normative group represents the U.S. population on three or four important demographic variables with SES included	Adequate
	Neither criterion is met	Inadequate
Reliability		
Internal consistency reliability coefficient (subtests and composites)	≥ 0.90	Good
	0.80–0.89	Adequate
	<0.80	Inadequate
Test–retest reliability coefficient (composites only)	≥ 0.90	Good
	0.80–0.89	Adequate
	<0.80	Inadequate
Test–retest reliability coefficient (subtests only)	≥ 0.80	Adequate
	<0.80	Inadequate
Test–Retest Sample		
Size and representativeness of test-retest sample	Sample contains at least 100 subjects and represents the U.S. population on at least five or more demographic variables	Good

	Sample contains at least 50 subjects and represents the U.S. population on three or four demographic variables	Adequate
	Neither criterion is met	Inadequate
Age range of the test–retest sample	Spans no more than a 1-year interval	Good
	Spans no more than 2 years	Adequate
	Spans more than 2 years or extends beyond the preschool age range (i.e., 2–5 yr), regardless of interval size	Inadequate
Length of test–retest interval[b]	Interval $\leq$3 months	Good
	Interval $>$3 and $\leq$6 months	Adequate
	Interval $>$6 months	Inadequate

Floors

Subtests[c]	Raw score of 1 is associated with a standard score $>$2 standard deviations below the normative mean	Adequate
	Raw score of 1 is associated with a standard score $\leq$2 standard deviations below the normative mean	Inadequate
Composites[d]	Composite standard score $>$2 standard deviations below the normative mean	Adequate
	Composite standard score $\leq$2 standard deviations below the normative mean	Inadequate

Item Gradients[e]

Item Gradient Violations	No item gradient violations occur *or* all item gradient violations are between 2 and 3 standard deviations below the normative mean *or* the total number of violations is $<$5% across the age range of the test	Good
	All item gradient violations occur between 1 and 3 standard deviations below the normative mean *or* the total number of violations is $\geq$5% $\leq$15% across the age range of the test	Adequate

(Continued)

Table 5.2
(Continued)

Technical Characteristic	Criteria	Evaluative Classification
	All or any portion of item gradient violations occur between the mean and 1 standard deviation below the normative mean *or* the total number of violations is >15% across the age range of the test	Inadequate
Validity[f]	Presence and quality of validity evidence 4 or 5 strands of validity evidence and the authors' evaluation of available data	Good
	3 strands of validity evidence and the authors' evaluation of available data	Adequate
	<3 strands of validity evidence and the authors' evaluation of available data	Inadequate

[a]An overall rating is obtained as follows: Good = All Goods; Adequate = Goods and Adequates; Inadequate = Goods and/or Adequates, and Inadequates.

[b]The criteria presented here regarding the length of the test-retest interval differ from traditional criteria used with school-age children because young children's abilities change rapidly.

[c]Assuming a scale having a mean of 100 and a standard deviation of 15, a raw score of 1 that is associated with a standard score of ≤69 would constitute an adequate floor.

[d]Floors are calculated based on the aggregate of the subtest raw scores that comprise the composites, where one item per subtest is scored correctly.

[e]An item gradient is defined as the increase in standard score points associated with a one point increase in raw score values. An item gradient violation occurs when a one point increase in raw score points is associated with a standard score increase of greater than one third of a standard deviation (Bracken, 1987).

[f]Ratings of "Good" or "Adequate" were made only when the available validity evidence was reviewed positively by the authors and corroborated by other reviews in the extant literature.

0.80 to 0.89), or *Inadequate* (coefficients less than 0.80). These evaluations provide the practitioner with an indication of the degree of confidence that can be placed in test score interpretation. Specifically, tests with good reliability yield scores that are sufficiently reliable for use in diagnostic decision making when supported with convergent data sources. Tests with adequate reliability yield scores that are moderately reliable and therefore are most appropriately used to make screening decisions. Tests with inadequate reliability yield scores are insufficiently reliable for most purposes and therefore should not be used to make either diagnostic or screening decisions.

Although the criteria for evaluating the reliability of psychometric tests described here are used widely, they are most appropriate for evaluating a test's *internal consistency* reliability and should not be confused with test-retest reliability coefficients. As with internal consistency coefficients, higher is generally better. However, whereas internal consistency coefficients provide information about a test's reliability or, conversely, unreliability (i.e., measurement error), it must be remembered that a test's stability not only reflects measurement error but also systematic changes, such as those due to development or prior exposure to test materials, and nonsystematic changes, such as unpredictable variations in trait level (e.g., verbal ability) over time (McGrew et al., 1991). Because test-retest reliability coefficients are confounded by trait stability (or conversely, instability), they may be *lower* than internal consistency coefficients (Cattell, 1957; McGrew et al., 1991). In such cases, they are often interpreted inappropriately as reflective of the quality of the instrument (for a more detailed discussion, see Flanagan & Alfonso, 1995, and McGrew et al.). See Table 5.2 for criteria and evaluative classifications for test–retest reliability coefficients.

In addition to evaluating the magnitude of test-retest reliability coefficients, other factors related to the quality of test-retest studies should be considered prior to using test-retest findings to inform interpretation. There are three factors in particular that directly affect the magnitude of test-retest reliability coefficients, including the size and representativeness of the test-retest sample, the age range of the sample, and the length of the test-retest interval. First, the *size of the test-retest sample* on which the stability coefficient is calculated should be sufficiently large to ensure that adequate representation is possible. Second, test-retest coefficients should be provided for the various *age levels* at which the test was normed (Anastasi & Urbina, 1997). For example, if a test was normed on individuals between the ages of 3 and 12 years, interpretations regarding a 4-year-old's expected performance based on stability information from a sample ranging in age from 3 to 10 years (mean age = 6.5 years) is likely to be misleading (Flanagan & Alfonso, 1995). Generalizations regarding this child's expected performance would be most accurate if they were based on stability estimates that were calculated on a representative sample of *4-year-olds only*. Third, because progressive developmental changes are discernible at early ages over a period of a month or less, the *test-retest interval* "should rarely exceed six months" (Anastasi & Urbina, 1997, p. 92). When practitioners are interested in expected stability of test performance, they should evaluate carefully the test-retest sample characteristics prior to using stability coefficients to inform interpretation. Table 5.2 lists the criteria and evaluative classifications for the reliability of norm-referenced tests as well as the test-retest sample characteristics included in their technical manuals.

TEST FLOORS

Instruments with adequate test floors will yield scores that effectively discriminate among various degrees of functioning at the extremes of an ability continuum. A test with an *inadequate floor*, or an insufficient number of easy items, will not distinguish adequately between individuals functioning in the average, low average, and deficient ranges of ability. For example, on the Stanford-Binet Intelligence Scales, 5th edition (Roid, 2003a) a preschooler aged 2 years, 1 month who earns a raw score of 1 on the Verbal Quantitative Reasoning (VQR) test earns a corresponding scaled score of 6, which is considered low average. A raw score of 1 should be associated with the deficient range of functioning (i.e., a scaled score ≤ 3). Thus, tests with inadequate floors will not provide sufficiently precise information for diagnostic and placement decisions, especially for children who function at or near the lower extreme of the ability continuum.

A simple raw score to standard score conversion for each norm table age grouping can be used to examine the adequacy of individual test floors across the age range of a test in a manner similar to that of Bracken (1987), Flanagan and Alfonso (1995), and McGrew and Flanagan (1998). For test floors, subtests, and composites for which a raw score of 1 is associated with a standard score that is *more than* 2 standard deviations below the normative mean of the test is considered *adequate*. If this condition is not met, the subtest floor is considered *inadequate*. For composites, floors are calculated based on the sum of subtest (test) raw scores that comprise the composite, where one item per subtest (test) is answered correctly (Flanagan & Alfonso). Table 5.2 lists the criteria and evaluative classifications for the tests floors of norm-referenced tests.

ITEM GRADIENTS

The information gained from examining a test's item gradient complements information related to the floor of the test. That is, the extent to which a test effectively differentiates among various ability levels at the low end of the ability continuum (e.g., low average, deficient) can be determined by examining test floors, whereas the extent to which a test effectively differentiates *within* various ability levels (e.g., within the low average range; within the deficient range) along the entire scale of the test can be determined by examining item gradients. In other words, item gradients are sensitive to *fine gradations* in ability across the scale of the test. *Item gradient* refers to the density of items across a test's latent trait scale. A test with good item gradient characteristics has items that are approximately equally spaced in difficulty along the entire scale of the test, and the distance between items is small enough to allow for reliable discrimination between individuals on the latent trait measured by the test (McGrew & Flanagan, 1998). Item gradient information is concerned with the extent to which changes in a single raw score point on a test result in excessively large changes in ability scores (or standard scores; Bracken, 1987).

Little attention has been paid to item gradients in the test development and evaluation literature. Among the first investigators to highlight the importance of item gradients and to present procedures for evaluating this test characteristic was Bracken (1987). Several years later, Flanagan and Alfonso (1995) updated the item gradient information for preschool intelligence tests offered by Bracken (1987) using a slight modification of his procedure. Flanagan and Alfonso posited that knowing the frequency of item gradient violations without reference to the mean of the test was limited because frequency data alone did not provide enough information to determine whether a subtest was useful for assessing fine gradations in ability within and across the various ranges of functioning. According to Flanagan and Alfonso, "A consideration of subtest floors, as well as an examination of the distance that item gradient violations occur from the mean of the subtest, is necessary to make informed decisions with regard to the utility of preschool intelligence tests" (1995, p. 71). Like Bracken, Flanagan and Alfonso defined an *item gradient violation* as a one unit increase in raw score points that resulted in a change of more than one-third standard deviation in standard score values.

McGrew and Flanagan (1998) and Oades-Sese and Alfonso (2003, 2008) used a system for evaluating the item gradients of intelligence tests that differed from the previous methods used by Bracken (1987) and Flanagan and Alfonso (1995). Briefly, they tallied the number of item gradient violations for intelligence and language tests, respectively, and compared these values to the total number of possible item gradient violations for the respective test. For example, if a test had two item gradient violations out of a possible 50 (i.e., 50 possible raw score changes across the entire scale), the test was characterized as having 4% (2 of 50) item gradient violations. McGrew and Flanagan calculated the total percent of item gradient violations for the major intelligence tests at every age level, including preschool (i.e., ages 2–5 years).

To establish a system for evaluating the item gradients of a test, McGrew and Flanagan (1998) examined the distribution of the percentage of item gradient violations for all subtests across all age levels and across all intelligence batteries included in their investigation. Results indicated that intelligence tests showed less than or equal to 5% item gradient violations approximately 80% of the time, 5–15% violations approximately 12% of the time, and greater than 15% violations approximately 8% of the time.

When combined with logical considerations, these data were used to categorize tests as having *good* ($\leq$ 5 % violations), *adequate* (> 5 % to $\leq$ 15 % violations), or *inadequte* (> 15 % violations) item gradient characteristics at each age level for which the test provided norms. Table 5.2 lists the criteria and evaluative classifications for item gradients of norm-referenced tests. It is important to note that when evaluating tests for preschoolers, one should pay attention to the number of violations that occur between the ages of 2 and 5 years.

VALIDITY

Much like the variable and complex nature of norm samples, validity is not an *all-or-nothing* condition, and the validity of one test is dependent on the validity of the criterion measure to which it is being compared (Bracken, 1987). Therefore, an acceptable validity criterion is difficult to establish. Because the concept of validity itself is more abstract than the concept of reliability, for example, it is difficult to agree on specific criteria that are appropriate for evaluating the adequacy of the validity evidence reported for any given test (Hammill et al., 1992). Because the criteria for specifying the conditions under which an instrument is determined to be valid were rather arbitrary and confusing, Flanagan and Alfonso (1995) reported on the presence or absence of content, criterion, and construct validity, since these three types of validity were among the traditional categories most often used in establishing the validity of psychometric instruments (Anastasi & Urbina, 1997). In order to identify the validity evidence that existed for the intelligence tests evaluated by Flanagan and Alfonso, each test's examiner's manual and technical manual was reviewed as well as the extant literature. Flanagan and Alfonso's overall review of a test's validity was based on the number and type of validity studies available as well as their own personal judgment regarding the quality of these studies.

In 1999, the new *Standards for Educational and Psychological Testing* were published and a new framework for understanding and evaluating validity evidence was discussed. The *Standards* suggested that validity can be classified according to *strands* of validity evidence including test content, response processes, internal structure, relations to other variables, and consequences of testing. Test authors and publishers are expected to provide evidence for these validity strands in their test manuals so that practitioners may familiarize themselves with the validity evidence "for the intended use and purposes of the tests and inventories selected" (AERA et al., 1999, p. 120). Because the *Standards* discuss five strands of validity evidence and more recent reviews of norm-referenced instruments have incorporated these strands in their evaluations (e.g., Flanagan, McGrew, & Ortiz, 2000; Floyd & Bose, 2003; Oades-Sese & Alfonso, 2003, 2008), we have revised the criteria put forth by Flanagan and Alfonso (1995) to be consistent with the *Standards*. That is, the presence or absence of the five validity strands and the authors' evaluation of available evidence of a test's validity have replaced the traditional categories of content, criterion, and construct validity. See Table 5.2 for the criteria and evaluative classifications for a test's validity. For further discussion of validity concepts, the reader is referred to AERA and associates (1999), Aiken (2000), Anastasi and Urbina (1997), Gregory (2000), and Salvia and Ysseldyke (1981).

AN EXAMPLE OF EVALUATING THE ADEQUACY OF THE TECHNICAL CHARACTERISTICS OF A NORM-REFERENCED INSTRUMENT: THE STANFORD-BINET INTELLIGENCE SCALES, 5TH EDITION

DESCRIPTION

The Stanford-Binet Intelligence Scales, 5th edition (SB5; Roid, 2003a) is an individually administered intelligence battery that is appropriate for use with individuals between the ages of 2 and 85+ years. The SB5 was published by Riverside Publishing in 2003, approximately 17 years after the publication of the SB4. The SB5 is composed of 10 subtests, 5 nonverbal (NV) and 5 verbal (V). The NV subtests combine to yield a NVIQ, the V subtests combine to yield a VIQ, and all 10 subtests combine to yield a Full Scale IQ (FSIQ). Two of the 10 subtests are *routing* subtests—one for the nonverbal domain and one for the verbal domain. The routing subtests assist examiners in determining where to begin the administration of the remaining eight subtests. An abbreviated IQ (i.e., ABIQ) may be obtained by combining the scaled scores earned on the routing subtests. In addition to IQs, the SB5 subtests are organized into five separate Cattell-Horn-Carroll (CHC) factors, including Fluid Reasoning (FR), Knowledge (K), Quantitative Reasoning (QR), Visual-Spatial Processing (VSP), and Working Memory (WM). Each factor is composed of one NV and one V subtest.

The SB5 subtests have a mean of 10 and standard deviation of 3; the composites (i.e., IQs and factors) have a mean of 100 and a standard deviation of 15. The reported range of standard scores for the FSIQ is 40–160 (Roid, 2003b). Derived scores that are available to assist in test interpretation include standard scores, percentiles, change-sensitive scores, and age equivalents. Administration time for the SB5 is 45–75 minutes, depending on the age and ability of the individual. The remainder of this chapter provides an evaluation of the adequacy of the test characteristics of the SB5, as specified in Table 5.2, specifically at the age range of 2–5 years.

EVALUATION OF SB5 STANDARDIZATION SAMPLE CHARACTERISTICS

The standardization sample included 4,800 individuals (1,400 were between the ages of 2 and 5 years), with 350 individuals per 1-year interval for ages 2–5 years and at least 200 individuals through age 16 years. Therefore, the standardization sample size was rated as *Good*. The SB5 standardization data were gathered in 2001-2002 and are considered recent, also resulting in a rating of *Good*. The norm tables of the SB5 are divided in 2-month age blocks for individuals between the ages of 2 and 4 years and 4-month intervals for age 5 years. This characteristic therefore is rated *Adequate to Good*. The sample closely approximated the U.S. population (2001 Census data) on the following variables: age, gender, geographic region, race/ethnicity, and SES (i.e., years of education completed by parents or guardians for children under 18 years) (see Tables 2.4–2.9 in Roid, 2003c). Therefore, the match between the demographic characteristics and the U.S. population is considered *Good*. Overall, the adequacy of the standardization sample of the SB5 is *Good*.

EVALUATION OF SB5 RELIABILITY

The SB5 subtests generally have *Adequate* (0.80-0.89) to *Good* ($\geq$ 0.90 or greater) internal consistency reliability at the preschool age range. Oddly, the Nonverbal Knowledge (NVK) and Nonverbal Quantitative Reasoning (NVQR) subtests have *Adequate to Good* reliability at ages 2–4 years and *Inadequate* reliability (i.e., < 0.80) at age 5 years. The SB5 IQs generally have *Good* internal consistency reliability coefficients. For example, all four IQs have *Good* internal consistency reliability coefficients at ages 2–5 years with the exception of the ABIQ, which has a reliability coefficient of 0.89 (*Adequate*) at age 3 years. The SB5 factors also have *Good* internal consistency reliability coefficients across the preschool age range with the exception of FR (0.86), QR (0.89), and VSP (0.89) at age 5 years, all of which are considered *Adequate*.

Test-retest reliability is *Adequate to Good* for half of the SB5 subtests at the preschool age range. All test-retest reliability coefficients for composites (i.e., IQs and factors) are *Adequate to Good*, with the majority being rated as *Good*. The sample from which the SB5 test-retest reliability coefficients were drawn included 96 children. The only demographic characteristics reported for this sample were gender and race/ethnicity and there was a poor match between these characteristics and the U.S. population estimates (see Figure 3.7 and Table 2.4 in Roid, 2003c). Therefore, the size and representativeness of the SB5 test-retest sample at the preschool age range was rated *Inadequate*. Also rated *Inadequate* is the age range of the test-retest sample (i.e., 2–5 years) because it spans more than two years. Although the length of the test-retest interval (median interval = 5 days; range = 1–36 days) is *Good*, the other test-retest sample characteristics render the overall adequacy of the SB5 test-retest sample for preschools *Inadequate*. As such, the test-retest reliability coefficients must be considered of minimal value when determining whether the SB5 measures the same constructs over time for children ages 2–5 years.

EVALUATION OF SB5 TEST FLOORS

In general, the SB5 subtests have *Adequate* floors. Although only three subtests have *Adequate* floors at age 2 years (i.e., Verbal Knowledge [VK], Nonverbal Visual-Spatial Processing [NVVS], Nonverbal Knowledge [NVK]), nearly all subtests have adequate floors by age 3 years, 6 months. Exceptions are NVQR, Verbal Fluid Reasoning (VFR), and Verbal Quantitative Reasoning (VQR), which do not have *Adequate* floors until age 3 years, 8 months.

All SB5 IQs have *Adequate* floors across the preschool age range. In general, the SB5 factors also have *Adequate* floors. The only exceptions are FR, which does not have an *Adequate* floor until age 3 years, 0 months; WM, which does not have an *Adequate* floor until age 2 years, 4 months; and QR, which does not have an *Adequate* floor until age 3 years, 4 months. Overall, the subtests, IQs, and factors of the SB5 are generally *Adequate* for the assessment of young children, especially ages 3–5 years.

EVALUATION OF SB5 ITEM GRADIENTS

The quality of the item gradients of the SB5 subtests was evaluated following Bracken's (1987) criterion for identifying item gradient *violations* as described above. Furthermore, we applied McGrew and Flanagan's (1998) system for evaluating item gradient violations by tallying the number if item gradient violations and comparing these values to the total number of possible item gradient violations for the respective subtest. For example, the VFR subtest had one item gradient violation at the 5:0–5:3 age division in the norm table. The total number of possible item gradient violations was 17. Therefore, there were four item gradient violations (one for each of the four 1-month intervals included in this age division) out of a possible 68 (i.e., $17 \times 4 = 68$). This same procedure was followed for the other age divisions in the 5-year range (i.e., 5:4–5:7 and 5:8–5:11). If the latter two age divisions also contained one item gradient violation each, then the total number of item gradient violations for 5-year-olds would be 12 (i.e., 4 [number of 1-month intervals in age division] $\times$ 3 [number of age divisions for 5-year-olds] = 12 out of a possible 204 [$68 \times 3 = 204$], resulting in approximately 6% item gradient violations [$12/204 = 0.058$]), which is considered *Adequate*. Note that this example is rather simplistic because the values remained constant across each age division. When values differ across age divisions, it is necessary to follow this example within age divisions and then sum across age divisions for each 1-year age range.

With the exception of age 2 years, most SB5 subtests have *Adequate* to *Good* item gradients. For example, at ages 4 and 5 years, all subtests were rated *Adequate* or *Good* with the exception of VQR, which was rated *Inadequate*. At age 3 years, all SB5 subtests were rated *Adequate* or *Good* with the exception of VFR and VQR, which were rated as *Inadequate*. The only subtests that had *Adequate* or *Good* item gradients at age 2 years were Nonverbal Fluid Reasoning (NVFR) and Verbal Knowledge (VK), respectively. Noteworthy is the fact that only one subtest (i.e., VQR) was rated *Inadequate* across the entire preschool age range.

Evaluation of SB5 Validity Evidence

Although the SB5 was published several years after the *Standards* (1999), the technical manual and interpretive manual of the SB5 refer to the traditional categories of validity (i.e., content, criterion, and construct), rather than the five strands or lines of validity evidence discussed in the *Standards*. Nevertheless, our discussion and evaluation of the SB5 validity evidence is in concert with the *Standards* and recent critical reviews of norm-referenced instruments for preschoolers (e.g., Alfonso, Russo, Fortugno, & Rader, 2005; Oades-Sese & Alfonso, 2003, 2008). That is, our evaluation of the SB5 validity evidence is presented according to the following five strands of validity evidence: (1) test content, (2) response processes, (3) internal structure, (4) relations to other variables, and (5) consequences of testing.

Evidence Based on Test Content   The *Standards* state that evidence supporting the test content of an instrument "refers to the themes, wording, and format of its items and tasks, as well as guidelines for procedures regarding administration and scoring" (AERA et al., 1999, p. 11). A description of the SB5 test development and standardization process is provided on pages 25–62 of the technical manual (Roid, 2003c). Details regarding each of the five major stages in the 7-year development of the SB5 including planning, pilot studies, tryout edition, standardization edition, and final published edition are provided in a very thorough, clear, and explicit manner. The names of the advisory panel members, site coordinators, principal investigators, field researchers, and examiners who participated in the SB5 standardization are provided in Appendix E of the technical manual (Roid, 2003c). Moreover, details regarding literature reviews, expert advice, user surveys, factor analyses of previous SB editions, pilot studies of new items and subtests, tryout edition studies, item development, design of functional levels and testlets, and the design of the standardization edition and final published edition are available. A thorough treatment of administration and scoring of the SB5 is provided in the *Examiner's Manual* (Roid, 2003b).

Roid (2003c) includes a discussion of three types of test content validity, namely, professional judgment of content, coverage of important constructs, and empirical item analysis. Regarding *professional judgment of content*, Roid stated, "a comprehensive item bank was assembled containing all items from previous editions including those of Binet and Simon" (2003c, p. 78), and these items were rated to determine the extent to which they were consistent with the SB5 design and coverage of important constructs. In addition, meetings of experts and an advisory panel met to discuss the planned subtests and other important features of the SB5, hundreds of professional examiners reviewed test items and completed questionnaires to provide feedback to the SB5 development team. Feedback on item fairness was provided by reviewers that represented different genders, racial/ethnic groups, and religious groups.

The second type of SB5 test content validity evidence provided by Roid (2003c) is that of *coverage of important constructs*. Here, the author discusses the selection of constructs to be measured and the items used to measure these constructs. Items were rated by experts in the CHC theory of cognitive abilities/processes to determine which factor or factors an item was measuring. These ratings and factor analyses based on previous editions of the SB were used to develop a test specification chart that was used to "match items to domains and factors, develop new items and subtests, and conduct item analyses and factorial studies" (Roid, 2003c, p. 79). As a result, the structure of the SB5 consists of two domains (i.e., NV and V) and five CHC cognitive factors (i.e., FR, K, QR, VSP, and WM).

Finally, *empirical item analysis* was used to provide evidence of SB5 test content validity. These analyses included item discrimination, percentage correct at successive age levels, a number of model-data-fit statistics, and differential item functioning. According to Roid (2003c), "these analyses and item studies created homogeneous, unifactor scales having consistent evidence of model-data-fit and content relevance" (p. 81).

The test content validity evidence of the SB5 is impressive overall. For example, the breadth and depth of test development and standardization is exemplary, the use of a variety of experts to review items as indicators of specific cognitive constructs and to identify unfair or biased items is consistent with cognitive test development, and the empirical item analyses are extensive and informative. However, the coverage and measurement of important cognitive constructs especially with respect to preschoolers is questionable. For example, according to Alfonso and Flanagan (2007) "the structure of the SB5 is different for preschoolers as compared to older samples simply because many of the activities administered to preschoolers appear to measure different abilities than those underlying activities more typically administered to older children" (p. 275). As such, Alfonso and Flanagan posited an alternative factor structure and interpretive system of the SB5 for young children that has yet to be tested empirically. Therefore, the content validity of the SB5 for very young children is equivocal.

Evidence Based on Response Processes   This strand of validity evidence provides support regarding "the fit between the construct and the detailed nature of performance or response actually engaged in by examinees" and is typically assessed via analyses of individual responses (AERA et al., 1999, p. 12). This strand of validity evidence is not addressed in the SB5 manuals and thus could not be evaluated directly.

Evidence Based on Internal Structure   According to the *Standards* (AERA et al., 1999), evidence based on internal structure indicates the "relationships among test items and test components that conform to the construct on which the proposed test score interpretations are based" (p. 13). Evidence based on the internal structure of the SB5 includes information regarding age trends, intercorrelations of the subtests, factors, and IQs, evidence for general ability or g, and various confirmatory factor analyses. Roid (2003c) provides evidence that the SB5 measures developmental growth and life-span change by demonstrating the "classic trend of increasing mean raw scores . . . until late adolescence or middle adult age, followed by a gradual decline in function for the elderly" (p. 103). This evidence is most clear by inspecting the norms tables found in the SB5 *Examiner's Manual* (Roid, 2003b). In addition, Roid (2003c) discusses and provides growth curves for the five SB5 factor index scores. These growth curves are consistent with those found on other cognitive tests (e.g., Woodcock-Johnson III Tests of Cognitive Abilities [WJ III COG]; Woodcock, McGrew, & Mather, 2001) and the extant research base on age changes of various cognitive abilities (e.g., Horn, 1985).

Intercorrelations of the SB5 subtests for children between the ages of 2 and 5 years range from a low of 0.30 between the NVVSP and NVK subtests to a high of 0.60 between the VVSP and NVQR subtests. Intercorrelations among the SB5 factors range from a low of 0.56 between the K and VSP factors to a high of 0.69 between the QR and WM factors. Finally, intercorrelations among the SB5 IQs are 0.80 between the NVIQ and VIQ, 0.94 between the NVIQ and FSIQ, and 0.96 between the VIQ and FSIQ. In addition, Roid provides a table of g loadings of the SB5 subtests based on unrotated first principal axis factor analysis and principal component analysis for 2- to 5-year-olds. The g loadings for SB5 subtests for children between the ages of

2 and 5 years range from a low of 0.55 for the NFR subtest to a high of 0.79 for the NVQR subtest indicating that the SB5 is a strong measure of *g* even for the youngest individuals included in the standardization sample. The correlations among the SB5 subtests and factors as well as the *g* loadings reported for subtests are generally consistent with what is expected in a multifactor cognitive battery (Alfonso & Flanagan, 2007; Carroll, 1993). However, the correlations among the SB5 IQs are uncharacteristically high. For example, the correlation between the NVIQ and VIQ (i.e., 0.80) is higher than any verbal-nonverbal scale intercorrelation associated with other intelligence tests (e.g., Wechsler scales).

Confirmatory factor analyses were conducted using split-half subtest scores to "confirm" the five-factor model of the SB5 for five different age groups, including a group of 1,400 children between the ages of 2 and 5 years. Roid (2003c) provides fit statistics for five SB5 factor models including a one-factor (*g*), two-factor (i.e., fluid versus crystallized factors), three-factor (i.e., nonverbal reasoning/visual, verbal comprehension, and memory factors), four-factor (i.e., abstract/visual, quantitative, verbal, and short-term memory factors), and a five-factor (the actual SB5 factor design). He concluded that the five-factor model provided a better fit to the data than all other models not only for preschoolers (ages 2–5 years) but for all ages. Nevertheless, in order to gain a better understanding of the factor structure of the SB5, the test author and publisher should have included subtest loadings on all factors, not just the factor on which the subtest theoretically belongs, as well as intercorrelations among the factors.

Similar to the content validity evidence discussed above, the construct validity evidence for the SB5 is impressive overall. Our strongest criticism of the construct validity evidence pertains to the factor structure of the SB5 for young children, which is directly related to the content validity of the test. Based on Alfonso and Flanagan's (2007) classifications of the SB5 subtests for preschoolers and rationale for those classifications, they suggested that the SB5 measures four, rather than five, CHC abilities at the preschool age range (i.e., K, VSP, QK, and WM). Given the limited amount of information available on the factor structure of the SB5 for ages 2–5 years, the viability of Alfonso and Flanagan's (2007) 4-factor model should be tested and compared to the recommended 5-factor model reported in the manual.

Evidence Based on Relations to Other Variables   External variables may include measures of some criterion that the rating scale is expected to predict, as well as relationships to other scales hypothesized to measure the same constructs and scales that measure related or different constructs (AERA et al., 1999). The SB5 technical manual contains detailed information regarding the relationship of the SB5 to other measures of cognitive abilities including previous editions of the SB, important outcomes such as achievement functioning, and membership in special groups.

A review of the correlations between various composite scores on the SB5 and previous versions of the SB and the Wechsler Preschool and Primary Scale of Intelligence-Revised (WPPSI-R; Wechsler, 1989) indicated high positive relationships as expected of similar constructs. For example, the FSIQ of the SB5 correlated 0.90 with the Composite Standard Age Score of the SB4, 0.85 with the FSIQ of the SB Form L-M, and 0.83 with the FSIQ of the WPPSI-R. In addition, Roid (2003c) provides numerous tables of data regarding SB5 performance of several special groups including, but not limited to, those with mental retardation, autism, and developmental delay. Patterns of means and standard deviations were generally consistent with the extant research base on clinical groups. For example, all factors and IQs were ≤ 65 for a sample of 119 individuals with mental retardation between the ages of 3 and 25 years.

The SB5's evidence based on its relations to other variables is comprehensive overall. However, evidence of its relationship to outcome measures for young children was absent. That is, the SB5 samples consisted mainly of individuals beyond 5 years of age, meaning that we do not know how the SB5 relates to other variables at the preschool age range only (i.e., 2–5 years of age).

Evidence Based on Test Consequences   Although the incorporation of the consequences of tests as validity evidence in the *Standards* (AERA et al., 1999) has raised considerable attention in recent years, test developers and publishers are required to demonstrate evidence that scores on cognitive tests and decisions made based on them produce the intended consequences. Treatment/utility studies are typically used to demonstrate this type of validity evidence. Roid (2003d) includes a chapter that addresses fairness and consequential validity of the SB5 for individuals with exceptionalities. Specifically, he states that "one research method that examines the consequences of test-score usage is classification analysis" (Roid, 2003d, p. 43). In a series of classification analyses with exceptional groups such as individuals with mental retardation, giftedness, and learning disabilities and using a variety of data sources (e.g., standardization and validity data), Roid concluded that the SB5 was highly accurate for screening and assessment of mental retardation and giftedness, but that caution should be used for identifying learning disabilities.

Although these classification studies are an important first step in providing validity evidence based on test consequences, much more evidence is necessary before drawing definitive conclusions. The SB5 should not be criticized too strongly, however, given that the test was published only 5 years ago and this strand of validity evidence requires many more years of test use to determine the consequences of using it.

Roid (2003c, 2003d) provides ample validity evidence, especially with respect to several strands of validity evidence recommended in the *Standards* (AERA et al., 1999). For example, Roid demonstrates that the SB5 measures the constructs it was intended to measure via careful and thorough item development, generally supportive factor analytic results, high intercorrelations among the SB5 subtests and composites, group difference data, and relations with measures of similar constructs that are significant and in the expected direction. Relatively weaker validity evidence is provided with respect to response processes and the consequences of testing. Given that the SB5 provides four strands of validity evidence in its various manuals and that the present authors have evaluated this evidence positively, the overall validity of the SB5 was rated *Good*.

Overall, the SB5 is a substantial improvement over its predecessor, particularly with respect to its utility for assessing the cognitive capabilities of young children ages 2–5 years (see also Alfonso & Flanagan, 2007). Because the five-factor structure purported to underlie the SB5 *total* standardization sample is unlikely to emerge as the best explanation of the structure of cognitive abilities in the SB5 *preschool* standardization sample, Alfonso and Flanagan proposed an alternative factor structure for the preschool age range. In addition, these authors provided an interpretive system that integrates information from both the published five-factor model and the alternative four-factor model. Also noteworthy is the method proposed by Flanagan et al. (2007) that allows practitioners to understand the extent to which a child's cultural and language differences have had a systematic and attenuating affect on test performance.

SUMMARY

This chapter provided a framework for evaluating the adequacy of the technical characteristics of norm-referenced tests for preschoolers. Because most reviews of norm-referenced tests tend to summarize information from the test's technical manual, rather than review the test independently, we specified herein specific criteria for reviewing the most important technical characteristics of tests, particularly as they apply to the preschool age range (i.e., 2–5 years). We applied these criteria to review critically the SB5. It is recommended that practitioners rely on evidence-based tests when evaluating the capabilities of very young children. In the area of cognitive assessment, the criteria specified herein should be adhered to when determining the utility of such tests for preschoolers.

REFERENCES

Achenbach, T. M., & Rescorla, L. A. (2000). *Manual for ASEBA Preschool Forms & Profiles.* Burlington, VT: University of Vermont Research Center for Children, Youth, & Families.

Aiken, L. R. (2000). *Psychological testing and assessment* (10th ed.). Boston: Allyn & Bacon.

Alfonso, V. C., & Flanagan, D. P. (1999). Assessment of cognitive functioning in preschoolers. In E. V. Nuttall, I. Romero, & J. Kalesnik (Eds.), *Assessing and screening preschoolers* (2nd ed., pp. 186–217). Boston: Allyn & Bacon.

Alfonso, V. C., & Flanagan, D. P. (2007). Best practices in the use of the Stanford–Binet Intelligence Scales, 5th edition (SB5) with preschoolers. In B. A. Bracken & R. Nagle (Eds.), *Psychoeducational assessment of preschool children* (4th ed., pp. 267–295). Mahwah, NJ: Erlbaum.

Alfonso, V. C., Russo, P. M., Fortugno, D. A., & Rader, D. E. (2005, Spring). Critical review of the Bayley Scales of Infant Development–Second Edition: Implications for assessing young children with developmental delays. *The School Psychologist, 59,* 67–73.

Allen, D. A. (1989). Developmental language disorders in preschool children: Clinical subtypes and syndromes. *School Psychology Review, 18,* 442–451.

American Association on Mental Retardation (2002). *Mental retardation, definition, classification, and systems of support* (10th ed.). Washington, DC: Author.

American Educational Research Association, American Psychological Association, & National Council on Measurement in Education (1999). *Standards for educational and psychological testing.* Washington, DC: American Educational Research Association.

Anastasi, A., & Urbina, S. (1997). *Psychological testing* (7th ed.). Upper Saddle River, NJ: Prentice Hall.

Bayley, N. (2006). *Bayley Scales of Infant and Toddler Development, 3rd ed.: Administration manual.* San Antonio, TX: Psychological Corporation.

Bracken, B. A. (1987). Limitations of preschool instruments and standards for minimal levels of technical adequacy. *Journal of Psychoeducational Assessment, 4,* 313–326.

Bracken, B. A., Keith, L. K., & Walker, K. C. (1998). Assessment of preschool behavior and social-emotional functioning: A review of thirteen third-party instruments. *Assessment in Rehabilitation and Exceptionality, 1,* 331–346.

Bracken, B. A., & Nagle, R. J. (Eds.). (2007). *Psychoeducational assessment of preschool children* (4th ed.). Mahwah, NJ: Erlbaum.

Bracken, B. A., & Pecyna-Rhyner, P. M. (1991, November). *Technical adequacy of preschool language and articulation assessments.* Paper presented at the American Speech–Language–Hearing Association's annual conference, Atlanta, GA.

Bracken, B. A., & Walker, K. C. (1997). The utility of intelligence tests for preschool children. In D. P. Flanagan, J. L. Genshaft, & P. L. Harrison (Eds.), *Contemporary intellectual assessment: Theories, tests, and issues* (pp. 484–502) New York: Guilford Press.

Bradley-Johnson, S. (2001). Cognitive assessment for the youngest of children: A critical review of tests. *Journal of Psychoeducational Assessment, 19,* 19–44.

Bradley-Johnson, S., & Johnson, C. M. (2007). Infant and toddler cognitive assessment. In B. A. Bracken & R. Nagle (Eds.), *Psychoeducational assessment of preschool children* (4th ed., pp. 195–218). Mahwah, NJ: Erlbaum.

Brassard, M. R., & Boehm, A. E. (2007). *Preschool assessment.* New York: Guilford Press.

Campbell, J. M., & James, C. L. (2007). Assessment of social and emotional development. In B. A. Bracken & R. Nagle (Eds.), *Psychoeducational assessment of preschool children* (4th ed., pp. 111–135). Mahwah, NJ: Erlbaum.

Campbell, F. A., & Ramey, C. T. (1994). Effects of early intervention on intellectual and academic achievement: A follow-up study of children from low-income families. *Child Development, 65,* 684–698.

Carroll, J. B. (1993). *Human cognitive abilities: A survey of factor-analytic studies.* Cambridge, UK: Cambridge University Press.

Casto, G., & Mastropieri, M. A. (1986). The efficacy of early intervention programs: A meta-analysis. *Exceptional Children, 52,* 417–424.

Cattell, R. B. (1957). *Personality and motivation structure and measurement.* New York: World Book.

Collier, V. P. (1992). A synthesis of studies examining long-term language minority student data on academic achievement. *Bilingual Research Journal, 16,* 187–212.

Conners, C. K. (2008). *Conners* (3rd ed.). North Tonawanda, NY: Multi-Health Systems.

Crocker, L., & Algina, J. (1986). *Introduction to classical and modern test theory.* New York: Holt, Rinehart, & Winston.

Daniel, M. H. (1997). Intelligence testing: Status and trends. *American Psychologist, 52,* 1038–1045.

Dockrell, J. E. (2001). Assessing language skills in preschool children. *Child Psychology & Psychiatry Review, 6,* 74–85.

Dunn, W. (1999). Assessment of sensorimotor and perceptual development. In E. V. Nuttall, I. Romero, & J. Kalesnik (Eds.), *Assessing and screening preschoolers* (2nd ed., pp. 240–261). Boston: Allyn & Bacon.

Evans, L. D., & Bradley-Johnson, S. (1988). A review of recently developed measures of adaptive behavior. *Psychology in the Schools, 25,* 276–287.

Flanagan, D. P., & Alfonso, V. C. (1995). A critical review of the technical characteristics of new and recently revised intelligence tests for preschool children. *Journal of Psychoeducational Assessment, 13,* 66–90.

Flanagan, D. P., McGrew, K. S., & Ortiz, S. O. (2000). *The Wechsler Intelligence Scales and Gf-Gc theory: A comprehensive approach to interpretation.* Boston: Allyn & Bacon.

Flanagan, D. P., Ortiz, S., & Alfonso, V. C. (2007). *Essentials of cross-battery assessment* (2nd ed.). Hoboken, NJ: Wiley.

Flanagan, D. P., Ortiz, S. O., Alfonso, V. C., & Dynda, A. M. (2008). Best practices in cognitive assessment. In A. Thomas & J. Grimes (Eds.), *Best practices in school psychology* (5th ed., pp. 633–659). Washington, DC: National Association of School Psychologists.

Flanagan, D. P., Ortiz, S. O., Alfonso, V. C., & Mascolo, J. T. (2002). *The achievement test desk reference (ATDR): Comprehensive assessment and learning disabilities*. Boston: Allyn & Bacon.

Flanagan, D. P., Ortiz, S. O., Alfonso, V. C., & Mascolo, J. T. (2006). *The achievement test desk reference (ATDR): A guide to learning disability identification* (2nd ed.). Hoboken, NJ: Wiley.

Fletcher, J. M., Lyon, G. R., Fuchs, L. S., & Barnes, M. A. (2007). *Learning disabilities: From identification to intervention*. New York: Guilford Press.

Floyd, R. G., & Bose, J. E. (2003). Behavior rating scales for assessment of emotional disturbance: A critical review of measurement characteristics. *Journal of Psychoeducational Assessment, 21*, 43–78.

Ford, L., & Dahinten, S. (2005). Use of intelligence tests in the assessment of preschoolers. In D. P. Flanagan & P. L. Harrison (Eds.), *Contemporary intellectual assessment: Theories, tests, and issues* (2nd ed., pp. 487–503). New York: Guilford Press.

Gitlin-Weiner, K., Sandgrund, A., & Schaefer, C. (Eds.). (2000). *Play diagnosis and assessment* (2nd ed.). New York: Wiley.

Gould, S. J. (1981). *The mismeasure of man*. New York: Norton.

Gregory, R. J. (2000). *Psychological testing: History, principles, and applications* (3rd ed.). Boston: Allyn & Bacon.

Guralnick, M. J. (1997). *The effectiveness of early intervention*. Baltimore: Brookes.

Hammill, D. D., Brown, L., & Bryant, R. (1992). *A consumer's guide to tests in print* (2nd ed.). Austin, TX: PRO-ED.

Harrison, P. L., & Oakland, T. (2003). *Adaptive Behavior Assessment System* (2nd ed.). San Antonio, TX: Psychological Corporation.

Harrison, P. L., & Raineri, G. (2007). Adaptive behavior assessment for preschool children. In B. A. Bracken & R. Nagle (Eds.), *Psychoeducational assessment of preschool children* (4th ed., pp. 195–218). Mahwah, NJ: Erlbaum.

Horn, J. (1985). Remodeling old models of intelligence. In B. B. Wolman (Ed.), *Handbook of intelligence* (pp. 267–300) New York: Wiley.

Jacobson, J. W., & Mulick, J. A. (1996). *Manual of diagnosis and professional practice in mental retardation*. Washington, DC: American Psychological Association.

Kamphaus, R. W. (2005). *Clinical assessment of child and adolescent intelligence* (2nd ed.). New York: Springer.

Kamphaus, R. W., & Frick, P. J. (2005). *Clinical assessment of child and adolescent personality and behavior*. New York: Springer.

Kaufman, A. S. (1979). *Intelligent testing with the WISC-R*, New York: Wiley.

Keith, T. Z. (1994). Intelligence *is* important, intelligence is complex. *School Psychology Quarterly, 9*, 209–221.

Kelley, M. F., & Surbeck, E. (2007). History of preschool assessment. In B. A. Bracken & R. Nagle (Eds.), *Psychoeducational assessment of preschool children* (4th ed., pp. 3–28). Mahwah, NJ: Erlbaum.

Knoff, H. M., Stollar, S. A., Johnson, J. J., & Chenneville, T. A. (1999). Assessment of social-emotional functioning and adaptive behavior. In E. V. Nuttall, I. Romero, & J. Kalesnik (Eds.), *Assessing and screening preschoolers* (2nd ed., pp. 126–160). Boston: Allyn & Bacon.

Lidz, C. S. (2003). *Early childhood assessment.* New York: Wiley.

Lord, F., & Novick, M. (1968). *Statistical theories of mental test scores.* Reading, MA: Addison Wesley.

Martin, R. P. (1988). *Assessment of personality and behavior problems.* New York: Guilford Press.

McCauley, R. J., & Swisher, L. (1984). Psychometric review of language and articulation tests for preschool children. *Journal of Speech and Hearing Disorders, 49,* 34–42.

McCloskey, G. (March, 2007). *Evaluation of processing integrities and deficiencies.* Paper presented at the "Response-to-Intervention, 'Intelligent Testing' and Specific Learning Disabilities Assessment" conference at Yale Child Study Center, Yale University School of Medicine, New Haven, CT.

McGrew, K. S., & Flanagan, D. P. (1998). *The intelligence test desk reference (ITDR): Gf-Gc cross-battery assessment.* Boston: Allyn & Bacon.

McGrew, K. S., Werder, J. K., & Woodcock, R. W. (1991). *Woodcock-Johnson technical manual.* Chicago: Riverside.

Merrell, K. W. (2003). *Behavioral, social, and emotional assessment of children and adolescents.* Mahwah, NJ: Erlbaum.

Nagle, R. J. (2000). Issues in preschool assessment. In B. Bracken (Ed.), *The psycho-educational assessment of preschool children* (3rd ed., pp. 19–32). Boston: Allyn & Bacon.

Nagle, R. J. (2007). Issues in preschool assessment. In B. A. Bracken & R. Nagle (Eds.), *Psychoeducational assessment of preschool children* (4th ed., pp. 29–48). Mahwah, NJ: Erlbaum.

Neisser, U., Boodoo, G., Bouchard, T. J., Boykin, A. W., Brody, N., Ceci, S. J., et al. (1996). Intelligence: Knowns and unknowns. *American Psychologist, 51,* 77–101.

Nelson, N. W., & Warner, C. (2007). Assessment of communication, language, and speech: Questions of what to do next? In B. A. Bracken & R. Nagle (Eds.), *Psychoeducational assessment of preschool children* (4th ed., pp. 361–395). Mahwah, NJ: Erlbaum.

Nunnally, J. S. (1978). *Psychometric theories.* New York: McGraw-Hill.

Oades-Sese, G., & Alfonso, V. C. (2003, August). *A critical review of the psychometric integrity of preschool language tests.* Poster presented at the annual meeting of the American Psychological Association, Toronto, Ontario, Canada.

Oades-Sese, G., & Alfonso, V. C. (2008). A critical review of the psychometric integrity of preschool language tests. Manuscript in preparation.

Paul, R. (1995). *Language disorders from infancy through adolescence.* St. Louis: Mosby-Year Book.

Plante, E., & Vance, R. (1994). Selection of preschool language tests: A data-based approach. *Language, Speech, and Hearing Services in Schools, 25,* 15–24.

Price, R. H., Cowen, E. L., Lorion, R. P., & Ramos-McKay, J. (Eds.). (1988). *14 ounces of prevention.* Washington, DC: American Psychological Association.

Ramey, C. T., & Ramey, S. L. (1998). Early intervention and early experience. *American Psychologist, 53,* 109–120.

Reynolds, C. R., & Kamphaus, R. W. (2004). *Behavior Assessment System for Children*. (2nd ed.). Circle Pines, MN: American Guidance Service.

Roid, G. (2003a). *Stanford–Binet Intelligence Scales* (5th ed.). Itasca, IL: Riverside.

Roid, G. (2003b). *Stanford–Binet Intelligence Scales* (5th ed.), *Examiner's manual*. Itasca, IL: Riverside.

Roid, G. (2003c). *Stanford–Binet Intelligence Scales* (5th ed.), *Technical manual*. Itasca, IL: Riverside.

Roid, G. (2003d). *Stanford–Binet Intelligence Scales interpretive manual: Expanded guide to the interpretation of SB5 test results*. Itasca, IL: Riverside.

Salvia, J., & Ysseldyke, J. E. (1981). *Assessment in special and remedial education* (2nd ed.). Boston: Houghton Mifflin.

Salvia, J., & Ysseldyke, J. E. (2004). *Assessment* (9th ed.). Boston: Houghton Mifflin.

Sattler, J. (1988). *Assessment of children's intelligence and special abilities* (2nd ed.). San Diego, CA: Author.

Saye, K. B. (2003). Preschool intellectual assessment. In C. R. Reynolds & R. W. Kamphaus (Eds.), *Handbook of psychological and educational assessment of children: Intelligence, aptitude, and achievement* (2nd ed., pp. 187–203). New York: Guilford Press.

Shands, E. I., Phillips, J. F., Autry, B. K., Hall, J. A., Floyd, R. G., Alfonso, V. C., et al. (2008, February). *A review of the technical characteristics of contemporary adaptive behavior assessment instruments: Preliminary results and conclusions*. Poster presented at the annual meeting of the National Association of School Psychologists, New Orleans.

Sparrow, S. S., Cicchetti, D. V., & Balla, D. A. (2005). *Vineland Adaptive Behavior Scales* (2nd ed.). Circle Pines, MN: AGS.

Thomas, W. P., & Collier, V. P. (1997). *School effectiveness for language minority students*. Washington, DC: National Clearinghouse on Bilingual Education.

Urbina, S. (2004). *Essentials of psychological testing*. New York: Wiley.

Vig, S., & Sanders, M. (2007). Cognitive assessment. In M. R. Brassard & A. E. Boehm, *Preschool assessment (pp. 383–419)*. New York: Guilford Press.

Wechsler, D. (1989). *Wechsler Preschool and Primary Scale of Intelligence–Revised*. San Antonio, TX: Psychological Corporation.

Weiner, P., & Hoock, W. (1973). The standardization of tests: Criteria and criticisms. *Journal of Speech and Hearing Research, 16,* 616–626.

Williams, H. G., & Monsma, E. V. (2007). Assessment of gross motor development. In B. A. Bracken & R. Nagle (Eds.), *Psychoeducational assessment of preschool children* (4th ed., pp. 397–433). Mahwah, NJ: Erlbaum.

Wilson, M. J., & Bullock, L. M. (1989). Psychometric characteristics of behavior rating scales: definitions, problems and solutions. *Behavioral Disorders, 14,* 186–200.

Woodcock, R. W., McGrew, K. S., & Mather, N. (2001). *Woodcock–Johnson III Test of Cognitive Abilities*. Itasca, IL: Riverside.

Wyatt, T. A., & Seymour, H. N. (1999). Assessing the speech and language skills of preschool children. In E. V. Nuttall, I. Romero, & J. Kalesnik (Eds.), *Assessing and screening preschoolers* (2nd ed., pp. 218–239). Boston: Allyn & Bacon.

CHAPTER 6

Neurodevelopmental Assessment

DEBORAH J. WALDER,
JANET COHEN SHERMAN, and
MARGARET B. PULSIFER

INTRODUCTION

Recently, there is an increased appreciation of the clinical value of assessing early development of the central nervous system (CNS) including structure–function relationships from neurobehavioral and neuropsychological perspectives. As reviewed by Aylward (2002, 2003), the reasons for this increase are multifold and include improved survival rates of extremely low birth weight (e.g., 800 grams at birth) and preterm infants (e.g., 23–24 weeks gestation) (Hack & Fanaroff, 1999) and rising rates of *high prevalence/low severity dysfunctions* such as learning disabilities, borderline mental retardation, attention deficit hyperactivity disorder (ADHD), specific neuropsychological deficits (e.g., visual motor integration), and behavioral problems. Despite relatively stable rates of major disabilities such as severe mental retardation and epilepsy, increasing high prevalence/low severity dysfunctions are noteworthy given that they occur in as many as 50–70% of very-low-birth-weight infants (<1,500 grams at birth) and tend to become more apparent as the child reaches school age (see Aylward). However, empirical evidence points to the efficacy of early intervention with children with neurodevelopmental disorders (e.g., Rogers & Vismara, 2008).

This chapter focuses on neurodevelopment assessments, performed on young children (usually <5 years of age), with the purpose of obtaining a snapshot of their current developmental functioning. Neurodevelopmental assessments at this early age play a critical role in guiding diagnosis and intervention. Assessment of CNS functioning varies across stages of early development. During neonatal/infant stages, assessment typically emphasizes motor responses, primitive behaviors, and vocalizations (i.e., cry and state regulation) (Lipkin & Allen, 2005). There is then a shift during maturation into the first year of life, to assessment of functional motor development and then more readily observable CNS skills, specifically component parts of cognition such as attention and language (Lipkin & Allen). The advent of sophisticated noninvasive assessment tools such as genetic testing provide additional means to understand the child's underlying neurologic impairment in relation to its functional consequences. The goal of the neurodevelopmental exam is to assess the child's level of functioning at a particular point in time and to conduct follow-up evaluations to chart the child's progress and developmental trajectory. The seven principal areas of assessment in preschool children include developmental and intellectual functioning, attention and memory, language, visual motor/fine and gross motor skills, school readiness, behavior, adaptive skills, and to some degree executive functioning. While sensorimotor development is assessed in young children even before age 2, neuropsychologists do not typically assess sensorimotor integration. Comprehensive formal sensorimotor-integration evaluations typically fall under the auspices of occupational therapists.

In contrast to the assessments of children less than 5 years of age, *neuropsychological assessments* for children 5 years and older typically assess the traditional areas of functioning. These areas include emerging higher order cognitive functions, such as executive functions (e.g., organization, planning, abstract problem solving and reasoning, mental flexibility, inhibitory control) (also see Lezak, Howieson, & Loring, 2004). One objective of the neuropsychological assessment for children over 5 years, rather than broadly assessing intellectual functioning and academic achievement, is to provide a finer delineation of a child's perception, integration and expression of information, and performance across a range of specific domains toward making inferences about brain functioning (Baron, 2004).

The rationale for assessing CNS integrity from infancy through preschool age is varied. The neuropsychologist uses early childhood assessment to establish a baseline level of functioning early in a child's life, particularly when neurological insult or disease is known or suspected. Assessment allows for careful longitudinal follow-up and monitoring of progress in neurocognitive and neurobehavioral weaknesses and the efficacy of interventions. In addition, Baron (2004) and Beers, Hammond, and Ryan (2005) suggest that early assessment is important with respect to: (1) aiding in early identification of individuals at greatest risk for developing neurodevelopmental disabilities; (2) assisting with differential diagnosis, establishing current developmental status, detecting delays, and quantifying deviations from normal development; (3) educating parents and teachers (e.g., enhancing comprehension of a child's strengths and weaknesses so they can better advocate for services that can lead to improvement); (4) implementing preventive strategies for those deemed to be at high risk; (5) formulating cognitive and behavioral profiles that identify strengths and weaknesses by integrating a multidisciplinary perspective (e.g., psychiatry, neurology, pediatrics, school setting); and (6) assessing at follow-up the effectiveness of program implementation and intervention services. Finally, early childhood assessment is necessary to determine a child's need and eligibility for early intervention and special education services. Under the provisions of the Individuals with Disabilities Education Improvement Act (IDEIA, 2004), preschool children ages birth to 5 years may be eligible for services if found delayed in one of five areas of development: physical, cognitive, speech and language, social and emotional, and adaptive/self-help skills. The definition of *delay* can vary by state, but is typically considered to be a 25% delay for age (adjusted for prematurity or chronological) in one of these five areas. Children born with known risk factors for developmental problems (e.g., very low birth weight, Down syndrome, prematurity) can be eligible for Early Intervention services (e.g., for children from birth through age 3) without evidence of delay.

CONSIDERATIONS IN THE ASSESSMENT OF CENTRAL NERVOUS SYSTEM DISRUPTION IN YOUNG CHILDREN

In assessing the infant and young child, it is important for the examiner to appreciate how disruption to the CNS impacts early brain maturation. There are qualitative and quantitative differences in brain–behavior relationships and the functional organization of the brain in the child compared to the adult (Baron, 2004; Riccio & Wolfe, 2003). Therefore, it follows that developmentally-based CNS insult yields impairment that is different from adult CNS disruption. This is partly because the young developing brain is still undergoing maturation (Beers et al., 2005). Brain maturation varies not only between children of similar age, but pace of maturation may vary across brain regions within the child (Beers et al.). Neuromaturation is a dynamic, ongoing process involving CNS functional development as influenced by prenatal and postnatal genetic and environmental factors (Allen, 2005). The postnatal development of the nervous system can be compartmentalized into four distinct phases, namely neurogenesis (generation/birth of neurons), cell migration (movement of neurons to appropriate locations), neuronal differentiation (nerve cell development of specialized properties), and pruning (adaptive reduction of unnecessary neurons) of cells and their interconnections (Kolb & Fantie, 1997). Spreen, Risser, & Edgell (1995) provide a more in-depth review of the principles of neural development. Each stage is contingent on growth factors, hormones, and proteins that guide cell development (Kolb & Fantie, 1997). The developing brain is not only characterized by this growth and differentiation, but also potential for plasticity, specifically, the capacity for reorganization of function (Baron, 2004; Kolb & Whishaw, 2003). By contrast, the adult brain is relatively developmentally static, resulting in the greater likelihood of permanent consequences to brain injury, although recent studies (Komitova, Johansson, & Eriksson, 2006) also provide evidence of greater reorganization after injury than was previously appreciated.

CNS maturation generally unfolds according to the dictates of time influenced by environmental factors (Kolb & Fantie, 1997). As a result, critical to infant and early child assessment is consideration of not only the nature/type, location, duration, and severity of potential CNS insult, but also the developmental timing of insult or age at injury as well as the age of the individual being assessed. Moreover, a more complex picture has replaced initial theories postulating better cognitive outcomes linked to earlier compared to later insult (Anderson & Moore, 1995; Taylor & Alden, 1997). For example, as reviewed by Baron (2004), there is now evidence that early compared to later damage to the CNS can have pervasive effects (Ewing-Cobbs, Fletcher, Levin, Francis, Davidson, & Miner, 1997). The functions associated with specific neural regions may change over time such that some functions may be transferred from one region to another through the normal course of development (see Kolb & Fantie, 1997). Therefore, damage or insult to the brain at early developmental stages may cause functions to be transferred to other regions not typically assuming such roles, a phenomenon that can lead to *crowding*, negatively impacting not only the function that is transferred, but also functions that are controlled by the region that is assuming new functions (Anderson, Northam, Hendy, & Wrennall 2001). Variability in the impact of early insult together with individual differences in cultural and life experience make it challenging to distinguish developmental delay from stable or progressive brain dysfunction, and to determine the nature and degree of deficit (Beers et al., 2005). An appreciation of these challenges is critical to understanding both the pattern of preserved and impaired functioning for the young child, as well as estimating the child's potential for remediation and subsequent development. Despite such complexities, there remain substantial benefits to assessment of young children with neurodevelopmental-based problems.

Neurodevelopmental findings resulting from assessment of the young child may help to determine the etiology of cognitive–behavioral impairments (e.g., maturational delays, neural dysfunction, motor deficits). Normal CNS development may be disrupted by a variety of endogenous and exogenous factors, including, but not limited to, environmental toxin/teratogen exposure (e.g., Dietrich et al., 2005), abnormalities in normal genetic programming, nutritional deficiencies (e.g., Dror & Allen, 2008), prenatal maternal stress/drug use (e.g., Laplante, Brunet, Schmitz, Ciampi, & King, 2008), obstetric complications (Boksa, 2004), sociocultural/socioeconomic factors, and the interplay of genetic and environmental factors (Fatjó-Vilas et al., 2008; see also Connors et al., 2008). While further discussion of all the possible factors that might disrupt CNS development is beyond the scope of this chapter, it is important to recognize that individually and/or collectively, such factors may yield detrimental cognitive and behavioral sequelae that are observable in the context of assessment. Moreover, the outcome following CNS disruption may vary depending on the degree of residual damage, neural reorganization, behavioral compensation, delayed emergence of insult sequelae, or a combination of such factors (Aylward, 1997).

In the remainder of this chapter, we will first review the initial steps in the assessment process, including the clinical interview and history taking, and the importance and role of behavioral observations, testing environment, and establishment of rapport. Next, we will provide an overview of key domains of neurodevelopmental functioning that are typically assessed, and a description of the measures utilized in clinical practice. We refer to contemporary research literature that illustrates the underpinnings of neurodevelopmental functioning from a developmental neuroscience perspective, with the caveat that relatively "little is known regarding the neural bases of cognition in normally developing children" (Casey, Giedd, & Thomas, 2000, p. 244). For example, we identify neuroanatomic substrates of key cognitive functions. Given the rapid expansion of the field of developmental and cognitive neuroscience, especially with the advent of novel, noninvasive neuroimaging techniques, we provide only a glimpse of cutting-edge findings, with the understanding that a comprehensive overview is beyond the scope of this chapter. We also describe the final steps of the assessment process, namely, interpretation of results, the recommendations that can be made to help guide both expectations for the child as well as intervention and educational strategies, and communication of results via the feedback process. Finally, we describe the role of the neuropsychologist beyond clinical evaluator, basic ethical and multicultural issues, and outline current training criteria.

INITIAL STEPS IN THE ASSESSMENT PROCESS

The initial phase of a comprehensive neurodevelopmental assessment involves several important steps that precede standardized test administration. It is critical to obtain a comprehensive history and behavioral observations of the child in order to understand the range of factors contributing to the child's current presentation and performance, as well as the child's behavior and underlying attitudes. It is also important to establish an age-appropriate testing environment, as well as trust and rapport with the child and the child's family, as these initial steps will help ensure collection of accurate information. The overarching goal of these procedures is to ensure that information gathered through structured, standardized, and less formal assessment methods is relevant, reliable, and valid (Sattler, 2008). A more extensive review of clinical interviewing/history taking, behavioral observations, the testing environment, and establishing rapport with the child can be found in the literature, which was used as a basis for the sections to follow (Baron, 2004; Beers et al., 2005; Lezak, et al., 2004; Sattler).

CLINICAL INTERVIEW/OBTAINING HISTORY

The process of clinical interviewing and history taking includes: (1) obtaining basic demographic information about the child, developmental, family, medical/psychiatric history, prematurity status, and results of any prior testing such as speech and language evaluations; (2) gaining insight into the child's behavior and underlying attitudes; (3) understanding the reason for referral and the presenting problem/complaint; and (4) clarifying with whom the parent would like results to be shared.

Multiple informants and sources of information are ideal (Beers, et al., 2005) to increase reliability of information. Informants may include the parent (s) (primary caregiver), child care provider, teacher (if child is in educational setting), and the referring physician. Because children under 10 years of age tend to be poor historians (Beers et al.), evaluators primarily rely on sources other than the child for information regarding prominent symptoms, chief complaint, and known developmental history. Of course, the child may supply important information, if appropriate. The neuropsychologist also typically reviews physician reports, medical records (e.g., medical, genetic, radiology test results), and information from any prior reports/evaluations (e.g., speech/language, early intervention or school assessments) as supplemental sources of information.

A *developmental history* should include birth history (e.g., prenatal teratogen exposure, maternal infection, illness, accident, medications, cigarette, drug and alcohol use, bleeding, falls, preeclampsia, hospitalization, gestational diabetes, premature birth), labor and delivery history (e.g., vaginal delivery versus caesarean section), duration of pregnancy, birth weight, Apgar scores, and whether and for what reason the child remained in the hospital following delivery. Information should be gathered regarding feeding (e.g., breast versus bottle fed), infant temperament/behavior (e.g., colicky, enjoyed cuddling, irritable, fussy), activity level, sleep or eating problems, and age at which primary developmental milestones were achieved (e.g., sitting, walking alone, first words, learning colors, writing his/her name), as well as whether there were any notable problems observed in the acquisition of any of these skills. Prior difficulties in day care or early educational settings should be identified, including behavioral symptoms, indication of irritability, mood/

behavioral regulation, excessive or extended tantrums, staring spells, attentional problems, relationship difficulties, and sensory integration issues. It is also important to ask about family composition, socioeconomic status, and adult and peer relations, as well as family history of learning problems or developmental delays/disabilities.

Family history should include parental and sibling history of medical, neurological, and psychiatric conditions. It is helpful to note differences in the child's development from other family members, especially siblings. If the child was adopted, the parent should be asked about what, if any, information is known regarding birth parents, birth history, and early developmental history.

Medical and psychiatric history should also be reviewed in order to determine whether the child experienced major illnesses, surgeries, hospitalizations, frequent ear infections, headaches, asthma, seizures, head injury with and without loss of consciousness, accidents, diagnostic procedures (e.g., genetic testing, neuroimaging findings), current medications, current and prior services (e.g., medical and mental health), and abuse/trauma. Vision and hearing problems need to be considered given that these impairments can compromise accuracy and reliability of test data. If the child has known vision or hearing problems, appropriate instruments should be selected accordingly to accommodate any hearing and vision problems.

The neuropsychologist carefully considers prematurity status in the assessment, and when conducting an assessment with a child under 2 years of age, uses this information in calculating a child's chronological age. Specifically, age at testing is adjusted for prematurity because it is assumed that the infant has been deprived of significant physical and neurologic growth during the last trimester of in-utero development. Correcting for prematurity is usually done until the child reaches 18–24 months of age. Serial assessments are important to determine if there is catch-up growth (i.e., a narrowing of the developmental gap between gestational and chronological ages).

Behavioral Observations and Testing Environment

Behavioral observations should include a brief description of the child's presentation and characteristics such as ability to separate from parent, temperament, frustration tolerance, motivation, energy level, response to feedback and encouragement, and attitude toward the assessment. The evaluator notes the child's language, motor coordination, sensory problems (e.g., visual and auditory), ability to remain on task, eye contact, affect, and social appropriateness (Beers et al., 2005). Assessments are best conducted in an age-appropriately designed testing room or private office that is quiet and free from distraction. For very young children (e.g., ages 3 years and under), it is often necessary for the parent to be present during the evaluation.

From the beginning of the assessment, it is important to establish positive rapport with the child and involved family members, and to maintain the child's interest, cooperation, and motivation throughout the assessment. The neuropsychologist must be sensitive to the child's level of attention, hunger, fatigue, and need for breaks. It is incumbent on the neuropsychologist to make accommodations during the testing session accordingly in order to allow for the child's optimal performance across tasks.

PRINCIPAL DOMAINS OF ASSESSMENT

While early neurodevelopmental assessments can be helpful in defining a child's pattern of strengths and weaknesses, it is important to appreciate the limitations of assessment at these early ages. Stability of indices and their predictive validity for children prior to 24 months of age are limited (Dietrich et al., 2005). Prediction of later intelligence improves after age 4 or 5 (McCall, 1979). It is critical that the neuropsychologist appreciates these predictive limitations, and assist parents to understand that these early test scores might not be predictive of their child's later performance across domains. However, lower scores are generally more predictive than higher scores; for example, low scorers (e.g., moderate to profoundly retarded range) on the Bayley Scales remain low 1–3 years after assessment (Brooks-Gunn & Lewis, 1983). However, as discussed by Bracken & Nagle (2007), to date there are very few studies on the predictive validity of the Bayley Scales.

This section describes the domains typically assessed in the neurodevelopmental assessment of a young child. Each subsection begins with reference to contemporary research findings describing underpinnings of neurodevelopmental functioning from a developmental neuroscience perspective. We provide only a cursory introduction to some neurobiological substrates, as a more comprehensive review is beyond the scope of this chapter. This is followed by an overview of key domains of neurodevelopmental functioning in early childhood, and respective measures used in clinical practice and research to index CNS integrity. The domains include intelligence, receptive and expressive language skills, visual motor–visual skills, spatial skills, attention, memory and executive functioning, school readiness, adaptive skills, and behavior. Many standardized tests are available to assess an infant and preschool child's developmental functioning. The tests described in this chapter are not exhaustive, but represent an overview of common currently used tests that are believed to have adequate reliability and validity, and have norms that reflect recent U.S. Census data. Table 6.1 provides a list of such frequently used tests for early neurodevelopmental childhood assessment,

Table 6.1
Frequently Used Tests for Early Childhood Assessment

Domain and Measure	Age Range	Description
Developmental–Cognitive		
Bayley Scales of Infant and Toddler Development-3rd ed.	0:16–42:15 months	Cognitive, language, motor, social–emotional, and adaptive skills
Differential Ability Scales, 2nd ed.	2:6–17:11 years	Verbal, nonverbal reasoning, spatial, school readiness, working memory, and processing speed
Mullen Scales of Early Learning	1:30–68:30 months	Gross motor, visual reception, fine motor, receptive and expressive language
NEPSY, 2nd ed.	3:0–16:11 years	Attention/executive functioning, language, memory/learning, sensorimotor, social perception, and visuospatial processing
Leiter International Performance Scale–Revised	2:0–20:11 years	Nonverbal intelligence, visuospatial memory, and attention
Stanford–Binet Intelligence Scales, 5th Edition	2:0–89:11 years	Fluid and quantitative reasoning, knowledge, visual–spatial, and working memory
Wechsler Preschool and Primary Scale of Intelligence, 3rd ed.	2:6–7:3 years	Verbal, nonverbal, processing speed, and expressive and receptive vocabulary
Language		
Clinical Evaluation of Language Fundamentals, 4th ed.	5:0–21:11 years	Expressive and receptive language, phonological awareness, rapid naming, and pragmatics
Comprehensive Test of Phonological Processing	5:0–24:11 years	Phonological awareness and memory, and rapid naming
Expressive One-Word Picture Vocabulary Test, 3rd ed.	2:0–18:11 years	Single-word expressive language
Expressive Vocabulary Test, 2nd ed.	2:6–90+ years	Expressive vocabulary and word retrieval
MacArthur Communicative Development Inventories	8:0–30:30 months	Written parent questionnaire for receptive and expressive language
Peabody Picture Vocabulary Test, 4th ed.	2:6–90+ years	Single-word receptive language
Preschool Language Scale, 4th ed.	Birth–6:11 years	Auditory comprehension and expressive communication

(Continued)

Table 6.1

(Continued)

Domain and Measure	Age Range	Description
Receptive One-Word Picture Vocabulary Test, 2nd ed.	2:0–18:11 years	Receptive vocabulary
Receptive-Expressive Emergent Language Scale, 3rd ed.	Birth–30:30 months	Parent report of expressive and receptive language
Test of Auditory Conceptualization of Language, 3rd ed.	3:0–9:11 years	Comprehension of vocabulary, grammatical morphemes, and sentences
Visual Motor–Visual Spatial		
Developmental Test of Visual–Motor Integration, 5th ed.	2:0–18:11 years	Visual perception/visual–motor coordination
Developmental Test of Visual Perception, 2nd ed.	4:0–10:11 years	Visual perception, visual–motor, and eye–hand coordination
Motor-Free Visual Perception Test, 3rd ed.	4:0–90+ years	Spatial relations, visual discrimination, closure, memory, and figure–ground
Purdue Pegboard Test	2:6–15:11 years	Fine motor speed/manual dexterity
Attention, Memory and Executive Functioning		
Children's Category Test	5:0–16:0 years	Nonverbal learning and memory, problem solving, concept formation
Children's Memory Scale	5:0–16:0 years	Auditory and visual memory, attention, and concentration
Conners' Kiddie Continuous Performance Test	4:0–5:11 years	7.5-minute computerized visual attention task
Wide Range Assessment of Memory and Learning, 2nd ed.	5:0–85+ years	Verbal and visual memory, attention, and concentration
School Readiness		
Bracken Basic Concept Scale–Revised	2:6–7:11 years	11 concept categories (e.g., numbers, shapes)
Slosson Test of Reading Readiness	5:0–7:11 years	Visual, auditory, and cognitive skills related to reading readiness
Test of Early Math, 3rd ed.	3:0–8:11 years	Informal and formal math skills
Wechsler Individual Achievement Test, 2nd ed.	4:0–19:11 years	Reading, math, written expression, and oral language

Wide Range Achievement Test, 4th ed.	5:0–94:11 years	Word recognition, spelling, and arithmetic
Adaptive Skills		
Adaptive Behavior Assessment System		Conceptual, social, and practical skills areas
Parent Form	Birth–21:11	
Teacher/Day Care Provider Form	2:0–21:11 years	
Scales of Independent Behavior–Revised	Birth–80+	Motor, language, social, daily living, and community living skills; maladaptive behavior; parent report
Vineland Adaptive Behavior Scale, 2nd ed.	Birth–90:11 years	Communication, socialization, and daily living. Motor skills before age 6.
Behavior		
Autism Diagnostic Observation Schedule	Toddler–adult	Assesses behaviors characteristic of autism and pervasive developmental disorder
Behavior Assessment System for Children, 2nd ed.	2:0–25:11 years	Attention, behavior, and emotional problems; parent and teacher forms
Behavior Rating Inventory of Executive Function–Preschool Version	2:0–5:11 years	Inhibition, shifting, emotional control, working memory, and planning/organizing; parent report
Child Behavior Checklist	1:6–5:11 years	Attention, behavior, and emotional problems; parent and teacher forms
Conners' Parent Rating Scale–Revised	3:0–17:11 years	Attention and behavior problems; parent and teacher forms
Early Childhood Inventory-4	3:0–5:11 years	Screens for DSM-IV emotional and behavioral
		Disorders; parent and teacher report
Gilliam Asperger's Disorder Scale	3:0–22:11 years	Social interaction; restricted patterns of behavior, cognitive patterns, and pragmatic skills
Gilliam Autism Rating Scale-2	3:0 22:11 years	Stereotyped behavior, communication, social interactions

organized by domains of functioning, with age ranges for appropriate usage and a description of each measure. Since domains develop at different rates, assessment tools emphasize different skills at different ages, and this affects predictive validity at young ages. Furthermore, young children are prone to developmental lags and spurts. These fluctuations reflect the nonuniform growth of the brain after birth including growth spurts marked by irregular increases in brain mass (Kolb & Fantie, 1997).

DEVELOPMENTAL AND INTELLECTUAL FUNCTIONING

Neurobiological Underpinnings   To date, there is limited research delineating the neuroanatomic substrate(s) of intelligence. In normal adults, structural brain imaging studies have revealed: (1) a link between intelligence and gray and white matter volumes in predominantly frontal, temporal and parietal regions (Haier, Jung, Yeo, Head, & Alkire, 2004); (2) that the relative regional contributions vary as a function of age; and (3) that there are likely sex differences in the pattern of brain regions utilized to achieve similar performance on measures of intellectual functioning, suggesting the absence of a unitary underlying neuroanatomic substrate to general intelligence (Haier, Jung, Yeo, Head, & Alkire, 2005).

Since the brain is known to differ across developmental stages from infancy/early childhood through adolescence and adulthood, it is not surprising that intelligence is associated with varying brain regions such as the anterior cingulate at different developmental stages in childhood (Wilke, Sohn, Byars, & Holland et al., 2003), the orbitofrontal and medial prefrontal cortices in adolescence (Frangou, Chitins, & Williams, 2004), and lateral prefrontal cortex in older adults (Haier, Jung, Yeo, Head, & Alkire, 2004; see Shaw et al., 2006). Recent longitudinal neuroimaging studies aim to capture neural correlates of intellectual ability during rapid brain maturation from early childhood to adolescence. In particular, Shaw et al. demonstrated that intelligence is linked with the dynamic and plastic nature of brain maturation and pattern of cortical growth. Specifically, the study results suggested: (1) a developmental shift whereby a negative association of cortical thickness with intelligence in early childhood transitions to a positive relationship in late childhood onward, and (2) that variability in cortical change is most salient in the prefrontal cortex. In addition, "more intelligent children demonstrate a particularly plastic cortex, with an initial accelerated and prolonged phase of cortical increase, which yields to equally vigorous cortical thinning by early adolescence" (Shaw et al. p. 676). The authors argue " . . . the prolonged phase of prefrontal and cortical gain in the most intelligent might afford an even more extended 'critical' period for the development of high-level cognitive cortical circuits" (Shaw et al. p. 678). In this way, "brainy" children are not more intelligent as a result of magnitude of gray matter, but rather "intelligence is related to dynamic properties of cortical maturation" (Shaw et al. p. 678). Future research is clearly necessary to discover more linkages between intelligence and early brain development.

Instruments that Measure Early Development and Intelligence   Early childhood assessment nearly always includes an individually administered, standardized measure of overall developmental status and intellectual functioning. The information obtained from this measure can be critical in determining whether any delays identified are isolated to a specific domain or are more global in nature.

The Bayley Scales of Infant and Toddler Development-3rd edition (Bayley-III; 2005) is the most widely used instrument of developmental functioning in young children, ages 1 to 42 months. This instrument is a measure of maturational growth and is not designed to be used as a measure of intelligence or to predict academic achievement (Bayley). The Bayley-III provides comprehensive information about a child's current developmental status, but like other infant measures, it is not a strong predictor of adult IQ (Bayley, 1969; McCall, 1979). The primary purpose of the Bayley-III is to identify developmental delay and to provide information for intervention planning. The Bayley-III consists of three administered scales: the Cognitive scale, the Language scale, and the Motor scale. The Cognitive scale assesses infants' memory and ability to habituate to novel stimuli, and young children's problem solving and quantitative skills. The Language scale measures expressive and receptive communication by observing the child's spontaneous use of communication during testing and by asking the child to name pictures and objects, follow directions, and answer questions. The Motor scale assesses quality of movement, sensory integration, perceptual–motor integration, and fine and gross motor skills. The Bayley-III consists of two additional scales that are completed by the parent or primary caregiver. The Social–Emotional scale assesses a child's interest in the world and the ability to self-regulate and engage with others. The Adaptive Behavior scale assesses a child's daily living skills in various areas, such as communication, self-care, and functional preacademics. One major advantage of the Bayley-III is that it provides normative scores for the five areas (e.g., motor, cognitive, communication, social and emotional, and adaptive development) specified by IDEIA (2004) for assessing the eligibility of young children for intervention services.

The Mullen Scales of Early Learning (Mullen; 1995) is an individually administered measure of cognitive functioning for infants and young children. The purpose of the instrument is to identify a child's strengths and weaknesses for learning and to provide specific information to guide individual educational programming. The instrument consists of five scales: the Gross Motor scale together with four cognitive scales that assess Visual Reception, Fine Motor, Receptive Language, and Expressive Language. The Gross Motor scale is administered from birth to 33 months. The cognitive scales are administered to children from birth to 68 months. The Mullen offers a single cognitive summary score, the Early Learning Composite, as a measure of general intelligence. In contrast to the Bayley-III, the Mullen can be administered until a child is nearly old enough for the Wechsler Intelligence Scale for Children-Fourth Edition (WISC-IV; Wechsler, 2003), although an examiner may want to transition to the *Wechsler Preschool and Primary Scale of Intelligence*, 3rd edition (WPPSI-III; Wechsler, 2002) when a child turns age 2½. The Mullen provides normative scores for three of the five areas (i.e., motor, cognitive, communication) specified by IDEIA for assessing the eligibility of young children for intervention services.

The Neuropsychological Test of Development for Children, 2nd edition (NEPSY-II; Korkman, Kirk, & Kemp, 2007) assesses neuropsychological development in children from 3–16 years. The NEPSY-II identifies cognitive deficits that may be related to childhood disorders, such as attention deficit hyperactivity disorder and pervasive developmental disorder. Six broad functional domains are assessed: Attention and Executive Functioning, Language, Memory and Learning, Sensorimotor, Social Perception, and Visuospatial Processing. The Social Perception domain is a new addition to the NEPSY-II that identifies cognitive deficits that can be associated with autism spectrum disorders. The examiner is not required to assess all domains or administer all subtests. The NEPSY-II is one of the few measures that allows the examiner to tailor the instrument to measure cognitive abilities specific to the referral question and diagnostic concern.

The WPPSI-III is a measure of intellectual ability for children ages 2:6 to 7:3. The WPPSI-III is well standardized, with good reliability and validity. The measure has been revised twice (1989, 2002) since it was first published in 1967 and now assesses a lower age range to assist with educational programming for young children. The current revision is better equipped to assess very low and very high functioning children. As with other Wechsler scales, the WPPSI-III provides an IQ score that represents the overall level of intellectual functioning. The test also yields a Verbal IQ score that is a measure of acquired knowledge, verbal reasoning, and word knowledge, and a Performance IQ score that primarily taps visual–spatial and visual–motor integration skills. In addition, the WPPSI-III assesses single-word receptive and expressive vocabulary beginning at age 2½ and information processing speed in children ages 4:0 to 7:3. The WPPSI-III overlaps with the WISC-IV (2003) between ages 6:0 to 7:3. The examiner must then decide which measure to administer based on the child's level of functioning (e.g., the WPPSI-III may be best for children with significant delay) and whether the child has received prior WPPSI-III testing.

ATTENTION, MEMORY, AND EXECUTIVE FUNCTIONING

This section reviews three component parts of higher order cognitive functions that, as previously discussed, cannot be fully assessed at young ages as compared to school-aged children, namely attention, memory, and executive functioning (i.e., the ability to control and direct one's own learning, thinking, and mental activity). These three processes are generally treated as separate cognitive constructs. However, components of these processes such as working memory (e.g., temporarily holding and manipulating information), response inhibition (suppression of a response in the face of competing information), and attention allocation have been linked to a single brain region, the prefrontal cortex (Diamond, 1988; Fuster, 1989; Goldman-Rakic, 1987; see also Casey, Giedd, & Thomas, 2000). Shared neuroanatomic substrates together with interrelated functional roles support the possibility that aspects of these processes "may be part of a single construct or common underlying circuitry" (Casey, Giedd, & Thomas, p. 244). As such, we discuss attention, memory, and executive functioning collectively.

Neurobiological Underpinnings Research examining neurobiological substrates of attention, memory, and executive functions is accelerating. As reviewed by Baron (2004), neuroimaging and neuropsychological findings together suggest attention involves intricate distributed neural networks, including involvement of the inferior parietal lobe, frontal, prefrontal, orbital frontal, striatal and occipital regions, limbic system, subcortical and midbrain systems, and corpus callosum. Research in these areas indicates that there is maturation of the frontal lobe at the end of the first year, particularly the prefrontal cortices. The hippocampus, with growth and differentiation of cortical pyramidal neurons and dendrites continue in the second year, and contribute to important changes in the child's attention and executive functioning, as well as to improvements in memory encoding, retention, and retrieval (Liston & Kagan, 2002). For example, studies indicate that between the ages of 7 months and 3:6 years, the child's ability to sustain attention increases linearly (Garon, Bryson, & Smith, 2008). Also, between 2 and 6 years, the young child becomes better able to focus on structured tasks, such as continuous performance measures (e.g., tasks that require sustained attention to continuously presented stimuli), a change that is argued to be due to maturation of the anterior attention subsystem over the more rudimentary orienting subsystem. This neural maturation allows the young child to be less tied to external factors directing attention and, instead, to be more flexible in his/her ability to shift attention, an achievement that is considered a milestone in the development of executive functioning (Garon et al.). Similarly, studies indicate that the changes that take place in memory development during the early years are also due to the differential rates of development of different neural substrates that contribute to memory processes. Specifically, while the rapid development of the cerebellum near the end of the prenatal period allows for different forms of memory that do not involve conscious mediation (e.g., procedural learning, instrumental conditioning referred to as *nondeclarative memory*), the ability to consciously form, maintain, and retrieve experiences, facts, or events (referred to as *declarative memory*) depends on the slower and longer development of temporal–cortical networks (Bauer, 2008).

Instruments that Measure Attention, Memory, and Executive Functioning   In the child's typical first formal school experience during the preschool years, the child who is unable to sit at circle time, who requires considerably more direct supervision than peers and prompts from a teacher to remain on task, who distracts other children, or who has difficulty transitioning from one activity to another is often referred for a neurodevelopmental evaluation. Not uncommonly, the referral question raised in such circumstances is whether the child might meet diagnostic criteria for ADHD, the most commonly diagnosed form of psychopathology in the preschool years (Armstrong & Nettleton, 2004; Mahone, 2005). In addressing the question of whether the child's inattentiveness and/or motor restlessness is due to an underlying attention problem, the neuropsychologist needs to determine whether there might be other cognitive factors, for example, a more generalized intellectual deficit, or a deficit within another cognitive domain (e.g., language processing) that might account for the child's behavior. In order to sort out such questions, the neuropsychologist needs to administer a battery of tests that assesses different domains of functioning, obtain information from a caregiver through behavioral rating scales (see descriptions in the Behavior section below), observe the child's ability to attend within the highly structured testing situation, and to present the child with direct tests of attention.

There are relatively few direct measures of attention available for the young child, and those that exist mainly target children age 4 and older (Mahone, 2005). As with school-age children and adults, a commonly used method to assess attention in the young child is continuous performance tests (e.g., Conners' Kiddie Continuous Performance Test (K-CPT); Gordon Diagnostic System; Conners, 2006). With such measures, the child views a number of sequentially presented stimuli and rapidly responds to all but one particular stimulus. The child's profile of responses on these measures, including his or her reaction time and accuracy, is helpful in distinguishing normal attention from inattentiveness and impulsivity. Although such measures can provide important information regarding specific difficulties within the realm of attention, their dependence on a rapid motor response, as well as the fact that performance on these measures correlates highly with overall level of intellectual functioning in young children makes them less useful in the determination of specific attention problems in the child under age 4 (Mahone; 2005). Measures of attention are also included within more generalized measures; for example, the NEPSY-II includes measures of both attention and executive functioning that can be administered to children age 5 and older. As both attention and executive functioning require the ability to self-regulate behavior, these are often assessed together (Korkman, Kirk & Kemp, 2007). While neurodevelopmental evaluations of young children may not always include an assessment of executive functioning, at this time, there is both increased awareness of the importance of this skill in terms of both the role it plays in behavior and in learning, and increased availability of measures of executive functions in children in the preschool years (Isquith, Crawford, Espy, & Gioia, 2005).

As described in more detail in the Behavior section below, measures of executive functioning include parent and teacher rating scales (e.g., Behavior Rating Inventory of Executive Functions-Preschool Version (BRIEF-P); Gioia, Espy, & Isquith, 2003). There are also direct measures of executive function. These include subtests from the NEPSY-II (Korkman, Kirk & Kemp, 2007), specifically, measures of behavioral initiation (e.g., word generation–semantic [ages 3–6], design fluency (ages 5 and up), and a measure of motor persistence and inhibition (ages 3 and up).

Memory is also central to the young child's ability to learn, with true learning only occurring when the child successfully encodes and retains information (Gathercole, 1998). As with attention and executive functioning, specific measures of memory are only available in the "later" preschool years, with the Wide Range Assessment of Memory and Learning, 2nd edition (WRAML-2; Sheslow & Adams, 2003) designed for administration for children age 5 and up. The WRAML-2 and instruments that assess more general cognitive functioning (e.g., NEPSY-II) include subtests that assess various aspects of the child's memory. Specifically, these subtests assess the child's ability to: (1) encode information, as measured by immediate recall tasks; (2) retain information over time, as measured by delayed recall tasks; and (3) retrieve information, with distinctions between difficulties with retention and retrieval assessed by administering measures of recognition and free recall, respectively.

Assessment measures also distinguish the child's ability to remember different types of information. For example, to learn and remember information that is presented in the verbal versus visual modality (e.g., stories versus pictures) and to determine whether the child is better able to learn and remember information that is more structured and contextually supported (e.g., stories) versus information that is less structured in its format (e.g., a list of words). More effective encoding that leads to better retrieval of information generally occurs when the material is meaningfully structured into smaller units (e.g., Delis, Freeland, Kramer, & Kaplan, 1988), although studies have found that young children (e.g., 5- to 8-year-olds) generally fail to spontaneously employ such strategies (e.g., Brown, Bransford, Ferrara, &

Campione, 1983; Schneider & Pressley, 1989). List learning measures, such as the CVLT-C (Delis, Kramer, Kaplan, & Ober, 1994), normed for children age 5 and older, allow the examiner to determine the type of learning strategy employed by the child, specifically, whether the child learns the list by actively chunking the randomly ordered items into semantic groups, or instead tries to remember them in the order presented. This enables the examiner to determine the extent to which the child's learning strategies impact their ability to retrieve information.

Language

A very common reason for a neurodevelopmental evaluation in a young child is delayed language development. Although once thought of as a skill learned through imitation and reinforcement (Skinner, 1957), language is now clearly appreciated as having a biological foundation, with children's brains hard-wired to acquire language (e.g., Chomsky, 1981). As such, its development, including the patterns and age of onset of infants' cooing and babbling, first words, and combination of words into phrases and sentences, unfolds in a highly predictable manner (e.g., Pinker, 1994). While the biological basis of language is clearly appreciated, so is the importance of environmental input (Hayiou-Thomas, 2008). Moreover, the role of enriched environmental input appears to be even more critical for the development of certain language skills (i.e., syntax) in children with pre- or perinatal injury than is the case for typically developing children (Rowe, Levine, Fisher, & Goldin-Meadow, in press).

When there is concern that either the pattern or rate of language development is abnormal, typically noticed by a child's parent or pediatrician, a neuropsychologist is often consulted to help determine the extent of delay relative to normative data, and to define the nature of the child's language difficulties. One very important question addressed through a neurodevelopmental evaluation is whether the child's delayed or atypical language is domain specific, or is consistent with the child's intellectual development more generally. In addition, for some disorders, the age at onset of language difficulties is important. For example, for the diagnosis of autism to be made, there not only needs to be evidence for a marked impairment in language and communication, along with other features of the disorder, but there also needs to be evidence that this core feature was present before age 3 (American Psychiatric Association [APA], 2000). While such information can be obtained retrospectively, early identification of language disorders is helpful, not only for precise diagnosis, but also to intervene at an early age, with studies indicating that early intervention for language disorders can lead to improvement (e.g., Rapin & Dunn, 2003).

Neurobiological Underpinnings Language is among the domains of functioning most closely examined in young children, with respect to neuroanatomic substrates. As outlined by Kolb & Fantie (1997), speech onset occurs during the first 3 years, and language depends on perceptual abilities (e.g., identification and categorization of speech sounds) and motor capacities (e.g., control of vocal cords, lips and tongue). These perceptual and motor abilities related to speech production are contingent on temporal and frontal lobe maturation. Given the variable rate of development of these brain regions, children may show delayed speech acquisition with subsequent normal intelligence, and skeletal and gross motor development. While it has been argued that language development depends on "some form of environmental stimulation," the emergence of speech and language is more likely accounted for by "maturational brain changes" (Kolb & Fantie, p. 31). To this end, the prominent changes between 2 and 12 years of age lie in neuronal interconnectivity, namely decreased synaptic number and increased dendritic arborization complexity. As such, "changes in synaptic density and dendritic detail may be logical candidates as constraints of speech development" (Kolb & Fantie, p. 31).

Instruments that Measure Language Measures designed to assess young children's language include tests directly administered to the child as well as parent questionnaires concerning a child's language development. The latter play an important role due to the limited opportunity that an examiner has to sample a child's language, as well as factors of temperament and personality that can impede a child's willingness to verbalize during a neurodevelopmental assessment (Fenson et al., 1994). Directly administered language tests include those that specifically assess expressive and receptive language. Also, as language is a complex system comprised of different forms used to convey meaning, language measures assess children's abilities at different levels of language, including their awareness of and ability to manipulate individual sounds or phonemes (tests of phonological development), to comprehend or produce individual lexical items (e.g., tests of vocabulary), and to comprehend or produce language at the sentence level (e.g., tests of syntactic development) (Caplan, 1987). The ability to utilize language appropriately, referred to as pragmatic language, is typically assessed through observation, as well as through informal and formal parent report, including questionnaires and rating scales. Identifying the level at which the child is experiencing difficulty is important in terms of addressing questions regarding etiology, with the DSM-IV-TR (APA, 2000) distinguishing expressive language disorders, mixed receptive/expressive disorders, phonological disorders, and providing information that allows the clinician to make specific recommendations regarding intervention.

As can be seen in Table 6.1, measures that assess language are included in both general measures of intellectual functioning as well as in domain specific measures. The fact that language is critical to early intellectual development is recognized in both infant and preschool general measures, with the Bayley-III, WPPSI-III and the Differential Ability Scales, 2nd edition (DAS-II; Elliot, 2007) including specific language scales with separate measures of receptive and expressive language. Within these general measures, the language measures vary according to the age parameters of the tests. For example, early items on the Bayley Scales of Infant Development-III assess the child's ability to engage in the foundations of communication, including orienting to person and reacting to sounds in the environment. At later ages, items assess whether the child is able to make further discriminations. For example, specifically associate meaning with different classes of words, including object names, action words, pronouns, prepositions, possessives, and words that denote size, quantity, categories, colors, mass, negation, and tense. Later items require the child to interpret concepts such as tense within a sentence context (e.g., show me "The boy washed his dog"). General measures that assess intellectual development in preschool age children (e.g., WPPSI-III, DAS-II) also include measures of receptive and expressive language skills, with word–picture matching and picture naming tests, respectively. The DAS-II (early years) additionally includes an assessment of the child's comprehension of sentences that include prepositions, inferences, and time-dependent clauses.

Specific language measures include those that assess language at the level of phonology (specifically discussed in the School Readiness section), vocabulary, and syntax. At the single word level, receptive vocabulary measures include the Peabody Picture Vocabulary Test, 4th edition (PPVT-4), which is appropriate for children age 2:6 and up (Dunn & Dunn, 2007), and the Receptive One-Word Picture Vocabulary Test, 2nd edition (ROWPVT-2), which is appropriate for children age 2 and up (Brownell, 2000) and rely on word–picture matching tasks. For these measures, the child hears a series of single words presented by the examiner, and for each, is asked to point to one of four pictures that matches the word's meaning. Although these tasks require the child to visually discriminate pictures, the task requirements are otherwise quite simple, relying on comprehension of the single word presented and a pointing response. Both of these measures are co-normed with expressive vocabulary measures; the PPTV-4 is co-normed with the Expressive Vocabulary Test, 2nd edition (EVT-2; Williams, 2007) and the ROWPVT-2 (Brownell, 2000b) is co-normed with the Expressive One-Word Picture Vocabulary Test, 3rd edition (EOWPVT-3; Brownell, 2000a). The co-norming of these measures allows the examiner to determine whether the child's difficulties are specific; for example, a statistically lower expressive than receptive language score suggests of an expressive language disorder, while impaired scores on measures of both receptive and expressive language tests is more suggestive of a mixed receptive–expressive language disorder. For both expressive measures, the child is presented with pictures for which he or she needs to provide a one-word spoken response. For the EVT-2, the child is asked to either name the picture or provide a synonym for a word provided by the examiner that describes some aspect of the picture. The synonym task allows for assessment of different word classes, including nouns, verbs, adjectives, and adverbs. The EOWPVT-3 (Brownell, 2000a) also samples the child's ability to name objects, actions, and category names. For both expressive and receptive vocabulary measures, the tests sample a broad range of vocabulary difficulty, with items ordered by increasing difficulty.

Measures that assess language at the sentence level include the Preschool Language Scale, 4th edition (PLS-4; Zimmerman, Steiner & Pond, 2002) and the Test of Auditory Comprehension of Language-3 (TACL-3; Carrow-Woolfolk, 1999), with the former including measures of both language expression and comprehension and the latter assessing comprehension only. The PLS-4 is designed to assess language development from birth through age 6:11. Like the Bayley-III, the PLS-4 includes items that assess the child's ability to engage in fundamental aspects of communication, with later items assessing the child's understanding of different classes of single words as well as a variety of sentence types. Expressive items require the child to verbally respond to different types of questions (e.g., where, why, what), to repeat different sentence types, to complete sentences, and to describe conceptual similarities. Like the PPVT-4 and the ROWPVT-2, the TACL-3, normed for children age 3:0 to 9:11, also includes a word–picture matching task to assess vocabulary. In addition, the TACL-3 includes subtests that assess the child's comprehension of grammatical morphemes, including prepositions, noun number and case, verb number and tense, noun–verb agreement, derivational suffixes and pronouns, and that assess elaborated phrases and sentences, including the ability simple sentences and a variety of complex sentences that require comprehension of adjective modification, conjoined sentences, negation, interrogatives, active and passive sentences, and embedded sentences. The test provides separate scores for each of the subtests as well as a total score allowing the examiner to pinpoint the aspect of language comprehension that may be impaired.

Assessment of the child's language ability often includes an assessment of pragmatic language, that is, the child's ability to engage and use language appropriately. This is particularly important when the referral question and/or the clinical history and behavioral observations raise the question of an autism spectrum disorder. Information regarding these aspects of language communication is often gleaned through direct observation of the child as well as through information provided by the parent, with rating scales, including the Gilliam Autism Rating Scale (Gilliam, 2001) and Gilliam Asperger's Disorder Scale-2 (Gilliam, 2006) which poses questions pertaining specifically to types of communication abnormalities characteristic of these disorders.

VISUAL PERCEPTUAL, VISUAL MOTOR, FINE AND GROSS MOTOR MEASURES

The DSM-IV-TR (APA, 2000) does not include a clinical taxonomy for disorders that impact either the child's visual perceptual abilities (e.g., their ability to appreciate and discriminate visual form), or the child's ability to integrate visual and motor skills (also referred to as visual motor skills; e.g., difficulties with eye–hand coordination that can impact a child's ability to learn important skills such as drawing, handwriting, tying shoes). Moreover, these disorders may be less apparent to the casual observer than disorders of language. Nevertheless, the acquisition of visual perceptual skills and the ability to integrate visual and motor skills (i.e., visual motor abilities) are central to the young child's ability to learn about the external world (Hammill, Pearson, & Voress, 1993). Difficulties with various aspects of visual perception and the ability to integrate visual and motor skills are often early signs of developmental disorders. For example, difficulty with visual motor tasks, such as constructing simple block towers or putting together simple puzzles, is often observed in children with nonverbal learning disabilities (Pennington, 1991). As these latter difficulties can be due to problems with visual perception, to problems with fine motor coordination, or to problems integrating visual and motor skills, it is important for the neuropsychologist to determine the locus and nature of the child's impairment in order to address questions regarding possible etiology of the child's difficulty, and to make appropriate recommendations to address the child's underlying deficit.

Neurobiological Underpinnings   Given motor functions are among the primary functions, it is not surprising that neuroimaging studies show that brain regions underlying motor and sensory functions mature first (Casey, Galvan, & Hare, 2005). For example, the infantile grasp, one of the earlier motor functions to emerge, has been correlated with myelin formation of motor cortex fibers (Kolb & Whishaw, 2003).

Instruments that Measure Visual Perception, Visual Motor, and Fine and Gross Motor Functions   As within the language domain, measures that assess the young child's visual and motor functions as well as their ability to integrate visual and motor skills (e.g., visual motor skills) are included in general cognitive measures (e.g., the Bayley-III, WPPSI-III, Stanford Binet Intelligence Scales, 5th edition (Stanford-Binet-V; Roid, 2003), DAS-II, NEPSY-II). For example, within the Bayley-III, many of the early items assess the infant's ability to orient to a visual stimulus, discriminate between visual stimuli, show preferences for particular visual stimuli, and notice and search for an object that has disappeared. Items are also included that assess the child's ability to manipulate visual stimuli. For example, items at an early age assess the child's ability to reach for objects in the environment, to bring objects together, and to use objects in an appropriate and intentional manner (e.g., pushing a car, feeding a baby doll). As discussed above, the Bayley-III also includes a separate motor scale, including separate measures of fine motor and gross motor abilities. Such infant measures, combined with less formal qualitative behavioral observations are the principal methods for measurement of fine and gross motor functions among younger children. Items included within these more general intellectual measures also assess early visual motor integration skills. Accordingly, the child is presented with form boards to complete, simple designs to imitate or copy, and towers or block designs to construct, with the required discriminations and motor manipulations becoming more complex with development.

Specific measures designed to assess the young child's abilities within this domain include those that assess visual perception, visual motor integration, motor coordination, and fine motor skills. Measures that assess visual perception in the young child, and that require only minimal motor skills (e.g., pointing response) include the Motor-Free Visual Perception Test, 3rd edition (MVPT-3; Colarusso & Hammill, 2003), normed for individuals from age 4:0 and extending through adulthood, and the Developmental Test of Visual Perception, 2nd edition (DTVP-2; Hammill, Pearson & Voress, 1993), with normative data for children ages 4–10 years old. The DTVP-2 includes two scales, one designed to assess motor-reduced visual perception and one designed to assess visual motor integration. Within the Motor Reduced Visual Perception scale of the DTVP-2 and the MVPT-3, the child points to the correct response within a multiple-choice format. Both measures provide an overall score of visual perception, and both include items that assess different aspects of visual perception, with the MVPT-3 including measures of visual discrimination, spatial relationships, figure–ground discrimination, visual closure, and visual memory, while the DTVP-2 including measures of position in space, figure–ground, spatial relations, and form constancy. Although visual perception encompasses these component skills, in order to perceive objects adequately in the world, these skills work in concert with one another. For example, in order to discriminate an object, the child must be able to determine its identity even when it is seen in a different orientation, when seeing only a part rather than the entire object, or seeing it among other objects. The DTVP-2 nonetheless provides individual age-equivalent and percentile scores for each subtest, allowing the examiner to help pinpoint which aspect of visual perception might be difficult for the child, while the MVPT-3 provides an overall score only.

Perhaps the most commonly used measure for the assessment of visual motor coordination in the young child is the Beery–Buktenica Developmental Test of Visual–Motor Integration, 5th edition (Beery VMI; Beery & Beery, 2004). This test, normed for individuals from ages 2 to 18 years includes 27 forms presented in order of increasing complexity that the individual is asked to copy. The 21-item short-form for children ages 2–7 includes six initial items in which the child is asked to imitate scribbles and basic forms produced by the examiner, and the remaining items require the child to copy a sequence of line drawings that progress from less to more complex. The child's drawings are scored according to a set of precise developmentally-normed criteria. Test scores from the Beery VMI are highly sensitive to development and correlate more highly with chronological age than with intelligence. The Beery VMI is more commonly included in the neuropsychological assessment than are motor-free measures of visual perception, as examiners often use copying tasks as a first pass at assessing both visual and motor skills. The rationale for using copy tasks as measures of visual perception is that the child's ability to perceive a stimulus is reflected in his/her ability to copy it (Hammill et al., 1993). When a child has difficulty with the Beery VMI, the examiner should back up and present measures that require more basic perceptual functioning (e.g., form discrimination) to help pinpoint if the reason for the child's impairment is visual perception or visual motor integration.

During the preschool years, children make significant gains in their visual motor coordination abilities. This is evidenced in Figure 6.1 which shows the developmental progression in a child's ability to copy common shapes over 3 years (from age 2–5). As the reader can see, there are advances in the child's fine motor coordination as well as in the child's appreciation of basic visual form.

SCHOOL READINESS

Although children are typically not exposed to formal academic teaching until school age, there are often signs before a child reaches kindergarten that a young child may go on to have academic difficulties (see Sherman, 2008 for a review). These signs include not only generalized deficiencies in intellectual functioning, but also more specific cognitive weaknesses. For example, numerous studies indicate that well before the child comes to the task of learning to read, those who go on to the diagnosis of developmental dyslexia display weaker phonological awareness skills than those who go on to become normal readers (e.g., see Adams, 1990; Castles & Coltheart, 2004 for a review). Neurobiological studies also support a fundamental

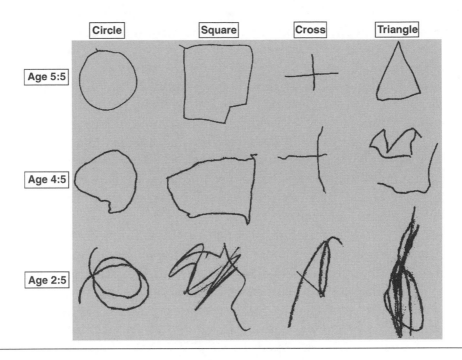

Figure 6.1 Work Sample This figure shows developmental changes in visual motor integration abilities as evidenced by one child's copies of four common shapes at different ages. The copies produced by the child at age 2:5 are all inaccurate. The improvement in accuracy provides an example of developmental progression that typically occurs in early childhood.

phonological processing deficit in dyslexia (e.g., Shaywitz et al., 1998; Shaywitz et al., 2002; Temple, 2002; Temple et al., 2001), with studies of both adult and childhood dyslexia providing evidence of decreased activation in the left temporoparietal cortex in adult dyslexics as well as in children with dyslexia, with this area critically involved in phonological processing. Similarly, within the nonverbal domain, early difficulties with fine motor skills (e.g., delayed acquisition of a pincer grasp) and in the development of spatial abilities can be observed in children who go onto a diagnosis of a nonverbal learning disorder (Pennington, 1991). Detection of these early difficulties can help guide recommendations as to the types of educational settings and services that may be most appropriate for the child, as well as recommendations for early intervention specifically directed at bolstering areas of weakness. Early intervention in areas of weakness has been shown to benefit the acquisition of academic skills (e.g., Bernhardt & Major, 2005). These researchers suggest, "Early phonological and meta-phonological intervention can promote normalization of speech development, and normal acquisition of literacy skills for children with severe phonological impairments" (Bernhardt & Major, p. 24).

Measures that are designed to assess school readiness skills include those that evaluate the child's knowledge of concepts that are an important foundation for academic achievement. They are the Bracken Basic Concept Scale–Revised (Bracken, 1998), the Slosson Test of Reading Readiness (Perry & Vitali, 1991), Test of Early Mathematics Ability, 3rd edition (TEMA-3; Ginsburg & Baroody, 2003), Wechsler Individual Achievement Test, 2nd edition (WIAT-II; Wechsler, 2005), as well as those that evaluate abilities that have been shown to be predictive of the ability to learn a particular academic skill, such as the Comprehensive Test of Phonological Processing (CTOPP; Wagner, Torgesen, & Rashotte, 1999). The Bracken provides the most comprehensive measure of concept categories, including an assessment of the young child's knowledge of colors, letters, numbers/counting, size, comparisons, shapes, direction/position, self/social awareness, texture/material, quantity, and time/sequence. Other measures assess skills that are more specific to foundations of a particular academic domain; for example, math (e.g., TEMA-3) or reading (e.g., Slosson Test of Reading Readiness). More generalized achievement measures (e.g., WIAT-II) also include items within each of the subtests that assess the young child's knowledge of concepts important to later development of academic skills. As described previously, early phonological awareness is highly predictive of reading development and is specifically assessed on the CTOPP.

While it is important to be aware of early signs of precursors for later learning difficulties, it is also important to appreciate that children can demonstrate different rates of development. Early difficulties are not always predictive of a later learning disability, as is evidenced in Figure 6.2, which

Figure 6.2 Work Sample These figures show responses by the same child at two different ages (age 5:5 and 6:5). The child's responses indicate significant development of fine motor control as well as academic achievement.

shows one child's progression in his writing of letters from the alphabet at age 5:5 and his at age 6:5. The child's written response indicates significant gains in his knowledge of letter form, with greater appreciation of lowercase letters at age 6 as well as qualitative improvements in fine motor control.

BEHAVIOR

Behavior problems are not uncommon in young children, with one recent study finding the overall rate of psychiatric disorders in preschool at approximately 19% (Egger & Angold, 2006). However, the exact number of children presenting serious emotional/behavioral problems is unknown, with estimated prevalence depending on the studies cited. A recent literature review revealed estimates ranging from 5% to 26% (Brauner & Stephens, 2006). ADHD is the most common diagnosis received by young children referred for mental health services (Gadow, Sprafkin, & Nolan, 2001; Keenan & Wakschlag, 2000; Wilens, Biederman, Brown, Monuteaux, Prince, & Spencer, 2002). Early childhood assessment is often requested of neuropsychologists to distinguish between normal individual differences and clinically significant behavior problems in a child. As with other disorders, the age of onset and current neuropsychological functioning are important factors for diagnosis. For example, diagnosis of ADHD is made if symptoms of inattention and/or hyperactivity are present before age 7 and symptoms are excessive for the child's current mental age (APA, 2000). Distinguishing between developmentally appropriate activity level in a young child and ADHD symptoms is critical to the diagnosis. Age of onset and current developmental functioning are also important in the diagnosis of autism spectrum disorders. Children with autism show disturbances in social interaction, communication, symbolic play, and imagination prior to age 3, whereas children with Asperger's disorder are typically recognized at a later age (APA, 2000).

Measures designed to assess behavior problems in young children include parent and teacher rating scales as well as rating scales based on observation of the child during the evaluation. As shown in Table 6.1, the assessment of behavior includes both broad measures of behavioral functioning as well as measures of specific behaviors. The Behavioral Assessment System for Children, 2nd edition (Reynolds & Kamphaus, (2004) is a frequently administered standardized measure that assesses broad behavioral disorders in children ages 2 to 5 years. The measure includes parent and teacher forms that have questions about inattention, hyperactivity, atypicality, withdrawal, anxiety, depression, aggression, and social skills. The Early Childhood Symptom Inventory, 4th edition (ECI-4; Sprafkin & Gadow, 2000) is a behavior rating scale that screens for DSM-IV-TR (APA, 2000) emotional and behavioral disorders in children ages 3 to 5. Disorders assessed include ADHD, oppositional defiant disorder, pervasive developmental disorder, Asperger's disorder, and separation anxiety sisorder. Parent and teacher checklists are available. Measures of specific behaviors include the BRIEF–Preschool (Gioia, Espy, & Isquith, 2003). The BRIEF–Preschool has subscales relevant to the assessment of attentional problems in young children, such as working memory and planning/organization. Parent and teacher forms of the BRIEF–Preschool (Gioia et al.) are available. Measures of behaviors characteristic of autism spectrum disorders include the Gilliam Asperger's Disorder Scale (GADS; Gilliam, 2001) and the Autism Diagnostic Observation Schedule (ADOS; Lord, Rutter, DiLavore, & Risi, 2001). These measures assess overt behaviors either reported by the parent or observed by the clinician. The GADS assesses four areas of behaviors characteristic of children with the disorder, including social interaction, pragmatic skills, and restricted patterns of behavior, and yields an overall score that determines the likelihood that a child has the disorder. Parents and professionals can complete the written measure. The ADOS is a standardized behavioral observation and coding measure completed by the clinician to assess autism and pervasive developmental disorder. It is a semistructured assessment that allows the clinician to observe social and communication behaviors in children across a wide age range of language functioning. The measure is appropriate for ages 14 months to adult and consists of four modules, with each higher module presenting progressively more complex language and developmental skills. Based on the child's age and an estimate of expressive language ability (ranging from nonverbal to verbally fluent), a module is selected for use. The ADOS is one of the few measures that involve direct assessment of autism spectrum disorders across such a wide developmental range. Intensive training is required to administer.

ADAPTIVE BEHAVIOR

Adaptive behavior refers to a child's functioning at a developmentally appropriate degree in such areas as communication, social skills, and daily living skills. In the past, mental retardation was based solely on the basis of intelligence test results. In 1959, the American Association on Mental Deficiency (now the American Association on Mental Retardation) published its first official manual and formally included deficits in adaptive behavior, in addition to significantly below average general intellectual functioning, as necessary for the diagnosis of mental retardation. More recently, IDEIA made assessment of adaptive functioning an important part of evaluations for children birth to age 5, with adaptive behavior being identified as one of five developmental domains assessed for eligibility of intervention. The

Vineland Adaptive Behavior Scales, 2nd edition (Vineland-II; Sparrow, Cicchetti, & Balla, 2005) and the Scales of Independent Behavior–Revised (Bruininks, Woodcock, Weatherman, & Hill, 1996) are two norm-referenced measures designed to document an individual's level of adaptive functioning from birth to adulthood. For children under age 7, the Vineland-II assesses everyday living skills in four domains: communication, daily living, socialization, and motor skills. The Vineland-II also includes a Maladaptive Behavior domain for ages 3+ to assess problem behaviors that may be interfering with adaptive functioning. Both a Survey Interview Form and a Parent/Caregiver Rating Form are available. Similar to the Vineland-II, the Scales of Independent Behavior–Revised measures both adaptive and maladaptive behaviors based on parent/caregiver report. Adaptive behaviors assessed include motor skills, social interaction/communication, personal living, and community living skills.

FINAL STEPS OF THE ASSESSMENT PROCESS

INTERPRETATION OF RESULTS, PROFILE SUMMARY, AND RECOMMENDATIONS

Strong and effective assessments aim to draw conclusions based on the integration of multidimensional comprehensive data, including information gathered from history taking, observations during task administration and clinical interviewing, and qualitative (e.g., integrity of handwriting) and quantitative (e.g., age-appropriate normative test scores) interpretation of performance. The clinician's skills are critical for interpretation of individual test results in the broader context of the child's history and functioning, with consideration of limits of the testing environment and behavioral observations. For example, a child's attention may fluctuate, in part, as a function of motivation, self-esteem, anxiety, mood, and effects of even mild illness (Baron, 2004), which can impact reliability and validity of testing results. As discussed previously, results need be interpreted with consideration of CNS maturation as a dynamic process, especially during infancy and early childhood. There is considerable heterogeneity in the pace of brain maturation, cultural background, and life experiences for each child (Beers et al., 2005). This is essential to consider when distinguishing potential delays in development from stable or even progressive brain dysfunction, as well as relative strengths and weaknesses for a given child.

The absence of an immediate observable weakness or deficit in the presence of a known neurological insult should be interpreted with caution, particularly with respect to understanding implications of the dynamic progression of brain development during early childhood. Depending on the nature of the insult, it is possible that instead of an acute loss of function, a child may fail to progress normally, resulting in later-onset of cognitive or behavioral deficits that may only be detected at a later chronological age (e.g., emergent in the form of a learning disability). For example, high-prevalence/ low-severity dysfunction associated with low birth weight and preterm status may not be detected early on in infancy or preschool, as deficits tend to become more apparent as the child advances in school age (see Aylward, 2002). Accordingly, follow-up assessment at school entry or beyond is critical. Likewise, the observation of acute loss of a previously acquired function does not necessarily dictate a child's expected developmental trajectory, in that some children recover functions either partially or in full over time (Baron). These represent situations where recommendation for close monitoring of the child's achievement of subsequent expected milestones or indications of recovery of function, and possibly a follow-up neurodevelopmental or neuropsychological assessment, may be warranted. Such decisions reside in the judgment of the expert clinician and should include consideration regarding who will be the recipient of feedback, as well as potential (long- and short- term) implications of the recommendations, including benefits and disadvantages regarding the child's future development and progress.

It is important to interpret test results in the context of the referral question, and to describe the child's areas of relative strength and weakness, in order to provide an overall neurodevelopmental/neurobehavioral profile that addresses functioning across domains. Critical to the summary within a report are recommendations that may help facilitate actualization of the child's development and success cognitively, academically, socially, emotionally, and functionally. Discussion of specific referrals and intervention services is beyond the scope of this chapter. However, recommendations may include referrals to, for example, psychologists (e.g., for psychotherapy, parent-management training), psychiatrists (for medication consultation), neurologists (for CNS workup), pediatricians (for medical evaluation), speech–language therapists, and other services aimed at remediation, rehabilitation, and treatment/intervention. Assessments may also include recommendations regarding educational placement and strategies to help address the child's relative areas of strength and weakness. Identification of individual strengths is particularly important as they may be used to help facilitate the development of relative areas of weakness. Ultimately, the goal is to make practical recommendations aimed at actualizing the child's potential and outcome through facilitation of remediation, rehabilitation, and treatment/intervention services.

Arguably, one of the most important elements of the assessment is communication of results via feedback. In addition to sharing results with parents, with parental consent and the clinical judgment of the evaluator, results may be shared with educators, physicians, psychologists, and others involved in the child's current and/or future treatment or care.

ETHICAL AND MULTICULTURAL ISSUES

Neuropsychologists have an ethical obligation to use reliable measures appropriately normed and validated for the preschool age group, and when reporting results to indicate any reservations they may have about the validity or reliability of the results because of circumstances during the assessment (e.g., difficult behavior), or the inappropriateness of the norms for the child tested. In addition, clinicians should be aware of cultural issues that may bias test results, and when available, should use measures that are normed on the appropriate populations. Consideration of bias is particularly important when assessing individuals from cultural backgrounds different from that of the test developer and the standardization population (see Lezak et al., 2004). Section 9 (Assessment) of the American Psychological Association's Ethical Principles of Psychologists and Code of Conduct (2002) outlines these issues in greater detail (see www.apa.org/ethics/code2002.html).

Language, culture, age, and education affect the neuropsychological functioning of children, but the specific effect of these variables is not well understood (Kestemberg, Silverman, & Emmons, 2007). Thus, Kestemberg and colleagues outline the key factors that need to be considered when assessing children who are culturally and linguistically diverse (CLD). They include: (1) underinclusion of individuals from diverse cultures in instrument standardization (Horton, Carrington, & Lewis-Jack, 2001), (2) issues pertaining to test translation (Ardilla, Rosselli, & Puente, 1994), and (3) lack of data regarding behavioral and social–emotional assessment of CLD individuals (Merrell, 2003). As a result, neuropsychological assessments should recognize the child's level of acculturation and language proficiency and development (Kestemberg et al.). Moreover, it is incumbent on the neuropsychologist to "define, measure, and adjust for racial/cultural group rather than merely assigning an individual to a race/ethnicity group and making a judgment without consideration of other relevant and more pertinent factors" (Baron, 2004, p. 23).

Kestemberg and colleagues (2007) also highlight that it is important for neuropsychologists to: (1) be flexible in approaching CLD cases, capitalizing on the utility of multiple methods of assessment, multiple sources of information, and multiple settings for data collection; (2) attend closely to neuropsychological assessment measures and manuals to determine their applicability to CLD individuals (Ochoa, Powell, & Robles-Pina, 1996); (3) be familiar with and accommodate the culture of the CLD child and family; and (4) seek professional consultation as needed in the assessment process. These steps will optimize accuracy and utility of the assessment.

VARIOUS ROLES OF THE NEUROPSYCHOLOGIST AND CLINICAL TRAINING CRITERIA

According to the APA Council of Representatives (1996, reapproved 2003), the Archival Description of Clinical Neuropsychology is as follows:

> Clinical neuropsychology is a specialty that applies principles of assessment and intervention based upon the scientific study of human behavior as it relates to normal and abnormal functioning of the central nervous system. The specialty is dedicated to enhancing the understanding of brain–behavior relationships and the application of such knowledge to human problems. (Appendix K, XVI.3)

Moreover, according to the APA Council of Representatives (1996, reapproved 2003), the Parameters to Define Professional Practice in Clinical Neuropsychology indicate that the practice of clinical neuropsychology is distinguished from clinical, counseling and school psychology, and other health-related specialties in that it, in part, builds specialized competencies in the following areas:

> . . . comprehensive history taking; identification of neurobehavioral problems/ issues to be addressed; application of a wide range of neuropsychological assessment procedures to multiple populations; test construction and validation; remedial and supportive intervention design and implementation; individual and agency consultation; and consumer education/ethics, specifically in a neuropsychological context/(Appendix K, XVI.3, c.)

More information can be found at the APA Division 40, Clinical Neuropsychology web site (http://www.div40.org/def.html).

In addition to serving a unique role with respect to conducting neurobehavioral and neuropsychological evaluations, marked by application of brain–behavior relationships to individual patients (Adams, 1996), child neuropsychologists make other important contributions to the field. As scientist–practitioners, neuropsychologists need to be trained to conduct research aimed at better understanding both normal brain development and etiological processes involved in disruptions of brain development and respective cognitive, behavioral and clinical sequelae. Exploration of etiological factors often includes identification of risk and protective factors. Research efforts also cover areas such as development of new, more ecologically valid measures and diagnostic methods, establishment of normative data to be used in interpreting clinical data, conduct of studies aimed at better integrating cross-cultural perspectives, and development of rehabilitation techniques (Baron, 2004).

SUMMARY

Neurodevelopmental assessment in young children plays an important role in early identification of cognitive, behavioral, and motor difficulties that can affect a child's development. Such an assessment can be important in determining current developmental status as well as in assisting with diagnostic clarification and in determining what types of early intervention services might be most helpful for a child. The information from the assessment is also critical in that it can be used to chart a child's progress and response to interventions, as well as to provide information that can be very helpful to parents in that it describes a child's areas of strength and weakness. This can be extremely beneficial in helping a parent understand the underlying reasons for why certain tasks may be difficult for their child. Ultimately, the parent plays a very important role as advocate for their child's needs. Providing parents and educators with a better understanding of a child's cognitive strengths and weaknesses helps guide them in terms of what types of educational services and environments might be most beneficial for a child. Assessment may also shed light on underlying CNS insult, with testing results, at times, suggesting that further investigation may be helpful and or necessary. These questions can be addressed with a careful neurodevelopmental assessment that is sensitive to the child's developmental stage, cultural background, medical history, and specific referral question.

REFERENCES

Adams, M. J. (1990). *Beginning to read: Thinking and learning about print*. Cambridge: MIT Press.

Adams, R. L. (1996). Introduction. In R. L. Adams, O. A. Parsons, J. L. Culbertson & S. J. Nixon (Eds.), *Neuropsychology for clinical practice* (pp. 1–5). Washington, DC: American Psychological Association.

Allen, M. C. (2005). Assessment of gestational age and neuromaturation. Mental retardation and developmental disabilities. *Research Reviews, 11*, 21–33.

American Psychiatric Association. (2000). *Diagnostic and statistical manual of mental disorders* (4th ed., Text Revision). Washington, DC: Author.

American Psychological Association Council of Representatives. (1996, reapproved 2003). *Archival description of clinical neuropsychology*. Retrieved from www.div40 .org/def.html.

American Psychological Association Ethical Principles of Psychologists and Code of Conduct. (2002). www.apa.org/ethics/code2002.html.

Anderson, V. & Moore, C. (1995). Age at injury as a predictor of outcome following pediatric head injury: A longitudinal perspective. *Child Neuropsychology, 1*, 187–202.

Anderson, V., Northam, E., Hendy, J., & Wrennall, J. (2001). *Developmental neuropsychology: A clinical approach*. East Sussex, UK: Psychology Press.

Ardilla, A., Rosselli, M., & Puente, A. E. (1994). Introduction: Neuropsychological assessment in different cultural contexts. In A. Ardilla, M. Rosselli, & A. E. Puente (Eds.), *Neuropsychological evaluation of the Spanish speaker* (pp. 1–6). New York: Plenum Press.

Armstrong, M. B., & Nettleton, S. K. (2004). Attention deficit hyperactivity disorder and preschool children. *Seminars in Speech and Language, 25,* 225–232.

Aylward, G. P. (1997). *Infant and early childhood neuropsychology.* New York: Plenum Press.

Aylward, G. P. (2002). Cognitive and neuropsychological outcomes: more than IQ scores. *Mental Retardation and Developmental Disabilities Research Reviews, 8,* 234–240.

Aylward, G. P. (2003). Neonatology, prematurity, NICU, and developmental issues. In Michael C. Roberts (Ed.), *Handbook of pediatric psychology* (3rd ed.). New York: Guilford Press.

Baron, I. S. (2004). *Neuropsychological evaluation of the child.* Oxford, UK: Oxford University Press.

Bauer, P. J. (2008). Toward a neurodevelopmental account of the development of declarative memory. *Developmental Psychobiology, 50,* 19–31.

Bayley, N. (1969). *Bayley Scales of Infant Development.* San Antonio, TX: Psychological Corporation.

Bayley, N. (2005). *Bayley Scales of Infant and Toddler Development: Administration manual* (3rd ed.). San Antonio, TX: Harcourt Assessment.

Beers, S. R., Hammond, K. & Ryan, C. M. (2005). General assessment issues for a pediatric population. In Snyder, P. J., & Nussbaum, P. D. (Eds.), *Clinical Neuropsychology: A pocket handbook for assessment.* Washington, DC: American Psychological Association.

Beery, K. E., & Beery, N. A. (2004). *The Beery–Buktenica Developmental Test of Visual-Motor Integration: Administration, scoring, and teaching manual* (5th ed.). Minneapolis, MN: NCS Pearson.

Bernhardt, B., & Major, E. (2005). Speech, language, and literacy skills 3 years later: A follow-up study of early phonological and metaphonological intervention. *International Journal of Language Communication Disorders, 40,* 1–27.

Boksa, P. (2004). Animal models of obstetric complications in relation to schizophrenia. *Brain Research Brain Research Reviews, 45,* 1–17.

Bracken, B. A. (1998). *Bracken Basic Concept Scale–Revised: Examiner's manual.* San Antonio, TX: Psychological Corporation.

Bracken, B. A., & Nagle, R. J. (2007). *Psychoeducational assessment of preschool children* (4th ed.). Mahwah, NJ: Erlbaum.

Brauner, C. B., & Stephens, C. B. (2006). Estimating the prevalence of early childhood serious emotional/behavior disorders: Challenges and recommendations. *Public Health Reports, 121*(3), 303–310.

Brooks-Gunn, J. & Lewis, M. (1983). Screening and diagnosing handicapped infants. *Topics in Early Childhood Special Education, 3,* 14–28.

Brown, A. L., Bransford, J. D., Ferrara, R. A., & Campione, J. C. (1983). Learning, remembering and understanding. In P. H. Mussen (Ed.), *Handbook of child psychology* (vol. III, pp. 77–166). New York: Wiley.

Brownell, R. (2000a). *Expressive One-Word Picture Vocabulary Test: Manual* (3rd ed.) Novato, CA: Academic Therapy.

Brownell, R. (2000b). *Receptive One-Word Picture Vocabulary Test: Manual* (2nd ed.). Novato, CA: Academic Therapy.

Bruininks, R. H., Woodcock, R. W., Weatherman, R. F., & Hill, B. K. (1996). *Scales of Independent Behavior–Revised*. Chicago: Riverside.

Caplan, D. (1987). *Language: Structure, processing, and disorders*. Cambridge, MA: MIT.

Carrow-Woolfolk, E. (1999). *Test of Auditory Conceptualization of Language: Examiner's manual* (3rd ed.) Austin, TX: PRO-ED, Inc.

Casey, B. J., Galvan, A., & Hare, T. A. (2005). Changes in cerebral functional organization during cognitive development. *Current Opinion in Neurobiology, 15,* 239–244.

Casey, B. J., Giedd, J. N., & Thomas, K. N. (2000). Structural and functional brain development and its relation to cognitive development. *Biological Psychology, 54,* 241–257.

Castles, A., & Coltheart, M. (2004). Is there a causal link from phonological awareness to success in learning to read? *Cognition, 91,* 77–111.

Chomsky, N. (1981). *Lectures on government and binding: The Pisa lectures*. Dordecht: Foris.

Colarusso, R. P., & Hammill, D. D. (2003). *Motor-Free Visual Perception Test: Manual* (3rd ed.) Novato, CA: Academic Therapy.

Conners, C. K. (2006). *Conners' Kiddie Continuous Performance Test: Technical guide and software manual*. North Tonawanda, NY: Multi-Health Systems.

Connors, S. L., Levitt, P., Matthews, S. G., Slotkin, T. A., Johnston, M. V., Kinney, H. C., et al. (2008). Fetal mechanisms in neurodevelopmental disorders. *Pediatric Neurology, 38,* 163–176.

Delis, D. C., Freeland, J., Kramer, J. H., & Kaplan, E. (1988). Integrating clinical assessment with cognitive neuroscience: Construct validation of the California Verbal Learning Test. *Journal of Consulting and Clinical Psychology, 56,* 123–130.

Delis, D. C., Kramer, J. H., Kaplan, E., & Ober, B. A. (1994). *California Verbal Learning Test–Children's Version*. San Antonio, TX: Psychological Corporation.

Diamond, A. (1988). The abilities and neural mechanisms underlying AnotB performance. *Child Development, 59,* 523–527.

Dietrich, K. N., Eskenazi, B., Schantz, S., Yolton, K., Rauh, V. A., Johnson, C. B., et al. (2005, October). Principles and practices of neurodevelopmental assessment in children: Lessons learned from the Centers for Children's Environmental Health and Disease Prevention research. *Environmental Health Perspectives, 113*(10), 1437–1446.

Dror, D. K., & Allen, L. H. (2008). Effect of vitamin B_{12} deficiency on neurodevelopment in infants: Current knowledge and possible mechanisms. *Nutrition Reviews, 66,* 250–255.

Dunn, L. M., & Dunn, D. M. (2007). *Peabody Picture Vocabulary Test: Manual* (4th ed.). Minneapolis, MN: NCS Pearson.

Egger, H. L., & Angold, A. (2006). Common emotional and behavioral disorders in preschool children: Presentation, nosology, and epidemiology. *Journal of Child Psychology and Psychiatry, 47,* 313–337.

Elliot, C. D. (2007). *Differential Ability Scales: Administration and scoring manual* (2nd ed.). San Antonio, TX: Harcourt Assessment.

Ewing-Cobbs, L., Fletcher, J. M., Levin, H. S., Francis, D. J., Davidson, K., & Miner, M. E. (1997). Longitudinal neuropsychological outcome in infants and preschoolers with traumatic brain injury. *Journal of the International Neuropsychological Society, 3*, 581–591.

Fatjó-Vilas, M., Gourion, D., Campanera, S., Mouaffak, F., Levy-Rueff, M., Navarro, M. E., et al. (2008). New evidences of gene and environment interactions affecting prenatal neurodevelopment in schizophrenia-spectrum disorders: a family dermatoglyphic study. *Schizophrenia Research, 103*, 209–217.

Fenson, L., Dale, P. S., Reznick, D. T., Bates, E., Hartung, J. P., Pethick, S., et al. (1994). *MacArthur Communicative Development Inventories: User's guide and technical manual.* San Diego: Singular.

Frangou, S., Chitins, X., & Williams, S. C. (2004). Mapping IQ and gray matter density in healthy young people. *Neuroimage, 23*, 800–805.

Fuster, J. M. (1989). *The prefrontal cortex: Anatomy, physiology and neuropsychology of the frontal lobe.* New York: Raven Press.

Gadow, K. D., Sprafkin, J. & Nolan, E. E. (2001). DSM-IV symptoms in community and clinic preschool children. *Journal of the American Academy of Child and Adolescent Psychiatry, 40*, 1383–1392.

Garon, N., Bryson, S. E., & Smith, I. M. (2008). Executive function in preschoolers: A review using an integrative framework. *Psychological Bulletin, 134*, 31–60.

Gathercole, S. E. (1998). The development of memory. *Journal of Child Psychology and Psychiatry, 39*, 3–27.

Gilliam, J. E. (2001). *Gilliam Asperger's Disorder Scale: Examiner's manual.* Austin, TX: PRO-ED.

Gilliam, J. E. (2006). *Gilliam Autism Rating Scale: Examiner's manual* (2nd ed.). Austin: PRO-ED.

Ginsburg, H. P., & Baroody, A. J. (2003). *Test of Early Mathematics Ability: Examiner's manual* (3rd ed.) Austin: PRO-ED.

Gioia, G. A., Espy, K. A., & Isquith, P. K. (2003). *Behavior Rating Inventory of Executive Function–Preschool Version: Professional manual.* Lutz: Psychological Assessment Resources.

Goldman-Rakic, P. S. (1987). Circuitry of primate prefrontal cortex and regulation of behavior by representational memory. In V. B. Mountcastle, F. Plum, & S. R. Geiger (Eds.), *Handbook of physiology (vol. V, pt. 1., sect. 1). The nervous system: Higher functions of the brain* (pp. 373–417). Bethesda: American Physiological Society.

Hack, M., & Fanaroff, A. A. (1999). Outcomes of children of extremely low birthweight and gestational age in the 1990s. *Early Human Development, 53*, 193–218.

Haier, R. J., Jung, R., Yeo, R., Head, K., & Alkire, M. T. (2004). Structural brain variation and general intelligence. *NeuroImage, 23*, 425–433.

Haier, R. J., Jung, R., Yeo, R. A., Head, K., & Alkire, M. T. (2005). The neuroanatomy of general intelligence: Sex matters. *NeuroImage, 25*, 320–327.

Hammill, D. D., Pearson, N. A., & Voress, J. K. (1993). *Developmental Test of Visual Perception: Examiner's manual* (2nd ed.). Austin, TX: PRO-ED.

Hayiou-Thomas, M. E. (2008). Genetic and environmental influences on early speech, language and literacy development. *Journal of Communication Disorders, 41*, 397–408.

Horton, A. M., Jr., Carrington, C. H., & Lewis-Jack, O. (2001). Neuropsychological assessment in a multicultural context. In L. A. Suzuki, J. J. Ponterotto, & P. J. Meller (Eds.), *Handbook of multicultural assessment: Clinical, psychological, and educational applications* (2nd ed., pp. 443–460). San Francisco: Jossey-Bass.

Individuals with Disabilities Education Improvement Act (IDEIA) of 2004. (2004). Public Law 108-446, *U.S. Statutes at Large, 118.*

Isquith, P. K., Crawford, J. S., Espy, K. A., & Gioia, G. (2005). Assessment of executive function in preschool-aged children. *Mental Retardation and Developmental Disabilities Research Reviews, 11*, 209–215.

Keenan, K. & Wakschlag, L. S. (2000). More than the terrible twos: The nature and severity of behavior problems in clinic-referred preschool children. *Journal of Abnormal Child Psychology, 28*, 33–46.

Kestemberg, L. A., Silverman, M. T., & Emmons, M. R. (2007). Neuropsychological assessment of culturally and linguistically diverse children: A review of relevant issues and appropriate methods. In G. B. Esquirel, E. C. Lopez, & S. Nahari (Eds.), *Handbook of multicultural school psychology: An interdisciplinary perspective.* New York: Routledge.

Kolb, B., & Fantie, B. (1997). Development of the child's brain and behavior. In C. R. Reynolds & E. Fletcher-Janzen (Eds.) *Handbook of clinical child neuropsychology* (2nd ed.). New York: Plenum Press.

Kolb, B., & Whishaw, I. Q. (2003). *Fundamentals of human neuropsychology* (5th ed.). New York: Worth.

Komitova, M., Johansson, B. B., & Eriksson, P. S. (2006). On neural plasticity, new neurons and the posticshemic milieu: An integrated view on experimental rehabilitation. *Experimental Neurology, 199*, 42–55.

Korkman, M., Kirk, U., & Kemp, S. (2007). *Neuropsychological Test of Development for Children (NEPSY): Clinical and interpretive manual* (2nd ed.). San Antonio, TX: Harcourt Assessment.

Laplante, D. P., Brunet, A., Schmitz, N., Ciampi, A., King, S. (2008). Project Ice Storm: Prenatal maternal stress affects cognitive and linguistic functioning in 5½-year-old children. *Journal of the American Academy of Child and Adolescent Psychiatry, 47*, 1063–1072.

Lezak, M. D., Howieson, D. B., & Loring, D. W. (2004). *Neuropsychological assessment* (4th ed.). Oxford, UK: Oxford University Press.

Lipkin, P. H., & Allen, M. C. (2005). Introduction: Developmental assessment of the young child. *Mental Retardation and Developmental Disabilities Research Reviews, 11*, 171–172.

Liston, C., & Kagan, J. (2002). Memory enhancement in early childhood. *Nature, 419*, 896.

Lord, C., Rutter, M., DiLavore, P. C., & Risi, S. (2002). *Autism diagnostic observation schedule.* Los Angeles: Western Psychological Services.

Mahone, E. M. (2005). Measurement of attention and related functions in the preschool child. *Mental Retardation and Developmental Disabilities Research Reviews, 11*, 216–225.

McCall, R. B. (1979). The development of intellectual functioning in infancy and the prediction of later I.Q. In J. D. Osofsky (Ed.), *Handbook of infant development* (pp. 704–741). New York: Wiley.

Merrell, K. W. (2003). *Behavioral, social, and emotional assessment of children and adolescents* (2nd ed.). Mahwah: Erlbaum.

Mullen, E. (1995). *Mullen Scales of Early Learning: Manual* (AGS ed.). Circle Pines, MN: AGS.

Ochoa, S. H., Powell, M. P., & Robles-Pina, R. (1996). School psychologists' assessment practices with bilingual and limited-English-proficient students. *Journal of Psychoeducational Assessment, 14*, 250–275.

Pennington, B. F. (1991). *Diagnosing learning disorders: A neuropsychological framework.* New York: Guilford Press.

Perry, L. A., & Vitali, G. J. (1991). *Slosson Test of Reading Readiness: Manual.* East Aurora, NY: Slosson Educational Publications.

Pinker, S. (1994). *The language instinct: How the mind creates language.* New York: Morrow.

Rapin, I., & Dunn, M. (2003). Update on the language disorders of individuals on the autistic spectrum. *Brain & Development, 25*, 166–172.

Reynolds, C. R., & Kamphaus, R. W. (2004). *Behavior Assessment System for Children: Manual* (2nd ed.). Circle Pines, MN: AGS.

Riccio, C. A., & Wolfe, M. E. (2003). Neuropsychological perspectives on the assessment of children. In C. R. Reynolds & R. W. Kamphaus (Eds.), *Handbook of psychological and educational assessment of children: Intelligence, aptitude, and achievement* (2nd ed., pp. 305–324). New York: Guilford Press.

Rogers, S. J., & Vismara, L. A. (2008). Evidence-based comprehensive treatments for early autism. *Journal of Clinical Child and Adolescent Psychology, 37*, 8–38.

Roid, G. H. (2003). *Stanford Binet Intelligence Scales: Examiner's manual* (5th ed.). Itasca, IL: Riverside.

Rowe, M. L., Levine, S. C., Fisher, J. A., and Goldin-Meadow, S. (in press). Does linguistic input play the same role in language learning for children with and without early brain injury? *Developmental Psychology.*

Sattler, J. M. (2008). *Assessment of children: Cognitive foundations* (5th ed.). San Diego: Sattler.

Schneider, W., and Pressley, M. (1989). *Memory development between 2 and 20.* New York: Springer-Verlag.

Shaw, P., Greenstein, D., Lerch, J., Clasen, L., Lenroot, R., Gogtay, N., et al. (2006). Intellectual ability and cortical development in children and adolescents. *Nature, 440*, 676–679.

Shaywitz, S. E, Shaywitz, B. A., Pugh, K. R., Fulbright, R. K., Constable, R. T., Mencl, W., et al. (1998). Functional disruption in the organization of the brain for reading in dyslexia. *Proceedings of the National Academy of Sciences of the United States of America, 95*(5), 2636–2641.

Shaywitz, B. A., Shaywitz, S. E., Pugh, K. R., Mencl, W. E., Fulbright, R. K., Skudlarski, P., et al. (2002). Disruption of posterior brain systems for reading in children with developmental dyslexia. *Biological Psychiatry, 52,* 101–110.

Sherman, J. C. (2008). Normal and LD development of academic skills. In L. E. Wolf, H. Schreiber, & J. Wasserstein (Eds.), *Adult learning disorders: Contemporary issues* (pp. 3–24). New York: Taylor & Francis.

Sheslow, D., & Adams, W. (2003). *Wide Range Assessment of Memory and Learning: Administration and technical manual* (2nd ed.). Lutz, FL: Psychological Assessment Resources.

Skinner, B. F. (1957). *Verbal behavior.* New York: Appleton.

Sparrow, S. S., Cicchetti, D. V., & Balla, D. A. (2005). *Vineland Adaptive Behavior Scales: Survey forms manual* (2nd ed.). Circle Pines, MN: AGS.

Sprafkin, J., & Gadow, K. D. (2000). *Early Childhood Inventory: Screening manual* (4th ed.). Stony Brook, NY: Checkmate Plus.

Spreen, O., Risser, A. H., & Edgell, D. (1995). *Developmental neuropsychology.* New York: Oxford University Press.

Taylor, H. G., & Alden, J. (1997). Age-related differences in outcomes following childhood brain insults: An introduction and overview. *Journal of the International Neuropsychological Society, 3,* 555–567.

Temple, E. (2002). Brain mechanisms in normal and dyslexic readers. *Current Opinion in Neurobiology, 12,* 178–183.

Temple, E., Poldrack, R. A., Salidis, J., Deutsch, G. K., Tallal, P., Merzenich, M. M., et al. (2001). Disrupted neural responses to phonological and orthographic processing in dyslexic children: An fMRI study. *NeuroReport, 12,* 299–307.

Wagner, R. K., Torgesen, J. K., & Rashotte, C. A. (1999). *Comprehensive Test of Phonological Processing: Examiner's manual.* Austin, TX: PRO-ED.

Wechsler, D. (2005). *Wechsler Individual Achievement Test: Scoring and normative supplement for grades preK–12* (2nd ed.). San Antonio, TX: Harcourt Assessment.

Wechsler, D. (2003). *Wechsler Intelligence Scales for Children: Administration and scoring manual* (4th ed.). San Antonio, TX: Psychological Corporation.

Wechsler, D. (2002). *Wechsler Preschool and Primary Scale of Intelligence: Administration and scoring manual* (3rd ed.) San Antonio, TX: Psychological Corporation.

Wilens, T., Biederman, J., Brown, S., Monuteaux, M.C., Prince, J., & Spencer, T. J. (2002). Patterns of psychopathology and dysfunction in clinically referred preschoolers. *Journal of Developmental and Behavioral Pediatrics, 23,* 531–537.

Wilke, M., Sohn, J. H., Byars, A. W., & Holland, S. K. (2003). Bright spots: Correlations of gray matter volume with IQ in a normal pediatric population. *NeuroImage, 20,* 202–215.

Williams, K. T. (2007). *Expressive Vocabulary Test: Manual* (2nd ed.). Minneapolis, MN: NCS Pearson.

Zimmerman, I. L., Steiner, V. G., & Pond, R. E. (2002). *Preschool Language Scale: Examiner's manual* (4th ed.). San Antonio, TX: Psychological Corporation.

CHAPTER 7

Parent Assessment and Intervention

BARBARA A. MOWDER
and RENEE SHAMAH

I N MEETING THE needs of young children, service providers are in a unique position. Unlike most other service recipients, infants and young children can neither identify their own needs nor present themselves for services; therefore, working with the individuals especially charged with youngster's health, safety, and general well-being is fundamental. Indeed, parents create the environment for young children to grow and develop, influencing virtually all aspects of their development including, for instance, adaptive behavior, language and communication, as well as social-emotional regulation and functioning. Thus, parents are critical in children's development (Bornstein & Bradley, 2003; Collins, Maccoby, Steinberg, Hetherington, & Bornstein, 2000) and represent essential individuals to work with in meeting infants' and young children's needs. In fact, parents are the means, and not infrequently the end, in providing those services.

Determining parenting practices resulting in positive child outcomes, as well as those associated with negative or problematic ones, guides much of service delivery. Fortunately, there is ample contemporary research on parenting and, setting aside the issue of developmental differences for the moment, the parenting research for the most part is consistent and persuasive. For example, Benjet, Azar, and Kuersten-Hogan (2003) contend that parenting research primarily focuses on two dimensions: control (e.g., authoritarianism, monitoring, restrictiveness) and responsiveness (e.g., involvement, warmth). Further, extremes of control, whether too permissive or overly restrictive, in conjunction with low responsiveness, compromise children's development.

Dallaire et al. (2006) generally concur with this position, comparing supportive–positive (e.g., responsive, warm) with harsh–negative (e.g., critical, hostile) parenting behaviors. Indeed, there is little question that supportive–positive parenting is associated with positive child developmental outcomes.

Ryan, Martin, and Brooks-Gunn (2006) maintain that maternal supportiveness is critical to early child cognitive development and, further, there is little question that factors such as involvement and warmth are related to positive early childhood outcomes. Thus, responsiveness, sensitivity, and stimulation, whether provided by the mother or father, contribute to positive child outcomes. For example, Radziszewska, Richardson, Dent, and Flay (1996) find that warm, controlling parents have children with fewer depressive symptoms than controlling parents who are not warm.

In terms of negative child developmental outcomes, there also is extensive recent research. Indeed, negative parenting (e.g, harshness, inconsistency) is associated with children's internalizing behavior problems (e.g., anxiety, depression) as well as externalizing difficulties (e.g., aggression, conduct disorders). With regard to internalizing problems, Dallaire et al. (2006) find that low rates of supportive-positive parenting, in tandem with high levels of harsh–negative parenting, contribute to children's depressive symptomatology. Consistent with negative parenting behaviors, parents' expression of negative emotions also place children at-risk for depression (Eisenberg et al., 2001).

With regard to externalizing problems, Del Vecchio and O'Leary (2006) suggest that two styles of parenting are likely culprits. First, meeting children's misbehavior with overreactive or harsh discipline encourages children's aggression. Second, aggression and misbehavior are likely fostered through lax parental disciplinary strategies, including capitulating and not following through on threats related to continued misbehavior. Lax discipline negatively as well as positively reinforces misbehavior; for example, ignoring noncompliance and overlooking prior demands provides negative reinforcement while providing attention when the misbehavior occurs offers positive reinforcement. Thus, excessively harsh, as well as excessively lax, parenting is significantly related to children's externalizing behaviors (Chang, Schwartz, Dodge, & McBride-Chang, 2003; Cunningham & Boyle, 2002; Romano, Tremblay, Farhat, & Cote, 2006).

Specific to young children, Brook, Zheng, Whiteman, and Brook (2001) determine that power-assertive discipline is associated with toddlers' aggression. As young as two years of age, aggression is stable and, further, early child aggression predicts negative adult behavioral outcomes (Del Vecchio & O'Leary, 2006). Consistent with these findings, Kim, Ge, Brody, Conger, Gibbons, & Simons (2003) maintain that unrelentingly harsh and hostile parents have children whose externalizing difficulties escalate over time. More specifically, negative parenting practices are implicated in the persistence of oppositional defiant disorder (ODD) (August, Realmuto, Joyce, & Hektner, 1999). Indeed, hostility is a primary overall factor related to children's behavior problems (Rhoades & O'Leary, 2007). Not only does harsh and coercive parenting contribute to the development of aggression, but also compromises academic achievement in school settings (Collins et al., 2000).

In summary, before discussing issues, such as parent definitions, theories, and measures, there are a number of consistent, identified themes. First, parents are critical in children's development, often serving as the intervention focus for early childhood services. Second, most research reveals two major parenting dimensions, control and responsiveness; for example, supportive, positive parenting is generally associated with positive child outcomes, and harshness and inconsistency with negative child outcomes.

PARENT DEFINITION ISSUES

Although extensive research relates parenting to various child developmental outcomes, applications to professional practice (e.g., assessment, consultation, intervention) are limited. Professional practice benefits from research, to be sure; however, there are few direct linkages. That is, for example, there are few parent assessment measures specifically designed for professional practice, regardless of whether the assessment focuses on the parent and/or the child.

One challenge is no common definition of who the parent is. Lest this seem a minor point, the ramifications can be significant, since there are a number of ways to define parent (e.g., biologically, legally, socially). For example, if a biological, nature-oriented definition is employed, the child's parent is defined genetically and by extension, no further action or behavior is necessarily implied. However, if a nurture-oriented, social, and/or legal definition is utilized, then the individual may be the biological parent, some other designated individual, or even the state. A more socially oriented definition inevitably incorporates responsibilities associated with being a parent inexorably tied to the cultural context. For example, Lamm, Keller, Yovsi, and Chaudhary (2008) contend that parenting is a cultural activity closely attuned to the sociocultural environment.

In an age when others (e.g., grandparents, surrogate parents) are involved in children's upbringing, the issue of what defines the parent is significant. Thus, there are real implications for professional practice. For instance, if there is no definition of *parent* from which service emanates, then individual providers ultimately rely on their own parenting beliefs, which may vary not only among professionals, but also between providers and the parents served. In other words, without definitional clarity, the opportunities for miscommunication are significant (Mowder, Harvey, Moy, & Pedro, 1995).

PARENTING THEORY

Related to definitions, there also are broader theoretical concerns. Theories are critical since they provide a logical, cohesive framework for conceptualizing issues, giving consistency and meaning not only to practice but also research. In this regard, Baumrind's (1971, 1991) work springs to mind for most developmentalists. She definitely provided seminal research on issues such as parental warmth and control; however, she neither defined parents nor provided a parenting theory. Indeed, her voluminous, thoughtful contributions generally constitute parenting types (Steinberg, Lamborn, Darling, Mounts, & Dornbusch, 1994) in contrast to a broader, generalizable parenting theory. Somewhat more recently, Galinsky (1987) proposed six stages of parenting, emanating mostly from an early childhood education perspective. Today, however, her theory is rarely mentioned in the contemporary research literature. A newer framework, the parent development theory (PDT; Mowder, 2005) offers a data-based, organized theoretical perspective for addressing and framing parent-related practice issues.

The PDT provides definitions as well as a developmentally, culturally sensitive context for examining parenting. Viewing parenting as consistent with social role performance, the *parent* is defined as one who recognizes, accepts, and performs the parent role and the *child* as the compliment to the dyadic relationship, the individual receiving parenting. Further, the parent role combines elements of bonding or love and affection, discipline, education, general welfare and protection, responsivity, and sensitivity (Mowder, 1993; Mowder et al., 1995), with the relative emphasis of each varying somewhat as children, from infancy through adulthood, grow and develop. As with most social roles, individuals' social cognitive parenting perspectives belie considerable variation. Some, for example, think bonding, warmth, and love crucial and key, while others might firmly embrace other parenting dimensions such as discipline and education. Like other social cognitions, parenting perceptions evolve over time, continuously developing based on multiple factors. Ultimately, parenting beliefs are founded on individuals' themselves (e.g., education, personality, prior experience in a parent–child relationship) and, after becoming a parent, those beliefs adjust to the child (e.g., age, gender, developmental difficulties), the emerging parent–child relationship, and family dynamics (e.g., extended family, siblings, spousal relationship), within the social–cultural environment. To be sure, the PDT conceptually relies on broader cognitive developmental and social learning theories, with the assumption that cognitions generally inform parenting behaviors (Mowder, 2005).

This chapter does not veer into debating parent definition or theory, although these issues are important to professional practice. The point of acknowledging definition and theory importance relates to practice issues since practice begs dimension clarification and specification. For example, questions such as with whom and what assessments might address, whom to consult with and why, and possible intervention targets abound. Without definition and theory, professional practice tends to lack overall coherence even though mostly based on extensive research data documenting significant parenting dimensions (e.g., warm–harsh, controlling–lax).

PARENTING MEASURES

Perhaps for definitional, theoretical, and/or other reasons, there are few comprehensive assessment instruments for use with parents. What measures there are tend to focus on specific parenting dimensions, often targeting the most problematic parenting behaviors rather than appreciating the broad range of parenting behaviors. The focus on negative parenting (e.g., child abuse, neglect) is not surprising given the multiple negative problematic consequences for children, parents, and society. Beyond the focus on specific aspects of parenting, the majority of parenting measures have been designed for research and are neither tailored for professional practice nor necessarily conform to standards for practice measures (e.g., *Standards for Educational and Psychological Testing*, 1999). Therefore, although the measures discussed in this chapter have evidence base, not all were especially developed or generally useful for professional practice purposes. The first measures discussed are used in clinical practice, while the second set is currently mostly for parenting research. The research-based measures are included for a number of reasons; for instance, some may develop further and become clinical measures while others have been employed to evaluate parent intervention programs.

CLINICAL PARENTING MEASURES

Parenting Scale One of the more prominent evidence-based assessment measures is the Parenting Scale (PS; Arnold, O'Leary, Wolff, & Acker, 1993), a brief measure of dysfunctional parenting. The PS is described as useful for both clinical and research purposes, particularly in detecting problematic parental discipline. The authors of this scale developed items based on parenting "mistakes" related to children's externalizing behaviors. Revisions were based on responses of mothers of 1½- to 4-year-olds and ultimately led to a 30-item measure. Parents respond to each item (e.g., "When my child misbehaves, I raise my voice or yell") on a 7-point scale, anchored on one end by effective and on the other by ineffective disciplinary strategies. The scale takes approximately 10 minutes to complete.

Early research (Arnold et al., 1993) determined three primary PS factors: laxness, overreactivity, and verbosity. Initial reliability (Arnold et al.), in terms of coefficient alphas, were laxness, 0.83; overreactivity, 0.82; verbosity, 0.63; and total, 0.84. Subsequent research (Reitman, Rhode, Hupp, & Altobello, 2002) confirmed the laxness and overreactivity factors, but failed to identify verbosity or another third factor. Recently, research by Rhoades and O'Leary (2007) indicates that the PS is a cost-effective, reliable measure of parental discipline. In their study of a large community sample of parenting 3- to 7-year-old children, laxness and overreactivity again were captured, but with one additional factor termed *hostility* (e.g., cursing, name-calling, physical punishment). Corrected coefficient alphas for mothers and fathers, respectively, were as follows: laxness, 0.85 and 0.82; overreactivity, 0.80 and 0.80; and hostility, 0.78 and 0.83. In terms of validity, all three factors are related to children's behavior problems as reported on the CBCL (Achenbach, 1991).

Parent Behavior Inventory   Not terribly dissimilar to the PS, the Parent Behavior Inventory (PBI; Lovejoy, Weis, O'Hare, & Rubin, 1999) also purports clinical, as well as research, use by measuring two parenting dimensions: supportive/engagement and hostile/coercive behaviors. This 20-item measure assesses parents' behavior toward preschool and young school-age children. After significant consideration of a wide range of behaviors, the authors determined 20 items to assess parents' hostile/coercive and supportive/engaged behavior toward preschool and young school-age children. The measure has parallel forms, utilizing the same items as those for parents, specifically addressed to observers as well as those knowledgeable about the parent. The authors state that overall PBI assessment fidelity is likely enhanced by the availability and use of multiple methods (e.g., self, observer), multiple sources (e.g., parent, spouse), and multiple settings (e.g., clinic, home).

Factor analysis confirmed the two primary PBI factors (i.e., hostile/coercive, supportive/engaged) and content validity was established through determination by members of a professional child development association; Cronbach's alpha was 0.81 for the hostile/coercive scale and 0.83 for the supportive/engaged scale. Test–retest reliability indications were 0.69 for the hostile/coercive scale and 0.74 for the supportive/engaged scale. Correlations with related constructs show that children's problem behavior is positively correlated with the hostile/coercive scale and inversely related to the supportive/engaged scale. Thus, the PBI is useful as a rating scale and has adequate internal consistency and test–retest reliability.

Parent Behavior Checklist   The Parent Behavior Checklist (PBC; Fox, 1994) was developed to contribute to the evaluation of families, determining strengths and needs. The PBC was derived empirically and is appropriate for parents of children from 1 through 4 years, 11 months of age. This paper-and-pencil measure is easily administered, taking only approximately 10–20 minutes to complete, and provides indications of parental expectations, discipline, and nurturance. The measure was developed in recognition of parents' contribution to children's experienced difficulties as well as in response to federal legislation (i.e., the Education for All Handicapped Children Act, Public Law 99-457) requiring appropriate comprehensive assessment for young handicapped children.

Unlike many parenting measures that do not necessarily rely on definitions or theory, the PBC is based on a specific definition:

> Parenting is a dynamic process that includes the unique behaviors of a parent that a child directly experiences and that significantly impact his or her development. Parenting also includes parental expectations that children indirectly experience through their parents' behaviors. (Fox, 1994, p. 3)

Further, depending on a developmental–environmental framework, the PBC rests on two major components: parental expectations and parental behaviors. Although based on two dimensions, Fox (1994) utilized factor analytic techniques and determined there were three primary factors. The first factor taps parental expectations and is labeled the *Expectation Factor*; the second factor identifies parental disciplinary behaviors and is termed the *Discipline Factor*; the third factor captures the extent to which parents foster children's psychological development and is called the *Nurturing Factor*.

Ultimately, potential items were generated from which 100 were selected; 50 items constitute the *Expectations Subscale*, 30 items make up the *Discipline Subscale*, and 20 items are included in the *Nurturing Subscale*. Each item utilizes a 4-point response scale, with parents indicating the frequency of each behavior (e.g., "I spank my child at least once a week," "My child and I play together on the floor") as A = always/almost always, F = frequently, S = sometimes, and N = never/almost never. The PBC has multiple uses, including identifying parenting strengths and needs as well as screening (e.g., in clinic, home, hospital, school settings) for parenting problems. Further, the PBC may be incorporated as part of a comprehensive family assessment, used in relation to legislative requirements for the development of family educational plans, and, with further research, may have specific diagnostic utility in determining the selection of appropriate parent and/or family interventions (Fox, 1994).

The PBC has received extensive psychometric attention. Internal consistency findings for the three subscales were 0.97, 0.91, and 0.82, respectively, test–retest results 0.98, 0.87, and 0.81. There were gender differences between mothers and fathers on the nurturing subscale, but not the two others; the author attributes the gender differences to perhaps scale development, which occurred exclusively with mothers and not fathers. Content validity was established through professional as well as parent review; further, PBC subscale responses varied among parents with young children of different ages, and item to construct correlations were strong, each of which offers additional support for content validity. Concurrent validity was established by using the Developmental Questionnaire (DQ: Peters & Fox, 1993), convergent validity established by relating the PBC to the Adult–Adolescent Parenting Inventory (AAPI: Bavoleck, 1984), and discriminant validity was established by comparing PBC scores with responses to the Child Behavior Checklist (CBCL; Achenbach, 1991).

Parent–Child Relationship Inventory   In contrast to the PS, PBI, and PBC, the Parent–Child Relationship Inventory (PCRI; Gerard, 1994) was designed, using empirical and rational approaches, to assess attitudes toward parenting and parents' children. The scale includes seven subscales; five of the subscales (i.e., Satisfaction with Parenting, Involvement, Communication, Limit Setting, Autonomy) relate to important aspects of the parent–child relationship (Coffman, Guerin, & Gottfied, 2006) and two additional subscales (i.e., Parental Support, Role Orientation) are less associated specifically with the parent–child relationship and tend to address other aspects of parenting. For example, Parental Support measures emotional support and practical assistance the parent receives and Role Orientation provides an indication of endorsement of shared or distinct roles for mothers and fathers. Finally, the PCRI provides an indication of respondent "defensive response set" (i.e., socially desirable responses) as well as inconsistency (i.e., inattentive responding).

The PCRI is a 78-item measure in which respondents utilize a 4-point scale ranging from *strongly agree* to *strongly disagree*. Items in six of the seven subscales (i.e., Satisfaction with Parenting, Involvement, Communication, Limit Setting, Autonomy, Parental Support) are keyed as positive or negative; for the positive items, a response of *agree* or *strongly agree* increases the score and if the item is negative, a response of *disagree* or *strongly disagree* decreases the score. High scores are associated with positive parenting and low scores with less than positive parenting. With the remaining subscale, Role Orientation, the items relate less to positive and negative parenting than the endorsement of distinct or shared parental roles. High scores on this subscale indicate shared responsibility attitudes and low scores traditional male and female parenting role points of view.

Gerard (1994) reports coefficient alpha levels are good, with no value below 0.70 and the median value at 0.82. More recently, Coffman et al. (2006) examined five of the seven subscales, finding that for their sample, coefficient alpha values of at least 0.70 were found for Satisfaction with Parenting, Involvement, and Limit Setting, but not for Communication or Autonomy. Further, they caution PCRI use in custody evaluations since their research reveals differences in the correspondence between how adolescents view their relationship with their mothers as opposed to their fathers; that is, there seems to be a relationship between adolescents and their mothers', but not fathers', perceptions of the dyadic relationship.

Parenting Stress Index   The Parenting Stress Index (PSI; Abidin, 1995) is a self-report Likert-type measure that includes 120 items related to parents and children. Considered too time consuming, the PSI was revised, becoming a 36-item PSI–Short Form (PSI-SF; Abidin, 1995). The PSI-SF has three subscales (i.e., Parental Distress, Parent–Child Dysfunction Interaction, Difficult Child), each with 12 items rated from 1 or *strongly disagree* to 5 *strongly agree*. Each subscale score may range from 12 to 60 and the overall score from 36 to 180. High scores on Parental Distress indicate stress related to issues such as parental competence and familial conflict, high scores on Parent–Child Dysfunction Interaction relate to stress associated with issues such as child failure to meet expectations, and high scores on the Difficult Child subscale indicate stress related to issues such as the child's temperament and demandingness. The PSI-SF also includes a Defensive Responding Scale, with seven items, to measure attempts to deny or minimize parenting difficulties.

Recently, Chang and Fine (2007) report PSI-SF coefficient alpha levels of 0.79, 0.82, and 0.84 for the three subscales. Considering additional PSI-SF psychometric qualities, Haskett, Ahern, Ward, and Allaire (2006) examined factor structure and validity, finding support for a two factor model including Parent Distress (PD) and Child-Rearing Stress (CS) (e.g., includes items from the Parent–Child Dysfunctional Interaction and Difficult Child subscales). In addition, these researchers report indications of PSI-SF construct and predictive validity as well as test–retest stability. In the end, Haskett et al. (2006) note that the CS scale, not the PD scale, predicts group status, since higher scores are associated with an increased chance of being in the abusive parent group.

ADDITIONAL PARENTING MEASURES

In addition to the clinical practice scales, a number of parenting measures have been used in parenting research and some, when supported psychometrically, may become relevant in clinical practice. For example, three research measures purport consistency with Baumrind's parenting styles (i.e., authoritative, authoritarian, permissive) and have been used primarily for research purposes. They are the Parental Authority Questionnaire (PAQ; Buri, 1991), the updated Parental Authority Questionnaire–Revised (PAQ-R; Reitman et al., 2002), and the Parenting Practices Questionnaire (Robinson, Mandleco, Olsen, & Hart, 1995). In addition, the Alabama Parenting Questionnaire (Shelton, Frick, & Wootton, 1996) and the Parent Behavior Importance Questionnaire

(Mowder, 2000; Mowder & Sanders, 2008) offer additional parent measurement choices.

Parent Authority Questionnaire The PAQ (Buri, 1991) was expressly developed as a research tool to measure Baumrind's (1971) authoritative, authoritarian, and permissive parenting styles. There are 30 items total, with 10 assessing authoritative, 10 authoritarian, and 10 permissive parenting styles. On one form individuals respond to each item regarding recollections of their mother's parenting and on another form their father's. Using a 5-point Likert-type scale ranging from strong disagreement to strong agreement, an indication of an individual's parenting experiences is derived; higher scores indicate greater consistency with a particular parenting style. Test–retest and internal consistency were generally in the moderate range and there are some indications of discriminant-related and criterion-related validity.

Reitman et al. (2002) revised the PAQ, changing the measure from a retrospective assessment of parenting received to a parental self-report inventory. Thus, the directions were changed from requesting responses according to how the statement applies to respondents and their mothers/ fathers (e.g., "As I was growing up, my mother seldom gave me expectations and guidelines for my behavior"; Buri, 1991) to how each statement describes the respondents' own beliefs about parenting (e.g., "I usually don't set firm guidelines for my children's behavior"; Reitman et al., 2002). Thus, the revision not only involved conversion of each item to refer to first person, but also expert review of each item to determine content validity with Baumrind's (1971) parenting styles. Ultimately, no original PAQ items were deleted, the reading level was determined to be approximately sixth grade, and, consistent with the PAQ, the measure is designed for use with parents of 3- to 8-year-old children.

Using three groups of participants, the PAQ-R was examined psychometrically and there is some doubt that the measure incorporates the three purported factors (i.e., authoritative, authoritarian, permissive). Indeed, the factor structure appears to vary according to sample characteristics (e.g., ethnicity, SES). The internal consistencies for the authoritarian and permissive subscales were modest and for the authoritative subscale weak. There are PAQ-R correlations with some PS subscales; for example, PAQ-R authoritativeness was associated with effective parent–child communication and authoritarian parenting was associated with overreactivity. With regard to the PCRI, however, authoritarian parenting was associated with communication and permissiveness was related to overreactivity. Clearly, additional research is indicated to determine the PAQ-R psychometric characteristics and usefulness as a parenting research measure.

Parenting Practices Questionnaire Also purporting to assess Baumrind's (1971) authoritative, authoritarian, and permissive parenting styles, the Parenting Practices Questionnaire (Robinson et al., 1995) was developed for research use with parents of preschool and school-age children. This measure has two forms, one for the parent respondent (e.g., "I am easy going and relaxed with our child") and the other for how the parent respondent views the spouse's parenting behavior (e.g., "S/he is easy going and relaxed with our child"). The 62-item instrument has 27 questions for authoritative parenting, 20 items for authoritarian, and 15 questions for permissive parenting; of these items, 19 came from an earlier measure (i.e., Block, 1965) and 43 items were new. Factor analyses revealed factors associated with authoritative parenting: warmth and involvement, reasoning/induction, democratic participation, and good natured/easy going. Authoritarian factors included: verbal hostility, corporal punishment, nonreasoning/punitive strategies, and directiveness. Permissive factors included behaviors such as a lack of follow-through and ignoring misbehavior. Recent research (Lagace-Seguin & d'Entremont, 2006), utilizing the Parenting Practices Questionnaire, indicates that authoritative parenting is negatively related to children's negative affect; in contrast, both authoritarian and permissive parenting styles are positively related to children's negative affect.

Another measure, also entitled the Parenting Practices Questionnaire (Gorman-Smith, Tolan, Zelli, & Huesmann, 1996), has been used to assess parenting. This measure is not based on Baumrind's (1971) parenting styles, rather uses questions from the Pittsburgh Youth Survey (Thornberry, Huizinga, & Loeber, 1995) to determine positive parenting, discipline effectiveness, avoidance of discipline, and monitoring/involvement. This measure has been used to assess the impact of family functioning and socialization processes (Robbins, Szapocznik, Mayorga, Dillon, Burns, & Feaster, 2007) as well as parenting associated with the September 11, 2001, terrorist attacks (Henry, Tolan, & Gorman-Smith, 2004).

Alabama Parenting Questionnaire The Alabama Parenting Questionnaire (APS; Shelton et al., 1996) is a 42-item measure of parenting associated with children's disruptive behavior. From the APQ, the APQ-Preschool Revision (APQ-PR) utilizes 32 items, deemed appropriate for parents of preschool children (Clerkin, Marks, Policaro, & Halperin, 2007). Research utilizing the APQ-PR with parents of hyperactive–inattentive and nonimpaired preschoolers highlights three main factors: positive parenting, negative/inconsistent parenting, and harsh parenting. The positive parenting factor (e.g., rewarding child) includes 12 items, the negative/inconsistent factor (e.g. threatening but not following through) has 7 items, and the punitive parenting factor (e.g., ignoring child when he or she is misbehaving) utilizes 5 items.

Parent Behavior Importance Questionnaire   Finally, the Parent Behavior Importance and Frequency Questionnaires (PBIQ, PBFQ; Mowder, 2000; Mowder & Sanders, 2008) and recently revised questionnaires (PBIQ-R, PBFQ-R; Mowder, 2007) have been utilized in a number of research studies (e.g., Mowder, Guttman, Rubinson, & Sossin, 2006). Based on prior research (Mowder, Harvey, Pedro, Rossen, & Moy, 1993) as well as the PDT, the questionnaires are based on a parenting definition and present specific parenting behaviors related to the parent role. The recently revised questionnaires include 73 items representing seven subscales (i.e., bonding, discipline, education, general welfare and protection, responsivity, sensitivity, negativity). The overall PBIQ-R has a coefficient alpha of 0.96 and all of the subscales, with the exception of discipline, have alpha values in the 0.80 range; the discipline subscale has an alpha value of 0.77. Factor analyses generally support the seven subscales; however, the discipline subscale appears to incorporate two disciplinary components including both the presentation of behavioral guidance as well as punishment related to non-compliance. Taken as a whole, using factor analysis, approximately 47% of the variance is accommodated for by the PBIQ-R subscales.

Thus, there are various parent assessment measures focusing on a range of issues including, for example, problematic parenting (e.g., PS), parenting stress (e.g., PSI-SF), and parenting behaviors (e.g., PBIQ-R). Some of the measures are reasonable for clinical use as well as research and others are currently primarily research instruments. From a review of the assessment instruments, clearly there is no one comprehensive instrument and, further, few are associated with parenting definitions and/or theory. As with other assessment areas, utilizing a multisource and multimethod of assessment is indicated.

PARENT INTERVENTION ISSUES

In terms of intervention, there are numerous issues beginning with who the parent is, who is in the parenting role, or, in other words, who will be treated (e.g., biological parent, foster parent, grandparent, step-parent)? In addition, those in the parent role may be at-risk for parenting difficulties due to a range of issues, including, for instance, poverty and lack of social support (Heinicke, Fineman, Ruth, Recchia, Guthrie, & Rodning, 1999). And, intervention programs may target parents of infants through adolescents (Heinicke et al.; Barnes, MacPherson, & Senior, 2006; Flynn, 1999; Valdez, Carlson, & Zanger, 2005) and be delivered in a variety of formats (e.g., home visits, group therapy, multi-media) (Heinicke et al.; Barnes, MacPherson, & Senior, 2006; Puckering, Rogers, Mills, Cox, & Mattsson-Graff, 1994; Segal, Chen, Gordon, Kacir, & Gylys, 2003) with advantages and disadvantages associated with each (Barnes et al. 2006; Heinicke et al.; Segal et al., 2003). In the end, there are a number of barriers regarding effective parent interventions (e.g., parents' earlier experiences, current behavioral dispositions, attrition, defensiveness, fear of judgment, transportation, motivation) (Letourneau, 2001; Olds, Sadler, & Kitzman, 2007; Segal et al., 2003).

TARGET OF TREATMENT

Who will be treated, including their characteristics and those of their children, is important since these issues inform a variety of decisions, such as the type of intervention selected and how the intervention is delivered. That is, for example, the target of the evaluation can vary based on a number of dimensions such as who is in the parenting role (e.g., adolescent parent, foster parent, surrogate parent). Thus, different issues may arise based on who is filling the role (e.g., parent developmental issues, permanency of the parent–child relationship) as well as establishing whether the treatment is preventive in nature (e.g., targeting at-risk parents) (Heinicke et al., 1999) or an intervention focusing on parents with identified difficulties. Another factor is the child's age. For example, some programs may focus on parents of children at a certain developmental age, such as infants and toddlers, preschoolers, elementary school aged children, or adolescents (Barnes et al., 2006; Flynn, 1999; Heinicke et al.; Valdez, Carlson, & Zanger, 2005). Finally, the targeted parent group may consist of parents of children with a particular disability (e.g., autism) (Brookman-Frazee, Stahmer, & Baker-Ericzen, 2006) and, most certainly, multicultural issues are a major consideration. For example, if the family has recently immigrated, they typically face unique social challenges, which may be significant based on their culture of origin (Ying, 1999).

WHO IS IN THE PARENTING ROLE?

Any parent intervention needs to be sensitive to the population meant to treat. For example, foster parents and biological parents face many common, but also unique challenges. For example, Linares, Montalto, MinMin, & Oza (2006) used the Incredible Years program in a foster care setting. Both the biological parent (to whom the child would return) and the foster parent experienced the intervention. Both parent groups received training in parenting and coparenting; the training was delivered in a group format and discussed four areas (i.e., play, praise and rewards, effective limit setting, handling misbehavior) through videotaped vignettes, role play, and home-work. Coparenting training occurred with the parent and foster-parent, working on expanding knowledge of each other and the child, open communication, and negotiating interpersonal conflict through lessons and re-enactment. The program was, for the most part, culturally sensitive as bilingual teams conducted the parent training sessions. Lenares and colleagues found improvement in positive and collaborative parenting for both biological and foster parents posttreatment. One year later, positive parenting gains were still evident, and the children had few externalizing problems. Parents also had clear expectations for their children. Thus, sensitivity to target groups (e.g., biological parent, foster parent) is an important issue to acknowledge and address.

PREVENTIVE PROGRAMS VERSUS INTERVENTION PROGRAMS

Olds and colleagues (2007) discuss the importance of delivering preventative programs (i.e., programs used proactively, not in response to an identified problem) especially to parents of young children. These programs can assist parents in understanding youngsters' communicative signals and responding appropriately, in an effort to promote children's health, development, and behavior. Other preventive programs, target "at-risk" parents in an effort to avoid the negative consequences associated with the population. For example, adolescent parents are frequently a population at risk (e.g., high incidence of infant mortality, low birth weights, child maltreatment) (Flynn, 1999) and, therefore, often are the focus of prevention efforts. Other at-risk parenting factors include issues such as poverty and lack of social support (Heinicke et al., 1999).

Heinicke et al. (1999) developed one such preventative program. They identified mothers at risk for inadequate parenting in the third trimester of pregnancy. Risk factors included poverty and lack of a support network. Once identified, the expectant mothers received weekly home visits and attended a mother–infant group. The focus of the intervention was to help the mother communicate effectively, teach her adaptation skills, help her in resolving her parenting concerns, and facilitate relating to children in effective ways. In addition, the home visitor focused on supporting and providing positive reinforcement for the mother as a way of developing mothers' self-confidence. As a result of the intervention, children tended to be secure and autonomous, their mothers responsive to their needs, and the mothers sensed support. Further, mothers' relationships with their partners became close, and, in addition, they became realistic about expectations related to partner support.

Other programs are implemented once dysfunction has emerged in the parent–child relationship or within the child. For example, Puckering et al. (1994) discussed a 4-month intervention for mothers with parenting difficulties, which was aimed at improving the quality of the mother–child interaction. This program had three components: psychotherapeutic groups focusing on past and present stressors and relationships, direct play for parents to practice new ways of interacting with their children, and group discussions of parenting topics. Parents were encouraged to try out solutions to their problems as homework. Worksheets and videos facilitated conversation and brought in the experiences mothers were having at home. Women were respected for their individuality and expert knowledge of their own children. As such, Puckering et al. did not use an expert model to facilitate parenting; instead, parenting advice was just as likely provided by another mother as a staff member. Parents reported that the intervention was helpful, and observers noted changes in parent interactions with their children. More specifically, parents reduced negative affect (e.g., criticizing, hitting) and increased positive affect (e.g., enjoying time with child, tuning in to child). Although their intervention was not compared to a control group, and thus lacks external validity, mothers reported an increase in their sense of parental competency.

ADDITIONAL INTERVENTION ISSUES

AGE OF THE TARGET PARENT

Parent training programs are also frequently used with at-risk adolescent parents. Flynn (1999) used the Adolescent Parenting Program to help adolescent mothers parent effectively and improve infant outcomes. Nursing paraprofessionals visited the mothers over the course of two years. At first, visits were weekly, then biweekly, monthly, and finally quarterly. Visits consisted of paraprofessionals going to mothers' home and discussing parenting skills and healthy behaviors (e.g., cessation of smoking, ages for immunizations). The visitor also provided social and emotional support, often accompanying the adolescent to doctor appointments. Further, the adolescents received assistance in setting and working toward goals. After two years, mothers who experienced this intervention had children with higher birth weights, and lower rates of mortality; there also were lower rates of child abuse and more age appropriate immunizations. Further, mothers were less likely to become pregnant again while in the program.

Barnet, Liu, DeVoe, Alperovitz-Bichell, & Duggan (2007) also used a home-visiting program with adolescent mothers. This program trained home visitors who began providing services in the mothers' third trimester and ended when the child was two years of age. Visits were biweekly in the first year and monthly in the second. During the home visits, two curricula were presented to the mothers, one for parenting and one for adolescents. The parenting curriculum spoke to information on child development, taught good parenting attitudes and skills, and encouraged appropriate use of health care services. The adolescent curriculum provided information on safe sex practices to prevent a repeat pregnancy, promote school completion, and improve communication skills. Barnet et al. found that this program improved maternal attitudes about parenting and decreased school drop out rate, but did not influence maternal depression or increase use of contraceptives.

CHILD'S AGE

Parent intervention programs also target parents of different age groups of children, including infants through adolescents. For example, Reid, Webster-Stratton, & Hammond (2007) were concerned with the social and emotional development of children, recognizing that an early prevention program might be especially effective at the time of child school entry. The program thus occurs at a time when children's behavior is malleable and most parents are motivated to be involved. Reid and his colleagues used the Incredible Years program in culturally diverse and disadvantaged elementary schools, beginning in kindergarten and lasting two years. While all children in their intervention group received the classroom intervention, only half also received the parent-training counterpart to the program as well. Through parent training, they focused on developing children's protective factors, such as supportive parenting. They found that children who had both types of intervention exhibited fewer externalizing problems and greater emotional regulation than children in the control group, or those with just the classroom intervention. Parents of children in this group were also more supportive, more involved in their child's school, and had a stronger bond with their child than those in the other groups.

PARENTS OF CHILDREN WITH DISABILITIES OR OTHER DIFFICULTIES

Not only are children's developmental stages important, but so too are children's special needs. For example, Sperling and Mowder (2006) found that parents of special needs preschoolers prioritize general welfare and protection as well as sensitivity when parenting. However, parents of typically developing preschoolers tend to embrace education. The differences in parenting concerns may influence parent-training programs.

Parents of children with special needs, for example, often require specific training to learn to effectively meet their children's needs. Brookman-Frazee et al. (2006) discuss parenting interventions for children with autism spectrum disorders. Operant conditioning techniques are often used with this population of children to reduce behavioral excess and decrease behavioral deficits (e.g., related to communication). Children with special needs are unique in that they may not respond to typical parenting strategies such as social praise and boundary setting, and, in addition, may experience a range of challenges (e.g., educational, social–emotional) over the course of their lives. Therefore, learning adaption and coping skills may assist parents of children with special needs.

The Incredible Years (Webster-Stratton, 2000) is a frequently used intervention for children with conduct problems; the program has been used preventatively to help parents develop positive parenting skills and foster children's social development. The program works with parents, teachers, and children to improve children's social competence. The program is delivered through collaborative group discussions, videotaped modeling, and rehearsal techniques. A troubleshooting book, home assignments, and "refrigerator notes" are also incorporated. There are five training programs within the Incredible Years. The first is a basic parenting program, teaching parents interactive play and reinforcement skills, discipline techniques, and problem solving strategies. Next is an advanced parent-training program, which acts as a supplement to the basic program; this program addresses parental interpersonal skills related to problem solving, anger management, communication, depression control, and giving/getting support. The third is an education program supplementing the basic program and speaking to developing children's academic competence. The purpose is to focus on and foster a strong relationship between the home and school. Thus, the goal is to help parents develop their positive parenting, communication, limit setting, and problem solving skills, and to involve the parents in school. Other training programs are available for the teacher and child. Webster-Stratton (2000) cites various research studies that provide efficacy data for the Incredible Years intervention.

MULTICULTURAL PARENTS

Immigrant parents face unique challenges in raising their children in America and their issues help highlight multicultural parenting concerns. For example, Ying (1999) notes that parent–child relationships are often strained in migrant families as a result of differential rates of acculturation; that is, typically the cultural gap between the country of origin's values and the dominant culture's values is significant. Prevailing parenting programs may not be responsive to differences in cultural values which impact parenting behaviors. The conflict may cause mental health problems as parents become confused, may sense betrayal, and children respond to differential demands causing confusion about their identity. As a result of some of these concerns, Ying developed a community-based prevention-based parenting program. She worked with Chinese-American immigrant families, helping them increase cross-cultural competence, their parenting skills (e.g., communication), and feelings of control over the parenting process; the program sought to assist these parents in coping with the stress of their position. The program used lectures, exercises, and homework over 16 biweekly classes. This intervention was deemed efficacious as parents reported a significant improvement in their relationship with their children as well as feelings of efficacy and responsibility related to their children's behavior.

INTERVENTION FORMATS

Interventions also embrace many different formats, each with associated advantages and disadvantages; for example, they occur in groups and during home visits, via videotape or interactive multimedia, and/or through printed material. Puckering et al. (1994), for instance, found success working with mothers identified on the Child Protection Register. They provided these mothers with psychotherapeutic services and, subsequently, parenting skills improved. In addition, some interventions combine different formats such as Sanders, Markie-Dadds, and Turner's (1996) Triple P Parenting Program. Their materials include a video, workbook, and tip sheet. The program is based on behavioral principles and informs parents about the causes of problems behavior, strategies for improving children's social competence, and ways to deal with difficult behavior. Parents also practice these new strategies using parenting checklists (Morawska & Sanders, 2006).

Allen (2007) discussed home-visiting programs, which are often used with children diagnosed with a disability or children at-risk for negative developmental outcomes. Further, Flynn (1999) and Barnet et al.'s (2007) home visiting programs were effective in working with at-risk adolescent parents. Allen (2007) evaluated factors related to home visitation interventions for young children. She found that the relationship between the parent and home visitor is a better predictor of the efficacy of the intervention than the amount of contact between the two or the level of need of the family. Barnes et al. (2006) reviewed the reasons parents may decline home visit interventions. They found they could predict 67.5% of program acceptance by reviewing several parent characteristics: if families were less disadvantaged, with no local support, several children in the family, a mother with educational qualifications, or parental health problems, they were more likely to accept support. Further, they found that parents at risk for parenting difficulties were less likely to accept support. Mothers also provided reasons for not participating; most felt that after birth they realized they did not need additional support. Many said they just changed their mind, and a few felt it was not the right type of support or they did not want a stranger working with them. Others reported that circumstances in their lives changed or that other commitments made participation too difficult. Other reasons for declining services include misperceptions about the service, issues with seeing self as vulnerable, concerns about building rapport or how the home will be perceived, or the parental perception that they do not need the help. Of note is that the most vulnerable parents are least likely to accept support. Reducing the stigma associated with parenting interventions (e.g., by offering support through existing services) may be necessary in order to increase parental participation.

Heinicke et al. (2000) looked at factors affecting the utility of home visits. They found certain characteristics often were associated with insecure attachment between the mother and child posttreatment. For example, a mother who was unable to work with the home visitor during the second half of the first year and was unresponsive to her child, also experienced low partner support, low confidence in herself, and difficulty forming stable relationships. Therefore, considering variables outside the delivery of parent information may be relevant for difficult to engage mothers.

ADVANTAGES AND DISADVANTAGES

Different approaches have different benefits and disadvantages. For example, use of interactive multimedia allows parents to determine their own learning pace and sequence of learning content, allowing them responsibility for their learning. Also, computers, used in a non-judgmental way when compared with receiving information in person, seems to circumvent parent defensiveness and allows them to repeat segments. This approach is also cost-effective, reduces the needed time commitment, and gives parents immediate results (Segal et al., 2003). Home visits are also effective and beneficial because they engage hard to reach families and reduce reluctance of discussing problems in a group. Further, problems related to transportation, child support, and motivation are alleviated with this type of intervention delivery (Barnes et al., 2006). Flynn (1999) also discussed the mechanisms that make home visits effective. Theories of mentorship and support are central to this type of intervention; home visitors act as parents' mentors and role models, providing information about child development and guiding parenting. Further, the visitor provides the parent with social and emotional support.

Although there is evidence-base for parent and family interventions (Kazdin & Weisz, 2003), Valdez et al. (2005) point out research often fails to consider or examine school related issues. That is, one important child intervention outcome is school functioning. They find current research gives children's adjustment and behavior in school little attention. The omission misses an important component of children's growth and development.

COMMONALITIES AMONG INTERVENTIONS

Though parenting intervention programs take on a variety of formats, some commonalities can be seen across most. Most programs tend to focus on teaching parents to discipline their children effectively. Maternal functioning, quality of mother–child relationship, and ultimately the child's development also tend to be common focuses of treatment. Finally, most practitioners using such interventions discuss the importance of developing a collaborative relationship with the parents. Allen (2007) even found that the nature of the parent–home visitor relationship was a better predictor of a positive outcome than the amount of contact or level of need.

One similarity among parenting programs is the lack of parenting measures to assess the efficacy of parent training programs. In most cases, efficacy is determined by measuring peripheral consequences (e.g., child externalizing problems, adolescent mother school continuation) (Barnet et al., 2007; Linares et al., 2006) instead of changes in the quality of the parenting. Thus, if evaluations measured, for instance, generalization of parenting interventions, effective practice might be identified.

INTERVENTION BARRIERS

Although parents obviously play an important role in children's developmental outcomes, there are many barriers to changing parenting behaviors. Barriers include different variables that influence how one cares for children, such as context or current situation, past experiences, current behavioral disposition, and genetic makeup (Olds et al., 2007). Attrition is also a problem with parenting interventions, particularly when the parent is an adolescent (Letourneau, 2001). Other barriers include parental defensiveness (e.g., parent does not want to be seen as vulnerable), fear of judgment, difficultly arranging transportation and child support, and motivation (Segal et al., 2003).

DEVELOPING AND EVALUATING INTERVENTION PROGRAMS

Intervention programs are most efficacious when they are based on a parenting model or theory since this allows for measuring parenting skills and focusing the intervention in meaningful ways (Puckering et al. 1994). Successful interventions address several areas of family functioning, such as the child, the parent, and those in the parents' support group. Further, changes in one parenting area are likely to affect other areas (Heinicke et al., 1999). When developing an intervention program, the targeted parenting behaviors must be related to empirical evidence regarding positive or facilitative parenting behaviors. Content relevance can first be gleaned from empirical literature, followed by expert judgment and agreement. For example, Segal et al. (2003) found evidence from previous studies that parenting interventions targeting the following behaviors reduce dysfunctional behaviors long term: facilitating pro-social behavior, monitoring the child's behavior, effective communication, reduced physical punishment, increased tangible and social reinforcement as established with the child, and learning to solve new conflicts.

Olds et al. (2007) discussed the important factors of developing appropriate and effective parenting programs, especially the grounding in theory and public health. This information can be used to determine an optimal target population, intervention focus, and method. Theory can also be used to determine an appropriate time to intervene, usually during a developmentally vulnerable time for the child, identifying target risk and preventative factors. Obstacles to developing these programs include issues such as choosing the aspects of parenting to work on, understanding what may impede behavioral change, engaging parents, and empirically evaluating the interventions. To be effective, interventions must engage parents by motivating them to participate; one way to do this is address issues that the parents see as relevant and fundamental. Once parents have accepted the intervention effort, the most important task is to motivate them to change (Olds et al., 2007). Particularly with home visits, there is a need for comprehensiveness, professional staffing, and frequent visits to increase effectiveness (Olds et al.; Heinicke et al., 1999).

Once parenting information has been used to determine the target behaviors and ways to change these behaviors, Olds et al. stress the importance of validating programs through randomized controlled trials. To be valid, the method and timing of randomization are critical. Practitioners must be sure there are procedures to ensure everything is evidence-based, and that reliable implementation can be assured in a variety of practice settings. Finally, replication of results is imperative (Olds et al., 2007).

When evaluating an intervention's validity, practitioners need to keep several factors in mind (Olds et al., 2007). Although there are standards, in reality few programs have met them. First, psychometrically sound measures with rigorous research design must be used, and a follow-up assessment at least 6 months after the intervention should continue to show effects. The program should be operationalized in manuals and training with a theory of causal mechanisms and practical value. Next, the samples on which the intervention was standardized should be specified, as well as the conditions in which the program can be expected to be effective. Finally, there needs to be replication, at least twice, with evaluation tools to assess progress.

MULTICULTURAL ISSUES

Professional practice with parents of young children necessitates keen cultural and diversity awareness, preparedness, and sensitivity. Definitions of parenting ultimately are housed within social-cultural contexts (Lamm et al., 2008) and diversity of parents as well as professionals lead to individual interpretations. The between and within group variability protend significant communication difficulties (Mowder et al., 1995). For example, the early childhood professional may believe positive parenting practice (e.g., warmth, consistency) are well recognized and accepted, yet other early childhood providers as well as parents may hold quite different beliefs (e.g., the worth of strong discipline).

To be sure, a number of professional organizations (e.g., American Psychological Association, 2002, 2003) require practitioner cultural competence. However, complete cultural competence is more of an aspiration than established reality (American Psychological Association, 2003). Although the breadth and depth of cultural competence may be daunting (Lopez & Rogers, 2001; Rogers & Lopez, 2002), the reality is that diversity is not a minor issue. Sable and Hoffman (2005) find that over 41% of public school children are identified as other than White non-Hispanic. As a result of increasing diversity, Ecklund and Johnson (2007) believe cultural competence is demographically necessary, professionally challenging, and ethically imperative. They suggest specific practices with child clients, such as communicating respect for clients' cultural context, avoiding culturally laden assumptions, and recognizing cumulative effects of prejudice and racism.

TRAINING

Different intervention programs are designed for a variety of practitioners (e.g., psychologists, social workers, nurse practitioners) and require various forms of training. For example, Flynn (1999) explained that home visitors need information on child development, stress management, and child abuse prevention. Nursing paraprofessionals usually deliver services for home visitations programs (Flynn, 1999). In general, for mental health professionals, there needs to be firm curricular mastery of child developmental principles and evidence-based parenting research. In addition, field training in working with parents and delivering parenting programs is indicated.

Barnet et al. (2007) pointed out that home visitors should have a high school degree and experiences related to health care, child development, or social work. They stressed the need for empathetic qualities, an ability to relate to teens and families, communication skills, and knowledge of the community they work with. Allen (2007) also focused on training home visitors in relationship development. Barnet and his colleagues trained their visitors with two days of initial training in the use of the curriculum, followed by ongoing training in depression, contraception, substance use, and domestic violence (Barnet et al., 2007). The Incredible Years Program, as mentioned previously, requires three day training from a certified trainer, peer reviews and self-evaluation before practicing. Practitioners then follow the "group leader manual" (Webster-Stratton, 2000).

Overall, some programs recommend specific training and field practice and others do not. Regardless of specific intervention or prevention program, however, sensitivity to family cultural and diversity issues is paramount. Often, mental health professional and the families they serve are from different backgrounds. Didactic training in cultural and diversity issues certainly is a starting point; fieldwork and culturally sensitive supervision obviously adds to appropriate preparation and training to serve young children and their families.

ETHICAL ISSUES

There are a variety of ethical issues to consider when working with parents regarding their young children (Harrison, 1997). First, many intervention programs require appropriate, mostly advanced training; practitioners need appropriate training before using particular interventions, seeking supervision until competence is established. Practitioners also require competence with different ethnicities as numerous parenting issues may arise based, at least to some extent, on cultural and/or diversity background. Best practice also involves using interventions that are evidence-based, thus practitioners need to be familiar with current research seeking out and providing such programs (American Psychological Association, 2002).

Informed consent is also an important issue. Especially if parent training is mandated by the court, psychologists must inform the individual of the type of anticipated service and confidentiality limits before proceeding. Informed consent for research also needs to be obtained if parent training data will be used for that purpose (American Psychological Association, 2002).

When delivering services through organizations, practitioners must be especially cautious. Before providing services, practitioners provide information to clients about, for example, the nature and objectives of the services, the intended recipients, which individuals are considered clients, the relationship the psychologist has with each person and the organization, the probable use of services provided, who has access to information, and the limits of confidentiality. Also, when therapy involves couples and families, practitioners need to clarify who the client is as well as the relationship the therapist has with each (American Psychological Association, 2002).

Finally, practitioners' confidentiality limits need discussion with families. This point is especially pertinent if, for example, the practitioner sees, or has a sense of, unsafe parental behavior. Such behavior must be reported to the appropriate authority; in other words, parents should be cautioned, in advance, regarding information offered to early childhood service providers. Confidentiality limits are not only relevant to parents and family members, but also to working with other early childhood practitioners (e.g., early childhood special educators, nutritionists); thus, confidentiality is important to keep in mind when consulting with other child and family service providers (American Psychological Association, 2002).

SUMMARY

Parent assessment and intervention is, without a doubt, a critical aspect of service provision for young children and their families. Indeed, parents often represent the primary individuals involved in service provision to young children and their families. Understanding parents, as well as the important role they serve in child development, is critical in the effective delivery of early childhood services. There is ample room for additional development of parent theory and practice. Training clearly is a requisite to the provision of effective parent services, especially in terms of cultural and diversity sensitivity. Finally, ethical issues regarding services to young children abound; these issues underlie all service provision. In the end, parent services represent one of the most important features of early childhood practice.

REFERENCES

Abidin, R. (1995). *Parenting stress index* (3rd ed.) Odessa, FL: Psychological Assessment Resources.

Achenbach, T. M. (1991). *Manual for the Child Behavior Checklist/4-19 and 1991 profile*. Burlington: University of Vermont Department of Psychiatry.

American Psychological Association. (2002). Ethical principles of psychologists and code of conduct. *American Psychologist, 57*, 1060–1073.

American Psychological Association (2003). Guidelines on multicultural education, training, research, practice, and organizational change for psychologists. *American Psychologist, 58*, 377–402.

Allen, S. F. (2007). Parents' perspective: An evaluation of case management intervention in home visiting programs for young children. *National Association of Social Workers, 29*(2), 75–85.

Arnold, D. S., O'Leary, S. G., Wolff, L. S., & Acker, M. M. (1993). The Parenting Scale: A measure of dysfunctional parenting in discipline situations. *Psychological Assessment, 5*(2), 137–144.

August, G. J., Realmuto, G. M., Joyce, T., & Hektner, J. M. (1999). Persistence and desistance of oppositional defiant disorder in a community sample of children with ADHD. *Journal of the American Academy of Child and Adolescent Psychiatry, 38* (10), 1262–1270.

Barnes, J., MacPherson, K., & Senior, R. (2006). Factors influencing the acceptance of volunteer home-visiting support offered to families with new babies. *Child and Family Social Work, 11*(2), 107–117.

Barnet, B., Liu, J., DeVoe, M., Alperovitz-Bichell, K., & Duggan, A. K. (2007). Home visiting for adolescent mothers: Effects on parenting, maternal life course, and primary care linkage. *Annals of Family Medicine, 5*(3), 224–232.

Baumrind, D. (1971). Current patterns of parental authority. *Developmental Psychology Monograph, 4.*

Baumrind, D. (1991). Parenting styles and adolescent development. In R. M. Lerner, A. C. Petersen, & J. Brooks-Gunn (Eds.), *Encyclopedia of adolescence* (vol. 2, pp. 746–758). New York: Garland Publishing.

Bavolek, S. J. (1984). *Handbook for the Adult–Adolescent Parenting Inventory*. Eau Claire, WI: Family Development Resources.

Benjet, G., Azar, S. T., & Kuersten-Hogan, R. (2003). Evaluating the parental fitness of psychiatrically diagnosed individuals: Advocating a functional–contextual analysis of parenting. *Journal of Family Psychology, 17*(2), 238–251.

Block, J. H. (1965). *The child-rearing practices report: A technique for evaluating parental socialization orientations*. Berkeley: University of California, Institute of Human Development.

Bornstein, M. H., & Bradley, R. H. (Eds.) (2003). *Socioeconomic status, parenting, and child development*. Mahwah, NJ: Erlbaum.

Brook, J. S., Zheng, L., Whiteman, M., & Brook, D. W. (2001). Aggression in toddlers: Associations with parenting and marital relations. *Journal of Genetic Psychology, 162*(2), 228–241.

Brookman-Frazee, L., Stahmer, A., & Baker-Ericzen, M. J. (2006). Parenting interventions for children with autism spectrum and disruptive behavior disorders: Opportunities for cross-fertilization. *Clinical Child and Family Psychology Review, 9*(3/4), 181–200.

Buri, J. R. (1991). Parental Authority Questionnaire. *Journal of Personality Assessment, 57*, 110–199.

Chang, Y. & Fine, M. A. (2007). Modeling parenting stress trajectories among low-income young mothers across the child's second and third years: Factors accounting for stability and change. *Journal of Family Psychology, 21*(4), 584–594.

Chang, Y., Schwartz, D., Dodge, K. A., & McBride-Chang, C. (2003). Harsh parenting in relation to child emotion regulation and aggression. *Journal of Family Psychology*, *17*(4), 598–606.

Clerkin, S. M., Marks, D. J., Policaro, K. L., & Halperin, J. M. (2007). Psychometric properties of the Alabama Parenting Questionnaire-Preschool Revision. *Journal of Clinical Child and Adolescent Psychology*, *36*(1), 19–28.

Coffman, J. K., Guerin, D. W., & Gottfied, A. W. (2006). Reliability and validity of the Parent–Child Relationship Inventory (PCRI): Evidence from a longitudinal cross-informant investigation. *Psychological Assessment*, *18*(2), 209–214.

Collins, W. A., Maccoby, E. E., Steinberg, L., Hetherington, E. M., & Bornstein, M. (2000). Contemporary research on parenting: The case for nature and nurture. *American Psychologist*, *55*(2), 218–232.

Cunningham, C. E., & Boyle, M. H. (2002). Preschoolers at risk for attention-deficit hyperactivity disorder and oppositional defiant disorder: Family, parenting, and behavioral correlates. *Journal of Abnormal Child Psychology*, *30*(6), 555–569.

Dallaire, D. H., Pineda, A. Q., Cole, D. A., Ciesla, J. A., Jacquez, F., LaGrange, B., et al. (2006). Relation of positive and negative parenting to children's depressive symptoms. *Journal of Clinical Child and Adolescent Psychology*, *35*(2), 194–202.

Del Vecchio, T., & O'Leary, S. G. (2006). Antecedents of toddler aggression: Dysfunctional parenting in mother–toddler dyads. *Journal of Clinical Child and Adolescent Psychology*, *35*(2), 194–202.

Ecklund, K., & Johnson, W. B. (2007). Toward cultural competence in child intake assessments. *Professional Psychology: Research and Practice*, *38*, 356–362.

Eisenberg, N., Losoya, S., Fabes, R. A., Guthrie, I. K., Reiser, M., Murphy, B., et al. (2001). Parental socialization of children's dysregulated expression of emotion and externalizing problems. *Journal of Family Psychology*, *15*, 183–205.

Flynn, L. (1999). The adolescent parenting program: Improving outcomes through mentorship. *Public Health Nursing*, *16*(3), 182–189.

Fox, R.A. (1994). *Parent Behavior Checklist*. Brandon, VT: Clinical Psychology.

Galinsky, E. (1987). *The six stages of parenting*. Reading, MA: Addison-Wesley.

Gerard (1994). *Parent–Child Relationship Inventory (PCRI): Manual*. Los Angeles: Western Psychological Services.

Gorman-Smith, D., Tolan, P. H., Zelli, A., & Huesmann, L. R. (1996). The relation of family functioning to violence among inner-city minority youths. *Journal of Family Psychology*, *10*, 115–129.

Harrison, H. (1997). Ethical issues in family-centered neonatal care. In A. H. Widerstrom, B. A. Mowder, & S. R. Sandall (Eds.), *Infant development and risk: An introduction* (2nd ed.). Baltimore: Brookes.

Haskett, M. E., Ahern, L. S., Ward, C. S., & Allaire, J. C. (2006). Factor structure and validity of the Parenting Stress Index-Short Form. *Journal of Clinical Child and Adolescent Psychology*, *35*(2), 302–312.

Heinicke, C. M., Goorsky, M., Moscov, S., Dudley, K., Gordon, J., Schneider, C., et al. (2000). Relationship-based intervention with at-risk mothers: Factors affecting variations in outcome. *Infant Mental Health Journal*, *21*(3), 133–155.

Heinicke, C. M., Fineman, N. R., Ruth, G., Recchia, S. I., Guthrie, D., & Rodning, C. (1999). Relationship based intervention with at risk mothers: Outcome in the first year of life. *Infant Mental Health Journal, 20*(4), 349–374.

Henry, D. B., Tolan, P. H., & Gorman-Smith, D. (2004). Have there been lasting effects associated with the September 11, 2001, terrorist attacks among inner-city parents and children? *Professional Psychology: Research and Practice, 35,* 542–547.

Kazdin, A. E., & Weisz, J. R. (Eds.) (2003). *Evidence-based psychotherapies for children and adolescents.* New York: Guilford Press.

Kim, I. J., Ge, X., Brody, G. H., Conger, R. D., Gibbons, F. X., & Simons, R. L. (2003). Parenting behaviors and the occurrence and co-occurrence of depressive symptoms and conduct problems among African American children. *Journal of Family Psychology, 17,* 571–583.

Lagace-Seguin, D. G., & d'Entremont, M-R. L. (2006). The role of child negative affect in the relations between parenting styles and play. *Early Child Development and Care, 176,* 461–477.

Lamm, B., Keller, H., Yovsi, R. D., & Chaudhary, N. (2008). Grandmaternal and maternal ethnotheories about early child care. *Journal of Family Psychology, 22,* 80–88.

Letourneau, N. (2001). Attrition among adolescents and infants involved in a parenting intervention. *Child: Care, Health, and Development, 27*(2), 183–186.

Linares, L. O., Montalto, D., MinMin, L., & Oza, V. S. (2006). A promising parenting intervention in foster care. *Journal of Counseling and Clinical Psychology, 74*(1), 32–41.

Lopez, E. C., & Rogers, M. R. (2001). Conceptualizing cross cultural school psychology competencies. *School Psychology Quarterly, 16,* 270–302.

Lovejoy, M., Weis, R., O'Hare, E., & Rubin, E. (1999). Development and initial validation of the Parent Behavior Inventory. *Psychological Assessment, 11*(4), 534–545.

Morawska, A., & Sanders, M. R. (2006). Self-administered behavioural family intervention for parents of toddlers: Effectiveness and dissemination. *Behaviour Research and Therapy, 44,* 1839–1848.

Mowder, B. A. (1993). Parent role research. *Early Childhood Interests, 8*(3), 6.

Mowder, B. A. (2007, April). Parenting Behavior Importance Questionnaire: A revised assessment instrument for use with parents. Invited presentation at the Fifth Annual Los Ninos/Fordham University Conference. New York City.

Mowder, B. A. (2000, March). *Parent role behaviors: Implications for school psychologists.* Paper presented at the annual meeting of the National Association of School Psychologists, New Orleans.

Mowder, B. A. (2005). Parent Development Theory: Understanding parents, parenting perceptions, and parenting behaviors. *Journal of Early Childhood and Infant Psychology, 1,* 45–64.

Mowder, B. A., Guttman, M., Rubinson, F., & Sossin, K. M. (2006). Parenting and trauma: Parents' role perceptions and behaviors related to the 9/11 tragedy. *Journal of Child and Family Studies, 15*(6), 730–740.

Mowder, B., Harvey, V. S., Moy, L., & Pedro, M. (1995). Parent role characteristics: Parent views and their implications for school psychologists. *Psychology in the Schools, 32*, 27–37.

Mowder, B. A., Harvey, V. S., Pedro, M., Rossen, R., & Moy, L. (1993). Parent Role Questionnaire: Psychometric Qualities. *Psychology in the Schools, 30*, 205–211.

Mowder, B. A., & Sanders, M. (2007). Parent Behavior Importance and Parent Behavior Frequency Questionnaires: Psychometric characteristics. *Journal of Child and Family Studies, 17*(5), 675–688.

Olds, D. L., Sadler, L., & Kitzman, H. (2007). Programs for parents of infants and toddlers: Recent evidence from randomized trials. *Journal of Child Psychology and Psychiatry, 48*(3/4), 355–391.

Peters, C. L., & Fox, R. A. (1993). Parenting Inventory: Validity and social desirability. *Psychological Reports, 72*, 683–689.

Puckering, C., Rogers, J., Mills, M., Cox, A. D., & Mattsson-Graff, M. (1994). Process and evaluation of a group intervention for mothers with parenting difficulties. *Child Abuse Review, 3*, 299–310.

Radziszewska, B., Richardson, J. L., Dent, C. W., & Flay, B. R. (1996). Parenting style and adolescent depressive symptoms, smoking, and academic achievement: Ethnic, gender, and sex differences. *Journal of Behavioral Medicine, 19*(3), 289–305.

Reid, M. J., Webster-Stratton, C., & Hammond, M. (2007). Enhancing a classroom social competence and problem-solving curriculum by offering parent training to families of moderate- to high-risk elementary school children. *Journal of Clinical Child and Adolescent Psychology, 36*(4), 605–620.

Reitman, D., Rhode, P. C., Hupp, S. D. A., & Altobello, C. (2002). Development and validation of the Parental Authority Questionnaire–Revised. *Journal of Psychopathology and Behavioral Assessment, 24*, 119–127.

Rhoades, K. A., & O'Leary, S. G. (2007). Factor structure and validity of the Parenting Scale. *Journal of Clinical Child and Adolescent Psychology, 36*(2), 137–146.

Robbins, M. S., Szapocznik, J., Mayorga, C. C., Dillon, F. R., Burns, M., & Feaster, D. J. (2007). The impact of family functioning on family racial socialization processes. *Cultural Diversity and Ethnic Minority Psychology, 13*, 313–320.

Robinson, C. C., Mandleco, B., Olsen, S. F., & Hart, C. H. (1995). Authoritative, authoritarian, and permissive parenting practices: Development of a new measure. *Psychological Reports, 77*, 819–830.

Rogers, M. R., & Lopez, E. C. (2002). Identifying critical cross cultural school psychology competencies. *Journal of School Psychology, 40*, 115–141.

Romano, E., Tremblay, R. E., Farhat, A., & Cote, S. (2006). Development and prediction of hyperactive symptoms from 2 to 7 years in a population-based sample. *Pediatrics, 117*, 2101–2110.

Ryan, R. M., Martin, A., & Brooks-Gunn, J. (2006). Is one good parent good enough? Patterns of mother and father parenting and child cognitive outcomes at 24 and 36 months. *Parenting: Science and Practice, 6*(2–3), 211–228.

Sable, J., & Hoffman, L. (2005). *Characteristics of the 100 largest public elementary and secondary school districts in the United States: 2002–03.* Retrieved from http://nces. ed.gov/pubsearch/pubsinfo and cited by Ecklund, K., Johnson, W.B., Sanders,

M.R., Markie-Dadds, C., & Turner, K. M. T. (1996). *Every parent's survival guide.* Brisbane, CA: Family International.

Segal, D., Chen, P. Y., Gordon, D. A., Kacir, C. D., & Gylys, J. (2003). Development and evaluation of a parenting intervention program: Integration of scientific and practical approaches. *International Journal of Human–Computer Interaction, 15*(3), 453–467.

Shelton, K. K., Frick, P. J., & Wootton, J. M. (1996). The assessment of parenting practices in families of elementary school aged children. *Journal of Clinical Child Psychology, 25,* 317–329.

Standards for Educational and Psychological Testing (1999). Washington, DC: American Educational Research Association.

Sperling, S., & Mowder, B. A. (2006). Parenting perceptions: Comparing parents of typical and special needs preschoolers. *Psychology in the Schools, 46*(3), 695–700.

Steinberg, L., Lamborn, S. D., Darling, N., Mounts, N. S., & Dornbusch, S. M. (1994). Over-time changes in adjustment from authoritative, authoritarian, indulgent, and neglectful families. *Child Development, 65,* 754–770.

Thornberry, T. P., Huizinga, D., & Loeber, R. (1995). The prevention of serious delinquency and violence: Implications from the program of research on the causes and correlates of delinquency. In J. C. Howell, B. Krisberg, J. D. Hawkins, & J. J. Wilson (Eds.), *Sourcebook on serious, violent, and chronic juvenile offenders* (pp. 213–237). Thousand Oaks, CA: Sage.

Valdez, C. R., Carlson, C., & Zanger, D. (2005). Evidence-based parent training and family interventions for school behavior change. *School Psychology Quarterly, 20,* 403–433.

Webster-Stratton, C. (2000). *Incredible years: The parents, teachers, and children training series.* Seattle, WA: Carolyn Webster-Stratton.

Ying, Y. (1999). Strengthening intergenerational/intercultural ties in migrant families: A new intervention for parents. *Journal of Community Psychology, 27*(1), 89–96.

CHAPTER 8

Family Assessment and Intervention

BARBARA A. MOWDER
and RENEE SHAMAH

T HIS CHAPTER DESCRIBES family dynamics in relation to young children and their families. Typically, children are born into families which themselves are part of broader social–cultural systems. Within each family, individuals have roles (e.g., parent, sibling) and relate to each member within their social–cultural environment. In fact, as soon as a child enters the family, parent–child interactions begin and those interactions become embedded in broader family dynamics. Professionals face many issues working with families (e.g., defining the family, explicating family functioning); further, not all family interactions are positive in nature (Hughes, Hedtke, & Kendall, 2008), such as when child maltreatment and neglect occur.

These issues as well as family assessment, consultation, and intervention in early childhood services, in the context of evidence-based practice, are presented. Analogous to some other topics in this book, evidence-based practice in early childhood family assessment and intervention is more developmental than established. Nonetheless, contemporary early childhood family assessment and intervention is presented with special attention given to appreciating family cultural and diversity issues (e.g., Celik, 2007), making training recommendations for professionals, and being sensitive to ethical issues.

FAMILY DEFINITION ISSUES

Bray (2004), as well as Glidden and Schoolcraft (2007), recently discussed many issues associated with family assessment, not the least of which is what constitutes a family. Reflecting on family composition issues, Bray observes that contemporary American families are increasingly diverse (e.g., extended families, single-parent families, stepfamilies) and no longer necessarily include biological relationships (Shellenberger, 2007). For instance, cohabiting gay, lesbian, bisexual, transgendered (GLBT) individuals develop families of choice not necessarily based on biological or legally recognized relationships. As a result, traditional biological and legal relationships are giving way to role relationships, which in turn evolve over time due to inevitable family change and circumstance (e.g., divorce, social supports, stress). Thus, a primary assessment challenge is determining the family constellation.

There certainly is more than one definition of family. A rather traditional notion involves considering the family in terms of at least two individuals, one of whom is an adult and the other a child, legally bound through birth, adoption, or legal guardianship (Mowder, 1997). In contrast, Pequegnat and Bray (1997) note the National Institute of Mental Health's (NIMH) definition of family as a network of mutual commitment. The NIMH definition underscores role relationships traditionally reserved for biological or legal relationships (Bray, 2004) and, if attended to, introduces significant complexity into clinical practice. That is, role relationships may be difficult to identify and assess, further they may change over time (e.g., grandparents assuming the parent role).

Because of the variable nature of contemporary families, Glidden and Schoolcraft (2007) think family assessment represents special difficulties. They point to definitional problems as well as an absence of an accepted, general, family functioning theory; in addition, assessment issues may be multiplied when the family includes a child with an intellectual or other developmental disability. Regardless of a particular definition, inevitably family assessment requires multiple informants; thus, any approach needs to account for shared and nonshared variability in family members' perspectives (Georgiades, Boyle, Jenkins, Sanford, & Lipman, 2008).

FAMILY ASSESSMENT ISSUES

Regarding assessment, Cook (2006) takes the position that families represent systems of interdependent individuals. Inevitably, individuals' adaptation, behavior, and overall functioning need to be considered from a family context. Due to the complexity inherent in family systems (e.g., interdependence), many assessment instruments fail to identify individual functioning in conjunction with overall family dynamics. Ultimately, Cook outlines four primary problems with traditional family assessment measures (e.g., Family Environment Scale (FES) (Moos & Moos, 1983)); Family Adaptability and Cohesion Scales (FACES III) (Olson, Portner, & Lavee, 1985):

- Each family member has a somewhat unique view of how the family functions; atypical scores may reflect the individual family member or, on the other hand, family functioning.

- The intended focus of family ratings may not be clear; individual members differentially conceptualize and present family functioning, emphasizing dyadic relationships rather than the whole.
- There are basic conceptual difficulties; individual indications of dyadic relationships and entire family functioning may not provide a composite picture of family patterns.
- Assessments of family functioning typically assume family member similarities; however, measures of overall functioning fail to appreciate different family member roles as well as individual family member personality.

Because of assessment issues, what begets healthy or unhealthy family functioning, using traditional measures, looms large.

Bray (2004) weighs in on these issues, asserting a major problem with current family assessment is the lack of agreement regarding a family diagnostic system analogous to the *Diagnostic and Statistical Manual of Mental Disorders*, 4th edition (DSM-IV) for individual psychological issues. Acknowledging this issue, he nevertheless maintains there are essentially five main characteristics of family functioning (i.e., family composition, family process, patterned relationships, family affect, family organization). Although each characteristic is important, all need to be understood with an appreciation for family complexity and diversity. Family composition refers to issues such as family membership (e.g., single parents), structure (e.g., divorced, step-family), and sexual orientation (e.g., bisexual, heterosexual). Family processes (e.g., conflict, problem solving) include the multitude of interactions, trans-actions, and patterns of family exchanges. Patterned relationships are inter-actions (e.g., contempt, defensiveness) developed over time, which may be associated with positive (e.g., marital satisfaction) or negative (e.g., divorce) consequences. Family affect captures emotional content (e.g., negative, positive) and expression (e.g., nonverbal, verbal); for example, the cumulative negative nature of family affect may result in debilitating consequences (e.g., alcoholism, mood disorders). Finally, family organization may reflect roles (e.g., child, parent), behavioral expectations, and underlying processes (e.g., decision-making hierarchies, emotionally supportive relationships).

Thus, although family assessment mostly relies on family systems theories (i.e., emphasizing the functioning of the family as a whole), criticism-free procedures or measures have proved elusive. Indeed, De Bruyn (2005) complains that FACES, a commonly used, respected measure, is problematic on a number of fronts (e.g., weak correspondence between family members' perceptions, the whole-family focus). Because of these and many other measurement issues, De Bruyn (2005) and Cook (2006) promote the Social Relations Model (SRM) (Cook & Kenny, 2004). The SRM benefits from a quantitative method of providing some sense of the family as well as how each individual fits within the complex whole (Cook, 2006).

The Round-Robin Family Assessment with SRM (RR-SRM) (Cook, 2007) is more a family assessment design than presentation of specific measures or instruments. That is, the system relies heavily on relationship-specific measures, determining each family member's behavior, feelings, perceptions or thoughts regarding each other. For example, according to Cook (2006), there are two primary aspects of interpersonal relationships, affiliation (e.g., acceptance, love) and control (e.g., autonomy, power). Psychometric instruments, such as the Interpersonal Sense of Control scales (Cook, 1993), or items from relatively well-established measures are used and compared across respondents. Indeed, impressive reliabilities are associated with control measures, averaged across family relationships. For families with young children, Cook (2006) recommends gleaning children's perspectives through interview techniques rather than administering psychometrically driven measures. However, introducing this variation inevitably creates conceptual and psychometric difficulties in capturing and evaluating dyadic and overall family functioning.

Hobbled by challenges regarding the definition of family as well as a widely accepted theory of family functioning, family assessment is difficult at best (Glidden & Schoolcraft, 2007). In fact, almost all the family assessment issues raised by Bray (2004), Cook (2006), and others (e.g., Glidden & Schoolcraft, 2007) are applicable to assessment of families with young children. For example, typically families with young children are adjusting to the addition of a dependent, often developmentally needy, family member. Further, if there are developmental issues, such as attention deficit hyperactivity disorder (ADHD), there may be many associated family problems (e.g., marital discord, parental adjustment) (Cunningham, 2007). To be sure, family assessment extends beyond the bounds of the identified family, including factors such as families' social support (e.g., extended family, grandparents, neighbors, religious groups) and level of stress (e.g., economic or financial loss, exposure to unsafe neighborhoods).

In summary, there is little agreement regarding standards for practice regarding family assessment, much less practice regarding families with young children. Most single methods (e.g., observational measures, self-report instruments) have drawbacks (e.g., ecological validity, reliance on individual family member perspective). Thus, best practice in the assessment of families with young children is far from established except for a decided appreciation for multimethod, systemically oriented, culturally sensitive approaches. Further, contemporary practice appropriately tends toward identifying family strengths rather than deficits, problems, or weaknesses and, further, increasingly recognizes wide and deep variations within ethnic and racial groups (Parke, 2000). Strength orientations provide, for example, potential avenues to develop, implement, and evaluate interventions. In addition, recognizing the ultimate uniqueness of each family assures sensitivity to individual, dyadic relationship, and group interactions without simplistic overgeneralizations based on ethnic, racial, or other group identified background.

FAMILY ASSESSMENT MEASURES

ESTABLISHED FAMILY MEASURES

Recognizing the many assessment challenges, there are some commonly utilized family instruments; the most frequently cited are the Family Adaptation and Cohesion Evaluation Scales (FACES; Olson, Portner, & Lavee, 1985), the Family Assessment Measure (FAM; Skinner, Steinhauer, & Sitarenios, 2000), the Family Environmental Scale (FES; Moos & Moos, 1983), and the McMaster Family Assessment Device (FAD; Epstein, Baldwin, & Bishop, 1983). A brief discussion of each measure highlights the evidence-base for family assessment practice.

Family Adaptability and Cohesion Evaluation Scales (FACES)   (Olson, Bell, & Portner, 1983; Olson, Portner, & Lavee, 1985; Olson, Tiesel, & Gorall, 1996). There are four versions of the self-report FACES (Craddock, 2001; Olson et al., 1996). The FACES III, for example, is a 20-item measure providing indications of adaptability (10 items) and cohesion (10 items). Respondents utilize a 5-point Likert-type scale to indicate *almost never* to *almost always* regarding each parenting statement. Olson et al. (1985) report internal reliability estimates as 0.62 for Adaptability and 0.77 for Cohesion, with negligible correlations between the two subscales.

All FACES versions rely on Olson's circumplex model (Olson, Sprenkle, & Russell, 1979), describing healthy families as having balanced adaptability and cohesion. Glidden and Schoolcraft (2007) comment that high or low FACES adaptability and/or cohesion may indicate problematic family issues (e.g., disengaged, enmeshed, rigid). Tolan, Gorman-Smith, Huesmann, and Zelli (1997) examined FACES, as well as other family functioning measures, finding three underlying dimensions (i.e., family beliefs, cohesion, structure). Family beliefs, for example, include importance of the family, purpose of the family, and child development expectations. Cohesion, although an important dimension, is considered an underlying, multicomponent characteristic of family functioning. Finally, family structure represents family organization in terms of predictability of expectations and family role dependability. FACES was not developed specifically for families with young children; therefore, although a

respected measure, FACES may not adequately assess relevant early childhood family variables putting into question its evidence base for this
population.

Family Assessment Measure (FAM)   (Skinner et al., 2000). Based on the Process
Model of Family Functioning (Steinhauer, 1984; Steinhauer et al., 1984), the
FAM (Skinner, Steinhauer, & Santa-Barbara, 1983) consists of 50 items, with
three levels of reporting (i.e., individual, dyadic, whole family), used for both
clinical and research purposes (Glidden & Schoolcraft, 2007). The FAM
General Scale consists of 50 items (9 subscales) scored on a 4-point Likert-
type scale from *strongly agree* to *strongly disagree*. As a measure of family
health, the FAM assesses the family in terms of role performance, communication, affective involvement, control, and task accomplishment subscales
(Tolan et al., 1997). An internal consistency estimate of 0.93 and median
internal consistency estimate of 0.73, with an average correlation of 0.36
across sources, have been found (Skinner et al., 1983).

Taken as a whole, seven subscales assess model constructs (e.g., Role
Performance, Communication, Affective Involvement), and two subscales
assess response style (i.e., Denial–Defensiveness, Social Desirability) (Jacob
& Windle, 1999). The FAM appears valid for assessing families with children
age 10 or older (Skinner et al., 2000), but may be questionable regarding
family functioning with younger age children. Thus, like FACES, the FAM
may lack adequate evidence base to support use in early childhood practice.

Family Environment Scale (FES)   The FES (Moos & Moos, 1983) consists of 90
items responded to in true–false format, measuring the family in terms of
three domains (i.e., family relationships, personal growth, system maintenance). Each domain has a minimum of two subscales; in total, there are 10
constructs measured. Moos and Moos (1983) report subscale coefficient *alphas*
range from 0.64 to 0.78 and subscale intercorrelations are generally low with
an average value of approximately 0.20.

The FES family relationship domain, for example, is measured by the
Family Relationships Index, consisting of three subscales (i.e., cohesion,
expressiveness, conflict). There is strong internal reliability (Cronbach's *alpha*
= 0.89), with each subscale consisting of 9 items and total family support
determined by averaging the three subscale scores (North, Holahan, Moos,
& Cronkite, 2008). Further, there is moderate to strong test–retest reliability
of 0.81 and construct validity reported (Moos & Moos, 1994). Glidden and
Schoolcraft (2007) find the FES is used in numerous studies, including
research focusing on families with developmentally disabled children (e.g.,
Rousey, Wild, & Blacher, 2002). However, there appears limited support for
use with families with young children.

McMaster Family Assessment Device (FAD)   The FAD (Epstein, Baldwin, & Bishop, 1983) is a 60-item self-report measure designed to assess family functioning consistent with the McMaster Model of Family Functioning (MMFF; Epstein et al., 1983), including six dimensions (i.e., problem solving, communication, roles, affective responsiveness, affective involvement, behavior control). Respondents indicate correspondence, using a 4-point scale, with statements regarding family functioning. For example, a problem-solving item is "We try to think of different ways to solve problems." Higher scores indicate stronger family functioning and fewer difficulties than lower scores. Some early research supported FAD reliability and validity (e.g., Kabacoff, Miller, Bishop, Epstein, & Keitner, 1990), but more recently there is considerable debate regarding its factor structure (Miller, Ryan, Keitner, Bishop, & Epstein, 2000) with suggestions that the FAD only consists of behavior control and general family functioning (Ridenour, Daley, & Reich, 1999).

Cunningham (2007) finds that the FAD provides a brief, easily administered and scored indication of family relationships, communication, and problem solving. However, issues have arisen regarding appropriate use with culturally diverse families. Aarons, McDonald, Connelly, and Newton (2007) examined the FAD in terms of reliability, validity, and factor structure, noting that despite extensive use, the FAD's psychometric properties with non-Caucasian families is not well established. As a consequence, Aarons et al. considered family functioning, measured by the FAD, in both Caucasian and Hispanic-American families. Results are quite mixed with Hispanic-American families stronger than Caucasian-American families in terms of roles, but weaker in terms of affective responsiveness and behavior control. In addition, FAD subscale reliabilities were strong when combining the two samples, but considered separately subscale reliabilities were lower for Hispanic-Americans on all subscales except behavior control. Thus, the cultural appropriateness of the FAD is questionable as well as its evidence-based use with families with young children.

Family assessment, in terms of frequently cited measures, falls short in terms of early childhood evidence-based practice. Instruments appear generally focused on measuring families with older children and adolescents. Thus, family measures may not be sensitive to younger family members or appreciate special family dynamics associated with parenting young children. Further, with regard to cultural issues, Aarons et al. (2007) conclude that either family assessment measures for Hispanic American families (and presumably other ethnic groups) need modification or additional, appropriate, psychometrically rigorous instruments developed. Regardless, there are strong implications for research as well as evidence-based clinical practice.

Far more attention, for example, appears necessary in conceptualizing and developing culturally sensitive, developmentally appropriate early childhood family measures. Turning away from standard psychometric measures, some recommend using observation techniques to discern family functioning (Janssens, De Bruyn, Manders, & Scholte, 2005).

OBSERVATION METHODS

Although most clinicians utilize observations (e.g., informal and formal interview schedules), few rely on structured observations of the family as a whole. Some of the reasons for the lack of direct, measurement-based observations are the financial and time constraints associated with obtaining and subsequently scoring observations. Further, there are difficulties in scheduling, problems determining consistent parameters in order to discern healthy functioning, problems with ecological validity if conducted in a therapy or other office-like setting, and psychometric considerations (e.g., weak agreement among observers).

One example of a family assessment observation system, albeit developed for older children and their parents, is described by Janssens et al. (2005). They observed parents and children during a conflict resolution task and subsequently rated parents' behavior toward their child and the child's behavior toward parents on four subscales: warmth, hostility, respect for autonomy, and setting limits. Each parent and child also completed questionnaires giving indications of the same constructs (e.g., warmth, hostility). In the end, Janssens et al. (2005) feel that observations capture information similar to that obtained from participant questionnaires; possibly, both methods generally reflect family climate. In contrast, microcoding (i.e., coding each family member's verbalizations into distinct categories) tends to fragment the family functioning picture, obscuring the overall quality of family relationships. The usefulness of observation notwithstanding, the reliance on psychometrically sound, coding-driven observation techniques, appear somewhat limited in providing additional, significantly different sources of information at this point in time.

CULTURAL AND DIVERSITY ASSESSMENT ISSUES

Cultural and diversity issues are a consistent theme in family assessment as well as intervention. Each family relates to family members in a social-cultural context, which in turn influences all aspects of family functioning. Indeed, what constitutes healthy and unhealthy functioning or notions of function and dysfunction are, to a great extent, culturally determined (Glidden

& Schoolcraft, 2007). For example, Shek (2001) actively explores Chinese family functioning, finding that family assessment research regarding Chinese populations tend to use a variety of translated instruments. Inevitably, however, research reveals significant differences in instrument factor structure. Different factor structures are not surprising, given Chinese families apparently are more hierarchical in structure than Western families, emphasize harmony, and involve face-saving problem solving; as a result, Siu and Shek (2005) recommend culture-specific family assessment measures.

More evidence of cultural family assessment issues is readily available. Ecklund and Johnson (2007) suggest an appreciation of structural family differences. They note numerous cultural differences including, for instance, communication patterns, gender roles, and power hierarchies. Further, as previously discussed, Aarons et al. (2007) found FAD psychometric differences when comparing Caucasian-American and Hispanic-American families. They recommend clinicians and researchers remain mindful of assessment cultural variations and suggest interventions be tailored for specific ethnic groups. Perhaps wishful thinking, they suggest "a single measure that functions psychometrically well and permits conceptually clear interpretations across multiple ethnic groups, in multiple translations, is clearly a goal for additional research" (p. 563). As a caution toward such aspirations, psychometric measures, like those who design and examine them, emanate from within a social–cultural framework. Therefore, a single psychometrically sound measure accommodating to all possible cultural and diversity variations seems quite unlikely.

For early childhood professionals, continuously being reminded of cultural perspectives is relevant. Although instruments may demonstrate psychometric strength, they might not be sensitive to cultural, diversity, and even developmental issues. This caution is offered in the context of intervention techniques as well. Evidence-based early childhood practice communicates assessment, consultation, and intervention activities that are sensitive to cultural nuances.

FAMILY INTERVENTION FOCUS

What constitutes a family, as discussed previously, and whom to treat when issues arise form significant concerns for early childhood professionals. Treatment may address parents and the identified child (Feinfield & Baker, 2004), the entire family (Shellenberger, 2007), family subsystems, or even different family dimensions at different points in time. The rationale for working with families as well as prevention, intervention, programs based on special issues (e.g., child disability, family trauma), and family multicultural and diversity are discussed next.

RATIONALE FOR WORKING WITH FAMILIES

Although there are many definitions of *family*, Snell-Johns, Mendez, and Smith (2004) consider family therapy as any intervention that "targets family interactions and conceptualizes problems as existing beyond individual clients" (p. 19). Likewise, many interventions use an ecological approach incorporating the identified individual along with broader systems in the individual's world (e.g., community, family, school). In this context, Dishion (2007a, 2007b) points out the importance of making at least one home visit, while treating a family, in order to assess the family in their natural environment.

Dishion (2007b) developed a program called EcoFIT, which supports change in family social interaction patterns to reduce children's problem behaviors. This intervention is tailored to specific family needs, with periodic interventions during developmental transitions (e.g., day care to preschool). This program is ecologically sensitive since the focus is not only on the child's family, but also social and community resources. For example for young children, EcoFIT therapists link family intervention services with educational services (e.g., Early Head Start). EcoFIT first targets reducing any immediate family risks and then shifts toward supporting family strengths, improving social interaction patterns, and finding appropriate interventions.

Family intervention programs inevitably recognize the importance of parent–child relationships. The parent–child relationship is certainly reciprocal; for example, parents' attitude and stress levels affect children and, in turn, children's behavioral difficulties affect parents. Fostering positive dyadic exchanges, however, has striking implications for the family (e.g., improving children's peer interactions and social status, enhancing parental satisfaction, warmth, and positive involvement with their child). Still, few programs have a parent–child relational component (Feinfield & Baker, 2004).

Combining parent and child treatments tends to address a broader range of risk factors (e.g., affect regulation, children's social skills, family problem solving, parents' disciplinary skills) than working with either the child or parent in relative isolation (Feinfield & Baker, 2004). For example, if untreated, family conflict can be predictive of child and adolescent externalizing problems (e.g., aggression, antisocial behavior, conduct disorders) as well as internalizing problems (e.g., depression, low self-esteem) (Yasui & Dishion, 2007). These problematic child development outcomes provide yet another reason for emphasizing treating families instead of individuals.

PREVENTATIVE AND INTERVENTION PROGRAMS

Many prevention programs are directed toward young children and their families. One program, Adults and Children Together Against Violence (ACT Against Violence) is a violence prevention program that targets adults raising children 0–8 years old. This program teaches parents violence prevention knowledge and skills (e.g., anger management, monitoring media violence). The goal is assisting parents to model and teach positive ways for children to deal with anger and resolve conflicts. Guttman, Mowder, & Yasik (2007) found this program effectively increased participant knowledge regarding violence in childhood.

WORKING WITH FAMILIES WITH CHILD MENTAL HEALTH AND OTHER DISABILITIES

Dishion (2007a) used family management therapy (FMT) as a means of treating child mental health problems. Initially the family is assessed to determine strengths, weaknesses, and develop intervention goals. Subsequently, there are five steps for treatment (i.e., establishing an agenda, affirming the parent–therapist collaboration toward a specified goal, providing a brief rationale for the new skill to be learned, introducing new activities or role-playing exercises, giving family homework to encourage practice). To be effective, therapists skillfully identify family strengths as well as deficits, continuously motivating parents to learn and practice new skills and effectively teaching (e.g., books, brochures, videotapes) parenting skills.

In contrast to Dishion (2007a), Feinfield and Baker (2004) used Project TEAM, a manualized, multimodal, 12-week family treatment program designed to help young children with externalizing problems and their parents. This intervention program has two primary components; first, parents and children attend their respective, separate groups. The parent group consists of parent training interventions, including developing parenting skills (e.g., behavior management principles) and addressing parenting difficulties (e.g., marital conflict, parental stress). In contrast, the children's group focuses on improving social skills, affect regulation, and problem solving. Second, families practice their new skills, work on collaborative tasks, and engage in relationship-building exercises during "together time." During this portion of the intervention, families have the opportunity to watch the therapist model skills (e.g., anger management, behavior management, communication, expression and acknowledgement of feelings, perspective taking, positive reinforcement). After treatment, Feinfield and Baker (2004) found that children had fewer behavioral problems; in addition, parenting practices improved, parents were less stressed, and parents felt more efficacious than those in the wait-list condition. Five months later the improvements were maintained.

Children's developmental disabilities also cause family stress with the entire family coping with the disorder in different ways. Addressing developmentally disabled children's concurrent behavioral difficulties, Roberts, Mazzucchelli, Studman, & Sanders (2006) designed a family intervention program. After 10 weeks of an individually administered, more or less psychoeducational parenting program (e.g., causes of child behavior problems, encouraging children's development, managing misbehavior), families participated in follow-up clinic appointments and home observations. Families in the intervention program experienced substantial benefits (e.g., decreased maternal stress, enhanced parenting styles, improvement in children's behavior) compared with families in the wait-list condition.

The Triple P Positive Parenting Program (TPPPP) is based on behavioral principles and informs parents about the causes of problem behavior, strategies for improving children's social competence, and ways to deal with difficult behavior. Stepping Stone Triple P (SSTP) represents a modification of the Triple P aimed at helping families of children with developmental disabilities. SSTP addresses issues (e.g., additional behavior problem causal factors, avenues to change common behavioral problems) associated with children's disabilities (Morawska & Sanders, 2006). Child mental health and other disabilities are but two early childhood practice issues; families also experience disturbances in family functioning subsequent to trauma.

WORKING WITH FAMILIES AFTER TRAUMA

Dyregrov (2001) discussed using early intervention for families after a traumatic event (e.g., death of a young child, fire destruction). Not only are crisis intervention skills essential, but also knowledge of family dynamics. Indeed, family trauma adaptation is influenced by many factors (e.g., access to support, coping resources, family members' developmental status, family's experience with past trauma, premorbid family functioning, type of stressor). Trauma can disturb parenting practices (e.g., withdrawal of physical support, reduction of parent–child communication) in parents' effort to shield children from what happened. One result may be that facts about the trauma are hidden and consequently trust and system stability is threatened. One major goal of trauma intervention is to be sensitive to the trauma, but assist in the prevention of secrets by establishing open family communication (Dyregrov).

WORKING WITH MULTICULTURAL FAMILIES

Similar to culturally sensitive family assessment, Yasui and Dishion (2007) discuss the importance of ethnic and diversity variables in treating minority youth, noting the strong influence ecology has on ethnic minority children. For instance, there are innumerable influential ecological variables (e.g., culturally specific values, experience of discrimination, level of acculturation) which interventions need to accommodate and integrate in a sensitive, understanding manner. Further, Dishion (2007a) discusses the importance of considering culture and diversity backgrounds in family management therapy stating that, "family management skills stem directly from culture and values and . . . cultural context affects the ability of families to use skills" (p. 172). Therefore, parenting skills need to be considered and, when necessary, taught in the context of the family's culture, with constant feedback between therapist and parent on culturally relevant skills. For example, Dishion finds Latino families typically use positive parenting and, in contrast, Asian-American families tend to emphasize guilt and shame to manage behavior.

INTERVENTION FORMATS

There are many intervention formats, such as that employed by Feinfield and Baker (2004) where parents and children have separate groups and then come together to practice skills and receive therapist feedback. Training programs, such as Behavioral Family Interventions (BFI), are a popular form of family intervention (Roberts, Mazzucchelli, Studman, & Sanders, 2006). Hudson et al. (2003) used a BFI called Signposts, an intervention system for families of children with an intellectual disability. This system may be delivered through groups, telephone support, or self-direction, and is effective in reducing behavioral problems in children aged 4–19.

Family interventions can also be self-administered. Morawska and Sanders (2006) used a BFI to demonstrate telephone counseling possibilities. Over a 10-week period, parents were instructed to read the TPPP materials and complete related workbook tasks. Parents engaged in weekly telephone consultations encouraging self-regulation in order to maintain and generalize new skills. Additionally, parents were encouraged to monitor their own performance and problem solve using their new skills. After treatment, parents reported decreased behavior problems in their children, less parenting conflict, and increased parenting confidence and maternal adjustment compared with before treatment; these results were maintained three months after program completion.

Shellenberger (2007) discusses the use of genograms in understanding, treating, and continuously evaluating family functioning. Genograms attempt to capture dates and circumstances of major family events, individual family member characteristics, and the overall quality of family social relationships. Especially useful with multiethnic families, the therapist and family together generate a template describing family history, crises, and ongoing challenges. The genogram may facilitate establishing family goals and modes of intervention, and form the basis for continuously evaluating family progress.

In the end, although methods such as telephone counseling have benefits (e.g., easy accessibility and anonymity, low cost, noninstitutional orientation), they are not without issue or concern (Morawska & Sanders, 2007). For example, telephone counseling obscures actual behavioral observation thus potentially missing important child, family, parent–child, and parent dynamics. To be sure, family services may be administered in numerous locations, including, for instance, agencies, clinics, and the home (Snell-Johns et al., 2004). The home location, for example, may seem ideal since this is the natural environment in which family interactions occur. Although incorporating ecological validity and convenience, the environment is decidedly difficult to control. Visitors, phone calls, and child care may disrupt treatment and compromise effectiveness (Dishion, 2007b).

INTERVENTION BARRIERS

Snell-Johns et al. (2004) discuss strategies to address barriers to treating underserved families (e.g., access, attrition, resistance to change). First, to overcome access barriers, therapists may offer child care, transportation, and low-cost services. Home-based, self-directed, and video-based interventions are also effective strategies for overcoming access barriers. By discussing the process of therapy early in the intervention process, issues preventing the family from attending may be addressed. Further, multiple-family therapy (MFT) groups are frequently able to decrease the stigma associated with receiving mental health services. In turn, social isolation is decreased and parents are exposed to effective skills and supportive feedback. In addition, since many families most in need of services are adverse to change, calling the family prior to the first session may be beneficial. That is, by establishing a relationship, even over the telephone, therapists may address at least some resistance issues. To increase attendance and decrease attrition, there are many options (e.g., decrease wait-list time, offer incentives for attendance, provide brief interventions, assure therapist availability, address parents' individual needs) with perhaps the most important being a focus on family strengths as well as therapist cultural and diversity competence (Snell-Johns et al.).

Dishion (2007a) concurs and points out that families often resist change by missing sessions, terminating treatment prematurely, or engaging in other negative therapeutic behaviors. To address these issues, numerous recommendations are made (e.g., genuine empathy and caring, listening to the family's concerns, normalizing the therapeutic experience, reflecting and paraphrasing, showing understanding, using humor, stories, and metaphors). Ultimately, the therapist needs to be prepared to structure and guide sessions as well as contextualize new skills in manageable ways (e.g., breaking content into teachable units, use of role-playing techniques). To facilitate change, Dishion also recommends using assessments to engage, motivate, and encourage family change as well as facilitate therapist–family collaboration. Once family skills are developed, therapists become less active and simply support family problem solving and overcoming barriers to progress.

TRAINING ISSUES

Training issues regarding early childhood family service provision are many. In terms of didactic knowledge, trainees need preparation in theories of family functioning (e.g., Grotevant, 1989; Kenny & LaVoie, 1984; Minuchin, 1974; Szapocznik & Kurtines, 1993; Walsh, 2003) and life span development. Major elements of family functioning include, for instance, roles and related expectations (Mowder, 2005), understanding families as interdependent systems (Cook, 2007) and subsystems (e.g, marital, parent-child) (Glidden & Schoolcraft, 2007) of individuals, family functioning (e.g., communication, family relationships, problem solving) (Cunningham, 2007), and family structure within a developmental context. Training in tests and measurement, especially test construction, evaluation, and standards (e.g., *Standards for Educational and Psychological Testing*, 1999) is essential as well as knowledge of major test instruments (e.g., FACES, FAD, FES) and observation techniques (e.g., behavioral observations, interviews) (Robbins, Hervis, Mitraini, & Szapocznik, 2001). Individual, family, and group therapeutic skills are essential. However, one of the most important aspects of training, which underlies all early childhood family practice issues, is appreciating cultural and other family diversity as well as professional ethics.

Together with academic preparation is fieldwork experience with families. Appropriate fieldwork experiences include the range of professional practice services, including assessment, consultation, and intervention with young children and their families. Multimethods, in the context of evidence-based practice, guide training in family assessment and intervention. Appropriate supervision, preferably from diverse points of view, also informs trainees and guides professional practice development. In the end, all training and supervisory activities by necessity follow ethical guidelines (e.g., American Psychological Association, 2002). Ethical guidelines, as well as training standards (e.g., American Psychological Association (APA) Committee on Accreditation Guidelines and Principles for Accreditation of Programs in Professional Psychology, 2008), assure that early childhood practice is grounded in evidence-based research, with every care toward those served.

ETHICAL ISSUES

Each early childhood professional discipline area follows their respective codes of conduct or ethical guidelines. For psychologists, the American Psychological Association (APA) has a formal code of conduct and ethical guidelines (APA, 2002). To be sure, the Preamble to the APA ethics code clearly begins with the statement that, "Psychologists are committed to increasing scientific and professional knowledge of behavior and people's understanding of themselves and others and to the use of such knowledge to improve the condition of individuals, organizations, and society." Thus, the indication, from the outset, is that professional practice follows scientific data. All psychologists and not simply researchers are charged with furthering professional knowledge of human interactions, encouraging all psychologists to be become involved in exploring human nature and improving human prospects as well as the psychology profession.

Not all ethical issues, in terms of working in early childhood family practice, are clear. Some of the more obvious issues include confidentiality (e.g., Donner, VandeCreek, Gonsiorek, & Fisher, 2008), dual-role relationships, and the necessity to follow evidence-based practice. Confidentiality issues arise almost immediately when working with families; for example, how does the early childhood practitioner respect each family member's privacy while at the same time conduct a family assessment, develop collaborative intervention options, and evaluate services? Working with families, indeed, begs the issue of limits of individual confidentiality. What, for instance, does the clinician do when discerning one family member's strong sense of family conflict in the face of another who believes family functioning is fine? Further, at what point does assessment become intervention; what are the boundaries in early childhood practice? The issue of who is the client also hovers over professional practice; are the parents the client and/or the child, parent–child dyadic relationship, siblings? Who determines what is best for the family and on what basis? How do cultural differences between the early childhood professional and the families served influence practice?

In other words, there are innumerable ethical issues regarding early childhood family practice (Lefaivre, Chambers, & Fernandez, 2007). Close attention to codes of conduct and ethical guidelines, along with skilled supervision, guide trainees and professionals alike in providing appropriate, sensitive services. There is no one manual for the professional to rely on, since ethical issues often arise in unique ways, consistent with the uniqueness associated with each individual, individuals' relationships, and their social–cultural context. Best practice, therefore, rests on appropriate knowledge, careful attunement to current evidence-based practice, reliance on ethical guidelines, and informed sensitivity to cultural and other diversity.

SUMMARY

In summary, there is little agreement regarding best practice in family assessment. To be sure, there are many methods (e.g., observation techniques,

RR-SRM) as well as measures (e.g., FACES, FES, FAD), all of which are subject to criticism. In fact, recently Park, Garber, Ciesla, and Ellis (2008) examine the convergence among multiple methods of measuring family functioning. More specifically, they considered the FES, FAD, and other family measures, ultimately making the assertion that there is convergence in the identification of positive and negative aspects of family functioning. In the end, working with families, and not simply the child in relative isolation, is essential to early childhood practice.

REFERENCES

Aarons, G. A., McDonald, E. J., Connelly, C. D., & Newton, R. R. (2007). Assessment of family functioning in Caucasian and Hispanic Americans: Reliability, validity, and factor structure of the Family Assessment Device. *Family Process, 46*(4), 557–570.

American Psychological Association (2008). *Committee on Accreditation Guidelines and Principles for Accreditation of Programs in Professional Psychology.* Washington, DC: Author.

American Psychological Association. (2002). Ethical principles of psychologists and code of conduct. *American Psychologist, 57*, 1060–1073.

Bray, J. (2004). Models and issues in couple and family assessment. In *Assessment of couples and families: Contemporary and cutting-edge strategies* (pp. 13–29). New York: Brunner-Routledge.

Celik, S. B. (2007). Family function levels of Turkish fathers with children aged between 0–6. *Social Behavior and Personality, 35*(4), 429–442.

Cook, W. L. (1993). Interdependence and the interpersonal sense of control: An analysis of family relationships. *Journal of Personality and Social Psychology, 64*, 587–601.

Cook, W. L. (2006). The Round Robin Family Assessment with Social Relations Model Analysis. In S. R. Smith and L. Handler (Eds.), *The clinical assessment of children and adolescents: A practitioner's handbook* (pp. 99–114). Mahwah, NJ: Erlbaum.

Cook, W. L., & Kenny, D. A. (2004). Application of the Social Relations Model to family assessment. *Journal of Family Psychology, 18*, 361–371.

Craddock, A. E. (2001). Family system and family functioning: Circumplex model and FACES IV. *Journal of Family Studies, 7*, 29–39.

Cunningham, C. E. (2007). A family centered approach to planning and measuring the outcome of interventions for children with attention-deficit/hyperactivity disorder. *Journal of Pediatric Psychology, 32*(6), 676–694.

De Bruyn, E. E. J. (2005). Family assessment and methodological issues: Introduction to the special section. *European Journal of Psychological Assessment, 21*(4), 213–215.

Dishion, T. J. (2007a). Family management therapy. In D. Thomas & A. Stormshak (Eds.), *Intervening in children's lives: An ecological, family-centered approach to mental health care* (pp. 163–181). Washington, DC: American Psychological Association.

Dishion, T. J. (2007b). The ecological family intervention and therapy model. In D. Thomas & A. Stormshak (Eds.), *Intervening in children's lives: An ecological, family-centered approach to mental health care* (pp. 49–67). Washington, DC: American Psychological Association.

Donner, M. B., VandeCreek, L., Gonsiorek, J. C., & Fisher, C. B. (2008). Balancing confidentiality: Protecting privacy and protecting the public. *Professional Psychology: Research and Practice, 39,* 369–376.

Dyregrov, A. (2001). Early intervention: A family perspective. *Advances in Mind–Body Medicine, 17*(3), 168–174.

Ecklund, K., & Johnson, W. B. (2007). Toward cultural competence in child intake assessment. *Professional Psychology: Research and Practice, 38,* 356–362.

Epstein, N., Baldwin, L., & Bishop, S. (1983). The McMaster Family Assessment Device. *Journal of Marital and Family Therapy, 9,* 171–180.

Feinfield, K. A., & Baker, B. L. (2004). Empirical support for a treatment program for families of young children with externalizing problems. *Journal of Clinical and Child Adolescent Psychology, 33*(1), 182–195.

Georgiades, K., Boyle, M. H., Jenkins, J. M., Sanford, M., & Lipman, E. (2008). A multilevel analysis of whole family functioning using the McMaster Family Assessment Device. *Journal of Family Psychology, 22,* 344–354.

Glidden, L. M., & Schoolcraft, S. A. (2007). Family assessment and social support. In J. W. Jacobson, J. A. Malick, and J. Rojahn (Eds.), *Handbook of intellectual and developmental disabilities* (pp. 391–422). New York: Springer.

Grotevant, H. D. (1989). The role of theory in guiding family assessment. *Journal of Family Psychology, 3,* 104–117.

Guttman, M., Mowder, B. A., & Yasik, A. E. (2007). The ACT against violence training program: A preliminary investigation of knowledge gained by early childhood professionals. *Professional Psychology Research and Practice, 37*(6), 717–723.

Hudson, A. M., Matthews, J. M., Gavidia-Payne, S. T., Cameron, C. A., Mildon, R. L., Radler, G. A., et al. (2003). Evaluation of an intervention system for parents of children with intellectual disability and challenging behavior. *Journal of Intellectual Disability Research, 47,* 238–249.

Hughes, A. A., Hedtke, K. A., & Kendall, P. C. (2008). Family functioning in families of children with anxiety disorders. *Journal of Family Psychology, 22*(2), 325–328.

Jacob, T., & Windle, M. (1999). Family assessment: Instrument dimensionality and correspondence across family reporters. *Journal of Family Psychology, 13,* 339–354.

Janssens, J. M. A. M., De Bruyn, E. E. J., Manders, W. A., & Scholte, R. H. J. (2005). The multitrait-multimethod approach in family assessment: Mutual parent–child relationships assessed by questionnaires and observations. *European Journal of Psychological Assessment, 21*(4), 232–239.

Kabacoff, R., Miller, I., Bishop, D., Epstein, N., & Keitner, G. (1990). A psychometric study of the McMaster Family Assessment Device in psychiatric, medical, and nonclinical samples. *Journal of Family Psychology, 3,* 431–439.

Kenny, D. A., & LaVoie, L. (1984). The social relations model. In L. Berkowitz (Ed.), *Advances in experimental social psychology* (vol. 18, pp. 141–182). New York: Academic Press.

Lefaivre, M., Chambers, C. T., & Fernandez, C. V. (2007). Offering parents individualized feedback on the results of psychological testing conducted for research purposes with children: Ethical issues and recommendations. *Journal of Clinical Child and Adolescent Psychology, 36,* 242–252.

Miller, I. W., Ryan, C. E., Keitner, G. I., Bishop, D. S., & Epstein, N. B. (2000). Why fix what isn't broken? A rejoinder to Ridenour, Daly, & Reich. *Family Process, 39,* 381–384.

Minuchin, S. (1974). *Families and family therapy.* Cambridge, MA: Harvard University Press.

Moos, R. H., & Moos, B. S. (1983). Clinical applications of the Family Environment Scale. In E. Filsinger (Ed.), *A sourcebook of marriage and family assessment* (pp. 253–273). Beverly Hills, CA: Sage.

Moos, R. H., & Moos, B. S. (1994). *Family Environment Scale manual* (3rd ed.). Redwood City, CA: Mind Garden.

Morawska, A., & Sanders, M. R. (2006). Self-administered behavioural family intervention for parents of toddlers; effectiveness and dissemination. *Behaviour Research and Therapy, 44*(12), 1839–1848.

Morawska, A., & Sanders, M. R. (2007). Are parent-reported outcomes for self-directed or telephone-assisted behavioral family intervention enhanced if parents are observed? *Behavior Modification, 31*(3), 279–297.

Mowder, B. A. (1997). Family systems and services. In A. Widerstrom, B. A. Mowder, & S. R. Sandall (Eds.), *Infant Development and Risk* (pp. 125–154). Baltimore: Brookes.

Mowder, B. A. (2005). Parent development theory: Understanding parents, parenting perceptions, and parenting behaviors. *Journal of Early Childhood and Infant Psychology, 1,* 45–64.

North, R. J., Holahan, C. J., Moos, R. H., & Cronkite, R. C. (2008). Family support, family income, and happiness: A 10-year perspective. *Journal of Family Psychology, 22,* 475–483.

Olson, D. H., Bell, R., & Portner, J. (1983). *FACES II manual.* St. Paul: University of Minnesota, Department of Family Social Sciences.

Olson, D. H., Portner, J., & Lavee, Y. (1985). *FACES III manual.* St. Paul: University of Minnesota, Department of Family Social Sciences.

Olson, D. H., Sprenkle, D. H., & Russell, C. S. (1979). Circumplex model of marital and family systems: 1. Cohension and adaptability dimensions, family types, and clinical application. *Family Process, 18,* 3–28.

Olson, D. H., Tiesel, J. W., & Gorall, D. (1996). *Family Adaptability and Cohesion Evaluation Scale IV.* Minneapolis: University of Minnesota, Department of Family Social Sciences.

Park, I. J. K., Garber, J., Ciesla, J. A., & Ellis, B. J. (2008). Convergence among multiple methods of measuring positivity and negativity in the family environment:

Relation to depression in mothers and their children. *Journal of Family Psychology*, 22, 123–134.

Parke, R. D. (2000). Beyond White and middle class: Cultural variations in families—assessments, processes, and policies. *Journal of Family Psychology*, 14(3), 331–333.

Pequegnat, W., & Bray, J. H. (1997). Families and HIV/AIDS: Introduction to the special section. *Journal of Family Psychology*, 11, 3–10.

Ridenour, T. A., Daley, J. G., & Reich, W. (1999). Factor analyses of the Family Assessment Device. *Family Process*, 38, 497–510.

Robbins, M. S., Hervis, O., Mitraini, V. B., & Szapocznik, J. (2001). Assessing changes in family interaction: The Structural Family Systems Ratings. In P. K. Kerig and K. M. Lindahl (Eds.), *Family observational coding systems: Resources for systemic research* (pp. 207–224). Hillsdale, NJ: Erlbaum.

Roberts, C., Mazzucchelli, T., Studman, L., & Sanders, M. R. (2006). Behavioral family intervention for children with developmental disabilities and behavioral problems. *Journal of Clinical Child and Adolescent Psychology*, 35(2), 180–193.

Rousey, A. M., Wild, M., & Blacher, J. (2002). Stability of measures of the home environment for families of children with severe disabilities. *Research in Developmental Disabilities*, 23, 17–35.

Shek, D. T. L. (2001). Psychometric properties of the Chinese version of the Self-Report Family Inventory: Findings based on a longitudinal study. *Research on Social Work Practice*, 11, 485–502.

Shellenberger, S. (2007). Use of the genogram with families for assessment and treatment. In *Handbook for EDMR and Family Therapy Processes* (pp. 76–94). Hoboken, NJ: Wiley.

Siu, A. M. H., & Shek, D. T. L. (2005). Psychometric properties of the Chinese family assessment instrument in Chinese adolescents in Hong Kong. *Adolescence*, 40, 817–826.

Skinner, H., Steinhauer, P., & Santa-Barbara, J. (1983). The Family Assessment Measure. *Canadian Journal of Community Mental Health*, 2, 91–103.

Skinner, H., Steinhauer, P., & Sitarenios, G. (2000). Family Assessment Measure (FAM) and Process Model of Family Functioning. *Journal of Family Therapy*, 22, 190–210.

Snell-Johns, J., Mendez, L., & Smith, B. H. (2004). Evidence based solutions for overcoming access barriers, decreasing attrition, and promoting change with underserved families. *Journal of Family Psychology*, 18(1), 19–35.

Standards for Educational and Psychological Testing (1999). Washington, DC: American Educational Research Association.

Steinhauer, P. D. (1984). Clinical applications of the process model of family functioning. *Canadian Journal of Psychiatry*, 29, 98–111.

Steinhauer, P. D., Santa-Barbara, J., & Skinner, H. A. (1984). The process model of family functioning. *Canadian Journal of Psychiatry*, 29, 77–88.

Szapocznik, J., & Kurtines, W. M. (1993). Family psychology and cultural diversity: Opportunties for theory, research and application. *American Psychologist*, 48, 400–407.

Tolan, P. H., Gorman-Smith, D., Huesmann, L. R., & Zelli, A. (1997). Assessment of family relationship characteristics: A measure to explain risk for antisocial behavior and depression among urban youth. *Psychological Assessment*, 9(3), 212–223.

Walsh, F. (2003). *Normal family processes: Growing diversity and complexity* (3rd ed.). New York: Guilford Press.

Yasui, M., & Dishion, T. J. (2007). The ethnic context of child and adolescent problem behavior: Implications for child and family interventions. *Clinical Child and Family Psychology*, 10(2), 137–179.

CHAPTER 9

Consultation

FLORENCE RUBINSON

T HE TRADITION IN psychological practice is to provide direct service to an individual child or groups of children, typically through assessment, counseling, and therapy (Brown, Pryzwansky, & Shulte, 2006; Donahue, Falk, & Provet, 2000; Erchul & Martens, 2006). Although psychologists continue to meet young children's needs for high-quality direct services, consultation as an indirect service model is gaining prominence as an adjunct and even alternative to traditional practice with young children (Buysse & Wesley, 2005; Donahue et al.; Gilliam & Shahar, 2006; Green, Everhart, Gordon, & Gettman, 2006). The major characteristic that distinguishes direct from indirect service delivery in early childhood settings is that rather than influencing a single child or group of children, the consultant works with the consultee (e.g., caregiver, parent, teacher, therapist) who then works to optimize the functioning of a child or group of children (clients) in their care (Buysse & Wesley; Donahue et al.).

In contrast to the traditional child-centered approach, consultation relies on the assumption that significant events, people, and settings are key factors in children's emotional and behavioral problems as well as vital resources in their resolution (Donahue et al., 2000). Indeed, early childhood practice has moved from focusing on individual children to appreciating the family and community influences on children's health and development (Shonkoff & Phillips, 2000). In the end, whether a psychologist is wedded to traditional practice or a combination of traditional practice and consultation, effective early childhood practice typically involves caregivers in some manner, since at no other time in young children's development will they depend more on caregivers' guidance, nurturance, and protection (Donahue et al.; Mowder, 1994). Therefore, practitioners in early childhood settings need a set of skills for working effectively with the significant adults in young children's lives.

This chapter examines the current literature on consultation in early childhood settings. Further, drawing on the larger body of theory and research with older children, a model of early childhood consultation appropriate for mental health and other early childhood, family-oriented practitioners is outlined. The chapter summarizes the literature on evidence-based practice in early childhood consultation as well as discusses issues regarding multicultural practice, training for students and practitioners, ethical issues, and suggests directions for future research. Readers interested in early childhood consultation practice specific to clinics, hospitals, and private practice are referred the literature on pediatric consultation and consultation in clinical psychology (e.g., Cates, Paone, Packman, & Margolis, 2006; Resnick & Kruczek, 1996).

INTERVENTION IN EARLY CHILDHOOD SETTINGS

Among the convincing reasons to support consultation in early childhood settings is evidence of the increasing number of young children in the United States exhibiting emotional and behavioral disorders (Keenan & Wakschlag, 2004; Mark-Wilson, Hopewell, & Gallagher, 2002; McDonnell & Glod, 2003). In addition, the increases in reported trauma within families and communities (e.g., child abuse, prolonged illness, substance abuse) can be especially difficult for young children. Infants, toddlers, and preschoolers exposed to trauma are particularly vulnerable since the resilient qualities necessary to defend against traumatic events are not fully developed (Donahue, 2002). Further, high prevalence/low severity disorders such as learning disabilities, borderline mental retardation, and attention deficit hyperactivity disorders are increasing (Aylward, 2002) and children with disabilities are at increased risk for behavior problems (Qi & Kaiser, 2003). With many children needing mental health services and instructional alternatives, consultation offers opportunities for individuals not previously viewed as potential resources (e.g. teachers, parents, social workers, therapists) to influence children's mental health and behavior (Parsons, 1996).

The prevalence of troubled young children in educational settings is unsettling. For example, Gilliam (2005) conducted a national study of expulsions from state-funded prekindergarten programs and found that approximately 10% of the teachers surveyed expelled at least one child due to behavioral concerns over the past 12 months, a rate 3.2 times higher than the kindergarten through grade 12 expulsion rates. The following year, Gilliam and Shahar (2006) examined preschool expulsions in a random sample of preschools in Massachusetts and discovered that during a 12-month period, 39% of teachers surveyed expelled at least one child. Clearly, exclusion from a child care and education program is an extreme sanction and unlikely to ameliorate challenging behaviors. In contrast, consultation with teachers may offer a better solution. In the nationwide study of 3,898 classrooms previously cited, pre-kindergarten teachers with access to a mental health consultant (e.g., psychiatrists, psychologists, social workers) were nearly half as likely to recommend expulsion (Gilliam). This finding is encouraging because teachers with ongoing access to mental health consultants indicated that they acquired classroom strategies for dealing with challenging behaviors.

Considering the prevalence of young children attending some type of early childhood program, these are ideal settings for consultants to use their skills for assisting young children, early childhood staff, and families (Knitzer, 2000). For example, many children in this country participate in some form of non-relative care (Capizzano & Adams, 2003). The U.S. Department of Education estimates that 43% of 3-year-olds and 69% of 4-year-olds are enrolled in center-based early childhood programs (U.S. Department of Education, 2006). Unlike clinics or private offices, preschools, nursery schools, and child care centers are environments that provide opportunities for interactions among all significant adults in children's lives (Donahue, 2002). Significant adults in young children's lives can influence academic achievement (Henderson & Mapp, 2002), behaviors (Bleecker & Sherwood, 2004; Field, Mackrain, & Sawilowsky, 2004), and mental health (Johns, 2003; Johnston & Brinamen, 2005), and their influence can be enhanced when consultants support caregivers and teachers (Donahue et al., 2000; Donahue, 2002). Support to caregivers often involves a number of activities, such as modeling strategies, verbal teaching, providing information, and providing opportunities for safe and open communication that promote problem solving (Caplan & Caplan, 1993; Hepburn, Kaufmann, Perry, Allen, Brennan, & Green, 2007), coaching/mentoring, supporting staff wellness (e.g., reducing stress), and training management teams (Green et al., 2006).

Some of the support for early childhood consultation comes from various difficulties associated with providing psychological therapy for young children. For example, traditional therapies can be poorly integrated in young children's lives (Donahue et al., 2000). That is, therapy typically provided in private office or clinic settings provides little opportunity for young children and their families to practice and generalize therapeutic gains. Early childhood settings provide young children with opportunities to learn new behaviors, receive positive feedback for changing behaviors, and practice appropriate behaviors in natural settings (Raver, Jones, Li-Grining, Metzger, Champion, & Sardin, 2008). Another difficulty is that services for atypically developing children are frequently fragmented, with each specialist concentrating on a single developmental area (e.g., fine motor development, speech and language) (Donohue et al.). Without linkages between early childhood services (e.g., education, speech and language therapy, occupational therapy), parents and professionals have limited opportunities to plan together or provide each other with ongoing feedback regarding children's progress. In contrast, consultation in child care and preschool settings brings together significant adults in children's lives and aims at a holistic and contextual understanding of early childhood problems (Hepburn et al., 2007).

CONSULTATION MODELS AVAILABLE FOR EARLY CHILDHOOD PRACTICE

Two models, mental health and problem-solving (formally called behavioral) consultation, make a significant contribution to consultation practice in early childhood settings. Although there are other models (e.g., Adlerian, Organizational), they are not discussed here (see Carlson, Watts, & Maniacci, 2006; McDowell, 1999). Mental health and problem-solving consultation share terminology and various aspects of practice, but also have distinct differences. Both consultation models are valuable and early childhood consultants should be skilled in both models, because consultants often need to determine which model of consultation or combination of models will be more effective for resolving a specific problem situation (Buysse & Wesley, 2005; Schulte & Osborne, 2003).

MENTAL HEALTH CONSULTATION

Caplan (1970) provided an early, albeit controversial, description of mental health consultation and continued to refine his consultation model for many years (Caplan & Caplan, 1999; Caplan, Caplan, & Erchul, 1995). Although Caplan did not directly apply his model to early childhood practice, his work is the basis of contemporary consultation practice (Buysse & Wesley, 2005; Donahue, 2000). The model, built on psychoanalytic theory, calls for a nonhierarchical or coequal relationship between the consultants (e.g., a mental health or other early childhood, family-oriented professionals) and consultees (e.g., person or persons who request help with a current work problem that is within consultants' scope of competence). At various points throughout the course of mental health consultation in early childhood settings, the target of an intervention may be the young child or group of children, significant adults in the child's world, settings in which the child participates, or some combination of the three. The predominant goals are to facilitate positive changes (e.g., behavioral, academic, social–emotional) for the child, but also to assist consultees in acquiring the knowledge, skill, objectivity, and confidence to address not only the current work related problem, but also better manage similar problems independently in the future. Consultants generally accomplish these goals through discussions with consultees as they move through a series of stages beginning with initial relationship building, to problem identification, to intervention design, implementation, and eventually to ending with evaluation and termination. The consultant remains active throughout the consultation process, but typically does not take an active role in implementation of the interventions that emerge from consultation. Thus, consultees are free to accept, reject, or modify the mutually generated interventions. The types of mental health consultation are client centered, consultee centered, and program centered.

Mental Health Client–Centered Consultation The most recognizable and commonly used type of mental health consultation is client centered (Dougherty, 2005). The focus for the consultant is on developing a plan with child care staff, teachers, and/or parents (consultees) to help a specific child or group of children (clients). The consultant and consultee discuss the problems, weigh options, establish objectives, design plans, and evaluate outcomes related to the best course of action to help the client. In addition to assessment of the client's difficulty or problem, the consultant also considers consultees' knowledge, skills, and motivation necessary to implement the intervention as well as the setting's capacity to support both the consultee and client. Although the main goal tends to be diagnosing and remediating the client's identified problem, an effective intervention requires a successful alliance between the consultant and consultee. Successful alliances are built on trust, and an ongoing supportive consultant–consultee relationship (Johns, 2003).

Mental Health Consultee–Centered Consultation In consultee-centered consultation, also based on the original work of Gerald Caplan (1970) and later with Ruth Caplan and Erchul (1995), the primary focus is on improving the consultee's ability to work successfully with specific client difficulties. The identified client, the child or group of children, remains the focus of discussion as in client-centered consultation, but the consultee's subjective story about the client becomes central to consultation. That is, the consultant uses the consultee's perspective to assess and increase the consultee's professional knowledge, skills, confidence, and/or objectivity as these relate to the client (Caplan & Caplan, 1999). In other words, the objective is to enhance specific areas of the consultee's professional practice that contribute to positive change with a particular case. Improvement in the client is a welcome side effect of consultee-centered consultation, but is not the prime objective (Caplan & Caplan).

Although Caplan's work (1970, 1993, 1999) involved relationships among professionals, many researchers now acknowledge the value of engaging in consultation with parents (Carlson & Christenson, 2005; Grissom, Erchul, &

Sheridan, 2003). Indeed, there is evidence for efficacy of consulting with parents in early childhood settings that involves identifying needs and resources, teaching advocacy skills to parents of children with disabilities, as well as providing parents with instructional methods, effective parenting strategies, information, and emotional support (Bailey et al., 2006; Kaczmarek, Goldstein, Florey, Carter, & Cannon, 2004). Unlike family therapy, or parent education (i.e., direct interventions) with a set agenda for presenting various parenting skills, consultee-centered consultation implies parents and consultants working together to understand unique problem situations and construct interventions related to children's specific academic, social-emotional functioning, and behavior (Brown et al., 2006). An in-depth discussion of consultation with parents of young children is presented later in this chapter.

Program-Centered Consultation   Caplan distinguishes two types of consultation at the program level that have the potential to influence entire systems (e.g., classrooms, schools, school districts) (Caplan, 1970, 1993, 1999). The consultant consults with program administrators in *program-centered administrative consultation,* focusing on supporting, improving, and developing systems within an organization, potentially serving all the children participating in a program. For example, work toward improving the emotional climate in an early childhood center affects staff and children attending the center. The essential and highly valuable aspect of engaging in the program-centered administrative consultation is that more than the individual child, teacher, or family potentially benefits from programmatic interventions. That is, program-centered consultation considers problems associated with organizational functioning, development of new programs, and promotion of overall organizational health (Erchul & Martens, 2006). The goal is to create, renew, or improve systems within the organization for the benefit of all children and their families. Thus, the organization or program becomes the client and program staff and administrators the consultees. Alternatively, *consultee-centered administrative consultation* is similar to consultee-centered consultation, but targets individual or groups of administrators with the goal of improving administrators' functioning.

PROBLEM-SOLVING CONSULTATION

Behavioral consultation more recently termed *problem-solving consultation,* (Kratochwill, 2008; Kratochwill, Elliott, & Callan-Stoiber, 2002) is based on the early work of Bergan (1977) and adheres to the principles of behavioral and social learning theory (Putnam, Handler, Rey, & McCarty, 2005). Broadly, problem-solving consultation is based on the assumption that human behavior is contextual, primarily a response to environmental factors. As such, behavioral change occurs when individuals change various aspects in the environment (e.g., adult response to a child's behavior, behavioral expectations in home or other settings). Problem-solving consultation has traditionally used applied behavioral analysis (ABA) strategies (e.g., systematic reinforcement, shaping, stimulus control) for designing and evaluating interventions. ABA relies on operational definitions of target behaviors, quantifiable goals, and quantitative data collection for establishing baselines and evaluation of interventions goals (Kratochwill et al.). However, a more current approach to problem-solving consultation is to use ABA techniques as well as a wide range of intervention techniques, specifically techniques that are evidence-based (Kratochwill; Sheridan & Kratochwill, 2008). For example, emerging from a consultation in a nursery school classroom participants might decide to use a common ABA strategy, immediate reinforcement (e.g., stickers or small snacks), to shape (e.g., reinforce for successive steps toward a goal) a young child's cooperative play behaviors. However, the participants in the consultation may also decide to teach the youngster to observe and label the emotions of self and peers (e.g., evidenced-based intervention), which may also help to increase cooperative play skills.

The most widely used consultation model in schools (Erchul & Martens, 2006), problem-solving consultation embodies the following specific characteristics. Problem-solving consultation is a structured problem solving process that involves assistance from consultants to consultee, who in turn works toward improving functioning for clients and programs. More specifically the goals are to provide interventions within a classroom, school, and home to influence children's behavior and academic problems (Watson & Sterling-Turner, 2008). This goal is accomplished by engaging in a series of interviews and observations as consultants and consultees move through a sequence of stages; consultees recognize the problem, consultants and consultees jointly define the problems and establish objectives for behavior change, consultees apply the intervention, and change is evaluated. As in mental health consultation, problem-solving consultants are concerned with building and maintaining collaborative relationships with consultees. Capacity building for consultees is also an expected outcome. That is, consultees will be better able to manage similar problems in the future. However, capacity building for consultees has not been supported consistently by research (Kratochwill, 2008; Putnam et al., 2005). Recently, problem-solving consultants have expanded their focus into organizational approaches designed to bring system-wide evidence-based programs to schools and school districts (Putnam, Luiselli, & Jefferson 2002; Zins & Erchul, 2002). For example, systemic application of evidence-based practices to improve overall discipline in an entire school has been found more effective than interventions designed for an individual student (Sugai, Horner, & Gresham, 2002; Putnam et al., 2005).

Conjoint behavioral consultation (CBC) is a consultation model in which consultants work with parents and teachers together to address the academic, mental health, and behavioral concerns of a youngster in their care. Parents and teachers are joint consultees working together in a collaborative manner. The critical aspects of CBC involve parents and early childhood professionals sharing their concerns, identifying common needs, establishing mutually agreed on goals, co-constructing intervention plans that can be implemented across settings (e.g., home, preschool, child care), and collecting data that determines goal attainment or the necessity for plan modification (Sheridan, Clarke, Knoche, & Edwards, 2006). Outcomes of CBC have been positive for creating effective interventions for academic and behavioral outcomes in school-age children (Guli, 2005; Sheridan, Eagle, Cowan, & Mickelson, 2001). Although the research on the effectiveness of CBC in early childhood settings is promising (Sheridan et al., 2006), more research needs to be done on joint parent–educator consultation in early childhood settings.

Another adaptation of problem-solving consultation is *direct behavioral consultation*, which originated in the school psychology literature with the work of Watson and Robinson (1996), and was expanded upon by Watson and Sterling-Turner (2008). This model is distinguishable from problem-solving consultation in the following way. Outcomes of problem-solving consultation typically rely on discussions between consultants and consultees, rather than consultants' direct treatment of clients to remediate clients' problems. Although the problem-solving approach may be appropriate for educators and parents with training in ABA strategies, in direct behavioral consultation there is an assumption that few teachers and even fewer parents possess behavioral analysis skills (Watson & Robinson). Indeed, Feldman and colleagues surveyed teachers and found that they considered ABA competence very important in their practice, and yet researchers found a significant difference between teacher ratings of importance and their ratings of competency (Feldman, Gordon, Merbler, & Tulbert, 1999). Therefore, in direct behavioral consultation consultants explain ABA techniques to consultees, model them with clients, provide consultees with opportunities to practice the skills with supervision from the consultant, and consultant and consultees evaluate outcomes together (Watson & Sterling-Turner). Thus, consultee training by consultants occurs at all stages of direct behavioral consultation process. Although, at this time, there is little direct evidence supporting the efficacy of direct behavioral consultation, research in staff development for early childhood educators suggests that teachers classroom management skills improve from a combination of mentoring and didactic instruction (Howes, James, & Ritchie, 2003; Raver et al., 2008).

COLLABORATION AND COLLABORATIVE RELATIONSHIPS IN SCHOOLS

Practitioners need to understand an important distinction between two terms frequently used in the consultation literature, *collaboration* and *collaborative relationships*. The term *collaboration* designates a form of consultative practice that can be used by mental health and problem-solving consultants (Erchul & Martens, 2006) while the term *collaborative* describes positive working relationships between consultants and consultees (e.g., coequal relationship, mutual sharing of expertise, open communication, trust) (Putnam et al., 2005; Schulte & Osborne, 2003). Collaboration as a form of consultation is described followed by a brief discussion of the collaborative relationships as they apply to consultation and collaboration.

Collaboration in Schools Collaboration as a form of consultative practice evolved as educators began to recognize the potential benefits of consultation. Consequently, schools and other institutions began to employ consultants on staff (Erchul & Martens, 2006; Welch & Tulbert, 2000). The realities of being an internal consultant (i.e., on the staff of a school) often requires a more direct style than the facilitative approach generally assumed by external consultants (i.e., consultants brought in from outside the school or organization to work with specific consultees or specific programmatic concerns). In early childhood settings, internal consultants typically assume an ethical and contractual responsibility for the social–emotional and behavioral concerns of the young children in their setting. As such, this role often necessitates a more directive approach to referral concerns than the supportive and encouraging approach often used by external consultants (Buysse & Wesley, 2005; Erchul & Martens, 2006). However for the external consultant, there may be a compelling reason to become directly involved in intervention or engage in direct service (e.g., counseling, therapy with clients) generally when consultees lack skill to implements interventions and timely intervention is a factor or when direct service is considered the most effective way to deliver treatment (Kratochwill & Pittman, 2002).

Collaborative Relationships in Schools Positive interpersonal relationships including qualities of openness, trust, and genuineness between consultants and consultees play an important role in the effectiveness of consultation particularly because consultation requires verbal communication and ongoing interactions between participants (Sheridan & Kratochwill, 2008). However, consultants have struggled with the assumption of coequal status between consultants and consultee, another aspect of collaborative relationships, for many years. The current assumption is that successful collaborative relationships may range from coequal to hierarchical depending on consultee characteristics (Kratochwill & Pittman, 2002). Indeed, participants in consultation possess different levels of experience, motivation, knowledge, and skills, which may result in natural disparities in status, potentially influencing the collaborative nature of relationships (Kratochwill & Pittman; Meyers, 2002). Donahue et al. (2000) points to significant challenges between the consultants and consultees in early childhood settings that might influence nonhierarchical or coequal relationships. Consultants generally have more education, typically receive a higher salary, and usually are afforded more professional respect than consultees, challenges that can potentially influence status and power relations. In the end, power differentials may be relatively unavoidable in early childhood settings, but nonetheless require consideration in building successful collaborative relationships.

Prevention/Capacity Building

Building capacity for consultees was first introduced into the literature by Gerald Caplan (1970), who envisioned his model would efficiently provide services for clients in need of mental health intervention, but also serve a preventative function by increasing the capacity of consultees to manage the mental health issues for their clients more effectively in the future. Thus, through their participation in consultation, the consultee develops skills, knowledge, confidence, and objectivity to function more effectively in the current case as well as the ability to manage similar future concerns that might arise in their care of young children. Although child care providers, early childhood educators, and parents often seek out immediate solutions, especially in crises and times of stress, consultants need to convey the importance of the consultee's contribution since consultees typically have a fuller understanding of the child's experience, more so than the consultant who observes children briefly (Johnston & Brinamen, 2005). Therefore, consultants and consultees explore one another's understanding of clients and consider each other's knowledge and ideas. The capacity to reflect on and manage the target child's academic and social-emotional behaviors increase for consultees, and perhaps generalizes to other young children in their care (Johnston & Brinamen). Said differently, the consultative approach with its use of discourse and active participation of consultees facilitates acquisition of new attitudes and skills (Knotek, Rosenfield, Gravois, & Babinski, 2003; Rosenfield, 2004). In a survey of Head Start programs, Green, Simpson, Everhart, Vale, & Gettman (2004), found that programs with integrated mental health consultation services had improved staff practices and overall program functioning. Further, consultees in early childhood settings offered consultative services reported improved self-efficacy in their ability to address the social–emotional needs of the children in their care

(Bleecker & Sherwood, 2005; Olmas & Grimmer, 2004; Perry, Dunne, O'Neil, & Campbell, 2005).

In addition to preparing consultees to be more effective in managing future problems with their clients, prevention can be also conceptualized as providing consultation services to individuals and groups at risk for a disorder or demonstrating early signs of a disorder (Meyers, 2002; Meyers & Nastasi, 1999). Another aspect of the preventive properties of consultation involves the strengthening of organizations. Providing organizations with programs and procedures to meet the needs of young children, their families, and staff is primary prevention in its most dynamic sense, because well functioning child care settings, preschools, and community programs attuned to the needs of young children and their families can do much to thwart the possibility of social-emotional and behavioral problems (Donahue, 2002; Huang et al., 2005).

CONSULTATION WITH PARENTS IN EARLY CHILDHOOD SETTINGS

Research findings consistently point to the importance of parent–school partnerships (Carlson & Christenson, 2005; Christenson & Carlson, 2005). Consultants, particularly, recognize the importance of partnerships with families, given that families represent a continuous resource in the prevention and intervention of problems for young children (Donahue et al., 2000). Although positive working relationships between educators and parents make both intuitive and empirical sense, in practice they are not so easy to achieve (Johns, 2003). Relationships between early childhood staff and families depend on a multitude of variables (Knopf & Swick, 2007). In order to create successful interventions for young children, parents and staff need to build genuine alliances that result from trust, positive social influence, and mutual respect for the expertise each brings to the process (Swick 2004). Productive relationships with parents require the consultant to do much the same. That is, demonstrate respect for families, build trust, encourage mutual communication, and display cultural sensitivity and competence (Blue-Banning, Summers, Frankland, Nelson, & Beegle, 2004; Donahue et al., 2000).

Evaluation studies in child care and preschool settings found that families reported positive changes in their child's behavior as well as increases in their own ability to manage their child after consultation (Bleecker & Sherwood, 2004; Bleecker, Sherwood, & Chan-Sew, 2005; Lehman, Lambarth, Friesen, MacLeod, & White, 2006). An interesting study involving conjoint behavioral consultation was conducted in several public and private early child care settings (Sheridanet al., 2006). Parents and teachers (joint consultees) participated collaboratively with the consultant throughout the process. Results suggested that joint decision making regarding the behavioral, social-emotional, and academic concerns shared by parents and educators resulted in successful interventions for the child. In addition, parents and educators reported high levels of acceptability and satisfaction with the process, while parents perceived improved communications with teachers.

Blue-Banning and her colleagues (2004) conducted numerous focus groups among families with children from 3 to 21 years and professional groups in order to develop indicators of professional practice behaviors associated with positive collaborative partnerships. Both parents and professionals, in separate groups, produced similar remarks. To varying degrees, each group expressed the importance of communication, commitment, shared involvement, professional competence, respect, and trust in order to achieve successful relationships. One interesting outcome of this research was the differing emphasis parents and professionals placed on shared involvement. Parents typically wanted professionals' unbounded involvement, while professionals were concerned about empowering families, that is, building capacity in families to solve their own problems. Professionals feared that becoming too involved created dependency in families that might actually harm them.

CULTURALLY COMPETENT CONSULTATION AND COLLABORATION

In consultation and collaboration, *cultural competence* refers to understanding, appreciating, and developing culturally sensitive consultation practices. Cultural competence in its broadest sense requires attention to the influences of many factors (e.g., culture, ethnicity, gender, race, religion, sexual identity) on relationships (e.g., parent–child, teacher–child, consultee–consultant), processes (e.g., type of consultation, nature of intervention), and outcomes (e.g., acceptable to consultee with differing perspectives) (Brown et al., 2006).

When consultants are unaware of, or insensitive to cultural differences influencing the relationship building process, problems can be defined incorrectly (Henning-Stout & Meyers, 2000). Awareness of and sensitivity to diversity are important since family structure, child-rearing practices, and language as well as beliefs and attitudes about education, mental health, and disabilities vary across cultures (Lynch, 2004). Research shows that accurate problem identification, an early stage in the consultation and collaboration process, is critical to the success of consultation (Welch & Tulbert, 2000) and requires mutual understanding between the consultant and consultee, while the nature of the problem is determined (Conoley & Conoley, 1992; Rosenfield & Gravios, 1996). In several studies, consultants who ignored cultural factors as well as individual differences within cultures were not successful in addressing relevant issues and ultimately the consultation was not effective (Ingraham, 2003; Maital, 2000; Sheridan, 2000).

There are many ways for consultants to achieve cultural competence. An important first step is consultants' awareness of their own culture (e.g., personal values, social interactions, worldview) (Rogers & Lopez, 2001; Wesley & Buysse, 2006). In addition, consultants need to acquire specific information about the consultees they serve. Consultants should understand the influence of acculturation, biculturalism, immigration status, communication patterns, and interpersonal skills unique to a specific culture (Rogers, 2000). Consultants should intentionally attempt to familiarize themselves with the values, beliefs, and attitudes of the population they serve since these variables are related to psychological functioning (Takushi & Uomoto, 2001), while concurrently reflecting on their own cultural-specific beliefs are in the best position to develop effective working relationships (Donahue et al., 2000; Soo-Hoo, 1998).

Based the work of Lopez and Rogers (2001) and Rogers and Lopez (2001), Nahari, Martines, and Marquez (2007) enumerate the research-based competencies to work effectively in a multicultural context. Taken as a whole, these competencies necessary suggest curricular and fieldwork training for consultants in order to become culturally competent. The competencies are:

1. Interpersonal skills to consult with others.
2. Knowledge of cultural differences that influence how problems are defined in consultation.
3. Knowledge of cultural and linguistic factors that influence the input, process, and outcome of consultation.
4. Skills in responding with sensitivity to cross-cultural differences.
5. Skills in using a variety of data collection techniques to identify client's problems.
6. Skills in recognizing how prejudice may influence the consultation process. (Nahari et al., 2007, p. 125)

CONSULTATION EFFECTIVENESS

Although not extensive, multiple sources provide the empirical evidence for effectiveness of consultation in child care and preschool settings. Evidence comes from scholars using quantitative and qualitative methodologies as well as evaluation studies (generally not peer reviewed). Additional evidence comes from the nation's Head Start programs that are required to provide mental health consultation along with continuous evaluation data. Perry, Brennan, Bradley, & Allen (2005) in their review of 31 mental health consultation studies between 1985 and 2005, pointed to promising evidence of effective teacher and program outcomes, and modest improvements for child-specific outcomes.

Consultation to assist young children and their families has great promise, but is not without its research challenges. Although the research presented below is compelling, there are important issues that influence our understandings of the literature. First, there is a vast consultation literature in many professions with numerous definitions and models of practice (Gutkin & Curtis, 1999; Buysse & Wesley, 2005), but as previously stated, few pertain directly to early childhood practice. In fact, much of the work done in consultation is located in the school psychology and special education literature and focuses on school-age children. Second is the nonuniformity in defining consultation and the resulting variations in consultant activities, training, and location (external/internal to the setting) across settings (Alkon, Ramler, & McLennan et al., 2003; Gilliam, 2007; Green et al., 2006). The lack of clear descriptions and the variable practice of consultation may indeed be responsible for disparate and limited outcome research (Gilliam, 2007; Zins, 2002). The third issue relates to the difficulty of measuring the influence of duration and intensity of consultation across settings (Hepburn et al., 2007). Studies differ in the time spent on cases and with consultees as well as the ongoing nature of the consultative relationship (directive versus coequal, trust, mutual decision making).

In spite of the caveats presented above, it seems that frequent contact with consultants is an important variable, which contributes to the overall success in client behavior and positive relationships among adults (Alkon et al., 2003; Green et al., 2004, 2006). Green et al. (2004) studied three large Head Start programs (urban, suburban, and rural) with variability in the mental health consultation services and found that teachers were more likely to report that consultation reduced young children's negative behaviors and increased their positive behaviors when, among other factors, the consultant was available to teachers when needed. Head Start staff believed that a high level of consultant involvement in the program was more likely to achieve child and family well-being. In addition, these authors determined that mental health consultants were more effective if their consultive relationship was ongoing, even when the actual time they spent in a program was minimal. Green et al. (2006) in their study of relationship characteristics of effective mental health consultation in early childhood settings found consultants who provided more frequent services had more positive relationships with staff. Therefore, there is evidence that the frequency and ongoing nature of consultation in early childhood settings contribute to teacher reported positive outcomes for young children and improved relationships among adults.

CLIENT IMPROVEMENT

Although consultation can influence adult behavior and program functioning, improvement in the young child is generally the primary goal and the major barometer used by staff and parents to measure success. Studies implementing consultation in early childhood settings emphasizing out comes with young children generally focus on increasing positive social behaviors, and decreasing externalizing, oppositional, and disruptive behaviors.

Various studies have reported increases in socialization and social skills, as well as improved global adjustment of young children in their child care and preschool settings as a result of consultative activities (Bleecker & Sherwood, 2003; Cagle, 2002; Elias, 2004; Field et al., 2004; Safford, Rogers, & Habashi, 2001). A number of studies relied on standardized rating scales completed by consultees, while others relied on observations by consultants and interviews with consultees. In various studies teachers' ratings pointed to improved social behaviors and global adjustment for the targeted client (Perry et al., 2005; Elias, 2004). A study using both teacher and parent reports of youngsters' social behavior and adjustment reported reliable changes in three of four children (Cagle, 2002). Han, Catron, Weiss, and Marciel (2005) found significant treatment effects for most social skills in teacher reports but not parent reports. These authors suggest that parent reports may reflect difficulties inherent in involving parents in school consultation efforts. Several studies use consultant report involving observation and interviews with consultees to affirm an increase in positive social behavior in young children (Bleecker & Sherwood, 2003; Field et al., 2004; Safford et al., 2001).

Externalizing behaviors have significant implications for young children, and without intervention generally increase as children get older (Lavigne, Arend, & Rosenbaum, 1998). Studies using parent and/or teacher reports found consultation effective in reducing externalizing behaviors of children in child care and preschool settings (Field et al., 2004; Han et al., 2005; Hennigan, Upshur, Wenz-Gross, 2004; Kupersmidt & Bryant, 2003; Shelton, Woods, Williford, Dobbins, & Neal, 2001). Researchers typically looked at aggression, emotional regulation, attention, and hyperactivity.

A few studies have addressed the issue of expulsion from early childhood settings. Gilliam (2007) in an evaluation of the Early Childhood Consultation Partnership in Connecticut found that mental health consultation for early education and child care classes throughout the state was successful at reducing oppositional behaviors, and significantly so, relative to classes not receiving consultation services. In this study, positive effects were greatest for decreased oppositional behaviors and hyperactivity. In a study of consultation outcomes with child care providers, young children 10 months to 7 years at risk of expulsion from child care for aggressive and hyperactive behaviors as well as anxious and depressive symptoms displayed decreased problem behaviors, and 79% of the at risk children were not expelled (Perry, Dunne, McFadden, & Campbell, 2007).

In a recent study, Williford and Shelton (2008), using training and consultation with teachers and training with parents of 96 preschoolers, researchers found reduced disruptive behavior in preschoolers and increased use of appropriate teacher strategies for managing disruptive behaviors in the classroom, after providing teachers with empirically-based strategies through training and consultation. Teachers and parents received training for implementing the *Incredible Years Parent and Teacher Training* (Webster-Stratton, Reid, & Hammond, 2001), but only teachers met weekly with consultants (4 months per child), while parents received only parent training. This study suggests that consultation combined with an evidence-based intervention was more effective than evidence-based strategies training.

Teacher and Program Outcomes

Teachers in early childhood settings were generally satisfied with mental health consultation services and tended to rate services as effective (Alkon et al., 2003; Elias, 2004; Green et al., 2004, 2006). Consultation with its capacity-building component aims to increase staffs' abilities to prevent and manage issues related to mental health. With this goal in mind, staff in several settings reported feeling more competent and having a greater sense of self-efficacy after participating in consultation (Alkon et al.; Field et al., 2004). In the Alkon et al. study teachers reported increases in understanding and empathy for difficult behaviors and greater knowledge of social-emotional development. They reported increased skill in working with parents, observation, reflection, and planning as a result of working with a mental health consultant. The most important variable that tends to moderate positive teacher outcomes for consultation was the quality of the relationship between staff and the consultants (Alkon et al.; Green et al., 2004, 2006). The more positive the relationship between the consultant and consultee in terms of trust and respect, the more likely the consultee reported feeling supported and the more likely the consultee believed the consultation was effective (Green et al., 2004, 2006). In addition, staff reports of lower stress levels (Alkon, et al.; Olmas & Grimmer, 2004) resulted from interactions with consultants.

Few studies address changes in overall program quality resulting from consultation. Using the Infant–Toddler Environment Rating Scale, the Early Childhood Environment Rating Scale, and the Family Day Care Rating Scale to measure changes in "poor to mediocre" child care environments at three points in time, researchers found that after consultation was introduced the majority of sites received ratings approaching "good" (Palsha & Wesley, 1998). As suggested earlier, it is difficult to determine program quality separate from duration of services, and from the quality of teacher competencies. However, controlling for duration of consultation services, researchers found that centers with teachers who had higher teacher competencies compared to centers with less competent teachers experienced significant positive changes in center quality (Alkon et al., 2003).

The efficacy of mental health consultation in early childhood settings is increasing the evidence base each year. However, a greater response to the rigors of evidence-based interventions would help consultants with decisions related to what tools and resources will be most effective with specific consultees and clients, and particularly helpful to evaluate their work (Wesley & Buysse, 2006).

ETHICAL CONCERNS AND TRAINING CONSIDERATIONS

RESPONSIBILITIES TO MULTIPLE CLIENTS

Helping professionals are always mindful of their ethical responsibilities to their clients. This is true for consultants who typically work with multiple clients in varied environments (Parsons, 1996). For example, in an attempt to create lasting change, a consultation or collaboration that begins with a child-centered issue (e.g., a child exhibiting aggressive behaviors in child care and at home) may evolve into interventions requiring changes in the physical setting, staff behavior, staff development, programmatic changes, and/or interventions for the home that involve family participation (Wesley & Buysse, 2006). To complicate matters further, family members, child care and educational staff, or program administrators, with potentially varied concerns and perspectives, may initially call on the consultant for assistance. Therefore, to whom is the consultant ultimately responsible, the referral source, the adults who must manage the problem, the child who has the problem, or the program who employs the consultant? With these complications in mind, it is often difficult to balance the requirements of all the participants involved in the process. The consultant must consider the impact on all those involved and resolve competing concerns related to the welfare of each participant on a case-by-case basis. Protecting the welfare of clients, a major principle of ethics in psychology, compels the consultant to anticipate the consequences of their practice on the all clients and consultees as well as individuals and institutions that may be affected by their services (American Psychological Association, 2002). However, when competing interests do emerge, The National Association of the Education of Young Children (2005) in their code of ethics suggests advocacy for children and families before advocacy for professionals (Dally, 2005).

COMPETENCE AND TRAINING

Professional codes of ethics recognize competence as a fundamental aspect of practice. The American Psychological Association's *Ethical Principles of*

Psychologists (2002) states, "Psychologists recognize the boundaries of their competence and the limitations of their techniques. They only provide services and only use techniques for which they are qualified by training and experience" (p. 2). At a basic level, consultants and collaborators working in early childhood settings must possess substantial knowledge of child development, children's mental health, and family systems. Strong foundations in these areas are required to assist child care and educational staff assess atypical behavior as well as promote healthy development (Johnston & Brinamen, 2005). Although possessing a substantial knowledge base is clearly important, successful consultation also depends on relationship-based processes. Simply providing information to staff and families is often not sufficient to affect change. Consultants need to combine knowledge of early childhood development and consultation practice with well-honed interpersonal and communication skills to solve problems (Erchul & Martens, 2006; Wesley & Buysse, 2006).

As a relatively new field, with limited research in the training of early childhood consultants, the school psychology literature can provide guidelines for training. Alpert and Taufique (2002) recommend that training of consultants should include didactic, practicum, and fieldwork experiences. This model allows trainees to integrate theory and practice. First, trainees acquire knowledge and skills in the classroom, then have opportunities to observe effective consultants, and finally refine their skills through guided practice under supervision. Meyers (2002) recommends trainees learn about and practice the different levels of consultation (child centered, consultee centered, program and administration centered). He believes that focus away from the more conventional child-centered approach encourages trainees to realize the strong potential consultation has as a preventive strategy, more common in consultee- and program-centered consultation.

Likely, many mental health professionals were not trained at the preservice level to consult with early childhood educators and therapists or families of young children (Klein & Harris, 2004). Indeed, in a survey of school psychologists certified in New York State and practicing in settings that serve young children, 70% of the respondents reported learning consultation/collaboration skills on the job (Rubinson, Sweeny, Mowder, & Sossin, 2003). Thus, issues of continuing education require exploration. In a study of school psychologists in New York State (Mowder, Goliger, Sossin, & Rubinson, 2003), using the same participants as the previous study, the overwhelming majority of those surveyed wanted additional training in intervention approaches. In their discussion of identifying content areas and methods of instruction for professional development, Wesley and Buysse (2001) made an interesting suggestion. They recommend that continuing education programs offer training to consultants and consultees together in order to promote a larger and common perspective pertaining to their roles and the process. No matter how the mental health professional is trained, it is up to individual consultants to determine whether their training is sufficient to deliver competent consultative services (Dougherty, 2005).

CONFIDENTIALITY

A major challenge for consultants and collaborators is establishing and main-taining a relationship with the consultee built on mutual trust. Trust is essential if consultees are to feel safe to share their concerns (Schulte & Osborne, 2003). Thus, consultants and consultees discussions need to remain confidential. However, consultants in early childhood settings come from many professions and confidentiality is not absolute; therefore, consultants need to be aware of exceptions to confidentiality (e.g., child abuse and neglect legislation) in their specific professional codes of ethics as well as exceptions mandated by the laws in their states. For example, potential harm to self or others and child abuse are not protected by confidentiality in most states. In consultative practice, the limits of confidentiality must be conveyed to all participants (Parsons, 1996) and this should be done during the entry stage (Buysse & Wesley, 2008).

The American Psychological Association's Ethical Principles for Psychologists (2002) addresses issues of confidentiality. However, other professionals in early childhood setting may not view confidentiality, a concept so familiar in mental health work, in the same way as mental health professionals. Certainly, families are not obliged to follow an ethical code. Mindful that others are not necessarily bound by ethical codes, consultants in early childhood settings, as in other school-type settings, generally disclose information on a need to know basis, which is often a confusing guideline (Wesley & Buysse, 2006). Newman and Robinson (1991) suggest the following framework that can help consultants make the difficult decisions related to confidentiality in early childhood settings since it is not simply the obligation of consultants to maintain confidentiality, but consultants must enlist the cooperative efforts of all participants in maintenance of confidentiality. The authors suggest that since participation of multiple consultees on a case can be variable, so should their access to information. Negotiate issues of confidentiality with each new case, so that participants do not assume that confidentiality is inherent in the process. Publicly express the limits of confidentiality to all participants, so each knows who has access to information. Lastly, encourage all parties to be respectful of the rights of colleagues, children, and families.

INFORMED CONSENT

Informed consent is the right of participants involved in the consultation process to have information in a context they can understand, that will enable them to make informed choices throughout the process (Parsons, 1996). A goal of informed consent is to encourage consultees to become active participants in the process. The consultant should discuss their respective roles and responsibilities throughout the various stages, the likely positive and negative impact of their actions, and the anticipated nature of the consultant/consultee relationship (Parsons, 1996; Wesley & Buysee, 2006).

CONSULTATION SUMMARIZED FOR PRACTICE EARLY CHILDHOOD SETTINGS

Mental health and problem-solving consultation and collaboration have made significant contributions to the contemporary practice of consultation and collaboration in early childhood settings (Buysse & Wesley, 2005; Cohen & Kaufmann, 2000, 2005; Donahue et al., 2000). Wesley & Buysse (2006) suggest that although there needs to be more evidence related to the roles, tasks, and skills necessary for effective consultation in early childhood settings, there are common elements central to effective consultation in early childhood education and care setting (Buysse & Wesley, 2005; Donahue et al., 2000). These elements require consultants' attention no matter their theoretical orientation.

Broadly, early childhood, family-oriented practitioners work directly with significant adults in young children's lives to influence young children's well-being. Consultation in early childhood settings is systematic problem-solving process in which consultants (e.g., mental health professionals, early childhood special educators, therapists) and consultees (e.g., early childhood professionals, parents) work together in a collaborative manner to address an area of concern or a common goal for change with individual children, groups of children, and institutions supporting young children. The consultant generally does not work directly with clients in consultation, but does work with individual young children when concerns call for the use of collaboration or direct intervention models. The primary purpose of the consultation is to address an immediate concern in the early childhood setting or home, as well as to prevent similar problems from occurring in the future (Buysse & Wesley, 2005).

FUTURE DIRECTIONS

Consultation and collaboration in K–12 settings enjoys a long history and large literature, unlike consultation in settings that serve young children. We have extrapolated much of what we know about consultation in early childhood settings from an extensive school-age literature. Much of the literature based on work with young children is practice-based and, although it is valuable work, it may not meet the rigorous standards for evidence-based interventions. As pointed out by Hepburn et al. (2007, p. 41), "Moving from 'service to science' has its challenges." However, as more young children enter early care outside their homes and the appreciation of early childhood as a significant time for building the foundations for later academic achievement and social-emotional health increases, the literature pertaining to child care and early education programs will continue to grow.

As we develop, the following questions require exploration:

1. What types of training and professional development activities are effective for consultant and consultees in early childhood settings? There is a need to explore multicultural perspectives and training requirements necessary for consultants to become more competent.
2. What specific services do child care and educational staff desire from consultants?
3. Is it possible to develop a common language, key components, and set activities that define consultation for early childhood professionals?
4. Since relationship variables appear to be vital aspects of consultation, we need more quantitative and qualitative program evaluations that demonstrate effectiveness but also define relationship variables. How does this material efficiently reach stakeholders in consultation?
5. It has been established that child care staff, families, and programs benefit from consultation. However, we need multiyear studies to determine the sustainability of consultee knowledge, skills, confidence building, and objectivity as well as the ongoing improvement in the client.

REFERENCES

Alkon, A., Ramler, M., & McLennan, K. (2003). Evaluation of mental health consultation in child care centers. *Early Childhood Education Journal, 13*(2), 91–99.

Alpert, J. L., Taufique, S. R. (2002). Consultation training: 26 years and three questions. *Journal of Educational and Psychological Consultation, 13*, 13–34.

American Psychological Association. (2002). Ethical principles of psychologists and code of conduct. *American Psychologist, 57*, 1060–1073.

Aylward, G. P. (2002). Cognitive and neuropsychological outcomes: more than IQ scores. *Mental Retardation and Developmental Disabilities Research Reviews, 8*, 234–240.

Bailey, D. B., Bruder, M. B., Hebbeler, K., Carta, J., Defosset, M., Greenwood, C., et al. (2006). Recommended outcomes for families of young children with disabilities. *Journal of Early Intervention, 28*, 227–251.

Bergan, J. R. (1977). *Behavioral consultation.* Columbus, OH: Merrill.

Bleecker, T., & Sherwood, D. L. (2004). *San Francisco high quality child care mental health consultation initiative*. San Francisco: Department of Public Health, Community Behavioral Services.

Bleecker, T., Sherwood, D. L., & Chan-Sew, S. L. (2005). *San Francisco high quality child care mental health consultation initiative*. San Francisco: Department of Public Health, Community Behavioral Services.

Blue-Banning, M., Summers, J. A., Frankland, L. L., Nelson, L. L., & Beegle, G. (2004). Dimensions of family and professional partnerships: Constructive guidelines for collaboration. *Exceptional Children, 70*, 167–184.

Brown, D., Pryzwansky, W. B., & Schulte, A. C. (2006). *Psychological consultation and collaboration: Introduction to theory and practice*. Boston: Allyn & Bacon.

Buysse, V., & Wesley, P. W. (2005). *Consultation in early childhood settings*. Baltimore: Brookes.

Buysse, V., & Wesley, P. W. (2008). A framework for understanding the consultation process: Stage-by-stage. *Young Exceptional Children, 7*(2), 2–9.

Cagle, M. L. (2002). Conjoint behavioral consultation with parents and teachers of Hispanic children: A study of acceptability, integrity, and effectiveness (doctoral dissertation, Oklahoma State University, 2002). *Dissertation Abstracts International 64*(2-A), 394.

Capizzano. J., & Adams, G. (2003). Children in low-income families are less likely to be in center-based care. Snapshots of American Families III No. 12. Washington, DC: Urban Institute.

Caplan, G. (1970). The theory and practice of mental health consultation. New York: Basic Books.

Caplan, G., & Caplan, R. B. (1993). *Mental health consultation and collaboration*. San Francisco: Jossey-Bass.

Caplan, G., & Caplan, R. B. (1999). *Mental health consultation and collaboration*. Prospect Heights, IL: Waveland Press. (Original work published in 1993.)

Caplan, G., Caplan, R. B., & Erchul, W. P. (1995). A contemporary view of mental health consultation: Comments on "Types of Mental Health Consultation" by Gerald Caplan. (1963). *Journal of Educational and Psychological Consultation 6*, 23–30.

Carlson, C., & Christenson, S. L. (2005). Evidence-based parent and family interventions in school psychology: Overview and procedures. *School Psychology Quarterly, 20*, 345–351.

Carlson, J., Watts, R. E., & Maniacci, M. (2006). Consultation and psychoeducation. In J. Carlson, R. E. Watts, & M. Maniacci (Eds.), *Adlerian therapy, theory, and practice* (pp. 251–273). Washington, DC: American Psychological Association.

Cates, J., Paone, T. R., Packman, J., & Margolis, D. (2006). Effective parent consultation in play therapy. *International Journal of Play Therapy, 15*, 87–100.

Christenson, S. L., & Carlson, C. (2005). Evidence-based parent and family interventions. *School Psychology Quarterly, 20*, 525–528.

Cohen, E., & Kaufmann, R. (2000). *Early childhood mental health consultation*. Washington, DC: U.S. Department of Health and Human Services.

Cohen, E., & Kaufmann, R. (2005). *Early childhood mental health consultation*. Promotion of mental health and prevention of mental and behavioral disorders (vol. 1). Washington, DC: U.S. Department of Health and Human Services, Substance Abuse and Mental Health Services Administration, Center for Mental Health Services.

Conoley, J. C., & Conoley, C. W. (1992). *School consultation: Practice and training* (3rd ed.). Boston: Allyn & Bacon.

Dally, K. (2005). Code of ethics literature review. Retrieved on September 1, 2008, from www.earlychildhoodaustralia.org.au.

Donahue, P. (2002). Promoting social and emotional development in young children: The role of mental health consultants in early childhood setting. In *The Kauffman Early Education Exchange* (vol. 1: L pp. 64–79). Kansas City, MO: Ewing Marion Kauffman Foundation.

Donahue, P. J., Falk, B., & Provet, A. G. (2000). *Mental health consultation in early childhood*. Baltimore: Brookes.

Dougherty, A. M. (2005). Psychological consultation and collaboration in school and community settings. Belmont, CA: Thomson Brooks/Cole.

Elias, C. F. (2004). Mental health consultation services in community based early childhood settings: A survey of preschool teachers (doctoral dissertation, Hartford University, 2004). *Dissertation Abstacts International, 64*(11-B), 5778.

Erchul, W. P., & Martens, B. K. (2006). *School consultation: Conceptual and empirical bases of practice*. New York: Springer.

Feldman, D., Gordon, P., Merbler, J., & Tulbert, B. T. (1999). Evaluations of the importance of applied behavior analysis competencies by teachers of students with emotional and behavioral disorders. *Teacher Educator, 35*(2), 15–29.

Field, S., Mackrain, M., & Sawilowsky, D. (2004). *Caring for Kids Initiative: Evaluation report*, May 1, 2003–April 30, 2004. Detroit, MI: Wayne State University, College of Education.

Gilliam, W. S. (2005) Prekindergarteners left behind: Expulsion rates in state prekindergarten systems. New Haven, CT: Yale University, Child Study Center.

Gilliam, W. S. (2007). Early childhood consultation partnership: Results of a random-controlled evalution. New Haven, CT: Yale University, Child Study Center.

Gilliam, W. S., & Shahar, G. (2006). Pre-kindergarten expulsion and suspension: Rates and predictors in one state. *Infants & Young Children, 19*, 228–245.

Green, B. L., Everhart, M. C., Gordon, L., & Gettman, G. M. (2006). Characteristics of effective mental health consultation in early childhood settings: Multilevel analysis of a national survey. *Topics in Early Childhood Special Education, 26*(3), 142–152.

Green, B. L., Simpson, J., Everhart, M. C., Vale, E., & Gettman, M. G. (2004). Understanding integrated mental health services in Head Start: Staff perspectives on mental health consultation. *National Head Start Association Dialogue, 7*(1), 35–60.

Grissom, P. F., Erchul, W. P., & Sheridan, S. M. (2003). Relationships among relational communication processes and perceptions of outcomes in conjoint behavioral consultation. *Journal of Educational and Psychological Consultation, 14*, 157–180.

Guli, L. A. (2005). Evidence-based parent consultation with school-related outcomes. *School Psychology Quarterly, 20,* 455–472.

Gutkin, T. B., & Curtis, C. R. (1999). School-based consultation theory and practice: The art and science of indirect service delivery. In C. R. Reynolds & T. B. Gutkin (Eds.), *The handbook of school psychology,* 3rd ed. (pp. 598–637). New York: Wiley.

Han, S. S., Catron, T., Weiss, B., & Marciel, K. K. (2005). A teacher consultation approach to social skills training for pre-kindergarten children: Treatment model and short-term outcome effects. *Journal of Abnormal Child Psychology, 33,* 681–693.

Henderson, A. T., & Mapp, K. L. (2002). A new wave of evidence: The impact of school family and community connections on student achievement. Austin, TX: Southwest Education Development Lab.

Hennigan, L., Upshur, C., & Wenz-Gross, M. (2004). Together for kids: Second year report. Worcester, MA: Health Foundation of Central Massachusetts. Retrieved June 16, 2008, from www.hfcm.org/CMS/images/TFK%20Year%20TWO%20 REPORT.pdf.

Henning-Stout, M., & Meyers, J. (2000). Consultation and human diversity: First things first. *School Psychology Review, 29,* 419–425.

Hepburn, K. S., Kaufmann, R. K., Perry, D. F., Allen, M. D., Brennan, E. M., & Green, B. L. (2007). *Early childhood mental health consultation: An evaluation tool kit.* Washington, DC: Georgetown University, Technical Assistance Center for Children's Mental Health; Johns Hopkins University, Women's and Children's Health Policy Center; and Portland State University, Research and Training Center on Family Support and Children's Mental Health.

Howes, C., James, J., & Ritchie, S. (2003). Pathways to effective teaching. *Early Childhood Research Quarterly, 18,* 104–120.

Huang, L., Stroul, B., Friedman, R., Mrazek, P., Friesen, B., Pires, S., & Mayberg, S. (2005). Transforming mental health care for children their families. *American Psychologist, 60,* 615–627.

Ingraham, C. L. (2003). Multicultural consultee-centered consultation: When novice consultants explore cultural hypotheses with experienced teacher consultees. *Journal of Educational and Psychological Consultation, 14,* 329–362.

Johns, B. (2003, January). The early childhood mental health project: Child care center consultation in action. San Francisco: Jewish Family and Children's Services.

Johnston, K., & Brinamen, C. (2005). Integrating and adapting infant mental health principals in the training of consultants to child care. *Infants & Young Children, 18* (4), 269–281.

Kaczmarek, L. A., Goldstein, H., Florey, J. D., Carter, A., & Cannon, S. (2004). Supporting families: A preschool model. *Topics in Early Childhood Special Education, 24,* 213–227.

Keenan, S. P., & Wakschlag, L. S. (2004). Are oppositional defiant and conduct disorder symptoms normative behaviors in preschoolers? A comparison of referred and nonreferred children. *American Journal of Psychiatry, 16,* 356–358.

Klein, M. D., Harris, K. C. (2004). Considerations in the personnel preparation of itinerant early childhood special education consultants. *Journal of Educational and Psychological Consultation, 15,* 151–166.

Knitzer, J. (2000). Early childhood mental health services: A policy and systems development perspective. In J. P. Shonkoff & J. S. Samuel (Eds.), *Handbook of early childhood intervention* (2nd ed., pp. 416–438). New York: Columbia University, National Center for Children in Poverty.

Knopf, H. T., & Swick, K. J. (2007). How parents feel about their child's teacher/ school? Implications for early childhood professionals. *Early Childhood Education Journal, 34,* 291–296.

Knotek, S. E., Rosenfield, S. A., Gravios, T. A., & Babinski, L. M. (2003). The process of fostering consultee development during instructional consultation. *Journal of Educational and Psychological Consultation, 14,* 303–328.

Kratochwill, T. R. (2008). Best practices in school-based problem-solving consultation: Applications in prevention and intervention systems. In A. Thomas & J. Grimes (Eds.), *Best practices in school psychology V* (pp. 1673–1688). Bethesda, MD: National Association of School Psychologists.

Kratochwill, T. R., & Pittman, P. H. (2002). Expanding problem-solving consultation training: Prospects and frameworks. *Journal of Educational and Psychological Consultation, 13,* 69–95.

Kratochwill, T. R., Elliott, S. N., & Callan-Stoiber, K. (2002) Best practices in school-based problem-solving consultation. In A. Thomas & J. Grimes (Eds.), *Best practices in school psychology IV* (pp. 283–608). Washington, DC: National Association of School Psychologists.

Kupersmidt, J. B., & Bryant, D. (2003, April). *The Preschool Behavior Project: Effectiveness of classroom and parenting interventions for aggressive preschoolers.* Paper presented at biennial meeting of the Society for Research in Child Development, Tampa, FL.

Lavigne, J, V., Arend, R., & Rosenbaum, D. (1998). Psychiatric disorders with onset in the preschool years: I. Stability of diagnosis. *Journal of the American Academy of Child & Adolescent Psychiatry* (vol. 3) 1246–1254.

Lehman, C., Lambarth, C. H., Friesen, B., MacLeod, M., & White, D. (2006). *Evaluation of the incredible years and mental health consultation to child care centers.* Unpublished manuscript. Portland, OR: Portland State University, Regional Research Institute for Human Services.

Lopez, E. C., & Rogers, M. R. (2001). Conceptualizing cross-cultural school psychology competencies. *School Psychology Quarterly, 16,* 270–302.

Lynch, E. W. (2004). Developing cross-cultural competence. In E. W. Lynch & M. J. Hanson (Eds.), *Developing cross-cultural competence: A guide for working with children and their families* (3rd ed., pp. 41–77). Baltimore: Brookes.

Maital, S. L. (2000). Reciprocal Distancing: A systems model of interpersonal processes in cross-cultural consultation. *School Psychology Review, 29,* 389–400.

Mark-Wilson, P., Hopewell, A., & Gallagher, J. (2002). Perceptions of child care professionals in California regarding challenging behaviors exhibited by young child in care: Findings and recommendations of focus group study. Washington, DC: Health Systems Research, Inc.

McDonnell, M. A., & Glod, C. (2003, October/December). The prevalence of psycho-pathology in preschool-aged children. *Journal of Child and Adolescent Psychiatric Nursing*, 1–13.

McDowell, T. (1999). Systems consultation in Head Start: An alternative to traditional family therapy. *Journal of Marital and Family Therapy, 25*, 155–168.

Meyers, J. (2002). A 30 year perspective on best practices for consultation training. *Journal of Educational and Psychological Consultation, 13*, 35–54.

Meyers, J., & Nastasi, B. (1999). Primary prevention in school settings. In C. R. Reynolds & T. B. Gutkin (Eds.), *The handbook of school psychology* (3rd ed., pp. 764–799). New York: Wiley.

Mowder, B. A. (1994). Consultation with families of young at-risk, and handicapped children. *Journal of Educational and Psychological Consultation, 5*, 309–320.

Mowder, B. A., Goliger, I., Sossin, K. M. & Rubinson, F. D. (2003). Continuing education interests and needs of New York State early childhood school psychologists. *The School Psychologist, 57*, 130–139.

Nahari, S. G., Martines, D., & Marquez, G. (2007). Consulting with culturally and linguistically diverse parents. In G. Esquivel, E. C. Lopez, & S. Nahari (Eds.), *Handbook of multicultural school psychology: An interdisciplinary perspective* (pp. 119–136). Mahwah, NJ: Erlbaum.

National Association for the Education of Young Children. (2005). *Code of Ethical Conduct and Statement of Commitment*, www.naeyc.org/about/positions/PSETH05.asp.

Newman, J. L., & Robinson, S. E. (1991). In the best interests of the consultee: Ethical issues in consultation. *Consulting Psychology Bulletin, 43*, 23–29.

Olmas, A., & Grimmer, M. (2005). PEARL: Lessons learned from collaboratively delivering mental health services in early childhood settings. In C. Newman, C. J. Liberton, K. Kutash, & R. M. Friedman (Eds.), *The 17th Annual Research Conference Proceedings: A system of care for children's mental health: Expanding the research base* (pp. 247–253). Tampa: University of South Florida, Louis de la Parte Florida Mental Health Institute, Research and Training Center for Children's Mental Health.

Palsha, S., & Wesley, P. W. (1998). Improving quality in early childhood environments through onsite consultation. *Topics in Early Childhood Special Education, 18*(4), 243–253.

Parsons, R. D. (1996). *The skilled consultant: A systematic approach to the theory and practice of consultation*. Boston: Allyn & Bacon.

Perry, D. F., Brennan, E., Bradley, J., & Allen, M. D. (2006, July). *Implementing mental health consultation: A promising practice for serving young children*. Paper presented at Georgetown Training Institutes 2006: Developing Local Systems of Care for Children and Adolescents with Emotional Disturbances and Their Families, Orlando, FL.

Perry, D. F., Dunne, M. C., McFadden, L., & Campbell, D. (2007). Reducing the risk for preschool expulsion: Mental health consultation for young children with challenging behaviors. *Journal of Family Studies, 17*, 44–54.

Perry, D. F., Dunne, M. C., O'Neil, M., & Campbell, D. (2005). Does mental health consultation increase social skills, decrease problem behaviors, and avoid expulsion for young children in child care? Unpublished manuscript. Washington, DC: Georgetown University, Center for Child and Human Development.

Putnam, R. F., Handler, M. W., Rey, J., & McCarty, J. (2005). The development of behaviorally based public school consultation services. *Behavior Modification. 29,* 521–538.

Putnam, R. F., Luiselli, J. K., & Jefferson, G. L. (2002). Expanding technical assistance consultation to public schools: District-wide evaluation of instructional and behavioral support practices for students with developmental disabilities. *Child & Family Behavior Therapy, 24,* 113–128.

Qi, C. H., & Kaiser, A. P. (2003). Behavior problems of preschool children from low-income families: Review of the literature. *Topics in Early Childhood Special Education, 23,* 188–216.

Raver, C. C., Jones, S. M., Li-Grining, C. P., Metzger, M., Champion, K. M. & Sardin, L. (2008). Improving preschool classroom processes: Preliminary findings from a randomized trial implemented in Head Start settings. *Early Childhood Research Quarterly, 23,* 10–26.

Resnick, R. J., & Kruczek, T. (1996). Pediatric consultation: New concepts in training. *Professional Psychology: Research and Practice, 27,* 194–197.

Rogers, M. R. (2000). Examining the cultural context of consultation. *School Psychology Review, 29,* 414–418.

Rogers, M. R., & Lopez, E. C. (2001). Identifying critical cross-cultural school psychology competencies. *Journal of School Psychology, 40,* 115–141.

Rosenfield, S. A. (2004). Consultation as dialogue: The right words at the right time. In N. M. Lambert, I. Hylander, & J. H. Sandoval (Eds.), *Consultee-centered consultation: Improving the quality of professional services in school and community organizations* (pp. 337–347). Mahwah, NJ: Erlbaum.

Rosenfield, S. A., & Gravios, T. A. (1996). *Instructional consultation teams.* New York: Guilford Press.

Rubinson, F. D., Sweeny, K. A., Mowder, B.A., & Sossin, K. M. (2003). Collaborative practices of New York State early childhood school psychologists. *The School Psychologist, 57,* 73–85.

Safford, P., Rogers, L., & Habashi, J. (2001). *A qualitative study of Day Care Plus: Children, providers, and the consultation process.* Cleveland, OH: Case Western Reserve University, Schubert Center for Child Development.

Schulte, A. C., & Osborne, S. S. (2003). When assumptive worlds collide: A review of definitions of collaboration in consultation. *Journal of Educational and Psychological Consultation, 14,* 109–138.

Shelton, T. L., Woods, J. E., Williford, A. P., Dobbins, T. R., & Neal, J. M. (2001). System of care interventions for hard to manage preschoolers in Head Start. In C. Newman, C. Liberton, K. Kutash, & R. Friedman (Eds.), *The 16th Annual Research Conference Proceedings: A System of Care for Children's Mental Health: Expanding the Research Base* (pp. 213–218). Tampa FL: University of South Florida, Louis de la Parte Florida Mental Health Institute, Research and Training Center for Children's Mental Health.

Sheridan, S. M. (2000). Considerations of multiculturalism and diversity in behavioral consultation with parents and teachers. *School Psychology Review, 29*, 344–353.

Sheridan, S. M., Clarke, B. L., Knoche, L. L., & Edwards, C. P. (2006). The effects of conjoint behavioral consultation in early childhood settings. *Early Education and Development, 17*, 593–617.

Sheridan, S. M., Eagle, J. W., Cowan, R. J., & Mickelson, M. (2001). The effects of conjoint behavioral consultation results of a 4-year investigation. *Journal of School Psychology, 39*, 361–385.

Sheridan, S. M., & Kratochwill, T. R. (2008). *Conjoint behavioral consultation: Promoting family-school connections and interventions.* New York: Springer.

Shonkoff, J., & Phillips, D. (2000). *From neurons to neighborhoods: The science of early childhood development.* Washington, DC: National Academy Press.

Soo-Hoo, T. (1998). Applying frame of reference and reframing techniques to improve school consultation in multicultural settings. *Journal of Educational and Psychological Consultation, 9*, 325–345.

Sugai, G., Horner, R. H., & Gresham, F. M. (2002). Behaviorally effective school environments. In M. R. Shinn, H. M. Walker, & G. Stoner (Eds.), *Interventions for academic and behavior problems II: Preventive and remedial approaches* (pp. 315–350). Washington, DC: National Association of School Psychologists.

Swick, K. (2004). Empowering parents, families, schools, and communities during the early childhood years. Champaign, IL: Stipes.

Takushi, R., & Uomoto, J. M. (2001). The clinical interview from a multicultural perspective. In L. L. A. Suzuki, J. G. Ponterotto, & R. J. Meller (Eds.), *Handbook of multicultural assessment: Clinical, psychological, and educational applications* (2nd ed., pp. 47–66). San Francisco: Jossey-Bass.

U.S. Department of Education, NCES 2006. *The condition of education in 2006, indicator 2: Enrollment in early childhood education programs.* Retrieved September 15, 2007, from http://nces.ed.gov/programs/coe/2006/pdf/02_2006.pdf.

Watson, T. S., & Robinson, S. L. (1996). Direct behavioral consultation: An alternative to traditional behavioral consultation. *School Psychology Quarterly, 11*, 267–278.

Watson, T. D., & Sterling-Turner, H. (2008). Best practices in direct behavioral consultation. In A. Thomas & J. Grimes (Eds.), *Best practices in school psychology V* (pp. 1661–1672). Bethesda, MD: National Association of School Psychologists.

Webster-Stratton, C., Reid, M. J., & Hammond, M. (2001). Preventing conduct problems, promoting social competence: A parent and teacher training partnership in Head Start. *Journal of Clinical Child Psychology, 30*, 283–302.

Welch, M., & Tulbert, B. (2000). Practitioners' perspectives of collaboration: A social validation and factor analysis. *Journal of Educational and Psychological Consultation, 11*, 357–378.

Wesley, P. W., & Buysse, V. (2006). Ethics and evidence in consultation. *Topics in Early Childhood Special Education, 26*, 131–141.

Williford, A. P., & Shelton, T. L. (2008). Using mental health consultation to decrease disruptive behaviors in preschool children. *Journal of Child Psychology and Psychiatry and Allied Disciplines, 49*, 191–200.

Zins, J. E. (2002). Outgoing editors farewell? Building a strong future for educational and psychological consultation. *Journal of Educational and Psychological Consultation, 13*, 5–6.

Zins, J. E., & Erchul, W. P. (2002). Best practices in school consultation. In A. Thomas & J. Grimes (Eds.), *Best practices in school psychology IV* (pp. 625–644). Bethesda, MD: National Association of School Psychologists.

CHAPTER 10

Play Therapy

ATHENA A. DREWES

T HE EARLY YEARS of infancy and toddlerhood are vulnerable times that can be significantly impacted upon by social, familial, environmental, physiological, and genetic factors. It is a time of rapid brain development in the areas of language, motor skills, emotions, reasoning, cognitive functioning, formation of social relationships and self-image, as well as impulse control. During the first three years of life, 90% of brain growth occurs and the experiences during these formative years are crucial in the way basic brain structures develop (Perlmutter, 2006; Siegel, 1999). High-risk factors of poverty, poor caretaking, lack of proper nourishment and medical care, abuse, and neglect significantly impact on brain development, as well as physical, emotional, cognitive and social growth. Chronic fear or stress increases cortisol hormone levels in the brain, which become toxic to brain growth and resulting self-control and regulation (Siegel).

Approximately 21% of the children in the United States under age 5 are living in poverty. High-risk children (children in poverty, experiencing neglect, abuse, abandonment, homelessness) under age 5 show signs of developmental and speech delays, difficulties with self-regulation, poor peer interactions and social skills, and an inability to learn (Osofsky, 2004; Siegel, 1999). In addition, poor relationships with adults, depression, and aggressive behaviors manifest (Aber, Jones, & Cohen, 2000). Kataoka, Zhang, and Wells (2002) found that close to 75–80% of children and youth in need of mental health services do not receive them, and that 88% (Ringel & Sturm, 2001) of minority children also have unmet mental health needs. Children who are at risk for social and emotional problems are often at risk for school failure and expulsion as early as preschool. Gilliam (2005) at Yale Child Study Center found the prekindergarten levels of school expulsion were three times higher than the rate for K–12 students. The type of future a child will have is often dependent on the outcome of these early formative years.

Early intervention can make a significant difference in remediating and lessening delays and limitations, while forestalling and even halting future secondary emotional or cognitive difficulties. The necessity for on-site mental health services and early intervention is underscored by a study conducted by Lavigne et al. (1996), which found 21% of the 3,800 preschool-age children studied met criteria for a psychiatric disorder and that 9.1% of this at-risk portion met criteria for a severe disorder.

Play is one way that children can process events, solve problems, create social contact and master tasks, and mediate the harmful effects of stress. The infant, through play, can acquire skills and strategies that assist in the development of representational thought about whom he or she is, along with object representation and self-other differentiation (Valentino, Cicchetti, Toth, & Rogosch, 2006). Play activities allow for the development of self-efficacy and social interactions with a significant other. They also allow for emerging peer relationships and a sense of mastery (Spinrad et al., 2004). Play allows for other benefits, such as physical development, relationship building, cognitive skill development (Pellegrini & Smith, 1998), self-regulation (Bodrova & Leong, 2003), as well as development of creativity (Howard-Jones, Taylor, & Sutton, 2002). There is also a positive relationship between exploratory play and that of secure attachment. Mother and toddler play with securely attached children has been found to result in increased exploration, competence, and symbolic play (Slade, 1987).

The Clinical Report of the American Academy of Pediatrics (2006) underscores the importance of play in a child's development, along with the importance of parental participation in child play. Play is as natural to children as breathing. It is the universal expression of children and it can transcend differences in ethnicity, language, or other aspects of culture (Drewes, 2005a).

PLAY THERAPY OVERVIEW

Play therapy utilizes the curative factors of play (Schaefer, 1993) along with play-based interventions as treatment with children and their families, from infancy on up through the life-span. Play therapists are able to utilize play therapy to strategically help young children to express themselves when their verbal language fails to communicate troubling thoughts and feelings. Through an emotionally supportive environment, toys with therapeutic value, along with specialized training in play therapy, the play therapist is able to respond to the child's metaphor and symbolism or through use of play-based interventions. The child's inner conflicts, cognitive distortions, and dysfunctional behaviors and interactions can be alleviated in a way that is consistent with his or her development and in an action-oriented way (Reddy, Files-Hall, & Schaefer, 2005).

DEFINITION OF PLAY THERAPY

Play therapy as defined by the Association for Play Therapy (APT, 2008) is:

> The systematic use of a theoretical model to establish an interpersonal process wherein trained play therapists use the therapeutic powers of play to help clients prevent or resolve psychosocial difficulties and achieve optimal growth and development (p. 2).

Play therapy is both a treatment modality and a term that encompasses a variety of treatment methods. Play can be used *as* therapy, as well as play being used *in* therapy.

Pretend play is a natural activity that most children engage. It involves symbolism along with the use of fantasy and make-believe (Russ, 2007). Play therapy helps children communicate through symbolism, the toys serve as the child's words and the play as their language (Landreth, 2002). Young children often lack the ability to verbally share how they are feeling and report disturbing and traumatic experiences and events. The use of play and art allows the young child to communicate in an effective way, as well as offers ways to help in self-soothing and self-regulating. Play and art also offer sensory experiences, which can benefit children with developmental delays and sensory integration difficulties. Being able to create a story using toy miniatures and mold sand in a sandtray or pound on clay helps a child therapeutically to connect and ground oneself to the present while dealing with emotionally charged material at a safe emotional distance.

Play therapy has also become an umbrella term that encompasses not only play *as* therapy but play *in* therapy. Art therapy, expressive arts therapy, drama, music, dance and narrative therapy, and sand-play therapy are utilized and may be considered as a part of play therapy.

PLAY THERAPY WITH THE YOUNG CHILD AND CAREGIVER

There are several play-based treatment approaches that have been researched as being effective with young children in conjunction with working with their caregiver. Among these are Theraplay (Jernberg, 1979), Developmental Play Therapy (Brody, 1997), Filial Therapy (Guerney, 1969; VanFleet, 1994), Child–Parent Relationship Therapy (Bratton & Landreth, 2005; Bratton, Landreth, Kellam, & Blackard, 2006), and Parent-Child Interaction Therapy (PCIT; Eyberg, 2004), to name a few. Play therapy can take the form and range from being child led in a nondirective approach to being therapist directed, child-involved, and parent coached.

For young children, play therapy is often used in building attachment and repairing relationships between the child and parent or caregiver, so that the caregiver is often an important component in the success of treatment. The use of toys, play and expressive arts materials within the clinician's room creates an inviting and comfortable place that conveys to the child that talk is not always necessary or expected in order to be understood (Drewes, 2001).

CURATIVE FACTORS OF PLAY

It is only in the past 25 years that child clinicians and researchers have looked closely at the specific qualities inherent in play behavior within therapy that makes it a therapeutic agent for change (Drewes, 2006; Russ, 2004). Schaefer (1993) identified 25 therapeutic factors: self-expression; access to the unconscious; facilitating learning; metaphorical insight; abreaction; catharsis; sublimation; alliance formation; attachment; relationship enhancement; moral judgment; stress inoculation; counter-conditioning; power/control; competence; self-control; creative problem-solving; fantasy compensation; reality testing; empathy; behavioral rehearsal; accelerated development; sense of self; physical health; and distraction.

THEORETICAL BASIS

The definition of play therapy includes a variety of theoretical approaches, which include child-centered play therapy (Axline, 1969; Landreth, 2002), Jungian play therapy (Allan, 1988), and sandtray therapy (Kalff, 1980), along with psychodynamic play therapy, which are childled and nondirective; cognitive-behavioral play therapy (Knell, 2003), a therapist directed and child-involved approach in which goals and objectives in symptom reduction drive the selection of the intervention and techniques to use; Adlerian play therapy (Kottman, 2002), which allows for a more combined and integrative approach with child-led and therapist-led approaches, as well as Ecosystemic play therapy (O'Connor & Ammen, 1997); and prescriptive play therapy (Schaefer, 2003), which allows the clinician to select the treatment approach that best meets the symptoms and situation of the child at the moment. More in-depth descriptions of these various theoretical approaches follow.

PSYCHOANALYTIC AND PSYCHODYNAMIC PLAY THERAPY

Play therapy and the use of play-based interventions dates back to the 1930s, when Hermione Hug-Hellmuth, Anna Freud, and Melanie Klein utilized toys as a way to adapt adult talk therapies for use with children as a means of engagement and treatment.

Play and toys were used as the treatment approach in order to access unconscious thoughts and feelings. They viewed change as coming through the power of play, in the safe and accepting therapeutic atmosphere with an empathic therapist who listens and responds to the child's play and metaphor. Through the formation of a therapeutic alliance and the process of transference and countertransference, the analysis of the transference relationship becomes important (Carmichael, 2006).

CHILD-CENTERED PLAY THERAPY

Later, the work of Carl Rogers was adapted by his student, Virginia Axline (1969) into a child-led, nondirective, child-centered play therapy. As was the case for the psychoanalytic and psychodynamic play therapy approach, the therapeutic environment and empathic therapist were considered crucial. The unconditional positive regard of the child, along with genuine concern and feedback from the therapist, allowed for transformation. Given the proper therapeutic environment, the child could flourish and develop a well-balanced, actualized personality (Axline & Carmichael, 1947). Landreth (2002) has extended Axline's views into a philosophical stance and life orientation that extends beyond the playroom. He postulates that children have an innate capacity for growth and resiliency so that they can direct and pace their own emotional growth and belief in self (Landreth, 1991). Consequently, "child-centered play therapy is an attitude, a philosophy, and a way of being" (Landreth, 1991, p. 55).

JUNGIAN PLAY THERAPY

Jungian theory, derived by Carl Gustav Jung, a Swiss psychiatrist and a contemporary of Freud and Adler, believes the central human drive is the individuation process that establishes one's unique personality and identity. Furthermore, there are both conscious (ego) and unconscious elements in the personality. These components and structures of the psyche strive to reconcile experiences and meaning with external reality (Carmichael, 2006). For children, play is viewed as having a curative component that allows the psyche to heal itself. The healing process is initiated by opening the dialogue with the ego-self through the symbolic language of the self. The creative processes of play, art, drama, poetry and stories, music, dreams, and sandtray facilitate the healing process.

ADLERIAN PLAY THERAPY

Adlerian play therapy follows Adler's theory that people are indivisible, social, decision-making beings whose actions and psychological movement have purpose (Dinkmeyer, Dinkmeyer, & Sperry, 1987). The child's play reflects inner characteristics and manner of behavior or style of life (Alfred Adler Institute, 2004). The child is helped to explore alternative perceptions about their life and experience, and utilize their goal-directed and purposeful behavior to move toward their desired goal. The playroom includes toys to assist the child to create rapport with the therapist, convey a variety of emotions, role-play situations and relationships that exist in their life, to provide a safe environment to test out behavioral and emotional limits, empower the child's sense of self, advance self-understanding, and improve the child's self-control and responsibility for his or her behavior and feelings (Kottman, 1995).

COGNITIVE-BEHAVIORAL PLAY THERAPY

Cognitive-behavioral play therapy is based on behavioral and cognitive theories of emotional development and psychopathology. It incorporates cognitive and behavioral interventions within a play therapy paradigm with verbal and nonverbal communication during play activities. Sessions include forming therapeutic goals, having both the child and therapist select materials and activities, using play to teach skills and alternative behaviors, having the therapist verbalize the conflicts and irrational logic to the child and use of praise by the therapist (Knell, 1993).

PRESCRIPTIVE PLAY THERAPY

Prescriptive play therapy is based on the premise of differential therapeutics (Frances, Clarkin, & Perry, 1984) and holds that some play interventions are more effective than others, for certain types of disorders (Schaefer, 2003). Thus, a child who does poorly in one type of play therapy may do well with another (Beutler, 1979). There is no "one size fits all" approach (Schaefer, 2003, p. 307), whereby one theoretical school is strong enough to make changes across all the many different and complex identifiable disorders. The prescriptive approach seeks to find the most effective play intervention for a specific disorder, matching the approach to the unique needs of the individual case (Schaefer, 2003). The prescriptive approach utilizes eclecticism, selecting from various theories and techniques to create a therapeutic strategy that is best for a particular child.

ASSESSMENT, CONSULTATION, AND INTERVENTION TECHNIQUES

Play therapy itself is process oriented, and assessment within play therapy should be ongoing and developmentally appropriate. A combination of play observations in naturalistic settings (classroom and playground, within the session with the parent and without the parent), along with full developmental and family histories, formal play diagnostic tools and observation in the playroom, should be used before proceeding with treatment. *Play Diagnosis and Assessment* (Gitlin-Weiner, Sandgrund, & Schaefer, 2000) is an exhaustive, comprehensive catalog of a variety of play diagnostics that are research-based and objective. The book is divided into sections covering developmental, diagnostic, parent-child interaction, and family play assessments, along with peer interaction and projective play assessments.

Play observation and informal play assessment can provide a wealth of information from children who especially may not be able to be evaluated in a more formal way. Play assessment also allows children to gain a safe distance from sensitive, threatening, or anxiety producing material through the use of toys. For example, puppets help engage a younger child, who may seem withdrawn or reluctant to participate. Interview questions can be given through the puppet, and the child's replies can also be given back through a puppet that they have selected to use.

Informal observation should focus on the quality of the child's play, age appropriateness and developmental level of play, and use and content of play materials. In addition the quality of interactions, frustration level, level of dependence and independence, cognitive and language skills, level of self-control, self-concept, and emotional awareness should also be assessed.

In assessing parent-child interactions in a more formal manner, the Marschak Interaction Method (MIM; Marschak, 1960; Jernberg & Booth, 1999) can be useful. It is a structured play-based means for observing and assessing caregiver and child interaction. The caregiver is given a series of simple structured play engagement tasks (e.g., the adult is given a card directing him/her to build a simple structure with one set of blocks and get their child to "build one just like mine") to carry out with their child, while the therapist or evaluator watches behind a one-way mirror. The tasks are designed to elicit a range of behaviors from the child in four dimensions: limit setting; providing structure; level of parental engagement with the child; and ability to meet the child's need for attention, soothing, and care (nurture), along with encouraging the child's effort to achieve at a developmentally appropriate level (Lindaman, Booth, & Chambers, 2000).

EVIDENCE-BASED SUPPORT FOR PLAY THERAPY

A review of outcome studies on play therapy reveals ample evidence that play therapy is an effective treatment for a variety of social-emotional disorders (Bratton & Ray, 2000; Bratton, Ray, Rhine, & Jones, 2005; Ray, Armstrong, Warren, & Balkin, 2005; Ray, Bratton, Rhine, & Jones, 2001). Over the past two decades well-designed, controlled play intervention studies have emerged. Meta-analytic reviews of play therapy and play counseling research (Bratton & Ray; Bratton et al.; Ray et al., 2005; Ray et al., 2001) have focused on the efficacy of play therapies and the combined effects of play therapies with children and families.

META-ANALYSES

The meta-analytic studies (Bratton et al., 2005; Leblanc & Ritchie, 2001; Ray et al., 2001) reported that play interventions produced large positive effects on treatment outcomes for children across treatment modalities (group and individual), age groups (3–16 years), gender, referred versus nonreferred populations, clinical setting, and treatment orientation (humanistic/non-directive, behavioral/directive). Play therapy has been extremely effective in addressing a wide variety of social, emotional, behavioral, and learning problems, including: posttraumatic stress disorder, conduct disorder, aggression, anxiety/fearfulness, depression, attention deficit hyperactivity disorder (ADHD), impulsivity, low self-esteem, reading difficulties, and social withdrawal. It has also been successfully used with children whose problems are related to life stressors, such as divorce, death, relocation, hospitalization, chronic illness, physical/sexual abuse, domestic violence, and natural disasters. Play therapy and play-based interventions can readily be paired with short-term treatments such as cognitive-behavioral and behavioral management techniques in a directive manner; as well as in long-term treatment exclusively using nondirective or a combination approach (Ray et al., 2001; Reddy et al., 2005).

EVIDENCE-BASED AND EMPIRICALLY-BASED TREATMENTS

Several empirically-based, play-based programs and interventions have been researched that are useful in the treatment of preschoolers both in the school setting and home setting (Barnett, 1991: Johnson, McLeod, & Fall, 1997; Knoblauch, 2001; Kot, Landreth, & Giordano, 1998; Reddy et al., 2005). Results of these studies have shown that use of play-based interventions have been successful in reducing separation anxiety, social skills deficits, internalizing behavior problems due to witnessing domestic violence, physical and sexual abuse, improving self-concept and facilitating children's expression of feelings. Two programs, The Primary Project and PCIT, are highlighted next.

The Primary Project   Among the empirically- and evidence-based treatments, the Primary Project (Cowen & Hightower, 1989) has been highlighted by the National Registry of Evidence-Based Programs and Practice (NREPP), a service of the Substance Abuse and Mental Health Services Administration (SAMHSA) (www.nrepp.samhsa.gov) as an evidence-based treatment that is effective in helping children through a child-led play-based approach. The Primary Project offers empirical evidence that a child-led play-based approach can help children with mild school adjustment difficulties become better socially and emotionally adjusted to school. This program will be more fully described in a later section.

Parent-Child Interaction Therapy (PCIT)   PCIT (Eyberg, 2004) has also been listed by SAMHSA as having shown through evidence-based practices that it is an effective treatment for parent–child interaction difficulties. Both of these treatments are described in more detail below.

INTERVENTIONS FOCUSING ON FAMILIES AND THE SOCIAL CULTURAL ENVIRONMENT

PARENT-CHILD INTERACTION THERAPY

PCIT is a behavioral intervention, with stated objectives of decreasing a child's disruptive behavior and improving parenting skills and attachment. PCIT is founded on social learning principles, along with behavioral and developmental principles. It was designed for children between 2 and 8 years of age with some type of externalizing disorders (Eyberg & Robinson, 1983; Hembree-Kigin & McNeil, 1995). The underlying model is that of a parent-training program in which the way a parent interacts with his or her child is modified, which results in child behavior problems diminishing and leads to more positive parenting (Borrego & Urquiza, 1998). PCIT is unique in that both the parent and child are together within the treatment sessions and it uses live and individualized therapist coaching. This coaching is geared toward changing dysfunctional aspects of the interaction within the parent-child relationship. Treatment is conducted in two phases with the first phase being child directed and focusing on enhancement of the parent-child relationship (Child-Directed Interaction or CDI). The second phase (Parent-Directed Interaction or PDI) focuses on improving child compliance and is parent-led. Treatment is approximately 20 sessions conducted within the therapist's office, with developmentally appropriate toys, such as blocks, cars, dollhouse, along with liberal positive reinforcement applied by the parent for child compliance.

What makes this parent-child play-based treatment most effective is that important shifts in cognition and attribution by both the parent and child occur along with a relationship shift. Along with the therapist coaching, in a way that allows for generalizability across all settings, PCIT serves to strengthen the parent-child relationship, which results in a closer attachment bond that supports a continuing healthy relationship. There are also additional parent-child play-based models with a similar format: Filial Therapy (Guerney, Guerney, & Andronico, 1999; VanFleet, 1994), and Child-Parent Relationship Therapy (Bratton & Landreth, 2005) that are empirically-based and relationship enhancing.

THERAPLAY

Theraplay (Munns, 2000) is a treatment ideally suited for the 0–3 population. The main goal is to enhance and/or repair a child's poor emotional bond, which then leads to a secure attachment with a primary caregiver. Without a strong, secure attachment with a significant caregiver, a child will more than likely develop future emotional, social, and behavioral problems unless it is remediated (Van Ijzendorn, Juffer, & Duyvesteyn, 1995; Webber-Stratton & Taylor, 2001). Theraplay also places an emphasis on physical contact with the child, along with activities that stimulate the vestibular system, allowing perception of body movement and balance. Activities, such as rocking, bouncing, and being carried, offer comfort through the repetitive motions that are conducted along with nursery rhymes.

Theraplay is a highly structured, caregiver-coached, short-term (12–16 weekly half-hour sessions) treatment. It is nonverbal, relying on touch, action, physical interaction, and fun. The therapist works with the caregiver to become more attuned to their child's needs, resulting in both caregiver's and young child's taking pleasure in one another. The child is able to become better self-regulated and attachment is strengthened (Gerhardt, 2004). Theraplay rests on attachment theory, the enhancement of attachment between caregiver and child. The treatment goes back to the stage at which the attachment process failed, and tries to replicate normal parenting for the child at that earlier stage. Regressive activities (e.g., feeding, rocking, caring for hurts) are used in order to guide the caregiver to become attuned to the child's cues and help regulate the child's emotional state, which results in the child's success in self-regulation (Booth, 2005). It has been used successfully with a wide spectrum of social, emotional, and behavioral difficulties, with minimal supplies and few toys.

RELATIONSHIP BETWEEN PLAY THERAPY AND YOUNG CHILDREN'S EDUCATIONAL ISSUES

Ray et al. (2001) found in a meta-analysis of play therapy studies, that there was a moderate to large effect size indicating that play interventions appear to be effective for children across treatment modalities (group, individual), age groups (3–16 years), gender, referred versus nonreferred populations, and treatment orientations (Reddy et al., 2005). Reddy et al. (2005) offer empirically-based, play-based programs and interventions that are useful in the treatment of children from preschool to adolescents. They report that through the review of the literature play interventions have shown success in treating children with disruptive behavior disorders, including ADHD, which results in improved social and academic functioning. Play-based interventions with children on the autism spectrum have resulted in significant improvement in symbolic play, social-emotional functioning, perceptual-fine motor skills, and language (Restal & Magill-Evans, 1994; Rogers & Lewis, 1989).

Young children's education can be negatively impacted by trauma. Its deleterious effects impact on cognition thereby affecting memory, school performance, and learning. Affect, interpersonal relations, impulse control, and behavior are also impacted and can in turn negatively impact on school performance and educational learning. Through play therapy and caregiver-child play-based interventions, young children can be taught more adaptive thoughts and behaviors, social skills, affect regulation, impulse control, mastery and coping skills, which in turn improve learning and educational performance (Russ, 2007). Play therapy has also been shown to be effective with preschoolers dealing with separation anxiety (Milos & Reiss, 1982).

PRIMARY PROJECT

The Primary Project is an on-site, school-based early detection and prevention program that helps to enhance social, emotional, behavioral, and learning skills. It also reduces social, emotional, and school adjustment difficulties in preschool through third-grade children. This developmentally appropriate, individual, child-led, nondirective, play-based approach is utilized as the vehicle to provide supportive treatment. The children receive an average of 25 forty-minute contacts over a 5- to 6-month span. The sessions are administered by a carefully selected and trained paraprofessional child associate, who is supervised regularly by school-based mental health professionals trained in play therapy (Wohl & Hightower, 2001). Introductory training is given over six to eight 2-hour sessions covering core components of relationship building, including unconditional positive regard, reflective listening, and verbal and nonverbal behaviors that enhance trust building.

Within the playroom the child communicates through play, in a nondirective way, with a warm, caring, and empathic child associate. Toys used in the playroom follow the selection used in Axline's child-centered approach (e.g., blocks, dolls, dollhouse, expressive arts materials, family figures).

Studies have shown that the Primary Project, an evidence-based program, is effective in helping children become more productive in school (Cowen, Hightower, Pedro-Carroll, Work, & Wyman, 1996; Nafpaktitis & Perlmutter, 1998).

MULTICULTURAL AND DIVERSITY ISSUES TO CONSIDER

IMPLICATIONS FOR CHILD CLINICIANS AND PLAY THERAPISTS

As the number of culturally diverse families increase, it is essential that child and play therapy clinicians become culturally competent in their work. Families should be asked about their upbringing and beliefs with regard to play, and what value play has for them. Negative cultural views or cultural beliefs about play can have serious impact on a clinician's success with use of play and play-based interventions and treatment. In addition, how children from diverse cultures play with peers or interact in groups can depend on cultural upbringing. It is important for the clinician to observe the child's play, without expectation or judgment, in light of the value the parent places on play and its cultural value (Drewes, 2005a).

It is important to remember that other cultures may not use verbal means for learning, but rather modeling and observational skills. In addition, a period of silence or a long pause may not signal a lack of attention or language problems, but perhaps a cultural norm for communication. Similarly, close physical proximity may be a necessity for communication and play, rather than an intrusion into the therapist's personal space (Drewes, 2005a). For example, a child from a Native American background may take a long pause in thinking through a response, as well as resent being touched, especially on the head or hair, by a nonfamilial adult, because in their culture only certain relatives may touch one's hair (Rettig, 2002).

We need to consider that play of children, regardless of type, may be strongly culturally defined, valued, interpreted, and perpetuated as a result of cultural practices. Similarly, Western theories of play as defined by Piaget, Smilansky, and others should be considered in light of the culture they were formulated in and may be inappropriate when applied to multicultural or indigenous peoples (Fleer, 1999).

CREATING A MULTICULTURAL PLAY ENVIRONMENT

Play materials, and the setting of the playroom, therapist office, and waiting area need to be set up in a way that respects and considers the cultural diversity of the clients served. Clinicians need not feel shy in asking their clients about their culture, use of metaphor, beliefs, religious views, and, in addition, asking about the family's country of origin and ancestry and languages spoken at home, as well as their view toward play.

Sensitivity is needed so that items are not included that might be taboo or considered bad luck or evil in the therapy space, office, and waiting area (Drewes, 2005b). Inclusion of paintings, prints, fabric, tapestries, rugs, and photos from various cultures that the clients come from should be considered

(Glover, 1999). Pottery, baskets, and cultural music in the waiting room make the environment inviting (Drewes, 2005b).

MULTICULTURAL PLAY THERAPY MATERIAL

Therapy supplies, such as arts and crafts materials, games, dolls, play foods, and books are now made reflecting multiculturalism and are available online (Drewes, 2005c). For example, given the nonverbal communication of emotionally-laden material that may be typical for many Asian cultures, it would be important to have available origami paper for folding, rice paper for painting, and red clay in the therapy room for the children to express themselves (Drewes, 2005b). Pencils, markers, crayons, and paints with multicultural skin tones are now available, which help children to draw and paint pictures more representative of their self-image and physical characteristics. Further, the inclusion of bibliotherapy books and stories that represent the different cultures served will help all children seen be able to learn and appreciate each other's diverse backgrounds as well as their own (Drewes, 2005b).

Dramatic play items, such as dishes, cooking utensils, and plastic food items representing various cultures are also available through catalogs and online (Drewes, 2005c). Empty tea boxes, tea tins, and plastic food containers from ethnic food can be obtained from stores within the communities of the families being served or by asking the families to bring in their empty containers. Dolls of all sizes, shapes, and ages can now be purchased in different skin colors as well as with realistic facial characteristics, realistic hair colors and styles, and culturally relevant clothing. Scraps of batik fabric, kente cloth, or other colorful woven fabric representative of various cultures can also be used as doll blankets, doll clothes, or even for dress-up (Drewes, 2005b).

The inclusion of a world globe or map in the therapy space can help spark discussion with the child and family about emigration, immigration and acculturation, or help clarify a family's point of origin (Martinez & Valdez, 1992).

It is also important that we as clinicians be able to be proactive in sharing our own cultural background, as well as in asking our clients about their multiculturalism in order to better meet their needs.

RECOMMENDATIONS FOR TRAINING IN EFFECTIVE USE OF PLAY THERAPY

In 1982, Dr. Charles Schaefer created the Association for Play Therapy (APT) for the purpose of promoting the healing powers of play, play therapy, and credentialed play therapists. Over the past 25 years the organization has grown to over 5,000 members, in 45 state branches as well as international organizations, who utilize play therapy in some form in their treatment of children and adolescents. Since 1990, national training and registration criteria were established by APT for earning the title of Registered Play Therapist (RPT), and Registered Play Therapist-Supervisor (RPT-S).

Qualifications for becoming an RPT or RPT-S include a master's or doctorate degree in a mental health field (e.g., clinical, counseling, school psychology), 2,000 hours of clinical experience, 500 hours of specific play therapy treatment experience along with 50 hours of direct supervision, a license or school certification, and 150 hours of play therapy specific training from an APT-approved provider. An RPT-S is required to have an additional 24 hours of supervision training and 5 years post-master's clinical experience. Annual renewal of the RPT and RPT-S is required, along with 36 hours of documented continuing education every 3 years, of which 18 hours are play therapy specific, and proof of a valid license or certification (see www.a4pt. org for more information regarding RPT & RPT-S training).

ETHICAL ISSUES PERTAINING TO PROVIDING PLAY THERAPY SERVICES

While many psychoanalysts and psychodynamically trained clinicians call themselves play therapists, the APT is the only organization to have a credentialing program that offers registration and use of the title Registered Play Therapist or Registered Play Therapist-Supervisor.

As is true for all clinical professionals, treating children and adolescents outside of one's scope of practice is unethical. Taking one course or a few workshops in play therapy does not make one a play therapist. And implementing some play-based techniques learned in a workshop without proper supervision and support can result in situations that could become harmful to the client. Therefore, a solid background in play therapy theory and practice, along with adequate supervision is necessary in order to competently practice play therapy.

In addition, the above-mentioned empirically- and evidence-based treatments require extensive training, application and supervision independently from obtaining the status of Registered Play Therapist. One should not attempt to utilize knowledge gained from training or workshops on these treatment methods without the proper qualified supervision.

OTHER PRACTICE ISSUES RELEVANT TO PLAY THERAPY

Play therapists today are subject to the same managed care mandates and professional best practices as other clinicians. Practitioners need to be aware of current research and trends, available evidence-based and empirically supported treatments, as well as aware of the underlying change mechanisms for effective treatment outcomes. Treatment goals and objectives need to be clearly delineated, along with a comprehensive assessment, in order to select the best treatment method to use. The play therapist must be familiar with the major theories of play therapy, have a clear understanding of play and how it is integrated into play therapy, the ways that play changes with development, and the many play materials and techniques currently available, along with the diverse ways these materials and techniques can be modified for a specific client and problem (Schaefer, 2003).

REFERENCES

Aber, J. L., Jones, S., & Cohen, J. (2000). The impact of poverty on the mental health and development of very young children. In C. H. Zeanah (Ed.), *Handbook of Infant Mental Health* (2nd ed., pp. 113–128). New York: Guilford Press.

Alfred Adler Institute. (2004). *Alfred Adler Institutes of San Francisco and Northwestern Washington.* Retrieved August 2007, from http://Ourworld.compuserve.com/homepages/hstein/homepage.htm.

Allan, J. (1988). *Inscapes of the child's world. Jungian counseling in schools and clinics.* Dallas, TX: Spring.

American Academy of Pediatrics (2006). *Clinical report: The importance of play in promoting healthy child development and maintaining strong parent-child bonds.* Elk Grove Village, IL: Author.

Association for Play Therapy. (2008). *About APT.* Retrieved May 1, 2008, from www.a4pt.org/ps.aboutapt.cfm?ID=1212.

Axline, V. M. (1969). *Play therapy* (rev. ed.). New York: Ballantine.

Axline, V. M., & Carmichael, L. (1947). *Play therapy: The inner dyanmics of childhood.* Boston: Houghton Mifflin.

Barnett, L. A. (1991). Developmental benefits of play for children. *Journal of Leisure Research, 27*(3), 245–263.

Beutler, L. E. (1979). Toward specific psychological therapies for specific conditions. *Journal of Consulting and Clinical Psychology, 47*, 882–897.

Bodrova, E., & Leong, D. J. (2003). *Educational Leadership, 60*(7), 50–53.

Booth, P. (2005). Current theraplay best practices: Focusing on attunement and regulation in play. *Theraplay Newsletter*, Summer, 5–8.

Borrego, J., & Urquiza, A. J. (1998). Importance of therapist use of social reinforcement with parents as a model for parent-child relationships: An example with parent-child interaction therapy. *Child and Family Behavior Therapy, 20*(4), 27–54.

Bratton, S., & Landreth, G. (2005). *Child parent relationship therapy: A 10 session filial therapy model.* New York: Brunner Routledge.

Bratton, S., Landreth, G., Kellam, T., & Blackard, S. (2006). *Child parent relationship therapy treatment manual: A 10 session filial therapy model for training parents.* New York: Brunner Routledge.

Bratton, S., & Ray, D. (2000). What the research shows about play therapy. *International Journal of Play Therapy, 9*(1), 47–88.

Bratton, S., Ray, D., Rhine, T., & Jones, L. (2005). The efficacy of play therapy with children: A meta-analysis review of treatment outcomes. *Professional Psychology: Research and Practice, 36*(4), 376–390.

Brody, V. (1997). *Dialogue of touch. Developmental play therapy.* New York: Aronson.

Carmichael, K. D. (2006). *Play therapy: An introduction.* Upper Saddle River, NJ: Pearson Prentice Hall.

Cowen, E. L., & Hightower, A. D. (1989). The primary mental health project: Thirty years after. *Prevention in Human Services, 6,* 225–257.

Cowen, E. L., Hightower, A. D., Pedro-Carroll, J. L., Work, W. C., & Wyman, P. A. (1996). *School-based prevention for children at risk: The Primary Mental Health Project.* Washington, DC: American Psychological Association.

Dinkmeyer, D. C., Dinkmeyer, J. D., & Sperry, L. (1987). *Adlerian counseling and psychotherapy* (2nd ed.). Columbus: Merrill.

Drewes, A. A. (2001). Play objects and play spaces. In A. A. Drewes, L. Carey, & C. Schaefer (Eds.), *School-based play therapy* (pp. 62–80). New York: Wiley.

Drewes, A. A. (2005a). Suggestions and research on multicultural play therapy. In E. Gil & A. A. Drewes (Eds.), *Cultural issues in play therapy* (pp. 72–95). New York: Guilford Press.

Drewes, A. A. (2005b). Play in selected cultures. Diversity and universality. In E. Gil & A. A. Drewes (Eds.), *Cultural issues in play therapy* (pp. 26–71). New York: Guilford Press.

Drewes, A. A. (2005c). Appendix. Multicultural play therapy resources. In E. Gil & A. A. Drewes (Eds.), *Cultural issues in play therapy* (pp. 195–206). New York: Guilford Press.

Drewes, A. A. (2006). Play-based interventions. *Journal of Early Childhood and Infant Psychology, 2,* 139–156.

Eyberg, S. (2004) The PCIT story—part one: The conceptual foundation of PCIT. *Parent-Child Interaction Therapy Newsletter, 1*(1), 1–2.

Eyberg, S., & Robinson, E. A. (1983). Conduct problem behavior: Standardization of a behavioral rating scale with adolescents. *Journal of Clinical Child Psychology, 12,* 347–354.

Fleer, M. (1999). Universal fantasy: The domination of Western theories of play. In E. Dau (Ed.), *Child's play: Revisiting play in early childhood settings* (pp. 67–79). London: Brookes.

Frances, A., Clarkin, J., & Perry, S. (1984). *Differential therapeutics in psychiatry.* New York: Brunner/Mazel.

Gerhardt, S. (2004). *Why love matters: How affection shapes a baby's brain.* New York: Brunner Routledge.

Gilliam, W. S. (2005). *Prekindergarteners left behind: Expulsion rates in state Prekindergarten program* (FCD Policy Brief Series No. 3). New York: Foundation for Child Development.

Gitlin-Weiner, K., Sandgrund, A., & Schaefer, C. (2000). *Play diagnosis and assessment.* New York: Wiley.

Glover, G. (1999). Multicultural considerations in group play therapy. In D. S. Sweeney & L. E. Homeyer (Eds.), *The handbook of group play therapy* (pp. 278–295). San Francisco: Jossey-Bass.

Guerney, B. (1969). Filial therapy: Description and rationale. In B. Guerney (Ed.), *Psycho-therapeutic agents: New roles for nonprofessionals, parents and teachers* (pp. 450–460). New York: Holt, Rhinehart & Wilson.

Guerney, B., Guerney, L., & Andronoico, M. (1999). Filial therapy. In C. Schaefer (Ed.), *The therapeutic use of child's play* (pp. 553–566). Northvale, NJ: Aronson.

Hembree-Kigin, T., & McNeil, C. B. (1995). *Parent-child interaction therapy.* New York: Plenum.

Howard-Jones, P. A., Taylor, J. R., & Sutton, L. (2002). The effect of play on the creativity of young children during subsequent activity. *Early Childhood Development and Care, 172*(4), 323–328.

Jernberg, A. M. (1979). *Theraplay: A new treatment for using structured play for problem children and their families.* Washington, DC: Jossey-Bass.

Jernberg, A. M., & Booth, P. B. (1999). *Theraplay: Helping parents and children build better relationships through attachment-based play* (2nd ed.). San Francisco: Jossey-Bass.

Johnson, L., McLeod, E., & Fall, M. (1997). Play therapy with labeled children in the schools. *Professional School Counseling, 1,* 31–34.

Kalff, D. (1980). *Sandplay: A psychotherapeutic approach to the psyche.* Santa Monica, CA: Sigo Press.

Kataoka, S., Zhang, L., & Wells, K. (2002). Unmet need for mental health care among U.S. children: Variation by ethnicity and insurance status. *American Journal of Psychiatry, 159*(9), 1548–1555.

Knell, S. M. (1993). *Cognitive-behavioral play therapy.* Northvale, NJ: Aronson.

Knell, S. M. (2003). Cognitive-behavioral play therapy. In C. Schaefer (Ed.), *Foundations of play therapy* (pp. 175–191). Hoboken, NJ: Wiley.

Knoblauch, P. J. (2001). Play therapy in a special education preschool. In A. A. Drewes, L. Carey, & C. Schaefer (Eds.), *School-based play therapy* (pp. 81–101). New York: Wiley.

Kot, S., Landreth, G., & Giordano, M. (1998). Intensive child-centered play therapy with child witnesses of domestic violence. *International Journal of Play Therapy, 7,* 17–36.

Kottman, T. (1995). *Partners in play: An Adlerian approach to play therapy.* Alexandria, VA: American Counseling Association.

Kottman, T. (2002). *Partners in play: An Adlerian approach to play therapy* (2nd ed.). Alexandria, VA: American Counseling Association.

Landreth, G. L. (1991). *Play therapy: The art of the relationship.* Muncie, IN: Accelerated Development.

Landreth, G. L. (2002). *Play therapy: The art of the relationship* (2nd ed.). New York: Brunner Routledge.

Lavigne, J. V., Gibbons, R. D., Christoffel, K. K., Arend, R., Rosenbaum, D., Binns, H., et al. (1996). Prevalence rates and correlates of psychiatric disorders among preschool children. *Journal of the American Academy of Child and Adolescent Psychiatry, 35,* 204–214.

Leblanc, M., & Ritchie, M. (2001). A meta-analysis of play therapy outcomes. *Counseling Psychology Quarterly, 14*(2), 149–163.

Lindaman, S. L., Booth, P. B., & Chambers, C. L. (2000). Assessing parent-child interactions with the Marschak Interaction Method (MIM). In K. Gitlin-Weiner,

A. Sandgrund, & C. Schaefer (Eds.), *Play diagnosis and assessment* (pp. 371–400). New York: Wiley.

Marschak, M. (1960). A method for evaluating child-parent interactions under controlled conditions. *Journal of Genetic Psychology, 97,* 3–22.

Martinez, K. J., & Valdez, D. M. (1992). Cultural considerations in play therapy with Hispanic children. In L. A. Vargas & J. D. Koss-Chioino (Eds.), *Working with culture* (pp. 85–102). San Francisco: Jossey-Bass.

Milos, M., & Reiss, S. (1982). Effects of three play conditions on separation anxiety in young children. *Journal of Consulting and Clinical Psychology, 50,* 389–395.

Munns, E. (Ed.), (2000). *Theraplay: Innovations in attachment enhancing play therapy.* Northvale, NJ: Aronson.

Nafpaktitis, M., & Perlmutter, B. F. (1998). School-based early mental health intervention with at-risk students. *School Psychology Review, 27,* 420–432.

O'Connor, K., & Ammen, S. (1997). *Play therapy treatment planning and interventions: The Ecosystemic model and workbook.* San Diego, CA: Academic Press.

Osofsky, J. D. (2004). *Trauma and the young child.* New York: Guilford Press.

Pellegrini, A. D., & Smith, P. K. (1998). The development of play during childhood: Forms and possible functions. *Child Psychology and Psychiatry, 3*(2), 51–57.

Perlmutter, D. (2006). *Raise a smarter child by kindergarten.* New York: Morgan Road.

Ray, D., Armstrong, S. A., Warren, S. E., & Balkin, R. S. (2005). Play therapy practices among elementary school counselors. *Professional School Counseling, 8*(4), 1096–2409.

Ray, D., Bratton, S., Rhine, T., & Jones, L. (2001). The effectiveness of play therapy: Responding to the critics. *International Journal of Play Therapy, 10,* 85–108.

Reddy, L. A., Files-Hall, T. M. & Schaefer, C. E. (2005). *Empirically based play interventions for children.* Washington, DC: American Psychological Association.

Restal, G., & Magill-Evans, J. (1994). Play and preschool children with autism. *American Journal of Occupational Therapy, 48*(2), 113–120.

Rettig, M. A. (2002). Cultural diversity and play from an ecological perspective. *Children and Schools, 24*(3), 189–199.

Ringel, J. S., & Sturm, R. (2001). National estimates of mental health utilization for children in 1998. *Journal of Behavioral Health Services and Research, 28*(3), 319–333.

Rogers, S., & Lewis, H. (1989). An effective day treatment model for young children with pervasive developmental disorders. *Journal of the American Academy of Child and Adolescent Psychiatry, 28*(2), 207–214.

Russ, S. W. (2004). *Play in child development and psychotherapy. Toward empirically supported practice.* Mahwah, NJ: Erlbaum.

Russ, S. W. (2007). Pretend play: A resource for children who are coping with stress and managing anxiety. *NYS Psychologist, XIX*(5), 13–17.

Schaefer, C. E. (1993). *The therapeutic powers of play.* Northvale, NJ: Aronson.

Schaefer, C. E. (2003). Prescriptive play therapy. In C. Schaefer (Ed.), *Foundations of play therapy* (pp. 306–320). Hoboken, NJ: Wiley.

Siegel, D. J. (1999). *The developing mind: How relationships and the brain interact or shape who we are.* New York: Guilford Press.

Slade, A. (1987). Quality of attachment and early symbolic play. *Developmental Psychology, 23*(1), 78–85.

Spinrad, T. L., Eisenberg, N., Harris, E., Hanish, L., Fabes, R. A., Kupanoff, K., et al. (2004). The relation of children's everyday nonsocial peer play behavior to their emotionality, regulation, and social functioning. *Developmental Psychology*: 40(1), 67–80.

Valentino, K., Cicchetti, D., Toth, S., & Rogosch, F. (2006). Mother-child play and emerging social behaviors among infants from maltreating families. *Developmental Psychology*, 42(3), 474–485.

VanFleet, R. (1994). *Filial therapy: Strengthening parent-child relationships through play.* Harrisburg, PA: Family Enhancement and Play Therapy Center.

Van Ijzendorn, M., Juffer, F., & Duyvesteyn, M. G. C. (1995) Breaking the intergenerational cycle of insecure attachment: A review of the effects of attachment-based interventions on maternal sensitivity and infant security. *Journal of Child Psychology and Psychiatry*, 36(2), 225–248.

Webber-Stratton, C., & Taylor, T. (2001). Nipping early risk factors in the bud: Preventing substance abuse, delinquency and violence in adolescence through interventions targeted at young children (0 to 8 years). *Prevention Science*, 2, 165–192.

Wohl, N., & Hightower, D. (2001). Primary Mental Health Project: A school-based prevention program. In A. A. Drewes, L. Carey, & C. Schaefer (Eds.), *School-based play therapy* (pp. 277–296). New York: Wiley.

PART III

EVIDENCE-BASED PRACTICE WITH YOUNG CHILDREN WITH SPECIAL NEEDS

CHAPTER 11

Self-Regulation

VIRGINIA SMITH HARVEY
and GAYLE L. MACKLEM

S ELF-REGULATION IS THE ability to suppress a preferred response in order to perform a less preferred response. This skill is evident when toddlers suppress the urge to be aggressive when angry, when preschoolers suppress self-interest and take turns, and when young children suppress the urge to play in order to complete challenging academic tasks. Throughout childhood and adolescence, developing self-regulation involves increasing planned, deliberate, and intentional inner and overt activity. It is associated with the maturation of the physical and neurological systems, and results in the ability to manage emotional reactions, control behavior, focus attention, learn, and participate in positive social interactions. Children must begin to develop self-regulation during the preschool years in order to learn and behave appropriately in school (Kopp, 2002; Thompson, 2002). Thus, fostering young children's ability to self-regulate is critically important.

Normally developing infants, toddlers, and young children systematically increase their ability to self-regulate affect, inhibit behavior, regulate arousal and attention, and monitor motivation. Bronson (2000) lists the milestones of self-regulation during the preschool period. In the emotional area, children become more able to control emotional intensity, talk about emotions, and recognize how others feel. Behaviorally, they improve their abilities to use language to regulate behavior and to control themselves in order to reach goals. Cognitively, children improve their ability to control attention and resist distractions. They increase self-regulation when they learn to evaluate their own performance and modify it accordingly.

Between infancy and the time the child enters formal schooling at age 5, the ability to self-regulate should be significantly transformed (Bronson, 2000; Brazelton & Sparrow, 2001; Knitzer, 2000; Shonkoff & Phillips, 2000). However, some children experience significant difficulty in developing self-regulatory strategies. Such difficulties create developmental anomalies and pose considerable challenges for parents and caregivers. When significant and unattended, disorders in self-regulation can persist across years and result in significant adjustment disorders. DeGangi, Breinbauer, Roosevelt, Porges, and Greenspan (2000) investigated the relationship of regulatory disorders during infancy with clinical status at age 3 and found that those who had significant difficulties with self-regulation as infants continued to do so as young children. In preschool and elementary school, well-adjusted children self-regulate emotions, behavior, motivation, attention, cognition, and context and consequently demonstrate personal, social, and academic adjustment. Those who cannot self-regulate face considerable challenges both inside and outside of school.

This chapter addresses the development of self-regulation in infants, toddlers, and children through age 8 years. Research related to physiological, neurological, temperamental, emotional, social, cognitive, attention, personality, and environmental etiologies for self-regulatory behaviors is presented, as well as implications of developmental anomalies and manifestations of multicultural issues. Methods to assess infants' and children's self-regulatory skills are presented, as are methods parents and caregivers can employ to facilitate children's self-regulatory strategies. The chapter concludes with a consideration of training needs and ethical considerations relevant to practitioners working in this area.

RESEARCH OVERVIEW

The topic of self-regulation has become recognized as key to our understanding of child development (Eisenberg, Champion, & Ma, 2004). The development of self-regulation involves all aspects of development, for it incorporates the dynamic interaction of genetic variables, neurology, early environment, later experiences, interpersonal interactions, and culture (Berger, Kofman, Livneh, & Henik, 2007; Davidson, 2001).

This topic has long been of considerable interest to research psychologists under the various terms of "self-regulation" (Kopp, 2002; Thompson, 1990, 1994), "effortful control" (Eisenberg, Champion et al., 2004; Kochanska & Knaack, 2003; Kochanska, Murray, & Harlan, 2000; Lieu, Eisenberg, & Reiser, 2004), and "executive function" (Zelazo, Muller, Frye, & Marcovitch, 2003). Among the domains over which young children gradually acquire self-control, *emotion regulation* has been of particular interest because of its relevance to social competence and psychological adjustment. The research on *effortful control* addresses increases in children's capacities for self-regulation and focusing attention throughout early and middle childhood, and is associated with social competence, emotion regulation, conscience development, psychological adjustment, social interactions, and academic success. Research on *executive function* focuses on problem-solving skills relative to self-regulation of both attention and cognitive processes. Thus, various abilities to self-regulate affect all areas of functioning.

PHYSIOLOGICAL ETIOLOGIES FOR SELF-REGULATORY BEHAVIORS

The first step is to master one's own physiology. During infancy and early childhood, children move from complete helplessness and dependency to "growing regulatory capacity" (Shonkoff & Phillips, 2000, p. 93). This process begins immediately after birth, when infants begin to regulate bodily functions by letting caretakers know what is needed and then responding to the help that is given. Major self-regulatory physiological milestones include regulation of arousal and sleep-wake cycles, maintaining a normal body temperature, learning to self-soothe, learning to quiet oneself after upset, feeding, sensory reactivity, and regulating mood (DeGangi et al., 2000). Newborns begin to adjust to wake and sleep cycles in the first few months of life as total sleep time decreases and sleep-awake cycles lengthen. To self-soothe and regulate their level of stimulation, typically developing infants suck on their thumbs or objects, and they learn to turn away from excessive stimulation by 3 months of age. Learning to regulate arousal (attention) depends on maturing brain areas. These functions are increasingly integrated as the infant develops neurologically, yet also interact with environmental experiences (Bronson, 2000). Infant crying peaks around 7 weeks of age and then declines, seemingly in response to physiological maturation manifested by more regulated sleep cycles and capacity for increased time between feedings. Crying also decreases when caretakers respond consistently and help infants acquire communication methods (gestures and vocalizations) that do not include crying.

Neurological development has considerable impact on the development of self-regulation. Different neurological areas develop at different rates and follow different pathways. As prefrontal areas of the brain develop, children increase their ability to control emotional expressions and are better able to inhibit behavior (Shonkoff & Phillips, 2000), yet these prefrontal areas of the brain do not reach full maturity until young adulthood. However, neurological development is not fixed. It is profoundly influenced by environmental factors such as nutrition and experience. There is considerable plasticity (changeability) in children's brains and interventions can have significant impact even on neurological structures (Davidson, Jackson, & Kalin, 2000; Davidson, Putnam, & Larson, 2000).

SELF-REGULATION AND TEMPERAMENT

Children differ in their thresholds for positive or negative emotions and ability to modulate behavior and intense feelings. Consequently, they have widely varied abilities in emotional self-regulation (Gross, 1998). These individual differences in reactivity, control mechanisms, and self-regulation are frequently defined as *temperament* (Rothbart, Ellis, Rueda, & Posner, 2003). Temperament can be considered relatively stable and enduring over time and place, as exemplified by trait theories such as the *Big Five Personality Dimensions* (openness to experience, conscientiousness, introversion, agreeableness, and neuroticism; McCrae & Costa, 2003). Temperament can alternatively be viewed as situational, as exemplified by social learning theories that emphasize personality changes in response to context (Bandura, 1986; Mischel & Shoda, 1995; Patrick & Middleton, 2002; Winne & Perry, 2000), or the integration of trait theories with contextual factors (McAdams & Pals, 2006). Although theories do not agree regarding temperament components, most include emotional processing, self-regulation, and activity level (Bussing, Lehninger, & Eyberg, 2006). Researchers in early childhood development have paid considerable attention to two components: effortful control and behavioral inhibition.

Effortful Control   Effortful control, the self-regulation portion of temperament, begins to be developed during the preschool period. It is a key player in emotion regulation (Eisenberg, Smith, Sadovsky, & Spinrad, 2004), develops in conjunction with attentional mechanisms (Calkins, 2004), and plays a role in the development of executive attention (Rothbart et al., 2003). Effortful control involves becoming aware of errors, planning, controlling attention, and inhibiting one's response to engage in an alternate response (Bunge & Wright, 2007). It is associated with the development of empathy, conscience, emotion modulation, interpersonal skills, and delaying gratification.

At the age of 3, children typically need adult support in managing their attention, feelings, and impulses. They show some effort at self-control (e.g., when required to wait their turn) but they easily lose control of their attention, feelings, and desires. In contrast, children age 4 typically and more consistently self-regulate their attention, thoughts, emotions, and impulses. They anticipate routines, follow rules with fewer reminders, more easily focus their attention on a task, and handle transitions more easily. They are increasingly capable of self-regulating their emotions and behavior, yet sometimes continue to need adult guidance (California Department of Education, 2008).

Children without adequate effortful control may either demonstrate externalizing behaviors or experience internalizing disorders. Children who externalize tend to be poor in inhibitory control and act impulsively (Eisenberg, Champion, et al., 2004). Children who exhibit high degrees of frustration can be less able to distract themselves from sources of frustration. Children who have problems voluntarily inhibiting behavior, or employing effortful control, are more likely to develop aggressive behavior (Dennis &

Brotman, 2003). In contrast, children with higher effortful control between ages 2 and 4 develop stronger consciences at 4½ years and fewer externalizing problems at 6 years (Kochanska & Knaack, 2003).

Behavioral Inhibition When some children encounter novel situations or unfamiliar individuals, they respond with behavioral inhibition or withdrawal. This is sometimes described as shyness or a lack of openness to experience, and can be a fairly stable temperamental characteristic. This trait is observable as early as the first year of life. Children who exhibit behavioral inhibition may experience a high level of negative emotions such as fear, anxiety, or distress (Fox, Henderson, Marshall, Nichols, & Ghera, 2005). They also may have lower levels of attentional and effortful control (Muris & Dietvorst, 2006). Children who become consistently behaviorally inhibited are at risk for developing anxiety or social withdrawal, possibly because they are biased to attend to negative emotions and find it difficult to self-distract from threatening stimuli (Fox et al.).

While the tendency toward behavioral inhibition appears to have some genetic and physiological components, environmental variables play a role. Overresponsive parents may prevent children from developing repertoires of appropriate self-regulation strategies because their children depend on them to provide external regulation (Fox & Calkins, 2003). Furthermore, different cultures variously value and devalue behavioral inhibition, and these values are reflected in parenting practices (Fox et al., 2005).

Neurological Foundations of Effortful Control and Behavioral Inhibition Neurological research suggests that there is a reciprocal influence between the areas of the brain that control reactivity and the areas associated with the effort a child exerts to attempt to control reactivity (Blair, 2003). To explain effortful control, research implicates both the ability to inhibit a pressing action tendency, and the ability to sustain attention. Inattention does not appear per se to be linked to effortful control (Dennis & Brotman, 2003).

Brass and Haggard (2007) investigated the neural correlates involved when a child intentionally tries to inhibit an act. A control structure in the fronto-median cortex allows the child to inhibit behavior or withhold actions that have been considered (Bunge & Wright, 2007). Different parts of the anterior cingulated cortex are involved in processing cognitive and emotional information. Actions of children are in turn monitored by other prefrontal areas. In young children, a broader area of these networks is activated than in older children, and these networks must be activated for a long time in order for the child to resolve conflicts. Rothbart and Rueda (2005) consider "effortful control as a central system for the successful development of cognitive and emotional regulation of children's behavior" (p. 183).

Infants who are described as showing negative emotional reactivity have a psychophysiological profile that includes high heart rate variability, high cortisol levels (Fox et al., 2005), heightened startle response, and right frontal electroencephalographic (EEG) asymmetry (Fox & Calkins. 2003). The reactivity, demonstrated in infancy by motor activities such as crying, converts to withdrawn behavior by middle childhood. This shift is in accord with the development of higher order cognitive activity (Pérez-Edgar & Fox, 2007).

It may be that children with left frontal EEG asymmetry are better able to employ attention and language strategies to self-regulate. A right frontal pattern of EEG asymmetry indicates that withdrawal is likely as well (Fox et al., 2005). Children with right frontal EEG asymmetry may be more susceptible to mild stress and react with avoidance and negative emotions. Henderson, Fox, and Rubin (2001) followed children whose mothers reported that they exhibited high rates of negative reactivity at 9 months of age until they were 4 years old. Boys whose mothers observed negative reactivity early on and who also had right frontal EEG asymmetry were rated as socially wary at 4 years. This was not found in the girls, who were more sociable at the same age.

Individual differences in behavioral inhibition are related to an overactive amygdala. This increased activity can lead to increased activity in several response systems, such as increased heart rate and secretion of the stress hormone cortisol. However, some children with these physiological reactions to their environments do not display behavioral inhibition. These children tended to have positive, growth-inducing experience with adults other than their parents (Fox et al., 2005). It is clear that biologically-based reactivity and regulation of emotions can be affected by environmental factors, particularly relationships (Blair, 2003).

SELF-REGULATION OF EMOTIONS

Eisenberg, Sadovsky, & Spinrad (2005) describe "emotion-related regulation" as the process children use to manage and modify emotions and emotion-related motivational and physiological states, as well as how they behaviorally express their emotions. Emotion-related regulation is accomplished through attentional and planning processes, inhibition or activation of behavior, and managing the external context. Behavioral responses to negative emotions involve: (1) active distraction (shifting attention away from the source of frustration by purposeful behaviors such as fantasy play, exploring the room, talking with a caregiver, singing or dancing); (2) focusing on the source of frustration in a constructive manner (speaking about, looking at, or trying to retrieve the desired object, or speaking about or trying to end the waiting period); (3) passive waiting (not engaging in any overt activity);

(4) information gathering (asking questions aimed at learning more about the waiting situation, but not aimed at changing the situation); and (5) comfort seeking. Use of *active* behavioral strategies when distressed results in better psychosocial adjustment (Grolnick, Bridges, & Connell, 1996).

Infants differ in the range of emotions they express, their ability to modulate their emotional states, and the fluidity with which they transition from one state to another. Emotions during infancy tend to be extreme because infants cannot regulate their responses (Shonkoff & Phillips, 2000). As they develop, infants expand their strategies and become increasingly able to stimulate themselves or quiet their own emotional states. By the time an infant is 3 months old, she can soothe herself by sucking, turning her head away from something that is bothering her, or signaling her caretaker by crying (Calkins, 2004). She progresses from thumb sucking, to hand clasping, to pushing away something or someone that is bothering her (Bronson, 2000). Caretakers help infants manage emotional distress by modeling and teaching self-comforting, help-seeking, and self-distraction strategies (Calkins). By the end of the first year of life, infants attend closely to the emotional signals of caretakers and respond accordingly, a process known as *social referencing* (Bronson; Shonkoff & Phillips).

Emotional responses are also context dependent. For example, at about a year of age the infant protests more upon his mother leaving when he is in unfamiliar settings, as compared with his response when he is in familiar settings (Fox, 1998). Toddlers most often use active engagement and distract themselves by refocusing their attention when attempting to modulate negative emotions (Silk, Shaw, Skuban, Oland, & Kovacs, 2006), yet vary strategies according to the context (Grolnick et al., 1996).

Young children can develop the ability to understand conflicting emotions by age 3, which affects their understanding of emotion by age 6. Understanding emotions is increased through participating in conversations with adults about causality, language, and positive interactions (Brown & Dunn, 1996). The ability to spontaneously name and recognize emotions predicts children's social functioning at school, including sociometric status, and peer victimization and rejection (Miller, Gouley, Seifer, Zakriski, Eguia, & Vergnani, 2005).

In later childhood, emotional regulation is critical to academic performance and motivation because strong negative emotions distract, interfere with learning, and cripple social interactions. Thus, Calkins (2004) points out that acquiring emotional self-regulation can be thought of as a "critical achievement of early childhood" (p. 38). Children who learn to appropriately manage their emotional response to frustration are able to successfully delay gratification, reduce focus on frustrating stimuli, refocus on soothing or more satisfactory stimuli, and appropriately persist when mildly frustrated when playing or learning.

Older children's emotional regulation is related to their knowledge of the range of emotions and language skills. Emotions affect, and are affected by, children's self-regulatory skills, feelings of competence, cognitive resources, and motivation (Linnenbrink & Pintrich, 2002; Pekrun, Goetz, Titz, & Perry, 2002). For example, school-age children often experience frustration and anger with challenging academic assignments. If they have not mastered emotional self-regulation, they are unlikely to persist enough to be successful.

Emotions can be negative and activating (anger, anxiety, shame), negative and deactivating (hopelessness and boredom), positive and activating (joy, hope, pride), or positive and deactivating (contentment, relief, relaxation). Negative activating emotions can be seriously detrimental to school success. During the early school years, heightened anxiety can result in school refusal and academic failure. Test anxiety affects one-third to one-half of children, and is particularly prevalent in certain subjects such as math even among gifted children (Betz, 1978). Excessive academic anxiety results in poor grades, presentations, and test performance (Beidel, Turner, & Taylor-Ferreira, 1999; Seipp, 1991). Negative deactivating emotions such as boredom and hopelessness can also be severely detrimental to academic motivation and achievement because they lead to superficial processing of information, increased irrelevant thoughts, and reduced attention to tasks. Boredom and frustration result when academic tasks are too easy or too difficult (Pekrun et al., 2002). Children who use strategies to control negative emotions such as frustration or fear can better deal with subsequent stress.

In addition to managing negative emotions, emotional self-regulation includes taking action to foster positive emotions. For example, a child who experiences frustration may manipulate the environment or engage in some activity that provides distraction or emotional relief. Strong learners deliberately induce and foster positive emotional states such as joy, pride, and hope as they learn. These positive activating emotions enhance academic motivation, improve achievement, facilitate the ability to think flexibly, and foster sophisticated learning strategies such as critical evaluation, elaboration, organization, metacognitive monitoring, intrinsic motivation, and the experience of "flow" (Csikszentmihalyi, 1990; Pekrun et al., 2002).

Neurological Foundations of Emotional Self-Regulation   Emotional self-regulation involves various prefrontal regions of the brain as well as subcortical limbic structures working as a complex circuit (Beauregard, Lévesque, & Bourgouin, 2001). This circuit includes the orbital frontal cortex, the amygdala, the anterior cingulate cortex, and their interconnections (Davidson, Putnam, et al., 2000). Each in turn influences various aspects of the child's experience.

The prefrontal cortex is involved with both positive and negative emotion and may also be involved in affective working memory, which allows a child to anticipate reward or punishment when concrete cues are absent. The orbital frontal cortex is activated when a child perceives increasingly intense anger in the environment. It also may suppress negative emotions and shorten the time they are experienced through connections with the amygdala (Davidson, Jackson, et al., 2000; Davidson, Putnam, et al., 2000).

The amygdala controls the ability to perceive danger, recognize threatening signals (visual and vocal expressions of fear and/or anger), detect ambiguity, and associate environmental events with reward or punishment (Davidson & Irwin, 1999; Davidson, Jackson et al., 2000). The amygdala quickly attends to threats in the environment because of extensive connections to brain regions that sense information, and is particularly and strongly triggered by others' facial expressions of threat or fear. The amygdala can also be triggered through both fear conditioning and bad feelings arising from watching a negative event (Davidson, Putnam, et al., 2000; Olsson & Phelps, 2007). Thus, one of the functions of the amygdala is to increase attention to potential threats (Phelps, 2006).

If the amygdala is overstimulated, the child may experience overwhelming negative emotion. If it is understimulated, the child may not respond to social signals to gain control (Davidson, Putnam, et al., 2000). Individual differences in the degree to which the amygdala is stimulated at baseline and after experiencing a negative event is related to speed of aversive conditioning, retrieval of negative emotional cues, and negative mood (Davidson, Jackson, et al., 2000). Thus, the action of the amygdala may explain individual differences between children in their reactions to punishment or negative incentives (Davidson & Irwin, 1999). Yet the action of the amygdala can be altered. The lateral prefrontal cortex region can inhibit the activity of the amygdala, so when a child employs the strategy of dealing with an emotional situation by thinking about it differently, amygdala activity is reduced (Phelps, 2006).

The anterior cingulated cortex is involved in cognitive control. It appears to be the error detection and correction system of the brain, and involves attention to regulate both cognition and emotion (Bush, Luu, & Posner, 2000). It seems to be activated when conflict is experienced (Botvinick, Braver, Barch, Carter, & Cohen, 2001). Brain mapping studies suggest that blood flow through the areas of the brain which are activated during emotional processing may be decreased when the child performs certain cognitive tasks demanding a high level of attention, and most likely vice versa. This suggests that cognitive activity (such as learning) is depressed when a child experiences intense fear or anxiety (Drevets & Raichle, 1998).

Children who withdraw when stressed may have extreme emotional reactivity. At the brain level, negative emotions such as anger and fear, and accompanying behaviors such as withdrawal, are associated with higher activation of the right frontal hemispheres. In contrast, positive emotions and approach behaviors are associated with higher activation of the left frontal hemispheres. Inhibited children with extremely fearful temperaments demonstrate a higher level of frontal EEG activity at baseline and a lower threshold for reactivity in the amygdala (Buss, Schumacheer, Dolski, Kalin, Goldsmith, & Davidson, 2003). Anxious children may have more than average difficulty disengaging their attention from threatening contexts or stimuli in their environment, resulting in yet greater wariness. Such children need to be taught to shift their attention away from these stimuli (Fox et al., 2005).

Other children react with intense frustration when prevented from doing something they desire. Infants with low frustration tolerance exhibit differences in activity level and attention control, in addition to differences in their abilities to control emotions and regulate physiologically. In the same way, toddlers who tend to act out demonstrate less ability to regulate emotions and poorer physiological regulation. These variations are reflected in differences in resting heart rate, which in turn predicts how well a child can regulate physiological responses to distress and frustration. Thus, there are clear links between negativity, resistance to control, activity level, and acting out behavior (Calkins, 2004).

Disorders in Emotional Self-Regulation   The relationship of children's (ages 4½ through 8½) negative emotion, regulation, and control with their internalizing and externalizing problem behaviors has been compared with behavioral observations and parent and teacher assessments. Children with externalizing problems are more prone to anger, impulsivity, and low regulation than either nondisordered children or children with internalizing problems. In contrast, children with internalizing symptoms are prone to sadness, low attentional regulation, and low impulsivity. The ability to shift attention away from a distressing stimulus is associated with decreased distress and lower levels of internalizing and externalizing symptomatology (Eisenberg et al., 2004). Therefore, children who direct sustained attention on sources of negative emotion may be using maladaptive strategies to regulate emotion, a tendency predictive of depressive symptoms and problem behavior (Silk et al., 2006).

SELF-REGULATION OF ATTENTION

Effortful control includes deliberate regulation of attention, which is critical for academic success. Duncan et al., (2007) analyzed six longitudinal data sets and found the strongest predictors of later academic achievement were school-entry math, reading, and attention skills, in that order. Internalizing, externalizing, and socializing behaviors were insignificant predictors, regardless of gender and socioeconomic background, even for children with high levels of problem behavior. Variations in the ability to self-regulate attention are due to individual differences in the abilities to attend to specific internal or external stimuli, concentrate for periods of time, shift attention, and inhibit thoughts or behavior.

Neurological Foundations of Attention Currently, significant research is focusing on defining the relationship between attention networks of the brain and self-regulation in children. Attention requires alerting, orienting, and executive control. *Alerting* comes into play when the child is attending closely to his or her environment or to specific stimuli in that environment. *Orienting* has to do with choosing what exactly to attend to among the choices that the child has available. *Executive control* has to do with checking and resolving any conflicts between various thoughts, feelings, and actions (Fan, McCandlis, Fossella, Flombaum & Posner, 2005; Rueda et al., 2004).

There is significant development of each of these three attentional networks after birth. Attention appears to control the activity levels of the child's sensory, cognitive, and emotional systems (Posner & Rothbart, 2007). This changes the affective experience of the child. At the neural level, orienting attention enhances whatever it may be that the child is paying attention to at the time. Thus, orienting skills help the child manage both positive and negative emotions and eventually these skills help the child control emotional experiences. In the first six months of life, as infants learn to focus their attention, they experience more positive feelings along with decreased distress. However, negative emotions interfere with infants' abilities to attend to and explore their environments.

Furthermore, maturation of the frontal lobes plays a critical role in children's ability to control attention, emotions, and behavior. Infants learn to attend and then disengage their attention from caretakers. Control of attention becomes more voluntary as the anterior cingulated cortex and the lateral prefrontal cortex mature, resulting in increased ability to flexibly focus and shift attention. This in turn contributes to improving self-regulation of thought, emotions, temperament, and behavior (Fox et al., 2005).

Disorders of Attention Regulation Attentional differences can be more extreme for some children. For example, attention deficit hyperactivity disorder (ADHD) is often cited in explanations of self-regulation failure. ADHD is a heterogeneous neurobiological disorder that has both genetic and environmental origins (Connor, 2002), and is manifested in problems alerting attention and executive control. Given the incidence of this disorder, there is significant interest in attempting to foster self-regulation by training attention or working memory, often depressed in those with ADHD.

Further, attention and emotion processes have overlapping neural circuitry in that attention can be used to regulate emotion, and emotions influence a child's ability to attend to stimuli under stress. Thus children who have weak attentional abilities, and who also cannot regulate anger easily, tend to exhibit behavior problems. Children who have weaknesses in attentional abilities, and who also have difficulty regulating sadness, are at risk for internalizing behaviors including depressive symptoms or shyness (Trentacosta & Izard, 2006).

SELF-REGULATION AND COGNITIVE AND ACADEMIC SKILLS

The rudiments of cognitive and academic self-regulatory strategies are evident at very early ages. Infants learn to anticipate and develop means-ends behavior, an early manifestation of executive functioning (Shonkoff & Phillips, 2000). The infant also begins to exhibit control over tasks that require working memory and inhibitory control at a simple level (Wolfe & Bell, 2007). Cognitive self-regulation milestones at the end of the first year include abilities to focus attention, note regularities and discrepancies, anticipate sequences, initiate behavior sequences, and recognize the impact of one's own actions on the environment (Bronson, 2000).

During the second year and beyond, toddlers and young children use private speech to guide their own behavior, an outward manifestation of cognitive self-regulation. However, use of private speech varies according to the immediate context. Children use more self-regulatory language when they are engaged in goal-directed task activities rather than during free play. They also display more private speech when adults provide an intermediate degree of external structure (Winsler & Diaz, 1995).

As they grow older, children who achieve academic success apply self-regulatory strategies when learning. Differences in self-regulation predict reading and math achievement in the early primary grades (Howse, Lange, Farran, & Boyles, 2003; NICHD Early Child Care Research Network, 2003). Even second grade children can profit from direct instruction in self-regulation processes in writing (Perry, 1998). Self-regulating children apply specific strategies as they learn, think about how well these strategies are working, and then modify strategies according to success (Peklaj, 2002; Schunk & Ertmer, 2000; Zeidner, Boekaerts, & Pintrich, 2000; Zimmerman, 2000). The ability to self-regulate is essential for academic success regardless of domain (Zimmerman, Bonner, & Kovach, 1996) and is, because of its link to sustained effort, more critical to success than innate ability (Ericsson & Charness, 1994). Successfully self-regulating children self-manage motivation. They select appropriate goals, accept responsibility for their own learning, select methods to maintain motivation, and modify future goals, attributions, emotions, and behaviors.

Models of cognitive self-regulation vary but agree that cognitive self-regulation involves at least three phases (Pintrich, 2000): (1) preparation (forethought, task definition, planning, goal setting, task analysis, strategy selection, selection of beliefs such as self-efficacy, outcome expectations, valuing, and intrinsic motivation); (2) performance (goal striving, strategy use, strategy monitoring and revision, self-monitoring, self-instruction, attention focus, self-recording, self-experimentation, and self-control); and (3) appraisal (self-reflection, self-judgment, performance evaluation, performance feedback, and self-satisfaction). The appraisal phase leads to subsequent modifications in preparation, performance and appraisal in a recurring cycle (Harvey & Chickie-Wolfe, 2007).

As they find success with their selection of learning strategies, children develop positive self-efficacy and attribution, link positive emotions to learning, improve their motivational states, and progress from lower to higher level cognitive skills. These experiences result in the development of cognitive self-regulation. Self-regulation is also fostered by positive beliefs about one's capabilities; experiencing and fostering positive emotions regarding learning; managing goal orientations; setting goals for learning; strategic planning; attending to and concentrating on instruction; using effective strategies to organize, code, and rehearse information to be remembered; employing metacognitive strategies to assess learning and the efficacy of learning strategies; monitoring performance; managing time effectively; establishing a congenial and productive work environment; using resources effectively; and seeking assistance when needed (Schunk & Ertmer, 2000; Zeidner et al., 2000).

Neurological Foundations of Cognitive Processes   Research identifies ages 3–5 as especially important for the development of executive function, since the ability to self-regulate attention and cognitive processes are tied to neurological development during this time period (Bunge & Zelazo, 2006; Diamond & Taylor, 1996; Gerstadt, Hong, & Diamond, 1994). Rueda, Posner, and Rothbart (2005) point out that functions connected to the executive attention network overlap with general functions including working memory, planning, switching, and inhibitory control. The neural network involved includes the anterior cingulated and lateral prefrontal areas of the brain, all of which undergo significant developmental changes throughout childhood. These changes are triggered by genetics and influenced by the child's environments. Children with ADHD often have deficits in working memory, inhibitory control, and short-term memory as compared to children who do not have the disorder (Stevens, Quittner, Zuckerman, & Moore 2002). These deficits have been attributed to impairment of the frontal lobe (Klingberg, Forssberg, & Westerberg, 2002).

Self-Regulation and Social Adjustment

Evidence exists that children's social and emotional competence (increased cooperation and decreased aggression) is integrally linked to the ability to learn and be successful at school (Knitzer, 2000; Raver, 2004). As children experience appropriate and supportive social interactions, they develop the self-regulation strategies essential to positive social interactions. For example, relative to younger children, typical 4-year-olds are more behaviorally competent, take greater active initiative in social interactions, have greater awareness of themselves and others, have increased self-control, and have more reciprocal social relationships. Socially competent kindergarteners demonstrate self-awareness, self-regulation, cooperation and responsibility, empathy and caring, social and emotional understanding, positive interactions with peers in the forms of friendship and group participation, learning initiative, and positive interactions and attachments to parents, teachers, and caregivers. However, individual differences are vast because children are so remarkably diverse in terms of temperament, personality, cognitive growth, language, and cultural background.

Social–emotional skills emerge through positive relationships with parents, teachers, and peers. These positive experiences are characterized by conversations, nurturance, guided instruction in taking responsibility and controlling oneself, being encouraged to be empathetic and understand other's feelings and needs, and direct instruction to self-regulate behavior both as an individual and as a responsible group member. Additionally, pretend, social, and structured play has a pivotal role in fostering the social-emotional development of young children (California Department of Education, 2008). High levels of pretend play are associated with enhanced emotional understanding for both boys and girls, and influence girls' emotional regulation and competence. For boys, physical play develops emotional competence (Linsey & Colwell, 2003).

Self-Regulation and Dysfunctional Social Adjustment   For a number of reasons, particular children may have greater than average difficulty with social skills, conflict management, emotional regulation, and making friends. For example, children with ADHD, those who have experienced abuse or conflict, and those with poor self-regulatory skills are at higher risk. Problem behaviors are evident in about 10% of young children and occur at a higher rate in children of low-income families (Webster-Stratton, Reid, & Hammond, (2001). Calkins,

Gill, Johnson, and Smith (1999) found that toddlers' emotional reactivity and emotion regulation were important predictors of conflict and cooperation.

Without intervention, emotional and behavioral problems in young children are less amenable to intervention after age 8 (Eron, 1990). Older children require more intensive and explicit training to learn the skills needed to be successful in their peer group. Thus, teaching young children skills such as how to play with others, recognize and express feelings, be friendly and talk to peers, exercise self-control, and negotiate conflict situations can result in fewer aggressive responses, more positive friendships, inclusion with prosocial peer groups, and increased school success.

ENVIRONMENTAL EFFECTS ON SELF-REGULATION

As should be evident from the foregoing discussion, self-regulation develops in a dynamic system in which every factor continually and mutually influences other factors in the system. Physiological, neurological, temperamental, attentional, behavioral, cognitive, social, familial, and instructional factors reciprocally and continuously interact (Bandura, 1986; Bronfenbrenner, 1979; Shapiro & Schwartz, 2000).

According to Zimmerman (2000), the ability to self-regulate is developed primarily through social cognition (Bandura, 1986). The child first observes self-regulation displayed by parents, siblings, peers, and teachers and thus discerns important strategies. The child imitates these strategies under the caretaker's guidance and thereby develops the ability to control emotions, motivation, cognitive strategies, and behavior under structured conditions. When the child is able to display these strategies independently, he or she has attained self-control. Eventually, the child generalizes these strategies to new and diverse situations, hopefully and eventually exhibiting self-regulation independently across settings.

Such learning usually occurs incidentally without direct or deliberate instruction. When a child is exposed to positive models, this can work quite well. However, many children are regularly exposed to models with poor self-control and self-regulation, such as a parent with poor emotional control or peers with poor self-regulatory skills. These experiences result in learning maladaptive strategies. Subsequently, interventions during which children are directly taught more productive and more appropriate self-regulatory strategies are required.

Parent-Child Relationships   Several familial factors influence children's learning skills in emotional self-regulation. First, they learn strategies through observational learning, modeling and social referencing. Second, parental practices regarding emotions, emotional expressiveness, and management of emotions affect the development of emotional self-regulation. Third, children's emotional self-regulation is affected by the familial emotional climate, parenting style, attachment relationships, family expressiveness, parental mental health, and parental marital relationship (Morris, Silk, Steinberg, Myers, & Robinson, 2007).

During infancy and the toddler years, infant–caregiver relationship quality sets the stage for the ability to self-regulate emotions. Children with predictable environments and secure attachments to their caregivers are much more likely to be able to soothe themselves when they encounter frustrations. For example, children who are able to trust that they will be fed and comforted in the future are more capable of dealing with hunger and temporary caregiver absence. They adopt self-soothing techniques such as employing a "lovey" to help themselves weather frustrating moments. In contrast, some children without predictable environments or a secure attachment to caregivers can be more difficult to soothe by an adult and also have more difficulty soothing themselves (Bronson, 2000; Calkins, 2004; Morris et al., 2007).

Thus, infants' self-regulation development is influenced by the quality of the environment they experience, including the quality of relationships with caregivers. Early efforts to regulate emotions, arousal, and behavior can be undermined by overstimulating environments, by inexperienced or inept caretakers who are fearful or angry, or an environment bereft of stimulation (Bronson, 2000). Parenting and the child's development of effortful control continue to be closely tied during the second year of life. Mothers who are characterized as using warm and supportive behaviors have children who can shift their attention away from sources of distress, delay gratification, and better control attention. Furthermore, the importance of parental responsiveness depends on the setting. Maternal oversolicitousness during unstructured free-play activities can result in shyness and social reticence. On the other hand, the emotionally dysregulated children whose mothers provide little guidance or control during a stressful teaching task can be more likely to be reticent (Rubin, Cheah, & Fox, 2001).

McDonough and Conway (2006) studied whether sensitive caregiving and temperament mutually influence each other during infancy, such that the children develop effective emotion regulation by the age of 3. In situations designed to elicit intense emotions, researchers observed the behaviors of mothers and their children at both 7 and 33 months of age. The children's emotional responses (anger, sadness, and joy intensities and the presence/ absence of regulation strategies) were coded on a second-by-second basis. Maternal sensitivity at 7 months predicted children's emotion regulation at 33 months. Infant temperament at 7 months did not. Children of more sensitive mothers were more likely to use behaviors to reduce negative emotions. They also took less time to demonstrate positive emotions following a challenge.

Stansbury and Sigman (2000) examined the emergence of strategies for emotion regulation in 3- and 4-year-olds. When frustrated, children tended to use the same strategies as their parents and even 3-year-old children could use a variety of methods to deal with frustration, including cognitive reappraisals. Thus, young children use strategies to organize emotional states before they can verbally report them.

Young children become aware of emotional states through direct conversations about emotions. An analysis of parent-child conversations about past emotional experiences with children age 4 years revealed that mothers talked more about emotions than did fathers. However, both fathers and mothers were more likely to discuss emotions when speaking with daughters than sons, particularly regarding sad events. They also were more likely to place emotional experiences in an interpersonal context (Fivush, Brotman, Buckner, & Goodman, 2000). Parental perceptions of and desire for change in their 6- to 11-year-old children's sadness behavior differs as a function of parent gender, child gender, and child age. Fathers indicate that they are likely to respond to their children's sadness with minimization, while mothers indicate that they are likely to respond with expressive encouragement and problem-focused strategies (Cassano, Perry-Parrish, & Zeman, 2007).

Negative familial experiences have been shown to have a detrimental impact on the development of self-regulatory skills. Interparental conflict appears to interact with young children's temperament and gender in impacting peer relationships. High parental conflict is associated with decreased peer interactions and increased problematic relations for preschoolers who have low effortful control, particularly for girls. In contrast, parental conflict is associated with increased peer interactions and decreased problematic relationships for children with high effortful control (David & Murphy, 2007). Maternal anger impacts preschoolers' emotional competence (situation knowledge, explanations of emotions, positive emotional expression during peer play, and emotional intensity) and social behavior (social initiations, positive social bids, anger-related reactions, and prosocial acts) (Garner & Estep, 2001). Increased maternal depression when their children were age 3 is associated with their children's emotional deregulation and behavior problems at age 4 (Hoffman, Crnic, & Baker, 2006). Apparently, depressed mothers can be less effective at providing the emotional, motivational, and technical scaffolding needed by children in order to develop the ability to self-regulate their emotional states.

Teacher–Child Relationships   The development of self-regulatory learning strategies is also affected by the social context provided by teachers and classmates, as well as by the learning environments created in classrooms and schools (Borkowski, Chan, & Muthukrishna, 2000; Puustinen & Pulkkinen, 2001).

Self-regulation is most likely learned in contexts that foster autonomy, and least likely learned in highly structured settings where goals are set by others, such as classrooms settings with teacher dictated learning experiences (Boekaerts & Niemivirta, 2000; Pintrich, 2000).

Although the quality of child–mother interactions is more strongly related to preschool and kindergarten adjustment than the quality of child–teacher relationships, children with secure relationships with their mothers also tend to have secure relationships with their teachers (Pianta, Nimetz, & Bennett, 1997). The quality of children's relationships with their early school teachers contributes to school adaptation (Birch & Ladd, 1997; Howes, 2000). For example, Pianta and Stuhlman (2004) assessed teacher–child relationships in preschool, kindergarten, and first grade. Moderate correlations among teachers' ratings of conflict, and slightly lower correlations among ratings of closeness, were found across years. Hierarchical regression analyses revealed that preschool and kindergarten teacher–child relationship quality can predict children's first-grade social and academic skills. Thus teacher–child relationships play pivotal roles in children's ability to acquire academic and social skills necessary for success. Similarly, Howes conducted a 5-year longitudinal study of children's teacher–child relationships and children's social-emotional competence. Children's second-grade social competence could be predicted by the social-emotional climate of their preschool experience, the degree to which they exhibited behavior problems at age 4, the quality of their relationship with their preschool teacher, and the quality of their relationship with their second-grade teacher. The effect has been found to extend for many years: conflicted or dependent kindergarten teacher–student relationships have been found to be predictive of eighth-grade academic outcomes, particularly for those children with behavior problems in kindergarten (Hamre & Pianta, 2001).

Cultural Context   There are wide variations among the environments that caretakers can provide for children utilizing different cultural practices, all of which can provide *good enough* enrichment for children (National Research Council and Institute of Medicine, 2000). There are many ways for caretakers to be successful in facilitating self-regulation in the children for whom they are responsible. As would be expected, environmental variables that affect the development of self-regulation naturally differ according to culture. Hofstede (1993) identified several dimensions on which cultures typically differ: the degree to which individuals act in their own interest as opposed to the interest of the group; the degree to which a culture attempts to reduce inequalities in power and wealth; the degree to which cultures deal with the unpredictability of the future by turning to technology, law, and/or religion; the extent to which traditionally male or female traits are valued; and, the degree to which the culture focuses on and plans for the future over short-term gains. Taking initiative and demonstrating other characteristics of self-regulation varies along each of these dimensions and is therefore valued to varying degrees in different cultures.

For example, many children are from cultures that discourage the level of assertiveness expected from middle-class English-speaking children. In mainland China, maternal reports of physical coercion, overprotection, shaming, directiveness, and encouragement of modesty were compared with teacher-rated reticent, solitary–passive, solitary–active, and modest behaviors. Nelson, Hart, Wu, Yang, Roper, and Jin (2006) found that: (1) maternal directiveness was correlated with reticent behavior in girls and negatively associated with solitary–passive behavior in boys; (2) for girls, maternal overprotection was positively related to both reticent behavior and solitary–passive behavior, and negatively related to modest behavior; (3) for girls, coercion was positively associated with solitary–active and reticent behavior; and (4) shaming was related to all forms of withdrawn behaviors in both sexes, and with modest behavior in boys. Chang, Schwartz, Dodge, and McBride-Chang (2003) studied the effects of harsh parenting on Chinese children's emotion regulation and aggression. They found that harsh parenting has both indirect and direct effects on child aggression through the mediation of child emotional regulation.

The relationship between African-American father involvement and pre-schoolers' school readiness has been investigated. Paternal involvement in child care and home-based educational activities are predicted by context and child attributes; father's involvement increased when they lived in the child's home, when a child was highly emotional, and when the fathers perceived a strong parenting alliance. In turn, paternal involvement was associated with higher levels of children's emotion regulation (Downer & Mendez, 2005).

ASSESSMENT

As indicated by the Temple University Forum on Preschool Assessment (Kochanoff, Hirsh-Pasek, Newcombe, & Weinraub, 2003), when working with preschoolers it is important to assess the constructs of emotional regulation, self-regulatory skills, prosocial and problem behaviors, and temperament. To facilitate prevention and early intervention, the forum recommended annual screenings for all preschoolers in programs such as Head Start, augmented by monthly monitoring for at-risk children and weekly monitoring for children exhibiting regulatory difficulties.

Valid approaches to assessment of self-regulation involve parents in the process, take setting and educational experiences into consideration, are culturally appropriate, reflect the child's developmental level, involve multiple sources of data over time, and utilize tools that are easy to understand and manage. Only those tools which specifically address self-regulation will be considered in this chapter; the reader is referred to Chapter 4 regarding the use of general developmental tools with infants and Chapter 12 for guidance in conducting functional assessment of behavior and the use of behavioral rating scales with preschoolers. In addition, the reader is referred to the Evaluation Data Coordination Project report (American Institutes for Research, 2004), the Temple University Forum on Preschool Assessment (Kochanoff et al., 2003), and Denham's work (2005a, 2005b) for more detailed information regarding tools for assessing self-regulation of young children.

There are a few tools of interest that are commercially available. These include the Brief Infant Toddler Social and Emotional Assessment (Briggs-Gowan & Carter, 2006) and the Social Skills Rating System (SSRS) (Gresham & Elliott, 1990), which has a self-control scale and is available in both preschool and elementary level forms. The Bayley Scales of Infant and Toddler Development (3rd ed.) (Bayley, 2005) has a social-emotional subtest, while the Devereux Early Childhood Assessment (LeBuffe & Naglieri, 2003) assesses protective factors and screens for social and emotional difficulties in children aged 2–5 years. The Vineland Social-Emotional Early Childhood Scales (Sparrow, Cicchetti, & Balla, 2006) identifies strengths and weakness in social and emotional behaviors and can be used for both planning and for monitoring children. Finally, the Social Competence and Behavior Evaluation, Preschool Edition (LaFreniere & Dumas, 1995) is a tool recommended by the Evaluation Data Coordination Project.

In addition, several research tools are in the public domain, including the Rothbart Child Behavior Questionnaire, Emotion Regulation Checklist, and Coping with Children's Negative Emotions Scale (Denham, 2005b). The Evaluation Data Coordination Project (American Institutes for Research, 2004) has a screening tool adaptation of Shields and Cicchetti's (1995) *Emotion Regulation Checklist* found at www.acf.hhs.gov/programs/opre/other_ resrch/eval_data/reports/common_constructs/com_ch5_low_inc_fam2. html. The Parenting Clinic provides evaluation tools and forms online at www.son.washington.edu/centers/parenting-clinic/forms.asp. A 12-item scale at this site, the Social Competence Scale (P-COMP), can be used to screen prosocial behavior.

FOSTERING THE DEVELOPMENT OF CHILDREN'S SELF-REGULATION

Efforts by parents and child care workers to facilitate young children's development of self-regulation are both necessary and important. Helping parents improve their relationships with their children and improve their skills at helping their children to self-regulate is important over the entire age range of childhood, but is particularly important when children are young (Karreman, van Tuijl, van Aken, & Dekovic, 2006). Colman, Hardy, Albert, Raffaelli, and Crockett (2006) looked at parent behavior in relation to their 4- and 5-year-old children and evaluated the children's ability to self-regulate 4 years later, at ages 8 and 9. Even when the children's initial abilities were taken into consideration, the degree to which children acquired the skills and abilities of self-regulation was related to parent practices.

Warm, responsive parenting early in life predicts later ability to regulate attention, emotions, and behavior. A meta-analysis of 41 studies looked at the relationships between parenting and self-regulation in preschoolers, and determined that caretaker discipline methods are related to children's self-regulation. Caretakers who set limits with mild to moderate power-assertion tactics while using clear guidance instructions have children who exhibit self-regulated behavior. Children's compliance was related to positive control. Although effect sizes between caretaker control and self-regulation were small, parental guidance, direct teaching, and encouragement were identified as related to higher levels of self-regulation in children (Karreman et al., 2006).

Both extreme overcontrol, and undercontrol, by parents has negative effects on children's development of self-regulation (Spinrad et al., 2006). Some parenting strategies that are negatively associated with the development of self-regulation in children include: inconsistent discipline practices (Garner, Spears & Garner, 2000); coercive, intrusive, restrictive, and over-stimulating parenting (Sonuga-Barke, Thompson, Abikoff, Klein, & Brotman, 2006); and harsh practices on the part of mothers (Chang et al., 2003). Therefore, parents need to learn how to control their own emotions while they learn to coach, instruct and model appropriate ways of responding in highly emotional contexts (Melnick & Hinshaw, 2000). Parental self-control may also need to be addressed in parent training efforts. Studies show that children with more extreme temperaments can learn to control negative traits when parents are effective and skilled (Knox, McHale, & Widon, 2004). It is most helpful when caretakers model a variety of strategies for their children to learn and imitate (Stansbury & Sigman, 2000). Passive regulation (such as waiting for help or continuing to focus on the distress source) is an inadequate strategy commonly used by children of depressed mothers. Active strategies such as self-distracting are most beneficial when needing to decrease negative affect (Silk et al., 2006).

Recent studies suggest specific training may be needed for particular children. Parents of more fearful children need to interact sensitively and use more subtle practices whereas children who are especially outgoing may need close and tight controls (Knox et al., 2004). Some children have challenging temperaments, while others have disabling conditions that interfere with the development of pre-requisite skills. Additionally, some families struggle with economic disadvantage and others experience family disruption, both of which can pose challenges for children in their development of self-regulation.

To some extent, high-quality preschool environments and positive child–teacher relationships can mitigate the effects of negative home experiences. Child development programs contribute to short- and long-term development and can ameliorate some effects of poverty (Schweinhart, 2001). Recent experimental studies, in which children and families have been randomly assigned to program and no-program groups, have provided unequivocal evidence of program effects. Additional quasi-experimental studies, in which the no-program group was not randomly assigned or in which there was no comparison group at all, cannot rule out alternative explanations, but they do provide additional evidence for the positive effect of preschool programs. Short-term studies provide guarded support for infant-toddler programs, and significant support for 4-year programs, in terms of the children's readiness to enter school and remain on grade. Most significantly, long-term studies have indicated that good preschool programs have far-reaching effects including improving high school graduation rates and reducing the criminal activity of participants.

FOSTERING EMOTIONAL SELF-REGULATION

Prevention and intervention programs that focus on teaching emotional knowledge and skills can foster children's emotional regulation. Ramona, Bisquerra, Agulló, Filella, and Soldevila (2005) advocate early childhood activities that focus on emotional awareness, emotional regulation, self-esteem, social competence, and life skills.

Emotion Labeling The ability to perceive and differentiate emotions is a necessary precursor for self-regulation of emotion, and the ability to spontaneously name and recognize emotions predicts children's social functioning at school (Miller et al., 2005). Nonetheless, many children have difficulty identifying their emotional states. Caregivers must help children learn to be able to identify when they feel angry, anxious, shameful, hopeless, bored, joyful, hopeful, proud, content, relieved, or relaxed. Through careful observation and listening to children's responses, adults can identify children's emotional states and engage children in conversations in which the emotions are labeled and processed. Bibliotherapy, or reading aloud books that describe emotional states with a child, can be a useful strategy to this end.

Promoting Alternative Strategies (PATHS; Greenberg, Kusché, & Mihalic, 1998) is an example of a *promising practices* curriculum designed to improve social competence and reduce problem behavior. Emotion labeling is a component of this curriculum (www.vanderbilt.edu/csefel/briefs/wwb21.pdf). Domitrovich, Cortes, and Greenberg (2007) implemented this curriculum in 10 preschool classrooms with children in Head Start. Participating children improved their emotion knowledge and were rated to have become more socially competent.

Reducing Behavior Withdrawal   Child care workers can help children reduce behavior withdrawal and overcome anxiety by (1) providing support to the (often anxious) parent; (2) ensuring that the child's school experience is warm, supportive, and positive; (3) employing systematic desensitization and helping the child progressively master the school environment; and (4) teaching the child to employ physiologically incompatible alternate responses to anxiety such as slow breathing, progressive muscle relaxation, and grounding. Children who are able to discuss emotion more easily and who can learn to understand emotional experiences are more skilled regulating their emotions when they are upset (Suveg, Zeman, Flannery-Schroeder, & Cassano, 2005). Unfortunately, the caretakers of anxious children appear to have difficulties helping their children develop these skills, and even demonstrate behaviors that are not helpful. They model anxiety in their own talk and behavior, and tend to interact with their children in overcontrolling ways that are intrusive and negative. They also model suppressing emotions by discouraging talking about negative experiences, using fewer words to describe emotions, and by appearing uncomfortable when conversations turn to emotional matters. Consequently, parent programs with this type of parent require helping them manage their own anxiety as well as their child's.

Facilitative parenting has been of considerable interest connected with behavioral inhibition. Reticent, shy, withdrawn, and anxious children need caretakers who provide opportunities to explore and who encourage exploring the environment (Rubin et al., 2001). Parents who encourage exploration and who provide opportunities to interact with peers help their wary children deal with inhibition that is driven by temperamental qualities. Parents who are intrusive in that they hover and remain close to their children when the context is not anxiety producing may actually exacerbate their child's wary tendencies. Parenting needs to change as inhibited children grow because sensitive support is needed early, but as soon as inhibited children are 2 years of age, parents need to encourage independence. Warm parenting can be insensitive, over-involved, over-directive, overly solicitous, and intrusive for children of 2 years of age and older if the child is easily upset, highly reactive, and difficult to soothe. In particular, a mother's oversolicitous behavior in nonstressful situations is associated with anxiety in her children. These inhibited children with over protective mothers are prevented from developing adequate coping strategies (Rubin et al.). Further, a recent study has found that when both mothers and fathers are very emotionally supportive, their children may be so protected from negative emotions that they do not learn how to handle them. McElwain, Halberstadt, and Volling (2007) found that when both parents provided a good deal of protective support, their youngsters did not understand their own emotions very well and experienced more upsets with peers.

Studies show that shyness is not predictive of internalizing symptoms or the development of social anxiety in those children who have the ability to shift their attention away from threatening stimuli (Fox et al., 2005). By gaining some mental distance from threatening or distressing situations the young child may be able to regain some cognitive flexibility. Engaging in play and creative activities when stressed is an adaptive emotion regulation strategy (Westphal & Bonanno, 2004).

Mindfulness practices are essentially attention enhancing techniques that have shown promise as clinical treatments for adult anxiety and depression. Semple, Reid, and Miller (2005) examined mindfulness training and found it could be successfully taught to 7- and 8-year-old children in order to increase their ability to focus attention and decrease their anxiety, although results suggested that clinical improvements were related to initial levels of attention.

Self-Monitoring   To foster emotional regulation, interventions should be designed such that children can take over and monitor their use. This is because the child must learn to determine when they are necessary and to ensure their ongoing use. Short-term interventions, such as deep breathing and progressive relaxation to control anxiety, deliberately focusing attention to induce flow, taking short breaks to reduce boredom, or breaking a task down into small bits to reduce frustration, require that children recognize emotional states on their own, determine that they need to employ a learned intervention because of a decrease in performance, perceive that their emotional state is contributing to their functioning, and actually use the intervention until the emotion dissipates. Ongoing interventions require long-term planning. These interventions, such as regular meditation or exercise, must be employed without the cue of discomfort, much like taking multivitamins without the cue of physical discomfort. To employ these measures on a preventative basis, children need to monitor implementation until habitual.

Once a strategy has been found to be effective under guided practice, adults can check with the child to ascertain whether and how well they continue to be practiced. Often, it is helpful for children to log their use on a calendar to facilitate remembering to use them. Initially, check-ins will need to be frequent, but as the child becomes autonomous, the frequency of the check-ins should be diminished. It can be very helpful for the adult to schedule a biannual preventative check-in to ensure that the child has transferred necessary skills to new situations.

FOSTERING ATTENTIONAL REGULATION

Because the function of attention is to affect other systems of the brain, and because attention networks overlap with brain areas involving intelligence, training attention is of particular interest. There is quite a bit of evidence that the executive attention network is strongly connected to academic learning (Posner & Rothbart, 2007). Attention skills, such as a child's ability to persist when working, increases engagement time (Duncan et al., 2007).

Sohlberg and Matee (2001) describe four approaches to managing attention impairments. These include attention process training, training children to use strategies, training the use of external aides, and providing environmental support. Tamm, McCandliss, Liang, Wigal, Posner, and Swanson (2006) additionally describe neurofeedback, cognitive training such as self-talk, and the use of electronic equipment to provide the child with a cue when he or she is off task. Kerns, Eso, and Thomson (1999) worked with school-age children from 5 to 10 years of age using materials designed to improve sustained, selective, alternating, and divided attention skills. This 8-week intervention called *Pay Attention!* affected selective attention and also improved academics, as rated by teachers.

Increasing numbers of preschoolers are being identified as children with ADHD. Nonpharmacological interventions for preschoolers with ADHD have been a priority among researchers for some time, albeit with limited success. Because these interventions do not wipe out the core symptoms, they are recommended primarily as part of multimodal treatments.

Unfortunately, parent training and family interventions used alone do not reduce ADHD symptoms (Sonuga-Barke et al., 2006), but parent-based therapies and interventions designed to assist caretakers manage the symptoms of their children with ADHD are considered "valuable" (Sonuga-Barke, Daley, Thompson, Laver-Bradbury, & Weeks, 2001), effective in the home setting (McGoey, Eckert, & DuPaul, 2002), empirically supported, and having a substantial evidence base (Chronis, Chacko, Fabiano, Wymbs, & Pelham, 2004).

Children with ADHD tend to become overstimulated when interacting in some contexts and may become aggressive, inflexible, and emotionally labile. They may disrupt group games, or they may withdraw when they are feeling out of control. These behaviors are indicative of difficulties with emotional regulation, lack of attentional flexibility, and poor behavioral inhibition. The more aggressive children with ADHD seem to be the most susceptible to emotional dysregulation. They are easily provoked, get stuck on the negative aspects of situations, have difficulty reinterpreting situations positively (reframing situations), and have particular difficulty *downregulating*. De-escalation is extremely difficult for this group and may be even more of a problem than their generally elevated intensity is for them. Disapproval from or control battles with mothers can contribute directly to their failed attempts to get back in control (Melnick & Hinshaw, 2000).

Recently, interventionists have focused on strengthening training for parents of children with ADHD. An example of this is the *New Forest Parenting Package*. This training package combines behavior management with parent training to help parents scaffold and motivate their children's attention and self-organization. Parents are taught to reduce negative interactions, utilize appropriate limit setting, and improve positive interactions. When compared to counseling and support or wait-listed children, as measured by parent support, there were strong effect sizes for the intervention group that were maintained for 15 weeks. However, the researchers pointed out that when parents who themselves exhibit symptoms of ADHD attempt to deliver the intervention it is "relatively less effective" (Sonuga-Barke et al., 2006, p. 149).

Reid, Trout, and Schwartz (2005) conducted a meta-analysis to determine the effectiveness of four self-regulation strategies for students with ADHD. These included self-monitoring, self-monitoring plus reinforcement, self-reinforcement, and self-management (self-evaluation). The researchers determined that training students to use self-regulation strategies produced large effects in on-task behavior, productivity/accuracy and also reduced interfering behaviors.

Fostering Self-Regulation of Behavior

Because the development of social skills is not automatic, intentional teaching is needed, particularly for at-risk children. Social-emotional curricula have been developed to teach young children prosocial skills and to decrease problem behavior. Social–emotional curricular programs are comprehensive, manualized curricula that focus on developing friendship skills, emotional recognition, problem-solving skills training, violence and substance abuse prevention, and social and anger coping skills training (Joseph & Strain, 2003). A typical curriculum covers basic conversation skills, self-assertiveness, and conflict solving (Ramona et al., 2005).

Parent training has been determined to be the most effective approach for reducing behavior problems in children (Keyes, 2004). Brotman, Gouley, Chesir-Teran, Dennis, Klein, and Shrout (2005) used the parent program (preschool version) of the *Incredible Years Series*, in addition to a classroom intervention with children, using the same program. Parents who participated were found to be less negative in their interactions with their children after training.

Webster-Stratton et al. (2001) explored interventions for children with conduct problems in the 4- to 8-year old age ranges. In particular, they investigated the efficacy of their own program, the *Incredible Years Dinosaur Social Skills and Problem Solving Curriculum*. They found that children demonstrated clinically significant positive behavior changes as measured by independent observations. Follow-up measures were also positive except for those children whose mothers continued to make critical statements and use physical force.

Shernoff and Kratochwill (2007) implemented the Incredible Years Classroom Management Program in four preschools. They identified some of the barriers involved in transferring interventions from a university setting or clinics to schools. Schools have time barriers, staff need to be trained, there can be mismatches of points of view between program developers and school staff, and school staff have difficulty persisting in their use of program strategies over the long run. This program is listed as receiving a *proven* rating on the Promising Practices Network (www.promisingpractices.net/program.asp?programid=134) because rigorous standards were utilized including control groups and researchers identified sizeable improvements in behavior and outcomes.

FOSTERING SELF-REGULATION IN COGNITIVE AND ACADEMIC SKILLS

To foster young children's development of self-regulation of cognitive and academic skills, it is best to provide an intermediate amount of structure and allow them to spontaneously engage in challenging goal-directed activities (Winsler & Diaz, 1995). When teaching children to self-regulate their behavior, it is helpful to follow the steps outlined by Harris, Friedlander, Saddler, Frizzelle, & Graham (2005), as follows:

1. An adult and the child discuss the importance of the behavior change.
2. The child agrees to use a new procedure to help improve behavior.
3. The child is taught to notate the occurrences of positive behavior.
4. The child graphs the number of positive occurrences.
5. Tally sheets are completed daily.

In addition, intervention programs for children at risk of developing conduct problems might effectively focus on promoting inhibitory skills (Dennis & Brotman, 2003).

Dysfunction in self-regulation relative to study skills can result from children's reactive rather than proactive approaches to studying, disinterest in a particular subject, or a trait such as a learning disability (Zimmerman, 2000). Self-regulation dysfunction often *appears* when a child moves from highly structured contexts to those that require increased self-regulation. Children can be assisted in developing these skills via daily or weekly coaching sessions during which the child reviews completed activities and applies the questions: "What did I do?", "How well did it work?", and "What do I need to change?" (Dawson & Guare, 2004). Interventions can be initiated by adults but their ongoing maintenance should be transferred to children as soon as possible to foster independence.

Self-regulatory skills are best taught in a problem-solving approach in which all concerned collaborate (Kampworth, 2006; Sheridan, Kratochwill, & Bergan, 1996). Children are included as *experts on themselves* to help collaboratively identify, analyze, and define a problem in specific, measurable, and behavioral terms. The group consider actions that have already been taken to address the problem; gather baseline data about the frequency, duration, and severity of the problem; identify time of day and conditions most associated with the problem; speculate on conditions most likely to alleviate the problem; identify consequences that are helping to maintain the behavior; enumerate consequences that could be used to reinforce improved perform-ance; assess other environmental variables such as expectations and attitudes of friends, peers, family members, and others; collaboratively agree upon the acceptable level of performance; and identify resources such as the child's strengths, materials, and supportive individuals. The team generates possible interventions, delineates positive and negative aspects of each possibility, determines implementation strategies, assigns responsibilities, and monitors progress. After a successful intervention has been implemented, strategies to promote generalization and child self-regulation are developed, implemented, and appraised.

TRAINING CONSIDERATIONS

Training needed in order to apply the information contained in this chapter must address both knowledge and skills in a number of areas. These include a foundational knowledge in psychology and education including pertinent theories, research, and techniques. An in-depth knowledge of infant and early childhood development regarding normally developing children, at-risk children, and children with disabilities, is necessary. In addition, knowledge and skills in the use of assessment tools and intervention programs described previously is important.

An additional critical area of expertise is behavioral consultation and collaboration, including those skills relevant to working with children and parents from diverse backgrounds. Given the importance of parental respon-siveness in developing self-regulation, practitioners will need expertise in working with parents such that they are able to provide parent education programs that effectively help parents provide a warm, responsive environment balancing overcontrol and undercontrol, and thereby help their children increase their self-regulation. The reader is referred to Chapters 7 and 8 for additional information regarding parent education.

Similarly, skill in providing consultation to school personnel is important. Just as is the case for parents, it is helpful when school personnel provide a warm, responsive environment balancing overcontrol and undercontrol. This environment will appropriately challenge children to learn self-control. In addition, educators should provide instruction in emotion labeling, self-monitoring self-talk, social skills, and attention regulation. Educators need to be able to identify areas of need, implement appropriate interventions with integrity, monitor their effectiveness, and modify them. Consultants can facilitate educators as they take these steps.

Finally, it is essential that practitioners have skills in designing, implementing, monitoring, and evaluating interventions provided both in educational settings and in the home. Coursework and field-based experiences must address the acquisition of skill in data-based decision-making in order to identify strengths and areas of needs in classrooms and for children and their families as well as monitor the outcomes of interventions.

ETHICAL CONSIDERATIONS

As in all areas, it is ethically important that professionals practice within their areas of expertise. This can be challenging in that many undergraduate and graduate programs provide insufficient preparation with preschool populations. In this eventuality, it is important for practitioners to attain appropriate supervision and mentoring to ensure that they attain the knowledge, skills, and expertise described above.

SUMMARY

Self-regulation is a broad and complex concept, not easily disaggregated. One reason for this is that there have been significant developments in our understanding of self-regulation in children that have not been widely disseminated. Another reason is that the ability to self regulate involves interactions between genes, physiology, neurology, and the environment. A third reason is the concept is so complex and affects all areas of development.

This chapter addressed the developing child's neurology, physiology, cognitive development, temperament, emotions, and attentional capacities, and how these factors interact with the child's environment as reflected in the child's relationship with her caregivers and her caregivers' management style, cultural beliefs, and competencies. Inadequacies in each of these variables can have consequences of poor preparation for formal schooling, poor social and emotional adjustment, and weak academic preparation and performance.

When there are concerns about young children, interventions can be considered at three levels. First, general parenting practices can be strengthened as long as cultural differences are respected. Second, child care agencies and preschools can provide climate and curricula to strengthen social-emotional learning and skills. Third, evidence-based interventions for children and their families can be tailored to meet specific needs.

Adequate self-regulation is essential for social, emotional, and academic adjustment. Although early intervention to strengthen a child's self-regulation is ideal, there is no doubt that attempts must be made whenever adults realize a child needs assistance in self-regulating or strengthening self-regulatory abilities. Improvement can occur at any age, and fostering youngsters' self-regulatory behaviors must be a priority.

REFERENCES

American Institutes for Research (2004). The Evaluation Data Coordination Project: Common constructs and measures across nine ACF studies and other key data collection efforts. Washington, DC: U.S. Department of Health & Human Services.

Bandura, A. (1986). Social foundations of thought and action: *A social cognition theory*. Englewood Cliffs, NJ: Prentice Hall.

Bayley, N. (2005). *Bayley Scales of Infant and Toddler Development* (3rd ed.). San Antonio, TX: Harcourt Assessment.

Beauregard, M., Lévesque, J., & Bourgouin, P. (2001). Neural correlates of conscious self-regulation of emotion. *Journal of Neuroscience, 21*(165), 1–6.

Beidel, D. C., Turner, S. M., & Taylor-Ferreira, J. C. (1999). Teaching study skills and test-taking strategies to elementary school students. *Behavior Modification, 23*, 630–646.

Berger, A., Kofman, O., Livneh, U., & Henik, A. (2007). Multidisciplinary perspectives on attention and the development of self-regulation. *Progress in Neurobiology, 82*, 256–286.

Betz, N. E. (1978). Prevalence, distribution, and correlates of math anxiety in college students. *Journal of Counseling Psychology, 25*, 441–448.

Birch, S. H., & Ladd, G. W. (1997). The teacher–child relationship and children's early school adjustment. *Journal of School Psychology, 35*, 61–79.

Blair, C. (2003). *Self-regulation and school readiness*. Champaign, IL: ERIC Clearinghouse on Elementary and Early Childhood Education. Eric Documentation ED477640.

Boekaerts, M., & Niemivirta, M. (2000). Self-regulated learning: Finding a balance between learning goals and ego-protective goals. In M. Boekaerts, P. R. Pintrich, & M. Zeidner (Eds.), *Handbook of self-regulation* (pp. 417–451). San Diego, CA: Academic Press.

Borkowski, J. G., Chan, L. K. S., & Muthukrishna, N. (2000). A process-oriented model of metacognition: Links between motivation and executive functioning. In G. Schraw & J. Impara (Eds.), *Issues in the measure of metacognition* (pp. 1–42). Lincoln, NE: Buros Institute of Mental Measurements, University of Nebraska.

Botvinick, M. M., Braver, T. S., Barch, D. M., Carter, C. S., & Cohen, J. D. (2001). Conflict monitoring and cognitive control. *Psychological Review, 108,* 624–652.

Brass, M., & Haggard, P. (2007). To do or not to do: The neural signature of self-control. *Journal of Neuroscience, 27,* 9141–9145.

Brazelton, T. B., & Sparrow, J. D. (2001). *Touchpoints three to six: Your child's emotional and behavioral development.* Cambridge, MA: Perseus.

Briggs-Gowan, M. J., & Carter, A. S. (2006). Social–emotional screening status in early childhood predicts elementary school outcomes. *Pediatrics, 121,* 957–962.

Bronfenbrenner, U. (1979). *The ecology of human development: Experiments by nature and design.* Cambridge, MA: Harvard University Press.

Bronson, M. B. (2000). *Self-regulation in early childhood: Nature and nurture.* New York: Guilford Press.

Brotman, L. M., Gouley, K. K., Chesir-Teran, D., Dennis, T., Klein, R. G., & Shrout. P. (2005). Prevention for preschoolers at high risk for conduct problems: Immediate outcomes on parenting practices and child social competence. *Journal of Clinical Child and Adolescent Psychology, 34,* 724–734.

Brown, J. R., & Dunn, J. (1996). Continuities in emotion understanding from three to six years. *Child Development, 67,* 789–802.

Bunge, S. A., & Wright, S. B. (2007). Neurodevelopmental changes in working memory and cognitive control. *Current Opinion in Neurobiology, 17,* 243–250.

Bunge, S. A., & Zelazo, P. D. (2006). A brain-based account of the development of rule use in childhood. *Current Directions in Psychological Science, 15,* 118–121.

Bush, G., Luu, P., & Posner, M. I. (2000). Cognitive and emotional influences in the anterior cingulate cortex. *Trends in Cognitive Science, 4,* 215–222.

Buss, K. A., Schumacheer, J. R., Dolski, I., Kalin, N. H., Goldsmith, H. H., & Davidson, R. J. (2003). Right frontal brain activity, cortisol, and withdrawal behavior in 6-month-old infants. *Behavioral Neuroscience, 117,* 11–20.

Bussing, R., Lehninger, F., & Eyberg, S. (2006). Difficult child temperament and attention-deficit/hyperactivity disorder in preschool children. *Infants & Young Children, 19,* 125–131.

California Department of Education (2008). *Preschool learning foundations.* Sacramento, CA: Author.

Calkins, S. D. (2004). Temperament and emotional regulation: Multiple models of early development. In M. Beauregard (Ed.), *Consciousness, emotional self-regulation and the brain* (pp. 35–60). Philadelphia, PA: John Benjamins.

Calkins, S. D., Gill, K. L., Johnson, M. C., & Smith, C. L. (1999). Emotional reactivity and emotional regulation strategies as predictors of social behavior with peers during toddlerhood. *Social Development, 8,* 310–334.

Cassano, M., Perry-Parrish, C., & Zeman, J. (2007). Influence of gender on parental socialization of children's sadness regulation. *Social Development, 16,* 210–231.

Chang, L., Schwartz, D., Dodge, K. A., & McBride-Chang, C. (2003). Harsh parenting in relation to child emotion regulation and aggression. *Journal of Family Psychology*, *17*, 598–606.

Chronis, A. M., Chacko, A., Fabiano, G. A., Wymbs, B. T., & Pelham.W. E. (2004). Enhancements to the behavioral parent training paradigm for families of children with ADHD. *Clinical Child and Family Psychology Review*, *7*, 1–27.

Colman, R. A., Hardy, S. A., Albert, M., Raffaelli, M., & Crockett, L. (2006). Early predictors of self-regulation in middle childhood. *Infant and Child Development*, *15*, 421–437.

Connor, D. (2002). Preschool attention deficit hyperactivity disorder: A review of prevalence, diagnosis, neurobiology, and stimulant treatment. *Journal of Developmental & Behavioral Pediatrics*, *23*(Suppl.) S1–S9.

Csikszentmihalyi, M. (1990). *Flow: The psychology of optimal experience*. New York: Harper.

David, K. M., & Murphy, B. C. (2007). Interparental conflict and preschoolers' peer relations: The moderating roles of temperament and gender. *Social Development*, *16*, 1–23.

Davidson, R. J. (2001). Toward a biology of personality and emotion. *Annals of the New York Academy of Sciences*, *935*, 191–207.

Davidson, R. J., & Irwin, W. (1999). The functional neuroanatomy of emotion and affective style. *Trends in Cognitive Sciences*, *3*, 11–21.

Davidson, R. J., Jackson, D. C., & Kalin, N. H. (2000). Emotion, plasticity, context and regulation: Perspectives from affective neuroscience. *Psychological Bulletin*, *126*, 890–909.

Davidson, R. J., Putnam, K. M., & Larson, C. L. (2000). Dysfunction in the neural circuitry of emotion regulation: A possible prelude to violence. *Science*, *289*, 591–594.

Dawson, P., & Guare, R. (2004). *Executive skills in children and adolescents: A practical guide to assessment and intervention*. New York: Guilford Press.

DeGangi, G. A., Breinbauer, C., Roosevelt, J. D., Porges, S., & Greenspan, S. (2000). Prediction of childhood problems at three years in children experiencing disorders of regulation during infancy. *Infant Mental Health Journal*, *21*, 156–175.

Denham, S. A. (2005a). *Assessing social–emotional development in children form a longitudinal perspective for the National Children's Study*. Columbus, OH: Battelle Memorial Institute. Retrieved June 29, 2008, from www.nationalchildrensstudy.gov/research/analytic_reports/.

Denham, S. A. (2005b). *Assessing social–emotional development in children from a longitudinal perspective for the National Children's Study*. Columbus, OH: Battelle Memorial Institute. Retrieved June 29, 2008, from www.nationalchildrensstudy.gov/research/analytic_reports.

Dennis, T. A., & Brotman, L. M. (2003). Effortful control, attention, and aggressive behavior in preschoolers at risk for conduct problems. *Annals of the New York Academy of Sciences*, *1008*, 1–4 (www.devereux.org/site/PageServer?pagename=deci_index).

Diamond, A., & Taylor, C. (1996). Development of an aspect of executive control: Development of the abilities to remember what I said and to "do as I say, not as I do." *Developmental Psychobiology, 29,* 315–334.

Domitrovich, C. E., Cortes, R. C., & Greenberg, M. T. (2007). Improving young children's social and emotional competence: A randomized trial of the preschool "PATHS" curriculum. *Journal of Primary Prevention, 28,* 67–91.

Downer, J. T., & Mendez, J. L. (2005). African–American father involvement and preschool children's school readiness. *Early Education and Development, 16,* 317–340.

Drevets, W. C., & Raichle, M. E. (1998). Reciprocal suppression of regional cerebral blood flow during emotional versus higher cognitive processes: Implications for interactions between emotion and cognition. *Cognition and Emotion, 12,* 353–385.

Duncan, G. J., Dowsett, C. J., Claessens, A., Magnuson, A., Huston, A. C., Klebanov, P., et al. (2007). School readiness and later achievement. *Developmental Psychology, 43,* 1428–1446.

Eisenberg, N., Champion, C., & Ma, Y. (2004). Emotion-related regulation: An emerging construct. *Merrill-Palmer Quarterly, 50,* 236–259.

Eisenberg, N., Sadovsky, A., & Spinrad, T. L. (2005). Associations of emotion-related regulation with language skills, emotion knowledge, and academic outcomes. *New Directions in Child and Adolescent Development, 109,* 109–118.

Eisenberg, N., Smith, C. L., Sadovsky, A., & Spinrad, T. L. (2004). Effortful control: Relations with emotion regulation, adjustment, and socialization in childhood. In R. F. Baumeister & K. D. Vohs (Eds.). *Handbook of self-regulation: Research, theory, and applications* (pp. 259–282). New York: Guilford Press.

Ericsson, K. A., & Charness, N. (1994). Expert performance: Its structure and acquisition. *American Psychologist, 49,* 725–747.

Eron, L. D. (1990). Understanding aggression. Bulletin of the International Society for Research on Aggression, *12,* 5–9.

Fan, J., McCandlis, B. D., Fossella, J., Flombaum, J. I., & Posner, M. I. (2005). The activation of attentional networks. *NeuroImage, 26,* 471–479.

Fivush, R., Brotman, M. A., Buckner, J. P., & Goodman, S. H. (2000). Gender differences in parent-child emotion narratives. *Sex Roles: A Journal of Research.* Retrieved February 16, 2007, from www.findarticles.com/p/articles/mi_m2294/is_2000_Feb/ai_63787373.

Fox, N. A. (1998). Critical importance of emotional development: Temperament and regulation of emotion in the first years of like. *Pediatrics, 102*(5 Suppl.), 1230–1235.

Fox, N. A., & Calkins, S. D. (2003). The development of self-control of emotion: Intrinsic and extrinsic influences. *Motivation and Emotion, 27,* 7–26.

Fox, N. A., Henderson, H. A., Marshall, P. J., Nichols, K. E., & Ghera, M. M. (2005). Behavioral inhibition: Linking biology and behavior within a developmental framework. *Annual Review of Psychology, 56,* 235–262.

Garner, P. W., Spears, F. M., & Garner, C. C. (2000). Emotion regulation in low-income preschoolers. *Social Development, 9,* 246–264.

Garner, P. W., & Estep, K. M. (2001). Emotional competence, emotion socialization, and young children's peer-related social competence. *Early Education and Development, 12,* 29–48.

Gerstadt, C., Hong, Y., & Diamond, A. (1994). The relationship between cognition and action: Performance of 3–7 year old children on a Stroop-like day–night test. *Cognition, 53,* 129–153.

Greenberg, M. T., Kusché, C., & Mihalic, S. F. (1998). *Promoting Alternative Thinking Strategies (PATHS): Blueprints for violence prevention* (book 10). Blueprints for Violence Prevention Series (D. S. Elliott, Series Editor). Boulder, CO: Center for the Study and Prevention of Violence, Institute of Behavioral Science, University of Colorado.

Gresham, F. M., & Elliott, S. N. (1990). *Social Skills Rating System* (SSRS). Circle Pines, MN: American Guidance Service.

Grolnick, W. S., Bridges, L. J., & Connell, J. P. (1996). Emotion regulation in two-year-olds: Strategies and emotional expression in four contexts. *Child Development, 67,* 928–941.

Gross, J. J. (1998). The emerging field of emotion regulation: An integrative review. *Review of General Psychology, 2,* 271–299.

Hamre, B. K., & Pianta, R. C. (2001). Early teacher–child relationships and the trajectory of children's school outcomes through eighth grade. *Child Development, 72,* 625–638.

Harris, K. R., Friedlander, B. D., Saddler, B., Frizzelle, R., & Graham, S. (2005). Self-monitoring of attention versus self-monitoring of academic performance: Effects among students with ADHD in the general education classroom. *Journal of Special Education, 39,* 145–156.

Harvey, V. S., & Chickie-Wolfe, L. A. (2007). *Fostering independent learning: Practical strategies to promote student success.* New York: Guilford Press.

Henderson, H. A., Fox, N. A., & Rubin, K. H. (2001). Temperamental contributions to social behavior: The moderating roles of frontal EEG asymmetry and gender. *Journal of the American Academy of Child and Adolescent Psychiatry, 40,* 68–74.

Hoffman, C., Crnic, K. A., & Baker, J. S. (2006). Maternal depression and parenting: Implications for children's emergent emotion regulation and behavioral functioning. *Parenting, 6,* 271–295.

Hofstede, G. (1993). Cultural constraints in management theories. *Academy of Management Executive, 7,* 81–90.

Howes, C. (2000). Social–emotional classroom climate in child care, child-teacher relationships and children's second grade peer relations. *Social Development, 9,* 191–204.

Howse, R. B., Lange, G., Farran, D. C., & Boyles, C. D. (2003). Motivation and self-regulation as predictors of achievement in economically disadvantaged young children. *Journal of Experimental Education, 71,* 151–174.

Joseph, G., & Strain, P. (2003). Comprehensive evidence-based social–emotional curricula for young children: An analysis of efficacious adoption potential. *TECSE, 23,* 65–76.

Kampworth, T. J. (2006). *Collaborative consultation in the schools: Effective practices for students with learning and behavior problems* (3rd ed.). Upper Saddle River, NJ: Merrill.

Karreman, A., van Tuijl, C., van Aken, M. A., & Dekovic, M. (2006). Parenting and self-regulation in preschoolers: A meta-analysis. *Infant and Child Development, 15,* 561–579.

Kerns, K. A., Eso, K., & Thomson, J. (1999). Investigation of a direct intervention for improving attention in young children with ADHD. *Developmental Neuropsychology, 16,* 273–295.

Keyes, A. W. (2004). *The enhanced effectiveness of parent education with an emotion socialization component.* Dissertation submitted to the University of New Orleans in partial fulfillment for the degree of doctor of philosophy in applied developmental psychology.

Klingberg, T., Forssberg, H., & Westerberg, H. (2002). Training of working memory in children with ADHD. *Journal of Clinical and Experimental Neuropsychology, 24,* 781–791.

Knitzer, J. (2000). Using mental health strategies to move the early childhood agenda and promote school readiness. New York: National Center for Children in Poverty.

Knox, S. S., McHale, S. M., & Widon, C. P. (Co-Chairs) (2004, October 4). *National children's study workshop: Measuring parenting from an epidemiologic perspective.* Meeting held at the Chevy Chase Pavilion, Washington, DC. Retrieved June 12, 2008 from http://www.nationalchildrensstudy.gov/research/workshops/Pages/measuring_parenting_102004.aspx

Kochanoff, A., Hirsh-Pasek, K., Newcombe, N., & Weinraub, M. (2003, January 30–31). *Using science to inform preschool assessment: A summary report of the Temple University forum on preschool assessment.* Center for Improving Resources in Children's Lives. Philadelphia, PA: Temple University. Retrieved June 25, 2008, from www.temple.edu/psychology/FacultyWebs/Weinraub/Links/CIRCL_PreSchAssesmt%20Final%20report%20paper%2010-03.pdf.

Kochanska, G., & Knaack, A. (2003). Effortful control as a personality characteristic of young children: Antecedents, correlates, and consequences. *Journal of Personality, 71,* 1087–1112.

Kochanska, G., Murray, K. T., & Harlan, E. T. (2000). Effortful control in early childhood: Continuity and change, antecedents, and implications for social development. *Developmental Psychology, 36,* 220–232.

Kopp, C. B. (2002). School readiness and regulatory processes. *Social Policy Report, 16,* 11.

LaFreniere, P. J., & Dumas, J. E. (1995). *The Social Competence and Behavior Evaluation–Preschool Edition.* Los Angeles: Western Psychological Services.

LeBuffe, P. A., & Naglieri, J. A. (2003). *Devereux Early Childhood Assessment Clinical Form* (DECA-C). Lewisville, NC: Kaplan Press.

Lieu, J., Eisenberg, N., & Reiser, M. (2004). Preschoolers' effortful control and negative emotionality, immediate reactions to disappointment, and quality of social functioning. *Journal of Experimental Child Psychology, 89,* 298–313.

Linnenbrink, E. A., & Pintrich, P. R. (2002). Achievement goal theory and affect: An asymmetrical bi-directional model. *Educational Psychologist, 37,* 69–78.

Linsey, E. W., & Colwell, M. J. (2003). Preschoolers' emotional competence: Links to pretend and physical play. *Child Study Journal, 33,* 39–52.

McAdams, D. P., & Pals, J. L. (2006). A new big five: Fundamental principles for an integrative science of personality. *American Psychologist, 61*, 204–217.

McCrae, R. R., & Costa, P. T. (2003). *Personality in adulthood: A five-factor theory perspective* (2nd ed.). New York: Guilford Press.

McDonough, S. C., & Conway, A. (2006, June). *Longitudinal predictors of emotion regulation from infancy to preschool.* Paper presented at the annual meeting of the XVth Biennial International Conference on Infant Studies, Westin Miyako, Kyoto, Japan. Retrieved September 27, 2007, from www.allacademic.com/meta/p94335_index.html.

McElwain, N. L., Halberstadt, A. G., & Volling, B. L. (2007). Mother- and father-reported reactions to children's negative emotions: Relations to young children's emotional understanding and friendship quality. *Child Development, 78*, 1407–1425.

McGoey, K. E., Eckert, T. L., & DuPaul, G. J. (2002). Early intervention for preschool-age children with ADHD. *Journal of Emotional and Behavioral Disorders, 10*, 14–28.

Melnick, S. H., & Hinshaw, S. P. (2000). Emotion regulation and parenting in AD/HD and comparison boys: Linkages with social behaviors and peer preference. *Journal of Abnormal Child Psychology, 28*, 73–86.

Miller, A. L., Gouley, K. K., Seifer, R., Zakriski, A., Eguia, M., & Vergnani, M. (2005). Emotion knowledge skills in low-income elementary school children: Associations with social status and peer experiences. *Social Development, 14*, 637–651.

Mischel, W., & Shoda, Y. (1995). A cognitive-affective system theory of personality: Reconceptualizing situations, dispositions, dynamics, and invariance in personality structure. *Psychological Review, 102*, 246–268.

Morris, A. S., Silk, J. S., Steinberg, L., Myers, S. S., & Robinson, L. R. (2007). The role of the family context in the development of emotion regulation. *Social Development, 16*, 361–388.

Muris, P., & Dietvorst, R. (2006). Underlying personality characteristics of behavioral inhibition in children. *Child Psychiatry and Human Development, 36*, 437–445.

National Research Council and Institute of Medicine (2000). From neurons to neighborhoods: The science of early childhood development. In J. P. Shonkoff & D. A. Phillips (Eds.) *Board on Children, Youth, and Families, Commission on Behavioral and Social Sciences and Education* (pp. 93–123). Washington, DC: National Academy Press.

Nelson, L. J., Hart, C. H., Wu, B., Yang, C., Roper, S. O., & Jin, S. (2006). Relations between Chinese mothers' parenting practices and social withdrawal in early childhood. *International Journal of Behavioral Development, 30*, 261–271.

NICHD Early Child Care Research Network (2003). Do children's attention processes mediate family predictors and school readiness? *Developmental Psychology, 39*, 581–593.

Olsson, A., & Phelps, E. A. (2007). Social learning of fear. *Nature Neuroscience, 10*, 1095–1102.

Patrick, H., & Middleton, M. J. (2002). Turning the kaleidoscope: What we see when self-regulated learning is viewed with a qualitative lens. *Educational Psychologist, 37*, 27–39.

Peklaj, C. (2002). Differences in students' self-regulated learning according to their achievement and sex. *Studia Psychologica, 44*, 29–43.

Pekrun, R., Goetz, T., Titz, W., & Perry, R. P. (2002). Academic emotions in students' self-regulated learning and achievement. *Educational Psychologist, 37*, 91–105.

Pérez-Edgar, K., & Fox, N. A. (2007). Temperamental contributions to children's performance and emotion-word processing task: A behavioral and electrophysiological study. *Brain and Cognition, 65*, 22–35.

Perry, N. E. (1998). Young children's self-regulated learning and contexts that support it. *Journal of Educational Psychology, 90*, 715–729.

Phelps, E. A. (2006). Emotion and cognition: Insights from studies of the human amygdala. *Annual Review of Psychology, 57*, 27–53.

Pianta, R. C., & Stuhlman, M. W. (2004). Teacher-child relationships and children's success in the first years of school. *School Psychology Review, 33*, 444–458.

Pianta, R. C., Nimetz, S. L., & Bennett, E. (1997). Mother-child relationships, teacher–child relationships, and school outcomes in preschool and kindergarten. *Early Childhood Research Quarterly, 12*, 263–280.

Pintrich, P. R. (2000). The role of goal orientation in self-regulated learning. In M. Boekaerts, P. R. Pintrich, & M. Zeidner (Eds.), *Handbook of self-regulation* (pp. 451–502). San Diego, CA: Academic Press.

Posner, M. I., & Rothbart, M. K. (2007). Research on attention networks as a model for integration of psychological science. *Annual Review of Psychology, 58*, 1–23.

Puustinen, M., & Pulkkinen, L. (2001). Models of self-regulated learning: A review. *Scandinavian Journal of Educational Research, 45*, 269–286.

Ramona, R., Bisquerra, R., Agulló, M. J., Filella, G., & Soldevila, A. (2005). An emotional curriculum proposal for early childhood education. *Cultura y Educación, 17*, 5–17.

Raver, C. C. (2004). Placing emotional self-regulation in sociocultural and socio-economic contexts. *Child Development, 75*, 346–353.

Reid, R., Trout, A. L., & Schwartz, M. (2005). Self-regulation interventions for children with attention deficit/hyperactivity disorder. *Council for Children, 71*, 361–377.

Rothbart, M. K., Ellis, L. K., Rueda, M. R., & Posner, M. I. (2003). Developing mechanisms of temperamental effortful control. *Journal of Personality, 71*, 1113–1143.

Rothbart, M. K., & Rueda, M. R. (2005). The development of effortful control. In U. Mayr, E. Awh, & S. W. Keele (Eds.), *Developing individuality in the human brain* (pp. 167–188). Washington, DC: American Psychological Association.

Rubin, K. H., Cheah, C. S., & Fox, N. (2001). Emotion regulation, parenting and display of social reticence in preschoolers. *Early Education & Development, 12*, 97–115.

Rueda, M. R., Fan, J., McCandliss, B. D., Halparin, J. D., Gruber, D. B., Lercari, L. P., & Posner, M. I. (2004). Development of attentional networks in children. *Neuropsychologia, 42*, 1029–1040.

Rueda, M. R., Posner, M. I., & Rothbart, M. K. (2005). The development of executive attention: Contributions to self-regulation. *Developmental Neuropsychology, 28*, 573–594.

Schunk, D. H., & Ertmer, P. A. (2000). Self-regulation and academic learning: Self-efficacy enhancing interventions. In M. Boekaerts, P. R. Pintrich, & M. Zeidner (Eds.), *Handbook of self-regulation* (pp. 631–649). San Diego, CA: Academic Press.

Schweinhart, L. J. (2001). Recent evidence on preschool programs. ERIC Digest (ED458046) ERIC Clearinghouse on Elementary and Early Childhood Education Champaign IL. Retrieved from www.ericdigests.org/2002-2/preschool.htm.

Seipp, B. (1991). Anxiety and academic performance. *Anxiety Research, 4,* 27–41.

Semple, R. J., Reid, E. F., & Miller, L. (2005). Treating anxiety with mindfulness. *Journal of Cognitive Psychotherapy, 19,* 379–392.

Shapiro, S. L., & Schwartz, G. E. (2000). The role of intention in self-regulation: Toward intentional systemic mindfulness. In M. Boekaerts, P. R. Pintrich, & M. Zeidner (Eds.), *Handbook of self-regulation* (pp. 255–273). San Diego, CA: Academic Press.

Sheridan, S. M., Kratochwill, T. R., & Bergan, J. R. (1996). *Conjoint behavioral consultation: A procedural manual.* New York: Plenum Press.

Shernoff, E. S., & Kratochwill, T. R. (2007). Transporting an evidence-based classroom management program for preschoolers with disruptive behavior problems to a school. *School Psychology Quarterly, 22,* 449–472.

Shields, A., & Cicchetti, D. (1995). *The development of an emotion regulation assessment battery: Reliability and validity among at-risk grade-school children.* Paper presented at the Society for Research in Child Development. Indianapolis, IN.

Shonkoff, J. P., & Phillips, D. A. (Eds.). (2000). *From neurons to neighborhoods: The science of early childhood development.* Committee on Integrating the Science of Early Childhood Development, National Research Council and Institute of Medicine. Washington, DC: National Academy Press.

Silk, J. S., Shaw, D. S., Skuban, E. M., Oland, A. A., & Kovacs, M. (2006). Emotion regulation strategies in offspring of childhood-onset depressed mothers. *Journal of Child Psychology and Psychiatry, 47,* 69–78.

Sohlberg, M. M., & Matee, C. A. (2001). Improving attention and managing attentional problems. *Annuals of the New York Academy of Sciences, 931,* 359–375.

Sonuga-Barke, E. J., Daley, D., Thompson, M., Laver-Bradbury, C., & Weeks, A. (2001). Parent-based therapies for preschool attention-deficit/hyperactivity disorder: A randomized, controlled trial with a community sample. *Journal of the American Academy of Child & Adolescent Psychiatry, 40,* 402–408.

Sonuga-Barke, E. J., Thompson, M., Abikoff, H., Klein, R., & Brotman, L. M. (2006). Nonpharmacological interventions for preschoolers with ADHD: The case for specialized parent training. *Infants & Young Children, 19,* 142–153.

Sparrow, S. S., Cicchetti, D. V., & Balla, D. A. (2006). *Vineland Adaptive Behavior Scales* (2nd ed.), *Teacher Rating Form* (Vineland II-TRF). Livonia, MN: Pearson Assessments.

Spinrad, T. L., Eisenberg, N., Cumberland, A., Fabes, R. A., Valiente, C., Shepard, S. A., et al. (2006). Relation of emotion-related regulation to children's social competence: A longitudinal study. *Emotion, 6,* 498–510.

Stansbury, K., & Sigman, M. (2000). Responses of preschoolers in two frustrating episodes: Emergence of emotion regulation. *Journal of Genetic Psychology, 161,* 182–202.

Stevens, J., Quittner, A. L., Zuckerman, J. B., & Moore, S. (2002). Behavioral inhibition, self regulation of motivation, and working memory in children with attention deficit hyperactivity disorder. *Developmental Neuropsychology, 21,* 117–139.

Suveg, C., Zeman, J., Flannery-Schroeder, E., & Cassano, M. (2005). Emotion social-ization in families of children with an anxiety disorder. *Journal of Abnormal Child Psychology, 33*, 145–155.

Tamm, L., McCandliss, B. D., Liang, B. A., Wigal, T. L., Posner, M. I., & Swanson, J. M. (2006). Can attention itself be trained? Attention training for children at-risk for ADHD. In K. McBurnett, L. Pfiffner, R. Schacher, & G. R. Elliott (Eds.), *Attention deficit/hyperactivity disorder: A 21st century perspective.* New York: Marcel Dekker.

Thompson, R. A. (1990). Emotion and self-regulation. In R. A. Thompson (Ed.), *Socioemotional development. Nebraska Symposium on Motivation* (vol. 36, pp. 383–483). Lincoln, NE: University of Nebraska Press.

Thompson, R. A. (1994). Emotion regulation: A theme in search of definition. In N. A. Fox (Ed.), The development of emotion regulation and dysregulation: Biological and behavioral aspects. *Monographs of the Society for Research in Child Development, 59* (2–3), 25–52.

Thompson, R. A. (2002). The roots of school readiness in social and emotional development. *The Kauffman Early Education Exchange, 1*, 8–29.

Trentacosta, C. J., & Izard, C. E. (2006). Children's emotional competence and attentional competence in early elementary school. *School Psychology Quarterly, 21*, 148–170.

Webster-Stratton, C., Reid, J., & Hammond, M. (2001). Social skills and problem-solving training for children with early-onset conduct problems: Who benefits? *Journal of Child Psychology and Psychiatry, 42*, 943–952.

Westphal, M., & Bonanno, G. A. (2004). Emotion self-regulation. In M. Beauregard. (Ed.). *Consciousness, emotional self-regulation and the brain* (pp. 1–33). Philadelphia, PA: John Benjamins.

Winne, P. H., & Perry, N. E. (2000). Measuring self-regulated learning. In M. Boekaerts, P. R. Pintrich, & M. Zeidner (Eds.), *Handbook of self-regulation* (pp. 531–566). San Diego, CA: Academic Press.

Winsler, A., & Diaz, R. M. (1995). Private speech in the classroom: The effects of activity type, presence of others, classroom context, and mixed-age grouping. *International Journal of Behavioral Development, 18*, 463–487.

Wolfe, C. D., & Bell, M. A. (2007). The integration of cognition and emotion during infancy and early childhood: Regulatory processes associated with the develop-ment of working memory. *Brain and Cognition, 65*, 3–13.

Zeidner, M., Boekaerts, M., & Pintrich, P. (2000). Self-regulation: Directions and challenges for future research. In M. Boekaerts, P. R. Pintrich, & M. Zeidner (Eds.), *Handbook of self-regulation* (pp. 749–768). San Diego, CA: Academic Press.

Zelazo, P. D., Muller, U., Frye, D., & Marcovitch, S. (2003). The development of executive function. *Monographs of the Society for Research in Child Development, 68*.

Zimmerman, B. J. (2000). Attaining self-regulation. In M. Boekaerts, P. R. Pintrich, & M. Zeidner (Eds.), *Handbook of self-regulation* (pp. 13–39). San Diego, CA: Academic Press.

Zimmerman, B. J., Bonner, S., & Kovach, R. (1996). *Developing self-regulated learners: Beyond achievement to self-efficacy.* Washington, DC: American Psychological Association.

CHAPTER 12

Attention Deficit
Hyperactivity Disorder

MARK D. TERJESEN and
ROBYN KURASAKI

ATTENTION DEFICIT HYPERACTIVITY disorder (ADHD) is a chronic behavior disorder typically characterized by abnormally high levels of impulsivity, inattention, and hyperactivity (Barkley, 1998; Colegrove, Homayounjam, Williams, & Hanken, 2001). Attention disorders, such as ADHD, have long been recognized with elementary school-age children and older individuals. Indeed, current conservative ADHD estimates are 3–7% of school-age children in the United States (American Psychiatric Association, 2000; Stevens, 2000). Prevalence studies of ADHD in young children, however, are only beginning to emerge. For example, international prevalence studies report ADHD estimates in young children from 2%, reported by primary care physicians, to 59%, reported by child psychiatric clinics (Connor, 2002).

Although the onset of ADHD symptoms typically occurs during the preschool years (Anastopoulos & Shelton, 2001), the diagnosis of ADHD often is made during middle childhood (e.g., 8 years of age) (Sonuga-Barke, Auerbach, Campbell, Daley, & Thompson, 2005). Currently, there appears to be somewhat of a shift, with a noticeable trend toward diagnosis and subsequent psychopharmacologic intervention in preschool-age children (Zito, Safer, dosRies, Gardner, Boles, & Lynch, 2000). Indeed, Wilens and colleagues (Wilens et al., 2002) assert that the symptom structure of preschool- and school-based ADHD are fairly equivalent in terms of symptomatic presentation, comorbidity, and social dysfunction.

Taking another point of view, Döpfner, Rothenberger, and Sonuga-Barke (2004) point out that differences may exist in early childhood ADHD. For example, in contrast to elementary school-aged presentation, factors associated with school failure (e.g., self-esteem and peer relationships) usually are not present. Consequently, symptoms may be more amenable to psychosocial treatment approaches (e.g., parent training). In the end, Döpfner and colleagues assert that research supports diagnosing ADHD during the preschool years, concluding that, "on the basis of this data one can start to make an argument about the utility of the preschool ADHD construct" (p. 130).

Despite the argued desirability of early childhood diagnosis, often attention disorders are not recognized as problematic until children reach school age. However, ADHD type behaviors observed at 30 months of age often are predictive of ADHD diagnoses at 5 and 8 years of age (Fewell & Mailman Center for Child Development, 1999). Further, there are links between early childhood ADHD symptoms and subsequent academic difficulties (e.g., emergent literacy and language skills) (Greenfield-Spira & Fischel, 2005). Therefore, identification of ADHD symptoms in early childhood may lead to intervention strategies that assist children in reaching their potential while also preventing the development of future difficulties.

This chapter provides an overview of ADHD difficulties in early childhood, with a focus toward evidence-based assessment and intervention. The issue of early childhood attention disorders is compared and contrasted with those of older children and recommendations for assessment and interventions are presented. ADHD difficulties within the family and cultural context are discussed in addition to training and ethical issues.

WHAT IS ADHD?

Traditionally, children with ADHD are thought to have difficulty in two major areas: hyperactivity-impulsivity and inattention (American Psychiatric Association [APA], 2000). More specifically, the difficulties include sustaining attention, completing assigned work, remaining in their seats, adhering to classroom rules, and refraining from interrupting (Netherton, Holmes, & Walker, 1999). However, some of these behaviors correspond more with school-based activities rather than early childhood activities. That is, some ADHD symptoms focus on behaviors that are apparent in school-age classrooms and not especially apparent in early childhood settings.

Often, diagnosticians rely on the *Diagnostic and Statistical Manual of Mental Disorders*, 4th edition, Text Revision (DSM-IV-TR; APA, 2000), which lists categories of mental disorders along with the criteria for diagnosis. The DSM-IV-TR describes three types of ADHD: ADHD, predominately inattentive type; ADHD, predominately hyperactive–impulsive type; and ADHD, combined type. Children presenting with symptoms consistent with ADHD inattentive type generally exhibit difficulty in organization, following directions, and sustaining attention. The child with hyperactive–impulsive ADHD is characterized by the aforementioned attentive difficulties, but in addition presents with hyperactive and impulsive behaviors (e.g., acting without thought, excessive fidgetiness) (Sagvolden, 1999). Finally, the combined type of ADHD incorporates the other two categories, as well as at least six symptoms associated with inattention, hyperactivity, and impulsivity (Reynolds & Gutkin, 1999). According to the DSM-IV-TR (APA), additional important factors regarding the diagnosis of ADHD are that symptoms should be present before age 7 and, in addition, there must be clear evidence of academic or social impairment. For a listing of the DSM-IV-TR symptoms of ADHD, see Figure 12.1.

Figure 12.1 DSM-IV Criteria for ADHD

I. **Either A or B:**
   A. Six or more of the following symptoms of inattention have been present for at least 6 months to a point that is disruptive and inappropriate for developmental level:
      1. Often does not give close attention to details or makes careless mistakes in schoolwork, work, or other activities.
      2. Often has trouble keeping attention on tasks or play activities.
      3. Often does not seem to listen when spoken to directly.
      4. Often does not follow instructions and fails to finish schoolwork, chores, or duties in the workplace (not due to oppositional behavior or failure to understand instructions).
      5. Often has trouble organizing activities.
      6. Often avoids, dislikes, or doesn't want to do things that take a lot of mental effort for a long period of time (such as schoolwork or homework).
      7. Often loses things needed for tasks and activities (e.g. toys, school assignments, pencils, books, or tools).
      8. Is often easily distracted.
      9. Often forgetful in daily activities.
   B. Six or more of the following symptoms of hyperactivity-impulsivity have been present for at least 6 months to an extent that is disruptive and inappropriate for developmental level:
      • Hyperactivity:
         1. Often fidgets with hands or feet or squirms in seat.
         2. Often gets up from seat when remaining in seat is expected.
         3. Often runs about or climbs when and where it is not appropriate (adolescents or adults may feel very restless).
         4. Often has trouble playing or enjoying leisure activities quietly.
         5. Is often "on the go" or often acts as if "driven by a motor."
         6. Often talks excessively.
      • Impulsiveness:
         1. Often blurts out answers before questions have been finished.
         2. Often has trouble waiting one's turn.
         3. Often interrupts or intrudes on others (e.g., butts into conversations or games).
II. **Some symptoms that cause impairment were present before age 7 years.**
III. **Some impairment from the symptoms is present in two or more settings (e.g. at school/work and at home).**
IV. **There must be clear evidence of significant impairment in social, school, or work functioning.**
V. **The symptoms do not happen only during the course of a pervasive developmental disorder, schizophrenia, or other psychotic disorder. The symptoms are not better accounted for by another mental disorder (e.g., mood disorder, anxiety disorder, dissociative disorder, or a personality disorder).**

Source: American Psychiatric Association (2000).

Hyperactivity–implusivity and inattention can be serious problems in early childhood. In a summary of the preschool ADHD literature, Sonuga-Barke and colleagues (2005) present three domains associated with preschool hyperactivity: (1) mild intellectual impairment, developmental deficits, and poor preacademic skills; (2) motor coordination difficulties; and (3) deficits in social skills and problems with close relationships. These areas warrant attention in assessment and become areas for intervention for young children with ADHD.

Considering inattentive behaviors, Connor (2002) summarizes research estimating up to 40% of young children present with problems of concern to their parents and preschool teachers. However, the majority of these concerns typically remit within 3–6 months. For young children with an ADHD designation, 48% retain that diagnosis later in childhood or adolescence. In the end, Connor maintains that although inattentiveness may interfere with development during this period, the associated behaviors by themselves may not indicate ADHD.

ISSUES IN DIAGNOSIS OF ADHD IN YOUNG CHILDREN

The diagnosis of ADHD and identification of inattentive and hyperactive–impulsive behavior in early childhood should stem from an evidence-based, empirically sound, multidimensional approach (Pelham, Fabiano, & Massetti, 2005). However, prior to discussing assessment of ADHD in early childhood, there are a number of important potential concerns to consider. These include the appropriateness of the current DSM-IV-TR diagnostic criteria for this age group, the context in which these behaviors occur, symptom overlap with other diagnoses, and referring agent expectations influencing reporting accuracy. Each concern is discussed in relation to the ADHD diagnosis.

Although DSM-IV-TR criteria assist in mental health diagnosis, in the case of young children with ADHD the criteria may also describe typical early childhood behaviors. For example, criteria include behaviors such as being easily distracted, fidgeting with hands or feet, or squirming in a seat. These behaviors are typical with young children and, therefore, may not necessarily reflect a clinical disorder. Thus, clinician awareness of age appropriate behavior is imperative in diagnosing young children (APA, 2000). Although many diagnostically pertinent behaviors are more-or-less typical, a related question or concern is at what level do behaviors become an area of clinical concern? In other words, accurate ADHD identification often requires infor-mation about the degree to which behaviors deviate from age-appropriate levels (Anastopoulos & Shelton, 2001).

Unfortunately, the DSM-IV-TR ADHD criteria were designed specifically for school-age children (i.e., 6- to 12-year-old) (Steinhoff et al., 2006) and not younger children. Steinhoff and colleagues suggest that the application of the DSM-IV criteria for young children is open to individual clinician "translation" of the symptoms. They offer as an example, "Often leaves seat in classroom," which may be translated to "Often leaves seat at the dinner table." However, caution is advised in making these translations since some criteria do not easily translate and caregiver expectations for young children are far from uniform. For example, in some homes young children are expected to sit at a table to eat, while in other homes this may not be an expectation. Therefore, even when modified, these criteria may not be appropriate in diagnosing ADHD.

Although there may be inherent difficulties in symptom translation, the necessity of translating or modifying ADHD symptoms for preschoolers is supported by research (Hardy et al., 2007). In fact, Hardy and colleagues determined a two-factor model of ADHD (inattention and hyperactivity–impulsivity) for preschoolers after removing some DSM-IV-TR symptoms (e.g., often leaves seat; easily distracted) (Hardy et al.). Given the research sorting through DSM-IV-TR ADHD symptoms, clinicians may want to use this classification system with caution with young children.

The context in which inattentive behaviors are seen as a problem is also a key diagnostic factor with young children. Indeed, these behaviors are only considered consistent with a disorder when they impair daily functioning in two or more settings (APA, 2000). This is an important consideration since Murray and colleagues (2007) find that preschool-age children's behaviors vary considerably across settings. As a consequence, they recommend collecting information from multiple informants to assist in obtaining a more complete perspective of young children's functioning in child care or educational settings.

A related question arises when young children do not attend an early childhood program and primarily reside in one environment, generally the home. In this case, clinicians may consider both the context in which children are exhibiting the behaviors as well as how individuals in that environment (e.g., parents, siblings, caregivers) respond to and influence the behaviors (APA, 2000). For example, if the behavior is considered impulsive, a clinician may wish to examine the child's context or related interaction activities. In addition, the clinician may also evaluate caregivers' responses to the child's behaviors. For example, if a young child attempts to leave a mildly frustrating task, and the caregiver provides redirection and assistance, does the child respond? This point highlights the importance of collecting information across situations as well as caregivers to glean a comprehensive understanding of the child's behavior.

Another difficulty in establishing an ADHD diagnosis is that there are overlaps with other childhood diagnoses. Recent research reports that 40% of children referred for ADHD have other disorders, for instance, mental retardation and learning disabilities (Kube, Petersen, & Palmer, 2002). Furthermore, Lewinsohn, Shankman, Gau, and Klein (2004) estimate that more than half of children with ADHD have at least one subthreshold disorder, and over half of the children diagnosed with ADHD have conduct disorder (CD) or oppositional defiant disorder (ODD) (APA, 2000). More specific to the preschool-age population, many studies indicate that preschool hyperactivity typically does not present in isolation. Instead, ADHD usually is accompanied by symptoms of other behavioral disorders (e.g., ODD) (DuPaul, McGoey, Eckert, & VanBrackle, 2001; Posner et al., 2007), and these oppositional and aggressive behaviors often are the reasons for initial referral (Keenan & Wakschlag, 2002).

Finally, although assessment is often associated with a diagnosis, diagnoses are not always necessary to inform and guide treatment with young children. That is, classification systems, for example, do not necessarily capture young children's difficulties. Therefore, a diagnosis may not be especially relevant; for example, parenting difficulties associated with child-rearing, leading to child mental health issues, would not be captured by diagnosing the child according to the DSM-IV-TR. Therefore, with young children, issues such as the need for treatment, case conceptualisation (e.g., background data, presenting concerns, underlying cause of problem), setting treatment goals and objectives, monitoring progress, and evaluating outcome are especially relevant (Pelham, Fabiano, & Massetti, 2005). Further, many ADHD symptoms that are diagnostic in nature (e.g., easily distracted, difficulty organizing) may not be seen by parents and teachers as important in contrast with other concerns (e.g., academic achievement, peer relationships) (Pelham et al.). In this regard, Tobin and colleagues (Tobin, Schneider, Reck, & Landau, 2008) posit that assessment should be geared to ADHD behaviors and their impact on preschool children's ability to function and perform routine and age-appropriate tasks, since these are often what initially led to the referral and require intervention.

ASSESSMENT OF ADHD IN EARLY CHILDHOOD

Interviews and Observations of Behavior

Interviews Structured, semistructured, and unstructured diagnostic interviews often are useful to the clinician in understanding the level of impairment and assisting in a differential diagnosis of ADHD. Structured and semistructured interviews are considered valid assessment tools (Goldman, Genel, Bezman, & Slanetz, 1998; Schwab-Stone et al., 1996; Shaffer et al., 1996), although Pelham and colleagues (2005) do not believe that they add much to validity beyond ratings scales, and most do not specifically consider the preschool-age child.

Recently, the Preschool Age Psychiatric Assessment (PAPA; Egger & Angold, 2004), a structured psychiatric assessment of the child's behavior accomplished by interviewing a parent, was constructed with consideration of young children (i.e., 2–5 years). The interview has a number of mandatory questions and probes and differentiates disruptive behaviors, oppositional defiant/conduct, hyperactivity–impulsivity, and inattention. This interview structure may capture some of the ADHD multidimensionality and hold important clinical implications for practitioners by providing one approach for better understanding symptom presentation. Although Pelham and colleagues (2005) report that structured diagnostic interviews do not provide any incremental validity or support for an ADHD diagnosis above ratings scales with school-age children, we argue that given the lack of assessment approaches for preschool-age children, structured interviews, supplemented by rating scales and direct observations, may be beneficial in that they allow clinicians to collect information on major areas of potential impairment.

Observation Direct of behavior is an integral part of developing an accurate diagnosis and may provide information that is unavailable through other assessment strategies (Anastopolous & Shelton, 2001). Observations may be less susceptible to bias than rating scales and prove useful in treatment planning (Sattler & Hoge, 2006). However, when conducting a behavioral observation, the context in which the behaviors occur requires thoughtful consideration. For example, one observational setting may require a greater need for the child to concentrate on a stimulus that is not interesting or even boring than another (Jensen & Cooper, 2002). Indeed, the observation location is also important to consider. Typically, observations of ADHD-type behaviors, for research purposes, occur in preschool settings and not the home environment (Stormont & Zentall, 1999). Given that ADHD crosses settings, practitioners may need to observe young children in their most natural environment, the home.

Utilizing specific ADHD observational measures, along with looking at how others respond to young children's behavior, may be important in helping understand ADHD and important influential factors. To this end, the ADHD Observational Rating Scale (ADHD-ORS; Deutscher & Fewell, 2001) was useful in predicting future (age 5 and 8) physician diagnosis of ADHD as well as future school difficulties. The ADHD-ORS was developed specifically as a screening tool of behaviors that are predictive of ADHD with 5- to 8-year-olds. Observers are asked to rate the child's behaviors on 12 items rated on a 5-point Likert scale with higher scores (4 or 5) reflective of ADHD-related behaviors. The authors report good interrater reliability, predictive validity, and describe support for a three-factor scale, including inattentiveness (e.g., acting before thinking, rushing), overactivity (e.g., always being on the go, moving fast), and impulsivity (e.g., not being able to wait and becoming easily frustrated), which match the three main ADHD attributes.

When conducting an observation of the child's ADHD behavior, a functional assessment of the behavior may be important. A functional assessment involves identifying (typically through observation) variables in the environment (e.g., attention from others, avoidance of undesirable tasks) that are maintaining/reinforcing the problem behavior (e.g., not attending to group activities). This knowledge may then be used to assist in the development of effective behavioral interventions. With younger children, Boyajian and colleagues conduct functional analysis procedures to develop interventions for preschool children at risk for ADHD (Boyajian, DuPaul, Wartel-Handler, Eckert, & McGoey, 2001). Results of the functional analysis indicate that these behaviors were maintained by environmental contingencies that were either positive (e.g., attention) or negative (e.g., escape). That is, the negative behaviors associated with ADHD symptoms continued to occur because they were reinforced by attention provided by the teacher. Conducting a functional assessment of the behavior may be an approach to consider in the assessment for ADHD, offering insight into the behavior as well as assisting the clinician in developing strategies with parents and teachers.

ASSESSMENT OF BEHAVIOR

Rating Scales   Although best practices stress the importance of a comprehensive evaluation, clinicians often rely heavily on behavior scales, which can be subjective in nature (Carey, 2002). The research on behavior rating scales suggests that over reliance at the expense of observation and clinical interviews may be due to their ease of use, and a lack of biological markers (i.e., genetic tests) for ADHD (Hermans, Williams, Lazzaro, Whitmont, Melkonian, & Gordon, 2004; Raz, 2004). Currently, a number of well-constructed and nationally standardized behavior rating scales aid clinicians in their assessment of ADHD (Terjesen & Sciutto, 2008). However, the majority of these measures focus on the assessment of ADHD in children above the age of five (Smith & Corkum, 2007), particularly problematic since ADHD symptoms typically emerge during the preschool years (Anastopoulos & Shelton, 2001).

Identifying specific ADHD preschool measures can guide clinicians. For preschoolers, among the measures used are the Conners' Rating Scales–Revised (CPRS-R; Conners, 1997), the Behavior Assessment System for Children-2 (BASC-2; Reynolds & Kamphaus, 2004), the Early Childhood Attention Deficit Disorders Evaluation Scale (ECADDES; McCarney, 1995), the Achenbach System of Empirically-Based Assessment, Child Behavior Checklist for Ages 1½–5 (CBCL; Achenbach & Rescorla, 2000), the Preschool Behavior Questionnaire (PBQ; Behar, 1977), the ADHD Rating Scale–IV (DuPaul, Power, Anastopoulos, & Reid, 1998), the Brown Attention Deficit Disorder Scales (Brown, 2001), the ACTeRS (Ullmann, Sleator, & Sprague, 2000), and the Home/School Situations Questionnaire (Barkley, 1990).

For assessing ADHD in preschoolers, there are a number of variables (e.g., psychometric properties, age range of items, gender norms) clinicians consider in selecting a rating scale (Smith & Corkum, 2007). Smith and Corkum and Terjesen and Sciutto (2008) contrasted behavior-rating scales for diagnosing preschoolers with ADHD, based on their psychometric characteristics and quality of guidelines for interpretation.

Given the aforementioned comordidity of ADHD, Terjesen and Sciutto (2008) recommend clinicians consider broad-band (e.g., assessing behavioral assets and deficits across a broad range of behavior) along with narrow-band (e.g., assessing a specific area of behavior, ADHD) instruments. The BASC-2, the Child Behavior Checklists, and the Conners' Rating Scales are broad-band rating scales that evaluate characteristics other than ADHD symptoms. In contrast, the narrow-band measures include the ADHD Rating Scale–IV, Brown Attention Deficit Disorder Scales, ACTeRS, and the ECADDES. The narrow-band may be preferable when only information about ADHD related symptoms is needed.

Overall, Terjesen and Sciutto (2008) report that the age ranges covered by scales vary considerably, with few (e.g., BASC-2, CBCL, ECADDES) providing norms across the entire 2- to 5-year range. For the most part, the standardization samples of the measures are generally of sufficient size and the respective test authors report attempts to be representative of the population in the United States. While all of the scales provide separate gender norms, only the BASC-2 provides clinical norms of an ADHD sample. One consistent concern among the scales noted by Terjesen and Sciutto was the tendency to pool normative data across the entire preschool-age range. That is, they did not provide separate normative data for each age within the preschool age, but rather pooled all of the preschool data together.

Not having separate norms for each age is problematic because the behavior of a 2-year-old may differ significantly from that of a 5-year-old. In some cases (i.e., ACTeRS, Brown ADD), normative information about preschool-age children was combined with information about older children (e.g., 4- to 11-year-olds). A problem inherent in pooling across age groups is that there is an assumption that the psychometric properties of the scale are consistent across children's development. While prior research (Connor, 2002; Sonuga-Barke et al., 2005) highlights developmental differences in patterns of impairment, why these differences exist is not clearly understood.

That is, are these differences in fact due to the different settings in which ADHD preschoolers versus adolescents reside (e.g., day care versus structured school setting), or are there differing patterns as a function of developmental level? Hinshaw (2002) argues that the lack of longitudinal investigations across the age span hinders an understanding of the severity of impairment with increasing age along with the mechanism of impairment. As such, measures that pool items across age groups may not provide useful information to the clinician.

The symptom description within the measure as well as the psychometric properties and logistics of the scale are all factors that may warrant consideration in selection of a measure of ADHD in early childhood (Smith & Corkum, 2007). Terjesen and Sciutto (2008) argue that the provision of separate inattention and hyperactivity-impulsivity scales may be important for making an accurate diagnosis of ADHD subtypes (e.g., hyperactive–impulsive; inattentive) as well as in treatment planning. Only the Child Behavior Checklist Ages 1½–5, from the ASEBA (Achenbach & Rescorla, 2000) fails to make this distinction, as this measure provides an attention problems scale but not an exclusively hyperactivity–impulsivity scale. Terjesen and Sciutto report that among the test manuals reviewed many provide sufficient evidence of reliability and validity for ages 5 and up; however, the manuals provide far less detail about psychometric data with preschoolers. As an example, some measures report internal consistency of the measure while others report test–retest reliability. These inconsistencies may provide a challenge for the clinician in choosing which measures are more psychometrically sound and appropriate for this age group or any age group for that matter. Furthermore, Terjesen and Sciutto recommend that because the scales used for diagnosing ADHD differ in terms of various special features (e.g., validity scales, clinical norms), clinicians should carefully and closely consider the match between the purpose of the assessment and the instrument used.

Academically Related, Sensory–Motor, Peers, and Family   With school-age children, much of the research links ADHD with specific academic work behavior. These issues also may warrant attention in early childhood. McClelland, Morrison, and Holmes (2000) report that work-related skills (e.g., following instructions and directions, compliance with teacher demands) seen in early childhood may serve as a precursor to subsequent academic success or failure. The clinician may wish to consider these factors when conducting an ADHD assessment.

Measures of sustained performance on an activity and vigilance tasks have become core components of an assessment protocol for school-age children with possible ADHD (Byrne, DeWolfe, & Bawden, 1998), but they have not been researched as much with the preschool-age population. These measures may serve as both a means to identify current ADHD behaviors in preschoolers (Smith & Corkum, 2007) as well as provide an opportunity to develop educational goals for the child and measure response-to-intervention. Attending behavior, as measured by a vigilance task, may impact the acquisition of concepts. Smith and Corkum report that the most commonly used measures of attention for preschool-age children by researchers were the Conners' Continuous Performance Test–Kiddie Version (KCPT; Conners, 2001) and the Gordon Diagnostic System (GDS; Gordon, 1996). These vigilance tasks assess a child's ability to demonstrate impulse control and maintain attention to a sequence of visual stimuli. Using a mouse, children respond by clicking whenever a target stimulus (e.g., picture or letter) appears. When children fail to respond to target stimuli (e.g., error of omission), this reflects inattention. In contrast, when they respond to nontarget stimuli, these errors of commission are thought to reflect impulsive tendencies.

The omission and commission variables discriminate between children with ADHD and normal controls (Losier, McGrath, & Klein, 1996). Smith and Corkum (2007) cite a number of studies that provide acceptable reliability and validity for these measures. Recently, the Pediatric Attention Disorders Diagnostic Screener (PADDS) has been used for screening ADHD symptoms in children ages 6–12. While not utilized at present with the preschool-age group, this measure integrates vigilance tasks with a structured interview and parent and teacher ratings and shows good reliability and validity (Reddy, Fumari, Pedigo, & Scott, 2008). This integrative approach may provide a model for how to conduct assessments with a younger age population.

Some children with ADHD may also have difficulties in the sensory motor area (Iwanaga, Ozawa, Kawasaki, & Tsuchida, 2006). Typically, sensory motor difficulties include over sensitivity or under reactivity to sensory stimulation (e.g., auditory, visual, tactile) and/or coordination (e.g., motor planning deficit) difficulties. While research with preschool-age children who demonstrate ADHD type behaviors seems limited, this area of functioning is still recommended for clinicians to consider in their evaluation of a child for a potential diagnosis of ADHD. Identification of possible strengths or weaknesses in this area may allow for effective educational recommendations. Among the measures in this area used for young children are the Miller Assessment for Preschoolers (Miller, 1988) and the Dean–Woodcock Neuropsychological Battery (Dean & Woodcock, 2003).

Peer relationships is another area that has been regularly examined in the ADHD literature, as there is a strong link between childhood ADHD and impaired peer relations (Hoza et al., 2005). Indeed, children whose problems persist tend not to see themselves as socially competent (Campbell, 1995). Therefore, clinicians often assess peer relationships as part of a multidimensional assessment. Focusing on peer relationships also may be meaningful for parents and teachers as this aspect of child functioning usually is meaningful and valued by them (Pelham et al., 2005). In terms of assessment, there are a number of approaches for measuring peer relations in early childhood. Among them are a sociometric/peer nomination approach (Balda, Punia, & Punia, 2002), rating scales of social behavior (Social Skills Rating System [SSRS]; Gresham & Elliott, 1990), and observational systems for behavior (Brotman, Gouley, & Chesir-Teran, 2005).

Finally, in terms of assessment, clinicians may wish to look at family dysfunction/discord as having a child with ADHD predisposes families to have more conflicts, increased stress, and increased marital discord (Hinshaw, 2002). A greater understanding of this area may assist in looking at any contributory factors towards the child's behavior as well as how this stress may interfere with accurate rating of behavior and follow-through of interventions.

CONSIDERATION OF CULTURE IN ASSESSMENT

Much like many areas of child behavior, culture can play a significant role in how symptoms present themselves and whether or not interventions for these behaviors are sought. Connor (2002) reports great variability in symptom presentation across cultures. The role of culture in understanding early childhood behavior may be a very complex process and may impact upon referral practices and adult perception of children's behavior. Multicultural issues, in conjunction with norming concerns (e.g., rating scales may not be particularly representative of all cultures), raise considerable assessment questions. Further, research with diverse preschool children is scant (Bain & Pelletier, 1999). Combined, these issues suggest concerns regarding the accuracy of identification of children of all ages with ADHD.

Regardless, among the factors to consider may be the variations in ratings of ADHD behavior as a function of culture. For example, a study in Hong Kong on rates of hyperactivity in children indicates prevalence rates twice as high as other studies (Ho, Leung, Luk, Taylor, Bacon-Shone, & Mak, 1996). The authors posit that, as a function of their culture, respondents may have a lower threshold for deviance and readily report ADHD-type behaviors. With regard to a cultural examination of preschool-age children, ADHD prevalence studies report prevalence rates of 18.2% in Colombia, South America (Pineda et al., 1999), 9.6% in Germany (Baumgaertel, Wolraich, & Dietrichm, 1995), and 5.2% in India (Bhatia, Nigam, Bohra, & Malik, 1991). Although there are variations in the rate of specific behaviors across cultures, the disorder presentation is considered valid and appropriate from both statistical and clinical perspectives (Bird, 2002). To be sure, interpretation of rating scale results, as indicated previously, needs to be made with caution and consideration of the normative base (Sattler & Hoge, 2006).

INTERVENTIONS FOR YOUNG CHILDREN WITH ADHD

The accurate identification and treatment of young children with ADHD is important for the prevention of problems in home, school, academic, and social domains (Posner et al., 2007). With more research in early identification and intervention, future prevention efforts may provide young children with or at risk for ADHD enhanced opportunities to achieve positive social-emotional and academic outcomes.

In their review of empirically supported interventions for school-age children and adolescents, Chambless and Ollendick (2001) report that parent training, behavioral, and multimodal interventions (e.g., stimulant medication, behavior modification) were efficacious treatments for children and adolescents with ADHD. Additional interventions used in the treatment of children ages 5–9 with ADHD include social skills training (Chronis, Jones, & Raggi, 2006) and psychopharmacology (Lerner & Wigal, 2008). However, the behavioral expectations, and educational demands of younger children by parents and teachers differ from those with school-age children (McGoey, DuPaul, Eckert, Volpe, & Brakle, 2005). Therefore, more studies with preschoolers are needed to build upon the existing research (Daly, Creed, Xanthopoulos, & Brown, 2007; Greenhill et al., 2006; McGoey & DuPaul, 2000; McGoey et al., 2005) to continue to evaluate the efficacy of parent training, behavioral interventions, psychopharmacology, and multimodal interventions.

Several studies evaluate the effectiveness of interventions with preschoolers and provide support for behavior management, parent training, and pharmacological interventions with younger children (McGoey, Eckert, & DuPaul, 2002). The description and applications of these interventions for preschoolers will be discussed within the context of the classroom and home environment. In addition, we agree with DuPaul and Ervin (1996) and recommend that when implementing interventions, clinicians need data to monitor the effectiveness of interventions. Tools or methods of data collection should be specific to the intervention targeted goals or behaviors. For example, when conducting parent behavioral training and classroom behavior management strategies, practitioners assess the frequency, intensity, and duration of the targeted child and parent behaviors from baseline, treatment, and follow-up to evaluate treatment effectiveness. In the end, developmental, practical, and multicultural considerations for interventions need to be addressed.

Behavior Management

Behavior management is a frequently used intervention to treat ADHD symptoms (Daly et al., 2007). Behavioral management programs reporting some success with preschoolers include the use of reinforcement programs (McGoey & DuPaul, 2000; McGoey et al., 2002), daily report cards (Chafouleas, Riley-Tillman, & Sassu, 2006; McCain & Kelly, 1993), response cost, and token economy procedures (McGoey & DuPaul).

Positive reinforcement is a component of most behavior management programs, providing young children with rewards after an appropriate behavior occurs and increasing the future frequency of that behavior (Cooper, Heron, & Heward, 2007). An important consideration is that reinforcers (e.g., rewards) are developmentally appropriate and appealing for preschoolers. Examples of common rewards used with young children include social praise, stickers, or privileges such as computer time. The rewards used in preschool studies include buttons on a chart, stickers, and stamps (McGoey & DuPaul, 2000), and attention (Kern et al., 2007). Typically, studies using positive reinforcement with preschoolers include reinforcement within a token economy system or as part of a multicomponent intervention. With multicomponent interventions (e.g., parent training, classroom-based interventions), sometimes discerning which component led to treatment change is difficult.

Preschool educators also utilize positive reinforcement, often choosing token economies or daily report cards to increase adaptive behaviors. Token economies are designed to increase appropriate behavior by giving students tokens (e.g., stars on a chart) when an appropriate behavior such as "being on task" occurs. An example of these tokens may be stickers or a poker chip. These tokens may then be subsequently exchanged for other objects or activities that the child finds desirable. In one of the preschool-based studies for treatment of ADHD related behaviors, tokens acquired by children were exchanged for tangible rewards. Results indicate that token economies are effective in reducing preschoolers' disruptive behavior (McGoey & DuPaul, 2000).

Daily report cards are another behavior management tool frequently used by classroom teachers to change children's behavior (Chafouleas et al., 2006). Daily report cards require the professional to monitor and rate the targeted behavior and share the data with someone other than the rater (e.g., the child's parent). The data collected then guides the delivery of consequences to the child (Chafouleas, Riley-Tillman, & McDougal, 2001). For example, a teacher may wish to increase the "turn-taking" behavior of preschool students. During play time, the teacher may rate preschoolers on turn-taking and at the end of the day shares this information with each preschooler's respective parent. Based on the teacher's feedback, the preschooler can be rewarded at home for reaching behavioral goals in the classroom. Daily report cards allow flexibility in implementation and can be modified to meet the needs of users. Like teachers at many levels, preschool teachers report widespread use of daily report cards and consider them as highly acceptable as behavior monitoring and intervention tools (Chafouleas et al., 2006). Importantly, reports can be used both individually and with groups, modifying a range of child behaviors (e.g., compliance) (Chafouleas et al., 2006; Chafouleas, Riley-Tillman, Sassu, LaFrance, & Patwa, 2007; McCain & Kelley, 1993). With regard to preschool-age children, daily report cards do not seem to be used as often, but have been shown to increase attentiveness and decrease disruptiveness (McCain & Kelley).

Response-cost programs are a combination of positive reinforcement and punishment. In response-cost programs, children earn points when they exhibit positive and prosocial behaviors (e.g., waiting their turn, attending in groups), but lose points or privileges when they display a disruptive or maladaptive behavior (e.g., pushing ahead of others, disrupting the group). For example, if a student breaks the rule "take your turn," the student loses a point and often the teacher makes a short specific statement informing the student they lost the point. These programs decrease impulsivity and increase attention and on-task behavior in preschoolers with ADHD (Fiore, Becker, & Nero, 1993; McGoey & DuPaul, 2000). Response-cost programs are time efficient and tend to be acceptable interventions by preschool educators (McGoey & DuPaul).

McGoey and colleagues (McGoey & DuPaul, 2000; McGoey et al., 2002) describe several important factors to consider when planning and implementing behavioral strategies in preschool-age settings. First, materials used for behavior plans that involve reinforcement need to be developmentally appropriate and appealing. Regular reinforcer preference assessments need to be conducted to ascertain children's motivation to complete tasks. Second, when choosing targeted behaviors to increase/decrease, developmental levels need strong consideration (e.g., expectations and desired behaviors developmentally appropriate and within the capability of the child). Especially for preschool-age children, visual and verbal cues are useful as reminders of consequences. Further, behavioral programs are enhanced when preschool children are provided with short, clear, and specific requests or task commands. For example, if compliance with classroom rules is the targeted behavior, rules need to be clear and repeated often. Third, to prevent treatment failure, reinforcement contingencies or behavioral strategies need to be implemented consistently, immediately, and frequently. Fourth, behavior plans created in collaboration with all parties facilitate plan compliance and success. Failure to have teacher collaboration and acceptability of the intervention may interfere with the implementation and overall effectiveness of the behavior plan.

PARENT TRAINING

Early intervention programs highlight the need to look beyond child-focused interventions and include family-based interventions targeting and supporting parents through education, enhanced parenting skills, and support (Fox, Dunlap, & Powell, 2002). The usual aim of parent training is to help parents change their parenting behavior to elicit positive changes in children's behavior. To facilitate parenting change, often parents are taught behavior management strategies as well as provided with information about ADHD and other child behavior problems (Daly et al., 2007). Many parent training programs focus on teaching parents principles of learning to help them understand the rationale behind, acquire, and apply effective child behavior management strategies. Parents are typically taught principles of contingency management (e.g., if a behavior is reinforced, the behavior is more likely to occur again) and discipline practices for dealing with ADHD related behaviors (Chronis, Chacko, Fabiano, Wymbs, & Pelham, 2004).

Parents also are specifically taught how to identify and modify antecedents and consequences of children's behavior, how to promote appropriate behavior, and identify methods for decreasing inappropriate behavior (Chronis et al., 2004). Through these training programs, parents receive direct instruction, participate in role plays, and have monitored parent-child interactions (e.g., immediate feedback provided regarding parent behavior). A combination of approaches may be particularly effective in keeping parents engaged in the training. Although not always the primary focus of parent training, helping parents manage their negative emotions through cognitive and behavioral techniques may be useful in reducing parents' stress and improving parenting behavior (Kurasaki, 2008). Additional benefits for participating in parent training programs include an increase in parents' sense of competence, reduction in parent stress, and improvements in parenting behavior (Anastopoulos, Shelton, DuPaul, & Gueveremont, 1993).

The aim of most parent training programs is to teach parents skills in intervening with children's ADHD symptoms, and promoting healthy environments allowing children to flourish academically and socially. Among the many approaches for treatment of ADHD, interventions with parents appear to be appropriate for several reasons. First, characteristic symptoms of ADHD such as inattention, hyperactivity, and impulsivity, have been associated with negative parent-child interactions and parent stress (Chronis et al., 2006). Parents may have difficulty coping with their child's behaviors and may be using maladaptive parenting strategies that negatively impact their child's behaviors (Chronis et al., 2006). Second, because parents contribute to and can control the environment in which many of the symptom/behaviors occur, parents are in a good position to implement behavior management strategies (e.g., positive reinforcement) to help their child decrease problematic (e.g., noncompliance) and increase appropriate and adaptive behaviors (Chronis et. al, 2004).

The effectiveness of parent training for school-age children with ADHD led to the evaluation of effectiveness with preschool children (Lundahl, Risser, & Lovejoy, 2006; Sonuga-Barke, Daley, Thompson, Laver-Bradbury, & Weeks, 2001). Studies with preschool-age children find that parent training for ADHD or disruptive behaviors led to improvements in child compliance (Pisterman, McGrath, Firestone, Goodman, Webster, & Malory, 1989), ADHD symptoms (Jones, Daley, Hutchings, Bywater, & Eames, 2007; Sonuga-Barke et al., 2001), disruptive behaviors (Bor, Sanders, & Markie-Dadds, 2002; Sonuga-Barke et al., 2005), and parent-child interactions (Hartman, Stage, & Webster-Stratton, 2002). Positive improvements in parent management skills (Bor et al., 2002), parent self-efficacy (Erhardt & Baker, 1990; Sonuga-Barke et al., 2001), and parent knowledge of behavior principles and child behavior problems (Erhardt & Baker) were also reported. Sonuga-Barke et al. (2001) evaluated the effectiveness of a parent training intervention comprised of child management strategies in decreasing ADHD symptoms and improving participating mothers' sense of well-being. The authors found that the parent training intervention is more effective on both child and parent outcomes than parent counseling (i.e., nondirective supportive counseling) and a wait-list control.

Relative to other interventions for ADHD, parent training may be seen as a cost-effective type of service delivery (Dretzke, et al., 2005). Although parents may need a "booster session" to reinforce learned strategies from time to time (Eyberg, Edwards, Boggs, & Foote, 1998), they are taught a life skill dealing with ADHD symptoms that may not warrant further, regular psychotherapeutic interventions (Sonuga-Barke et al., 2001). Second, parent training may also be conducted in group settings. In addition to less of a financial cost, group interventions often provide parents with a source of support, recognition that they are not alone, and an opportunity to learn from others effective parenting practices (Terjesen & Esposito, 2005).

When working with families, clinicians consider the impact of several key factors on treatment outcome. First, awareness of cultural and linguistic client background, as well cultural norms, is essential. Further, clinicians implement appropriate interventions taking into account the family's traditions, perceptions of child development and mental health services, and expectations of themselves as parents (Kazdin & Weisz, 2003; Mattox & Harder, 2007). For example, families who have negative perceptions of mental health services (e.g., parent training) may avoid involvement and participation in carrying out interventions. Further, some cultures have a communal approach to child rearing, suggesting involvement by other members of the household (e.g., grandparents) who may assist parents in the caregiving role and have a significant impact on managing children's behaviors (Mattox & Harder). In addition to having knowledge of the client's background, Ortiz, Flanagan, and Dynda (2008) recommend that developing cultural competency requires practitioners' self-awareness. That is, professionals working with children with ADHD and their families need first and foremost to examine how their own views and values may impact intervention service delivery and the working relationships among young children, families, and practitioners (Ortiz et al.).

PSYCHOPHARMACOLOGY

Psychopharmacology has been a common treatment for the symptoms of ADHD in children and adolescents. The most frequently used medications are stimulants, which include methylphenidate (e.g., Ritalin, Concerta, Focalin) and amphetamines (e.g., Dexedrine, Adderall) (Barbaresi, 2003). Stimulant medications operate by increasing the levels of neurotransmitters in the brain which typically improves children's classroom behavior, academic efficiency, and social functioning (Hoza et al., 2005) as well as task completion, behavior during parent-child interactions, and attentiveness (Lerner & Wigal, 2008). Criticism of the use of stimulants with children stems from the lack of long-term evidence supporting improvement in student academic achievement (Daly et al., 2007) and peer relationships (Chronis et al., 2006). In addition, approximately 30% of children do not respond to stimulant medication; indeed, medication treats the symptoms of the disorder and when the medication is removed, behaviors such as impulsivity and hyperactivity reemerge (Reiff & Tippins, 2004).

Although the use of stimulants with children and adolescents has received considerable attention and support over the years (Greenhill et al., 2006; Musten, Firestone, Pisterman, Bennett, & Mercer, 1997), use with younger children is more controversial. Currently, d-amphetamine (Dexedrine) is the only approved short-term treatment of ADHD in children 3–6 years of age (Kratochvil, Greenhill, March, Burke, & Vaughn, 2004). However, recent studies investigating the long-term safety of the stimulant medication methylphenidate (Ritalin) in preschool-age children are inconsistent (Heriot, Evans, & Foster, 2008). In preschool-age children, methylphenidate use leads to significant improvements in attention, impulsivity, compliance with requests, and on-task behavior (Barkley, 1988; Greenhill et al., 2006; Musten et al., 1997). In particular, the Preschool ADHD Treatment Study (PATS) found in their clinical trials that low dosages of methylphenidate lead to clinically significant improvements in ADHD symptoms of preschool children 3–5.5 years of age (Greenhill et al.).

The use of stimulants with children and adolescents warrant careful monitoring due to the potential for adverse side effects. Common stimulant side effects among children and adolescents include headaches, abdominal pain, repetitive movements/tics, decreased appetite, weight loss, jitteriness, and insomnia (Lerner & Wigal, 2008). Many of the side effects reported in school-aged populations are mild, short-lived, and may be ameliorated by changes in medication dosage and timing. Similar side effects have also been reported in preschool populations (Greenhill et al., 2006). However, more severe, variable, and additional side effects such as dullness, fatigue, listlessness, social withdrawal, repetitive movements, and reductions in expected growth have been observed (Firestone, Musten, Pisterman, Mercer, & Bennett, 1998; Greenhill et al.; Lerner & Wigal). Given these possibilities, caution in the use of stimulants and psychopharmacologic approaches with younger children is recommended until additional research examining the effectiveness and safety of medication with this population is conducted. In light of the potential for adverse side effects and the limited clinical trials supporting the use of medication in younger children, careful consideration and application of other interventions such as behavior management and parenting training both prior to and in conjunction with medication is recommended.

COMBINED INTERVENTIONS

Since children with ADHD demonstrate symptoms and impairment across settings (e.g., home, school), a combination of interventions operating in both home and school settings may help to address impairments across all domains. As findings appear promising for multicomponent interventions for school-age children (Fabiano et al., 2007), few studies have examined the effectiveness of combined interventions for ADHD for preschool-age children (Henry, 1987; Kern et al., 2007; McGoey et al., 2005). In one of the earlier studies, Henry evaluated the effectiveness of medication, parent training, and symbolic modeling (i.e., child watches videotape of child performing desired behavior) with preschool children receiving stimulant medication for ADHD. Although some methodological concerns exist, including small sample size, results suggest that the combination of interventions is more effective than stimulant medication and symbolic modeling alone.

McGoey and colleagues (2005) evaluated a multicomponent treatment package with preschoolers at risk for ADHD. Results indicate that preschoolers in the multicomponent condition, which consisted of school-based consultation, parent training, and, when needed, medication, had a greater decrease in inappropriate behaviors and showed improvements in self-control, on task performance, and social skills. In addition, parents of these preschoolers also demonstrated increases in positive parenting behaviors.

In a more recent study with children ages 3–5, Kern et al. (2007) evaluated the effectiveness of a multicomponent intervention combining parent education and an individualized assessment-based intervention in home and in preschool/day care settings. Parent education in the multicomponent intervention involved teaching parents behavior management strategies, child safety, and preacademic readiness skills. Participants in the multicomponent intervention also received home and school behavioral interventions based on data collected from functional analytic assessments. Both the participants in the multicomponent intervention and the comparison group, who received only parent education, demonstrated improved child behavior and preacademic skills. However, no differences in a 1-year follow-up between intervention groups were found. Although multicomponent interventions for younger children with or at risk for ADHD are being developed, more comparative studies (e.g., Kern et al., 2007) are needed to determine the efficacy of multicomponent treatments above and beyond single interventions (i.e., parent training alone) and determine moderating and/or mediating variables (e.g., socioeconomic status) that may influence treatment outcomes.

CONSIDERATIONS OF ETHICS IN ASSESSMENT, DIAGNOSIS, INTERVENTION, AND TRAINING

Unfortunately, in comparison with the school-age population, clinicians do not have as much research to guide professional practice and training when working with ADHD behaviors in early childhood. Although research to guide clinical practice is emerging, ethically responsible clinicians should continue to make themselves aware of current research and related limitations. Clinicians should exercise caution when using standard ADHD assessment and interventions practices that lack evidence-based support for use with young children.

With regard to assessment, the *Standards for Educational and Psychological Testing* (Standards; American Educational Research Association [AERA], American Psychological Association [APA], National Council on Measurement in Education [NCME], 1999), and the National Association of School Psychologists (NASP, 2008) provide guidelines in test development and test use reflecting changes in law as well as the ethical codes. Among the areas addressed are standards for testing individuals with disabilities or different linguistic backgrounds, fairness in testing and test use, and educational testing and assessment. Therefore, when conducting assessments for ADHD, clinicians need to examine and be informed about the psychometric characteristics and the applicability of the tool with the individual or population being tested.

The same concerns for ethical practice are considered with regard to treatment implementation. In 2005, The APA Presidential Task Force on Evidence-Based Practice was convened to develop a definition of evidence-based psychological practice that would become policy to promote sound psychological practice (APA Presidential Task Force on Evidence-Based Practice, 2006). The definition of evidence-based practice in psychology (EBPP) stems from the best available research in the context of client characteristics, culture, and preferences and aims to promote effective psychological practice and enhance public health by applying empirically supported principles of psychological assessment, case formulation, therapeutic relationship, and intervention. The task force proposed that "clinical decisions should be made in collaboration with the patient, based on the best clinically relevant evidence, and with consideration for the probable costs, benefits, and available resources and options" (APA Presidential Task Force on Evidence-Based Practice, p. 280). Interventions are to "be appropriate to the presenting problems and are consistent with the data collected" (NASP, 2008, pp. xxvi) and, essentially, science is the guide to training (Leffingwell & Collins, 2008) and clinical practice (Forman & Burke, 2008) and, at the same time, informs others about the limits of science in a specific area (e.g., preschool ADHD symptoms).

SUMMARY

A common theme across both assessment and intervention components of this chapter is the need for more research with younger children who present with ADHD or ADHD-related behaviors. That is, the means for identifying, measuring, and intervening with ADHD behaviors, in an evidence-based manner, is still developing. In addition, the field would substantially benefit from the development of more culturally representative and sensitive measures of ADHD with younger children. Further, insufficient taxonomy, especially regarding parent and family dynamics, and measures may hinder our ability to appropriately identify and subsequently treat behaviors associated with ADHD.

At present, we do have some evidence-based, empirical support for the use of pharmacology, parent training, and behavior modification to reduce the symptoms and problems characteristic of ADHD. For younger children, many practitioners suggest that parent training and behavior modification is the first line of intervention before turning to medication (Kratochvil, Egger, Greenhill, & McGough, 2006). When medication is sought out, careful monitoring of side effects as well as the introduction of other empirically supported interventions is indicated. Furthermore, recent studies also highlight the importance of multimodal intervention plans with varied combinations of treatment components (Gureasko-Moore, DuPaul, & White, 2006). Consistent with ADHD diagnostic criteria, specifying ADHD symptoms should occur across settings; treatments need to be carried out in both home and classroom environments to facilitate greater change and generalizability of effects across settings (Chronis et al., 2006; McGoey et al., 2005).

On the whole, the treatment literature is lacking in representative samples for measuring ADHD as well as larger, randomized control trials for treatment outcome. Furthermore, more comparative and component analysis studies are needed to determine what interventions and which components of treatment packages contribute to treatment gains with this age group. Additional research is also needed to further investigate the effectiveness of social skills training, academic interventions, and cognitive–behavioral interventions as part of a treatment package with younger children. Finally, development and evaluation of treatments among culturally diverse populations is absolutely essential.

REFERENCES

Achenbach, T. M., & Rescorla, L. A. (2000). *Manual for the ASEBA preschool forms & profiles*. Burlington, VT: University of Vermont, Research Center for Children, Youth, & Families.

AERA, APA, & NCME. (1999). *Standards for educational and psychological testing*. Washington, DC: Author.

American Psychiatric Association. (2000). *Diagnostic and statistical manual of mental disorders* (4th ed., Text revision). Washington, DC: Author.

Anastopoulos, A. D., & Shelton, T. L. (2001). *Assessing attention-deficit/hyperactivity disorder*. New York: Kluwer Academic/Plenum.

Anastopoulos, A. D., Shelton, T. L., DuPaul, G. J., & Guevremont, D. C. (1993). Parent training for attention-deficit hyperactivity disorder. *Journal of Abnormal Child Psychology, 21*, 581–596.

APA Presidential Task Force on Evidence-Based Practice. (2006). Evidence-based practice in psychology. *American Psychologist, 61*(4), 271–285.

Bain, S.K., & Pelletier, K. A. (1999). Social and behavioral differences among a predominantly African American preschool sample. *Psychology in the Schools, 36*, 249–259.

Balda, S., Punia, S., & Punia, D. (2002). Peer Rating Scale: A reliable sociometric measure for preschool children. *Journal of Psychometry, 15*(1), 21–28.

Barbaresi, W. J. (2003). Use of psychotropic medications in young, preschool children. *Archives of Pediatric and Adolescent Medicine, 157*, 121–123.

Barkley, R. A. (1988). Child behavior rating scales and checklists. In: M. Rutter, H. Tuma, & I. Lann (Eds.), *Assessment and diagnosis in child psychopathology* (pp. 113–155). New York: Guilford Press.

Barkley, R. A. (1990). *Attention-deficit hyperactivity disorder: Handbook for diagnosis and treatment* (2nd ed.). New York: Guilford Press.

Barkley, R. A. (1998). *Attention-deficit hyperactivity disorder: A handbook for diagnosis and treatment* (2nd ed). New York: Guilford Press.

Baumgaertel, A., Wolraich, M., & Dietrichm, M. (1995). Comparison of diagnostic criteria for attention deficit disorders in a German elementary school sample. *Journal of American Academy of Child and Adolescent Psychiatry, 34,* 629–638.

Behar, L. B. (1977). The Preschool Behavior Questionnaire. *Journal of Abnormal Child Psychology, 5*(3), 265–275.

Bhatia, M. S., Nigam, V. R., Bohra, N., & Malik, S. C. (1991). Attention deficit disorder with hyperactivity among pediatric outpatients. *Journal of Child Psychology and Psychiatry, 32,* 297–306.

Bird, H. R. (2002). The diagnostic classification, epidemiology, and cross-cultural validation of ADHD. In P. S. Jensen & J. R. Cooper (Eds.), *Attention deficit hyperactivity disorder state of science-best practices* (pp. 2-1–2-16). Kingston: Civic Research Institute.

Bor, W., Sanders, M. R., & Markie-Dadds, C. (2002). The effects of the Triple P-Positive Parenting Program on preschool children with co-occurring disruptive behavior and attention/hyperactive difficulties. *Journal of Abnormal Child Psychology, 30,* 571–587.

Boyajian, A. E., DuPaul, G. J., Wartel-Handler, M., Eckert, T. L., & McGoey, K. E. (2001). The use of classroom-based brief functional analyses with preschoolers at-risk for attention deficit hyperactivity disorder. *School Psychology Review, 30,* 278–293.

Brotman, L., Gouley, K., & Chesir-Teran, D. (2005). Assessing peer entry and play in preschoolers at risk for maladjustment. *Journal of Clinical Child & Adolescent Psychology, 34*(4), 671–680.

Brown, T. E. (2001). *Brown Attention-Deficit Disorder Scales: For children and adolescents.* Dallas, TX: Psychological Corporation.

Byrne, J. M., DeWolfe, N. A., & Bawden, H. N. (1998). Assessment of attention deficit hyperactivity disorder in preschoolers. *Child Neuropsychology, 4,* 49–66.

Campbell, S. B. (1995). Behavior problems in preschool children: A review of recent research. *Journal of Child Psychology & Psychiatry & Allied Disciplines, 36,* 113–149.

Carey, W. B. (2002). Is ADHD a valid disorder? In P. S. Jensen & J. R. Cooper (Eds.), *Attention deficit hyperactivity disorder: State of the science—best practices* (pp. 3-1–3-19). Kingston, NJ: Civic Research Institute.

Chafouleas, S. M., Riley-Tillman, T. C., & McDougal, J. (2001). Good, bad, or in-between: How does the daily behavior report card rate? *Psychology in the Schools, 39,* 157–169.

Chafouleas, S. M., Riley-Tillman, T. C., Sassu, K. A. (2006). Acceptability and reported use of daily behavior report cards among teachers. *Journal of Positive Behavior Interventions, 8*(3), 174–182.

Chafouleas, S. M., Riley-Tillman, T. C., Sassu, K. A., LaFrance, M. J., & Patwa, S. S. (2007). Daily behavior report cards: An investigation of the consistency of on-task data across raters and methods. *Journal of Positive Behavior Interventions, 9*(1), 30–38.

Chambless, D. L., & Ollendick, T. H. (2001). Empirically supported psychological interventions: Controversies and evidence. *Annual Review of Psychology, 52,* 685–716.

Chronis, A. M., Chacko, A., Fabiano, G. A., Wymbs, B. T., & Perlham, W. E. (2004). Enhancements to the behavioral parent training paradigm for families of children with ADHD: Review and future directions. *Clinical Child and Family Psychology Review, 7,* 1–27.

Chronis, A. M., Jones, H. A., & Raggi, V. L. (2006). Evidence-based psychosocial treatments for children and adolescents with attention-deficit/hyperactivity disorder. *Clinical Psychology Review, 26,* 486–502.

Colegrove, R., Homayounjam, H., Williams, J., & Hanken, J. (2001). Reducing the overidentification of childhood ADHD: A stepwise diagnostic model. *ADHD Report, 9,* 11–16.

Conners, C. K. (1997). *Conners' Rating Scales-revised technical manual.* New York: Multi-Health Systems.

Conners, C. K. (2001). *Conners' Kiddie Continuous Performance Test.* Toronto: Multi-Health Systems.

Connor, D. (2002). Preschool attention deficit hyperactivity disorder: A review of prevalence, diagnosis, neurobiology, and stimulant treatment. *Journal of Developmental and Behavioral Pediatrics, 23*(18), S1–S9.

Cooper, J. O., Heron, T. E., & Heward, W. L. (2007). *Applied Behavior Analysis* (2nd ed.). Upper Saddle River, NJ: Pearson.

Daly, B. P., Creed, T. A., Xanthopoulos, M., & Brown, R. T. (2007). Psychosocial treatments for children with attention deficit/hyperactivity disorder. *Neuropsychology Review, 17,* 73–89.

Dean, R. S., & Woodcock, R. W. (2003). *Dean-Woodcock Neuropsychological Battery.* Itasca, IL: Riverside.

Deutscher, B., & Fewell, R. R. (2001). The development and use of the Attention Deficit Hyperactivity Disorder-Observational Rating Scale: Factor analysis and a preliminary investigation of predictive validity. *Journal of Psychoeducational Assessment, 19*(4), 317–329.

Döpfner, M., Rothenberger, A., & Sonuga-Barke, E. (2004). Areas for future investment in the field of ADHD: Preschoolers and clinical networks. *Journal European Child & Adolescent Psychiatry, 13*(1), 130–135.

Dretzke, J., Frew, E., Davenport, C., Barlow, J., Stewart-Brown, S., Sandercock, J., et al. (2005). The effectiveness and cost-effectiveness of parent training/education programmes for the treatment of conduct disorder, including oppositional defiant disorder, in children. *Health Technology Assessment, 9*(50), 1–250.

DuPaul, G. J., & Ervin, R. A. (1996). Functional assessment of behaviors related to attention-deficit/hyperactivity disorder: Linking assessment to intervention design. *Behavior Therapy, 27*(4), 601–622.

DuPaul, G. J., Power, T. J., Anastopoulos, A. D., & Reid, R. (1998). *ADHD-IV rating scale: Checklists, norms, and clinical interpretation.* New York: Guilford Press.

DuPaul, G. J., McGoey, K. E., Eckert, T. L., & VanBrackle, J. (2001). Preschool children with attention deficit/hyperactivity disorder: Impairments in behavioral, social, and school functioning. *Journal of the American Academy of Child and Adolescent Psychiatry, 40,* 508–515.

Egger, H. L., & Angold, A. (2004). The Preschool Age Psychiatric Assessment: A structured parent interview for diagnosing psychiatric disorders in preschool children. In R. DelCarmen-Wiggins & A. Carter (Eds.), *The handbook of infant, toddler, and preschool mental health assessment* (pp. 223–246). New York: Oxford University Press.

Erhardt, D., & Baker, B. L. (1990). The effects of behavior parent training on families with young hyperactive children. *Journal of Behavior Therapy and Experimental Psychiatry, 21,* 121–132.

Eyberg, S. M., Edwards, D., Boggs, S. R., & Foote, R. (1998). Maintaining the treatment effects of parent training: The role of booster sessions and other maintenance strategies. *Clinical Psychology Science and Practice, 5,* 544–554.

Fabiano, G. A., Pelham, W. E., Gnagy, E. M., Burrows-MacLean, L., Coles, E. K., Chacko, A., Wymbs, B. T., Walker, K. S., Arnold, F., Garefino, A., Keenan, J. K., Onyango, A. N., Hoffman, M. T., Massetti, G. M., & Robb, J. A. (2007). The single and combined effects of multiple intensities of behavior modification and multiple intensities of methylphenidate in a classroom setting. *School Psychology Review, 36,* 195–216.

Fewell, R.R. (1999 January 1). *Attention deficit hyperactivity disorder early identification research project.* (ERIC Document Reproduction Service No. ED463594) Retrieved July 30, 2008, from ERIC database.

Fiore, T. A., Becker, E. A., & Nero, R. C. (1993). Educational interventions for students with attention deficit disorder. *Exceptional Children, 60,* 163–173.

Firestone, P., Musten, L. M., Pisterman, S., Mecer, J., & Bennett, S. (1998). Short-term side effects of stimulant medication are increased in preschool children with ADHD: A double-blind placebo-controlled study. *Journal of Child and Adolescent Psychopharmacology, 8,* 13–25.

Forman, S. G., & Burke, C. R. (2008). Best practices in selecting and implementing evidence-based school intervention. In A. Thomas & J. Grimes (Eds.), *Best practices in school psychology V* (pp. 799–811). Bethesda, MD: National Association of School Psychologists.

Fox, L., Dunlap, G., & Powell, D. (2002). Young children with challenging behaviors: Issues and considerations for behavior support. *Journal of Positive Behavior Interventions, 4,* 208–218.

Goldman, L. S., Genel, M., Bezman, R. J., & Slanetz, P. J. (1998). Diagnosis and treatment of attention-deficit/hyperactivity disorder in children and adolescents. *Journal of the American Medical Association, 279,* 1100–1107.

Gordon, M. (1996). Administrative manual for the Gordon diagnostic system. DeWitt, New York: Author.

Greenfield-Spira, E., & Fischel, J. E. (2005). The impact of preschool inattention, hyperactivity, and impulsivity on social and academic development: A review. *Journal of Child Psychology & Psychiatry, 46*(7), 755–773.

Greenhill, L., Kollins, S., Abikoff, H., McCracken, J., Riddle, M., Swanson, J., et al. (2006). Efficacy and safety of immediate-release methylphenidate treatment for preschoolers with ADHD. *Journal of the American Academy of Child and Adolescent Psychiatry, 45,* 1284–1293.

Gureasko-Moore, S., DuPaul, G. J., White, G. P., (2006). The effects of self-management in general education classrooms on the organizational skills of adolescents with ADHD. *Behavior Modification, 30*(2), 159–183.

Hardy, K. K., Kollins, S. H., Murray, D. W., Riddle, M. A, Greenhill, L., Cunningham, C., et al. (2007). Factor structure of parent- and teacher-rated attention-deficit/hyperactivity disorder symptoms in the preschoolers with attention-deficit/hyperactivity disorder treatment study (PATS). *Journal of Child and Adolescent Psychopharmacology, 17*(5), 621–634.

Hartman, R. R., Stage, S., & Webster-Stratton, C., (2002). A growth curve analysis of parent training outcomes: Examining the influence of child risk factors (inattention, impulsivity, and hyperactivity problems), parental and family risk factors. *Journal of Child Psychology and Psychiatry, 43*(7), 388–298.

Henry, G. K. (1987). Symbolic modeling and parent behavioral training: Effects on noncompliance of hyperactive children. *Journal of Behavior Therapy and Experimental Psychiatry, 18,* 105–113.

Heriot, S. A., Evans, I. M., & Foster, T. M. (2008). Critical influences affecting response to various treatments in young children with ADHD: A case series. *Child: Care, Health, and Development, 34*(1), 121–133.

Hermans, D. F., Williams, L. M., Lazzaro, I., Whitmont, S., Melkonian, D., & Gordon, E. (2004). Sex differences in adult ADHD: A double dissociation in brain activity and autonomic arousal. *Biological Psychology, 66,* 221–233.

Hinshaw, S. P. (2002). Is ADHD an impairing condition in childhood and adolescence? In P. S. Jensen & J. R. Cooper (Eds.), *Attention deficit hyperactivity disorder: State of the science—best practices* (pp. 5-2–5-21). Kingston, NJ: Civic Research Institute.

Ho, T. P., Leung, P. W., Luk, E. S., Taylor, E., Bacon-Shone, J., & Mak, F. L. (1996). Establishing the constructs of childhood behavioral disturbances in a Chinese population: A questionnaire study. *Journal of Abnormal Child Psychology, 24,* 417–431.

Hoza, B., Mrug, S., Gerdes, A. C., Hinshaw, S. P., Bukowski, W. M., Gold, J. A., et al. (2005). What aspects of peer relationships are impaired in children with attention deficit hyperactivity disorder? *Journal of Consulting and Clinical Psychology, 73,* 411–423.

Iwanaga, R., Ozawa, H., Kawasaki, C., & Tsuchida, R. (2006). Characteristics of the sensory-motor, verbal and cognitive abilities of preschool boys with attention deficit/hyperactivity disorder combined type. *Psychiatry and Clinical Neurosciences, 60,* 37–45.

Jensen, P.S., & Cooper, J. R. (2002). *Attention deficit hyperactivity disorder: State of the science—best practices.* Kingston, NJ: Civic Research Institute.

Jones, K., Daley, D., Hutchings, J., Bywater, T., & Eames, C. (2007). Efficacy of The Incredible Years basic parent training programme as an early intervention for children with conduct problems and ADHD. *Child: Care, Health, & Development, 33,* 749–756.

Kazdin, A. E., & Weisz, J. R. (2003). Context and background of evidence-based psychotherapies for children and adolescents. In A. Kazdin, & J. Weisz (Eds.), *Evidence-based psychotherapies for children and adolescents* (pp. 21–40). New York: Guilford Press.

Keenan, K., & Wakschlag, L. S. (2002). Can a valid diagnosis of disruptive behavior disorder be made in preschool children? *American Journal of Psychiatry, 159,* 351–358.

Kern, L., DePaul, G., Volpe, R., Sokol, N., Lutz, G., Arbolino, L., et al. (2007). Multisetting assessment-based intervention for young children at risk for attention deficit hyperactivity disorder: Initial effects on academic and behavioral functioning. *School Psychology Review, 36,* 237–255.

Kratochvil, C., Egger, H., Greenhill, L. L., & McGough, J. J. (2006). Pharmacological management of preschool ADHD. *Journal of the American Academy of Child & Adolescent Psychiatry, 45,* 115–118.

Kratochvil, C. J., Greenhill, L. L., March, J. S., Burke, W. J., & Vaughn, B. S. (2004). The role of stimulants in the treatment of preschool children with attention-deficit hyperactivity disorder. *CNS Drugs, 18,* 957–966.

Kube, D. A., Petersen, M. C., & Palmer, F. B. (2002). Attention deficit hyperactivity disorder: Co-morbidity and medication use. *Clinical Pediatrics, 47,* 461–470.

Kurasaki, R. K. (2008, May). REBT with parents. In M. D. Terjesen (Chair), *Unique applications of cognitive behavioral interventions with children and adolescents.* Symposium conducted at the meeting of the New York State Psychological Association, Cooperstown, NY.

Leffingwell, T. R., & Collins, F. (2008) Graduate training in evidence-based practice in psychology. In R. G. Steele, T.D. Elkin & M.C. Roberts (Eds.), *Handbook of Evidence-Therapies for Children and Adolescents: Bridging Science and Practice* (551–568). New York: Springer.

Lerner, M., & Wigal, T. (2008). Long-term safety of stimulant medications used to treat children with ADHD. *Psychiatric Annals, 38,* 43–51.

Lewinsohn, P. M., Shankman, S. A., Gau, J. M., & Klein, D. (2004). The prevalence and co-morbidity of sub threshold psychiatric conditions. *Psychological Medicine, 34,* 613–622.

Losier, B. J., McGrath, P. J., & Klein, R. M. (1996). Error patterns on the continuous Performance Test in non-medicated and medicated samples of children with and without ADHD: A meta-analytic review. *Journal of Child Psychology and Psychiatry, 37,* 971–987.

Lundahl, B., Risser, H. J., & Lovejoy, C. (2006). A meta-analysis of parent training: Moderators and follow-up effects. *Clinical Psychology Review, 26,* 86–104.

Mattox, R., & Harder, J. (2007). Attention deficit hyperactivity disorder (ADHD) and diverse populations. *Child and Adolescent Social Work Journal, 24,* 195–207.

McCain, A. P., & Kelley, M. L. (1993). Managing the classroom behavior of an ADHD preschooler: The efficacy of a school-home note intervention. *Child and Family Behavior Therapy, 15,* 33–34.

McCarney, S. B. (1995). Early childhood attention deficit disorders evaluation scale (ECADDES). Columbia, MO: Hawthorne Educational Services.

McClelland, M. M., Morrison, F. J., & Holmes, D. L. (2000). Children at risk for early academic problems: The role of learning related social skills. *Early Childhood Research Quarterly, 15,* 307–329.

McGoey, K. E., & DuPaul, G. J. (2000). Token reinforcement and response cost procedures: Reducing the disruptive behavior of preschool children with attention-deficit/hyperactivity disorder. *School Psychology Quarterly, 15,* 330–343.

McGoey, K. E., DuPaul, G. J., Eckert, T. L., Volpe, R. J., & Brakle, J. V. (2005). Outcomes of a multi-component for preschool children at-risk for attention-deficit/hyperactivity disorder. *Child & Family Behavior Therapy, 27,* 33–56.

McGoey, K. E., Eckert, T. L., & DuPaul, G. J. (2002). Early intervention for preschool-age children with ADHD: A literature review. *Journal of Emotional & Behavioral Disorders, 10,* 14–29.

Murray, D. W., Kollins, S. H., Hardy, K. K., Abikoff, H. B., Swanson, J. M., Cunningham, C., et al. (2007). Parent versus teacher ratings of attention-deficit/hyperactivity disorder symptoms in the preschoolers with attention-deficit/hyperactivity disorder treatment study (PATS). *Journal of Child and Adolescent Psychopharmacology, 17*(5), 605–620.

Musten, L. M., Firestone, P., Pisterman, S., Bennett, S., & Mercer, J. (1997). Effects of methylphenidate on preschool children with ADHD: Cognitive and behavioral functions. *Journal of the American Academy of Child and Adolescent Psychiatry, 36*(10), 1407–1415.

National Association of School Psychologists. (2008). NASP Principles for Professional Ethics. In A. Thomas & J. Grimes (Eds.), *Best practices in school psychology V* (pp. xxi–xxx). Bethesda, MD: National Association of School Psychologists.

Netherton, S. D., Holmes, D., & Walker, C. E. (1999). *Child and Adolescent Psychological Disorders.* New York: Oxford University Press.

Ortiz, S., Flanagan, D., & Dynda, A. (2008). Culturally diverse children and families. In A. Thomas & J. Grimes (Eds.), *Best practices in school psychology V* (pp. 1721–1738). Bethseda, MD: National Association of School Psychologists.

Pelham, W. E., Fabiano, G. A., & Massetti, G. M. (2005). Evidence-based assessment of attention deficit hyperactivity disorder in children and adolescents. *Journal of Clinical Child and Adolescent Psychology, 34,* 449–476.

Pineda, D., Ardila, A., Rosselli, M., Arias, B. E., Henao, G. C., Gomez, L. F., et al. (1999). Prevalence of attention-deficit/hyperactivity disorder symptoms in 4- to 17-year-old children in the general population. *Journal of Abnormal Child Psychology, 27,* 455–462.

Pisterman, S., McGrath, P., Firestone, P., Goodman, J. T., Webster, I., & Malory, R. (1989). Outcome of parent-mediated treatment on preschoolers with attention deficit disorder with hyperactivity. *Journal of Consulting and Clinical Psychology, 57,* 628–635.

Posner, K., Melvin, G. A., Murray, D. W., Gugga, S. S., Fisher, P., Skrobala, A., et al. (2007). Clinical presentation of attention-deficit/hyperactivity disorder in preschool children: The preschoolers with attention-deficit/hyperactivity disorder treatment study (PATS). *Journal of Child and Adolescent Psychopharmacology, 17*(5), 547–562.

Raz, A. (2004). Brain imaging data of ADHD. *Adolescent Psychiatry, 34*, 987–1000.

Reddy, L. A., Fumari, G., Pedigo, T. K., & Scott, V. (2008). Pediatric attention disorders: Diagnostic screener for children at risk for attention-deficit/hyperactivity disorder. *School Psychologist, 62*(3), 93–98.

Reiff, M. I., & Tippins, S. (2004). *ADHD: A complete and authoritative guide.* Elk Grove Village, IL: American Academy of Pediatrics.

Reynolds, C. R., & Gutkin, T. B. (1999). *The handbook of school psychology.* New York: Wiley.

Reynolds, C., & Kamphaus, R. (2004). *Behavior assessment system for children (BASC-2).* Circle Pines, MN: American Guidance Service.

Sagvolden, T. (1999). Attention deficit/hyperactivity disorder. *European Psychologist, 4*(2), 109–114.

Sattler, J. M., & Hoge, R. D. (Eds.), (2006). *Assessment of children: Behavioral, social, and clinical foundations.* (5th ed.). San Diego, CA: Sattler.

Schwab-Stone, M., Shaffer, D., Dulcan, M. K., Jensen, P. S., Fisher, P., Bird, H. R., et al. (1996). Criterion validity of the NIMH Diagnostic Interview Schedule for Children Version 2.3 (DISC-2.3). *Journal of the American Academy of Child and Adolescent Psychiatry, 35*, 878–888.

Shaffer, D., Fisher, P., Dulcan, M. K., Davies, M., Piacentini, J., Schwab-Stone, M., et al. (1996). The NIMH Diagnostic Interview Schedule for Children Version 2.3 (DISC-2.3): Description, acceptability, prevalence rates, and performance in the MECA study. *Journal of the American Academy of Child and Adolescent Psychiatry, 35*, 865–877.

Smith, K. G., & Corkum, P. (2007). Systematic review of measures used to diagnose attention-deficit/hyperactivity disorder in research on preschool children. *Topics in Early Childhood Special Education, 27*(3), 164–173.

Sonuga-Barke, E. J., Auerbach, J., Campbell, S. B., Daley, D., & Thompson, M. (2005). Varieties of preschool hyperactivity: Multiple pathways from risk to disorder. *Developmental Science, 8*, 141–150.

Sonuga-Barke, E., Daley, D., Thompson, M., Laver-Bradbury, C., & Weeks, A. (2001). Parent-based therapies for preschool attention-deficit/hyperactivity disorder: A randomized, controlled trial with a community sample. *Journal of the American Academy of Child & Adolescent Psychiatry, 40*(4), 402–408.

Steinhoff, K. W., Lerner, M., Kaplinsky, A., Kotkin, R., Wigal, S., Steinberg-Epstein, R., et al. (2006). Attention deficit/hyperactivity disorders. In Luby, J. L. (Ed.), *Handbook of preschool mental health: Development, disorders, and treatment* (pp. 63–79). New York: Guilford Press.

Stevens, L. J. (2000). *12 effective ways to help your ADD/ADHD child.* New York: Penguin.

Stormont, M., & Zentall, S. S. (1999). Assessment of setting in the behavioral ratings of preschoolers with and without high levels of activity. *Psychology in the Schools, 36*, 109–155.

Terjesen, M. D., & Esposito, M. A. (2005). Rational emotive behavior group therapy with children and adolescents. In A. Ellis, & M. E. Bernard (Eds.). *Rational emotive behavior approaches to childhood disorders* (pp. 385–413). New York: Springer.

Terjesen, M. D. & Sciutto, M. J. (2008). Behavior rating scales and the assessment of ADHD in early childhood: A review of psychometric properties and scale features. Manuscript submitted for publication.

Tobin, R. M., Schneider, W. J., Reck, S. G., & Landau, S. (2008). Best practices in the assessment of children with attention deficit hyperactivity disorder: Linking assessment to response to intervention. In A. Thomas & J. Grimes (Eds.), *Best practices in school psychology V* (pp. 617–631). Bethesda, MD: National Association of School Psychologists.

Ullmann, R. K., Sleator, E. K., & Sprague, R. L. (2000). *ACTeRS Teacher, Parent, and Self-Report Forms Manual* (2nd ed.). Champaign, IL: MetriTech.

Wilens, T. E., Biederman, J., Brown, S., Tanguay, S., Monuteaux, M. C., Blake, C., & Spencer, T. J. (2002). Psychiatric comorbidity and functioning in clinically referred preschool children and school-age youths with ADHD. *Journal of the American Academy of Child and Adolescent Psychiatry, 41*(3), 262–268.

Zito, J. M., Safer, D. J., dosRies, S., Gardner, J. F., Boles, M., & Lynch, F. (2000). Trends in prescribing the psychotropic medications to preschoolers. *Journal of the American Medical Association, 283*, 1025–1030.

CHAPTER 13

Social-Emotional Issues

SUSAN CHINITZ
and RAHIL BRIGGS

S OCIAL-EMOTIONAL DEVELOPMENT REFERS to feelings and competencies that reflect children's sense of themselves, their expectations of others, and their growing abilities to understand and manage emotions and to interact successfully with adults and other children. Accumulated knowledge derived from interrelated disciplines, including attachment research, developmental psychopathology, and neuroscience, has powerfully converged to highlight the importance of children's social and emotional competencies for mastery across all developmental domains, and for establishing the foundation for well-being throughout life (Shonkoff & Phillips, 2000). The nature and quality of the social-emotional competencies established in infancy and early childhood set a strong or shaky foundation for competencies that are needed throughout the lifespan—being in close relationships with other people, possessing a sense of security and positive self-regard, managing anxiety and coping with stress, resolving conflict and working cooperatively with others, and mastery motivation—as important examples. The social-emotional development of young children has, therefore, attained elevated importance in contemporary theories of child development. Whereas cognitive development was previously considered the key event of early childhood and efforts to better the life chances of vulnerable children aimed to improve their cognitive functioning, social-emotional competencies are increasingly found to be the bedrock for successful adaptation (Schore, 2005). As a result of this very significant paradigm shift, it is currently recommended that the social-emotional development of young children be a focused target for increased resource allocation in public policy, in program development across child serving systems, and in interventions with vulnerable or high-risk infants, toddlers, and preschool-age children (Center on the Developing Child, 2007).

THE CONTEXT FOR YOUNG CHILDREN'S SOCIAL-EMOTIONAL DEVELOPMENT

Social-emotional development is a multifaceted, formative process best understood through a transactional-ecological framework that acknowledges the multitude of influences on development, including the child's genetic and temperamental constitution, characteristics of parents and their own relationship and life histories, family composition, stability and resources, the characteristics of neighborhoods and communities, and the way that each of these shapes and impacts the others (Bronfenbrenner, 1979; Sameroff, 1993). Under markedly varying circumstances, young children form attachments; construct internal representations of themselves and others; generate expectations of the social world; regulate impulse, affect, and behavior; engage in relationships with other children and adults outside of the home and family context; and embark on the road to formal learning in structured school settings. The nature and quality of these emerging competencies, whether they are adaptive or maladaptive, is highly dependent on children's experiences in the first years of life (Center on the Developing Child, 2007).

Much is known about the factors that promote positive outcomes and those that derail social-emotional development, referred to, respectively, as protective and risk factors (Rutter, 1987; Sameroff & Chandler, 1975). A burgeoning research base affirms that the young child's social environment, particularly that created and mediated by primary caregivers, directly affects not only the child's observable behaviors, but, in a more fundamental way, the brain structures that support emerging and future capacities, thereby constituting a source of protection and resilience, or one of risk and dysfunction (National Scientific Council on the Developing Child, 2004). Children's healthy relationships with parents and other caregivers and the development of secure attachments are the basis for social and emotional competence (Shonkoff & Phillips, 2002). Secure attachment to a primary caregiver imbues the infant and toddler with multiple competencies that have enduring benefit throughout life. Other protective factors include an easy temperament, and good cognitive and language competencies (Rutter).

RISK FACTORS FOR SOCIAL-EMOTIONAL DEVELOPMENT

Contemporary models of developmental psychopathology underscore the interplay between children's constitutional vulnerabilities and parenting behaviors in establishing the developmental pathways toward social-emotional disorders. Risk factors may be posed by biological or constitutional vulnerabilities in the child or parent, stressors in the environment, or by combinations of these, mediated by patterns of parent-child affect regulation.

Children's inborn temperamental or regulatory difficulties may pose elements of risk due to the caregiving and interactive challenges they present, especially in the context of parenting stress. The literature on the development of disruptive behavior disorders in young children, for example, suggests that children's oppositional and aggressive behaviors often result from the interplay between the temperamental profile of high child emotional reactivity and highly controlling and coercive parenting styles (Greene & Doyle, 1999). Disability poses risks for social-emotional development as children with disabilities often have cognitive or linguistic skill deficits, and/or impairment in one or more of the sensory or motor modalities that support interactive behaviors, social competencies, and children's sense of agency and efficacy. This is compounded by the stress on parents in adjusting to the birth of, and caring for, a child with special needs (Foley, 2006).

Maternal depression, a high incidence condition, particularly in poverty-affected communities (Lanzi, Pascoe, Keltner, & Ramey, 1999; Petterson & Albers, 2001), is a serious risk factor that affects both the emotional availability of the mother to her infant, and the emotional tenor of her interactions with her child. Depressed mothers are more likely either to withdraw from their children and to respond to them with little emotion or energy, or to be irritable, with high rates of intrusiveness and hostility (Belsky, 1984). The effects of maternal depression on parenting behaviors contribute to the increased rates of attachment insecurity in infants and toddlers with depressed mothers (Murray, 1992) and to problems with the regulation of negative affect, with some children showing affect-related helplessness or flat affect (Kelley & Jennings, 2003) and others showing increased aggression.

Prolonged separation from primary caregivers, whether in the context of military deployment, incarceration, or death of a parent, may trigger intense grief reactions in infants and young children, especially when compounded by the stress and/or bereavement of the remaining parent which may limit his or her ability to be physically or psychologically present for the child (Lieberman, Compton, Van Horn, & Ghosh Ippen, 2003). Internationally adopted children whose early months or years were spent in orphanages, with limited stimulation, and deprived of opportunities to establish a relationship with a consistent caregiver, often have developmental delays and deficits in regulatory and social-emotional competencies, and show varying degrees of recovery usually dependent upon their age at adoption. Residual problems in social-emotional adjustment are often reported, even when greater gains are made in other developmental domains (Rutter & the English and Romanian Adoptees [ERA] Study Team, 1998).

Of greatest concern are those young children who experience physical or sexual maltreatment, and/or exposure to domestic or community violence. Occurring separately, or too often in conjunction with one another, these constitute extremely traumatic experiences for young children and often occur in the context of parental substance abuse, mental illness, and/or intergenerational histories of neglect or abuse. When abuse or violence is perpetrated by a parent or otherwise occurs in the context of children's important relationships, a situation referred to as complex trauma (Cook et al., 2005) may occur, children show patterns of disorganized attachment sometimes accompanied by developmental delays, and almost always accompanied by problems in emotion and behavioral regulation due to the chronic activation of their brain-based fear/stress systems (Center on the Developing Child, 2007). As a result of the danger they experience in the context of their families, many children who have such experiences are ultimately placed in foster care, adding attachment disruption, sometimes of a repeated nature, to their traumatic experiences. Children under 5 years old are currently the largest cohort of children in the foster care system (U.S. Department of Health and Human Services, 2003). Often considered the most vulnerable segment of the early childhood population, these children's social-emotional profiles are characterized by mistrust, deficits in empathy and emotional competence, poor peer relationships, and elevated levels of both internalizing (e.g., anxiety, depression) and externalizing (e.g., aggression, oppositional) symptoms (Wiggins, Fenichel, & Mann, 2007). Young children in foster care have high rates of mental health disorders including attachment disorders and post-traumatic stress disorder (PTSD) (Vig, Chinitz, & Shulman, 2005).

Poverty is an extremely strong risk factor for children's social and emotional development, constituting the umbrella under which multiple risk factors (e.g., family instability, parental stress and psychopathology, parental substance abuse, exposure to violence and trauma, intergenerational transmission of relationship discord) cluster and impact on young children's development in a cumulative manner (McLoyd, 1998). Poverty is considered to have its most adverse effect during infancy and early childhood due to the detrimental impact of *toxic stress* on the brain-based structures and processes, pivotal to children's social and emotional health, that are in formation during this developmental period (Center on the Developing Child, 2007).

THE SOCIAL-EMOTIONAL FOUNDATIONS OF SCHOOL READINESS

School readiness is a complex construct that has multiple determinants and incorporates diverse developmental processes, many of which have their origins in infancy (Andreassen & West, 2007). While research and public policy continue to underscore the cognitive underpinnings of school readiness, most contemporary formulations of school readiness are now much broader and encompass a wide range of social and emotional competencies that have been found to support young children's positive adjustment to school and subsequent academic success (Thompson & Raikes, 2007). School entry places many demands on young children's social and emotional abilities. They must separate from their parents, relate to and cooperate with teachers and other adults, make friends, resolve conflicts adaptively, listen attentively, and demonstrate impulse control while also coping with the challenges of acquiring new academic skills (Raver, Garner, & Smith-Donald, 2007). Teachers affirm the primary importance of these competencies for success in the classroom. In the National Center for Educational Statistics' (1993) survey of teachers' ratings of child characteristics essential for kindergarten readiness, teachers endorsed the greater importance for early learning of social-emotional competencies over traditional academic readiness skills.

In recent years, there has been concern about increasing numbers of children in early childhood programs who have emotional and behavioral problems that make it difficult for them to participate in and benefit from these programs (Carnegie Corporation of New York, 1994; Rimm-Kaufman, Pianta, & Cox, 2000). In one study, Head Start teachers reported that a significant number of preschool age children exhibited signs of serious emotional distress including depression, withdrawal, aggression, and anti-social behavior (Yoshikawa & Knitzer, 1997). In another study of nearly 4,000 children in pre-K classrooms randomly selected across the country, over 10% of teachers reported at least one expulsion in their classes during the previous year (Gilliam, 2005).

Consequently, there is substantial focus in the school readiness literature on children's self-regulation, encompassing such competencies as emotion regulation, behavior regulation, effortful control, inhibition, focused and sustained attention, and the ability to delay gratification (Blair, 2002). Children's self-regulatory capacities are central to school readiness due to their positive association with the development of cognitive and academic skills (McClelland et al., 2007; NICHD Early Child Care Research Network, 2003), as well as with the social competence and cooperation required of children in the classroom. Chapter 11 presents an in depth discussion of children's self-regulatory abilities.

While studies consistently demonstrate that children's emotional dysregulation is predictive of problematic school performance (Ladd, Birch, & Buhs, 1999; McClelland, Morrison, & Holmes, 2000), research also shows that contextual variables have a powerful effect on behavior and that supportive teachers and classrooms can play an important moderating function in shifting children from negative educational trajectories to more positive ones (Hamre & Pianta, 2005; Mashburn et al., 2008; McCabe & Brooks-Gunn, 2007).

School readiness, therefore, is not just a matter of qualities inherent in the child, nor does it simply refer to the acquisition of cognitive skills. It is significantly influenced by the relationships and social contexts that shape early social-emotional and cognitive growth in homes, schools, and communities (Knitzer & Lefkowitz, 2006). Enhancing school readiness requires careful consideration of the multiple challenges that exist within the child, family, and learning environments, especially for children at socio-demographic risk of subsequent school failure (Blair, 2002; Thompson & Raikes, 2007).

PREVALENCE AND PRESENTATION OF SOCIAL-EMOTIONAL DISORDERS IN YOUNG CHILDREN

Studies have demonstrated high prevalence rates of mental health problems in children under 5 years of age, reaching as high as 25% overall and as high as 9% for mental health problems considered to be severe (Lavigne et al., 1996; Powell, Fixsen, & Dunlap, 2003). Low-income children (Qi & Kaiser, 2003) and young children in foster care (Harman, Childs, & Kelleher, 2000) have the highest rates of mental health disorders. Research consistently shows that behavior problems in early childhood often persist into later years (Campbell & Ewing, 1990), rendering more compelling the need for early identification and intervention.

Symptoms of social-emotional disturbance in young children may be different than their presentation in older children. In infants and toddlers, emotional distress may present in the form of failure to thrive, sleep or feeding disorders, flat affect, lethargy, gaze aversion, irritability or excessive crying, marked separation anxiety, aggression, or self-injurious behavior (Zero to Three, 2005). In preschool-age children, symptoms may include developmental regression, tantrums, social withdrawal, difficulty getting along with other children, hyperactivity, impulsivity, or aggressive behavior (Task Force on Research Diagnostic Criteria: Infancy and Preschool, 2003).

The primary diagnostic system used for young children, *Diagnostic Classification of Mental Health and Developmental Disorders in Infancy and Early Childhood-Revised* (DC:0-3R; Zero to Three, 2005), was developed to frame those mental health conditions found primarily in early childhood and not adequately represented in the current *Diagnostic and Statistical Manual of Mental Disorders*, 4th edition, Text Revision (DSM IV-TR; APA, 2000), and to describe the different ways that symptoms, or manifestations of disorders found in older children, can present in very young children. Clinical disorders described range from those that have a primary constitutional etiology, such as the Regulation Disorders of Sensory Processing and Disorders of Relating and Communicating, to those that have a strong experiential component such as PTSD and Grief and Bereavement Disorder. The DC:0-3R provides a multiaxial framework that underscores the importance of children's biology, relationships, and psychosocial context in the formation of and intervention for mental health and behavioral disorders.

SCREENING AND ASSESSMENT

Early identification and assessment of social-emotional problems is of paramount importance. While practitioners in fields such as pediatrics, education, and mental health often conduct informal assessments, data shows that such informal assessments do not adequately identify the presence of social-emotional difficulties in young children. As such, only approximately 30% of children with developmental and social-emotional problems are detected prior to school entrance (King & Glascoe, 2003), versus a much higher reported rate (i.e., 70–90%) of sensitivity (percentage of children with true problems identified by the screening test) and specificity (percentage of children without problems who correctly "pass" a screening test) for many social-emotional screening tools available for use today. Therefore, the case is clearly made for the inclusion of validated screening instruments in all child-serving systems to greatly enhance the ability to detect those children in need, to refer them for services when necessary, and to connect families to relevant resources (McCann & Yarbrough, 2006).

Beyond screening, when relevant, programs should also participate in monitoring and assessment. *Screening* is a one-time event, likely brief, meant to identify any children who may need further assessment. Generally, large numbers of children may be screened, and they are usually thought to be asymptomatic for the presence of a particular trait. *Monitoring* refers to repeated and ongoing screening, conducted at relevant times. Best practice suggests that a monitoring system is most effective to address longitudinal changes and age-appropriate/specific social-emotional development. Once a child has been screened and found to be at risk for a particular problem, *assessment* becomes relevant in order to determine the degree of impairment. Assessment refers to a more in-depth analysis of a particular set of concerns, and is often more time consuming, more expensive, and more accurate than screening alone.

Best practice requires the use of validated and normed instruments with good to excellent psychometric properties (Halfon, Regalado, McLearn, Kuo, & Wright, 2003; see also Chapter 5). When choosing a screening or assessment instrument, practitioners must become familiar with basic psychometric standards of validity, reliability, sensitivity, and specificity, and attempt to adhere to instruments validated in populations similar to those in question. However, the field of early childhood social-emotional assessment is still a nascent one, and there are some areas in which it is not yet possible to use validated and normed instruments. In these circumstances, findings must be interpreted with caution, and should be augmented by additional sources of information.

The remainder of this section will highlight those instruments considered to adhere most closely to gold standard criteria of reliability and validity, in addition to some tools not yet subjected to reliability and validity testing yet especially relevant to the field. Screening tests will be described first, after which will follow a discussion of more in-depth assessment tools.

SCREENING

Social-emotional screening tests are ideally brief; easily administered, scored and interpreted; validated for the age group in question; not prohibitively expensive; used by a broad range of professionals, not dependent on a particular educational background; multifaceted, with focus on developmental concerns that may overlap with social-emotional concerns; reliable and valid; with sensitivity and specificity in the 70–80% range; validated on diverse populations; and available in multiple languages (Bergman, 2004; Sosna, 2005) (see Table 13.1).

One of the most widely used social-emotional screening tools for young children is the Ages & Stages Questionnaire: Social-Emotional (ASQ:SE; Squires, Bricker, & Twombly, 2002). The ASQ:SE is a parent-completed questionnaire, available in English and Spanish at a fifth-grade reading level, with questions specific to age intervals that correspond to well child visits, from 3 to 66 months. Each age range questionnaire has an empirically derived cut-off score, at or above which children should be assessed further. The questions assess seven characteristics of development and behavior, including self-regulation, compliance, communication, adaptive functioning, autonomy, affect, and interaction with others. Psychometrics of the questionnaire are consistently high to strong, including test-retest reliability, internal consistency, and concurrent and predictive validity.

ASSESSMENT

Assessment of social-emotional development is indicated when screening results are concerning or when there is a parental or professional concern serious enough to warrant more in-depth analysis. Social-emotional assessment should incorporate a variety of methods, including clinical interviews, parental reports, Q-sort measures, structured situations involving observation and/or inquiry, naturalistic observation, and paper-and-pencil checklist

Table 13.1

Social-Emotional Screening Tools for Infants and Toddlers

	Time to complete	Age	Cost	Training req. for admin?	Areas of focus	Psychometrics	Languages
Ages and Stages Questionnaire: Social-Emotional (ASQ:SE)	10–15 minutes	3–66 mos.	$190	No	Self-regulation, compliance, communication, adaptive functioning, autonomy, affect, and interaction with people	Acceptably High, with the exception of the normative sample, which was not nationally representative	English, Spanish
Brief Infant-Toddler Social-Emotional Assessment (BITSEA)	10 minutes	12–36 mos.	$99	Yes	Social emotional and behavioral delays and problems	Acceptably High	English, Spanish, French, Hebrew, Dutch
Child Behavior Checklist (CBCL)	20–30 minutes	18–60 mos.	$195	Yes	Behavioral, emotional, and social functioning, including language development	Acceptably High (although only English-speaking parents)	English, Spanish
Devereux Early Childhood Assessment (DECA)	10 minutes	1–60 mos.	$200	Yes	Strengths-based assessment of resilience and protective factors (initiative, self-control, and attachment), and screener for behavioral concerns	Moderate to Acceptably High	English, Spanish
Eyberg Child Behavior Inventory (ECBI)	10 minutes	24 mos. to 16 years	$174	Yes	Frequency and severity of disruptive behaviors in home/school	Moderate to Acceptably High	English

(Continued)

Table 13.1

(Continued)

	Time to complete	Age	Cost	Training req. for admin?	Areas of focus	Psychometrics	Languages
Functional Emotional Assessment Scale	20 minutes	7–48 mos.	$40	Yes	Emotional and social functioning and caregiver capacity to support development	Moderate to Acceptably High	English
Infant/Toddler Symptom Checklist	10–20 minutes	7–30 mos.	$80	Yes	Sensory and regulatory disorders	Moderate	English
Parents' Evaluation of Developmental Status (PEDS)	10 minutes	Birth to 8 years	$30	No	Developmental and behavioral-emotional problems	Moderate to Acceptably High	English, Spanish, Vietnamese
Pediatric Symptom Checklist	10–15 minutes	4–16 years	No cost	No	Social-emotional delays or disorders	Moderate to Acceptably High	English, Spanish, Japanese, Chinese, Dutch, German, Hmong, French, Haitian-Creole, Hindi, Portuguese
Temperament And Atypical Behavior Scales (TABS)	5 minutes	11–71 mos.	$95	No	Atypical temperament and self-regulatory behaviors	Acceptably High	English
Vineland Social-Emotional Early Childhood Scales	25 minutes	Birth to 72 mos.	$88	Yes	Social-emotional functioning (interpersonal relationships, play and leisure time, and coping skills)	Moderate to Acceptably High	English

measures. Many note that it is of utmost importance to add observational measures to parent report when completing an assessment battery, as observational measures may provide a less biased account of the behavior in question (Martin McDermott & Fox, 2007). However, observational measures are not standardized, they are time consuming, and have limited generalizability, thus exemplifying the trade-off often considered when designing an assessment battery. Fitzgerald (2007) suggests that "a comprehensive assessment of child development may involve measures of child characteristics, parent characteristics, parent-child relationships, parent-parent relationships, family conflict and resources, and the rearing environment" (p. 285).

The remainder of this section will present three social-emotional assessment measures, including one parental report of behavior, one structured situation with observation, and one structured situation with questions. These measures are presented as high-quality options in the realm of social-emotional assessment, yet they are by no means an exhaustive presentation of the available tools. Readers are directed to a recent issue of the *Infant Mental Health Journal* (2007, vol. 28) and the seminal *Handbook of Infant, Toddlers, and Preschool Mental Health Assessment* (Del-Carmen-Wiggins & Carter, 2004) for a more comprehensive review.

The Infant–Toddler Social and Emotional Assessment (ITSEA; Carter & Briggs-Gowan, 2006) is a parent report instrument developed to measure social-emotional competencies and problem behaviors in children 12–36 months. A parent or caregiver completes 139 items covering the domains of Externalizing behaviors (i.e., overactivity, aggression, and defiance), Internalizing behaviors (i.e., anxiety, depression, inhibition to novelty), Dysregulation (i.e., eating and sleeping problems, negative emotionality, and sensory activities), and Competencies (i.e., behaviors that reflect the achievement of age-expected social-emotional skills, such as attention and empathy). The ITSEA has acceptably high scores on relevant psychometrics, and normative data was collected from a community birth cohort of more than 1,300 families representative of the national population. ITSEA questions are answered on a 3-point Likert scale, written at approximately a sixth-grade reading level, and require roughly 30 minutes to complete. Score interpretation depends on *T* scores, indicating whether a child falls in the *of concern* area, determined via cut-off points related to age and sex.

The Nursing Child Assessment Satellite Training (NCAST) Feeding and Teaching Scales (Kelly & Barnard, 2000) are structured situations with observation, used with infants from birth to 12 months (Feeding Scale) or 36 months (Teaching Scale). Both scales have four subscales that describe the parent: Sensitivity to Cues, Response to Distress, Social-Emotional Growth

Fostering, and Cognitive Growth Fostering, and two subscales to describe the child: Clarity of Cues and Responsiveness to Caregiver. The Feeding Scale is administered during a regular feeding, and thus administration time will vary according to feedings. The Teaching Scale is scored following the observation of a session in which the caregiver is asked to teach the child a defined age-appropriate activity, and can generally be completed within 5 minutes. The NCAST is unique in terms of observational tools as it has standardized training for trainers and coders, and offers standardized norms against which findings can be compared. Furthermore, it is flexible enough that it may be coded *in vivo* or via videotape.

The MacArthur Story Stem Battery (MSSB) is a structured situation with questions to the child, resulting in a child narrative revealing understanding and representation of his or her social-emotional world (Bretherton & Oppenheim, 2003). Children aged 3–7 are presented with the beginnings of 14 stories concerned with parent-child attachment, marital and peer conflict, competence and mastery, and moral rules and emotions, and are asked to complete the story, relying on their linguistic and imaginative skills (Bettmann & Lundahl, 2007). Trained coders then examine the completed stories to identify risks related to social-emotional development, such as anxiety/worry and conflict/aggression. Competencies, such as prosocial/ affiliation, are also coded (Holmberg, Robinson, Corbitt-Price, & Wiener, 2007). Although training for coding the MSSB is rigorous, and numerous scoring systems make conventional psychometrics difficult to report, many investigators report high levels of interobserver reliability and internal consistency (Holmberg et al.).

The three assessment measures presented here demonstrate the wide variety available to the clinician seeking to gain comprehensive insight into the social-emotional functioning of an infant or toddler. The tools highlight the trade-off presented to the clinician or researcher when choosing an assessment tool, as they may be rich with observational insight yet lacking in standardization, or normed and reliable yet dependent upon (possibly biased) parental report.

Regardless of challenges inherent in the social-emotional screening and assessment of young children, it is incumbent on all those in a position to enhance our ability to identify and treat children at risk of problems in this area to become sophisticated users of the tools available. In order to find the largest number of vulnerable children, it is recommended that screening occur in all settings where young children are seen, including primary pediatric care, early care and education programs, family support programs, and the child welfare system (Zeanah, Nagle, Stafford, Rice, & Farber, 2005).

CREATING SYSTEMS OF SUPPORT FOR YOUNG CHILDREN'S SOCIAL-EMOTIONAL DEVELOPMENT

Comprehensive systems of support for young children's social-emotional development should include efforts and initiatives at three different levels. *Promotion* includes those activities directed at the entire population, regardless of risk status, aimed at benefiting all young children and their families. Examples include public awareness campaigns, anticipatory guidance provided by pediatricians in well-child visits, and the provision of high-quality early care and education programs for young children. *Prevention* refers to those activities that are targeted to young children who are at risk for social-emotional disorders. Such efforts aim to reduce the occurrence or impact of mental health disorders through early identification and intervention. Many prevention programs are specifically designed for low-income children and families due to the high level of risk in this population. *Treatment* refers to those specialized interventions that are provided for young children with identified social-emotional or mental health disorders, and are typically more intensive and individualized services designed for a relatively small percentage of children.

Best practice dictates that social-emotional support services for young children be family centered and relationship-based, with a focus on support to both the child and his or her primary caregivers. Services should also be integrated into settings where children and families receive other services to ensure access. Services may be delivered via consultation to other practitioners involved with the child or family or may be delivered directly to the child and family. Service providers must be respectful of and responsive to cultural differences among families, often reflected in child-rearing practices and approaches to help seeking, and should receive reflective supervision due to the strong emotional response often elicited in this work (Shahmoon-Shanok, 2006).

Programs that Support Parent-Child Relationships

The proliferation of research attesting to the profound impact of early caregiving experiences on children's social, emotional, behavioral, and academic development has generated an array of interventions aimed at strengthening the relationship between parents and their young children. Some of these work at the level of prevention, while others are targeted interventions for children with established disorders. While these services are delivered in a variety of sites, and by practitioners from different disciplines, their overarching goal is to enhance the ability of caregivers to nurture young children more effectively, thus enhancing opportunities for successful social-emotional development

(Zeanah, Stafford, & Zeanah, 2005). The empirical support for parenting interventions suggests that parenting is open to change. A number of carefully evaluated interventions have successfully improved various dimensions of parenting, and some have linked these changes to improved child outcomes. The literature also suggests, however, that changing parenting behaviors is difficult, and that not all programs designed to improve parenting or child outcomes accomplish these goals (Shonkoff & Phillips, 2000). Successful programs typically have a two-generation focus, with services provided to parents as well as to children, are sufficiently intense to address the multiple risk factors facing families, invest in staff training and supervision, and ensure consistent and well-implemented service delivery (Center on the Developing Child, 2007). The following is a selective review of programs that have empirical support in the program evaluation literature.

EVIDENCE-BASED PREVENTION PROGRAMS

The Nurse Family Partnership Home-Visiting Program   Developed by David Olds in 1977, and guided by theory and research, the Nurse Family Partnership is a program that targets first-time, low-income mothers who are primarily young (mostly adolescent) and unmarried (Olds, 2002). The program aims to modify parental behaviors and environmental conditions early in an infant's life in order to improve birth outcomes, reduce child abuse and neglect (by increasing parents' empathic and sensitive care), and improve parents' life course and self-sufficiency. Beginning in the second trimester of pregnancy and continuing until the child's second birthday, each mother receives regularly scheduled visits from a trained registered nurse at her home, usually weekly or biweekly. Each home visitor follows a standardized curriculum, the content of which is organized around the challenges that mothers encounter during pregnancy, and as the infant develops. Nurses were selected to be the home visitors because of their formal training in women's and children's health, their competence in managing the complex clinical situations often presented by high-risk families, and their credibility in the community. Nurses undergo specialized training throughout their work in the program and receive regular clinical supervision.

The Nurse Family Partnership has been tested in two separate large-scale randomized controlled trials (Olds, 2002) with different populations in different contexts, and continues to be studied via coordinated, national research protocols. It has successfully improved parental care of the child, reflected in fewer injuries and ingestions related to neglect or abuse; has improved cognitive and social behavior of the child; and has improved the life course and self-sufficiency of parents reflected in fewer subsequent pregnancies, greater workforce participation, and reduced use of public assistance and food stamps. In one of the studies, the program also reduced criminality, substance abuse, and promiscuous sexual activity in adolescents who were visited as infants (Olds, 2006). The program is currently widely disseminated throughout the country, financed through a variety of public and private funding sources (www.nursefamilypartnership.org).

Early Head Start Early Head Start, established in 1994, was created as a comprehensive, two-generation program that targets low-income pregnant women and families of infants and toddlers (U.S. Department of Health and Human Services, 1994). The program has four cornerstones including: *Child Development; Family Development,* incorporating a focus on specific supports for parents and for the parent-child relationship; *Staff Development;* and *Community Development,* inclusive of partnerships and linkages to support families. Services for children and families are provided through a combination of center-based and home-based program components. The program is governed by a comprehensive set of performance standards that reflect best practice and articulate the scope of services each program is expected to provide (Head Start Bureau, 1996). Among these are the requirement that programs have consistent mental health consultation that supports children, parents, and staff. The Early Head Start Program has, from its inception, had an extensive, national evaluation. Data collected from the initial 17 programs indicated that Early Head Start participants performed significantly better than nonparticipating children on measures of cognitive, language, and social-emotional development. Parents also demonstrated a variety of positive benefits, including more emotionally supportive interactions with their children, more support for learning in the home, and less inclination toward spanking (Administration on Children, Youth, and Families, 2002). In a follow-up study, these cumulative benefits were thought to have contributed to findings of decreased parental depression 2 years after the completion of the program when children were entering kindergarten (Chazan-Cohen, Ayoub, et al., 2007). In 2000, in response to staff and family feedback, and as part of its commitment to continuous improvement, the Head Start Bureau launched an initiative specifically focused on programmatic and research efforts to even further support the mental health of participating children and parents (Chazan-Cohen, Stark, Mann, & Fitzgerald, 2007).

The Incredible Years Parent Program The Incredible Years Parent Program addresses risk factors posed by young children's vulnerabilities in the areas of temperament and self-regulation toward the goal of preventing the development of conduct disorder or other disruptive behavior disorders. It does so by helping parents learn systematic approaches to positive behavior management in order to avoid the negative outcomes that often result when children's proclivity toward difficult behavior, including high emotional intensity and reactivity, and impulsivity and hyperactivity, are met with parental criticism, harshness, coercion, or corporal punishment (Webster-Stratton & Reid, 2007).

The BASIC program targets parents of children from 3 to 6 years of age, and consists of a series of 12 sessions in which groups of parents view videotapes of parent-child interactions, learn principles of positive behavior management, role-play, and report back on homework assignments given to reinforce parents' new skills. Session content is manualized and includes materials and activities that support the development of new parenting skills. Multiple randomized control group evaluations have shown the program to be effective in increasing parent positive affect, increasing parental use of effective limit setting, reducing harsh and physical discipline, reducing parental depression, increasing parental self-confidence, increasing positive family communication and problem solving, increasing child compliance, and decreasing conduct problems (Webster-Stratton & Hancock, 1998). Supplemental programs, including the ADVANCE program for school-age children and Supporting Your Child's Education, have been developed to address more complicated family risk factors as well as risk factors posed by children's academic problems and weak home–school connections. Most recent additions to the series are an Incredible Years Parents and Babies Program and Incredible Years Parents and Toddler Program (www.IncredibleYears.org).

EVIDENCE-BASED INTERVENTION PROGRAMS FOR CHILDREN WITH ESTABLISHED DIFFICULTIES

Child-Parent Psychotherapy (CPP)   Initially developed for very young children with relationship disorders and their parents (Fraiberg, 1980; Lieberman, 1991), CPP is now, with modifications, an intervention of choice for preschool-age children who have experienced trauma, particularly exposure to domestic violence. This dyadic intervention (Lieberman & Van Horn, 2005) uses both an attachment and a trauma perspective to treat young children's symptoms of trauma, with the theoretical rationale that children's relationships are inevitably affected when interpersonal violence is perpetrated by attachment figures, and that a strengthened child-parent relationship, in which the mother is more competent in responding to the child's emotional needs, provides the best mechanism for behavioral change and for ongoing therapeutic protection for the child.

Child and mother are seen in joint sessions in which guided therapeutic play and therapist-child-parent dialogue are used to create a joint trauma narrative that addresses and clarifies the traumatic event(s) and restores trust in the parent-child relationship. Sessions are also used to promote safety planning; to support the child's and parent's affect regulation; to foster parents' use of positive, developmentally appropriate strategies for behavior management; and to put the traumatic event in perspective and restore hope for the future. The therapeutic manual provides guidance on intervening with children's regulatory problems, fearfulness, self-endangering behaviors, aggression and defiance, critical or punitive parenting, and feelings about the perpetrating parent. It addresses the importance of crisis intervention, case management, and assistance with daily living in fostering families' trust and stability.

CPP, provided in 1-hour weekly sessions over the course of approximately 1 year, has shown efficacy in randomized trials in decreasing behavior problems and symptoms of PTSD in both children and their mothers in a culturally diverse, low-income group of preschoolers exposed to marital violence (Lieberman, Van Horn, & Ghosh Ippen, 2005). A follow-up study (Lieberman, Ghosh Ippen, & Van Horn, 2006) found that improvements in children's behavior problems and maternal symptoms were evident 6 months after termination of the treatment. Empirical support is also evident for the use of CPP to improve the attachment status of maltreated infants and preschoolers (Cicchetti, Rogosch, & Toth, 2006; Toth, Maughan, Manly, Spagnola, & Cicchetti, 2002).

Parent-Child Interaction Therapy (PCIT) PCIT (Hembree-Kigin & McNeil, 1995) is a dyadic intervention designed for young children aged 2–7 with disruptive behavior disorders that result from a variety of etiological circumstances, including children's temperamental proclivities, parent-child relationship problems, and trauma. Integrating behavioral and play therapy techniques, PCIT aims to improve the parent-child relationship, and to teach parents to use developmentally sound and positive strategies for behavior management. Intervention usually occurs over a course of 12 weekly sessions. The first stage, Child Directed Interaction, teaches parents how to play with their child in a nondirective manner using praise, imitation, and descriptive commenting. These skills help to build a positive relational foundation for the discipline strategies that parents will learn in the second stage of intervention. In the second stage, Parent-Directed Interaction, parents learn to give clearly stated instructions, set limits, and deliver consistent consequences for child compliance. Active, in-the-moment parent coaching is the core feature of PCIT throughout both components of the intervention. The therapist's observations of the parent and child in session and the immediate feedback provided to parents helps shape desired parental behaviors by rewarding successive approximations, permits modifications in parenting techniques in response to specific child characteristics, corrects parent errors promptly, and provides parents with confidence to practice and use new skills. In a review and meta-analysis of outcome studies, PCIT reduced parent-reported child behavior and parenting problems noteworthy for its large effect size (Thomas & Zimmer-Gembeck, 2007) and stability of improvement over a 2-year period of time (Eyberg et al. 2001).

Interventions in Other Child-Serving Systems

Growing awareness of the importance of young children's healthy social and emotional development, the knowledge that many children at risk for social-emotional disturbance will not readily access specialized services, and best-practice recommendations that call for the provision of mental health services and supports for children and families in other child-serving systems, have resulted in the development of models of consultation and direct service delivery outside of traditional clinical settings. Services infused into natural environments or other child-serving systems permit the greatest access to all levels of intervention, and have the additional benefit of enhancing the perspectives and capacities of others who care for children (e.g., pediatricians, early childhood teachers, child care providers, foster parents, foster care caseworkers, family court judges) to support young children's healthy social-emotional development (Kaufmann & Hepburn, 2007).

Interventions in Primary Pediatric Care Settings   With a recommended schedule of 10 well-baby visits within the first 3 years, pediatric providers are often the first, if not the only, professionals who have regular contact with infants, toddlers, and their parents. These contacts occur in a setting that is non-stigmatizing, typically imbued with trust by families, and universally accessed (recent studies reveal that at least 95% of children regularly visit a pediatrician; Newacheck, Hung, Hochstein, & Halfon, 2002). For these reasons, the pediatric practice is a unique and important resource for screening and assessment of children's social and emotional development and for the provision of support via consultation, facilitated referrals or direct service provision. In a national survey conducted by the Commonwealth Foundation in 1996, almost 80% of parents of young children said they wanted more information from their pediatricians related to their children's sleep, crying, toilet training, and discipline, and significant numbers of parents endorsed feelings of frustration, parenting stress, and symptoms of depression (Young, Davis, Schoen, & Parker, 1998). Several models have been developed to enhance the capacity of primary pediatric care to promote young children's social-emotional well-being and to screen and address child and adult risk factors (Rosman, Perry, & Hepburn, 2005).

Healthy Steps for Young Children In this program, developed at the Boston University School of Medicine, initially funded by the Commonwealth Foundation, and currently implemented in more than 50 sites throughout the country, a developmental specialist (Healthy Steps Specialist) is an integral part of the health care team and provides enhanced behavioral and developmental guidance and support services to families of infants from birth to 3 years of age in the context of their well child care. Via joint office visits with the pediatrician and/or home visits, the Healthy Steps Specialist provides screening for developmental and behavioral concerns; helps parents manage common behavioral concerns related to sleep, feeding, crying, toilet training, and tantrums; answers a telephone information and *warm-line* for parents; shares written materials with parents; facilitates parent groups; and assesses more serious concerns and provides referrals to, and follow-up with, community and therapeutic support services. An evaluation of the impact of the Healthy Steps program revealed that parents who received these services reported high levels of satisfaction with their pediatric care, better understood their children's behavior and development and thereby used more favorable (less physical) discipline practices, spent more time discussing their own emotional status, and played with and read more to their children (Minkovitz et al., 2003). Children in Healthy Steps programs were also more likely to have had developmental screenings. Studies also show lasting benefits more than 2 years postintervention, including sustainment of more favorable parental discipline practices (Minkovitz et al., 2007).

Bright Futures Developed by the Maternal and Child Health Bureau and the Medicaid Bureau, and endorsed by the American Academy of Pediatrics, Bright Futures is a set of practice guidelines for pediatric providers that expand the view of children's health to one that is inclusive of psychosocial and environmental factors that influence health and development. These guidelines promote mental health as an essential component of overall health and well-being, address prevention and early identification of childhood psychological problems, include topics for anticipatory guidance, and provide tools for health professionals and families for use in screening, care management, and health education. Recommendations for the 1-month visit, for example, include discussion of parental (maternal) well-being including postpartum depression, substance abuse, and other issues for new mothers such as breast-feeding, plans to return to work or school, and child care. The 18-month visit includes adaptation to non-parental care, anticipation of return to clinging behaviors, and the early identification of autistic spectrum disorders. The topics, provider- and family-oriented materials, and interventions that comprise the multiple components of Bright Futures are evidence-driven and are now integrated into professional training programs, community-based pediatric care, state policy, plans, and standards for health care provision, and as a requirement for health-related grant programs (Zimmerman, Gallagher, Botsko, Ledsky, & Gwinner, 2005; Zimmerman et al., 2006).

INTERVENTIONS IN EARLY CHILD CARE AND EDUCATION PROGRAMS

Increasing numbers of infants, toddlers, and preschool-age children are spending extended hours in child care and preschool programs (Cohen & Kaufmann, 2000). The care that children receive in these settings, therefore, plays a major role in shaping children's social and emotional development. As a result of their increased prominence in the lives of children and families, early childhood programs feel the impact of family stresses, and staff report that they are serving growing numbers of children with significant emotional and behavioral problems connected to the complex array of difficulties faced by families and communities across the socioeconomic spectrum (Donahue, Falk, & Provet, 2007). As cornerstones of their communities, early child care and education programs are critical venues for the promotion of children's healthy social-emotional development, and for intervention for emerging concerns about the child and/or family. The following interventions have strong empirical support in early childhood settings.

Mental Health Consultation   In Gilliam's 2005 study of the rate of preschool expulsions, the one factor that reduced the number of expulsions for disruptive behavior was the presence of an on-site mental health or behavioral consultant who provided support for preschool teachers. Mental health consultation in child care and preschool programs is a vital service for programs and for children and families (Knitzer, 2000), and has long been a component of the performance standards for Head Start programs (Powell et al., 2003). Mental health consultation in early childhood programs is a problem-solving and capacity-building intervention implemented within a collaborative relationship between a consulting mental health professional and early childhood program staff, and is aimed at improving the ability of staff, families, and programs to prevent, identify, and treat mental health and behavioral difficulties in young children (Cohen & Kaufmann, 2000). Mental health consultation may be child centered, programmatic, or a combination of both (see Chapter 9).

Social-Emotional Curricula   Many curricula have been developed for use in groups to improve the emotional regulation and pro-social behaviors of young children with impulsive behaviors, or those who have experienced life adversities that have negatively affected their behavior. These curricula systematically and intentionally teach children skills of emotion recognition, appropriate expression of emotion, friendship skills, problem-solving skills, conflict resolution, and stress management. Several have shown empirical support in randomized control trials (Joseph & Strain, 2003). The Incredible Years Child Training Program, called Dinosaur School (Webster-Stratton, 2000), is a program that uses puppets and other techniques to teach social-emotional competencies over the course of approximately 20 weekly sessions to small groups of children with behavior problems. Dinosaur School is also being used as a universal intervention in Head Start and other early childhood classrooms, implemented for whole classes via 60 lesson plans delivered one to three times a week in 45-minute class periods. Evaluations of both applications of this program have shown improvement in children's social problem-solving skills and pro-social behaviors as well as a reduction in disruptive behaviors (Joseph & Strain; Webster-Stratton, Reid, & Stoolmiller, 2008). Other curricula include First Step to Success for at-risk kindergarteners with externalizing behavior problems (Walker et al., 1998), Second Step (Frey, Nolan, Van Schoiack-Edstrom, & Hirschstein, 2005), and Promoting Alternative Thinking Skills (PATHS; Kusche & Greenberg, 1994).

INTERVENTIONS IN THE CHILD WELFARE SYSTEM

Children known to the child welfare system often have multiple layers of risk factors for social-emotional disorders, including prenatal exposure to teratogens, maltreatment or other forms of trauma, and attachment disruptions. Several interventions for abused or maltreated children, usually those requiring the most intensive services (Shonkoff & Phillips, 2000), have now been empirically validated.

Attachment and Biobehavioral Catch-up This intervention, developed for foster parents of very young children, targets three needs identified as critical to help children cope with disruptions in care: the regulatory problems that accompany prenatal exposures and neglectful or abusive early experiences, the need for nurturing parenting regardless of the avoidant or resistant behaviors children often manifest, and the need to address the barriers to the provision of nurturing care often faced by foster parents (Dozier, Dozier, & Manni, 2002). Ten sessions are provided for foster parents in their homes, several of which incorporate the use of videotape and parent-child play as learning aids. In the first two sessions, foster parents are taught to see children's alienating behaviors as reflecting their strategies for coping with

402 EVIDENCE-BASED PRACTICE WITH YOUNG CHILDREN WITH SPECIAL NEEDS

previous relationship failures, and learn skills for providing nurturance even when children fail to ask or even spurn their efforts. Sessions three and four address difficulties the caregiver may have that interfere with his or her ability to sense the child's distress, or to respond in positive ways to the child's needs. Subsequent sessions address the importance of touch for distressed children, and the importance of other caregiving practices that support children's regulation, sense of efficacy, and emotion understanding. The final session is a review of what has been learned and an opportunity to pinpoint progress and ongoing goals. In an outcome study conducted 1 month following the completion of the training, children in the experimental group had lower stress hormone values than children in the control group, and experimental intervention parents reported fewer behavior problems, providing preliminary evidence of the effectiveness of the intervention (Dozier et al., 2006).

Miami Court Team Program   This program, an outgrowth and continuation of Florida's Infant and Young Child Mental Health Pilot Project for children under 3 years of age at risk for out-of-home placement due to abuse or neglect or already in foster care, links an evidence-based relational psychotherapy program, conducted at the University of Miami's Linda Ray Intervention Center, to the Miami Dade County Juvenile Court, enabling judges to readily obtain therapeutic services for families, and to use the feedback from this program to make permanency decisions for young children.

Children and their biological parents are seen for approximately 25 therapy sessions, using the techniques of CPP (Lieberman & Van Horn, 2005), toward the goals of improving the parent-child relationship, reducing the recurrence of abuse and neglect, expediting permanency, and enhancing child development outcomes. The underlying assumption of this service is that the child has been hurt in the context of the parent-child relationship and must be healed in this relational context. Information about the status and progress of the parent-child dyad toward improved interactions, derived from standardized empirically supported relational assessments, is shared with judges and is an important factor in planning for these infants and toddlers. Preliminary data from the pilot project, conducted in three different sites within Florida, indicate a reduction in further reports of abuse or neglect, improved health and developmental status of children, decreased rates of parental depression, and improved parent-child relationship functioning based on both observational assessments and parental reports. Limitations of these studies include the lack of a control group and the fact that many parents in this high-risk sample did not complete treatment or postintervention measures (Osofsky et al., 2007).

CULTURAL COMPETENCY IN CLINICAL PRACTICE WITH CHILDREN AND FAMILIES

The increase in immigration and the growing diversity of ethnicities and cultures represented in communities require that clinicians develop competence in culturally sensitive practice. Culture impacts all aspects of a family's functioning, behavior, and interactions. This is especially the case in patterns of child rearing, families' expectations and goals for their children, and in their approach to help seeking when a child has a developmental or behavioral problem. Some aspects of culture are readily observable, while others, including values, belief systems, and worldview are less apparent, though often the driving force behind families' behaviors. Families often straddle the interface between two cultures—the one of their heritage and homeland, and that of their newly adopted home—creating tensions, conflicts, and adaptations that families cope with more or less successfully. In addition, culture interacts with the broader social context in which families live, including communities' acceptance or rejection of specific ethnic groups, their economic opportunities or insecurities, differences in perceived or real power, and families' consequent access to resources, all of which play a part in families' options, decisions and the manner in which they raise their children (Huang & Issacs, 2007).

In order to avoid a disconnect between families and practitioners that is antithetical to the nature and goals of intervention around children's social-emotional disorders, clinicians must be aware of the ways in which culture affects family structure and decision making, including the role of women; approaches to children's feeding, sleeping, and proximity seeking; negotiation of children's needs for dependency and autonomy; approaches to discipline; the selection of programs; and, ultimately, the child's sense of self (Recchia & Williams, 2006). Professional competence in culturally sensitive practice—the ability of the provider to understand, respect, and build on the cultural and linguistic practices of the family to promote young children's healthy growth and development—is facilitated by personal tolerance of diversity, an open and inquiring stance with families, self-reflection and examination, and reflective supervision. Cultural sensitivity is reflected not only in personal behaviors, but also in organizational practices as well as in a flexible interpretation of existing models of child development that are drawn primarily from studies of the dominant population.

TRAINING AND WORKFORCE ISSUES

The professional capacity to deliver services to infants, toddlers, and pre-school-age children with social-emotional and behavioral disorders does not meet the demand and is one of the greatest challenges currently facing this field (Meyers, 2007; Shonkoff & Phillips, 2000). Working with infants, toddlers, and preschool-age children requires a knowledge base and competencies that differ from those of practitioners who work with older children. First, these include a strong foundation in relationship-based practice that acknowledges the primary importance of parents and caregivers in young children's social and emotional development and that addresses and supports the relationship as a critical component of the intervention. Second, infant mental health requires a transdisciplinary, integrative perspective that appreciates the contributions of many scientific and developmental disciplines (e.g., genetics, neurology, speech and language, physical and occupational therapy) to the understanding of young children's developing capacities, as well as to the individual and systemic interventions that best support their development (Shahmoon-Shanok, Henderson, Grellong, & Foley, 2006).

Training in children's social-emotional development is needed across child-serving systems and will naturally differ whether one's efforts are at the level of promotion, prevention, or intervention for established problems. Pediatricians and providers of early care and education, for example, require competencies at the level of promotion, screening, and other methods of early identification and referral, while mental health practitioners need specialized training in those clinical interventions that are specifically designed for very young children with identified disorders. Several states across the country are working to define the different levels of competencies in social-emotional support needed by practitioners who interface with young children and families across systems, and to link these to training recommendations and opportunities. The Michigan Association for Infant Mental Health has made the most progress in developing competencies that lead to endorsement at one of four professional levels and could be a resource to other localities or the springboard for a national model. At the present time, the Harris Foundation has been the main force in developing a cadre of clinicians to provide specialty services for infants and young children through its funding of 15 programs nationwide that comprise the Harris Infancy and Early Childhood Professional Development Network. Each of these programs provides training for professionals from a variety of disciplines in evaluation and intervention with infants, toddlers, and families. It is also recommended that university-based professional education programs in fields such as clinical psychology, school psychology, social work, and education include specializations in the field of infancy and early childhood, and that such training be readily available in community-based in-service programs (Meyers, 2007).

REFERENCES

Administration on Children, Youth and Families. (2002). *Making a difference in the lives of infants and toddlers and their families: The impact of Early Head Start* (Executive Summary), Washington, DC: Department of Health and Human Services.

American Psychiatric Association (2000). *Diagnostic and statistical manual of mental disorders* (4th ed., text revision). Washington, DC: Author.

Andreassen, C., & West, J. (2007). Measuring socio-emotional functioning in a national birth cohort study. *Infant Mental Health Journal, 28*(6), 627–646.

Belsky, J. (1984). The determinants of parenting: A process model. *Child Development, 55*, 83–96.

Bergman, D. (2004). *Screening for behavioral developmental problems: Issues, obstacles, and opportunities for change.* Retrieved April 20, 2008, from the National Academy for State Health Policy Web site: http://www.nashp.org.

Bettmann, J. E., & Lundahl, B. W. (2007). Tell Me a Story: A review of narrative assessments for preschoolers. *Child and Adolescent Social Work Journal, 24*, 455–475.

Blair, C. (2002). School readiness: Integrating cognition and emotion in a neuro-biological conceptualization of children's functioning at school entry. *American Psychologist, 57*(2), 111–127.

Bretherton, I., & Oppenheim, D. (2003). The MacArthur Story Stem Battery: Development, directions for administration, reliability, validity, and reflections about meaning. In R. N. Emde, D. P. Wolf, & D. Oppenheim (Eds.), *Revealing the inner worlds of young children: The MacArthur Story Stem Battery and parent–child narratives* (pp. 55–80). New York: Oxford University Press.

Bronfenbrenner, U. (1979). *The ecology of human development: Experiences by nature and design.* Cambridge, MA: Harvard University Press.

Campbell, S. B., & Ewing, L. J. (1990). Hard to manage preschoolers: Adjustment at age nine and predictors of continuing symptoms. *Journal of Child Psychology and Psychiatry, 31*, 871–889.

Carnegie Corporation of New York. (1994). *Starting points: Meeting the needs of our youngest children.* New York: Author.

Carter, A. S., & Briggs-Gowan, M. J. (2006). *Manual for the Infant-Toddler Social-Emotional Assessment (ITSEA), version 2.* San Antonio, TX: Psychological Corporation, Harcourt Press.

Center on the Developing Child. (2007). *A science-based framework for early childhood policy: Using evidence to improve outcomes in learning, behavior and health for vulnerable children.* Cambridge, MA: Harvard University.

Chazan-Cohen, R., Ayoub, C., Alexander Pan, B., Roggman, L., Raikes, H., McKelvey, L., et al. (2007). It takes time: Impacts of Early Head Start that lead to reductions in maternal depression two years later. *Infant Mental Health Journal, 28*(2), 151–170.

Chazan-Cohen, R., Stark, D. R., Mann, T. L., & Fitzgerald, H. E. (2007). Early Head Start and infant mental health [Special issue]. *Infant Mental Health Journal, 28*(2), 99–105.

Cicchetti, D., Rogosch, F. A., & Toth, S. L. (2006). Fostering secure attachment in infants in maltreating families through preventive interventions. *Development and Psychopathology, 18*, 623–650.

Cohen, E., & Kaufmann, R. (2000). *Early childhood mental health consultation*. Washington, DC: Georgetown University, National Technical Assistance Center for Children's Mental Health, Center for Child and Human Development.

Cook, A., Spinazzola, J., Ford, J., Lanktree, C., Blaustein, M., Cloitre, M., et al. (2005). Complex trauma in children and adolescents. *Psychiatric Annals, 35*, 390–398.

Del-Carmen-Wiggins, R., & Carter, A. (Eds.). (2004). *Handbook of infant, toddler, and preschool mental health assessment*. New York: Oxford University Press.

Donahue, P. J., Falk, B., & Provet, A. G. (2007). Promoting social-emotional development in young children: Mental health supports in early childhood environments. In D. F. Perry, R. K. Kaufmann, & J. Kintzer (Eds.), *Social and emotional health in early childhood: Building bridges between services and systems* (pp. 281–312). Baltimore: Brookes.

Dozier, M., Dozier, D., & Manni, M. (2002). Attachment and biobehavioral catch-up: The ABC's of helping infants in foster care cope with early adversity. *Zero to Three*, April/May, 7–13.

Dozier, M., Peloso, E., Lindhiem, O., Gordon, K. M., Manni, M., Sepulveda, S., et al. (2006). Developing evidence-based interventions for foster children: An example of a randomized clinical trial with infants and toddlers. *Journal of Social Issues, 62* (4), 767–785.

Eyberg, S. M., Funderburk, B. W., Hembree-Kigin, T. L., McNeil, C. B., Querido, J. G., & Hood, K. K. (2001). Parent-Child Interaction Therapy with behavior problem children: One and two year maintenance of treatment effects in the family. *Child & Family Behavior Therapy, 23*(4), 1–20.

Fitzgerald, H. E. (2007). Commentary: Difficulties assessing social and emotional behavior in large-scale national studies. *Infant Mental Health Journal, 28*, 685.

Foley, G. M. (2006). The loss grief cycle: Coming to terms with the birth of a child with a disability. In G. M. Foley & J. D. Hochman (Eds.), *Mental health in early intervention* (pp. 227–243). Baltimore: Brookes.

Fraiberg, S. (1980). *Clinical studies in infant mental health*. New York: Basic Books.

Frey, K. S., Nolan, S. B., Van Schoiack-Edstrom, L., & Hirschstein, M. K. (2005). Effects of a school-based emotional competence program: Linking children's goals, attributions, and behavior. *Journal of Applied Developmental Psychology, 26*, 171–200.

Gilliam, W. S. (2005). *Prekindergartners left behind: Expulsion rates in state prekindergarten systems*. New Haven, CT: Yale University Child Study Center.

Greene, R. W., & Doyle, A. E. (1999). Toward a transactional conceptualization of oppositional defiant disorder: Implications for assessment and treatment. *Clinical Child and Family Psychology Review, 2*(3), 129–148.

Halfon, N., Regalado, M., McLearn, K. T., Kuo, A. A., & Wright, K. (2003). *Building a bridge from birth to school: Improving developmental and behavioral health services for young children* (Publication No. 564). New York: The Commonwealth Fund.

Hamre, B. K., & Pianta, R. C. (2005). Can instructional and emotional support in the first grade classroom make a difference for children at risk for school failure? *Child Development, 76*, 949–967.

Harman, J. S., Childs, G. E., & Kelleher, K. J. (2000). Mental health utilization and expenditures by children in foster care. *Archives of Pediatric and Adolescent Medicine, 154*, 1114–1117.

Head Start Bureau. (1996). *Head Start program performance standards* (45 CFR Part 1304). Washington, DC: U.S. Department of Health and Human Services, Administration on Children, Youth, and Families.

Hembree-Kigin, T. L., & McNeil, C. B. (1995). *Parent–Child Interaction Therapy.* New York: Plenum Press.

Holmberg, J., Robinson, J., Corbitt-Price, J., & Wiener, P. (2007). Using narratives to assess competencies and risks in young children: Experiences with high risk and normative populations. *Infant Mental Health Journal, 28,* 647–666.

Huang, L. N., & Issacs, M. R. (2007). Early childhood mental health: A focus on culture and context. In D. F. Perry, R. K. Kaufmann, & J. Knitzer (Eds.), *Social and emotional health in early childhood: Building bridges between services and systems* (pp. 37–59). Baltimore: Brookes.

Joseph, G. E., & Strain, P. S. (2003). Comprehensive evidence-based social-emotional curricula for young children: An analysis of efficacious adoption potential. *Topics in Early Childhood Special Education, 23,* 65–76.

Kaufmann, R. K., & Hepburn, K. S. (2007). Early childhood mental health services and supports through a systems approach. In D. F. Perry, R. K. Kaufmann, & J. Knitzer (Eds.), *Social and emotional health in early childhood: Building bridges between services and systems* (pp. 63–96). Baltimore: Brookes.

Kelley, S. A., & Jennings, K. D. (2003). Putting the pieces together: Maternal depression, maternal behavior, and toddler helplessness. *Infant Mental Health Journal, 24,* 74–90.

Kelly, J. F., & Barnard, K. E. (2000). Assessment of parent–child interaction: Implications for early intervention. In J. P. Shonkoff & S. J. Meisels (Eds.), *Handbook of early childhood intervention* (pp. 258–289). New York: Cambridge University Press.

King, T., & Glascoe, F. (2003). Developmental surveillance of infants and young children in pediatric primary care. *Current Opinion Pediatrics, 15,* 624–629.

Knitzer, J. (2000). Early childhood mental health services: A policy and systems development perspective. In J. P. Shonkoff & S. J. Meisels (Eds.), *Handbook of early childhood intervention* (2nd ed., pp. 416–438). New York: Cambridge University Press.

Knitzer, J., & Lefkowitz, J. (2006). *Pathways to early school success: Helping the most vulnerable infants, toddlers and their families.* New York: National Center for Children in Poverty.

Kusche, C. A., & Greenberg, M. T. (1994). *The PATHS curriculum.* Seattle, WA: Developmental Research and Programs.

Ladd, G. W., Birch, S. H., & Buhs, E. S. (1999). Children's social and scholastic lives in kindergarten: Related spheres of influence? *Child Development, 70,* 1373–1400.

Lanzi, R. G., Pascoe, J. M., Keltner, B., & Ramey, S. L. (1999). Correlates of maternal depressive symptoms in a national Head Start program sample. *Archives of Pediatric and Adolescent Medicine, 153,* 801–807.

Lavigne, J. V., Gibbons, R. D., Christoffel, K. K., Arend, R., Rosenbaum, D., Binns, H., et al. (1996). Prevalence rates and correlates of psychiatric disorders among preschool children. *Journal of the American Academy of Child and Adolescent Psychiatry, 35*(2), 204–214.

Lieberman, A. F. (1991). Attachment theory and infant–parent psychotherapy: Some conceptual, clinical and research considerations. In D. Cicchetti & S. Toth (Eds.), *Models and integrations* (vol. 3, pp. 261–287). Rochester Symposium on Developmental Psychopathology. Hillsdale, NJ: Erlbaum.

Lieberman, A. F., Compton, N. C., Van Horn, P., & Ghosh Ippen, C. (2003). *Losing a parent to death in the early years.* Washington, DC: Zero to Three Press.

Lieberman, A. F., Ghosh Ippen, C., & Van Horn, P. (2006). Child-parent psychotherapy: 6 month follow-up of a randomized control trial. *Journal of the American Academy of Child & Adolescent Psychiatry, 45*(8), 913–918.

Lieberman, A. F., & Van Horn, P. (2005). *"Don't hit my mommy!": A manual for child–parent psychotherapy with young witnesses of family violence.* Washington, DC: Zero to Three Press.

Lieberman, A. F., Van Horn, P., & Ghosh Ippen, C. (2005). Toward evidence-based treatment: Child–parent psychotherapy with preschoolers exposed to marital violence. *Journal of the American Academy of Child and Adolescent Psychiatry, 44* (12), 1241–1248.

Martin McDermott, J. N., & Fox, N. A. (2007). Conundrums in the use of observational measures. *Infant Mental Health Journal, 28,* 667–681.

Mashburn, A. J., Pianta, R. C., Hamre, B. K., Downer, J. T., Barbarin, O. A., Bryant, D., et al. (2008). Measures of classroom quality in pre-kindergarten and children's development of academic, language and social skills. *Child Development, 79*(3), 732–749.

McCabe, L. A., & Brooks-Gunn, J. (2007). With a little help from my friends?: Self-regulation in groups of young children. *Infant Mental Health Journal, 28*(6), 584–605.

McCann, C. E., & Yarbrough, K. (2006). *Snapshots: Incorporating comprehensive developmental screening into programs and services for young children.* Chicago: Ounce of Prevention Fund.

McClelland, M. M., Cameron, C. E., Connor, C. M., Farris, C. L., Jewkes, A. M., & Morrison, F. J. (2007). Links between behavioral regulation and preschoolers' literacy, vocabulary, and math skills. *Developmental Psychology, 43*(4), 947–959.

McClelland, M. M., Morrison, F. J., & Holmes, D. L. (2000). Children at risk for early academic problems: The role of learning related social skills. *Early Childhood Research Quarterly, 15,* 307–329.

McLoyd, V. C. (1998). Socioeconomic disadvantage and child development. *American Psychologist, 53*(2), 185–204.

Meyers, J. C. (2007). Developing the workforce for an infant and early childhood mental health system of care. In D. F. Perry, R. K. Kaufmann, & J. Knitzer (Eds.), *Social and emotional health in early childhood: Building bridges between services and systems* (pp. 97–120). Baltimore: Brookes.

Minkovitz, C., Hughart, N., Strobino, D., Scharfstein, D., Grason, H., Hou, W., et al. (2003). A practice-based intervention to enhance quality of care in the first 3 years of life: The healthy steps for young children program. *Journal of the American Medical Association, 290*(23), 3081–3091.

Minkovitz, C. S., Strobino, D., Mistry, K. B., Sharfstein, D. O., Grason, H., Hou, W., et al. (2007). Healthy steps for young children: Sustained results at 5.5 years. *Pediatrics, 120*(3), e658–e668.

Murray, L. (1992). The impact of postnatal depression on infant development. *Journal of Child Psychology and Psychiatry, 33*, 543–561.

National Center for Educational Statistics (1993). *Public school kindergarten teachers' views on children's readiness for school* (NCES 94–193). Washington, DC: U.S. Department of Education.

National Scientific Council on the Developing Child (2004). *Young children develop in an environment of relationships* (Working Paper #1). Retrieved June 2008 from www .developingchild.net.

Newacheck, P. W., Hung, Y., Hochstein, M., & Halfon, N. (2002). Access to health care for disadvantaged young children. *Journal of Early Intervention, 25*(1), 1–11.

NICHD Early Child Care Research Network. (2003). Do children's attention processes mediate the link between family predictors and school readiness? *Developmental Psychology, 39*, 581–593.

Olds, D. (2002). Prenatal and infancy home visiting by nurses: From randomized trials to community replication. *Prevention Science, 3*(3), 153–172.

Olds, D. (2006). The Nurse-Family Partnership. In N. F. Wyatt, C. Ayoub, R. H. Bradley, J. E. Puma, & W. A. LeBoeuf (Eds.), *The crisis in youth mental health: Early intervention programs and policies* (pp. 147–180). Westport: Praeger.

Osofsky, J. D., Kronenberg, M., Hammer, H. H., Lederman, C., Katz, L., Adams, S., et al. (2007). The development and evaluation of the intervention model for the Florida Infant Mental Health Program. *Infant Mental Health Journal, 28*(3), 259–280.

Petterson, S. M., & Albers, A. B. (2001). Effects of poverty and maternal depression on early child development. *Child Development, 72*(6), 1794–1813.

Powell, D., Fixsen, D., & Dunlap, G. (2003). *Pathways to service utilization: A synthesis of evidence relevant to young children with challenging behavior. Center for Evidence-based Practice: Young Children with Challenging Behaviors.* University of South Florida, University of Colorado at Denver.

Qi, C. H., & Kaiser, A. P. (2003). Behavior problems of preschool children from low income families: Review of the literature. *Topics in Early Childhood Special Education, 23*(4), 188–216.

Raver, C. C., Garner, P. W., & Smith-Donald, R. (2007). The roles of emotion regulation and emotion knowledge for children's academic readiness. In R. C. Pianta, M. J. Cox, & K. L. Snow (Eds.), *School readiness and the transition to kindergarten in the era of accountability* (pp. 121–147). Baltimore: Brookes.

Recchia, S. L., & Williams, L. R. (2006). Culture, class and diversity: Implications for practice. In G. M. Foley & J. D. Hochman (Eds.), *Mental health in early intervention* (pp. 267–294). Baltimore: Brookes.

Rimm-Kaufman, S. E., Pianta, R. C., & Cox, M. J. (2000). Teachers' judgments of problems in the transition to kindergarten. *Early Childhood Research Quarterly, 15*, 147–166.

Rosman, E. A., Perry, D. F., & Hepburn, K. S. (2005). *The best beginning: Partnerships between primary health care and mental health and substance abuse services for young children and their families.* Georgetown: Georgetown University National Technical Assistance Center for Children's Mental Health.

Rutter, M. (1987). Psychosocial resilience and protective mechanisms. *American Journal of Orthopsychiatry, 57,* 316–331.

Rutter, M., & the English and Romanian Adoptees (ERA) Study Team (1998). Developmental catch-up, and deficit, following adoption after severe global privation. *Journal of Child Psychology and Psychiatry, 39,* 465–476.

Sameroff, A. J. (1993). Models of development and developmental risk. In C. H. Zeanah, Jr. (Ed.), *Handbook of infant mental health* (pp. 3–13). New York: Guilford Press.

Sameroff, A. J., & Chandler, M. J. (1975). Reproductive risk and the continuum of caretaking casualty. In F. D. Horowitz, E. M. Hetherington, S. Scarr-Salapatek, & G. Siegel (Eds.), *Review of child development research* (pp. 187–244). Chicago: University of Chicago Press.

Schore, A. N. (2005). Attachment, affect regulation, and the developing right brain: Linking developmental neuroscience to pediatrics. *Pediatrics in Review, 26*(6), 204–217.

Shahmoon-Shanok, R. (2006). Reflective supervision for an integrated model. In G. M. Foley & J. D. Hochman (Eds.), *Mental health in early intervention* (pp. 343–381). Baltimore: Brookes.

Shahmoon-Shanok, R., Henderson, D., Grellong, B., & Foley, G. M. (2006). Preparation for practice in an integrated model. In G. M. Foley & J. D. Hochman (Eds.), *Mental health in early intervention* (pp. 383–422). Baltimore: Brookes.

Shonkoff, J., & Phillips, D. (2002). Nurturing relationships. In K. Jones (Ed.), *Readings in human behavior* (vol. II, pp. 171–209). Lakewood, CO: Thomas Learning.

Sosna, T. (2005). *Mental health screening and referral capacity for children 0–5.* Sacramento: California Institute for Mental Health.

Squires, J., Bricker, D., & Twombly, E. (2002). *Ages and Stages Questionnaire: Social Emotional* (ASQ:SE). Baltimore: Brookes.

Task Force on Research Diagnostic Criteria: Infancy and Preschool. (2003). Research diagnostic criteria for infants and preschool children: The process and empirical support. *Journal of the American Academy of Child and Adolescent Psychiatry, 42*(12), 1504–1512.

Thomas, R., & Zimmer-Gembeck, M. J. (2007). Behavioral outcomes of Parent–Child Interaction Therapy and Triple P–Positive Parenting Program: A review and meta-analysis. *Journal of Abnormal Child Psychology, 35*(3), 475–495.

Thompson, R. A., & Raikes, H. A. (2007). The social and emotional foundations of school readiness. In D. F. Perry, R. K. Kaufmann, & J. Knitzer (Eds.), *Social and emotional health in early childhood: Building bridges between services and systems* (pp. 13–35). Baltimore: Brookes.

Toth, S. L., Maughan, A., Manly, J. T., Spagnola, M., & Cicchetti, D. (2002). The relative efficacy of two interventions in altering maltreated preschool children's representational models: Implications for attachment theory. *Developmental Psychopathology, 14,* 877–908.

U.S. Department of Health and Human Services, Administration for Children, Youth and Families, Children's Bureau. (2003). *AFCARS report: Current estimates as of March* 2003. Washington, DC: Author.

U.S. Department of Health and Human Services. (1994). *The statement of the advisory committee on services for families of infants and toddlers.* Washington, DC: Author.

Vig, S., Chinitz, S., & Shulman, L. (2005). Young children in foster care: Multiple vulnerabilities and complex service needs. *Infants & Young Children, 18*(2), 147–160.

Walker, H. M., Kavanaugh, K., Stiller, B., Golly, A., Severson, H. H., & Feil, E. (1998). First Step to Success: An early intervention approach for preventing school antisocial behavior. *Journal of Emotional and Behavioral Disorders, 6*(2), 66–80.

Webster-Stratton, C. (2000). *How to promote children's social and emotional competence.* London: Sage Publications.

Webster-Stratton, C., & Hancock, L. (1998). Training for parents of young children with conduct problems: Content, methods, and therapeutic processes. In C. E. Schafer & J. M. Briesmeister (Eds.), *Handbook of parent training* (pp. 98–152). New York: Wiley.

Webster-Stratton, C., & Reid, J. M. (2007). The Incredible Years parents and teachers training series: A Head Start partnership to promote social competence and prevent conduct problems. In. P. Tolan, J. Szapocznik, & S. Sambrano (Eds.), *Preventing youth substance abuse: Science-based programs for children and adolescents* (pp. 67–88). Washington, DC: American Psychological Association.

Webster-Stratton, C., Reid, J. M., & Stoolmiller, M. (2008). Preventing conduct problems and improving school readiness: Evaluation of the Incredible Years teacher and child training programs in high-risk schools. *Journal of Child Psychology and Psychiatry, 49,* 471–480.

Wiggins, C., Fenichel, E., & Mann, T. (2007). *Literature review: Developmental problems of maltreated children and early intervention options for maltreated children.* Retrieved June 2008 from http://aspe.hhs.gov/hsp/07/Children-CPS/litrev.htm.

Yoshikawa, H., & Knitzer, J. (1997). *Lessons from the field: Head Start mental health strategies to meet changing needs.* New York: National Center for Children in Poverty.

Young, K. T., Davis, K., Schoen, C., & Parker, S. (1998). Listening to parents: A national survey of parents with young children. *Archives of Pediatric and Adolescent Medicine, 152,* 255–262.

Zeanah, P., Nagle, G., Stafford, B., Rice, T., & Farber, J. (2005). Addressing socioemotional development and infant mental health in early childhood systems: Executive summary. In N. Halfon, T. Rice, & M. Inkelas (Eds.), *Building state early childhood comprehensive systems series* (No. 12). Los Angeles: National Center for Infant and Early Childhood Health Policy at UCLA.

Zeanah, P., Stafford, B., & Zeanah, C. (2005). *Clinical interventions to enhance infant mental health: A selective review.* Los Angeles: National Center for Infant and Early Childhood Health Policy at UCLA.

Zeroto Three (2005). *Diagnostic Classification of mental health and developmental disorders of infancy and early childhood* (rev. ed.). Washington, DC: Zero to Three Press.

Zimmerman, B., Gallagher, J., Botsko, M. A., Ledsky, R., & Gwinner, V. (2005). *Assessing the bright futures for infants, children, and adolescents initiative: Findings from a national process evaluation.* Washington, DC: Health Systems Research.

Zimmerman, B., Gallagher, J., Gwinner, V., Ferreira, M., Ledsky, R., & Sternesky, L. (2006). *Using Bright Futures in public health efforts to promote child health: Findings from six case studies.* Washington, DC: Health Systems Research.

CHAPTER 14

Aggression

GRETA L. DOCTOROFF
and RACHELLE THEISE

E XTERNALIZING PROBLEMS REPRESENT one of the most common reasons that young children are referred to mental health clinics (Egger & Angold, 2006; Wilens, et al., 2002). Families of toddlers and preschoolers are often confronted with a range of challenging child behaviors, including aggression, noncompliance, defiance, tantrums, and disruptive behavior. These behaviors tend to occur in concert with other difficulties. For instance, even 1- to 2-year-old children with elevated behavior problems tend to show lags in social-emotional competence and disrupted family functioning (Briggs-Gowan, Carter, Skuban, & Horwitz, 2001). For most children, these behavior problems represent normative, transient difficulties, but for some children these behaviors forecast developing mental health problems. Young children experiencing these difficulties are at elevated risk for severe impairments in functioning, such as preschool expulsion (Gilliam, 2005). Unfortunately, the vast majority of children in need of mental health services lack adequate access; this is particularly true for ethnic minority children (Kataoka, Zhang, & Wells, 2002). While empirically validated interventions exist to serve young children and their families, lack of access to these services is a considerable challenge.

The present chapter includes a discussion of the development, assessment, and treatment of early childhood disruptive behavior disorders with a focus on empirically supported practices. While hyperactivity and impulsivity are often comorbid with early externalizing problems (Egger & Angold, 2006), the current discussion focuses on aggression and disruptive behavior disorders excluding attention deficit hyperactivity disorder due to distinct differences in these forms of developmental psychopathology.

Longitudinal studies have indicated that conduct problems typically originate during early childhood. In particular, research suggests that lifetime aggressive behavior peaks not in adolescence as previously thought, but during children's second year (Tremblay, 2000). Subsequently, aggressive behavior tends to decrease from the ages of 2 to 5 years, so that children tend to have low levels of aggression by school entry. Instead of learning to be aggressive, it is likely that children learn to inhibit aggression and engage in other forms of self-regulation and communication. Even though early childhood behavior problems are often normative and tend to decline, approximately half of children with behavior problems continue to have difficulties (Campbell, Ewing, Breaux, & Szumowski, 1986; Campbell, Pierce, Moore, & Marakovitz, 1996), and the most critical behavioral risk factor for adolescent antisocial behavior is early onset oppositional defiant disorder or conduct disorder (Yoshikawa, 1994).

It is not surprising that toddlers would experience a surge of aggressive behavior, noncompliance, and temper tantrums. In early childhood, toddlers acquire frustration tolerance, learn to delay gratification, begin to control impulses, use verbal communication skills, and become sensitive to the needs and desires of others. These developments occur in a climate of rapidly changing cognitive, language, motor, and social-emotional development. As children gain mobility and show increasing desire for exploration and autonomy, responsive parents must adjust to new demands for close monitoring, structuring of the environment, and limit setting.

For young children, noncompliance is a key early behavior that predicts later externalizing problems (Shaw, Keenan, & Vondra, 1994). In order to distinguish clinically significant from normative noncompliance, the developmental and relational context must be examined. Noncompliance may represent an active resistance of authority, or a more circumscribed effort to maintain autonomy when adults intervene. Children with clinically significant disruptive behavior disorders tend to show more consistent defiance, seek a reaction from caregivers, and have less positive caregiver relationships (Keenan & Wakschlag, 2002). While mild aggression is typical for young children, more intense, hostile aggression that is pervasive across contexts represents a potential cause for concern (Campbell, 1995; Hay, Castle, & Davies, 2000). Caution is warranted because similar behavior problems may have different etiologies; for instance, behavior problems may stem from an underlying behavior disorder or a young toddler's limited repertoire of language or self-regulation skills.

RISKS AND PREDICTORS OF BEHAVIOR PROBLEMS

Ecological and transactional models (Bronfenbrenner, 1986; Sameroff, 1995) provide an understanding of how risk and protective factors across multiple systems impact child and family functioning. With an accumulation of child, family, and community risk factors, children show more negative cognitive and social–emotional outcomes (Sameroff, Seifer, Zax, & Barocas, 1987). A constellation of risk factors has been linked to the development of externalizing and other forms of child psychopathology, including maternal depression, parental antisocial behavior, family conflict, child maltreatment, lack of social support, neighborhood violence, socioeconomic disadvantage, and minority status (Campbell, 2002).

Similar to findings with older children, young ethnic minority children growing up in poverty show elevated rates of disruptive behavior disorder symptoms. Unfortunately, children from ethnic minority backgrounds are disproportionately represented within samples of children living in poverty. Across a range of assessment methods and informants, preschoolers from low-income families show significantly higher rates of conduct problems and lower rates of social competence in comparison to community samples (Keenan, Shaw, Walsh, Delliquadri, & Giovannelli, 1997; Webster-Stratton & Hammond, 1998). Preschool children growing up in poverty face higher child and parenting risk factors, such as low soothability, high parental stress, and poor physical surroundings (Klebanov, Brooks-Gunn, & Duncan, 1994; Wakschlag & Keenan, 2001). Chronic poverty is associated in longitudinal studies with lower child cognitive skills and higher behavior problems, with parenting playing an important role (Allhusen et al., 2005). Neighborhood disadvantage can increase the strength of links between risk factors and conduct problems in older African-American children (Brody et al., 2003). For instance, in the context of neighborhood disadvantage, lack of nurturant-involved parenting and sibling behavior problems can have deleterious effects on child conduct problems. Some longitudinal evidence with American Indian and non-Indian school-age children suggests that while poverty and associated factors place children at risk, gains in family income are associated with reductions in oppositional defiant and conduct disorder symptoms (Costello, Compton, Keeler, & Angold, 2003). While race and ethnicity have traditionally been controlled for within research studies, a growing literature is examining how neighborhood disadvantage, perceived discrimination, and acculturation impact parents and children (e.g., Prelow, Danoff-Burg, Swenson, & Pulgiano, 2004; Szalacha et al., 2003). Further research on the development of behavior problems in context is needed for infants and young children from diverse racial, ethnic, and cultural backgrounds.

Despite limitations in the existing literature, a number of child, family, and community factors have been identified as important in the etiology of early behavior problems (Campbell, 2002). For instance, maternal depression and parental antisocial behavior present environmental and genetic risks for the development of aggressive behavior (Keenan & Shaw, 1994). Biological and genetic factors have been implicated in children's risk for impulsivity and negative emotionality (Moffitt, 1993; Raine, 2002). The biological and social environments interact to impact outcomes; for instance, genetic variations have been identified that increase children's risk of aggression within the context of specific early relational experiences, such as maltreatment (Jaffee, Caspi, Moffitt, & Taylor, 2004).

Temperament has also been implicated as a factor in the development of behavioral problems. Definitions of temperament have varied, but commonalities include emotional and behavioral patterns that emerge early in development and are influenced by environmental and biological processes (Eisenberg, Smith, Sadovsky, & Spinrad, 2004; Kagan, 1998; Rothbart & Bates, 2006). Thomas and Chess (1977) defined temperament using the following dimensions: activity level, rhythmicity of body functions, approach to novel situations, adaptability to change and transitions, intensity of behavior, mood, persistence in the face of challenge, distractibility or ability to be soothed, and sensory threshold to garner a response. While findings have been mixed, aspects of temperament in infancy, such as negative emotionality, may predict adolescent conduct problems (Caspi, Henry, McGee, Moffit, & Silva, 1995; Keenan, Shaw, Delliquadri, Giovannelli, & Walsh, 1998). Researchers have identified that the goodness of fit between parenting style and infant temperament is important in influencing whether a child is at risk for psychopathology (Seifer, 2000). On a related note, a number of studies suggest that aspects of early emotional regulation and behavioral control play an important role in the development of externalizing problems. Specifically, early manifestations of dysregulated noncompliance, hostility, attention seeking, and impulsivity have been associated with later externalizing problems (Calkins, 1994; Kuczynski & Kochanska, 1990; Shaw, Gilliom, Ingoldsby, & Nagin, 2003; Shaw et al., 1998). In the area of cognitive development, children with early behavior problems show deficits in social cognition, such as hostile attributional biases in ambiguous situations (Dodge & Pettit, 2003).

There is strong evidence that parenting plays an important role in the development and maintenance of child behavior problems. When children receive sensitive caregiving in early childhood, they are at reduced risk for school-age behavior problems (Pettit, Bates, & Dodge, 1997). Observational research suggests that infants who receive responsive mothering and share positive infant–mother interactions derive significant benefits for socialization, impacting parenting interactions, and child distress upon violating behavioral expectations (Kochanska, Forman, & Coy, 1999). Positive parent-child relationships are critical in supporting behavioral and emotional regulation. Parents of children with externalizing problems tend to hold more negative child perceptions and have fewer positive family cognitions (Zeanah, Larrieu, Heller, & Valliere, 2000). Inconsistent, lax, harsh, and overreactive parenting behaviors have consistently been identified as strong predictors of conduct problems (Acker & O'Leary, 1996;

Dodge & Pettit, 2003; Shaw et al., 1998). Patterson's coercive model (1982) is a critical theory with empirical support that describes how parents and children develop escalating cycles of coercive interactions in which the child responds to demands with resistance, and the parent responds to resistance with escalating negativity, until the parent acquiesces to avoid the aversive interaction. These parent-child patterns likely play a role in promoting young children's emotional dysregulation and poor peer relationships (Scaramella & Leve, 2004).

While authoritative parenting styles characterized by high warmth and sensitivity and firm limits have been documented to be advantageous for European-American children from middle-class or upper-class backgrounds, there is evidence that this form of parenting may not be equally effective for children from varying racial, ethnic, and cultural backgrounds. For instance, research suggests that nonabusive physical discipline in the context of warm relationships with caregivers may benefit African-American children, highlighting the need for research that considers discipline in context for ethnically diverse families (Deater-Deckard, Dodge, Bates, & Pettit, 1996). Authoritarian strategies that focus on control and compliance and cultivate respect may protect children growing up in dangerous neighborhoods. Further research is needed to understand cultural differences in parenting to inform assessment and treatment.

ASSESSMENT OF EARLY BEHAVIOR PROBLEMS

There is an understandable reluctance to diagnose young children with behavior disorders due to challenges distinguishing normative from abnormal behavior in early childhood, few contexts to assess development outside the family during this developmental period, rapid growth across developmental domains, and the potential for stigmatizing children. At the same time, delaying assessment presents an ethical dilemma because prevention of conduct problems is critical and supports should not be withheld from children and families at risk. Another challenge is that few assessment tools with strong psychometric properties exist for young children, particularly for ethnically diverse children (Carter, Briggs-Gowan, & Ornstein Davis, 2004).

It is now widely accepted that young children's social, emotional, and behavioral competence impacts learning and social development (Shonkoff & Phillips, 2000), and these areas are as worthy of assessment as cognitive and language skills. Nevertheless, disagreement exists about whether disruptive behavior disorders should be conceptualized from a dimensional or categorical standpoint (Silk, Nath, Siegel, & Kendall, 2001). Dimensional assessment involves a "bottom-up" approach in which children's symptoms are rated on a continuum and the scores are combined into scales and compared with standardized samples to determine deviance by gender and age. Strong research evidence with behavior rating scales supports dimensional conceptualizations of externalizing behavior (Briggs-Gowan, et al., 2001). In contrast, categorical conceptualizations involve a "top-down" approach, operationalizing symptoms based on clinical diagnoses to determine who meets criteria for a disorder, such as with a clinical diagnostic interview. While oppositional defiant disorder and conduct disorder can be diagnosed in early childhood based on the *Diagnostic and Statistical Manual of Mental Disorders*, 4th edition, *Text Revision* (DSM-IV-TR; American Psychiatric Association, 2000), the DSM-IV-TR has been criticized for being based largely on research with older children and reflecting a lack of developmental sensitivity. Despite these criticisms, a burgeoning evidence base suggests that oppositional defiant disorder and conduct disorder are valid diagnoses in early childhood (Keenan & Wakschlag, 2002; Speltz, McClellan, DeKlyen, & Jones, 1999). A recent set of diagnostic guidelines specific to young children, the *Diagnostic Classification of Mental Health and Developmental Disorders of Infancy and Early Childhood: DC:0-3R* (Zero to Three, 2005), has the advantage of conceptualizing child behavior problems in a relational context, but this system has limited research support at present.

A number of authors describe key challenges in the multicultural assessment of children and considerations in adapting assessment procedures to children's needs (Dana, 2000). There is a need for resources to be developed to guide assessment practices for cultural groups (Canino & Guarnaccia, 1997) and to help clinicians increase their multicultural competence. Despite increased attention to concerns about assessment for children from diverse backgrounds, a limited amount of research has focused on these issues specifically in early childhood (Christensen, Emde, & Fleming, 2004). There is a growing literature examining cross-cultural use of various measures with school-age children. Achenbach and colleagues (2008) advocate for the use of dimensional multicultural assessment approaches that rely on empirical techniques to evaluate the use of measures of psychopathology for large, diverse samples of children. Findings from this research with behavior rating scales suggest that while there are variations across multicultural groups, scale scores tend to show greater variation within a given population than between populations. At the same time, there is concern about potential sources of bias in the assessment of multicultural children, and researchers have argued that when assessments with strong psychometric properties are used, there is evidence that true disparities exist that place children at risk for negative outcomes (Brown, Reynolds, & Whitaker, 1999; Mayfield & Reynolds, 1998).

Much of the research concerning bias includes reference to cognitive performance and academic achievement gaps, and controversy regarding the reason for these discrepancies between European-American and ethnic minority children. Historically, multicultural assessment concerns have included questions regarding adequate representation of minority groups in normative samples, language bias, differential predictive validity, construct validity, and varying social consequences for children based on testing. There is increasing evidence that complex processes influence children's performance in assessment contexts. For example, with school-age children from academically stigmatized groups, there is initial evidence that impairments in academic performance occur when underachieving stereotypes are made salient for children (McKown & Weinstein, 2003). In addition, there is the concern that informants and examiner bias may impact assessment (Epstein et al., 2005).

Ethical issues are particularly relevant to the assessment of disruptive behavior problems in early childhood. Beyond using empirically-based assessment practices and techniques, attention must be given to examiner bias, values, and decision making (Evans, 2008). Within early childhood, ethical issues arise because informants may vary in their level of concern and motivation to pursue an evaluation. While a preschool teacher may have serious concerns about the well-being of a child, a child's parents or caregivers may disagree or may be reluctant to accept a referral because of other stressors that are demanding their attention or limiting resources, such as financial difficulties, family conflict, or the behavioral challenges of an older child. In addition, young children with disruptive behavior may present a number of challenges in participating in assessment, such as limited attention, noncompliance, or fatigue with assessment procedures. While a developmentally appropriate assessment can alleviate these difficulties, multiple appointments may need to be scheduled, and this requires more of families who are already stressed in many cases. Some of the procedures developed within research contexts may be time intensive and overwhelming for families. For example, completing a clinical interview, multiple questionnaires, and participating in an observational assessment likely represents only part of a comprehensive assessment, and yet this can require hours of effort as well as the coordination of transportation and child care. In addition, ethically, examiners must wrestle with questions of labeling children as well as the potential risk of under identifying children with critical needs.

While children may show similar behavioral symptoms, the causal factors underlying these symptoms may be quite different, depending on the context. A child with a language delay that interferes with communication may have intense tempter tantrums, while another child may be reacting to family discord. A comprehensive assessment should include the following domains: cognition, language, motor, behavior, and social-emotional skills, family functioning, parenting practices, risk factors, and child and family strengths. Problems in early childhood, as in psychopathology in older children, are often comorbid (Thomas & Guskin, 2001). A comprehensive assessment must include a clinical interview to assess developmental and medical history, temperament, attachment relationships, family relational history, family medical history, family history of psychopathology, parenting, caregiving routines, parent perceptions about the child, and social supports.

Assessments should integrate screening and broadband measures, and more comprehensive forms of assessment should be conducted as warranted. For a review of social-emotional and behavioral screening instruments, consult Carter (2002). Ideally, a comprehensive evaluation should include clinical interviewing of the family and other caregivers, behavior rating scales completed by multiple caregivers, semistructured or structured diagnostic interviews with caregivers, and observation (Doctoroff & Arnold, 2004). There is no standard method of integrating information from these methods and informants, so considerable clinical expertise and developmental understanding is required. A comprehensive review of all assessment methods is beyond the scope of this chapter, but a selection of measures with adequate psychometric properties to assess early behavior problems will be described. Two key limitations are that most of these measures are not designed for children younger than 18 months of age, and for the most part the measures were developed in the context of clinical research and adapted for clinical use, so further work is needed to increase the ease of administration and the utility of these measures in clinical settings.

Behavior Rating Scales

Behavior rating scales are brief and easy to administer and score, allow comparison of a child's behavior to a normative sample of age-matched children, and provide a cost-effective opportunity to obtain the viewpoints of multiple caregivers. These scales typically focus on the frequency of behaviors rather than antecedents; consequences; and the intensity, severity, onset, and duration of the behavior. Concerns have been raised when there is a modest level of agreement across informants reporting on behavior rating scales (Achenbach, McConaughy, & Howell, 1987). These differences may represent measurement error, rating bias, or true differences between children across relational contexts. Nevertheless, parent perceptions may be impacted by other factors, such as parental depression or fears about the potential use of medication treatment.

In order to utilize behavior-rating scales, mental health professionals require training and knowledge of standardized assessment theory and procedures; typically, at least a master's degree in a mental health field is recommended. Knowledge of psychological assessment is required to choose which assessments are most appropriate for a given child and referral concerns. Clinicians must understand the goals and limits of an assessment based on research to support its use. Supervision should be provided to support clinicians in administering, scoring, and interpreting behavior-rating scales in context, and to communicate effectively with the family regarding findings. A thorough reading of the manual is a standard aspect of training.

For children between the ages of 12 and 36 months, the Infant–Toddler Social and Emotional Assessment (ITSEA; Briggs-Gowan & Carter, 1998) is a 169-item questionnaire that has strong empirical support for its use. Multiple studies provide a growing evidence base for the reliability and validity of this measure for use with young children (Carter, Little, Briggs-Gowan, & Kogan, 1999; Carter, Briggs-Gowan, Jones, & Little, 2003). This scale has the advantage of assessing deficits (internalizing, externalizing, dysregulation) and competencies, as well as low-base-rate behaviors that may be cause for concern.

The Achenbach System of Empirically-Based Assessment (ASEBA; Achenbach & Rescorla, 2000, 2007; Rescorla, 2005) has a strong research base for use with diverse samples of children and is available in multiple languages. The parent and teacher rating forms for young children from the ASEBA, the Child Behavior Checklist (CBCL), and the Caregiver–Teacher Report Form (C-TRF) for ages 1.5–5, are 99-item scales. This measure has empirical support for its sensitivity to intervention effects (Webster-Stratton, 1994). Clinical cutoffs exist that discriminate referred from nonrefer_red children and identify children at significant risk for psychopathology (Achenbach & Rescorla, 2000). This scale does not include adaptive scales focused on competence.

Other behavior-rating scales focus more specifically on disruptive behavior problems, providing more in-depth information. For instance, the Eyberg Child Behavior Inventory and the teacher completed Sutter–Eyberg Student Behavior Inventory–Revised (Eyberg & Pincus, 1999) are behavior-rating scales used to evaluate preschool and school-age children (ages 2–16). These short scales are brief to administer and can be easily scored. Assessments of the frequency of behaviors are included in addition to whether the informant considers these behaviors to be a problem. This scale is sensitive to the effects of treatment (Nixon, Sweeney, Erickson, & Touyz, 2003). There has been some criticism of the normative sample used, particularly that the number of children at each age range was limited, but a larger, more representative sample has been obtained (Burns & Patterson, 2001; Eyberg & Pincus). This scale has shown discriminative validity for clinic-referred versus nonreferred children with conduct problems (Rich & Eyberg, 2001). The combination of frequency and intensity ratings provides unique information regarding the level of behavior problems and caregiver reaction to these behaviors.

Diagnostic Interviews with Caregivers

Semistructured and structured diagnostic interviews provide comprehensive and systematic methods of assessment relevant to diagnosis. While these interviews are commonly used with older children (e.g., National Institute of Mental Health Diagnostic Interview Schedule for Children Version IV [NIMH DISC-IV]; Shaffer, Fisher, Lucas, Dulcan, & Schwab-Stone, 2000), few measures are available with adequate research support to warrant their use in the assessment of disruptive behavior disorders in early childhood. Existing diagnostic interviews tend to be adaptations of interviews used in clinical research with school-age children, making them less user friendly for clinical practice with young children. While these interviews provide opportunities to probe about onset, frequency, duration, intensity, and impairment, there is concern about the validity of the responses. Diagnostic interviews tend to be long and to involve screening questions that lead to more intensive probes if a caregiver endorses a particular child symptom. Over the course of a diagnostic interview, the number of symptoms endorsed by caregivers tends to decline, even when the order of symptoms within the interview is varied (Jensen, Watanabe, & Richters, 1999). For example, when clinicians inquire about symptoms in the middle or end of a long interview, tired and stressed parents may be less likely to elaborate because they know that the interview is likely to continue.

While structured respondent-based interviews do not require intensive training to administer, semistructured, interviewer-based interviews require examiners to make specific decisions about probing and clinical interpretations that require more intensive training and supervision. Training often involves reading resources, didactic seminars, observing interview techniques, supervised administration and scoring, and checks for reliability of administration and scoring. These training procedures can be costly and time intensive for clinicians, and diagnostic interviews can be taxing for families due to the time commitment involved and the repetitive nature of structured interviews that do not allow caregivers leeway for elaboration. Some interviews require training by the developers, whereas others distribute materials to support training with credentialed trainers.

Recent research has resulted in a growing evidence base for caregiver diagnostic interviews in early childhood. The Preschool-Age Psychiatric Assessment (PAPA) is designed for children ages 2–5 years old (Egger & Angold, 2004) and was based on review of DSM-IV-TR criteria, DC:0-3 criteria, and additional symptoms based on early childhood research.

Assessment of family relationships and the family environment are incorporated into the interview. There is initial support for the PAPA's test–retest reliability and validity (Egger et al., 2006). Aspects of this interview that may be prohibitive include the intensive training required, financial cost of the interview, and time burden.

OBSERVATIONAL MEASURES

Observation is a critical aspect of assessment in early childhood, but there tend to be few empirically-based methods of observation validated for use in clinical settings. Observational measures in naturalistic settings or analogue tasks in the clinic can be advantageous for understanding early childhood behavior and the caregiving context. Analogue observational tasks often involve situations that increase the likelihood of seeing certain behaviors of interest within a short time period. Observation typically includes structured and unstructured interactions derived from research tasks (e.g., free play, feeding, cleanup, parent-directed play). A key weakness of observational assessment is that it tends to lack normative data and there are often concerns about reliability and validity (Roberts, 2001). At the same time, these measures seem to be useful for monitoring treatment changes (Frick & Loney, 2000), provide rich information, and may be useful for building rapport with families.

Clinicians require training in administration of observational procedures and coding of affect, behavior, and other aspects of parent-child interaction. Within the context of working in a training clinic or under supervision, mental health trainees become familiar with various forms of observational assessments, such as observed free play, or family negotiation of a separation from the caregiver. Within certain treatments, observations of compliance and parenting strategies are completed to assess baseline functioning and treatment gains. Training for these procedures requires an understanding of the goals of the treatment and reliable coding of interactions. Training typically follows an apprentice model, with the trainee comparing ratings with an experienced coder to eventually achieve independence. Within the context of research, examiners engage in intensive training to reach an acceptable level of reliability with an expert observer. This training may involve viewing of videotapes, readings, coding with an expert observer, and coding independently once reliability has been reached.

One form of observation that may be advantageous for use in clinical settings is the Parent Daily Report (Chamberlain & Reid, 1987). This measure has been used in clinical research to assess conduct problems and parent discipline practices with telephone interviews. This measure has the advantage of training parents to serve as the observers for the previous

24-hour period. Parents are asked which behaviors of concern have occurred and provide information about how the behavior was handled. The Behavioral Coding System (BCS; Forehand & McMahon, 1981; McMahon & Forehand, 2003) and the Dyadic Parent-Child Interaction Coding System II (DPICS-II; Eyberg, Bessmer, Newcomb, Edwards, & Robinson, 1994) have been utilized with young children and their parents to examine child and parent behaviors related to externalizing difficulties. These coding systems provide opportunities for parents and children to engage in structured and unstructured activities together. These systems have successfully discriminated between referred and nonreferred samples of children and have been utilized in clinical settings (McMahon & Frick, 2005). Another structured observation, the Compliance Test, shows increasing evidence supporting its validity for use with young children (Roberts, 2001; Roberts & Powers, 1988). Within these observational systems, clinical cutoffs are not clearly specified.

A recent development in observational research is a systematic observational procedure to assess disruptive behavior in early childhood based on a similar assessment model to assess autism, which relies on clinical judgment in concert with standardized observational tasks and a diagnostic interview with caregivers (Lord, Risi, & Lambrecht, 2000). The Disruptive Behavior Diagnostic Observation Schedule (DB-DOS; Wakshlag et al., 2007) is a 50-minute structured clinical observation procedure that provides structured and unstructured situations with a child, caregiver and an examiner. Behavioral regulation and anger modulation are examined, as well as emotional responsiveness to the child, parent flexibility, and behavior management practices. Preliminary findings have demonstrated adequate reliability and validity, with DB-DOS scores predicting child impairment over time (Wakschlag et al., 2008a, 2008b).

INTERVENTIONS FOR EARLY BEHAVIOR PROBLEMS

While literature has indicated that many factors contribute to the development of child behavior problems, parents have uniquely influential roles in molding young children's behavior and influencing their likelihoods of developing conduct disorders (Brestan & Eyberg, 1998). While a number of promising parenting therapies exist, certain programs have been identified as best practices for the treatment of behavior problems, as these programs have a strong empirical evidence base. Additionally, some programs have focused interventions on teacher classroom management. Finally, it is less common to directly target preschool children for treatment in isolation because of their limited cognitive and developmental capabilities; however, some direct skills training programs have been developed.

The present discussion of treatment will mainly focus on empirically-based parent-training programs. For a program to be considered empirically-based, there must be rigorous, scientific evidence for the program's efficacy and, ideally, effectiveness. It is important to note that the majority of programs that have undergone rigorous, scientific testing are based on behavioral and social-learning principles, and that this creates a bias in what is presented.

In addition to this strong research base, these programs have many other important commonalities. First, they utilize treatment manuals that outline the goals of each session and the content that should be reviewed. Treatment manuals are helpful tools in enhancing fidelity and accuracy of delivering the intervention; however, at times, they may feel constricting for therapists. It is important to remember that manuals are best utilized when therapists can integrate their clinical skills to deliver content that will be acceptable and appropriate (Kendall, Chu, Gifford, Hayes, & Nauta, 1998). Supervision is a useful tool to ensure that therapists are true to the interventions, while still tailoring their approaches to the immediate needs of the family. Second, these programs often have credentialing processes to help clinicians receive recommended training, supervision, and feedback. Clinicians should undergo intensive training in which they learn the content, process, and techniques of how to tailor the intervention effectively to a given family, and then evaluated on their competency to deliver the intervention. Typically, clinicians engaged in parent training have a master's or doctoral degree in a mental health field, and have extensive experience working with young children and families.

While these therapeutic programs have demonstrated promise in treating early childhood externalizing behavior, it is essential to note that the majority were developed based on research with Caucasian, middle-class families (Forehand & Kotchick, 1996). In order to appropriately use empirically-based programs with diverse, multicultural families from a range of socioeconomic backgrounds, clinicians must adapt their treatment to fit with important cultural and societal values. At this point, there are not strong empirical guidelines for this process. While this task presents a challenge for researchers and clinicians, they have an ethical responsibility to create programs that incorporate relevant standards of cultural and racial sensitivity. Additionally, programs that lack this sensitivity may not be as successful in engaging families, promoting satisfaction, generating treatment gains, and generalizing from clinic to home (Forehand & Kotchick, 1996). Researchers are beginning to highlight the necessity of incorporating racial sensitivity within existing evidence-based programs (Coard, Wallace, Stevenson, & Brotman, 2004). Further work is needed to define the most effective ways to create programs that generate family satisfaction and acceptability for diverse populations while still achieving the goal of treating conduct problems. It is also important to attend to pragmatic factors that may impede parents from attending treatment. Spoth, Redmond, Hockaday, & Shin (1996) discuss the importance of addressing barriers to treatment such as parents' transportation to the center, lack of child care, financial constraints, and hectic work schedules. Furthermore, parents may not be willing to come to a clinic if they are uncomfortable with the stigma derived from the location (e.g., a hospital versus a church or preschool).

PREVENTION OF CONDUCT PROBLEMS

The prevention of conduct disorders has been highlighted as one of the nation's most critical areas for research (National Institute of Mental Health, 1996). The Nurse–Family Partnership (NFP; Olds, Henderson, Chamberlin, & Tatelbaum, 1986) is an exemplary prevention program aimed at combating risks related to the development of conduct disorder and delinquency. In the program, nurses make home visits to pregnant first-time mothers to try to improve maternal prenatal health and maternal life circumstances such as employment and education. When children are born, nurses teach mothers how to give proper emotional and physical care to their children, facilitate positive parent–infant interactions, and provide practical guidance in acquiring stable employment, finishing their education, and planning subsequent pregnancies. Short and long-term evidence has showed promising results in several areas of parent and child functioning for up to 15 years of maintenance (Olds et al., 1998).

INFANT AND TODDLER ATTACHMENT-BASED PARENT-TRAINING PROGRAMS

Various programs integrate attachment theory, as they focus on improving the parent-child relationship by helping parents be more sensitive to children's cues, increase warmth and responsiveness, have more appropriate developmental expectations, and reframe challenging behavior. These interventions stress the need to spend time building a positive relationship with one's child, typically through play. Lieberman's Child–Parent Psychotherapy (CPP; Lieberman & Van Horn, 2005) derives from the work of Stern (1985) and the "ghosts in the nursery" (Fraiberg, Adelson, & Shapiro, 1975). CPP incorporates attachment, psychodynamic, and behavioral theories in order to improve the relationship between parents and their young children. The efficacy of CPP has been supported in a study of low-income, ethnically diverse preschoolers and their mothers (Lieberman, Van Horn, & Ghosh Ippen, 2005).

While infants and toddlers may not necessarily display overt acts of aggression and disruptive behavior, they are likely to present with challenging behavior that may be more often described as *difficult* or *fussy*. Because infant behaviors stemming from temperament and attachment patterns are strong precursors of disruptive behavior problems during the preschool period, it is important to intervene to prevent relationship problems from escalating. Unfortunately, little empirical evidence from rigorous scientific trials that target the infant–parent relationship exist; however, certain programs have a growing evidence base [e.g., Circle of Security Project (Marvin, Cooper, Hoffman, & Powell, 2002), and Video-feedback Intervention to Promote Positive Parenting (VIPP; Juffer, Bakermans-Kranenburg, & Van IJzendoorn, 2005)].

PRESCHOOL BEHAVIORAL AND ATTACHMENT-BASED PARENT-TRAINING PROGRAMS

Parent–Child Interaction Therapy(PCIT) Derived from instrumental research on parent training principles, Eyberg's Parent-Child Interaction Therapy (Brinkmeyer & Eyberg, 2003; Hembree-Kigin & McNeil, 1995) is designed for children ages 2–6 and consists of 13 one-hour sessions that are divided into two phases over the course of treatment. The first phase, Child Directed Interaction (CDI), focuses on building positive relationships between parents and children by encouraging positive parent-child interactions. During this time, the parent uses descriptive commenting to follow the child's lead during play, and does not give commands or ask questions. Parents use PRIDE skills, in which they *praise* the child's behavior, *reflect* the child's statements, selectively *imitate* the child's play, *describe* the child's behavior like a sports commentator, and play with *enthusiasm*. Parents are also taught differential ignoring procedures, that is, to ignore minor inappropriate behavior that is not dangerous and return attention using PRIDE skills as soon as the child's behavior is appropriate.

Phase 2 is Parent-Directed Interaction (PDI), in which the parent takes the lead to deliver appropriate commands and set clear limits for the child's behavior. From the behavioral perspective, the critical goal during this phase is to change difficult behavior by setting clear limits for behaviors, delivering explicit and direct commands, and following through by delivering specific praise and rewards or implementing consequences such as time-out.

Each phase begins with a didactic session in which the therapist teaches skills using modeling, discussion, role-play, and behavioral rehearsal. In coaching sessions, the therapist communicates with the parent through a *bug in the ear* device, which allows the therapist to unobtrusively coach parents to increase positive interactions during play. Additionally, the therapist observes the parent-child play interactions in the first 5 minutes of every session, provides feedback on the parent's implementation of the skills, and keeps track of the parent's successes and struggles with the program material.

To extend PCIT principles outside of the clinic, the therapist and parent collaborate to increase instances of nurturance provided at home and establish clear rules that delineate appropriate behavior. The parent reviews these "House Rules" with the child, and discusses what will happen if rules are not followed.

Evidence from randomized controlled trials supports PCIT's efficacy. A randomized controlled trial is a quantitative, controlled experimental research design in which participants are randomly assigned to treatment versus control or comparison conditions to evaluate the impact of the intervention. Children who received PCIT demonstrate significantly less oppositionality when compared with waiting-list control groups and children whose parents enrolled in a parent education group (Eyberg & Matarazzo, 1980; Nixon, et al., 2003; Schuhmann, Foote, Eyberg, Boggs, & Algina, 1998). Furthermore, effects generalized to other settings. Children participating in the treatment were rated as displaying fewer conduct problems in school, and their untreated siblings demonstrated less problem behavior as well (McNeil, Eyberg, Eisenstadt, Newcomb, & Funderburk, 1991; Brestan, Eyberg, Boggs, & Algina, 1997). Importantly, PCIT has shown long-term efficacy, as children participating in the intervention continued to show positive gains at 1 and 2 years post-follow-up (Boggs et al., 2004), as well as long-term maintenance 6 years after treatment (Hood & Eyberg, 2003).

In order to address the need for culturally sensitive treatment programs, efforts have been made to adapt PCIT for ethnic minority families. An adapted version of the program that incorporated values of respect, loyalty, and the importance of the extended family was implemented with 15 families living in Puerto Rico. Results suggest that the program was acceptable to parents and helped reduce reports of children's behavior problems (Matos, Torres, Santiago, Jurado, & Rodriguez, 2006). Similarly, a randomized controlled trial testing an adapted version of PCIT for Mexican American parents has shown positive changes when compared to delivering the original treatment program to a control group of Mexican American parents (McCabe, Yeh, Garland, Lau, & Chavez, 2005).

The Incredible Years Series The Incredible Years Series (IYS; Webster-Stratton, 2005; Webster-Stratton & Hancock, 1998) is designed for parents of children ages 3–8, and is based on social learning and attachment theories. IYS is comprised of a BASIC program that includes review of brief video vignettes demonstrating positive and negative parenting strategies that are used as the basis for discussion in a group of 10–14 parents and 2 leaders, and lasts for 12–16 weekly 2-hour sessions. Parents who are identified as being especially at risk can receive an additional 8–10 weeks of group therapy with video-taped modeling (the ADVANCE program). All family members involved in caregiving are encouraged to attend groups. Content covered includes building positive relationships with children, providing effective praise, using rewards to motivate children, effective limit setting, techniques to handle challenging behavior (e.g., ignoring, redirection, natural and logical consequences), and time-out techniques.

The therapist works in a collaborative model, viewing the parents as experts and participating by guiding the discussion, keeping the group on track, facilitating frequent role plays, and highlighting principles relevant to child development and parenting strategies. The discussion can be altered and tailored to each parent's situation, and more or less time is spent on topics depending on the parents' needs. Parents share concerns and ideas about disciplining children and ways of responding to children's behavior. Importantly, parents help each other work through difficult situations by exchanging ideas and giving each other advice as parenting experts. In addition to supporting parents gain behavioral skills, the groups support parents in recognizing and reducing negative attributions about themselves and their children, understanding child development, and finding ways to cope with their emotional reactions to parenting. Parents in the group provide support to each other through weekly "buddy calls." The program also encourages parents to be more involved with children at home through play and daily activities. Additional research has also been conducted to support the use of the IYS Teacher-Training Program to train teachers in classroom management techniques (Webster-Stratton & Reid, 2004), and the Dina Dinosaur Child Program to support children's emotional regulation and social skills (Webster-Stratton & Reid, 2003b).

The Incredible Years Series has been identified as a well-established treatment for conduct-disordered children (Brestan & Eyberg, 1998). The parent program has been tested in randomized controlled trials by the developer as well as through independent replications (for reviews, see Webster-Stratton, 2000; Webster-Stratton & Reid, 2003a). Effects have been documented in decreasing harsh, and critical parenting practices, increasing positive parenting strategies, and placing children in the nonclinical range for their behavior. When the parent-training program is combined with a parallel program for children delivered by preschool teachers, significant decreases were found in children's behavior problems (Webster-Stratton, Reid, & Hammond, 2001).

The program has demonstrated success with various samples. When delivered as a selected preventive intervention in a Head Start setting, two randomized controlled trials of the IYS series demonstrated success with parents of ethnic minority backgrounds (Webster-Stratton, 1998; Webster-Stratton, Reid, & Hammond, 2001). Additionally, the program has shown success with parents of low-income, African-American toddlers (Gross, et al.,

2003), and a higher risk subgroup of a Head Start population (Baydar, Reid, & Webster-Stratton, 2003). A comparison of the interventions delivered to multiple racial groups yielded support for the program's effectiveness for use with low-income European-American, African-American, Hispanic, and Asian-American parents (Reid, Webster-Stratton, & Beauchaine, 2001). Brotman and colleagues (Brotman, Gouley, Chesir, et al., 2005; Brotman, Gouley, Huang, et al., 2007; Brotman et al., 2008) have shown that an adapted version of the IYS program led to long-term benefits for children at familial risk for antisocial behavior. This program generated positive effects on parenting practices, promotion of school readiness, child social competence, stress responses, and physical aggression.

PARENT MANAGEMENT TRAINING

With roots in Patterson's seminal work on coercion theory (1982), a well-established behavioral program is Parent Management Training (PMT; Kazdin, 1997; 2005). In this treatment, therapists work individually with parents for 6–8 weeks. Treatment begins by clearly defining the child's problem behaviors and specifically outlining antecedents that lead to such behaviors. Furthermore, an important piece of the intervention is altering the consequences of these behaviors. Through role play, practice, and rehearsal, the therapist works with parents to change existing harsh and coercive parenting practices to methods that incorporate positive reinforcement, ignoring, and mild or non-harsh punishment.

PMT has proven to be efficacious for children displaying defiant behavior, and has demonstrated efficacy when compared to waiting-list controls and other therapeutic treatments for parents. Several randomized controlled trials have shown that children receiving the treatment display improvements measured by parent, teacher, and independent rater observations (Graziano & Diament, 1992; Kazdin, 1997), but almost all studies are focused on European-American samples and children across a broad age range. Improvements have also been noted in untreated sibling functioning and maternal psychopathology (Kazdin, 1995). Long-term studies have found that children maintain treatment gains up to 1, 3, and 10–14 years post follow-up (Long, Forehand, Wierson, & Morgan, 1994).

SUMMARY

Advances in empirically-based assessment for toddlers and preschoolers allow children at risk for negative outcomes and externalizing disorders to be identified at an early age. A focus on evidence-based practices and prevention is essential. With parenting interventions, approximately two-thirds of children with clinically significant early behavior problems can move into the normal range of functioning (Webster-Stratton, 1990). Several evidence-based programs have been created to treat conduct problems in young children. These programs incorporate similar principles of behavior modification and relationship building, and differ in ways that make certain programs more useful in various contexts, or with certain families. It is important for clinicians to have knowledge of these programs and the many options available in order to provide efficacious treatment to children and families. Clinicians require training and support to understand the principles that make these interventions effective and the techniques that support effectiveness. At this point, the research literature has not "unpacked" interventions to help to identify active components. In addition, the development of culturally sensitive and responsive interventions for children and families experiencing early childhood behavior problems is in its infancy and research must focus on moving beyond surface adaptations to understanding and addressing assessment and treatment needs for ethnically, racially, and culturally diverse children and families.

REFERENCES

Achenbach, T. M., Becker, A., Dopfner, M., Heiervang, E., Roessner, V., Steinhausen, H., et al. (2008). Multicultural assessment of child and adolescent psychopathology with ASEBA and SDQ instruments: Research findings, applications, and future directions. *Journal of Child Psychology and Psychiatry, 49*, 251–275.

Achenbach, T. M., McConaughy, S. H., & Howell, C. T. (1987). Child/adolescent behavioral and emotional problems: Implications of cross-informant correlations for situational specificity. *Psychological Bulletin, 101*, 213–232.

Achenbach, T. M., & Rescorla, L. A. (2000). *Manual for the ASEBA preschool forms and profiles*. Burlington, VT: University of Vermont, Research Center for Children, Youth, & Families.

Achenbach, T. M., & Rescorla, L. A. (2007). *Multicultural understanding of child and adolescent psychopathology: Implications for mental health assessment*. New York: Guilford Press.

Acker, M. M., & O'Leary, S. G. (1996). Inconsistency of mothers' feedback and toddlers' misbehavior and negative affect. *Journal of Abnormal Child Psychology, 24*, 703–714.

Allhusen, V., Belsky, J., Booth-LaForce, C., Bradley, R., Brownell, C. A., Burchinal, M., et al. (2005). Duration and developmental timing of poverty and children's cognitive and social development from birth through third grade. *Child Development, 76*, 795–810.

American Psychiatric Association. (2000). *Diagnostic and statistical manual of mental disorders* (4th ed., Text Revision). Washington, DC: Author.

Baydar, N., Reid, M., & Webster-Stratton, C. (2003). The role of mental health factors and program engagement in the effectiveness of a preventive parenting program for Head Start mothers. *Child Development, 74,* 1433–1453.

Boggs, S. R., Eyberg, S. M., Edwards, D., Rayfield, A., Jacobs, J., Bagner, D. et al. (2004). Outcomes of parent-child interaction therapy: A comparison of dropouts and treatment completers one to three years after treatment. *Child and Family Behavior Therapy, 26,* 1–22.

Brestan, E. V., & Eyberg, S. M. (1998). Effective psychosocial treatments for children and adolescents with disruptive behavior disorders: 29 years, 82 studies and 5272 kids. *Journal of Clinical Child Psychology, 27,* 179–188.

Brestan, E. V., Eyberg, S. M., Boggs, S. R., & Algina, J. (1997). Parent-child interaction therapy: Parents' perceptions of untreated siblings. *Child and Family Behavior Therapy, 19,* 13–28.

Briggs-Gowan, M. J., & Carter, A. S. (1998). Preliminary acceptability and psychometrics of the Infant-Toddler Social and Emotional Assessment (ITSEA): A new adult-report questionnaire. *Infant Mental Health Journal, 19,* 422–445.

Briggs-Gowan, M. J., Carter, A. S., Skuban, E. M., & Horwitz, S. (2001). Prevalence of social-emotional and behavioral problems in a community sample of 1- and 2-year-old children. *Journal of the American Academy of Child and Adolescent Psychiatry, 40,* 811–819.

Brinkmeyer, M., & Eyberg, S. M. (2003). Parent-child interaction therapy for oppositional children. In A. E. Kazdin & J. R. Weisz (Eds.), *Evidence-based psychotherapies for children and adolescents* (pp. 204–223). New York: Guilford Press.

Brody, G. H., Ge, X., Kim, S. Y., Murry, V. M., Simons, R. L., Gibbons, F. X., et al. (2003). Neighborhood disadvantage moderates associations of parenting and older sibling problem attitudes and behavior with conduct disorders in African American children. *Journal of Consulting and Clinical Psychology, 71,* 211–222.

Bronfenbrenner, U. (1986). Ecology of the family as a context for human development: Research perspectives. *Developmental Psychology, 22,* 723–742.

Brotman, L. M., Gouley, K. K., Chesir-Teran, D., Dennis, T., Klein, R. G., & Shrout, P. (2005). Prevention for preschoolers at high risk for conduct problems: Immediate outcomes on parenting practices and child social competence. *Journal of Clinical Child & Adolescent Psychology, 34,* 724–734.

Brotman, L. M., Gouley, K. K., Huang, K.-Y., Kamboukos, D., Fratto, C., & Pine, D. S. (2007). Effects of a psychosocial family-based preventive intervention on cortisol response to a social challenge in preschoolers at high risk for antisocial behavior. *Archives of General Psychiatry, 64,* 1172–1179.

Brotman, L. M., Gouley, K. K., Huang, K.-Y., Rosenfelt, A., O'Neal, C., Klein, R. G., & Shrout, P. (2008). Preventive intervention for preschoolers at high risk for antisocial behavior: Long-term effects on child physical aggression and parenting practices. *Journal of Clinical Child & Adolescent Psychology, 37,* 386–396.

Brown, R. T., Reynolds, C. R., & Whitaker, J. S. (1999). Bias in mental testing since "Bias in Mental Testing." *School Psychology Quarterly, 14,* 208–238.

Burns, L. G., & Patterson, D. R. (2001). Normative data on the Eyberg Child Behavior Inventory and Sutter-Eyberg Student Behavior Inventory: Parent and teacher rating scales of disruptive behavior problems in children and adolescents. *Child and Family Behavior Therapy, 23*, 15–28.

Calkins, S. D. (1994). Origins and outcomes of individual differences in emotion regulation. In N. A. Fox (Ed.), The development of emotion regulation: Biological and behavioral considerations. *Monographs of the Society for Research in Child Development, 59*, 53–72.

Campbell, S. (1995). Behavior problems in preschool children: A review of recent research. *Journal of Child Psychology and Psychiatry, 36*, 113–149.

Campbell, S. (2002). *Behavior problems in preschool children: Clinical and developmental issues* (2nd ed.). New York: Guilford Press.

Campbell, S. B., Ewing, L. J., Breaux, A. M., & Szumowski, E. K. (1986). Parent-referred three-year-olds: Follow-up at school entry. *Journal of Child Psychology and Psychiatry, 27*, 473–488.

Campbell, S. B., Pierce, E. W., Moore, G., & Marakovitz, S. (1996). Boys' externalizing problems at elementary school age: Pathways from early behavior problems, maternal control, and family stress. *Development and Psychopathology, 8*, 701–719.

Canino, G. & Guarnaccia, P. (1997). Methodological challenges in the assessment of Hispanic children and adolescents. *Applied Developmental Science, 1*, 124–134.

Carter, A. S. (2002). Assessing social-emotional and behavior problems and competencies in infancy and toddlerhood: Available instruments and directions for application. In B. Zuckerman, A. Lieberman, & N. Fox (Eds.), *Emotion regulation and developmental health: Infancy and early childhood* (pp. 277–299). New York: Johnson & Johnson Pediatric Institute.

Carter, A. S., Briggs-Gowan, M. J., Jones, S. M., & Little, T. D. (2003). The Infant-Toddler Social and Emotional Assessment (ITSEA): Factor structure, reliability, and validity. *Journal of Abnormal Child Psychology, 31*, 495–514.

Carter, A. S., Briggs-Gowan, M. J., & Ornstein Davis, N. (2004). Assessment of young children's social-emotional development and psychopathology: Recent advances and recommendations for practice. *Journal of Child Psychology and Psychiatry, 45*, 109–134.

Carter, A. S., Little, C., Briggs-Gowan, M. J., & Kogan, N. (1999). The infant-toddler social and emotional assessment (ITSEA): Comparing parent ratings to laboratory observations of task mastery, emotion regulation, coping behaviors and attachment status. *Infant Mental Health Journal, 20*, 375–392.

Caspi, A., Henry, B., McGee, R. O., Moffitt, T. E., & Silva, P. A. (1995). Temperamental origins of child and adolescent behavior problems: From age three to fifteen. *Child Development, 66*, 55–68.

Chamberlain, P., & Reid, J. B. (1987). Parent observation and report of child symptoms. *Behavioral Assessment, 9*, 97–109.

Christensen, M., Emde, R., & Fleming, C. (2004). Cultural perspectives for assessing infants and young children. In R. Del-Carmen-Wiggins & A. Carter (Eds.), *Handbook of infant, toddler, and preschool mental health assessment* (pp. 7–23). New York: Oxford University Press.

Coard, S. I., Wallace, S. A., Stevenson, H. C., & Brotman, L. M. (2004). Towards culturally relevant preventive interventions: The consideration of racial socialization in parent training with African American families. *Journal of Child and Family Studies, 13*, 277–293.

Costello, E. J., Compton, S. N., Keeler, G., & Angold, A. (2003). Relationships between poverty and psychopathology: A natural experiment. *Journal of the American Medical Association, 290*, 2023–2029.

Dana, R. H. (2000). Multicultural assessment of child and adolescent personality and psychopathology. In A. L. Comunian & U. P. Gielen (Eds.), *International perspectives on human development* (pp. 233–258). Lengerich, Germany: Pabst Science.

Deater-Deckard, K., Dodge, K. A., Bates, J. E., & Pettit, G. S. (1996). Physical discipline among African American and European American mothers: Links to children's externalizing behaviors. *Developmental Psychology, 32*, 1065–1072.

Doctoroff, G. L., & Arnold, D. H. (2004). Parent-rated externalizing behavior in preschoolers: The predictive utility of structured interviews, teacher reports, and classroom observations. *Journal of Clinical Child and Adolescent Psychology, 33*, 813–818.

Dodge, K. A., & Pettit, G. S. (2003). A biopsychosocial model of the development of chronic conduct problems in adolescence. *Developmental Psychology, 39*, 349–371.

Egger, H. L., & Angold, A. (2004). The Preschool Age Psychiatric Assessment (PAPA): A structured interview for diagnosing psychiatric disorders in preschool children. In R. Del-Carmen-Wiggins & A. Carter (Eds.), *Handbook of infant, toddler, and preschool mental health assessment* (pp. 223–243). New York: Oxford Press.

Egger, H. L. & Angold, A. (2006). Common emotional and behavioral disorders in preschool children: presentation, nosology, and epidemiology. *Journal of Child Psychology and Psychiatry, 47*, 313–337.

Egger, H. L., Erkanli, A., Keeler, G., Potts, E., Walter, B. K., & Angold, A. (2006). Test-retest reliability of the Preschool Age Psychiatric Assessment (PAPA). *Journal of the American Academy of Child and Adolescent Psychiatry, 45*, 538–549.

Eisenberg, N., Smith, C. L., Sadovsky, A., & Spinrad, T. L. (2004). Effortful control: Relations with emotion regulation, adjustment, and socialization in childhood. In R. F. Baumeister & K. D. Vohs (Eds.), *Handbook of self-regulation: Research, theory, and applications* (pp. 259–282). New York: Guilford Press.

Epstein, J. N., Willoughby, M., Valencia, E. Y., Tonev, S. T., Abikoff, H. B., Arnold, L. E., et al. (2005). The role of children's ethnicity in the relationship between teacher ratings of attention-deficit/hyperactivity disorder and observed classroom behavior. *Journal of Consulting and Clinical Psychology, 73*, 424–434.

Evans, I. M. (2008). Ethical issues. In M. Hersen & D. Reitman (Eds.), *Handbook of psychological assessment, case conceptualization, and treatment: Children and adolescents* (vol. 2, pp. 176–195). Hoboken, NJ: Wiley.

Eyberg, S., Bessmer, J., Newcomb, K., Edwards, D., & Robinson, E. (1994). *Dyadic Parent-Child Interaction Coding System: II. A. manual.* Unpublished manuscript. University of Florida, Gainesville.

Eyberg, S. M., & Matarazzo, R. G. (1980). Training parents as therapist: A comparison between individual parent-child interaction training and parent group didactic training. *Journal of Clinical Psychology, 26*, 492–499.

Eyberg, S., & Pincus, D. (1999). *Eyberg Child Behavior Inventory & Sutter-Eyberg Student Behavior Inventory-Revised: Professional manual.* Odessa, FL: Psychological Assessment Resources.

Forehand, R., & Kotchick, B. A. (1996) Cultural diversity: A wake-up call for parent training. *Behavior Therapy, 27,* 187–206.

Forehand, R., & McMahon, R. J. (1981). *Helping the noncompliant child: A clinician's guide to parent training.* New York: Guilford Press.

Fraiberg, S., Adelson, E., & Shapiro, V. (1975). Ghosts in the nursery: A psycho-analytic approach to the problems of impaired infant-mother relationships. *Journal of the American Journal of Child Psychiatry, 14,* 387–422.

Frick, P. J., & Loney, B. R. (2000). The use of laboratory and performance-based measures in the assessment of children and adolescents with conduct disorders. *Journal of Clinical Child Psychology, 29,* 540–554.

Gilliam, W. S. (2005). *Prekindergarteners left behind: Expulsion rates in state pre-kindergarten systems.* New Haven, CT: Yale University, Child Study Center.

Graziano, A. M., & Diament, D. M. (1992). Parent behavioral training: An examination of the paradigm. *Behavior Modification, 16,* 3–38.

Gross, D., Fogg, L., Webster-Stratton, C., Garvey, C., Julion, W., & Grady, J. (2003). Parent training of toddlers in day care in low-income urban communities. *Journal of Consulting and Clinical Psychology, 71,* 261–278.

Hay, D., Castle, J., & Davies, L. (2000). Toddlers' use of force against familiar peers: A precursor of serious aggression? *Child Development, 71,* 457–467.

Hembree-Kigin, T. L., & McNeil, C. (1995). Parent-Child Interaction Therapy. In M. C. Roberts & A. M., LaGreca (Eds.), *Clinical child psychology library.* New York: Plenum Press.

Hood, K., & Eyberg, S. M. (2003). Outcomes of parent-child interaction therapy: Mothers' reports on maintenance three to six years after treatment. *Journal of Clinical Child and Adolescent Psychology, 32,* 419–429.

Jaffee, S. R., Caspi, A., Moffitt, T. E., & Taylor, A. (2004). Physical maltreatment victim to antisocial child: Evidence of an environmentally mediated process. *Journal of Abnormal Psychology, 113,* 44–55.

Jensen, P. S., Watanabe, H. K., & Richters, J. E. (1999). Who's up first? Testing for order effects in structured interviews using a counterbalanced experimental design. *Journal of Abnormal Child Psychology, 27,* 439–445.

Juffer, F., Bakermans-Kranenburg, M. J., VanIJzendoorn, M. H. (2005). The importance of parenting in the development of disorganized attachment: Evidence from a preventive intervention study in adoptive families. *Journal of Child Psychology and Psychiatry, 26,* 263–274.

Kagan, J. (1998). Biology and the child. In W. Damon & N. Eisenberg (Eds.), *Handbook of child psychology: Social, emotional, and personality development* (5th ed., vol. 3, pp. 177–235). Hoboken, NJ: Wiley.

Kataoka, S. H., Zhang, L., & Wells, K. B. (2002). Unmet need for mental health care among U.S. children: Variation by ethnicity and insurance status. *American Journal of Psychiatry, 159,* 1548–1555.

Kazdin, A. E. (1995). Child, parent, and family dysfunction as predictors of outcome in cognitive-behavioral treatment of antisocial children. *Behaviour Research and Therapy, 33*, 271–281.

Kazdin, A. E. (1997). Parent Management Training: Evidence, outcomes, and issues. *Journal of the American Academy of Child and Adolescent Psychiatry, 36*, 1349–1356.

Kazdin, A. E. (2005). *Parent management training.* New York: Oxford University Press.

Keenan, K. & Shaw, D. S. (1994). The development of aggression in toddlers: A study of low-income families. *Journal of Abnormal Child Psychology, 22*, 53–77.

Keenan, K., Shaw, D., Delliquadri, E., Giovannelli, J. & Walsh, B. (1998). Evidence for the continuity of early problem behaviors: Application of a developmental model. *Journal of Abnormal Child Psychology, 26*, 441–452.

Keenan, K., Shaw, D., Walsh, B., Delliquadri, E. & Giovannelli, J. (1997). DSM-III-R disorders in preschool children from low-income families. *Journal of the American Academy of Child & Adolescent Psychiatry, 36*, 620–627.

Keenan, K. & Wakschlag, L. (2002). Can a valid diagnosis of disruptive behavior disorder be made in preschool children? *American Journal of Psychiatry, 159*, 351–358.

Kendall, P., Chu, B., Gifford, A., Hayes, C., & Nauta, M. (1998). Breathing life into a manual: Flexibility and creativity with manual-based treatments. *Cognitive and Behavioral Practice, 5*, 177–198.

Klebanov, P. K., Brooks-Gunn, J., & Duncan, G. J. (1994). Does neighborhood and family poverty affect mothers' parenting, mental health, and social support? *Journal of Marriage and the Family, 56*, 441–455.

Kochanska, G., Forman, D. R., & Coy, K. C. (1999). Implications of the mother-child relationship in infancy: Socialization in the second year of life. *Infant Behavior and Development, 22*, 249–265.

Kuczynski, L., & Kochanska, G. (1990). Development of children's noncompliance strategies from toddlerhood to age 5. *Developmental Psychology, 26*, 398–408.

Lieberman, A. F., & VanHorn, P. (2005). *Don't hit my mommy.* Washington, DC: Zero to Three Press.

Lieberman, A. F., Van Horn, P. J., Ghosh Ippen, C. (2005). Toward evidence-based treatment: Child-parent psychotherapy with preschoolers exposed to marital violence. *Journal of the American Academy of Child and Adolescent Psychiatry, 44*, 1241–1248.

Long, P., Forehand, R., Wierson, M., Morgan, A. (1994). Does parent training with young noncompliant children have long-term effects? *Behaviour Research and Therapy, 32*, 101–107.

Lord, C., Risi, S., & Lambrecht, L. (2000). The Autism Diagnostic Observation Schedule—Generic: A standard measure of social and communication deficits associated with the spectrum of autism. *Journal of Autism and Developmental Disorders, 30*, 205–223.

Marvin, R. S., Cooper, G., Hoffman, K., Powell, B. (2002). The Circle of Security project: Attachment-based intervention with caregiver-preschool child dyads. *Attachment & Human Development, 4*, 107–124.

Matos, M., Torres, R., Santiago, R., Jurado, M., Rodriguez, I. (2006). Adaptation of parent-child interaction therapy for Puerto Rican families: A preliminary study. *Family Process, 45,* 205–222.

Mayfield, J. W. & Reynolds, C. R. (1998). Are ethnic differences in diagnosis of childhood psychopathology an artifact of psychometric methods? An experimental evaluation of Harrington's hypothesis using parent-reported symptomatology. *Journal of School Psychology, 36,* 313–334.

McCabe, K. M., Yeh, M., Garland, A. F., Lau, A. S., & Chavez, G. (2005). The GANA program: A tailoring program to adapting parent-child interaction therapy for Mexican Americans. *Education and Treatment of Children, 28,* 111–129.

McKown, C., & Weinstein, R. S. (2003). The development and consequences of stereotype consciousness in middle childhood. *Child Development, 74,* 498–515.

McMahon, R. J., & Forehand, R. L. (2003). *Helping the noncompliant child: Family-based treatment for oppositional behavior* (2nd ed.). New York: Guilford Press.

McMahon, R. J., & Frick, P. J. (2005). Evidence-based assessment of conduct problems in children and adolescents. *Journal of Clinical Child and Adolescent Psychology, 34,* 477–505.

McNeil, C. B., Eyberg, S. M., Eisenstadt, T. H., Newcomb, K., & Funderburk, B. W. (1991). Parent-child interaction therapy with behavior problem children: Generalization of treatment effects to the school setting. *Journal of Clinical Child Psychology, 20,* 140–151.

Moffitt, T. E. (1993). Adolescence-limited and life-course-persistent antisocial behavior: A developmental taxonomy. *Psychology Review, 100,* 674–701.

National Institute of Mental Health. (1996). *A plan for prevention research for the National Institute of Mental Health: A report to the National Advisory Mental Health Council* (Rep. No 96–4093). Washington, DC: Author.

Nixon, R. D. V., Sweeney, L., Erickson, D. B., & Touyz, S. W. (2003). Parent-child interaction therapy: A comparison of standard and abbreviated treatments for oppositional defiant pre-schoolers. *Journal of Consulting and Clinical Psychology, 71,* 251–260.

Olds, D. L., Henderson, C. R., Chamberlin, R., & Tatelbaum, R. (1986). Preventing child abuse and neglect: A randomized trial of nurse home visitation. *Pediatrics, 78,* 65–78.

Olds, D., Henderson, C. R., Jr., Cole, R., Eckenrode, J., Kitzman, H., Luckey, D., et al. (1998). Long-term effects of nurse home visitation on children's criminal and antisocial behavior: 15-year follow-up of a randomized controlled trial. *Journal of the American Medical Association, 280,* 1238–1244.

Patterson, G. R. (1982). *Coercive family process.* Eugene, OR: Castalia.

Pettit, G. S., Bates, J. E., & Dodge, K. A. (1997). Supportive parenting, ecological context, and children's adjustment: A seven-year longitudinal study. *Child Development, 68,* 908–923.

Prelow, H. M., Danoff-Burg, S., Swenson, R. R., & Pulgiano, D. (2004). The impact of ecological risk and perceived discrimination on the psychological adjustment of African American and European American youth. *Journal of Community Psychology, 32,* 375–389.

Raine, A. (2002). Biosocial studies of antisocial and violent behavior in children and adults: A review. *Journal of Abnormal Child Psychology, 30,* 311–326.

Reid, J. M., Webster-Stratton, C., Beauchaine, T. P. (2001). Parent training in Head Start: A comparison of program response among African American, Asian American, Caucasian, and Hispanic mothers. *Prevention Science, 2,* 209–227.

Rescorla, L. A. (2005). Assessment of young children using the Achenbach System of Empirically-Based Assessment (ASEBA). *Mental Retardation and Developmental Disabilities Research Reviews, 11,* 226–237.

Rich, B. A., & Eyberg, S. M. (2001). Accuracy of assessment: The discriminative and predictive power of the Eyberg Child Behavior Inventory. *Ambulatory Child Health, 7,* 249–257.

Roberts, M. W. (2001). Clinic observations of structured parent-child interaction designed to evaluate externalizing disorders. *Psychological Assessment, 13,* 46–58.

Roberts, M. W., & Powers, S. W. (1988). The Compliance Test. *Behavioral Assessment, 10,* 375–398.

Rothbart, M. K., & Bates, J. E. (2006). Temperament. In W. Damon & R. M. Lerner (Eds.), *Handbook of child psychology: Social, emotional, and personality development* (6th ed., vol. 3, pp. 177–235). Hoboken, NJ: Wiley.

Sameroff, A. J. (1995). General systems theories and developmental psychopathology. In D. Cicchetti & D. J. Cohen (Eds.), *Developmental psychopathology, vol. 1: Theory and methods* (pp. 659–695). Oxford, UK: Wiley.

Sameroff, A., Seifer, R., Zax, M., & Barocas, R. (1987). Early indicators of developmental risk: Rochester longitudinal study. *Schizophrenia Bulletin, 13,* 383–394.

Scaramella, L. V., & Leve, L. D. (2004). Clarifying parent-child reciprocities during early childhood: The early childhood coercion model. *Clinical Child and Family Psychology Review, 7,* 89–107.

Schuhmann, E. M., Foote, R. C., Eyberg, S. M., Boggs, S. R., & Algina, J. (1998). Efficacy of parent-child interaction therapy: Interim report of a randomized trial with short-term maintenance. *Journal of Clinical Child Psychology, 27,* 34–45.

Seifer, R. (2000). Temperament and goodness of fit: Implications for developmental psychopathology. In A. J. Sameroff, M. Lewis, & S. Miller (Eds.), *Handbook of developmental psychopathology* (2nd ed., pp. 257–276). Dordrecht, Netherlands: Kluwer Academic Publishers.

Shaffer, D., Fisher, P., Lucas, C. P., Dulcan, M. K., & Schwab-Stone, M. E. (2000). NIMH Diagnostic Interview Schedule for Children Version IV (NIMH DISC-IV): Description, differences from previous versions, and reliability of some common diagnoses. *Journal of the American Academy of Child and Adolescent Psychiatry, 39,* 28–38.

Shaw, D. S., Gilliom, M., Ingoldsby, E. M., & Nagin, D. (2003). Trajectories leading to school-age conduct problems. *Developmental Psychology, 39,* 189–200.

Shaw, D. S., Keenan, K., & Vondra, J. I. (1994). Developmental precursors of externalizing behavior: Ages 1 to 3. *Developmental Psychology, 30,* 355–364.

Shaw, D. S., Winslow, E. B., Owens, E. B., Vondra, J. I., Cohn, J. F., & Bell, R. Q. (1998). The development of early externalizing problems among children from low-income families: A transformational perspective. *Journal of Abnormal Child Psychology, 26*, 95–107.

Shonkoff, J. P., & Phillips, D. A. (2000). *From neurons to neighborhoods: The science of early childhood development.* Washington, DC: National Academy Press.

Silk, J. S., Nath, S. R., Siegel, L. R., & Kendall, P. C. (2000). Conceptualizing mental disorders in children: Where have we been and where are we going? *Development and Psychopathology, 12*, 713–735.

Speltz, M. L., McClellan, J., DeKlyen, M., & Jones, K. (1999). Preschool boys with oppositional defiant disorder: Clinical presentation and diagnostic change. *Journal of the American Academy of Child and Adolescent Psychiatry, 38*, 838–845.

Spoth, R., Redmond, C., Hockaday, C., Shin, C. Y. (1996). Barriers to participation in family skills preventive interventions and their evaluations: A replication and extension. *Family Relations, 45*, 247–254.

Stern, D. N. (1985). *The motherhood constellation: A unified view of parent-infant psychotherapy.* New York: Basic Books.

Szalacha, L. A., Erkut, S., Coll, C. G., Alarcon, O., Fields, J. P., & Ceder, I. (2003). Discrimination and Puerto Rican children's and adolescents' mental health. *Cultural Diversity and Ethnic Minority Psychology, 9*, 141–155.

Thomas, A. & Chess, S. (1977). *Temperament and development.* New York: Brunner/ Mazel.

Thomas, J. M., & Guskin, K. A. (2001). Disruptive behavior in young children: What does it mean? *Journal of the American Academy of Child and Adolescent Psychiatry, 40*, 44–51.

Tremblay, R. E. (2000). The development of aggressive behaviour during childhood: What have we learned in the past century? *International Journal of Behavioral Development, 24*, 129–141.

Wakschlag, L. S., Briggs-Gowan, M. J., Carter, A. S., Hill, C., Danis, B., Keenan, K., et al. (2007). A developmental framework for distinguishing disruptive behavior from normative misbehavior in preschool children. *Journal of Child Psychology and Psychiatry, 48*, 976–987.

Wakschlag, L. S., Briggs-Gowan, M. J., Hill, C., Danis, B., Leventhal, B. L., Keenan, K., et al. (2008a). Observational assessment of preschool disruptive behavior, Part II: Validity of the Disruptive Behavior Diagnostic Observation Schedule (DB-DOS). *Journal of the American Academy of Child and Adolescent Psychiatry, 47*, 632–641.

Wakschlag, L. S., Hill, C., Carter, A. S., Danis, B., Egger, H. L., Keenan, K., et al. (2008b). Observational assessment of preschool disruptive behavior, Part I: Reliability of the Disruptive Behavior Diagnostic Observation Schedule (DB-DOS). *Journal of the American Academy of Child and Adolescent Psychiatry, 47*, 622–631.

Wakschlag, L. S., & Keenan, K. (2001). Clinical significance and correlates of disruptive behavior in environmentally at-risk preschoolers. *Journal of Clinical Child Psychology, 30*, 262–275.

Webster-Stratton, C. (1990). Long-term follow-up of families with young conduct problem children: From preschool to grade school. *Journal of Clinical Child Psychology, 19*, 144–149.

Webster-Stratton, C. (1994). Advancing videotape parent training: A comparison study. *Journal of Consulting and Clinical Psychology, 62,* 583–593.

Webster-Stratton, C. (1998). Preventing conduct problems in Head Start children: Strengthening parenting competences. *Journal of Consulting and Clinical Psychology, 66,* 715–730.

Webster-Stratton, C. (2000). The Incredible Years Training Series. *Office of Juvenile Justice and Delinquency Prevention Bulletin,* 1–24.

Webster-Stratton, C. (2005). The Incredible Years: A training series for the prevention and treatment of conduct problems in young children. In E. D. Hibbs & P. S. Jensen (Eds.), *Psychosocial treatments for child and adolescent disorders: Empirically-based strategies for clinical practice* (2nd ed., pp. 507–555). Washington, DC: American Psychological Association.

Webster-Stratton, C., & Hammond, M. (1998). Conduct problems and level of social competence in Head Start children: Prevalence, pervasiveness and associated risk factors. *Clinical Child Psychology and Family Psychology Review, 1,* 101–124.

Webster-Stratton, C., & Hancock, L. (1998). Training for parents of young children with conduct problems: Content, methods, and therapeutic processes. In C. E. Schaefer & J. M. Briesmeister (Eds.), *Handbook of parent training* (pp. 98–152). New York: Wiley.

Webster-Stratton, C., Hollinsworth, T., & Kolpacoff, M. (1989). The long-term effectiveness and clinical significance of three cost effective training programs for families with conduct-problem children. *Journal of Consulting and Clinical Psychology, 57*(4), 550–553.

Webster-Stratton, C. & Reid, M. J. (2003a). The Incredible Years Parents, Teachers and Child Training Series: A multifaceted treatment approach for young children with conduct problems. In A. Kazdin & J. Weisz (Eds.), *Evidence-based psychotherapies for children and adolescents* (pp. 224–240). New York: Guilford Press.

Webster-Stratton, C., & Reid, M. J. (2003b). Treating conduct problems and strengthening social and emotional competence in young children: The Dina Dinosaur Treatment Program. *Journal of Emotional and Behavioral Disorders, 11,* 130–143.

Webster-Stratton, C., & Reid, M. J. (2004). Strengthening social and emotional competence in young children—the foundation for early school readiness and success: Incredible Years Classroom Social Skills and Problem-Solving Curriculum. *Journal of Infants and Young Children, 17,* 96–113.

Webster-Stratton, C., Reid, M. J., & Hammond, M. (2001). Preventing conduct problems, promoting social competence: A parent and teacher training partnership in Head Start. *Journal of Clinical Child Psychology, 30,* 283–302.

Wilens, T. E., Biederman, J., Brown, S., Monuteaux, M., Prince, J., & Spencer, T. J. (2002). Patterns of psychopathology and dysfunction in clinically referred preschoolers. *Journal of Developmental & Behavioral Pediatrics, 23,* S31–S36.

Yoshikawa, H. (1994). Prevention as cumulative protection: Effects of early family support and education on chronic delinquency and its risks. *Psychological Bulletin, 115,* 28–54.

Zeanah, C. H., Larrieu, J. A., Heller, S. S., & Valliere, J. (2000). Infant-parent relationship assessment. In C. H. Zeanah, Jr. (Ed.), *Handbook of infant mental health* (2nd ed., pp. 222–235). New York: Guilford Press.

Zero to Three, National Center for Clinical Infant Programs. (2005). *Diagnostic Classification: 0–3R, Diagnostic classification of mental health and developmental disorders of infancy and early childhood.* Washington, DC: Zero to Three.

CHAPTER 15

Anxiety and Depression in Early Childhood

MARK D. TERJESEN
and ROBYN KURASAKI

W HEN CONSIDERING EARLY childhood mental disorders, externalizing behaviors (e.g., attention deficit hyperactivity disorder [ADHD], aggression) get much of the attention, although internalizing behaviors and disorders (e.g., anxiety, depression) are still problematic to child development. Since externalizing behaviors are far more overt to an observer, many children with internalizing behaviors may go underidentified and receive no psychological intervention or treatment (Chavira, Stein, Bailey, & Stein, 2004; Greenbaum & Dedrick, 1998; Molins & Clopton, 2002). Although many children, including preschool-age children, may not meet strict diagnostic criteria, many display clinically significant symptoms of depression and/or anxiety (Kessler, Avenevoli, & Merikangas, 2001). Given the potential chronic nature of these conditions, unidentified and untreated children with internalizing behaviors may suffer long-term negative outcomes (Cicchetti & Toth, 1998; Ferdinand, Barrett, & Dadds, 2004; Warren & Sroufe, 2004). Unfortunately, at present, the research on internalizing disorders in early childhood remains limited (Bayer & Sanson, 2003).

With regard to young children's mood disorders, understanding the developmental trajectory of the basic emotional processes is important (Luby & Belden, 2006). One question is whether sufficient emotional development has taken place for the specific internalizing symptoms to manifest themselves and, at the same time, to distinguish between normative experiences of early childhood and clinically significant difficulties? In contrast to externalizing behaviors, internalizing behaviors are believed to be under-identified in school-age children; this state-of-affairs is potentially more problematic with younger children, especially given the lack of overt behavior associated with internalized disorders (Bayer & Sanson, 2003).

To highlight the importance of the preschool period, Bayer and Sanson (2003) present a number of reasons why the identification and prevention of the development of internalized emotional difficulties (e.g., anxiety, depression) is necessary. First, research reveals that emotional difficulties persist beyond the preschool period for both those children treated and those who were not. Second, the building blocks of future risk or resilience factors may develop during this period. For example, the early formation of negative, unhealthy ways of youngsters' viewing themselves and their world may become more rigidly held if intervention is not received. In light of these factors, Bayer and Sanson stress the importance of developing preventive measures as well as engaging in early identification to reduce the development of more severe emotional difficulties.

Before specifically discussing anxiety and depression in early childhood, there are a number of factors that complicate the study of psychopathology during this age period that warrant discussion (Stalets & Luby, 2006; Warren, 2007). First, young children have to adjust to numerous developmental challenges. For example, children often have their first experience with a structured preschool or day care environment and interactions with same age-peers at a young age. Some young children may not have the requisite skills to manage these new and varied contexts and the challenges they present (Stalets & Luby). Further, although the early childhood period is associated with rapid cognitive and other developmental growth, preschoolers remain heavily reliant on their caregivers.

On the caregiver end of the dyadic relationship, there may be increased parental expectations for maturity, further contributing to stress for preschoolers (Stalets & Luby, 2006). The complexity of these factors make discerning what is a true negative affective early childhood experience and what may be a consequence of other contextual factors (e.g., excessive family expectation) a challenge for the clinician. Finally, Stalets and Luby posit that clinically relevant behaviors and emotions may be difficult to discern given typical developmental variations. The question for the practitioner is when does behavior become clinically significant and, in addition, when is intervention indicated? Although negative affective symptoms and behaviors are common and sometimes healthy in children, we posit that clinicians need not necessarily wait to intervene. For example, with behavioral inhibition and social withdrawal in preschoolers as risk factors for a subsequent diagnosis of anxiety (Rapee, Kennedy, Ingram, Edwards, & Sweeney, 2005), these symptoms may be targeted for change even before a diagnosis is offered.

This chapter provides an overview of internalizing behaviors in early childhood. More specifically, through examining the mental health disorders related to anxiety and depression in early childhood, this chapter defines these disorders by discussing risk factors and prevalence, presenting diagnostic issues related to the disorders, and offering evidence-based and valid assessment and interventions. Developmental considerations are discussed along with the role of family and culture in both the genesis of these behaviors and in treatment.

DEFINING ANXIETY AND DEPRESSION

Anxiety has been described as negative affect, including feelings of uneasiness, tension, apprehension, and worry that a negative event or situation will occur in the future, and is often expressed through cognitive, physiological, emotional, and behavioral responses (Ramirez, Feeney-Kettler, Flores-Torres, Kratochwill, & Morris, 2006). Although the diagnostic classifications of anxiety disorders are discussed later in the chapter, the common symptomology seen across anxiety disorders is characterized by the experience of developmentally excessive fear or worry (American Psychiatric Association [APA], 2000). Although one of the most common psychiatric problems in school-age children (Ford, Goodman, & Meltzer, 2003), anxiety disorders are not well understood in younger children. Therefore, difficulties exist in discerning whether anxiety problems of older children are similar in presentation to those in younger children (Spence, Rapee, McDonald, & Ingram, 2001).

Recently, an Angold, Egger, Erkanli, and Keeler (2006) study (as cited in Egger & Angold, 2006a) reports that approximately 9.4% of preschoolers in a community-based sample met DSM-IV criteria for an anxiety disorder. Along with significant preschool prevalence rates, lifetime estimates indicate that if untreated, symptoms persist well into adulthood and can lead to future mental health issues and impairments in emotional, social, and academic development (Ferdinand et al., 2004). Since anxiety is one of the most prevalent and enduring mental health problems in young children (Angold et al., 2006; Feng, Shaw, & Silk, 2008), a persistent effort toward developing evidence-based diagnostic criteria, assessment measures, and treatments for younger children is warranted.

Depression in children has been described as an unhappy, sad mood, or as a syndrome including other symptoms (Roberts, Bishop, & Rooney, 2008). Typically, the symptoms associated with depression are anhedonia (i.e., absence of pleasure), negative self-evaluations, difficulty concentrating, indecisiveness, fatigue, and psychomotor disturbance. These factors can lead to decreased academic performance (e.g., poor performance on standardized tests) (Reinemann, Stark, Molnar, & Simpson, 2006) with school-age children. Although some related symptoms (e.g., cognitive processes, motivation, social relationships) may be present in early childhood, academic ramifications are more associated with school-age rather than young children.

Essentially, when depressive symptoms occur for two weeks or more, and are associated with functional impairment, they constitute clinical disorders (APA, 2000). Prevalence estimates for depression with school-age children are highly variable with prevalence rates varying as a function of age and developmental level. Most research estimates that the prepubertal prevalence rate is 1–3% for experiencing their first episode of depression (Garber & Horowitz, 2002; Lewinsohn & Essau, 2002). Although there is not as much research for prevalence rates of depression in early childhood, most estimates range from 0.9% to 2.7% (Stalets & Luby, 2006).

The symptoms of anxiety and depression, given their internalized nature, may be difficult to identify in young children (Bayer & Sanson, 2003). That is, young children may be more subtle than older children in how they present with the symptoms of depression or sadness. For example, younger children may show changes in temperament (e.g., behavioral inhibition to the unfamiliar), whereas older preschool-age children may withdraw socially (Bayer & Sanson).

Some basic emotional development research occurred over 20 years ago, but the findings still retain important implications for understanding affective development. Rotenberg and colleagues demonstrated that young children tend to report less intense feelings of sadness in comparison with older children (Rotenberg, Mars, & Crick, 1987). Whether or not young children are actually experiencing sadness to a lesser degree or just reporting sadness as less severe may, in part, be attributed to difficulties in verbal expression.

Differences in expression of affective states begin during infancy and are displayed throughout early childhood. Research indicates that sadness can be differentiated from other negative affective states as young as 2 months of age (Izard, Hembree, & Huebner, 1987) and that facial expressions can be linked to negative events between 2 and 6 months of age (Izard, Fantauzzo, Castle, Haynes, Rayias, & Putnam, 1995). Luby and Belden (2006) point out that beginning around 4 years of age, children become increasingly aware of social events (e.g., loss of social events) and subsequently begin experiencing sadness. Further, early childhood is also a time when youngsters engage in behaviors (e.g., seeking hugs) to regulate their affect. These early self-regulatory behaviors may be important for mental health clinicians and educators to consider in assessing and intervening with young children and their families.

RISK FACTORS

Research reveals many potential biological and environmental risk factors related to the development of internalizing disorders in young children (Bayer & Sanson, 2003; Biederman et al., 1993; Boer, Stegge, & Akyuz, 2008; Donovan &

Spence, 2000; Rapee et al., 2005). In fact, risk factors may predict the onset, severity, and duration of psychopathology (Coie et al., 1993). In preschool-age children, biological risk factors (e.g., genetic vulnerability, temperament) and environmental characteristics (e.g., parent affect) are identified in the early childhood research on development of internalizing disorders (Biederman et al., 1993; Boer et al., 2008; Rapee et al., 2005). If recognized early, these risk factors may lead to preventative planning which subsequently may reduce the short and long-term consequences of anxiety and depression (Bayer & Sanson). Although risk factors alone may not necessarily contribute to the development of anxiety and depression, in combination they may interact and lead to negative outcomes for children and families (Donovan & Spence, 2000; Ramirez et al., 2006). Therefore, additional research directed toward identifying risk factors and developing explanatory integrated models is needed (Bayer & Sanson; Albano, Chorpita, & Barlow, 2003).

Biological and genetic factors play central roles in the development of internalizing problems (Bayer & Sanson, 2003; Greenberg, Domitrovich, & Bumbarger, 2001). Although a review of all possible genetic components is beyond the scope of this chapter, clinicians must be aware of the genetic predisposition of internalizing disorders. For example, anxiety and depression heritability estimates range from 11% to 72% (Wambolt & Wambolt, 2000), and children whose parents are anxious and depressed are at a higher risk to develop mood and anxiety disorders than their peers (Beidel & Turner, 2007; Hammen, Shih, & Brennan, 2004; Warner, Mufson, & Weissman, 1995).

In addition to heritability estimates, biological risk factors (e.g., behavioral inhibition, negative affectivity) also are associated with the later development of anxiety disorders (Bierdeman et al., 1993; Boer et al., 2008). For example, behavioral inhibition is characterized as the propensity to withdraw in response to unfamiliar people, situations, or objects (Kagan, 1997). Negative affectivity is characterized as the inability to regulate negative emotion (Axelson & Birmaher, 2001; Kovacs & Devlin, 1998). Careful consideration of these factors when assessing young children's background, family, and developmental history is important.

In addition to biological/genetic risk factors, many environmental risk factors and child characteristics variables also are linked to internalizing disorders (Bayer & Sanson, 2003). Environmental risk factors include issues such as marital and family discord (Roberts et al., 2008), parent psychopathology (e.g., anxiety, depression) (Mulvaney, Mebert, & Flint, 2007; Verdeli, Ferro, Wickramaratne, Greenweald, Blanco, & Weissman, 2004), and parent behaviors (e.g., punitive/coercive discipline, over-control parenting) (Feng et al., 2008; Lovejoy, Graczyk, O'Hare, & Neuman, 2000; Shamir-Essakow, Ungerer, & Rapee, 2005; Wood, McLeod, Sigman, Hwang, & Chu,

2003). Child characteristics also may act as potential risk factors, including, for instance, prolonged physical illness (Reinherz, Giaconia, Pakiz, Silverman, Frost, & Lefkowitz, 1993), the occurrence of negative life events in childhood (Bruce, Cole, Dallaire, Jacques, Pineda, & LaGrange, 2006), the presence of an existing psychological disorder (Avenevoli, Stolar, Li, Dierker, & Merikangas, 2001), and social and interpersonal difficulties (Bayer & Sanson, 2003; Cole, 1990; Rudolph, Hammen, & Burge, 1994).

DIAGNOSTIC CONSIDERATIONS

The diagnosis of anxiety and depression in younger children has received considerable debate (Carter, Briggs-Gowan, & Davis, 2004; Stalets & Luby, 2006) and is complicated by a number of variables that make an accurate diagnosis difficult. Several authors have proposed a number of concerns about the clinical diagnoses of internalizing disorders in early childhood. First, Stalets and Luby argue that diagnoses may pathologize what are actually normal and transient variations in behaviors and emotional expression. Second, they posit that establishing a diagnosis can be damaging, creating an unnecessary stigma for the child and family. Third, diagnoses may not be appropriate at this age as behaviors may originate more from the caretaking environment (e.g., relationship between the parent and the child) rather than the young child (Egger & Angold, 2006a). Therefore, a formal diagnosis may not always be warranted and sometimes treatment may be more appropriately geared towards the family than the child (Rapee et al., 2005). Finally, Stalets and Luby point out that there may be a dichotomy between expectations and practice associated with a diagnosis of depression. They speculate that clinicians and society may consider early childhood as a carefree time of joy, and therefore there may be an inherent reluctance to recognize mood disorders in early childhood. However, despite reluctance, Stalets and Luby point out prescriptions for medication (e.g., antidepressants) with the preschool-age group doubled in a 4-year span of time and clinicians seem to be treating young children with depression increasingly with pharmacological interventions.

Some of the obstacles and criticisms in diagnosing young children with anxiety or depression (Egger & Angold, 2006b; Ronan, 1996) include (1) difficulties distinguishing between developmentally appropriate and adaptive affective states (e.g., concern, sadness), and those that are maladaptive, cause unwanted distress, and lead to avoidant behavior for the child; (2) the transitory nature of the preschool developmental period; (3) diagnostic classification systems that fail to take into account developmental variations; and (4) shortages of evidence-based, empirically validated, psychometrically sound measures for young children's internalizing disorders (Warren, 2007).

In light of such challenges, several leaders in the field have focused on identifying clinically significant anxiety in preschool children (Albano, Causey, & Carter, 2001; Egger & Angold, 2006a) that warrant intervention. When assessing young children's clinically significant anxiety, Egger and Angold recommend that clinicians look for disproportionate reactions to stimuli, frequent, involuntary, or uncontrollable reactions, impairments in development or functioning, avoidant behavior, and pervasiveness. These symptoms are important not only for diagnostic purposes, but also in the development of appropriate treatment strategies.

Currently, the *Diagnostic and Statistical Manual of Mental Disorders,* 4th ed., Text Revision (DSM-IV-TR; APA, 2000) contains nine types of anxiety disorders, with four disorders having typical age of onset in childhood: generalized anxiety disorder, selective mutism, separation anxiety disorder, and specific phobia (APA, 2000). Furthermore, selective mutism and separation anxiety disorder are the only two anxiety disorders specific to children and adolescents. In an attempt to define developmentally appropriate criteria for preschoolers, the American Academy of Child and Adolescent Psychiatry proposed changes to the DSM-IV criteria. Modifications for separation anxiety disorder were recommended by the 2003 Task Force on Research and Diagnostic Criteria: Infancy and Preschool, outlining how separation anxiety symptoms specifically may manifest in young children (as cited in Warren, 2007).

Although more research is needed, there is support for the differentiation of anxiety disorders in preschool-age children (Egger & Angold, 2006a; Spence et al., 2001). Through factor analytic procedures, five factors representing social phobia, separation anxiety, generalized anxiety, obsessive–compulsive disorder, and specific fears such as fear of physical harm emerge for children 2.5–6.5 years of age (Egger Erkanli, Keeler, Potts, Walter, & Angold, 2006; Spence et al., 2000). If these disorders are able to be differentiated effectively with this age group, then this may assist in efficient implementation of targeted interventions.

Much of the recent work on identifying symptoms of early childhood depression comes from the work of Luby and colleagues from the Washington University School of Medicine Early Emotional Development Program (EEDP). Luby and colleagues (Luby & Belden, 2006; Luby, Belden, & Spitznagel, 2006; Stalets & Luby, 2006) present data validating the presence of early childhood depression, propose a modification to diagnostic schemes, offer caution, and describe the challenges to the identification of depression in preschool-age children.

In terms of classification systems, the DSM-IV-TR (APA, 2000) and the International Classification and Diagnostic System (ICD; World Health Organization, 2004), were developed primarily for an adult population and, thus, lack developmental sensitivity in considering symptom presentation

(Stalets & Luby, 2006). Unlike the DSM-IV-TR, the *Diagnostic Classification of Mental Health and Developmental Disorders of Infancy and Early Childhood* (Zero to Three, 1994, 2005) was developed to consider developmental variables in application of symptoms for diagnosis; however, although the system offers operational definitions of anxiety and depression, the validity of these constructs has yet to be demonstrated.

One DSM-IV-TR developmentally sensitive exception is the inclusion of irritability and sadness as components in the diagnosis of depression in children. Given the lack of other clear, developmentally appropriate diagnostic criteria for depression, Luby and colleagues (Luby, Mrakotsky, Heffelfinger, Brown, Hessler, & Spitznagel, 2003) offer suggestions as to how the current diagnostic criteria may be modified for the preschool-age group. These modifications may be important for early childhood mental health providers to consider not necessarily for a diagnosis, but rather to better understand depressive behaviors with young children. Among Luby et al.'s recommended modifications, is the proposal that rather than requiring symptoms be persistent over 2 weeks, as in the DSM-IV-TR, they simply need to be present. This recommendation is made because of the high variability of preschool children's moods. In addition, Luby et al. offer modifications to the DSM-IV-TR symptoms. For example, because young children lack adult verbal skills, they suggest the consideration of play-based assessment. They maintain symptoms of depression can be "translated" to address age appropriate manifestations of the DSM-IV criteria; by using the translation, symptoms are identifiable in the preschool-age population.

Among the more interesting, potentially clinically significant, translations offered was their translation of anhedonia (e.g., the inability to enjoy activities and play) (Luby et al., 2003). The belief is that anhedonia is associated with more severe depression and related to children's inability to positively respond to joyful events. Indeed, anhedonia may be useful in screening for depression in early childhood and also hold important implications for treatment. For example, depressed adults who experience anhedonia tend to respond to pharmacologic treatments (Luby & Belden, 2006).

The proposed revised DSM-IV-TR criteria were validated with a group of 54 depressed preschoolers; that is, a pattern of specific, stable depressive symptoms differentiated the depressed youngsters from another clinical sample (ADHD) and a normal control condition (Luby, Mrakotsky, Heffelfinger, Brown, & Spitznagel, 2004). All depressive symptoms occurred more often in the depressed group with anhedonia being the most frequent. Further, the proposed depressive symptoms tend to cluster together and demonstrate strong internal consistency. The results provide preliminary evidence for depression as a valid clinical syndrome with the preschool-age population. In addition, Luby et al.'s research seems to refute the popular notion that symptoms of depression at young ages are more "masked" in nature rather than presenting as typical symptoms (Luby & Belden, 2006).

The theory behind the masked presentation of symptoms proposes that, because of developmental limitations, children mask their depressive symptoms and likely show regression or somatization. Luby and colleagues report that these masked symptoms are present, by determining somatization occurs in approximately 40% of preschoolers with depression; however, this symptom does not occur at a higher rate than the more typical symptoms of depression. Therefore, although masked symptoms may be important to assess, the typical symptoms of depression (e.g., sadness, irritability) may be the best clinical markers and remain an important part of any mental health screening. Although there are issues in applying the diagnostic criteria of depression to early childhood, the work of Luby and colleagues demonstrates that, at the very least, these behaviors occur in early childhood and whether or not part of a formal diagnosis, often warrant intervention.

ASSESSMENT CONSIDERATIONS

As previously discussed, the identification of anxiety and depression in early childhood is complicated by young children's limited verbal skills, as well as frequent comorbidity with other disorders, high levels of emotional variability at this age, and lack of clear developmentally sensitive diagnostic criteria. Therefore, accurate assessment of anxiety and depression in early childhood is often difficult. An overview of current assessment approaches for identifying symptoms and behaviors associated with anxiety and depression in young children is presented.

Egger and Angold (2006a) describe the goals of comprehensive assessment with preschool children, including identifying clinically significant levels of symptoms as well as assessing the levels of possible functional impairment in the child and family. To obtain a comprehensive assessment, several methods (e.g., behavior rating scales, observation systems) from different sources (e.g., parents, teachers), across different settings (e.g., home, school), are employed. This multidimensional approach allows clinicians opportunities to understand young children's behaviors. For example, data gathered from multiple methods (e.g., interviews, rating scales, observations) can be beneficial as young children often are unable to report their own symptoms (Carter et al., 2004).

In addition to employing several methods, the assessment process should involve multiple informants. Parents, child care professionals, preschool teachers, and/or professionals who interact with children, as well as the individual child, can all provide valuable information regarding issues such as symptoms, context, and behavior maintenance. For example, parents who speak for a child with selective mutism may be reinforcing the behavior, making mutism more likely to occur again. Information gathered through a multimethod/source approach may not only provide a more complete picture of the child's symptomatology and behaviors (Langley, Bergman, & Piacentini, 2002), but also assist in the development of clinical interventions.

Assessment of Behavior: Rating Scales

Rating scales provide valuable means to gather information about the child from several sources (Sattler & Hoge, 2006). Use of behavior rating scales as part of an evaluation or screening for internalizing symptomatology are among the most frequently used assessment tools (Miles, 2000; Shapiro & Heick, 2004); however, their applicability is limited for early childhood. Many of the measures were developed with older children in mind and, for the most part, normative ages were simply extended to cover early childhood. This downward extension may not accurately reflect the developmental differences in symptoms and behavior (Stalets & Luby, 2006). Further, caregivers and early childhood educators may not be well informed or observant regarding developmentally appropriate and inappropriate anxious and depressive related behaviors. Therefore, they may not accurately identify the nature and occurrence of clinically relevant behaviors. As a result, given the internalizing nature of these behaviors (e.g., symptoms not readily observable as aggressive behaviors), anxious and depressive symptoms often are underreported (Barrett, 2001; Bayer & Sanson, 2003).

Since symptoms and behaviors of anxiety and depression are present in young children, discussing rating scales and their associated psychometric properties is important. The broad-band measures which assess a range of behaviors, symptoms, and diagnoses, are the Behavior Assessment System for Children-2 (BASC-2; Reynolds & Kamphaus, 2004), the Achenbach System of Empirically-Based Assessment (ASEBA; Achenbach & Rescorla, 2000), the Conners' Rating Scales (Conners, 2008), and the Early Childhood Inventory–Parent Checklist (ECI-PC; Gadow & Sprafkin, 1997). These rating scales include subscales for depression and anxiety that may assist in differential diagnosis from other childhood behaviors and diagnoses.

In looking at specific attributes of the broad-band measures, the BASC-2 has both a teacher and parent version covering the age span of 2–5 years and excellent reliability and validity (Reynolds & Kamphaus, 2004). The ASEBA system consists of the Child Behavior Checklist (CBCL) and Caregiver–Teacher Report Form (C-TRF), covering ages 1½–5 years (Achenbach & Rescorla, 2000). The authors report, through large national normative and clinical samples, that they developed seven cross-informant syndromes, including an anxious/depressed syndrome. Both the CBCL and the C-TRF also provide DSM-oriented scales, rated by experts to be consistent with DSM-IV diagnostic categories. The proposed DSM category of Affective Problems differs from the Anxiety problem category, suggesting something clinicians may wish to consider in differentiating anxiety and depression from other disorders as well as from each other. The Conners' Rating Scales have screening items for anxiety and depression, with normative data down to 3 years of age (Conners, 2008). Finally, a more diagnostically derived measure, the ECI is a checklist reflecting the specific domains for the DSM, useful in screening for early childhood anxiety and depression.

Bayer, Sanson, and Hemphill (2006b) review a number of other published measures specifically for internalizing problems in early childhood. Among them are Squires, Bricker, Heo, and Twombly's (2001) Ages and Stages Questionnaire: Social-Emotional (as cited in Bayer, Sanson, & Hemphill, 2006b) and Carter, Briggs-Gowan, and Davis's (2004) Infant–Toddler Social and Emotional Assessment (ITSEA; as cited in Bayer et al., 2006b). Although both are considered by Bayer et al. as developmentally sensitive to childhood internalizing problems, the authors prefer the ITSEA primarily due to related psychometric characteristics, especially item development.

There have been recent attempts to develop rating scales specifically for internalizing disorders in younger children. Bayer et al. (2006b) developed the Children's Moods, Fears, and Worries, a parent report for preschoolers with internalizing difficulties. The test developers followed a sample of 112 children and their parents over a 2-year period from the age of 2. Results indicate stability in early internalizing difficulties and the measure demonstrates high intercorrelations regarding a number of early childhood internalizing difficulties (i.e., anxiety, depression, inhibition, peer withdrawal), all of which are consistent with the symptom presentation (Bayer et al.).

In addition to the broad-band measures and measures of internalizing behavior, more narrow-band (i.e., assessing a specific area of behavior) instruments also may be useful to the clinician in understanding anxiety and depression. Egger and Angold (2004) describe some rating scales for preschool-age children specific to anxiety: the Preschool Anxiety Scale (Spence et al., 2001), Fear Survey Schedule for Infants–Preschoolers (Warren, 2007; Warren, Ollendick, & Simmons, 2007), and the Infant–Preschool Scale for Inhibited Disorders (Warren, 2004). Although preschool normative data exists for these checklists, more psychometric data to confirm the reliability and validity of these measures, especially with regard to culturally diverse samples, is needed (Carter et al., 2004).

With regard to well-established, narrow-band measures specific to depression in early childhood, Luby, Heffelfinger, Koenig-McNaught, Brown, and Spitznagel (2004) developed the Preschool Feelings Checklist (PFC). This 20-item parent report checklist was administered to 174 parents of preschoolers, between the ages of 3 and 5.5 years, and results indicate that the measure is a good screener for depression in early childhood with strong reliability and discriminative validity. Clinicians may want to consider making the PFC part of early childhood mental health screening.

Assessment of Behavior: Interviews and Observations

Rating scales may be efficient and help determine severity level, but clinical interviews and observations of the child provide additional information not obtained by rating scales. Clinical interviews are a widely used tool for gathering information from children and parents through structured or unstructured formats to help better understand child behavior and provide a reliable means for obtaining a diagnosis (Langley et al., 2002). One interview approach specific to this developmental age is the Preschool-Age Psychiatric Assessment (PAPA; Egger & Angold, 2004).

The PAPA is a structured psychiatric interview assessment of children's behavior as reported by parents. The interview has a number of questions which probe responses, utilizing the developmentally modified DSM-IV criteria proposed by Luby et al. (2003). A number of statistical models provided lend support for a differentiation of emotional syndromes into three factors, one of which was depression/generalized anxiety. The overlap of these two syndromes is consistent with patterns seen in other parent-report measures along with the high comorbidity of both (Egger & Angold, 2006a). Although a broad measure of preschool psychopathology, the PAPA includes several sections particularly related to anxiety including separation anxiety, anxious affect, worries, and depression. The authors conclude that for the most part the DSM-IV nosology is applicable to preschoolers and this interview may be one means for understanding internalizing symptom presentation.

Despite young children's less advanced language sophistication and cognitive developmental level, information may be obtained from young children themselves. The Berkeley Puppet Interview (BPI; Luby, Belden, Sullivan, & Spitznagel, 2007) has shown that young children (i.e., 4.0–5.6 years) can be helpful informants, contributing to a valid assessment of some key aspects of depression and anxiety. An additional means of assessing personality and internalizing behaviors may be through the use of narrative assessments. Narrative assessments represent a qualitative approach towards understanding child affective states and involve children telling or completing a story (Esquivel & Flanagan, 2007). The stories may be elicited through play, dolls, puppets, pictures, or story stems (Bettmann & Lundahl, 2007). Bettmann and Lundahl provide a thorough review and critique of 13 empirically validated narrative assessments for preschoolers. Clinicians who work with young children may wish to consider integrating some of these narrative-based approaches into their assessment for anxiety and depression in early childhood. Consideration of the constructs assessed within the narrative assessment and the stimuli involved may help guide the selection of which measure may yield the most beneficial information.

The evaluation of anxiety and depression in preschool-age children also typically includes behavioral observations of children in multiple contexts (Egger & Angold, 2004). Specific to anxiety in preschool-age children, the Glennon and Weisz (1978) Preschool Observational Scale of Anxiety (POSA; as cited in Egger & Angold, 2006a), although relatively old, can help clinicians compare parent, teacher, and child reports of anxiety, observe the child's behaviors firsthand, and determine the impact that anxious symptoms and behaviors may have on children's daily functioning (Velting, Setzer, & Albano, 2004).

For depression, Luby and colleagues stress the importance of conducting an observation as part of the assessment process for preschoolers (Luby et al., 2006b). Observations of children's behavior assist in identifying and validating early-onset depression (Luby et al.). Observations of parents and children together also may offer additional insight into the experience of depression with this age group. Their research demonstrates that observations allow for differentiation among clinical subgroups (e.g., depressed, disruptive). Furthermore, their research points toward some significant differences between the anhedonically depressed group and the nonanhedonically depressed group. As discussed previously, the differentiation may hold important clinical implications for practitioners, as adults with anhedonia respond more often to pharmacologic interventions. In addition, when assessing for anxiety or depression, observational systems assessing parent-child interactions may provide useful information on parental behaviors and how parents may be unintentionally modeling or reinforcing anxious or depressive behaviors in their children.

For internalizing disorders in early childhood, in addition to a multi-method approach, clinicians often adopt functional analytic procedures (Ramirez et al., 2006). Functional-based assessments help gather information about problem behaviors, antecedents and consequences triggering or maintaining the problems, and provide information about the behavioral, physiological, and cognitive responses of the child (Ronan, 1996). An example of the utility of a functional assessment for anxious behaviors may be seen with preschoolers who have difficulty separating from parents to the preschool classroom. The early childhood clinician examines the function (e.g., attention seeking, avoidance, escape) for anxious behavior by identifying the feared stimuli, triggers, and reinforcers that may be maintaining the child engaging in these anxiety-related behaviors. Although more research is needed with early childhood internalizing behaviors, functional-based measures may assist in the assessment of the behaviors and in the design of treatment plans (Ramirez et al.).

In summary, despite difficulties in the identification of internalizing symptoms in early childhood, the problematic symptoms and behaviors can be assessed. Given their insidious nature, symptoms of anxiety and depression need to be identified through a comprehensive multimethod, multiple informant approach in early childhood so that clinically specific interventions can reduce the likelihood of further difficulties, and promote healthy social-emotional development. In addition, clinicians should consider assessment as an ongoing and continuous process to examine persistence and severity of anxious and depressive symptoms as well as see if the child is responsive to treatment.

INTERVENTIONS FOR INTERNALIZING DIFFICULTIES

The preschool years are a critical time for cognitive and interpersonal development (Rapee et al., 2005) as children begin establishing peer relationships and start developing early cognitive schemata (Bayer & Sanson, 2003). Early identification of young children experiencing excessive and unhealthy levels of anxiety and depressive symptoms may allow clinicians to effectively employ preventative strategies and early intervention efforts to alleviate symptoms and improve overall functioning (Bayer & Sanson, 2003).

The early childhood treatment outcome literature for internalizing disorder is lacking in comparison with older children and externalizing behaviors (Bayer & Sanson, 2003). Chambless and Ollendick (2001), in their review of empirically supported interventions for children and adolescents, did not differentiate effectiveness for treatment of internalizing disorders with early childhood and school-age children. This is consistent with other reviews of depression (David-Ferdon & Kaslow, 2008; Kaslow & Thompson, 1998) that do not address the important period of early childhood.

Although the intervention literature for anxiety and depression have made significant strides in evidence-based treatments for older children (e.g., Kendall's Coping Cat program, parent training programs) (Brent et al., 1997; Ginsburg & Schlossberg, 2002; Kendall & Hedtke, 2006; King, Heyne, & Ollendick, 2005; Moore & Carr, 2000), there are significantly fewer studies with preschool-age children (Egger & Angold, 2004). The effectiveness of these school-age interventions appears promising; however, more research is needed to modify, develop, and empirically evaluate the application of these interventions with younger children.

One of the few intervention studies with preschoolers exhibiting a number of withdrawal/inhibited behaviors was conducted by Rapee et al. (2005).

These researchers implemented an early intervention program designed to prevent the development of anxiety in a sample of 146 preschool-age children. The children's parents received six sessions of parent education covering topics about the nature of anxiety, parent-management techniques with an emphasis on educating parents on the relationship between overprotective parenting and child anxiety, exposure hierarchies (i.e., a list of feared stimuli), and cognitive restructuring of parents' worries (Rapee et al.). Those who received the parent education intervention had a greater decrease in children anxiety diagnoses at a 12-month follow-up than parents who did not receive treatment (Rapee et al.).

Recently, several other researchers have begun to design and evaluate interventions for anxiety and depression in preschool-age children. For example, researchers at the Center for Anxiety and Related Disorders conducted a randomized clinical trial to evaluate the efficacy of Parent-Child Interaction Therapy (PCIT) for young children with separation anxiety disorder, 4–8 years of age (Pincus, Santucci, Ehrenreich, & Eyberg, 2008). PCIT is designed to help parents develop a warm and responsive parent-child relationship through teaching parents parenting skills and positive behavior management strategies (e.g., reinforcement) (Pincus et al.). Preliminary data demonstrated that children and parents who received PCIT experienced fewer child anxious symptoms at the termination of treatment (Pincus et al.). Furthermore, parents reported an increase in child academic performance, improvements in relationships with siblings, and reductions in parent stress.

Considering depression, Stalets and Luby (2006) report that no studies have been conducted that efficaciously support psychopharmacologic or therapeutic treatment of depression in preschoolers. Luby and colleagues at the Early Emotional Development program are in the process of investigating the effectiveness of a dyadic psychotherapy program with children and parents. The program aims to utilize parent-child interactions to teach preschool children with depression strategies for emotional development; more specifically, they teach the management of negative emotions and promotion of positive emotions (Washington University in St. Louis, 2008). Finally, Gleason and colleagues (2007), in their development of psychopharmacologic practice guidelines with young children, point out that the effectiveness of nonpharmacologic treatment is highly variable and that there is no research at present that supports their use in treatment of depressive symptoms in young children.

Unfortunately, the lack of evidence-based interventions for young children causes problems for the clinician providing services to young children who are anxious and/or depressed. Guided by the preliminary results of recent intervention studies, several treatment considerations for young children are proposed. Preventative or early interventions for young children who are experiencing internalizing symptoms need to be guided by data gathered from a comprehensive assessment and case conceptualization (Egger & Angold, 2004). Interventions selected and implemented for young children uniformly need to be based on evidence-based principles. Given the lack of large outcome studies with this age group, even single-case designs may assist in the assessment of treatment outcomes (Egger & Angold).

Further, clinicians working with children and families who are culturally and linguistically diverse need to be sensitive not only to their own cultural beliefs, but also need to educate themselves on cultural norms (e.g., parent perceptions, expectations of child development, service delivery) (Mattox & Harder, 2007; Ortiz, Flanagan & Dynda, 2008). For example, as a function of culture, some families may differ in their expectations as to what their role is to be in the therapeutic process and although they may be willing to have their child engage in treatment parents themselves may not be willing to participate in the intervention (McMiller & Weisz, 1996). The recommendation is that clinicians consider the role of culture as influencing the participation of parents and the outcome of implemented interventions.

Consideration of Ethics in Assessment, Diagnosis, Intervention, and Training

From an examination of the history of anxiety and depression in early childhood, clearly research and practice has been building. Collectively, the research helps define, refine, and understand the validity and the appropriateness of diagnoses as well as the development of strategies to effectively intervene with these disorders. Clinicians have numerous important ethical responsibilities to consider in practice with young children who experience internalizing difficulties and there are training issues associated with practice as well. First, clinical practice should rely on evidence-base to guide and support diagnosis, assessment, and intervention (APA Presidential Task Force on Evidence-Based Practice, 2006). As mentioned throughout the chapter, in comparison with school-age children, the research to guide early childhood practice is limited. Despite the relative paucity of research, clinicians need to stay abreast with existing research and the findings of future investigations as they contribute to and guide clinical practice. In addition, clinicians should embrace current practice and studiously avoid using assessment and intervention practices that are out of date or designed for older children (APA Presidential Task Force on Evidence-Based Practice).

With regard to assessment, clinicians should adhere to best practice for psychological testing in consideration of the age group for which they work. The *Standards for Educational and Psychological Testing* (Standards; American Educational Research Association [AERA], American Psychological

Association [APA], National Council on Measurement in Education [NCME], 1999) provides clinicians with guidelines for interpreting and understanding the psychometric properties constituting appropriate measures. As previously mentioned, although the measures for early childhood anxiety and depression are still developing, clinicians should take care in test selection, ensuring that selected measures are developmentally appropriate and psychometrically sound for the young child (AERA, 1999).

More specifically, it is recommended that clinicians routinely review the validity and reliability of the instruments chosen. Furthermore, trainers of early childhood practitioners need to be aware of and inform practitioners of appropriate measures and interventions for early childhood to guide professional practice. Current, evidence-based practice is indicated in assessment, consultation, and intervention. That is, trainers consistently need to link evidence-based practices in the curriculum presented and in professional preparation (e.g., fieldwork experiences). When training practitioners in assessment of early childhood anxiety and depression, not only are age appropriate, multiculturally sensitive measures important to teach, but also strategies for evaluating the suitability of current and future measures of anxiety and depression.

Ethical standards and training implications standards are also important in early childhood clinical interventions, as research is lacking in this professional practice area. There is no question that clinical interventions are to be evidence-based (APA Presidential Task Force on Evidence-Based Practice, 2006) and each clinician's responsibility is to be active consumers of the research to remain current regarding effective interventions with this younger population (National Association of School Psychologists [NASP], 2008). Finally, although informing practitioners as to what is best science for assessment and intervention is important, we argue that it is equally important for clinicians to apply this knowledge to their practice with young children and their families.

SUMMARY

Throughout this chapter, challenges in the early childhood assessment, diagnosis, and intervention for anxiety and depression were highlighted. The current taxonomy that exists for identifying these early childhood disorders often is not reflective of the unique developmental characteristics and presentation of these disorders with this age group. The use of multiple means for identifying, measuring, and differentiating anxiety and depression from other disorders of early childhood is essential; further, the role of culture and family in the development and maintenance of symptoms or behaviors associated with these disorders is undeniable. Thus, parent and familial involvement is important to reduce the likelihood of development of anxiety and depression in early childhood. It is our hope that current studies underway and future investigations will expand the assessment and intervention research with young children to guide training and practice.

REFERENCES

Achenbach, T. M., & Rescorla, L. A. (2000). *Manual for the ASEBA preschool forms & profiles*. Burlington: University of Vermont, Research Center for Children, Youth, & Families.

AERA, APA, & NCME. (1999). *Standards for educational and psychological testing*. Washington, DC: Author.

Albano, A. M., Causey, D., & Carter, B. (2001). Fear and anxiety in children. In C. E. Walker & M. E. Roberts (Eds.), *Handbook of clinical child psychology* (3rd ed., pp. 291–316). New York: Wiley.

Albano, A. M., Chorpita, B. F., & Barlow, D. H. (2003). Childhood anxiety disorders. In E. J. Mash & R. A. Barkley (Eds.), *Child psychopathology* (2nd ed., pp. 279–329). New York: Guilford Press.

American Psychiatric Association. (2000). *Diagnostic and statistical manual of mental disorders* (4th ed., Text Revision). Washington, DC: Author.

Angold, A., Egger, H. L., Erkanli, A., & Keeler, G. (2006). *Prevalence and comorbidity of psychiatric disorders in preschoolers attending a large pediatric service*. Unpublished manuscript.

APA Presidential Task Force on Evidence-Based Practice. (2006). Evidence-based practice in psychology. *American Psychologist, 61*(4), 271–285.

Avenevoli, S., Stolar, M., Li, J., Dierker, L., & Merikangas, K. R. (2001). Comorbidity of depression in children and adolescents: Models and evidence from a prospective high-risk family study. *Society of Biological Psychiatry, 49*, 1071–1081.

Axelson, D., & Birmaher, B. (2001). Relation between anxiety and depressive disorders in childhood and adolescence. *Depression and Anxiety, 14*, 67–78.

Barrett, P. M. (2001). Current issues in the treatment of childhood anxiety. In M. W. Vasey & M. R. Dadds (Eds.), *The developmental psychopathology of anxiety* (pp. 304–324). London, UK: Oxford University Press.

Bayer, J. K., & Sanson, A. V. (2003). Preventing the development of emotional mental health problems from early childhood: Recent advances in the field. *International Journal of Mental Health Promotion, 5*, 4–16.

Bayer, J. K., Sanson, A. V., & Hemphill, S. A. (2006). Children's moods, fears, and worries: Development of an early childhood parent questionnaire. *Journal of Emotional and Behavioral Disorders, 14*, 41–49.

Beidel, D. C., & Turner, S. M. (2007). *Shy children, phobic adults: The nature and treatment of social anxiety disorder* (2nd ed.). Washington, DC: American Psychological Association Books.

Bettman, J. E., & Lundahl, B. W. (2007). Tell me a story: A review of narrative assessments for preschoolers. *Child & Adolescent Social Work Journal, 24*, 455–475.

Bierdeman, J., Rosenbaum, J. F., Bolduc-Murphy, E. A., Faraone, S. V., Chaloff, J., Hirshfield, D. R., & Kagan, J. A. (1993). A 3-year follow-up of children with and without behavioral inhibition. *Journal of the American Academy of Child and Adolescent Psychiatry, 32,* 814–821.

Boer, F., Stegge, H., & Akyuz, H. (2008). Recognition of children of preschool age at risk for internalizing disorders in mainstream and Islamic primary care. *International Journal of mental Health Promotion, 9,* 17–24.

Brent, D. A., Holder, D., Kolko, D., Birmaher, B., Baugher, M., Roth, C., & Johnson, B. (1997). A clinical psychotherapy trial for adolescent depression comparing cognitive, family, and supportive treatments. *Archives of General Psychiatry, 54,* 877–885.

Bruce, A. E., Cole, D. A., Dallaire, D. H., Jacques, F. M., Pineda, A. Q., & LaGrange, B. (2006). Relations of parenting and negative life events to cognitive diathesis for depression in children. *Journal of Abnormal Child Psychology, 34,* 321–333.

Carter, A. S., Briggs-Gowan, M. J., & Davis, N. O. (2004). Assessment of young children's social-emotional development and psychopathology: Recent advances and recommendations for practice. *Journal of Child Psychology and Psychiatry, 45,* 109–134.

Chambless, D. L., & Ollendick, T. H. (2001). Empirically supported psychological interventions: Controversies and evidence. *Annual Review of Psychology, 52,* 685–716.

Chavira, D. A., Stein, M. B., Bailey, K., & Stein, M. T. (2004). Child anxiety in primary care: Prevalent but untreated. *Depression and Anxiety, 20,* 155–164.

Cicchetti, D., & Toth, S. L. (1998). The development of depression in children and adolescents. *American Psychologist, 53*(2), 221–241.

Coie, J. D., Watt, N. F., West, S. G., Hawkins, J. D., Asarnow, J. R., Markman, et al. (1993). The science of prevention: A conceptual framework and some directions for a national research program. *American Psychologist, 48,* 1013–1022.

Cole, D. A. (1990). The relation of social and academic competence to depressive symptoms in childhood. *Journal of Abnormal Psychology, 99,* 422–429.

Conners, C. K. (1997). *Conners' Rating Scales-Revised: Technical manual.* New York: Multi-Health Systems.

Conners, C. K. (2008). *Conners' 3rd edition: Technical manual.* New York: Multi-Health Systems.

David-Ferdon, C., & Kaslow, N. J. (2008). Evidence-based psychosocial treatments for child and adolescent depression. *Journal of Clinical Child & Adolescent Psychology, 37,* 62–104.

Donovan, C. L., & Spence, S. H. (2000). Prevention of childhood anxiety disorders. *Clinical Psychology Review, 20,* 509–531.

Egger, H. L., & Angold, A. (2004). The Preschool Age Psychiatric Assessment: A structured parent interview for diagnosing psychiatric disorders in preschool children. In R. Del-Carmen-Wiggins & A. Carter (Eds.), *The handbook of infant, toddler, and preschool mental health assessment* (pp. 223–246). New York: Oxford University Press.

Egger, H. L., & Angold, A. (2006a). Anxiety disorders. In J. Luby (Ed.), *Handbook of preschool mental health assessment* (pp. 137–164). New York: Guilford Press.

Egger, H. L., & Angold, A. (2006b). Common emotional and behavioral disorders in preschool children: Presentation, nosology, and epidemiology. *Journal of Child Psychology and Psychiatry*, *47*(3), 313–337.

Egger, H. L., Erkanli, A., Keeler, G., Potts, E., Walter, B. K., & Angold, A. (2006). Test-retest reliability of the preschool age psychiatric assessment (PAPA). *Journal of the American Academy of Child and Adolescent Psychiatry*, *45*(5), 538–549.

Esquivel, G. B., & Flanagan, R. (2007). Narrative methods of personality assessment in school psychology. *Psychology in the Schools*, *44*(3), 271–280.

Feng, X., Shaw, D., & Silk, J. S. (2008). Developmental trajectories of anxiety symptoms among boys across early and middle childhood. *Journal of Abnormal Psychology*, *117*, 32–47.

Ferdinand, R. F., Barrett, P. M., & Dadds, M. R. (2004). Anxiety and depression in childhood: Prevention and intervention. In T. Ollendick & J. S. March (Eds.), *Phobic and anxiety disorders in children and adolescents: A clinician's guide to effective psychosocial and pharmacological interventions* (pp. 459–475). New York: Oxford University Press.

Ford, T., Goodman, R., & Meltzer, H. (2003). The British child and adolescent mental health survey 1999: The prevalence of DSM-IV disorders. *Journal of the American Academy of Child & Adolescent Psychiatry*, *42*, 1203–1211.

Gadow, K. D., & Sprafkin, J. (1997). *Early Childhood Inventory: Norms manual*. Stony Brook, NY: Checkmate Plus.

Garber, J., & Horowitz, J. L. (2002). Depression in children. In I. H. Gotlib & C. L. Hammen (Eds.), *Handbook of depression* (pp. 510–540). New York: Guilford Press.

Ginsburg, G. S., & Schlossberg, M. C. (2002). Family-based treatment of childhood anxiety disorders. *International Review of Psychiatry*, *14*, 143–154.

Gleason, M. M., Egger, H. L., Emslie, G. J., Greenhill, L. L., Kowatch, R. A., Lieberman, A. F., et al. (2007). Psychopharmacological treatment for very young children: Contexts and guidelines. *Journal of the American Academy of Child and Adolescent Psychiatry*, *46*, 1532–1572.

Greenbaum, P. E., & Dedrick, R. F. (1998). Hierarchical factor analysis of the Child Behavior Checklist/4–18. *Psychological Assessment*, *10*(2), 149–155.

Greenberg, M. T., Domitrovich, C., & Bumbarger, B. (2001). The prevention of mental disorders in school-aged children: Current state of the field. *Prevention & Treatment*, *4*, 1–62.

Hammen, C., Shih, J. H., & Brennan, P. A. (2004). Intergenerational transmission of depression: Test of an interpersonal stress model. *Journal of Consulting and Clinical Psychology*, *59*, 341–345.

Izard, C. E., Fantauzzo, C. A., Castle, J. M., Haynes, O. M., Rayias, M. F., & Putnam, P. H. (1995). The ontogeny and significance of infants' facial expressions in the first nine months of life. *Developmental Psychology*, *31*, 997–1013.

Izard, C., Hembree, E., & Huebner, R. (1987). Infants' emotional expressions to acute pain: Developmental change and stability in individual differences. *Developmental Psychology*, *23*, 105–113.

Kagan, J., (1997). Temperament and the reaction to unfamiliarity. *Child Development*, *68*, 139–143.

Kaslow, N. J., & Thompson, M. P. (1998). Applying the criteria for empirically supported treatments to studies of psychosocial interventions for child and adolescent depression. *Journal of Clinical Child Psychology, 27,* 146–155.

Kendall, P. C., & Hedtke, K. A. (2006). *Cognitive-behavioral therapy for anxious children: Therapist manual* (3rd ed.) Ardmore, PA: Workbook.

Kessler, R. C., Avenevoli, S., & Merikangas, K. R. (2001). Mood disorders in children and adolescents: An epidemiological perspective. *Biological Psychiatry, 49,* 1002–1014.

King, N. J., Heyne, D., & Ollendick, T. H. (2005). Cognitive-behavioral treatments for anxiety and phobic disorders in children and adolescents: A review. *Behavioral Disorders, 30,* 241–257.

Kovacs, M., & Devlin, B. (1998). Internalizing disorders in childhood. *Journal of Child Psychology & Psychiatry Allied Disciplines, 39,* 47–63.

Langley, A. K., Bergman, L., & Piacentini, J. C. (2002). Assessment of childhood anxiety. *International Review of Psychiatry, 14,* 102–113.

Lewinsohn, P. M., & Essau, C. A. (2002). Depression in adolescents. In I. H. Gotlib & C. L. Hammen (Eds.), *Handbook of depression* (pp. 541–559). New York: Guilford Press.

Lovejoy, M. C., Graczyk, P. A., O'Hare, E., & Neuman, G. (2000). Maternal depression and parenting behavior: A meta-analytic review. *Clinical Psychology, 20*(5), 561–592.

Luby, J. *Early Emotional Development Program.* (2008). Retrieved September 8, 2008, from Washington University in St. Louis School of Medicine Web site: http:// research.medicine.wustl.edu/ocfr/Research.nsf/s/ D68C113BAF9182E98625677D005931C7.

Luby, J. L., & Belden, A. C. (2006). Mood disorders: Phenomenology and a developmental emotion reactivity model. In Luby, J. L. (Ed.), *Handbook of preschool mental health: Development, disorders, and treatment* (pp. 209–29). New York: Guilford Press.

Luby, J. L., Belden, A. C., & Spitznagel, E. (2006). Risk factors for preschool depression: The mediating role of early stressful events. *Journal of Child Psychology and Psychiatry, 47,* 1292–1298.

Luby, J. L., Belden, A., Sullivan, J., & Spitznagel, E. (2007). Preschoolers' contribution to their diagnosis of depression and anxiety: Uses and limitations of young child self-report of symptoms. *Child Psychiatry and Human Development, 38,* 321–338.

Luby, J. L., Heffelfinger, A., Koenig-McNaught, A. L., Brown, K., & Spitznagel, E. (2004). The preschool feelings checklist: A brief and sensitive screening measure for depression in young children. *Journal of the American Academy of Child and Adolescent Psychiatry, 43,* 708–717.

Luby, J. L., Mrakotsky, C., Heffelfinger, A., Brown, K., Hessler, M., & Spitznagel, E. (2003). Modification of DSM-IV criteria for depressed preschool children. *American Journal of Psychiatry, 160,* 1169–1172.

Luby, J. L., Mrakotsky, C., Heffelfinger, A., Brown, K., & Spitznagel, E. (2004b). Characteristics of depressed preschoolers with and without anhedonia: Evidence for melancholic depressive subtype in young children. *American Journal of Psychiatry, 161,* 1998–2004.

Luby, J. L., Sullivan, J., Belden, A., Stalets, M., Blankenship, S., & Spitznagel, E. (2006b). An observational analysis of behavior in depressed preschoolers: Further validation of early-onset depression. *Journal of the American Academy of Child and Adolescent Psychiatry, 45*, 203–211.

Mattox, R., & Harder, J. (2007). Attention deficit hyperactivity disorder (ADHD) and diverse populations. *Child and Adolescent Social Work Journal, 24*, 195–207.

McMiller, W. P., & Weisz, J. R. (1996). Help-seeking preceding mental health clinic intake among African-American, Latino, and Caucasian youths. *Journal of the American Academy of Child and Adolescent Psychiatry, 35*, 1086–1094.

Miles, D. (2000, March). Critical issues in assessing AD/HD: A survey of current practices. *NASP Communique, 28*, 15.

Molins, N. C., & Clopton, J. R. (2002). Teachers' reports of the problem behavior of children in their classrooms. *Psychological Reports, 90*, 157–164.

Moore, M. & Carr, A. (2000) Depression and grief. In A. Carr (Ed.), *What works with children and adolescents? A critical review of psychological interventions with children, adolescents and their families* (pp. 203–232). London, UK: Routledge.

Mulvaney, M. K., Mebert, C. J., & Flint, J. (2007). Parental affect and childrearing beliefs uniquely predict mothers' and fathers' ratings of child behavior problems. *Journal of Applied Developmental Psychology, 28*, 445–457.

National Association of School Psychologists. (2008). NASP Principles for Professional Ethics. In A. Thomas & J. Grimes (Eds.), *Best practices in school psychology V* (pp. xxi-xxx). Bethesda, MD: National Association of School Psychologists.

Ortiz, S., Flanagan, D., & Dynda, A. (2008). Culturally diverse children and families. In A. Thomas & J. Grimes (Eds.), *Best practices in school psychology V* (pp. 1721–1738). Bethesda, MD: National Association of School Psychologists.

Pincus, D. B., Santucci, L. C., Ehrenreich, J. Y., & Eyberg, S. M. (2008). The implementation of modified parent-child interaction therapy for youth with separation anxiety disorder. *Cognitive and Behavioral Practice, 15*, 118–125.

Ramirez, S. Z., Feeney-Kettler, K. A., Flores-Torres, L., Kratochwill, T. R., & Morris, R. J. (2006). Fears and anxiety disorders. In G. G. Bear & K. M. Minke (Eds.), *Children's needs III: Development, prevention, and intervention* (pp. 267–279). Bethesda, MD: NASP.

Rapee, R. M., Kennedy, S., Ingram, M., Edwards, S., & Sweeney, L. (2005). Prevention and early intervention of anxiety disorders in inhibited children. *Journal of Consulting and Clinical Psychology, 73*, 488–497.

Reinemann, D. H. S., Stark, K. D., Molnar, J., & Simpson, J. (2006). Depressive disorders. In G. G. Bear & K. M. Minke (Eds.), *Children's needs III: Development, prevention, and intervention* (pp. 199–210). Bethesda, MD: NASP.

Reinherz, H. Z., Giaconia, R. M., Pakiz, B., Silverman, A. B., Frost, A.K., & Lefkowitz, E. S. (1993). Psychosocial risks for major depression in late adolescence: A longitudinal community study. *Journal of the American Academy of Child and Adolescent Psychiatry, 32*, 1159–1164.

Reynolds, C., & Kamphaus, R. (2004). *Behavior Assessment System for Children (BASC-2)*. Circle Pines, MN: American Guidance Service.

Ronan, K. (1996). Building a reasonable bridge in childhood anxiety assessment: A practitioner's resource guide. *Cognitive and Behavioral Practice, 3*, 63–90.

Roberts, C., Bishop, B., & Rooney, R. (2008). Depression and bipolar disorder in childhood. In T. P. Gullotta & G. M. Blau (Eds.), *Handbook of childhood disorders* (pp. 239–271). New York: Routledge.

Rotenberg, K., Mars, K., & Crick, N. R. (1987). Development of children's sadness. *Psychology and Human Development, 2,* 13–25.

Rudolph, K. D., Hammen, C., & Burge, D. (1994). Interpersonal functioning and depressive symptoms in childhood: Addressing the issues of specificity and comorbidity. *Journal of Abnormal Child Psychology, 22,* 355–371.

Sattler, J. M., & Hoge, R. D. (Eds.). (2006). *Assessment of children: Behavioral, social, and clinical foundations* (5th ed) San Diego, CA: Sattler.

Shamir-Essakow, G., Ungerer, J. A., & Rapee, R. M. (2005). Attachment, behavioral inhibition, and anxiety in preschool children. *Journal of Abnormal Child Psychology, 33,* 131–143.

Shapiro, E. S., & Heick, P. F. (2004). School psychologist assessment practices in the evaluation of students referred for social/behavioral/emotional problems. *Psychology in the Schools, 42,* 551–561.

Spence, S. H., Rapee, R., McDonald, C., & Ingram, M. (2001). The structure of anxiety symptoms among preschoolers. *Behaviour Research and Therapy, 39,* 1293–1316.

Stalets, M. M., & Luby, J. L. (2006). Preschool depression. *Child and Adolescent Psychiatric Clinics of North America, 15,* 899–917.

Velting, O. N., Setzer, N. J., & Albano, A. M. (2004). Update on the advances in assessment and cognitive-behavioral treatment of anxiety disorders in children and adolescents. *Professional Psychology Research and Practice, 35,* 42–54.

Verdeli, H., Ferro, T., Wickramaratne, P., Greenweald, S., Blanco, C., & Weissman, M. M. (2004). Treatment of depressed mothers of depressed children: Pilot study of feasibility. *Depression and Anxiety, 19,* 51–58.

Wambolt, M. Z., & Wambolt, F. W. (2000). Role of the family in the onset and outcome of childhood disorders: Selected research findings. *Journal of the American Academy of Child and Adolescent Psychiatry, 39*(10), 1212–1219.

Warner, V., Mufson, L., & Weissman, M. M. (1995). Offspring at high and low risk for depression and anxiety: Mechanisms of psychiatric disorder. *Journal of the American Academy of Child and Adolescent Psychiatry, 34*(6), 786–797.

Warren, S. (2004). Anxiety Disorders. In R. DelCarmen-Wiggins & A. Carter (Eds.), *Handbooks of infant, toddler, and preschool mental health* (pp. 355–376). New York, NY: Oxford University Press.

Warren, S. L. (2007). Diagnosis of anxiety disorders in infants, toddlers, and preschool children. Age and gender considerations in psychiatric diagnosis. In Narrow, W. E., First, M. B., Sirovatka, P. J., & Regier, D. A. (Eds.), *Age and gender considerations in psychiatric diagnosis: A research agenda for DSM-V* (pp. 201–214). Washington, DC: American Psychiatric Association.

Warren, S. L., Ollendick, T. H., Simmens, S. J. (2007). Reliability and validity of the Fear Survey Schedule for infants- preschoolers. *Depression and Anxiety, 25,* 205–207.

Warren, S. L., & Sroufe, L. A. (2004). Developmental issues. In T. Ollendick & J. S. March (Eds.), *Phobic and anxiety disorders in children and adolescents: A clinician's guide to effective psychosocial and pharmacological interventions* (pp. 92–115). New York: Oxford University Press.

Washington University in St. Louis. Research: Coping with anxiety, depression, schizophrenia. Retrieved September 8, 2008, from the Newswise web site: http://newswise.com/p/articles/view/541311/.

Wood, J. J., McLeod, B. D., Sigman, M., Hwang, W., & Chu, B. C. (2003). Parenting and childhood anxiety: Theory, empirical findings, and future directions. *Journal of Child Psychology & Psychiatry, 44*, 134–151.

World Health Organization. (2004). *ICD-10: International statistical classification of diseases and health problems* (10th revision, 2nd ed.). Geneva: Author.

Zero to Three. (1994). *Diagnostic classification of mental health and developmental disorders of infancy and early childhood.* Washington, DC: Zero to Three: National Center for Infants, Toddlers, and Families.

Zero to Three. (2005). Diagnostic Classification: 0–3R: *Diagnostic classification of mental health and developmental disorders of infancy and early childhood* (rev. ed.). Washington, DC: Zero to Three Press.

CHAPTER 16

Pervasive Developmental Disorders

GERARD COSTA and
MOLLY ROMER WITTEN

WHILE OUR KNOWLEDGE about the *spectrum* of disorders now considered under the category of the *Pervasive Developmental Disorders* or PDD (American Psychiatric Association [APA], 2000) has grown, there remains considerable and heated debate about how best to understand the *core deficits* involved in PDD, the most productive ways to diagnose and classify the *spectrum* or range of disorders within the category, and the most effective interventions. Currently, the diagnosis of PDD covers a range of childhood issues, and connotes a more behavioral perspective. That is, current use of PDD provides a description of a constellation of behaviors, rather than a set diagnosis.

Rimland (1993) suggests that PDD is not a diagnosable disorder, but a category of disorders. The definition provided by various clinics that specialize in assessment and treatment of PDD (including the M.I.N.D. Institute at UC Davis, the Mayo Clinic, Kennedy Krieger Institute, and the Yale Child Study Center) suggest that PDD represents a spectrum of *brain-based* behavioral disorders that involve impairments in social, communicative, cognitive, physical, and motor development. During infancy, these impairments are subtle, and the nature of the impairments changes over time. Although more is known now than ever before, the issue of what is and what is not a PDD during infancy is quite complex and not easy to resolve. This chapter attempts to provide structure to the complexity and make sense of this rapidly changing field.

BRIEF REVIEW OF THE PERVASIVE DEVELOPMENTAL DISORDERS

The *Diagnostic and Statistical Manual of Mental Disorders*, 4th ed., Text Revision (DSM-IV-TR; APA, 2000) employs the term *pervasive developmental disorders* as a grouping of Axis I disorders first diagnosed in infancy, childhood, or

467

adolescence. Disorders listed under this category all share certain observable, severe, and intensifying impairments in the areas of (1) reciprocal social interaction; (2) communication skills; and (3) stereotypical behaviors, interests, and activities. The DSM-IV-TR further identifies five variations, or subtypes of PDD: autistic disorder, Rett's disorder, childhood disintegrative disorder, Asperger's disorder, and pervasive developmental disorder not otherwise specified (PDD-NOS), including atypical autism. Each subtype is considered briefly next (summarized from the DSM-IV-TR; APA, 2000).

AUTISTIC DISORDER

The key features of this diagnosis are impaired social interactions and communication and a restricted repertoire of activities and interests. Children with this diagnosis often engage in repetitive or stereotypic movements, are resistant to change, and are fascinated with parts of objects and movement. Mild to profound mental retardation co-occurs in most cases. A range of other behavioral symptoms may be present, including poor attention, impulsivity, aggressiveness, and self-injurious behaviors. Abnormalities in response to sensations, eating, and mood may also be present. Seizures have been reported in 25% of cases (APA, 2000). Autistic disorder occurs prior to age 3, and there is an increased risk among siblings. The DSM-IV-TR assigns this diagnosis when delays occur in social interaction, social communication, and imaginative play. Specifically, a total of six symptoms is required for diagnosis, with at least two involving impairments in social interaction (e.g., poor eye contact, impaired peer relationships, lack of reciprocity) and at least one involving impaired communication and one involving stereotypic behaviors or interests (APA, 2000).

RETT'S DISORDER

Rett's disorder is a genetic disorder that affects only girls and is characterized by typical prenatal and early development, followed by marked deceleration in head circumference between 5 and 48 months. This is associated with a loss of hand skills and the development of stereotypic hand movements resembling hand washing, and subsequent motor coordination. Expressive and receptive language delays also occur. The disorder begins prior to 4 years of age and is considered lifelong and progressive. While there is an initial early loss of social engagement, social interaction can develop later (APA, 2000).

CHILDHOOD DISINTEGRATIVE DISORDER

Childhood disintegrative disorder is diagnosed when a period of normal development occurs in the first 2 years of life, followed by a significant loss or regression (before the age of 10) in at least two of the following areas of development: language, social skills or adaptive behavior, bowel or bladder control, play, or motor skills. In most cases skills are lost in all areas. This disorder is associated with severe mental retardation. An increased frequency in electroencephalographic (EEG) abnormalities and seizures has been reported. One hypothesis suggests that childhood disintegrative disorder is the result of an unidentified insult to the developing central nervous system. When the period of normal development has been long (e.g., > 5 years), an increased search for a medical/neurological cause should occur. Usually, the loss of skills plateaus, and improvement may occur (APA, 2000).

ASPERGER'S DISORDER

The essential features of Asperger's disorder are significant impairments in social interactions and restrictive/repetitive patterns of behavior, interests, and activities. Language and cognitive development are usually typical, although *pragmatic* use of language is impaired. Social and peer relationships are the principal areas of impairment, such as a lack of social referencing and sharing, impairments in participating in social games, and a frequent one-sided approach to others. Children assigned this diagnosis often show encompassing preoccupation, and accumulate much knowledge, about a narrow topic of interest. They may demonstrate poor social judgment, fail to read nonverbal cues, and have limited self-monitoring (APA, 2000; Wing, 1981).

PERVASIVE DEVELOPMENTAL DISORDER NOT OTHERWISE SPECIFIED (PDD-NOS)

This diagnosis is assigned when the three, shared characteristics (i.e., impaired reciprocal social interaction, impaired communication skills, and stereotypical behaviors) of PDD are present and none of the other subtypes or another diagnosis applies. PDD-NOS would also include a diagnosis of atypical autism, which is utilized when the child is older than the typical age of onset for autism, has an atypical symptom presentation, and/or has subthreshold symptoms.

ISSUES OF TERMINOLOGY

It is important to note that the terms *pervasive developmental disorders* and *autistic spectrum disorder* (ASD) are often used interchangeably. As previously described, the classification scheme employed in the DSM-IV-TR, pervasive developmental disorders (note the plural) refers to the overall category of developmental impairments of which autism is one subtype. However, the range of disorders considered under PDD has now been referred to as *autistic spectrum disorders* in both professional and consumer media. To further add to this confusion, the term *autism* as a public health concern likely refers not just to persons assigned the specific PDD-subtype diagnosis from DSM-IV-TR, but to individuals on the *spectrum* or within the range of PDD.

The subtypes of PDD provide at best, a clumping of descriptive symptoms that serve as convenient shorthand for communication among families and practitioners. In theory and practice, it seems more effective for treatment planning to differentiate the specific deficits that comprise the constellation of symptoms, rather than clump them together under the single label of PDD. Clinically, practitioners and families often seem to believe the diagnosis of *autism* is used when there is a greater level of impairment than PDD-NOS, for example (Klin & Volkmar, 1995). However, in practice the actual term applied to a child is less important than a comprehensive assessment of his or her *profile* of core deficits and strengths.

Regardless of the term, what we do know about the number of children affected is quite startling. The prevalence rates of the range of disorders subsumed under PDD have tripled over the last 25 years, and have now been reported as *1 in 150* (Centers for Disease Control and Prevention [CDC], 2007), with boys more likely to be diagnosed than girls. Reasons for this increase are unclear and likely include better diagnostic assessments, a broader definition of the characteristics that define PDD, and earlier detection. Lord and McGee (2001) note that the "label of autism was associated with the provision of intensive services," suggesting that the numbers may reflect some labeling as a precipitant for enhanced services, "highlight(ing) the need for further, well-designed investigations" (p. 25). Nonetheless, there is a consensus in the field that aside from artifactual influences on prevalence rates, there is a genuine increase in the children seen for spectrum-related disorders (e.g., Greenspan & Wieder, 1998; Rutter, 2005). Causal theories abound, but there are no clear answers.

DEVELOPMENTAL PROCESS AS A PARADIGM FOR PERVASIVE DEVELOPMENTAL DISORDERS

PDD constitutes a set of conditions in which many facets of an infant's development seem to occur out of developmental sequence, usually more slowly, but also in a different or unusual manner. This type of disorder requires the clinician to examine closely the pattern of developmental processes that the baby demonstrates. As a developmental condition, it unfolds in accord with the principles of development, meaning that the complexity of the developmental impairment follows predictable patterns, just like typical developmental changes do. The developmental process is built into the functioning of humans as a set of species preserving behavioral patterns. While development may be perceived as a set of discrete steps with ages or stages that occur on some impersonal timetable, it is also a process, a set of sequences of accomplishments in interaction between the caregivers and baby initially, then the external environment, and simultaneously within the individual child (Greenspan, 1989).

However, for most of the last century, the belief that individual differences observed in children with PDD are permanent and lifelong has been widespread. It has led to an assumption regarding the permanence of developmental delay as exceptions that prove the rule of the normal distribution, in that the *normal* range of developmental levels in a population calls for the *necessity* that some of the population be at the extremes. However, any child with characteristics of a PDD is different from any other child with the same diagnosis, and it is our contention that permanency of the disorder has not been empirically established (Greenspan & Wieder, 1998; Howard, Sparkman, Cohen, Green, & Stanislaw, 2005).

ALTERNATE DIAGNOSTIC CLASSIFICATIONS

While PDD is the overall category employed in the DSM-IV-TR, with *autism* as one subtype used when the criteria have been met, both scientific and popular publications have increasingly used ASD to refer to the wide range of individual differences that exist among those with the core deficits cited earlier. If a child under age 2 clearly meets criteria for a DSM-IV-TR PDD diagnosis, the use of the DSM-IV-TR criteria can be used. Greenspan (1992) and the *Diagnostic Classification of Mental Health and Developmental Disorders of Infancy and Early Childhood* (DC:0-3; Zero to Three, 1994, 2005) proposed a diagnosis of *multisystem developmental disorder* (MSDD) as an alternate formulation for children before 2 years of age.

MSDD does not require the range of relationship and communication difficulties observed in clinical populations of children with PDD. MSDD overlaps with the DSM-IV-TR categories of PDD-NOS and the concept of a broader autistic spectrum phenotype. While the DSM-IV-TR considers the child with a PDD as having a *primary* deficit in relating and communicating, the diagnosis of MSDD (with defined *patterns* or subtypes reflecting individual profiles) proposed that for many children, the common deficits of impaired relating and communicating were "*secondary* to motor and sensory processing deficits, such as difficulties in regulating, comprehending and responding to different types of sensations (including auditory and visual) and affects" (Zero to Three, 2005, p. 42)

This new proposal marked three important advances in the field. First, the new classification signaled a move toward etiological, not just descriptive, considerations. Second, in contrast to PDD, where impairments in relatedness are viewed as relatively fixed and permanent, a diagnosis of MSDD considers the range of difficulties in communication and relatedness seen in young children. Such an acknowledgment of the range of possible capacities signals the intervention potential, since they were secondary to potentially identifiable and treatable deficits, as open to change and growth. Children with MSDD are not seen on a continuum of those with a primary deficit in relatedness. Finally, the implication of a MSDD diagnosis is that disorders in relating and communicating could be identified and treated before 2 years of age. Indeed, there is mounting evidence (e.g., ICDL Clinical Practice Guidelines, 2000) that the deficits that come to define PDD can be identified and targeted for intervention prior to 2 years of age. Clinicians might employ MSDD, rather than PDD-NOS as a diagnosis for infants or toddlers less than 2 years of age, because, among other criteria, there is a significant deficit in sensory processing and motor planning (seen as leading to secondary deficits in impaired relatedness; Schoen, Miller, & Brett-Green, in press).

Reflecting this last assertion, the DC:0-3R (Zero to Three, 2005) diagnosis of MSDD is associated with four areas of difficulty. The first two are familiar: impairments in relatedness and communication. However, a third area of difficulty viewed as critical to the classification is impairment in affect. The fourth and final area defining MSDD is deficits in sensory processing. In contrast to a diagnosis of PDD, a diagnosis of MSDD suggests that stereotypies are derivatives of sensory impairments.

In 1997, Stanley Greenspan and Serena Wieder formed the Interdisciplinary Council on Developmental and Learning Disorders (ICDL; www.icdl.com), in an attempt to synthesize and integrate the remarkable contributions of the various allied pediatric disciplines in understanding the sensory, regulatory, and motor difficulties that contribute to problematic development in children diagnosed with PDD, MSDD, and other developmental and learning disorders. In 2000, ICDL published a multidisciplinary manual, *ICDL Clinical Practice Guidelines: Redefining the Standards of Care for Infants, Children and Families with Special Needs*, in which formulations regarding core deficits in children with disorders of relating and communicating were examined by contributors from a wide range of disciplines including psychology, psychiatry, pediatrics, education, occupational therapy, physical therapy, optometry, audiology, and speech and language pathology. Notably, Tsakiris (2000) advised that treatment planning that involved addressing the various individual differences in sensory perceptual and motor processing seemed more effective than the more conventional behavioral approach of clumping individual differences under the rubric of delayed development.

In 2005, ICDL also published the *Diagnostic Manual for Infancy and Early Childhood* (ICDL-DMIC), in which an eight-axial system of diagnosis was proposed, reflecting the range of contributing (secondary) influences on the observed deficits.

The range of disorders in relatedness and communication considered in this chapter are generally, although not universally, held to be the result of an interaction between biological factors, factors of interpersonal fit between the caregivers and baby, and environmental factors. This is in contrast to the assertions made by Kanner (1943), and then later unfortunately popularized by Bettleheim (1967), that autism was psychogenic, specifically due to the aloofness and coldness of maternal care, the *refrigerator mother*. Recent advances regarding the neuroscientific correlates of autism (e.g., Williams, 2008), notably with regard to impairments in the *mirror neuron* system in persons with autism, and the *Autism Genome Project* within the National Institutes of Health (www.nlmn.nih.gov) have provided remarkable clues about the potential biological deficits (discussed further in a later section of this chapter).

Theories of *parental cause* may obfuscate the distinction between cause and effect. Whereas gross parental failure in omissions and commissions can certainly lead to psychopathology and developmental derailment, it is equally plausible to suggest that observable parental difficulties (e.g., aloofness, detachment) may, in fact, be responses to a child with biologically-based difficulties that render him or her less available for human engagement. The intense transactional nature of the unfolding infant–parent relationship also implies that the nature of this relationship may both suffer from, and be ameliorative to, the observed deficits in relatedness and communication. This multifocal perspective as an organizing frame is particularly helpful as the field investigates the earliest deficits in infants and children and their caregiver responses, in an attempt to disentangle both the course of unfolding development (in child and family) and the optimal kinds of intervention (Nelson, 2007).

INTERVENTIONS IN THE PDDs: A COMPARATIVE ANALYSIS

COMPARING THEORETICAL APPROACHES

In order to assess the current state of the field, one must consider the historical and methodological context, as well as the complex relationships among (1) how and what to identify and measure with regard to developmental impairments, (2) the focus or *port of entry* for intervention, and (3) the ways to assess validation and evidentiary support. It is critical to review the integral relationships among theory, data, and interpretation. Overton and Reese (1973; Reese & Overton, 1970) present a *philosophy of science* that addresses methodological issues to consider when evaluating theories of development that can also be applied in analyzing theoretical approaches to PDD. Similarly, Maddi (1980, 1988, 1995) presents an approach to conducting comparative analyses of theories.

Table 16.1 provides an overview of the concepts proposed by Maddi (1980, 1988, 1995) that can be used to compare theoretical and intervention approaches for PDD. *Models* and root *metaphors* allow theorists to draw from knowledge domains that are well known in attempting to explain domains that are less well known. For example, concepts in behavioral theory, such as stimulus–response, are rooted in the notion that humans can at times be viewed *as if* (metaphorically) they are *machines* which are

Table 16.1

Key Concepts in Conducting a Comparative Analysis of Theories

---

Models of Development

A *model* stands for, or represents, something else. The most general models—sometimes called *world views*, *world models* or *paradigms*—offer statements and ideas about *the nature of human life*. These models rely on *metaphors* to describe human nature, and such models are rooted in philosophical beliefs. These models are metatheoretical and are rooted in pretheoretical origins—meaning that while the models may generate more specific theories, and even testable propositions, the general models themselves are not open to empirical test.

Metaphors Used in Theories

A metaphor is the use of a better known area of knowledge, to explain a lesser known area of knowledge. Metaphors generate terms that are useful in describing an unknown, or lesser known, domain.

There are general levels of models, and these can lead to specific theories of development, which lead to ideas in research and to ideas in therapy and intervention. This is based on literature in the philosophy of science. Primary sources are *World Hypotheses* (1942/1972) by Stephen Pepper; *The Structure of Scientific Revolutions* (1962/1996) by Thomas Kuhn; and the writings of Willis Overton and Hayne Reese, notably, Reese and Overton (1970) and Overton and Reese (1973).

Core Tendency: What the theory or approach postulates as the overall direction, purpose, and function of living.

Core Characteristics: What the theory or approach suggests are the concepts or descriptions that can be used to describe an individual and differences among individuals.

Peripheral Characteristics: What the theory or approach suggests are the smallest units of personality (e.g., traits) that can be organized into personality types.

Developmental Statement: What the theory or approach describes as the way a personality is formed when the environment interacts with the core tendency and core characteristics, to form the peripheral characteristics.

What you do in a therapy is decided (implicitly or explicitly) on the basis of your view of human nature (core beliefs) and your ideas about development.

Note. This categorization is based on the work of Salvatore Maddi (1968, 1980, 1995), *Personality Theories: A Comparative Analysis.* Homewood, IL: Dorsey Press.

governed by *inputs* and *outputs*. Maddi proposed that theories could also be described by an examination of what proponents considered as the *core* tendency of human functioning, the core characteristics or structural elements of human personality proposed by the particular theory, and peripheral characteristics (traits or describable qualities). Each theory also proposes a *developmental statement* that explains how the core tendency and characteristics lead to the observable peripheral qualities or traits a person possesses.

COMPARISON OF BEHAVIORAL AND RELATIONSHIP-BASED THEORETICAL APPROACHES

With regard to PDD, these concepts (Maddi, 1980, 1988, 1995) are useful in examining differences among approaches that offer ideas about assessing and treating the observable characteristics that fit the diagnostic criteria of the various subtypes of PDD. The concepts Maddi proposed (Table 16.1) can be applied to the different approaches that guide current formulations about and treatments of PDD. An analysis of the two traditions (i.e., behavioral and relationship-based approaches) that currently dominate the field of assessment and intervention of PDD is presented in Table 16.2. What becomes apparent from this analysis is that what behaviorists consider important to measure and teach (e.g., eye contact, reduction of stereotypies, verbal greetings) are not consider as primary targets of developmental/relational approaches. This difference is not simply one of emphasis but of semantics.

Behavioral approaches regard target behaviors as *primary* to the restoration of human development, whereas the developmental/relational approaches regard these behaviors as *secondary* or *derivative* observable behaviors that reflect underlying, internal, developmental, constitutional (biologic) and relational processes. The former approach might be described as targeting intervention (i.e., what is the *port of entry* for clinical treatment as *back-end*), meaning that the observable behavior is the back-end of a chain of internal processes. In contrast, the latter formulation considers the legitimate *port* as the *front-end* process, such as internal/biological sensory, regulatory processing characteristics. Perhaps, no better example of this distinction is the phenomenon of *stereotypes*, such as hand flapping, toe walking, or squealing. Approaches guided by behavioral models, regard such behaviors as undesirable, have no position regarding the origins or meanings of such behaviors, and approach them, like other *target behaviors* of primary concern, and are ones to be treated through extinction and replacement learning (Siegel, 2003). In contrast, approaches that regard such behaviors as reflecting unmet needs or deficiencies in neurosensory modulation or processing, attempt to understand the meaning and function/purpose of the behaviors, and rather than attempting to alter the behavior, therapists would employ treatment approaches to address the underlying needs or deficiencies (Tsakiris, 2000).

Table 16.2

A Comparison Between Behavior-Based and Relationship-Based Therapeutic Approaches to
the Treatment of Pervasive Developmental Disorders

Comparative Concepts	Treatment Approach	
	Behavior-Based	Relationship-Based
General **Model** of Development	Mechanistic	Organismic
Basic **Metaphor** of Human Nature	Machine—Reactive—Input/Output	Organism—Active—*A-priori* qualities
Core Tendency	To maximize reinforcement.	To establish relatedness through the achievement of developmentally organized goals.
Core Characteristics	Primary Drives	Constitutional/Sensory Profile
	Reinforcement	Stages of Functional-Emotional Development
Peripheral Characteristics	Learned Behaviors, Discriminative Control	Stage of Development Sensory/Constitutional Profile
	Secondary Reinforcement	
	Response Generalization	
Developmental Statement	Development is the product of learned behaviors, discrimination, and generalization. Principles of classical and operant conditioning explain behavioral change. Development is continuous and quantitative.	Development is a process of the the unfolding capabilities of the person, unique sensory and constitutional characteristics, and the caregiving environment. Development is discontinuous (e.g., stages) and qualitatively different over time (ontogeny).
Principal Behavioral Focus	The "what" of behavior.	The "how" and "why" of behavior

SPECIFIC INTERVENTION APPROACHES

In general, there are four approaches to treating PDD. Specifically, this section provides a brief summary of behavioral, relationship-based, sensory modulation/processing-based, and attachment related approaches. Table 16.3 provides a comparison of approaches on the key factors noted by Maddi (1980, 1988, 1995). A discussion of the essential elements of an intervention and the evidentiary base of interventions will be presented in the next sections of this chapter.

Table 16.3

A Comparison of Selected Interventions for Pervasive Developmental Disorders

Type of Intervention	Underlying Developmental Model	Principal Proponents	Evidentiary Base	Evaluation of Evidentiary Base	Exemplars (Same Class of Approaches; Not Identical)
Applied Behavioral Analysis (ABA)	Mechanistic	Lovaas, Smith, Rutter, Schopler, Carbone, Koegel, and Koegel	• Animal, laboratory and classroom research - foundation in learning theory • Structured, relative ease of intervention and measurement of progress • Experimental research	• Identified "target behaviors" may be trivial and "fragmented"; "splinter skills" • Treatment setting is artificial and directed by interventionist with recent "naturalistic" approaches • Generally poor generalization • Few long term studies • Few randomized control studies	• Discrete Trials Learning • TEACCH • Applied Verbal Behavior (AVB) • Pivotal Response Treatment • Incidental Teaching
Affect/Social/ Relational/ Developmental Based	Organismic/ Developmental	Greenspan and Wieder, Kaufman, Gutstein, Prizant, & Wetherby	• Multidisciplinary clinical case studies • Individualized profile of client determines unique treatment program • Naturalistic research; quasi-experimental	• Lack of randomized, control studies • Few trained practitioners • Difficult to measure progress • No long-term research program	• Developmental, Individual-difference, Relationship-based (DIR)/Floortime • Social-Pragmatic/ Communication-based • Options Therapy/ Son-Rise • Relational Development Intervention (RDI)

(Continued)

Table 16.3
(Continued)

Type of Intervention	Underlying Developmental Model	Principal Proponents	Evidentiary Base	Evaluation of Evidentiary Base	Exemplars (Same Class of Approaches; Not Identical)
Sensory Modulation/ Processing-Based Sensory Integration Training (SIT) Auditory Integration Training	Organismic/ Biological	Lucy Miller, Ayres, Berard, Miller & Miller	• Clinical descriptions of sensory integration disorders (SID) • Empirical studies on sensory processing disorders (SPD) • Emerging empirical support for efficacy of certain occupational therapy interventions leading to symptom reduction	• Emerging research program within OT/SLP/ Audiology, not yet widely accepted and integrated into mainstream mental health, medical and educational treatment protocols • Mental Health and Educational interventionists not trained in this area of assessment, intervention and research • Lacking controlled research studies	• Sensory Integration Therapy • Sensory Processing Disorder (SPD) Treatment • Auditory Integration Training • The Miller Method
Pharmacological	Biological	Various	• Published reports of targeted symptom reduction for specific medications • Medication selected on basis of symptom profile, not diagnosis	• Ever-changing field without "user-friendly" guidance; lack of unanimity on recommendations. • Concerns about side-effects	• Various classes of medications that target symptoms (e.g., Secretin for gastrointestinal disorders) • Dietary/allergens

For decades, the clinical field of treatment for PDD has been dominated by interventions derived from learning theory, collectively known as applied behavioral analysis (ABA). Lord and McGee (2001) reported that a review of 19,000 published journal articles yielded 500 papers on ABA and autistic spectrum disorders. Ninety of these were studies using single-subject designs examining specific interventions. While this approach has therefore been described and recommended as rooted in a strong evidentiary basis (Cohen, Amerine-Dickens, & Smith, 2006), the evidence could be considered weak, and what constitutes *evidence* can be called into question (e.g., Greenspan & Wieder, 1998, 2006; Schopler, Short, & Mesibov, 1989; Short & Schopler, 1987).

Within the class of approaches that share the same underlying model of development and mechanisms for change as ABA, treatment approaches have emerged which appear less prescribed and *robotic*, but which retain their fundamental adherence to mechanistic models of development. Applied Verbal Analysis (Carbone et al., 2006) and Pivotal Response Treatment (Koegel & Koegel, 2006) are two examples of behavioral interventions that are delivered in naturalistic settings and that promote use of the child's spontaneous intentional behavior. These interventions are included within the *mechanistic* model of approaches (Table 16.2) because proponents adhere to a shared set of underlying principles of change and measurement.

Another class of approaches, called the *Affect/Social/Relational/Developmental–Based* approach, is rooted in a different philosophical tradition in science, with a different common underlying model of development and concomitant methodology. The Developmental, Individual-difference, Relationship-based (DIR; Greenspan & Wieder, 1998, 2006) approach to assessment and treatment is presented as the exemplar of this approach. Other interventions regarded as of the same philosophical tradition, such as Options Therapy/Son-Rise (Kaufman, 1976), Social/Pragmatic Communication approaches (Prizant & Wetherby, 1987), and the Relational Development Intervention (RDI) approach (Gutstein, 2000) are subsumed under this class of approaches (Table 16.2). However, such groupings of treatment programs invariably obscure the very real differences among the approaches that appear to share the same underlying paradigm.

Those interventions grouped as *Sensory Modulation/Processing–based* all share preference to the biologically-based, sensory–motor systems that are intrinsically affected in the symptom profile of persons diagnosed with a PDD. While many of these proponents share conceptual frameworks with others (e.g., the Miller Method, Miller & Eller-Miller, 2000; DIR, Greenspan & Wieder, 1998, 2006), the categorizations in Table 16.2 were made on the basis

of the primary *port of entry* or focus of therapeutic intervention as conceptualized by the approach.

Additionally, as is evident in the controversy surrounding the class of
treatments known as *attachment therapy* some approaches will appear to
employ the theoretical and conceptual literature and language of one paradigm (e.g., attachment theory), but employ strategies that are neither supported nor validated by that approach (e.g., coercive holding, *rebirthing*
approaches) (See Costa, 2003; Mercer, Sarner, & Rosa, 2003).

Approaches rooted in ABA regard the symptoms evident in children
diagnosed with PDD as behaviors which must be treated in accord with
principles of learning theory, meaning that undesirable behaviors must be
extinguished or inhibited while new *target* behaviors are learned, through
principles of learning, involving structure and reinforcement. The origins or
meanings of the problematic behavior—whether they be lack of eye contact,
poor receptive and expressive language, hand flapping, or toe walking
(stereotypies)—are irrelevant. What is critical is the teaching of new, competing behaviors.

In contrast, the approach to assessment and intervention developed by the
DC:0-3R Work group (2003) as well as by Greenspan, Wieder, and colleagues
(Greenspan & Wieder, 1998, 2006; ICDL Clinical Practice Guidelines, 2000;
Wieder & Greenspan, 2001; Wieder, Greenspan, & Kalmanson, 2008), known
originally as the *floortime* approach, but formally referred to as the "Developmental, Individual-difference, Relationship-based" (DIR) approach, consider the understanding of the origins and functions of symptomatic behavior
as a goal of assessment and essential to the development of individualized
intervention planning.

These real differences are not simply convenient descriptive distinctions,
but represent the varying ways that each theoretical approach conceptualizes
core characteristics, developmental processes, and the processes of change/
therapeutic action (e.g., Maddi, 1995). Furthermore, the underlying philosophical tradition that underlies each approach has a defining effect on what
are defined as *methods* of change and *data* to measure (e.g., Overton & Reese,
1973; Pepper, 1972; Reese & Overton, 1970).

Lord and McGee (2001) suggest that the gaps between the two principal
approaches (i.e., behavioral and relationship-based), at least in practice, are
narrowing. An emerging trend in the field is the recognition that a *one size fits
all* approach to PDD is proving ineffective, and there is an increasing
realization that some children's *profiles* or symptoms may be more amenable
to certain treatment approaches than others. The National Research Council
(NRC; Lord & McGee) report, *Educating Children with Autism*, concludes that
because of the wide range of individual differences that exist in "language

development, verbal and non-verbal communication, sensory or motor skills, adaptive behavior, and cognitive abilities . . . the most important considerations in programming have to do with the strengths and weaknesses of the individual child . . . " (p. 212). They question any real educational and clinical benefit for the creation of further subclasses or types of PDD (while acknowledging research benefits), suggesting that individual profiles, not diagnoses, should drive intervention. This *aptitude by treatment effects* approach that can inform which treatment is best for which kind of child or profile, provides much heralded and cutting edge progress in the field.

These differences are fundamental to understanding both the current nature of the field and critical to understanding that the matter of *evidence* is not so easily resolvable, because what one approach *measures* is not considered proper *data* from the alternative perspective. Nonetheless, each approach must subject its theoretical frame to a research program or *context of justification* (Pepper, 1972). The NRC (Lord & McGee, 2001) attempted the difficult task of evaluating evidence regarding the varied approaches in the field of autism/PDD. The Council's committee established guidelines "to achieve a systematic and rigorous assessment of research studies . . . (to) evaluat(e) areas of strength, limitations and the overall quality of evidence" (p. 104). Rogers (1998) also recognized the wide differences among approaches, but reported that, nonetheless, "successful" programs with "better outcomes" shared a similar emphasis on addressing the "core neuropsychological difficulties" (p. 104). When we consider each of these reports and then consider some very recent neuropsychological findings, we can contextualize the assertion made by Rogers. We consider the emphasis on the underlying neurological processes, and the advances made in identifying and assessing these processes extremely encouraging.

ESSENTIAL INTERVENTION PROGRAM ELEMENTS

The NRC noted that "wide use and respect [for a particular intervention approach] cannot be interpreted as clear evidence of effectiveness" (Lord & McGee, 2001, p. 14). Nonetheless, the NRC reviewed the literature on a diverse set of approaches in search of empirical findings to discern supportable conclusions. As the way in which each approach defines *data* differs, this effort is quite complex and difficult, but still necessary as a way of approaching the need for validation in the field. Accordingly, the NRC report addresses the evidence question for each approach, rather than seeking a comparative approach, noting that no such *approach-to-approach* study exists. Given that children with a diagnosis of PDD vary widely in their individual profiles, and that an extraordinary range of approaches and claims have been made regarding treatment, there is no standard treatment protocol on which all researchers and practitioners can agree, and imprecise descriptions of the samples of children evaluated make generalization to other populations of children difficult (e.g., a threat to external validity). Further complications in evaluating evidence in the field are the virtual absence of randomized, control studies for any approach and the varied use of group and single-subject/case study research.

The NRC considered 10 program models (presented in Table 16.4), which all originated in university settings, to identify common elements of programs, across all noted variations in theory, population, and methodology. According to the NRC, these programs, 7 of which are behavioral in orientation and 3 of which are developmental, share some common emphases:

- Intervention should begin at the earliest possible age.
- There is a general consensus that comprehensive programs must deliver at least 20 hours of intervention per week, and that intensity may also involve longer duration programs (e.g., multiple years).
- Family involvement is critical, and all approaches promote parent training. Some require intensive one-to-one work with the child. Most identify the need for parent emotional support.
- Staff must be highly trained. All programs considered were led by doctoral-level, very experienced professionals. Most emphasized interdisciplinary staff, and most involved elaborate training and supervisory systems.
- Ongoing assessment of a child's progress is critical.
- Systematic, planful teaching curricula are important.
- Therapeutic environments vary (e.g., home, school, community) but attention to environmental elements (e.g., distractions, arrangements) is required.
- Programs share a focus in communication, and while not sharing the term *engagement*, all model programs emphasize its importance.
- Increasingly, all programs involve social interactions; an emphasis on play skills; and attention to cognitive, academic, and/or self-help skills.
- Most programs address the need to reduce challenging behaviors, and a few identify motor skills and motor planning (e.g., DIR) as essential to assessment and treatment.
- Generalization of progress outside of the original treatment program and maintenance of progress are critical to success. Programs vary in their success, and the move (even among behavioral approaches) towards naturalistic approaches is encouraging.

Table 16.4

University Based Intervention Programs Evaluated by NRC

Program	Description
Children's Unit at the State University of Binghamton	ABA principles and subsequent naturalistic procedures
Denver Model at the University of Colorado Health Sciences Center	*Playschool Model*: developmentally/play-based that evolved into a naturalistically delivered (e.g., home, preschool) approach
Developmental Intervention at the George Washington University School of Medicine	*Floortime Model*: relationship-based, developmental approach involving home and program therapies. Utilizes affect and engagement to facilitate growth through six stages of emotional development (current DIR model)
Douglass Developmental Center at Rutgers University	Developmentally sequenced based on ABA principles with segregated and integrated programs, and shift to naturalistic procedures.
Individualized Support Program at the University of South Florida at Tampa	Based on parent-training program, delivered in homes and community settings, emphasizing functional communication and social inclusion.
Learning Experiences, an Alternative Program for Preschoolers and their Parents (LEAP); Preschool at the University of Colorado School of Education	Based on federal demonstration project in Pittsburgh, involving behavioral skill training for parents, inclusion settings, and peer-mediated social skills training. *Blended* behavioral and developmentally appropriate practices.
Pivotal Response Model at the University of California at Santa Barbara	Parent education based on ABA principles/discrete trials with recent shift to naturalistic interventions delivered at clinic, home, and school settings.
Treatment and Education of Autistic and Related Communication Handicapped Children (TEACCH) at the University of North Carolina School of Medicine at Chapel Hill	Structured teaching approach with clear visual cues and parents as co-therapists. Communication curriculum based on behavioral procedures with naturalistic adjustments.
University of California at Los Angeles (UCLA) Young Autism Project	Based on behavioral/discrete-trial format delivered by parents and trained therapists. Initial focus on responding to requests, then imitation, then interaction and language. Recent shift to emotional discriminations.
Walden Early Childhood Programs at the Emory University School of Medicine	Initially developed at the University of Massachusetts–Amherst. Based on behavioral model-incidental learning, but with developmental influences. Focus on engagement and functional language. Integrated school settings.

- Individual intervention plans require that each program be *custom-designed* for each child.
- Most programs planned transitions to preschool and school settings.

This report suggests directions for critically evaluating the effectiveness of various intervention strategies. Since the release of this report, Miller (e. g., Miller & Fuller, 2006) has published compelling evidence for the utility of understanding and addressing a wide range of sensory processing disorders (SPDs) in children diagnosed with a PDD. The DIR model (Greenspan & Wieder, 1998, 2006) is unique in attending to the child's distinctive *individual differences* (sensory/motor/regulatory profile) as essential to assessment and intervention planning. This issue relates to understanding the distinction between *back-end* and *front-end* approaches, and the associated difference between symptoms being seen as primary problems, or as secondary/derivative problems emerging from other core deficits (e.g., sensory dysfunction).

CURRENT STATE OF EVIDENCE BASE

To date, virtually no outcome study has been published in a peer-reviewed journal establishing empirical support for one approach over another (Lord & McGee, 2001). This is less surprising given the differences in underlying theoretical models, and in how each approach defines quite differently, the process, outcomes, and assessment of therapeutic change. Nonetheless, claims about the evidentiary basis of particular approaches are often made. As noted earlier, there is a considerable history of empirical research for behavioral approaches. Rogers (1998) cited the Early Autism Project at UCLA as having the strongest scientific evidence for effectiveness of any model at that time. Published long-term studies (Cohen et al., 2006; Lovaas, 1987; McEachlin, Smith, & Lovaas, 1993) reported significant effects in higher IQ scores and measures of adaptive functioning and school placement for 19 experimental group participants who received intensive (e.g., 40 hour per week) behavioral therapy for 2 years at 6 and 7 years of age, and then were assessed in early adolescence and compared to two matched control groups. The total number of participants (19), however, limits the generalizability of these results.

Rogers (1998) cautioned that these findings have not been replicated, that the original Lovaas sample did not contain randomized controls, and that there were other threats (e.g., lack of standardized clinical intervention, lack of standardized data collection, inadequate history of the subject pool) to the internal validity of the study. Gernsbacher (2002) also noted that the Lovaas study excluded children with more severe forms of autism, and used only post IQ scores and public school placement (which may be related to many other factors including parental advocacy and school policies, as noted by Brandsma & Herbert, 2001), and not a broad range of outcome measures. Gernsbacher reported that of 232 articles reviewed that employed behavioral and educational interventions for children with autism, 5 articles (based on 4 studies which did not employ randomized controls) reported higher evidentiary levels than others. Smith, Groen, and Wynn (2000) published the results of a randomized controlled study with children diagnosed with PDD and reported that 13% of children (2 of 15) receiving intensive ABA approaches met the criteria used by the Lovaas (1987) and McEachin et al. (1993) for the "best outcome," much lower than the 47% rate reported by the Lovaas study. Furthermore, the treatment and control groups showed no differences in the two language scales used to assess change, and no difference in social-emotional functioning assessed by the Child Behavior Checklist (CBCL), and other measures. There were slight but nonsignificant differences on measures of academic achievement and intelligence between the groups.

Lord and McGee (2001) present summaries of the research conducted by the 10 program models reviewed in the NRC report. While virtually every model reports supportive evaluation studies, with the Denver, Douglass Development Center, and UCLA Young Autism models each publishing findings in peer-reviewed journals, there remains little unanimity on the particulars of what is most effective, although the 13 characteristics noted earlier point to a consensus across models about essential program elements.

What appears critical for the field is a clear determination about the source of therapeutic gain, which is invariably defined by the conceptual framework of the researcher and the practitioner. For example, even if the Lovaas long-term studies suggest genuine, long-lasting therapeutic benefits, the actual source of the benefit remains unclear. Would 40 hours per week of intensive DIR/floortime-guided engagement for 2 years, or any other guided model, have had similar benefit (albeit measured using different "data" and instruments)?

In a seminal article entitled *The End of Ideology in Behavior Modification*, London (1972) suggested that the *theory* that guides behavior modification, is more properly viewed as a *paradigm* or an *analogy*. Within this framework, it is plausible to suggest that effective treatments, whether they be behavioral or relational/developmental, *may be effective for actual reasons **other** than those described by proponents of the approach*. Thus, an approach may suggest ideas on how autistic symptoms could be ameliorated by suggesting an analogy (i.e., *as if*) to the way behaviors can be learned (e.g., through operant learning). This does not, however, mean that this is the way all behavior develops—only that it is one possible way it can. Such a framework may help reduce the contentious debate that occurs surrounding the differences in approaches, and may lead to progress in identifying elements that many can agree on. Advances in the brain sciences provide a useful illustration.

NEUROLOGICAL FINDINGS RELATED TO PDD

Recent neurological studies on the brain (e.g., Williams, 2008) using fMRI (functional magnetic resonance imaging) are helping to map brain differences that exist between persons with and without autism. Preliminary evidence suggests that the brains of persons with autism are related to a host of differences that are primarily reflected in poor synchronization among the various brain regions, with more severely disabled, lower functioning persons, and those with mental retardation, showing more impairment in synchronization. Information processing and the capacity to attach meaning to sensory information is severely compromised (Williams, 2008). These differences occur early in development and demand early intervention, this brain mapping suggests certain structured environmental interventions (also see Minishew & Williams, in press, cited by Williams, 2008). Williams writes, "What should the environmental input be? Interventionists should start by thinking about what a typically developing brain can do. Next, they should consider what a brain with autism cannot do" (2008, p. 15). Williams, a speech pathologist, offers an example regarding language development suggesting that the typical child's capacity to attach meaning to single words and their referent objects is more difficult for the child with autism, so that language learning may require *chunking* (Prizant & Wetherby, 1993) in which children with autism are thought to learn language by treating a phrase or sentence as if it were a word. Accordingly, working at single-word levels may initially help.

In a similar manner, if the brain of a child with autistic spectrum disorder is compromised with regard to auditory processing but is better at certain kinds of visual processing (e.g., Williams, 2008) visual supports, such as photographs or a picture of the word being learned, may be helpful. Williams reports that the brains of children with autism appear to form very strong local connections, with difficulty in connectedness and synchrony across various brain regions. This strength in local connections may be why children with autism succeed at learning through associations. However, this ability may lead to difficulty if the interventionists use "rote or highly structured teaching methods" (Williams, 2008, p. 16) because these children may, "'overlearn' or create connection between information that will interfere with the development of flexible use of cognition or language" (Williams, 2008, p. 16).

Van Kooten et al. (2008) reported that the portion of the brain involved in processing of faces had significant neural differences in persons with autism, compared to persons without the diagnosis. Recent research regarding mirror neuron systems, brain cells that are activated in comparable regions when one performs an action, and watches it being performed (also likely implicated in facial processing), suggests that persons with autism have deficiencies in this area (Society for Neuroscience, 2007). Such findings may lead to the identification of certain biological and therapeutic interventions designed to address these differences (e.g., *affect-rich* interactions may activate the amygdala/ mirror neuronal systems). This shift suggests that adherents of various approaches may discern common findings that may not entirely eliminate differences in perspective, but may suggest areas of shared ideas and strategies.

EDUCATIONAL CONSIDERATIONS FOR INFANTS AND TODDLERS

Education for infants and toddlers identified as having PDD requires a thoughtful acknowledgment of the principle of multifactor causation (Shonkoff & Meisels, 2000). Because infants and toddlers diagnosed with PDD are so different from each other, and vary so greatly according to their individual differences, it is unlikely that their educational needs are the result of one or only a few factors. Nor are the educational needs of children with PDD understood as a unitary set of preacademic skills. As a result, educational programs run a continuum of theories and strategies. The theoretical orientations have already been identified and discussed from the perspective of intervention paradigms in Tables 16.1 and 16.2.

However, the current range of theories does not begin to address the social and preacademic capacity of children with a PDD to function in a group setting. In 1986, the federal government created Part C of the Individuals with Disabilities Education Act (IDEA), "a federal grant program that assists states in operating a comprehensive statewide program of early intervention services for infants and toddlers with disabilities, aged birth through age 2 years, and their families" (Shonkoff & Meisels, 2000, p. 20). Part C mandates the following goals: (1) enhance the development of infants and toddlers with disabilities; (2) reduce educational costs by minimizing the need for special education through early intervention; (3) minimize the likelihood of institutionalization, and maximize independent living; and (4) enhance the capacity of families to meet their child's needs (Danaher & Goode, 2008). This legislation provides opportunities for inclusion of children with PDD in

Early Head Start center-based programs that serve infants and toddlers under 3 years of age. Within the context of Early Head Start, provision of educationally structured day care expands the focus of early intervention for children with PDD.

Early Head Start programs typically provide play-based day care in a center-based setting. This cognitively-based approach to education provides inclusive opportunities for incidental learning, mediated learning, and direct instruction, depending on the age and developmental status of the infant or toddler. Unlike Early Intervention that focuses on the provision of comprehensive services and individual interventions such as occupational therapy, developmental therapy and speech therapy, Early Head Start provides the opportunity for a child with PDD to be included in small group settings organized with typically developing infants and toddlers. The groups are generally between 6 and 8 children each, and are organized by chronological age rather than developmental ability level. A strength of this approach is that it provides services even when parents cannot be involved in each session of an intervention program because of the necessity of full-time employment. The provision of Early Head Start services also insures *wrap-around* services that theoretically provide a seamless transition from early intervention into preschool special educational services beginning at age 3 years, should that be indicated.

Part C programs maintain the service delivery unit as the family. When an infant enters the early intervention system, their parents and the educational professionals collaborate to identify each child's educational needs and create a service delivery plan in the form of a document referred to as the Individualized Family Service Plan (IFSP). The IFSP lists all the services that a child can receive under the canopy of early intervention and, if planned so, Early Head Start services. Elements of effective infant–toddler child care include small groups, high staff-to-child ratios, continuity of care, primary caregiver assignments so that each child is assured a consistent caregiver to relate to, health and safety, and cultural and linguistic continuity (Shonkoff & Phillips, 2000). Outcome research supports the effectiveness of early child care that provides a group milieu for young children with autism, and supports their capacity to develop peer relationships and learn pro-social, pre-academic behaviors (Shonkoff & Meisels, 2000; Shonkoff & Phillips). The National Academies of Science, Committee on Educational Interventions for Children with Autism, and NRC recommend that:

> . . . educational services begin as soon as a child is suspected of having a [pervasive developmental] disorder. Those services should include a minimum of 25 hours a week, 12 months a year, in which the child is engaged in

systematically planned, and developmentally appropriate educational activity toward identified objectives. The priorities of focus include functional sponta- neous communication, social instruction delivered throughout the day in various settings, cognitive development and play skills, and proactive approaches to behavior problems. To the extent that it leads to the acquisition of children's educational goals, young children with an autistic spectrum disorder should receive specialized instruction in a setting in which ongoing interactions occur with typically developing children (Lord & McGee, 2001, p. 23).

It is a paradox that the individual therapies that are advocated to help push development along for children with multiple developmental deficits and provide a process for teaching the infant's brain to engage in ways not initially accessible to the infant, do not provide the necessary early group experiences. Early Head Start and other educational models actually provide an opportu- nity in which infants and toddlers can learn to share their minds and develop an appreciation for shared meaning with peers in a naturalistic setting (Nelson, 2007). Group play experiences during infancy and toddlerhood also support the development and expansion of imitative capacities. Research has shown that imitation constitutes the first invitation for joint play (Wittmer & Petersen, 2006). So, the *educational* experience of Early Head Start, when executed in a developmentally appropriate way, supports the play skills and social capacities of children with a PDD in a manner that no individual therapies could provide.

FAMILIES OF CHILDREN WITH PERVASIVE DEVELOPMENTAL DISORDERS

To this point, our examination of the PDDs has addressed the complex issues associated with theoretical and diagnostic formulations, advances in our understanding of the neuroscientific mechanisms and correlates to the symp- tom profile, and the host of therapeutic interventions and evidentiary claims proponents have made. We now consider the very personal and unique impact of the diagnoses on the family.

In describing an infant mental health model of consultation to early intervention programs, Costa (2006) applied Stern's (1995) *motherhood con- stellation* as a helpful frame in understanding the impact that the arrival of an infant with a developmental disability might have on the parent. The motherhood constellation (Bruschweiler-Stern, 1998; Stern) is proposed as a constellation of feelings and themes emerging around motherhood that have great bearing on the unfolding parenting journey when infants are disabled. Stern describes four core themes that assume center stage, preoccupying the mother, as her parenthood unfolds. These are:

- *The Life theme:* Can she promote life and growth in her child?
- *The Relatedness theme:* Can she emotionally engage the baby and ensure mental/emotional development?
- *The Support Matrix theme:* Can she create the necessary support systems to meet these themes?
- *The Identity Reorganization theme:* Will she be able to transform her self-identity to meet these themes?

In considering the birth and parenting of a child with a PDD, all four themes might pose challenges to the mother and family at the very time these themes are preoccupying needs. If her child is not developing well (life), or has an impairment in social and emotional relatedness (relatedness), available resources and support systems may be stressed (support matrix) and resolution of the normal ambivalence that comes with the new identity of motherhood (identity reorganization) may be compromised. These insights may help practitioners in their work with families by leading the practitioner to wonder about, be with and *learn at the feet of parents* (Trout & Foley, 1989) about how they are doing and what they may need to feel, say, and do, without judgment or criticism.

Two characteristics have been particularly evident in families with children diagnosed with a PDD:

- The experience of loss of their child's *personhood,* in which their child may not smile, communicate, play, reference, miss them on separation and have unclear responses on reunions. Rones (2008) wrote a series of poignant articles about the impact of autism on a mother and family members, reporting that one mother described her day "filled with silence," noting that she initially felt she had "lost" her child.
- The response to a dramatic increase in diagnosed cases of PDDs. Families can feel anger at *belonging to a club* they would never have chosen to join, but also can be overwhelmed by the vast number of web sites with varying degrees of accurate information; differing professional recommendations and claims for *cure*; concerns about diet, immunizations, and holistic approaches; and a host of attractive but unvalidated treatment programs. It is recommended that clinicians *sit* with families and uncritically present the need to search for scientific validation for treatment options, but never criticizing their search for answers. For example, Rones (2008) told a story of a parent who had tried many conventional therapies and then learned about the *GFCF*

(gluten-free, casein-free) diet, which proved helpful. Similarly, Exkorn (2005) wrote a comprehensive guide for other families in *The Autism Sourcebook*, written "from a mother whose child recovered." Such assertions may represent hopefulness for many, particularly as a record of a parent. Professionals must always recognize however that profiles and symptom severity vary, so treatments that are effective for one child, may be less so for another.

Collectively, these themes and responses serve as defining experiences. Each family's response is unique, and families respond with enormous strength and adaptation. These insights however can provide a useful framework for those who work with families around the birth and care of their child with PDDs. Shahmoon-Shanok (2000) described the following six core tasks that families of children with developmental difficulties must seek to *master*:

1. Parents must come to recognize the precipitous risks of their child's disability.
2. Parents must overcome the sense of mystification, distance, and rejection.
3. Parents must learn to notice, observe, and read their child's odd and frustrating behaviors as individual differences.
4. Parents need to recognize themselves as the central, organizing, and contingent force on behalf of their child.
5. Parents must recognize, welcome, and respond contingently to their child's increasingly complex functional communicative, cognitive, and emotional needs.
6. Parents must become knowledgeable, effective, and engaged advocates for their child.

Practitioners must support parents in their struggle to master a new set of knowledge as they grapple to come to know their own child, who is not necessarily the child they expected. Catalano, Hernandez, and Wolters (2002) formulated an elegant and family-friendly tool to help parents develop their child's own unique *self-statement,* in which a narrative is created as if the child could speak for him- or herself. Integrated into the narrative are the insights from multidisciplinary assessments; interpretations about the *language of behavior;* how the child might respond to certain interpersonal, sensory and environmental situations; and, of course, the parent's own personal and loving insights. Hirschland (2008) also provides a remarkably integrated, hopeful consultation guide for parents and teachers, rich with carefully detailed and discussed case illustrations about children with a wide range of developmental, emotional, and behavioral disorders. These serve as models of support and intervention for families. The NRC recommendations (Lord & McGee, 2001) serve as important guidelines about the critical needs that families have, and the ways in which educational and therapeutic delivery systems must support family strengths and family involvement.

A useful framework for assessment and intervention planning incorporates *two critical questions* and *six organizing principles*. The *two questions*, considered essential in understanding a child's symptom profile and in reflecting with families about the nature of their child's difficulties, are:

1. What are the child's behavior and affect attempting to communicate?
2. What factors in the child's biology (e.g., sensory, regulatory, constitutions, state), psychology (e.g., history, experiences, developmental level), and social experiences (e.g., environment, family, culture) can we address to enhance the child's communication?

These questions are rooted in the view that what is observable in affect and behavior is the result of a long chain of internal (biological and experiential) and external influences. Accordingly, the *six principles* to consider are:

1. The distinction between competence and performance.
2. Internal and external factors can moderate performance.
3. All behavior is meaningful and occurs within a context. Not all meaning is inherently clear.
4. Behavioral and affect regulation are enhanced through primary caring relationships.
5. Misbehavior is not always *misbehavior*.
6. Purposeful, organized, and shared behavior requires the integration and cooperation of biological, psychological, and social factors.

CULTURAL AND ETHICAL CONSIDERATIONS

The unfortunate reality within general and special education is the disparity in conditions and resources that exists, which affect both educational opportunities and available effective interventions for children with disabilities. While the diagnoses subsumed under the PDDs cut across all demographics, the standards reviewed earlier (Lord & McGee, 2001) for the children and the complex treatment programs reviewed, require resources and strong advocacy. Local school districts vary with regard to training and support for staff development and educational services, and poorer districts often have fewer resources than more affluent communities. The clear message from the literature is children with PDD need early, multidisciplinary identification and intensive, early, and long-term intervention, for the child and family. This requires resources that, at present, appear inconsistently available. The documented increase in cases of PDD (e.g., CDC, 2007) and the emergence of public figures from entertainment and government who are parents of children with autism, has raised awareness, raised necessary research and programming funding, and may help those with fewer resources. Nonetheless, we must issue a clarion call for all local educational authorities to dedicate staff, child, and family resources to addressing the needs of children with PDDs.

The lack of any randomized control comparative studies, or studies designed to assess the needed aptitude by treatment effects are, in part, due to funding and the pragmatic difficulties of training researchers and tracking families in longitudinal studies. Lord and McGee (2001) note that, "Unless two treatments of equal vale can be compared, . . . (random) assignment creates the ethical issue of not providing the most promising treatment to children who might benefit" (p. 201). Large-scale treatments that are promising and that have demonstrated value and support require more research support and families who participate require the availability of equally appealing and helpful treatment options. Such research designs make randomized control studies more difficult, but still possible.

As we have examined the array of developmental difficulties associated with the spectrum of disorders in relating and communicating, caution about accurate and principled assessments must be issued. Children whose primary language may not be the dominant one in their culture, or whose cultural practices of relatedness differ from the dominant practices, may mistakenly be viewed as having communicative or interpersonal deficits that may originate from cultural differences instead. Children with limited English proficiency (LEP) are often disproportionately placed in special education programs, and schools must constantly assess and safeguard against such practices and errors. While the CDC (2007) prevalence studies look at ethnic and regional differences, economic and environmental differences are often confounded and further investigation is needed to ensure that all children with developmental difficulties are properly identified.

Concern for equal provision of services throughout diverse ethnic groups and across both genders as well as ethical considerations around assessment and intervention for children with pervasive developmental disorders can boggle the mind and confuse issues with outcomes. For example, during infancy and early childhood, we know that early intervention can dramatically change the future of children. However, early intervention is only selectively available. A 2007 study looked at the estimated differences by ethnicity in the diagnoses assigned prior to the diagnosis of autism. Compared with whites, black children were 5.1 times more likely to receive a diagnosis of adjustment disorder compared with ADHD, and 2.4 times more likely to receive a diagnosis of conduct disorder compared with a diagnosis of ADHD, when accounting for age, gender, and time on welfare. Boys were 8.9 times more likely than girls to receive a diagnosis of adjustment disorder compared with ADHD, and 3.5 times more likely to receive a diagnosis of conduct disorder compared with ADHD when accounting for age, race, and the time for which they were Medicaid eligible prior to diagnosis (Mandell, Ittenbach, Levy, & Pinto-Martin, 2007, p. 1799).

Further, the authors caution that "[i]t is possible that the presentation of autism differs among poorer children, perhaps because of environmental causes or mediators" (Mandell et al., p. 1799).

Technically, and philosophically, both issues of diversity and ethics in service provision attempt to acknowledge, explore, and provide solutions for the assumption of *ceilings* in the developmental outcome for children with the conditions involving varying degrees of PDD. The term *ceiling* refers to the level of functioning above which a child is predicted to not develop. For example, in the case of Rett's syndrome a condition with a known genetic base, and an outcome of death by the early 40s, a girl's functional capacities begin to deteriorate between 6 and 18 months of age, along with physiological changes that then provoke behaviors often associated with autism, including microcephaly and breathing irregularities as well (Hagerman, 1999). It is unclear why the DSM-IV-TR classifies Rett's syndrome as a pervasive developmental disorder rather than a medical and or genetically-based disorder in which the common triadic constellation of symptoms (i.e., cognitive, communication, and social/emotional delays), characteristic of autism are also prominent such as Fragile X, Down's syndrome, and Turner's syndrome. There are implicit assumptions regarding the likely developmental outcomes for children with these and other genetically loaded disorders. Such assumptions have little empirical research behind them and use outdated theoretical constructs, such as genetic determinism, linear thinking, and lack the insights gained from understanding multifactor causation (Shonkoff & Phillips, 2000). Additionally, the distinction exists between genetic loading for a disability and the level of functional capacities.

The issue becomes not whether there is disparity among diagnoses provided in various ethnic groups or between genders, but how to find an overarching principle to prevent the disparities from occurring in the first place. One potent solution is to use the structure of a developmentally-appropriate, individual differences–based, relationship-focused intervention paradigm to provide the bulk of intervention services. For example, regardless of the origin of issues, every evaluation process and intervention plan needs to include a statement of the child's developmental capacities as well as deficits. In addition, intervention must occur across a range of core capacities, including those listed previously. In order that the child engage in the interventions, research has demonstrated that early intervention needs to occur with the active participation of the child's parents or primary care providers, to the extent that the provider can participate (Lord & McGee, 2001). Illness, incarceration, or other forms of absence require that temporary and foster parents pick up the burden and responsibility for maintaining the child's capacity to engage in the intervention services. By requiring all three facets of growth (i.e., rate of development, sensory–perceptual individual differences, and relational resources available to the child) be included, issues of unfair provision of services as well as to whom to provide services become a moot point.

SUMMARY

This chapter began with a review of the theoretical underpinnings of assessment and intervention programs for children diagnosed within the spectrum of disorders considered under the pervasive developmental disorders. Diagnostic frameworks were reviewed, approaches to assessment and intervention were compared, and emergent commonalities about features and recommendations were reviewed. The issue of "evidentiary" support was carefully examined and advances in the neurobiology of autism were identified as promising paths to new treatment protocols.

Families need the principled, thoughtful help of clinicians. The chapter considered frameworks to organize and understand the ways in which those in the allied fields can support families. The increased prevalence rates of PDD have led to a dramatic national research program, and in the next 20 years, research and knowledge will surely grow about the neurobiological correlates and effective intervention programs.

Finally, the need for comprehensive and multidisciplinary training for the professional community from the varied disciplines involved in assessment and intervention must be emphasized. Prevailing models and approaches must be informed by the advances in our understanding of the core deficits and neurobiological underpinnings of the PDDs. The fact that approaches have been used for years is insufficient support for continuing to utilize them. Training programs for physicians, psychologists, educators, occupational therapists, physical therapists, speech–language pathologists, and the host of other staff who work with children and families affected by the PDDs, must be comprehensive and monitored to ensure that children and families are provided the earliest and best support available.

REFERENCES

American Psychiatric Association. (2000). *Diagnostic and statistical manual of mental disorders* (4th ed., Text Revision). Washington, DC: Author.

Bettleheim, B. (1967). *The empty fortress: Infantile autism and the birth of self.* London, UK: Collier-Macmillan.

Brandsma, L. L., & Herbert, J. D. (2001). Applied behavior analysis for childhood autism: Does the emperor have clothes? *Behavior Analyst Today, 3,* 45.

Bruschweiler-Stern, N. (1998). Early emotional care for mothers and infants. *Pediatrics, 102,* 1278–1281.

Carbone, V. J., Lewis, L., Sweeney-Kerwin, E. J., Dixon, J., Louden, R., & Quinn, S. (2006). A comparison of two approaches for teaching VB functions: Total communication vs. vocal-alone. *Journal of Speech–Language Pathology and Applied Behavior Analysis, 1*(3), 181.

Catalano, C., Hernandez, P. R., & Wolters, P. (2002, April). A child's self-statement: Who am I? *Exceptional Parent Magazine,* 60–65.

Centers for Disease Control (CDC) and Prevention. (2007). *Report from the Autism and Developmental Disabilities Monitoring (ADDM) Network.* Retrieved August 2008 from www.cdc.gov/ncbddd/dd/addmprevalence.htm.

Cohen, H., Amerine-Dickens, M., & Smith, T. (2006). Early intensive behavioral treatment: Replication of the UCLA model in a community setting. *Journal of Developmental & Behavioral Pediatrics, 27*(2), 145–155.

Costa, G. (2003). Better treatment for Candace: How trained psychotherapists would have approached this case. In J. Mercer, L. Sarner, & L. Rosa (Eds.), *Attachment therapy on trial: The torture and death of Candace Newmaker* (pp. 135–160). Westport, CT: Praeger.

Costa, G. (2006). Mental health principles, practices, strategies and dynamics pertinent to early intervention practitioners. In G. M. Foley & J. D. Hochman (Eds.), *Mental health in early intervention: Achieving unity in principles and practice* (pp. 113–138). Baltimore MD: Brookes.

Danaher, J., & Goode, S. (Eds.) (2008). *National Early Childhood Technical Assistance Center,* www.nectac.org/partc/partc.asp?text=12008.

Exkorn, K. S. (2005). *The autism sourcebook: Everything you need to know about diagnosis, treatment, coping and healing.* New York: Regan Books.

Gernsbacher, M. A. (2002). *A re-analysis of the outcome literature for autistic spectrum disorders.* Presentation at the Annual Interdisciplinary Council on Developmental and Learning Disorders Conference, Tysons Corner, VA.

Greenspan, S. I. (1989). The development of the ego: Biological and environmental specificity and the psychopathological developmental process. *Journal of the American Psychoanalytic Association, 37*(3), 605–638.

Greenspan, S. I. (1992). *Infancy and early childhood: The practice of clinical assessment and intervention with emotional and developmental challenges.* Madison, CT: International Universities Press.

Greenspan, S. I., & Wieder, S. (1998). *The child with special needs: Encouraging intellectual and emotional growth.* Reading, MA: Perseus Books.

Greenspan, S. I., & Wieder, S. (2006). *Engaging autism: The floortime approach to helping children relate, communicate, and think.* Reading, MA: Perseus Books.

Gutstein, S. E. (2000). *Autism/Asperger's: Solving the relationship puzzle.* Arlington, TX: Future Horizons.

Hagerman, R. J. (1999). *Neurodevelopmental disorders: Diagnosis and treatment.* New York: Oxford University Press.

Hirschland, D. (2008). *Collaborative intervention in early childhood: Consulting with parents and teachers of 3–7 year olds.* New York: Oxford University Press.

Howard, J. S., Sparkman, C. R., Cohen, H. G., Green, G., & Stanislaw, H. (2005). A comparison of intensive behavior analytic and eclectic treatments for young children with autism. *Research in Developmental Disabilities, 26*(4), 359–383.

Interdisciplinary Council on Development and Learning Disorders. (2000). *ICDL clinical practice guidelines: Redefining the standards and care for infants, children and families with special needs.* Bethesda, MD: Author.

Interdisciplinary Council on Developmental and Learning Disorders. (2005). *Diagnostic manual for infancy and early childhood.* Bethesda, MD: Author.

Kanner, L. (1943). Autistic disturbances of affective contact. *Nervous Child, 2,* 217–250.

Kaufman, B. N. (1976). *Son-Rise.* New York: Harper & Row.

Klin, A., & Volkmar, F. R. (1995). Autism and the pervasive developmental disorders. *Child and Adolescent Psychiatric Clinics of North America, 4,* 617–630.

Koegel, R. L., & Koegel, L. K. (2006). *Pivotal response treatment for autism.* Baltimore MD: Brookes.

London, P. (1972). The end of ideology in behavior modification. *American Psychologist, 27,* 913–920.

Lord, C., & McGee, J. (Eds.). (2001). *National research council educating children with autism.* Washington, DC: National Academy of Sciences.

Lovaas, O. I. (1987). Behavioral treatment and normal educational and intellectual functioning in young autistic children. *Journal of Consulting Clinical Psychology, 55,* 3–9.

Maddi, S. (1980, 1988, 1995). *Personality theories: A comparative analysis.* Homewood, IL: Dorsey Press.

Mandell, D. S., Ittenbach, R. F., Levy, S. E., & Pinto-Martin, J. (2007). Disparities in diagnoses received prior to a diagnosis of autism spectrum disorder. *Journal of Autism and Developmental Disorders, 37,* 1795–1802.

McEachlin, J. J., Smith, T., & Lovaas, O. I. (1993). Long-term outcome for children with autism who received early intensive behavioral treatment. *American Journal of Mental Retardation, 97,* 359–372.

Mercer, J., Sarner, L., & Rosa, L. (2003). *Attachment therapy on trial: The torture and death of Candace Newmaker.* Westport, CT: Praeger.

Miller, A., & Eller-Miller, E. (2000). A cognitive-developmental systems approach for children with body organization, social and communication issues. In *ICDL clinical practice guidelines: Redefining the standards and care for infants, children and families with special needs.* Bethesda, MD: Interdisciplinary Council on Development and Learning Disorders.

Miller, L. J., & Fuller, D. A. (2006). *Sensational kids: Hope and help for children with sensory processing disorders*. New York: Perigree-Penguin Books.

Minishew, N. J., & Williams, D. L. (in press). Brain behavior connections in autism. In K. D. Buron & P. Wolfberg (Eds.), *Educating learners on the autism spectrum: Translating theory into meaningful practice*. Shawnee, KS: Autism Asperger Publishing Company.

Nelson, K. (2007). *Young minds in social worlds: Experience meaning and memory*. Cambridge, MA: Harvard University Press.

Overton, W., & Reese, H. (1973). Models of development: Methodological implication. In J. R. Nesselroade & H. W. Reese (Eds.), *Life-span developmental psychology: Methodological issues* (pp. 65–86). New York: Academic Press.

Pepper, S. C. (1942/1972). *World hypotheses*. Los Angeles: University of California Press.

Prizant, B. M., & Wetherby, A. N. (1987). Communication intent: A framework of understanding social–communicative behavior in autism. *Journal of the American Academy of Child and Adolescent Psychiatry, 26*, 472–279.

Prizant, B. M., & Wetherby, A. N. (1993). Communication in preschool autistic children. In E. Schopler, M. E. Vann Bourgondien, & M. M. Bristol (Eds.), *Preschool issues in autism* (pp. 95–128). New York: Plenum Press.

Reese, H., & Overton, W. (1970). Models of development and theories of development. In L. R. Goulet & P. B. Baltes (Eds.), *Life-span developmental psychology* (pp. 115–145). New York: Academic Press.

Rimland, B. (1993). Autism. *Research Review International, 7*, 2.

Rogers, S. J. (1998). Neuropsychology of autism in young children and its implications for early intervention. *Mental Retardation and Developmental Disabilities Research Reviews, 4*, 104–112.

Rones, N. (2008). What autism does to a mother. *Redbook* (various issues). New York: Hearst Communications.

Rutter, M. (2005). Incidence of autism spectrum disorders: Changes over time and their meaning. *Acta Paediatrica, 94*, 2–15.

Schoen, S. A., Miller, L. J., & Brett-Green, K. (2008). Psychophysiology of children with autism spectrum disorder. *Research in Autism Spectrum Disorders, 2*, 417–429.

Schopler, E., Short, A., & Mesibov, G. (1989). Relation of behavioral treatment to "normal functioning": Comment on Lovaas. *Journal of Consulting and Clinical Psychology, 57*, 162–164.

Shahmoon-Shanok, R. (2000). The action is the interaction: Clinical practice guidelines for work with parents of children with developmental disorders. In *ICDL clinical practice guidelines: Redefining the standards and care for infants, children and families with special needs* (pp. 333–373). Bethesda, MD: Interdisciplinary Council on Development and Learning Disorders.

Shonkoff, J. P., & Meisels, S. J. (2000). *Handbook of early childhood intervention* (2nd ed.). Cambridge UK: Cambridge University Press.

Shonkoff, J. P., & Phillips, D. A. (2000). *From neurons to neighborhoods: The science of early childhood development*. Washington DC: National Academy Press.

Short, A., & Schopler, E. (1987). Recovery in autistic children: Comment on Lovaas study. *Spectrum, 1*(2), 4, 8.

Siegel, B. (2003). *Helping children with autism learn: A guide to treatment approaches for parents and professionals*. New York: Oxford University Press.

Smith, T., Groen, A. D., & Wynn, J. W. (2000). Randomized trial of intensive early intervention for children with pervasive developmental disorder. *American Journal of Mental Retardation, 105*, 269–285.

Society for Neuroscience (2007, November 7). *Mirror, mirror in the brain: Mirror neurons, self-understanding and autism research*. ScienceDaily. Retrieved February 2009, from http://www.sciencedaily.com/releases/2007/11/071106123725.htm.

Stern, D. (1995). *The motherhood constellation*. New York: Basic Books.

Trout, M., & Foley, G. (1989). Working with families of handicapped infants and toddlers. *Topics in Language Disorders, 10*(1), 57–67.

Tsakiris, E. (2000). Evaluating effective interventions for children with autism and related disorders: Widening the view and changing the perspective. In *ICDL clinical practice guidelines: Redefining the standards and care for infants, children and families with special needs* (pp. 725–766). Bethesda, MD: Interdisciplinary Council on Development and Learning Disorders.

Van Kooten, I., Palmen, S., von Cappelin, P., Steinbusch, H., Korr, H., Heinsen, H., et al. (2008). Neurons in the fusiform gyrus are fewer and smaller in autism. *Brain, 131*, 987–999.

Wieder, S., & Greenspan, S. I. (2001). The DIR (developmental, individual-difference, relationship-based) approach to assessment and intervention planning. *Zero to Three, 21*, 11–19.

Wieder, S., Greenspan, S., & Kalmanson, B. (2008). Autism assessment and intervention: The developmental, individual-difference, relationship-based/"floortime" model. *Zero to Three, 28*, 31–37.

Williams, D. (2008). What neuroscience has taught us about autism. *Zero to Three, 28*, 11–15.

Wing, L. (1981). Asperger's syndrome: A clinical account. *Psychological Medicine, 11*, 115–130.

Wittmer, D. S., & Petersen, S. H. (2006). Routines, environments, and opportunities: Day to day the relationship way. In D. Wittmer & S. Petersen (Eds.), *Infant and toddler development and responsive program planning: A relationship-based approach* (pp. 274–306). Columbus, OH: Pearson Merrill Prentice Hall.

Zero to Three. (1994). *Diagnostic classification of mental health and developmental disorders of infancy and early childhood*. Washington, DC: Author.

Zero to Three. (2005). *Diagnostic classification of mental health and developmental disorders of infancy and early childhood* (rev. ed.). Washington, DC: Author.

CHAPTER 17

Autism Spectrum Disorders

DIANNE ZAGER,
CAROL SOBER ALPERN, and
E. AMANDA BOUTOT

A
S THE FIELD of early childhood psychology has matured over the past
two decades, autism spectrum disorders have moved steadily to the
forefront of attention. Parents of young children have become
increasingly concerned about the alarming rise of autism, and discussion
and debate pertaining to underlying etiologies abound. The call to action by
advocacy groups has resulted in legislative initiatives, leading to increased
funding and research. New information pertaining to physiological differences in the brains of individuals with autism, pharmacological treatment,
and educational intervention continues to be reported. We read about genetic
studies, as well. Yet, even as we are bombarded with more information, we
see that the incidence of this disorder has continued to rise, reaching one in
150 children today (Autism Society of America [ASA], 2008).

Some possible explanations for the dramatic increase in attention to autism
spectrum disorders (ASDs) may be that (1) the lay public has become more
sophisticated about autism (Volkmar & Klin, 2005), (2) autism presently is
considered a spectrum disorder with broader diagnostic criteria that includes
a wide range of individuals (Bregman, 2005), and (3) there actually is a higher
incidence (ASA, 2008) of classic autism, as well as Asperger's syndrome.
Given this rise in prevalence, a textbook on infant and early childhood
psychology would be incomplete without a chapter on autism. This chapter
presents an overview of autism spectrum disorders, including diagnostic

Author's Note: This chapter was supported by the Pace University Center for Teaching and Research in Autism and Michael C. Koffler. Appreciation is extended to Nicole Mucherino for research assistance.

characteristics, identification, assessment, and evidence-based treatment with a specific focus on issues related to young children and autism.

Because autism is a continuing public health concern (Centers for Disease Control and Prevention [CDC], 2007), efforts are needed to educate professionals and families, to improve early identification, and to provide needed treatment. It is crucial that we provide effective early intervention in autism. We know that early intervention can lead to significant improvement in communication, behavior, and cognition; and that these gains are more difficult to accomplish in later years (Lord & McGee, 2001; Simpson, 2005).

DIAGNOSTIC CRITERIA FOR AUTISM SPECTRUM DISORDER

Autism is a spectrum disorder. This means that it is a set of neurobiological conditions that share underlying characteristics, including impairments in social interaction, communication and language development, responses to environmental stimuli, and restricted interests. A broad range of cognitive, social, and communicative functioning can be seen among individuals on the autism spectrum. In addition, there are great differences in the types and forms of behaviors exhibited. In spite of the broadening range of individuals being classified as autistic and controversy over diagnostic criteria for ASD, the clarity of the fundamental characteristics (Bregman, 2005) places these disorders among the most reliably diagnosed conditions in neurodevelopment and psychiatry.

Autism is a complex developmental disability that typically appears during the first three years of life and affects a person's ability to communicate and interact with others. The disorder is defined by a certain set of behaviors and affects individuals differently and to varying degrees. The disorder occurs in boys three to four times more often than in girls (World Health Organization [WHO], 2005). There is no known single cause for autism (ASA, 2008). The two most widely accepted definitions of autism can be found in the *Diagnostic Statistical Manual of Mental Disorders,* 4th ed., *Text Revision* (DSM-IV-TR; American Psychiatric Association [APA], 2000) and in the *International Classification of Diseases* (ICD-10; WHO, 2005).

Autism was first included in DSM-III in 1980 in a new class of conditions—the Pervasive Developmental Disorders. The most widely used definition of Autistic Disorder in the United States still can be found in the DSM-IV (APA, 1994). This definition essentially has remained unchanged from the DSM-IV to the DSM-IV-TR (APA, 2000). DSM-IV diagnostic criteria include characteristics related to impairment in social interaction, communication, symbolic play, and restricted repetitive or stereotyped patterns of behavior. The characteristics are similar to, and may be cross-referenced with, those listed in the ICD-10.

ETIOLOGY

Research has yet to yield a specific theory that can explain the etiology of autism. Information that has been gathered has, at times, been contradictory and confusing. The measurement of brain structure has yielded controversial findings because of limited sample sizes that have been spread across a wide age range and have included an even broader variety of symptoms. Brain imaging studies have shown that there is an increased volume of the total brain with abnormalities in the cerebellum, frontal lobe, amygdala, and hippocampus in young children with autism (e.g., Hardan, Minshew, Mallikarjuhn, & Keshavan, 2001; Sparks et al., 2002). Structural imaging studies have indicated that in some cases early brain growth acceleration has coincided with symptom onset (Minshew, Sweeney, Bauman, & Webb, 2005). Other studies have indicated that autism may be caused by an abnormal interaction between frontal and parietal brain areas (e.g., Damasio & Maurer, 1978; Haas et al., 1996). It should be noted that, according to Minshew et al., abnormalities of gross brain structure have not been identified in postmortem studies.

Courchesne, Carper, and Akshoomoff (2003) report that in a study of children with ASD ages 2–5, head size was reduced at birth and increased rapidly and excessively between 1 and 2 months and again between 6 and 14 months. Following this period of abnormal enlargement, head growth is reported to plateau, resulting in head size approximating that of adults without ASD (Belmonte, Allen, Boulanger, Carper, & Webb, 2004; Redcay & Courchesne, 2005). Increases in volume of the frontal cortex have been found to be correlated with measures of cerebellar abnormality in some children with ASD (Carper & Courchesne, 2000).

Pharmacological and neurochemical studies have examined factors including serotonin (e.g., Geller, Yuwiler, Freeman, & Ritvo, 1988), dopamine (Tsai, 2005), peptides and brain opoids (Hunter, O'Hare, Herron, Fisher, & Jones, 2003). However, there is not yet a definitive answer as to the roles or possible interaction of these factors.

Family studies have provided evidence that genetic factors play a role in autism. Chromosomal abnormalities have been noted (e.g., Ghaziuddin, Sheldon, Tsai, & Alessi, 1993) and some genetic syndromes have been associated with autism (e.g., Baker, Piven, & Sato, 1998). It also has been reported that relatives of children with autism, who themselves may not meet the criteria of autism, often exhibit mild characteristics (Tsai, 2005), particularly in social skills and communication.

VACCINES

Media reports have cited the MMR vaccine and thimerosal (a mercury-based preservative) as possible factors in the increase of autism. However, scientific studies (e.g., Madsen et al., 2003; Taylor et al., 2002) have failed to show a causal link between the MMR vaccination or thimerosal and autism (Verstraeten et al., 2003). Despite the lack of confirmed scientific evidence, due to the large number of parents and advocates who are convinced that vaccines are significant factors in the etiology of autism, this issue remains under debate.

In summary, there have been numerous studies over the past two decades attempting to determine possible causes of autism. These studies have investigated brain physiology, neurochemistry, pharmacology, genetics, and environmental factors. Yet definitive answers still elude scientists. Because autism is on the rise, attention is being directed toward meeting the pressing need for better services and more research funding. Recent legislation creating federal initiatives is encouraging biomedical research in autism, as well helping to improve educational and treatment services (Combating Autism Act, 2006). In addition, foundations and advocacy groups, such as Autism Speaks, Foundation for Autism Research, and Organization for Autism Research are encouraging and supporting research in the hope of identifying underlying causes and providing effective treatments.

HISTORY AND OVERVIEW

Autism is not a single disorder, but a complex diagnostic category based on a combination of characteristics that are behaviorally observed. The term *autism* is derived from the Greek word *autos*, meaning *self*, and was used by Leo Kanner (1943) in a report describing 11 children with disturbances of affective contact. Kanner coined the term *autism* to describe the withdrawn behavior that he observed in these children. He noted that these children demonstrated a profound lack of social engagement, failed to use language to communicate, and had an obsessive need for sameness. In the 1960s, Bruno Bettleheim (1967) proposed that these problems might be due to difficulties in the parent-child relationship, blaming poor parenting for the development of autism in young children. These poorly conceptualized ideas had disastrous effects on families of individuals with ASD. Over the past several decades, research has indicated that particular interventions can significantly improve functioning in children with autism, especially if treatment is delivered in the early years.

Early Intervention

Early intervention (EI) refers to services delivered to young children to facilitate development of age-appropriate abilities and behaviors, ameliorate or reduce deficits due to conditions that interfere with functioning and learning, and to support them in overcoming neurobiological challenges.

Developmental abilities that are addressed in early intervention programs for children with ASD generally fall into one or a combination of the following domains: (1) communication, (2) cognition, (3) motor skills, (4) behavior, and (5) sensory integration. According to Rogers (2000), desired outcomes of early intervention for children with ASDs include the development of verbal skills, an increase in social interactions, and a decrease in stereotypies characteristic of autism.

LEGISLATION

The creation of Head Start, under the Economic Opportunity Act of 1964 (PL 88-452), directed attention to preschool education and intervention. Although the act was not initially proposed for children with autism, it served to increase awareness of the importance of positive educational environments for all children, especially those in high need communities. The Handicapped Children's Early Education Act of 1968 (PL 90-538) was the first act to address early intervention, putting into place the fundamental elements of EI, such as parent involvement, professional development, and model programs (Scott & Baldwin, 2005). Then in 1975, the Education Act for All Handicapped Children (PL 94-142) was passed, serving as the Magna Carta for special education. This groundbreaking legislation changed forever the face of education by guaranteeing the right to a *free and appropriate public education* for all children, including those with disabilities. The act mandated the provision of EI services for infants and toddlers, including those with autism and other developmental disabilities (Gerhardt & Holmes, 2005). As a result, several states followed by developing guidelines for service provision for children with autism, beginning at birth.

When IDEA was reauthorized in 1997, a section devoted strictly to autism was incorporated, mandating specific services to children with autism (McGee & Morrier, 2005). Further, it was stated under IDEA Part C that early intervention services must be provided to children with disabilities in natural environments. A natural environment is considered one where typically developing individuals engage in real-life activities. According to the *Twenty-Fourth Annual Report to Congress on the Implementation of the Individuals with Disabilities Education Act*, in the 1999–2000 school year, 68% of all EI (Part C) under IDEA took place within the home setting as opposed to 53% in 1995–1996 school year, which was before IDEA was reauthorized in 1997 (United States Department of Education, 2002). Rapin (2005) has reported that today EI services are more readily available to children with autism than to youngsters with many other childhood disorders because of a belief that children with autism have a limited window of time in which to make developmental gains.

ASSESSMENT OF YOUNG CHILDREN WITH AUTISM

Diagnostic Screening

Diagnosing autism before age three historically has been difficult due to a lack of norm-referenced and reliable screening instruments. However, with increased awareness of the manifestation of autism in infants and toddlers, instruments specifically designed for this age group are emerging. Information about screening and diagnostic instruments that can be used with infants and toddlers is necessary in order that children in need of EI services can be identified. As more precise and clinically relevant diagnostic information becomes available, children in need of EI services will be detected with more reliability and early intervention should yield even stronger results.

Diagnosis and assessment should be carried out by a multidisciplinary team that includes but is not limited to pediatricians, neurologists, psychologists, special educators, and speech-language pathologists. It is crucial that the diagnosis be made by individuals knowledgeable and experienced in using diagnostic classification systems such as the DSM-IV-TR (APA, 2000). This section will discuss the American Academy of Pediatrics' First Signs effort at earlier detection of autism as well as review several instruments specific to infants and toddlers: the Checklist for Autism in Toddlers (CHAT; Baron-Coehn, Allen, & Gillberg, 1992), Modified Checklist for Autism in Toddlers (M-CHAT; Robins, Fein, Barton, & Green, 2001), Autism Diagnostic Observation Schedule (ADOS; Lord, Rutter, DiLavore, & Risi, 1999), Screening Tool for Autism in Two-Year-Olds (STAT; Stone & Ousley, 1997), and the Pervasive Developmental Disorders Screening Test-II (PDDST-II; Siegel, 2004). Some traditional screeners, which may be used for toddlers as well as older children, include the Gilliam Autism Rating Scale, 2nd edition (GARS-2; Gilliam, 2006) and the Childhood Autism Rating Scale (CARS; Schopler, Reichler, & Renner, 1986). Use of many of the tools described below requires specific training and certification.

First Signs   The American Academy of Pediatrics (AAP) has launched an effort to improve and increase early identification of infants and toddlers who may have autism through its First Signs initiative. First Signs provides information for parents and health care providers on early autism symptoms, as well as suggested Next Steps for intervention. Based on absolute indicators and other warning signs, First Signs provides a vehicle for early identification of autism. In addition to a website dedicated to information (www.firstsigns. org), the initiative includes books, brochures, and videos for use by families, health care providers, and early intervention professionals to improve awareness of autism and its symptoms. Among the information provided are *red flags* that may signal a child's risk for ASD or other developmental delay. Parents are urged to contact their health care provider if their child exhibits 2 or more of the 10 signs listed. Areas of concern are social interaction (e.g., eye gaze, response to name), communication (e.g., nonverbal communication, unusual prosody), and repetitive and restricted behaviors and interests (e.g., stereotypical mannerisms). The mission of the initiative is to increase early intervention for youngsters at risk for ASD through better screening and identification.

Checklist for Autism in Toddlers (CHAT) and Modified Checklist for Toddlers (M-CHAT) The CHAT, developed and initially tested in the United Kingdom, was designed for use by pediatricians as a means of quickly screening for the possibility of autism during routine well-baby visits (Baron-Cohen et al., 1992). The CHAT consists of a series of questions that the physician asks of the child's caregiver during office visits at 18 months of age. Physicians may also conduct observations in order to assess the child's abilities directly. Children who fail two or more of these questions are referred to an appropriate agency or professional for further assessment. The CHAT takes approximately 5 minutes to complete. Questions from the CHAT are available online at several websites, including the National Autistic Society. A follow-up study of children 6 years after screening on the CHAT found that this instrument did not identify many children who were later diagnosed with ASD. While the CHAT had a specificity of 98%, sensitivity was only 38% and the positive predictive power (PPV) was only 4.7% (Baird et al., 2000). The M-CHAT (Robins et al., 2001), utilizes the first nine items from the CHAT. The M-CHAT screens children at 24 months, rather than 18, in consideration of those children who regress after a period of typical development. Another difference in the modified version is that the M-CHAT uses only parent interview, often conducted by telephone (for a copy of the M-CHAT, the reader is referred to Robins et al., 2001). The M-CHAT is completed in 10–15 minutes. Kleinman et al. (2008) used the M-CHAT to screen children aged 16–30 months and again at 42–54 months. Initial screening resulted in a PPV of 36%; however, with a follow-up phone interview the PPV increased to 74%. The authors concluded that the M-CHAT has promise as a screening instrument for ASD.

Autism Diagnostic Observation Schedule (ADOS) The ADOS is a standardized instrument used for screening for autism in persons of various ages. Four modules make up the ADOS, with the first module appropriate for children under age three (Lord et al., 1999). The ADOS takes approximately 30–40 minutes to complete, and extensive training is required to give the test *presses* or probe the various domains. In Module One, there are 10 presses: Free Play, Response to Name, Response to Joint Attention, Bubble Play, Anticipation of a Routine with Objects, Responsive Social Smile, Anticipation of Social Routine, Functional and Symbolic Imitation, Birthday Party (pretend play), and Snack. Each press is designed to assess particular skills such as eye contact, repetitive patterns of interest or behavior, and language. The examiner makes notes to score the child on each skill area using a scale of 0–3. Cutoff scores are available for autism as well as PDD-NOS. Unlike screeners, the ADOS incorporates interactions and direct observations of children into the assessment measure. This instrument is routinely used as a diagnostic tool in establishing a diagnosis of autism for EI services. Lord et al. (2000) found that the ADOS demonstrated sensitivity ranging from 90% to 97% (depending on the module) and specificity ranging from 87% to 93% in discriminating individuals with ASD from those without ASD. The ADOS is presently considered one of the best measures for diagnosis of ASD in research protocols because of its strong psychometric features (American Speech–Language–Hearing Association [ASHA], 2006a, 2006b).

Screening Tool for Autism in Two-Year-Olds (STAT)   The STAT is used to screen for autistic symptoms in play, imitation, and communication in children aged 24–35 months (Stone & Ousley, 1997). The STAT was designed to be used as a follow-up screening instrument for differentiating autism from other developmental disorders, after initial screeners have identified the potential for autism (Stone & Ousley, 1997). This instrument utilizes interaction with the child, and can be completed in approximately 20 minutes. The STAT has been found to be an effective tool for identifying children with autism. Stone, Coonrod, Turner, and Pozdol (2004) found a sensitivity of 0.92; specificity of 0.85; and PPV of 0.86. The STAT demonstrates concurrent validity with clinical diagnosis of autism as well as with the ADOS.

Pervasive Developmental Disorders Screening Test-II (PDDST-II)   The PDDST-II (Siegel, 2004) is used to screen for autism, PDD, and Asperger syndrome in children between 12 and 48 months of age. The PDDST-II is a parent-report instrument, which takes approximately 10–20 minutes to complete. The test was norm-referenced on over 1,000 individuals. A review of test instruments (ASHA, 2006a, 2006b) states that although preliminary results suggest the usefulness of this test, further research is needed.

Gilliam Autism Rating Scale 2 (GARS-2)   The GARS-2 (Gilliam, 2006) is based on the diagnostic criteria in the DSM-IV-TR (APA, 2000) and is appropriate for use with children beginning as young as age three. Taking approximately 10 minutes to administer, the GARS-2 is a norm-referenced screening instrument, which includes 42 questions regarding communication, social interaction, and stereotypical behavior. The first edition of the GARS (Gilliam, 1995) was found to significantly underestimate which children in a sample had autism (South et al., 2002). Peer reviews of the second edition are not available at this time.

Childhood Autism Rating Scale (CARS) The CARS (Schopler et al., 1986) is a 15-item screener designed for use with children aged 2 years and older. Designed to be used as a follow-up to child observation, the CARS is a norm-referenced Likert-type scale comparing the child's behavior to that of typically developing children of the same age. It takes approximately 10 minutes to complete following the observation period. The CARS has a considerable number of studies attesting to its reliability and validity (Eaves & Milner, 1993; Garfin, McCallon, & Cox, 1988; Schopler, Reichler, DeVellis, & Daly, 1980; Sevin, Matson, Coe, Fee, & Sevin, 1991; Teal & Wiebe, 1986). Recent research revealed a 100% sensitivity within a sample of 65 children referred to a hospital-based clinic for ASD (Rellini, Tortolani, Trillo, Carbone, & Montecchi, 2004). However, a review of test instruments by Lord and Corsello (2005) indicates that the CARS may overidentify autism in children with low verbal or cognitive skills.

ASSESSING COMMUNICATION

A delay in the acquisition of communication and language is one of the hallmarks in identification of ASD (Woods & Wetherby, 2003). Children with ASD are often initially referred for testing because of delayed language development (Wetherby, Prizant, & Hutchinson, 1998). Therefore, this section will focus on the assessment of communication abilities of children diagnosed with or at risk for a diagnosis of ASD. About 50% (Lord & Paul, 1997) to 70% (Seltzer et al., 2003) of children with ASD develop some functional speech. Some children later diagnosed with ASD acquire a few words age-appropriately but then lose them or fail to develop more (Lord, Shulman, & DiLavore, 2004). Children who do develop functional speech typically demonstrate fewer delays in the areas of syntax (e.g., word order, sentence structure) and phonology (e.g., speech sound production) than in the areas of semantics (i.e., word meaning) and pragmatics (i.e., social communication). Most notably, speech may be characterized by a limited verbal repertoire, reduced spontaneity, and poor conversational skills including topic initiation, maintenance, relevance, turn-taking, and taking the perspective of the listener (Paul, 2007).

Echolalia is demonstrated in the early stages of language acquisition by many children with ASD (Wetherby, Prizant, & Schuler, 2000). Deficits in pitch and intonation have also been noted. Sheinkopf, Mundy, Oller, and Steffens (2000) compared vocalizations of preschool children with ASD to those of children with other developmental delays and found significant differences in the vocalizations of the two groups. Those with ASD demon-strated a greater proportion of atypical vocalizations such as squeals, growls, and yells. A comparison of the proportion of well-formed consonant–vowel syllables was not significant.

Communication Versus Language   It is important to note that the deficits seen in children with ASD can best be characterized as deficits in communication rather than language. Given this perspective, children at risk can be identified before speech fails to emerge through observation of developmental delays, many of which have been shown to predict later communication develop-ment. Wetherby et al. (1998) found that although children with ASD and nonspectrum developmental delays (DD) both demonstrate language delays, those with ASD had a pattern of deficits that distinguished them from other children. These behaviors included poorer scores on communicative func-tions, gestural communication, reciprocity, social/affective signaling, and symbolic behaviors. More specifically, these children showed deficits in joint attention, sociability of function, gaze shifts, and symbolic play. Strengths were seen in behavior regulation and constructive play. It is therefore essential that assessment of prelinguistic children identified as either at risk or with ASD focus on the core deficits of joint attention and symbol use (Wetherby et al., 2000; Woods & Wetherby, 2003).

Joint Attention   Joint attention deficits are reflected in difficulty shifting attention between people and objects. By 12 months, most infants share attention using alternating eye gaze, and follow the eye gaze or point of others (Toth, Munson, Meltzoff, & Dawson, 2006). Numerous studies have identified joint attention as a significant predictor of language acquisition (Anderson et al., 2007; Bono, Daley, & Sigman, 2004; Charman et al., 2003; Smith, Mirenda, & Zaidman-Zait, 2007; Toth et al., 2006; Wetherby et al., 2004).

Most recently, Anderson et al. (2007) studied 206 children with a diagnosis of autism, PDD-NOS, or DD. The children were followed from the ages of 2 to 9. Joint attention and nonverbal IQ were strong positive predictors of later verbal outcome. Charman et al. (2003) assessed children with ASD at 20 months and again at age 42 months. Language outcome was positively associated with earlier measures of joint attention. Smith et al. (2007) found that vocabulary growth was associated with a greater number of gestures to initiate joint attention. Toth et al. (2006) found that the ability to imitate pointing and showing for joint attention was strongly associated with lan-guage ability at 3–4 years of age. Toth et al. state that "[t]hrough joint attention interactions, infants begin to link words and sentences with objects and events" (2006, p. 994). It has been suggested that language deficits result because children are not tuned in to the speech directed at them and therefore do not make relationships between verbal input and the context (Carpenter & Tomasello, 2000).

Use of Symbols   The capacity for symbol use is essential for the development of conventional communication, both verbal and nonverbal (Wetherby et al., 2000). Conventional hand symbols such as waving, showing, and pointing may be absent or late to develop. The observation that nonverbal children with ASD do not substitute gestural communication in the face of speech deficits as do children with other communication disorders is probably explained by this deficit in symbol use. Various forms of unconventional verbal and vocal behaviors such as echolalia and perseveration may also have their roots in symbol deficits (Wetherby et al., 2000; Woods & Wetherby, 2003). Echolalic utterances, both immediate and delayed, are often in the form of unanalyzed chunks of speech that represent a situation or event but that may serve a communicative function. Wetherby et al. provide the example of a child saying, "Do you want a piece of candy?" to request candy. The child was echolalic in that he was repeating the question that was addressed to him in a particular situation; however, the child was using it for a different communicative function.

   A limitation in the capacity to use symbols is also reflected in limitations in object use and pretend play. Play skills and language are related in that both require the ability to make one thing stand for another. Furthermore, successful play interactions with peers require well developed communication skills. Deficits in symbolic play in children with autism have been documented by Wetherby et al. (1998). Smith et al. (2007) also demonstrated an association of vocabulary development with pretend play skills. Toth et al. (2006) found that toy play and imitation were most strongly associated with rate of communication development at age 4–6.5. Similarly, Charman et al. (2003) and Turner, Stone, Pozdol, and Coonrod (2006) found toy play and imitation to be associated with language.

Components of Comprehensive Communication Evaluation   A complete communication evaluation for a child at risk or diagnosed with ASD should examine both prelinguistic and linguistic communicative strengths and weaknesses. In the prelinguistic child, the following should be examined: gestural communication, the ability to respond to and initiate joint attention, the variety and frequency of communication intents, symbolic skills such as play and imitation of sounds, and response to verbal input. In the child who is demonstrating some verbal skills, the above skills may be assessed in addition to the comprehension and production of conventional meanings at the word, sentence, and discourse level. Nonconventional communication strategies such as echolalia and maladaptive communicative strategies such as tantrums to express rejection should also be assessed (Paul, 2007; Wetherby et al., 2000).

The purpose of assessment after a diagnosis of autism has been made is for intervention planning (ASHA, 2006a, 2006b). Therefore, an important component of the assessment process is to determine what supports might facilitate more successful communication and decrease maladaptive forms of communication such as tantrums and head banging. Exploration of visual supports such as Augmentative/Alternative Communication (AAC) systems or signing, for example, might be carried out in the form of a dynamic assessment. Buschbacher and Fox (2003) describe a process of functional assessment in which negative behaviors are analyzed to determine their communicative intent. Interventions can then be designed to replace these forms of communication with more positive behaviors. Assessment of interactions between the child and caregivers may also provide information about what facilitates or interferes with successful communication (ASHA, 2006a; Prelock, Beatson, Botner, Brodner, & Drucker, 2003).

ASSESSMENT METHODOLOGY

Although numerous standardized, norm-referenced tests of receptive and expressive language abilities are available, these traditional forms of testing should not be relied upon to provide the information needed to assess communication in children with ASD. Such assessment instruments usually focus on the form of language, such as syntax and phonology. As pointed out above, communication deficits are evident at the prelingustic stage of development in children with ASD, and therefore these instruments will be of limited usefulness in that population. Even for children who have developed verbal communication, such instruments do not typically assess the social-pragmatic functions of speech. For an accurate picture of a child's communication skills, assessment should be carried out in natural contexts, in a variety of situations, and with a variety of interactants such as caregivers or peers. Assessment tools such as observational checklists and caregiver interviews may provide a more accurate picture of the child's communication strengths and weaknesses (ASHA, 2006a; Wetherby et al., 2000).

Communication Assessment Instruments   Some instruments which have been utilized to measure social–communicative functions include the Communication and Symbolic Behavior Scales–Developmental Profile (CSBS-DP; Wetherby & Prizant, 2003), Early Social Communication Scales (ESCS; Mundy, Hogan, & Doelring, 1996), Assessing Linguistic Behavior (ALB; Olswang, Stoel-Gammon, Coggins, & Carpenter, 1987), and the MacArthur–Bates Communicative

Development Inventories (Fenson et al., 2003). For older, more verbal children, Paul and Sutherland (2003) recommend use of the Comprehensive Assessment of Spoken Language (CASL; Carrow-Woolfolk, 1999) and the Test of Language Competence (TLC; Wiig & Secord, 1989). The CASL includes measures of language structure, pragmatic functioning, and inferencing abilities. The TLC includes measures of figurative language and inferencing, areas that continue to be problematic even in individuals with relatively good language skills.

Related Assessment Domains   Other areas that are of interest to the practitioner include possible motor and sensory deficits. Motor planning deficits are often seen in children with ASD (Anzalone & Williamson, 2000; Rogers & Bennetto, 2000), and these can affect speech development in the form of apraxia (Wetherby et al., 2000). Rogers et al., (2006) suggest that it is important to determine if motor deficits underlie problems with speech development. If this is the case, treatments such as the PROMPT approach might be the more efficacious approach. In their intervention study, using a small sample of children, 4 out of the 5 nonverbal children with ASD developed some verbal communication after PROMPT treatment. However, other research on the use of this approach is limited.

   Feeding problems may be related to both motor and sensory issues. Research on prevalence of these problems is limited (ASHA, 2006b). The results of Sheinkopf et al. (2000) suggest that autism is not a problem of fine motor control for speech since babbling was found to be similar in children with both ASD and DD. However, Schreck, Williams, and Smith (2004) found more feeding problems in children with ASD than typical developing children, and parents reported that children ate a smaller variety of foods than other members of the family. Ho, Eaves, and Peabody (1997) studied a group of children with ASD in Canada and found that few of the children had diets that met the recommendations of the Canadian Food Guide. It is not clear whether feeding problems are related to sensory, motor, or behavioral issues.

CHARACTERISTICS OF EFFECTIVE INTERVENTION

EVIDENCE-BASED PRACTICES

In the field of autism there are a great many *fad* treatments that have come and gone over the years (Scheuermann & Webber, 2002). Green (2007) describes evidence-based practice as "using the best available evidence, combined with clinical expertise and consumer preferences, to guide practice" (p. 4). She further confronts *fad* treatments stating that, "popularity should not be mistaken for proof; enthusiasm is no substitute for evidence; (and) it just does not stand to reason that all interventions are comparably effective" (Green, 2007, p. 6). While there are many options for practice, only those that have strong research-based evidence are considered to be evidence-based, and only evidence-based practices should be used with children with autism (IDEA, 2004).

What, then, constitutes strong research-based evidence? According to Green (2007), studies that include direct intervention testing, controlled comparisons, systematic selection of participants, objective and reliable measurement of treatment effects, have been replicated by multiple researchers, and that have been published in peer-reviewed scientific journals meet the criteria for evidence-based. Examples of evidence-based practices in autism include: Applied Behavior Analysis (ABA), Discrete Trial Teaching (DTT), and Pivotal Response Training (PRT) (Simpson, 2005).

Though true evidence-based practices, as described by Green (2007), are recommended wherever possible, it is recognized that a great many promising practices exist, which have yet to meet the criteria to be considered evidence-based (Simpson, 2005). Promising practices, according to Simpson are those that "have (1) been widely used for several years without any or with few adverse outcomes, and/or (2) undergone research that suggests that children and youth with ASD respond favorably and display skill acquisition as a consequence of the intervention" (2005, p. 11). Examples of practices considered as promising, include: play-based interventions, DIR/Floortime, incidental teaching, and structured teaching (TEACCH Model) (Simpson). Other methods, such as the Picture Exchange Communication System (PECS; Bondy & Frost, 1994) and Carol Gray's (2000) Social Stories are also often considered promising practices.

Simpson (2005) further describes practices that are considered to have limited supporting evidence as well as those that are not recommended. Those with limited supporting evidence may be too new to the field to have warranted sufficient research, may have shown very limited effectiveness, or they may rely solely on less rigorous forms of research such as case study and anecdotal reports. Examples of limited supporting evidence strategies include: Gentle Teaching, Relationship Development Intervention (RDI), Music Therapy, Art Therapy, and Pet Therapy (Simpson, 2005). Treatments that are not recommended typically have either been proven to have little to no effectiveness through rigorous research, or have been shown to cause harm to the individual receiving the treatment. There are two examples, Holding Therapy and Facilitated Communication, that are not recommended practices according to Simpson (2005).

Hewitt (2005) believes that the highest level of evidence is a group design that follows a medical model. This model consists of random assignment to treatment condition, double-blind placebo controls and use of inferential statistics to interpret findings. In the field of ASD, however, it is difficult to find appropriate placebos; random assignment to treatment group can be a problem because of parental consent issues; and controlling for factors such other treatments provided at the time of the study, longitudinal changes in children during a developmental period, and differences in family characteristics is difficult. Most important, because of the many varied characteristics of children with ASD, no one methodology can be identified as best for an individual child (National Research Council [NRC], 2001).

Although results of single case studies that use multiple baseline design research cannot be generalized, they may represent a better approach for determining effectiveness of intervention approaches for individual children. Odom et al., (2003) reviewed 37 single subject research studies from 1990 to 2002 and divided his findings into three levels of evidence: Well-Established; Emerging and Effective; and Probably Efficacious. In the first category were techniques that used adult prompting and differential reinforcement. In the second category, he included peer-mediated interventions, visual supports such as PECS, self-monitoring techniques, and parent and other caregiver involvement. Finally, the third category included use of technology such as video modeling and embedding choice and child preferences into instructional tasks. Howlin (2005) suggests that randomized controlled trials (RCTs) provide the strongest evidence base for the effectiveness of a treatment. However, few RCTs have been carried out for communicative interventions in preschoolers with ASD (Aldred, Green, & Adams, 2004; Howlin, Gordon, Pasco, Wade, & Charman, 2007; Kasari, Freeman, & Paparella, 2006; Yoder & Stone, 2006a, 2006b).

Because of the emphasis in the literature and legislation on utilizing those practices that are considered to be most evidence-based, we will discuss only those that have been identified as either evidence-based or promising practices. Further, we will only focus on those that have implications for young children with autism.

FAMILY-CENTERED TREATMENT

Parents are considered by most educators, and early childhood professionals, as the *experts* on their children. Therefore, family involvement in the treatment process should be highly valued. Families have perspectives, insights, and historical knowledge of the child that professionals may not have. In addition, if the family does not support a particular treatment or skill for instruction, the chances of the skill generalizing to the natural environment of the home is unlikely. For these reasons, the literature is filled with studies on the importance of family involvement in the education and treatment of children with autism. In early intervention, Part C, of the Individuals with Disabilities Education Act (IDEA, 2004), not only is family involvement integral, but the individualized plan of service includes family as well as child needs.

The Individualized Family Service Plan (IFSP) requires that service providers assess and plan for meeting the needs of the family along with those of the child. In this way, the IFSP is inherently family-focused. In Part B of the IDEA, which serves children ages 3–21, families are required to be a part of the planning, but their needs are no longer a focus of the service plan. Under Part B, the plan that is developed is called the Individualized Education Plan (IEP) and, while family opinion is valued and parents or their representatives must sign that they agree with the service plan, their needs are not considered nor are they provided for as part of the plan for treatment. It is important that professionals working with families in Part C services prepare the families for this change in focus, and empower the families to take responsibility for their own needs when Part C is no longer there to do so for them. Professionals working in Part B service settings (e.g., schools) should consider the family's past involvement with Part C and the fact that they may have had more support through those services, and be prepared with supports, such as community resources, to help families take care of their own needs.

Cultural and Linguistic Sensitivity

Effective programs must be embedded within the natural environment and therefore must address not just the skills or deficits of the child but also address communication within the family system (Woods & Wetherby, 2003). As described earlier, family-centered principles also require that the families be included in both the assessment and planning process. Respect for family values is required by law in early intervention and is recommended at all levels of practice (Prelock et al., 2003). Family beliefs, perceptions of autism, and needs may vary by culture. For example, in some cultures, a disability in a child may be seen as a blessing indicating that the family is worthy of the challenge or has been given an opportunity to better themselves. Alternatively, having a child with a disability may be seen as punishment for misdeeds or a result of witchcraft (Wilder, Dyches, Obiakor, & Anzelone, 2004). Parents who see the child as being in need of *fixing* may be more proactive in seeking services than those who are more accepting. The value that parents place on early speech, talkativeness, and independence may affect rates of early identification and may be in conflict with therapeutic goals set by mainstream service providers (van Kleek, 1994).

Dyches, Wilder, Sudweeks, Obiakor, and Algozzine (2004) note that there are different prevalence rates for autism among different cultural/linguistic groups. The percentage of African-American and Asian-Pacific children identified with autism is disproportionately high and the percentage of Native-Americans identified with ASD is disproportionately low. Linguistic differences must also be addressed. Some languages do not have a word for autism so must adapt the English word, as in the Spanish word *el autismo*. Evaluations must be done by bilingual providers, and educational materials must be provided in the families' language. Little research exists document-ing differences in cultures in their perceptions of autism and the culturally appropriate intervention methods or materials. Santarelli, Koegel, Casas, and Koegel (2001) describe a case study of a Mexican-American child whose parents spoke little English but also had poor literacy skills in Spanish. Service providers therefore developed family training and information materials using the *fotonovela,* a method used throughout Central and South American to educate Spanish-speakers on health issues. Fotonovelas use photos illustrating a short, easy-to-follow drama. Since Latino children often live with extended families, this approach was able to educate all members of the household. More research on adaptations such as these would allow more culturally appropriate interventions.

TRANSDISCIPLINARY APPROACH

Initially, EI services were delivered by therapists who addressed only their own area of expertise, with little or no communication to share information and coordinate progamming. Eventually, providers recognized that they could increase program efficacy by sharing information through planned meetings and multidisciplinary cooperation. As this information sharing proved beneficial, the transdisciplinary model emerged, wherein professio-nals and parents collaborate in planning and delivery of services, actually teaching each other so that all stakeholders are familiar with the range of program goals and strategies, and may reinforce learning in multiple domains.

EARLY AND INTENSIVE INTERVENTION

In children with autism, early intervention is essential. Upon observation of a developmental delay (i.e., failure to meet a recognized benchmark) or if maladaptive behaviors are persistent (Scott & Baldwin, 2005), a plan for diagnosis and assessment should be initiated leading to a comprehensive intervention program plan. According to the NRC (2001), outcomes are best for children who begin intervention before age three. Furthermore, instruc-tional programming should be provided for a minimum of 25 hours a week (NRC, 2001) although this may include parent-mediated interactions.

APPROACHES TO INTERVENTION

THE DEVELOPMENT OF EARLY INTERVENTION MODELS

Prior to the 1970s, children with severe autism were often placed in institu-tional settings, isolated from society. With the deinstitutionalization and normalization movements (Wolfensberger, 1972), more children with severe disabilities began residing at home with their families. Early intervention home-based and center-based programs emerged to address the treatment needs of these young children and their families. Parents were able to receive training so that they could implement particular practices and reinforce learning at home. Center-based programs for infants and very young children, as well as school programs designed specifically for children with autism, provided a means to maintain consistency of intervention methods, therein enhancing treatment efficacy and facilitating development of skill maintenance and generalization.

One of the pitfalls of many intensive programs in the 1970s and 1980s was the absence of typically developing peers to emulate. In response to this concern, Strain and his colleagues established an alternative Learning Experience Program for Preschoolers and Their Parents (LEAP) at the University of Pittsburgh in 1982. This program was one of the first within the country to place children with autism into a preschool setting that included typically developing children (Dawson & Osterling, 1997). The program combined behavior therapy with social skill development to create a unique approach (Harris, Handelman, & Jennet, 2005).

As the inclusion movement gained momentum in the 1990s, children with disabilities began to spend more time in settings with their nondisabled peers, often with the support of paraprofessionals. School-based therapeutic settings for young children with ASD provided more opportunities to learn and socialize. Overall, positive behavior supports and system-wide change to accommodate children with autism in inclusive settings (Harris et al., 2005; Odom et al., 2003: Simpson & Myles, 1993) have made it possible for children with significant disabilities to spend more time interacting with typically developing children during the school day.

Historical and Philosophical Perspectives on EI Approaches

Approaches to ASD have been characterized in a number of reviews as moving on a continuum from traditional discrete trial approaches to more naturalistic, social pragmatic, developmentally-based approaches (Woods & Wetherby, 2003; Prizant, Wetherby, & Rydell, 2000; ASHA, 2006a, 2006b). Along this continuum one can find more contemporary behavioral approaches that focus less on speech and more on social-communicative goals than did some of the earlier behavioral programs (Lovaas, 1977). By focusing on more child initiated interests, embedding the interventions in natural environments, and using more reinforcement related to the child's communication attempts, the newer approaches have attempted to address the lack of generalization and spontaneity observed in children trained in earlier programs (Woods & Wetherby, 2003). Some examples of approaches that fulfill these criteria are the

Natural Language Paradigm (NLP; Koegel, O'Dell, & Koegel, 1987), pivotal response training (PRT; Koegel, Camarata, Koegel, Ben-Tall, & Smith, 1998), time delay (Charlop & Walsh, 1986), and Responsive Education and Prelinguistic Milieu Teaching (RPMT; Yoder & Stone, 2006a). These approaches have been successfully used to teach a variety of linguistic skills. For example, parents were trained to use the NLP to increase the frequency of their children's verbalizations (Laski, Charlop, & Schreibman, 1988). PRT has been used to teach grammatical morphemes (Koegel, Carter, & Koegel, 2003), to improve speech intelligibility (Koegel et al., 1998), to increase complex social interactions (Pierce & Schriebman, 1995), and to develop symbolic play skills (Stahmer, 1995). Time delay has been used to increase spontaneous verbalizations (Charlop & Trasowech, 1991), to increase the use of requests (Charlop, Schreibman, & Thibodeau, 1985), and to use question forms (Taylor & Harris, 1995). RPMT was effective in increasing turn taking and initiating joint attention (Yoder & Stone, 2006a, 2006b).

Interventions based on more developmental approaches in communication training have much in common with the naturalistic, behavioral models described above. However, they tend to be even more child directed in that the adult follows the child's lead, responds to all of the child's communicative attempts as if they were meaningful, and models more mature forms of communication. By arranging the environment (e.g., putting desired objects out of reach) communication is encouraged. Programs which utilize developmental, social, pragmatic interventions include the floortime approach used in the DIR model (Greenspan & Wieder, 1997; Ingersoll, Dvortcsak, Whalen, & Sikora, 2005); the Hanen More Than Words program (McConachie, Randle, Hammal, & Le Couteur, 2005; Sussman, 1999); and the Social, Communication, Emotional Regulation, and Transactional Support model (SCERTS; Prizant, Wetherby, Rubin, & Laurent, 2003). The following section will describe in greater detail some of the programs and strategies discussed above and others that are commonly used in intervention.

EVIDENCE-BASED INTERVENTION STRATEGIES

ASD can affect sensory and information processing, cognition and communication in very different ways and with vastly different levels of severity. Individuals on the spectrum may be functioning from a severely intellectually impaired level to an intellectually gifted level. In order to meet the needs of the diverse group of individuals affected, intervention strategies must be individualized and systematically delivered. The methods described in this section are not exclusive to children with autism and may be employed when building new skills or ameliorating behavioral excesses in individuals with other challenging learning and behavior needs, as well.

Applied Behavior Analysis   Applied Behavior Analysis (ABA) is defined as "the process of applying sometimes tentative principles of behavior to the improvement of specific behaviors, and simultaneously evaluating whether or not any changes noted are indeed attributed to the process of application" (Baer Wolf & Risley, 1968, p. 91, as cited in Simpson, 2005, p. 87). In essence, ABA involves the arrangement of the environment to increase the likelihood and strength of a desired response. Individualized strategies may be developed to build or strengthen behaviors, as well as to ameliorate maladaptive behaviors. Systematic administration of prompts and reinforcement to establish behaviors, followed by the fading of prompts and thinning reinforcement as mastery occurs add to program effectiveness. Ongoing assessment and data collection are key components of ABA. The Lovaas treatment applied Skinner's (1938) theory to intensive one-on-one behavioral intervention in the home for 40 hours per week. A key component of early ABA intervention involved training adults within the household in the method, so that the child would be provided with a structured setting at all times (Harris et al., 2005). In 1981, Lovaas published *Teaching Developmentally Disabled Children: The Me Book,* describing his treatment approach. Today the utilization of ABA intervention is the most commonly administered treatment for young children with severe autism, and it remains the most thoroughly researched and best-documented education approach in the field of autism (Cohen, Amerine-Dickens, & Smith, 2006; Eikeseth, Jahr, & Eldevik, 2007; Remington et al., 2007; Rosenwasser & Axelrod, 2001). In fact, the U.S. Surgeon General in 1999 recommended ABA as the treatment of choice for ASD (U.S. Department of Health and Human Services, 1999). In an effort to ensure provision of high-quality behavioral intervention, the Behavior Analyst Certification Board has developed a voluntary international certifying program for behavior analyst practitioners.

Discrete trial instruction, also known as discrete trial teaching (DTT), falls under the umbrella of ABA. It is useful for building new skills that require intensive direct instruction with many learning opportunities. A trial is defined as "a single teaching unit . . . that consists of the following components: presentation of a discriminative stimulus (teacher's instruction), the child's responses, and the consequence" with a pause between trials (Simpson, 2005, p. 98).

Structured teaching (TEACCH)   Structured teaching began as part of the TEACCH Program of North Carolina (Treatment and Education of Autistic and Related Communication Handicapped Children) (Simpson, 2005). There are four components to structured teaching: (1) physically organizing the layout of the educational setting so that students can better understand what activities and expectations for behavior occur when in the room, (2) using visual schedules to aid students with predicting activities, thereby lessening their anxiety, (3) designing work systems that aid students in working independently, and (4) establishing task organization systems that assist students in knowing steps of a task and completing that task independently. The goal of visual supports and structured teaching is to promote independence and lessen anxiety and other issues arising from the characteristics of autism. Training in the structured teaching methods is available through the TEACCH Program.

Incidental Teaching   Incidental teaching "involves taking advantage of a naturally occurring teaching opportunity (although it can also occur in situations staged by the teacher)" (Scheuermann & Webber, 2002, p. 150), and involves four components: (1) positive interactions between student and teacher that are of short duration, (2) interactions that occur in the setting in which the behavior would most likely occur (e.g., natural setting), (3) instruction in functional skills, and (4) student-centered interactions that follow the child's lead and interests. Incidental is also commonly referred to as milieu teaching and naturalistic instruction.

DIR/Floortime Approach   The Developmental, Individual-difference, Relationship-based approach (Greenspan & Wieder, 2006) is based on recognition of individual differences in processing information and in learning relationships. Greenspan and Wieder created a model that refers to six stages of development: shared attention and regulation, engagement and relating, purposeful emotional interactions, emotional signaling and problem-solving, creating ideas, and logical thinking. Floortime is a component of the DIR model, in which emotionally meaningful interactions to the child are encouraged by the parent or teacher. Training of parents is especially helpful in floortime because the difficulty of communicating with children with ASD may cause untrained parents to become more didactic and controlling rather than child-initiated and reciprocal in their communication. As parents are trained to become more sensitive and responsive to their children's communicative attempts, children will generally increase their communicative initiations (Aldred et al., 2004). The DIR model began as a home-based early childhood model. In the past few years, it has gained limited acceptance and use in school programs, primarily with young children. Evidence for its effectiveness has been demonstrated in studies by Greenspan and Wieder (1999) and Ingersoll et al. (2005).

Play-Based Strategies   Play is considered "the very fabric of childhood culture" (Quill, 1995, p. 214). The inability of most children with autism to participate in play prevents them from experiencing the typical culture of early childhood, and sets them apart from their peers. Play-based strategies use natural learning opportunities within the context of playful situations to teach various skills such as language and socialization to children with autism. Particularly for very young children, the use of play may be more appropriate than more traditional DTT due to the lack of attention span and ability to sit for long periods of time inherent in the average 2 year old (Boutot, 2008). An example of a play-based strategy used with young children is PRT (Koegel & Koegel, 2006), considered an evidence-based practice (Simpson, 2005). PRT uses motivation and responses to a wide variety of cues to increase communication. The model is based on the principles of ABA. The goal of PRT is for the child to generalize skills outside the training conditions. PRT may be used to teach language, social, behavioral, and play skills.

Social Stories   Social Stories, were developed specifically for children with autism by Carol Gray (2000), and have several uses:

> (1) describing a situation, including social cues and responses, in a nonthreatening manner; (2) personalizing social skills instruction; (3) teaching routines or student adjustment to routine changes; (4) teaching academic material in a realistic social setting; and (5) addressing a myriad of behaviors, such as aggression, obsessive behavior, and fear. (Simpson, 2005, p. 144)

For young children, Social Stories may be drawn, though they can also be written for children who can read. The use of scripts and Social Stories are especially useful in communication development. Social Stories have been used to help children with ASD who can read to initiate verbal communication and to engage in conversational exchanges with partners. Social Stories have also been used to provide scripts for socially appropriate behaviors and interactions (ASHA, 2006a). A review of the empirical research literature on Social Stories (Reynhout & Carter, 2006) concludes that it is a promising approach but in need of further research to document efficacy of the various components of the methodology.

Alternatives to Clinician/Teacher Directed Intervention   Models of intervention in the area of social communication that differ from the traditional clinician/ teacher directed format include peer-mediated interventions, parent-mediated interventions, and video modeling. Peers have been trained successfully to serve as models and to interact with children with autism (Prendeville, Prelock, & Unwin, 2005). Improved communication between children with ASD and their trained peers were found in studies by Pierce and Schreibman (1995) and Kalyva and Avramidis (2005). Parents have been trained to increase speech using the NLP (Laski et al., 1988) and to improve joint attention using both developmental (Schertz & Odom, 2007) and behavioral models (Rocha, Schreibman, & Stahmer, 2007). A strength of both peer and parent mediation is that the intervention is provided by the communication partners with whom the child interacts on a daily basis.

The video modeling methodology takes advantage of the relative strength in visual learning observed in many children with ASD (ASHA, 2006a). A number of studies have shown that social communicative skills can be taught by having the child watch a video that demonstrates an individual, or the child, engaging in appropriate social interactions (Buggey, 2005; Charlop & Milstein, 1989; Maione & Mirenda, 2006). Video modeling was used by Charlop-Christy and Daneshvar (2003) to teach perspective taking in children with autism.

Augmentative/Alternative Communication Use of the visual modality to develop communication has been especially successful for children who have not yet or cannot develop spoken communication. Augmentative/alternative communication (AAC) approaches include both unaided approaches such as sign language, and aided approaches such as the use of pictures, symbols, or written cues. Aided approaches include voice output communication aids (VOCAS). A meta-analysis of studies using AAC concluded that most of these interventions were effective in producing positive behavioral change and generalization (Schlosser & Lee, 2000). A systematic review of 9 single-subject and 2 group studies of AAC (Schlosser & Wendt, 2008) concluded that the use of AAC does not impede the development of speech, and may in fact, lead to modest increases in speech production in children with ASD. Mirenda (2003) points out that although numerous studies have supported the use of these approaches for children with ASD, decisions for which approach is best for a particular child must be measured in "specific contexts, with specific children, and to meet specific needs" (p. 212).

The most frequently used AAC system is the Picture Exchange Communication System (PECS; Bondy & Frost, 1994). Through PECS children learn to exchange a picture for what they want or need. The PECS system involves 2–3 days' worth of training and the protocol is based on the principles of ABA. PECS is effective at teaching early- or non-communicators the basic concepts of getting attention and initiating communication while also teaching them an alternative or augmentative form of communication.

Research suggests that the use of the PECS system can increase speech production (Ganz & Simpson, 2004; Tincani, Crozier, & Alazett, 2006). PECS training results in more spontaneous communication because it teaches communicative functions rather than response to an adult request for a label. The earliest goal is to teach requesting behaviors. The child is physically prompted to pick up a picture of an item; when s/he hands it to the adult, and s/he receives the item requested. Items available for request had already been identified as desired by the child, so motivation is present to request the item. Physical prompts are eventually faded, and as the child progresses, tasks are made more complex. In the final stages, the program teaches the child to produce word combinations such as "I want_____" and to initiate and respond to a wider range of communicative functions. A number of benefits to use of the PECS program have been documented. One benefit has been the emergence or increase in the use of spoken communication (Charlop-Christy, Carpenter, Le, LeBlanc, & Kellet, 2002; Ganz & Simpson, 2004). The effectiveness of PECs in developing speech may vary as a function of the individual. Yoder and Stone (2006b) compared the efficacy of PECS with Responsive Education and Prelinguistic Milieu Teaching (RPMT) in 36 preschoolers with ASD. For children with a certain level of play skills, PECS training resulted in more rapid skill acquisition.

Effective Intervention for Communication Development A number of conclusions can be drawn about effective interventions for developing social communication in children with ASD. Goals for communication should be based on the core challenges of ASD such as joint attention, language and related symbolic skills such as play, and communication skills for behavioral regulation and social interaction (Anderson et al., 2007; ASHA, 2006a, 2006b; Charman et al., 2003; Toth et al., 2006; Woods & Wetherby, 2003). These behaviors have been successfully targeted in recent studies using a variety of intervention approaches (Ingersoll & Schreibman, 2006; Kasari et al., 2006; Rocha et al., 2007; Yoder & Stone, 2006b). Furthermore, specific goals addressing these core challenges must be adapted as communication abilities develop. ASHA (2006) describes different goals for individuals prior to the emergence of symbolic language, at emerging language stages, and at more advanced stages of conversational discourse.

Communication interventions should lead to increased initiation of spontaneous communication in multiple contexts and with a range of social partners, improved comprehension of verbal and nonverbal discourse, an increased range of communicative functions, and both verbal and nonverbal means of communication (ASHA, 2006; Woods & Wetherby, 2003). Goals should be individualized for children after carrying out an ecologically appropriate assessment of abilities. The presence of fluent speech before the age of 5 is a significant predictor of future functioning socially and academically (Lord & Paul, 1997) and the presence of functional communication is associated with both reduction in problematic behavior and in family stress levels. "Therefore enhancement of communication and language abilities needs to be a major focus in education and clinical intervention for children with autism and their families" (Wetherby et al., 2000, p. 109).

SUMMARY

This chapter has provided a discussion of historical and philosophical perspectives of ASD, including diagnostic criteria, assessment, and intervention options, with an emphasis on social communication development. Research was reviewed to illustrate the level of support for a variety of teaching methodologies and approaches for intervention in autism (Goldstein, 2002; Hwang & Hughes, 2000; NRC, 2001; Odom et al., 2003). Some reviews highlighted limitations to practice, suggesting that parents and professionals exercise caution and seek information when selecting programs and approaches. Many studies are "designed to assess the effect of a restricted set of treatment components" (Goldstein, 2002, p. 392), although language is a multifaceted, complex process. Too often interventions target isolated behaviors in controlled settings (Hwang & Hughes).

The use of patchwork approaches to intervention (Prizant et al., 2003), in which various service providers use different models that are not well-integrated, is not recommended. Coordination of home-based services and school programs that will deliver consistent programming across providers remains a challenge to be met. Further research is necessary in order to predict which approach is best for individual children; what behaviors to include in a comprehensive program; how to determine and teach priority skills in the most efficacious sequence; and how to adapt intervention to the child's age, culture, family wishes, and educational environment.

REFERENCES

Aldred, C., Green, J., & Adams, C. (2004). A new social communication intervention for children with autism: Pilot randomized controlled treatment study suggesting effectiveness. *Journal of Child Psychology and Psychiatry, 45,* 1420–1430.

American Psychiatric Association. (1994). *Diagnostic and statistical manual of mental disorders* (4th ed.). Washington, DC: Author.

American Psychiatric Association. (2000). *Diagnostic and statistical manual of mental disorders* (4th ed., Text Revision). Washington, DC: Author.

American Speech–Language–Hearing Association. (2006a). *Guidelines for speech–language pathologists in diagnosis, assessment, and treatment of autism spectrum disorders across the lifespan* [Guidelines]. Available from www.asha.org/policy.

American Speech–Language–Hearing Association. (2006b). Principles for speech-language pathologists in diagnosis, assessment, and treatment of autism spectrum disorders across the life span [Technical Report]. Available from www.asha.org/policy.

Anderson, D., Lord, C., Risi, S., DiLavore, P. C., Shulman, C., Thurm, A., et al. (2007). Patterns of growth in verbal abilities among children with autism spectrum disorder. *Journal of Counseling and Clinical Psychology, 75,* 594–604.

Anzalone, M. E., & Williamson, G. G. (2000). Sensory processing and motor performance in autism spectrum disorders. In A. M. Wetherby & B. M. Prizant (Eds.), *Autism spectrum disorders: A transactional developmental perspective* (pp. 143–166). Baltimore, MD: Brookes.

Autism Society of America. (2008, January). *About autism*. www.autism-society.org.

Baird, G., Charman, T., Baron-Cohen, S., Cox, A., Swettenham, J., Wheelwright, S., et al. (2000). A screening instrument for autism at 18 months of age: A 6-year follow-up study. *Journal of the American Academy of Child and Adolescent Psychiatry, 39,* 694–702.

Baker, P., Piven, J., & Sato, Y. (1998). Autism and tuberous sclerosis complex: Prevalence and clinical features. *Journal of Autism and Developmental Disorders, 28,* 279–285.

Baron-Cohen, S., Allen, J., & Gillberg, C. (1992). Can autism be detected at 18 months? The needle, the haystack, and the CHAT. *British Journal of Psychiatry, 161,* 839–843.

Belmonte, M. K., Allen, G., Boulanger, L. M., Carper, R. A., & Webb, S. J. (2004). Autism and abnormal development of brain connectivity. *Journal of Neuroscience, 24,* 9228–9231.

Bettleheim, B. (1967). *The empty fortress: Infantile autism and the birth of the self.* New York: Plenum Press.

Bondy, A., & Frost, L. (1994) The Picture-Exchange Communication System. *Focus on Autistic Behavior, 9,* 1–19.

Bono, M., Daley, T., & Sigman, M. (2004). Relations among joint attention, amount of intervention and language gain in autism. *Journal of Autism and Developmental Disorders, 34,* 495–505.

Boutot, E. A. (2008). *Development of play, language, and social interaction in young children with autism.* Paper presented at the Young Child with Special Needs Conference, Las Vegas, NV.

Bregman, J. D. (2005). Definitions and characteristics of the spectrum. In D. Zager (Ed.), *Autism spectrum disorders: Identification, education, and treatment* (3rd ed., pp. 3–46), Mahwah, NJ: Erlbaum.

Buggey, T. (2005). Video self-modeling applications with students with autism spectrum disorder in a small private school setting. *Focus on Autism and Developmental Disabilities, 20,* 52–63.

Buschbacher, P. W., & Fox, L. (2003). Understanding and intervening with the challenging behavior of young children with autism spectrum disorder. *Language, Speech, and Hearing Services in Schools, 34,* 217–227.

Carpenter, M., & Tomasello, M. (2000). Joint attention, cultural learning, and language acquisition: Implications for children with autism. In A. M. Wetherby & B. M. Prizant (Eds.), *Autism spectrum disorders: A transactional developmental perspective* (pp. 31–54). Baltimore, MD: Brookes.

Carper, R. A., & Courchesne, R. A. (2000). Inverse correlation between frontal lobe and cerebellum sizes in children with autism. *Brain, 4,* 836–844.

Carrow-Woolfolk, E. (1999). *Comprehensive assessment of spoken language.* Circle Pines, MN: AGS Publishing.

Centers for Disease Control and Prevention (CDC). (February 9, 2007). Autism and developmental disabilities monitoring network. *Morbidity and Mortality Weekly Report, 6,* 12–28.

Charlop, M. H., & Milstein, J. P. (1989). Teaching autistic children conversational speech using video modeling. *Journal of Applied Behavior Analysis, 22,* 275–285.

Charlop, M. H., Schreibman, L., & Thibodeau, M. (1985). Increasing spontaneous verbal responding in children using a time delay procedure. *Journal of Applied Behavior Analysis, 18,* 155–166.

Charlop, M. H., & Trasowech, J. E. (1991). Increasing children's daily spontaneous speech. *Journal of Applied Behavior Analysis, 24,* 747–761.

Charlop, M. H., & Walsh, M. E. (1986). Increasing children's spontaneous verbalizations of affection: An assessment of time delay and peer modeling procedures. *Journal of Applied Behavior Analysis, 19,* 307–314.

Charlop-Christy, M., Carpenter, M., Le, L., LeBlanc, L., & Kellet, K. (2002). Using the Picture Exchange System (PECS) with children with autism: Assessment of PECS acquisition, speech, social-communicative behavior, and problem behavior. *Journal of Applied Behavioir Analysis, 35,* 213–231.

Charlop-Christy, M., & Daneshvar, S. (2003). Using video modeling to teach perspective taking to children with autism. *Journal of Positive Behavior Interventions, 5,* 12–21.

Charman, T., Baron-Cohen, S., Swettenham, J., Baird, G., Drew, A., & Cox, A. (2003). Predicting language outcome in infants with autism and pervasive developmental disorder. *International Journal of Language and Communication Disorders, 38*(3), 265–285.

Cohen, H., Amerine-Dickens, M., & Smith, T. (2006). Early intensive behavioral treatment: Replication of the UCLA model in a community setting. *Journal of Developmental & Behavioral Pediatrics, 27,* S145–S155.

Combating Autism Act. (2006). Pub. L. No. 109-416.

Courchesne, E., Carper, R., & Akshoomoff, N. (2003). Evidence of brain overgrowth in the first year of life in autism. *The Journal of the American Medical Association, 290,* 337–344.

Damasio, A. R., & Maurer, R. G. (1978). A neurological model for childhood autism. *Archives of Neurology, 35,* 777–786.

Dawson, G., & Osterling, J. (1997). The effectiveness of early intervention in autism. In M. J. Guralnick (Ed.), *The effectiveness of early intervention* (pp. 307–326). Baltimore, MD: Brookes.

Dyches, T. T., Wilder, L. K., Sudweeks, R. R., Obiakor, F. E., & Algozzine, B. (2004). Multicultural issues in autism. *Journal of Autism and Developmental Disorders, 34,* 211–222.

Eaves, R. C., & Milner, B. (1993). The criterion-related validity of the Childhood Autism Rating Scale and the Autism Behavior Checklist. *Journal of Abnormal Child Psychology, 21,* 481–491.

Eikeseth, S., Smith, T., Jahr, E., & Eldevik, S. (2007). Outcome for children with autism who began intensive behavioral treatment between ages 4 and 7: A comparison of controlled study. *Behavior Modification, 31,* 264–278.

Fenson, L., Dale, P., Reznick, S., Thal, D., Bates, E., Hartnug, J., et al. (2003). *The MacArthur–Bates Communicative Development Inventories*. Baltimore, MD: Brookes.

Garfin, D. G., McCallon, D., & Cox, R. (1988). Validity and reliability of the Childhood Autism Rating Scale with autistic adolescents. *Journal of Autism and Developmental Disorders, 21,* 417–432.

Ganz, J. B., & Simpson, R. L. (2004). Effects on communicative requesting and speech development of the picture exchange communication system in children with characteristics of autism. *Journal of Autism and Developmental Disorders, 34*(4), 395–409.

Geller, E., Yuwiler, A., Freeman, B. J., & Ritvo, E. (1988). Platelet size, number, and serotonin content in blood of autistic, childhood schizophrenic and normal children. *Journal of Autism and Developmental Disorders, 18,* 119–126.

Gerhardt, P. F., & Holmes, D. L. (2005). Employment: Options and issues for adolescents and adults with autism spectrum disorders. In F. R. Volkmar, R. Paul, A. Klin, & D. Cohen (Eds.), *Handbook of autism and pervasive developmental disorders: Vol. 2. Assessment, interventions, and policy* (3rd ed., pp. 1087–1101). Hoboken, NJ: Wiley.

Ghaziuddin, M., Sheldon, S., Tsai, L., & Alessi, N. (1993). Abnormalities of chromosome 18 in a girl with mental retardation and autistic disorder. *Journal of Intellectual Disability Research, 37,* 313–317.

Gilliam, J. E. (1995). *Gilliam Autism Rating Scale*. Austin, TX: PROED.

Gilliam, J. E. (2006). *Gilliam Autism Rating Scale* (2nd ed.). Austin, TX: PRO-ED.

Goldstein, H. (2002). Communication intervention for children with autism: A review of treatment efficacy. *Journal of Autism and Developmental Disorders, 32*(3), 373–396.

Gray, C. (2000). *The original social story^{TM} book: Illustrated edition*. Arlington, TX: Future Horizons.

Green, G. (2007). *Evidence-based practice and the California ASD guidelines/national standards projects*. Paper presented at the 2008 Autism Education Conference, Atlanta, GA.

Greenspan, S. I., & Wieder, S. (1997). Developmental patterns and outcomes in infants and children with disorders in relating and communicating: A chart review of 200 cases of children with autistic spectrum diagnoses. *Journal of Developmental and Learning Disorders, 1,* 87–141.

Greenspan, S. I., & Wieder, S. (1999). A functional developmental approach to autism spectrum disorders. *Journal of the Association for Persons with Severe Handicaps, 24,* 147–161.

Greenspan, S. I., & Wieder, S. (2006). *Review of engaging autism: Using the floortime approach to help children relate, communicate, and think*. Cambridge: De Capo Press.

Haas, R. H., Townsend, J., Courchesne, E., Lincoln, A. J., Schreibman, L., & Yeung-Courchesne, R. (1996). Neurological abnormalities in infantile autism. *Journal of Child Neurology, 11,* 84–92.

Hardan, A. Y., Minshew, N. J., Mallikarjuhn, M., & Keshavan, M. S. (2001). Brain volume in autism. *Journal of Child Neurology, 16,* 421–424.

Harris, S., Handelman, J., & Jennet, H. (2005). Models of education intervention for students with autism: Home, center, and school based programming. In

F. R. Volkmar, R. Paul, A. Klin, & D. Cohen (Eds.), *Handbook of autism and pervasive developmental disorders: Vol. 2. Assessment, interventions, and policy* (3rd ed., pp. 1043–1054). Hoboken, NJ: Wiley.

Hewitt, L. E. (2005). Evaluating treatment efficacy for language facilitation in autism. *Perspectives on School Based Issues, 6,* 21–25.

Ho, H. H., Eaves, L., & Peabody, D. (1997). Nutrient intake and obesity in children with autism. *Focus on Autism and Other Developmental Disabilities, 12,* 187–192.

Howlin, P. (2005). The effectiveness of interventions for children with autism. *Journal of Neural Transmission, 69* (Suppl.), 101–119.

Howlin, P., Gordon, R. K., Pasco, G., Wade, A., & Charman, T. (2007). The effectiveness of Picture Exchange Communication System (PECS) training for teachers of children with autism: A pragmatic, group randomized controlled trial. *Journal of Child Psychology and Psychiatry, 48*(5), 473–481.

Hunter, L. C., O'Hare, A., Herron, W. J., Fisher, L. A., & Jones, G. E. (2003). Opioid peptides and dipeptidyl peptidase in autism. *Developmental Medicine & Child Neurology, 45,* 121–128.

Hwang, B., & Hughes, C. (2000). The effects of social interactive training on early social communicative skills of children with autism. *Journal of Autism and Developmental Disorders, 30*(4), 331–343.

Individuals with Disabilities Education Improvement Act of 2004, Public Law 108–446 (IDEA Reauthorized). U.S. Statutes at Large 118 (2004), 2647.

Ingersoll, B., Dvortcsak, A., Whalen, C., & Sikora, D. (2005). The effects of a developmental, social-pragmatic language intervention on rate of expressive language production in young children with autistic spectrum disorders. *Focus on Autism and other Developmental Disabilities, 20,* 213–222.

Ingersoll, B., & Schreibman, L. (2006). Teaching reciprocal imitation skills to young children with autism using a naturalistic behavioral approach: Effects on language, pretend play, and joint attention. *Journal of Autism and Developmental Disorders, 36,* 487–505.

Kalyva, E., & Avramidis, E. (2005). Improving communication between children with autism and their peers through the "Circle of Friends": A small-scale intervention study. *Journal of Applied Research in Intellectual Disabilities, 18*(3), 253–261.

Kanner, L. (1943). Autistic disturbances of affective contact. *Nervous Child, 2,* 217–250.

Kasari, C., Freeman, S., & Paparella, T. (2006). Joint attention and symbolic play in young children with autism: A randomized controlled intervention study. *Journal of Child Psychology and Psychiatry, 47*(6), 611–620.

Kleinman, J. M., Robins, D. L., Ventola, P. E., Pandey, J., Boorstein, H. C., Esser, E., et al. (2008). The Modified Checklist for Autism in Toddlers: A follow-up study investigating the early detection of autism spectrum disorders. *Journal of Autism and Developmental Disorders, 38,* 827–839.

Koegel, R., Camarata, S., Koegel, L. B., Ben-Tall, A., & Smith, A. (1998). Increasing speech intelligibility in children with autism. *Journal of Autism and Developmental Disorders, 28,* 241–251.

Koegel, L. K., Carter, C., & Koegel, R. L. (2003). Teaching children with autism self-initiations as a pivotal response. *Topics in Language Disorders, 23*(2), 134–145.

Koegel, R. L., & Koegel, L. K. (2006). *Pivotal response treatments for autism*. Baltimore, MD: Brookes.

Koegel, R., O'Dell, M. C., & Koegel, L. K. (1987). A natural language paradigm for teaching nonverbal autistic children. *Journal of Autism and Developmental Disorders, 17*, 187–199.

Laski, K. E., Charlop, M., & Schreibman, L. (1988). Training parents to use the Natural Language Paradigm to increase their autistic child's speech. *Journal of Applied Behavior Analysis, 21*, 391–400.

Lord, C., & Corsello, C. (2005). Diagnostic instruments in autistic spectrum disorders. In F. Volkmar, R. Paul, A. Klin, & D. Cohen (Eds.), *Handbook of autism and pervasive developmental disorders, Vol. 2: Assessment, interventions, and policy* (pp. 730–731). Hoboken, NJ: Wiley.

Lord, C., & McGee, J. P. (2001). *Educating children with autism*. Washington, DC: National Academy Press.

Lord, C., & Paul, R. (1997). Language and communication in autism. In D. Cohen & F. Volkmar (Eds.), *Handbook of autism and pervasive developmental disorders* (2nd ed., pp. 195–225). New York: Wiley.

Lord, C., Risi, S., Lambrecht, L., Cook, E. H., Leventhal, B. L., DiLavore, P. C., et al. (2000). The Autism Diagnostic Observation Schedule–Generic: A standard measure of social and communication deficits associated with the spectrum of autism. *Journal of Autism and Developmental Disorders, 30*, 205–223.

Lord, C., Rutter, M., DiLavore, P., & Risi, S. (1999). *Autism Diagnostic Observation Schedule (ADOS) manual*. Los Angeles: Western Psychological Services.

Lord, C., Shulman, C., & DiLavore, P. C. (2004). Regression and word loss in autistic spectrum disorders. *Journal of Child Psychology and Psychiatry, 45*(5), 936–955.

Lovaas, V. (1977). *The autistic child: Language development through behavior modification*. New York: Irvington Press.

Madsen, K. M., Haviid, A., Vesteraard, M., Schendel, D., Wohlfart, J., Thorsen, P., Olsen, J., & Melbye, M. (2003). A population-based study of measles, mumps, and rubella vaccination and autism. *New England Journal of Medicine, 19*, 1477–1482.

Maione, L., & Mirenda, P. (2006). Effects of video modeling and video feedback on peer-directed social language skills of a child with autism. *Journal of Positive Behavior Interventions, 8*(2), 106–118.

McConachie, H., Randle, V., Hammal, D., & Le Couteur, A. (2005). A controlled trial of a training course for parents of children with suspected autism spectrum disorder. *Journal of Pediatrics, 147*(3), 335–340.

McGee, G. G., & Morrier, M. J. (2005). Preparation of autism specialists. In F. R. Volkmar, R. Paul, A. Klin, & D. Cohen (Eds.), *Handbook of autism and pervasive developmental disorders: Vol. 2. Assessment, interventions, and policy* (3rd ed., pp. 1123–1160). Hoboken, NJ: Wiley.

Minshew, N. J., Sweeney, J. A., Bauman, M. I., & Webb, S. J. (2005). Neurological aspects of autism. In F. R. Volkmar, R. Paul, A. Klin, & D. Cohen (Eds.), *Handbook of autism and pervasive developmental disorders: Vol. 2. Assessment, interventions, and policy* (3rd ed., pp. 473–514). Hoboken, NJ: Wiley.

Mirenda, P. (2003). Toward functional augmentative and alternative communication for students with autism: Manual signs, graphic symbols, and voice output communication aids. *Language, Speech, and Hearing Services in the Schools, 34,* 203–216.

Mundy, P., Hogan, A., & Doelring, P. (1996). *A preliminary manual for the abridged early social communication scales.* Coral Gables, FL: University of Miami.

National Research Council. (2001). *Educating children with autism.* Washington, DC: National Academy Press, Committee on Educational Interventions for Children with Autism, Division of Behavioiral and Social Sciences and Education.

Odom, S. L., Brown, W. H., Frey, T., Karasu, N., Smith-Canter, L. L., & Strain, P. S. (2003). Evidence-based practices for young children with autism: Contributions for single-subject design research. *Focus on Autism and Other Developmental Disabilities, 18*(3), 166–175.

Olswang, L., Stoel-Gammon, C., Coggins, T., & Carpenter, R. (1987). *Assessing prelinguistic and early linguistic behaviors in developmentally young children.* Seattle: University of Washington Press.

Paul, R. (2007). *Language disorders from infancy through adolescents: Assessment and intervention* (3rd ed.). St. Louis, MO: Mosby Elsevier.

Paul, R., & Sutherland, R. (2003). Asperger's syndrome: The role of speech-language pathologists in schools. *Perspectives on Language Learning and Education, 10*(3), 9–5.

Pierce, K., & Schreibman, L. (1995). Increasing complex social behaviors in children with autism: Effects of peer-implemented pivotal response training. *Journal of Applied Behavior Analysis, 23,* 265–295.

Prelock, P., Beatson, J., Botner, B., Brodner, C., & Drucker, A. (2003). Interdisciplinary assessment of young children with autism spectrum disorder. *Language, Speech, and Hearing Services in the Schools, 34,* 194–202.

Prendeville, J., Prelock, P. A., & Unwin, G. (2005). Peer play interventions to support the social competence of children with autism spectrum disorders (ASD). *Seminars in Speech and Language, 27*(1), 32–46.

Prizant, B. M., Wetherby, A. M., Rubin, E., & Laurent, A. C. (2003). The SCERTS Model: A transactional, family centered, approach to enhancing communication and socioemotional abilities of children with autism spectrum disorder. *Infants and Young Children, 16*(4), 296–316.

Prizant, B. M., Wetherby, A. M., & Rydell, P. J. (2000). Communication intervention issues for children with autism spectrum disorders. In A. M. Wetherby & B. M. Prizant (Eds.), *Autism spectrum disorders: A transactional developmental perspective* (pp. 193–224). Baltimore, MD: Brookes.

Quill, K. A. (1995). Enhancing children's social-communication in verbal children. In K. A. Quill (Ed.), *Teaching children with autism: Strategies to enhance communication and socialization* (pp. 163–184). New York: Delmar.

Rapin, I. (2005). Autism: Where we have been, where we are going. In F. R. Volkmar, R. Paul, Klin, & D. Cohen (Eds.), *Handbook of autism and pervasive developmental disorders: Vol. 2. Assessment, interventions, and policy* (3rd ed., pp. 1304–1317). Hoboken, NJ: Wiley.

Redcay, E., & Courchesne, E. (2005). When is the brain enlarged in autism? A meta-analysis of all brain size reports. *Biological Psychiatry, 58*, 1–9.

Rellini, E., Tortolani, D., Trillo, S., Carbone, S., & Montecchi, F. (2004). Childhood Autism Rating Scale (CARS) and Autism Behavior Checklist (ABC): Correspondence and conflicts with DSM-IV criteria in the diagnosis of autism. *Journal of Autism and Developmental Disorders, 34*, 703–708.

Remington, B., Hastings, R. P., Kovshoff, H., degli Espinosa, F., Jahr, E., et al. (2007). Early intensive behavioral intervention: Outcomes for children with autism and their parents after two years. *American Journal of Mental Retardation, 112*, 418–438.

Reynhout, G., & Carter, M. (2006). Social Stories for children with disabilities. *Journal of Autism and Developmental Disorders, 36*, 445–469.

Robins, D. L., Fein, D., Barton, M. L., & Green, J. A. (2001). The Modified Checklist for Autism in Toddlers: An initial study investigating the early detection of autism and pervasive developmental disorders. *Journal of Autism and Developmental Disorders, 31*, 131–144.

Rocha, M., Schreibman, L., & Stahmer, A. (2007). Effectiveness of training parents to teach joint attention in children with autism. *Journal of Early Intervention, 29*(2), 154–172.

Rogers, S. J. (2000) Interventions that facilitate socialization in children with autism. *Journal of Autism and Developmental Disorders, 30*, 399–409.

Rogers, S. J., & Bennetto, L. (2000). Intersubjectivity in autism: The roles of imitation and executive function. In A. M. Wetherby & B. M. Prizant (Eds.), *Autism spectrum disorders: A transactional developmental perspective* (pp. 79–108). Baltimore, MD: Brookes.

Rogers, S. J., Hayden, D., Hepburn, S., Charlifue-Smith, R., Hall, T. & Hayes, A. (2006). Teaching nonverbal children with autism useful speech: A pilot study of the Denver Model and PROMPT. *Journal of Autism and Developmental Disorders, 36*, 1007–1024.

Rosenwasser, B., & Axelrod, S. (2001). The contributions of applied behavior analysis to the education of people with autism. *Behavior Modification, 25*, 671–677.

Santarelli, G., Koegel, R., Casas, J. M., & Koegel, L. K. (2001). Culturally diverse families participating in behavior therapy parent education programs for children with developmental disabilities. *Journal of Positive Behavior Interactions, 3*(2), 120–123.

Schertz, H. H., & Odom, S. L. (2007). Promoting joint attention in toddlers with autism: A parent-mediated developmental model. *Journal of Autism and Developmental Disorders, 37*(8), 1562–1575.

Scheuermann, B., & Webber, J. (2002). *Autism: Teaching does make a difference.* Belmont, CA: Wadsworth/Thomson.

Schlosser, R. W., & Lee, D. L. (2000). Promoting generalization and maintenance in augmentative and alternative communication: A meta-analysis of 20 years of effectiveness research. *AAC: Augmentative and Alternative Communication, 16*(4), 208–226.

Schlosser, R. W., & Wendt, O. (2008). Effects of augmentative and alternative communication intervention on speech production in children with autism: A systematic review. *American Journal of Speech-Language Pathology, 17,* 212–230.

Schopler, E., Reichler, R. J., DeVellis, R. F., & Daly, K. (1980). Toward objective classification on childhood autism: Childhood Autism Rating Scale (CARS). *Journal of Autism and Developmental Disorders, 10,* 91–103.

Schopler, E., Reichler, R. J., & Renner, B. R. (1986). *The Childhood Autism Ratings Scale (CARS) for diagnostic screening and classification of autism.* New York: Irvington.

Schreck, K. A., Williams, K., & Smith, A. F. (2004). A comparison of eating behaviors between children with and without autism. *Journal of Autism and Developmental Disorders, 34,* 433–438.

Scott, J., & Baldwin, W. (2005). The challenge of early intensive intervention. In D. Zager (Ed.), *Autism spectrum disorders: Identification, education, and treatment* (3rd ed., pp. 173–228). Mahwah, NJ: Erlbaum.

Seltzer, M. M., Krauss, M. W., Shattuck, P. T., Orsmond, G., Swe, A., & Lord, C. (2003). The symptoms of autism spectrum disorders in adolescence and adulthood. *Journal of Autism and Developmental Disorders, 33,* 565–581.

Semel, E., Wiig, E. H., & Secord, W. (1987). *Clinical Evaluation of Language Fundamentals-Revised.* Dallas, TX: Psychological Corporation.

Sevin, J. A., Matson, J. L., Coe, D. A., Fee, V. E., & Sevin, B. M. (1991). A comparison and evaluation of three commonly used autism scales. *Journal of Autism and Developmental Disorders, 21,* 417–432.

Sheinkopf, S., Mundy, P., Oller, D. K., & Steffens, M. (2000). Vocal atypicalities of preverbal autistic children. *Journal of Autism and Developmental Disorders, 28,* 15–23.

Shriberg, L. D., Paul, R., McSweeny, J. L. Klin, A., Cohen, D. J., & Volkmar, F. R. (2001). Speech and prosody characteristics of adolescents and adults with high-functioning autism and Asperger syndrome. *Journal of Speech, Language and Hearing Research, 44,* 1097–1115.

Siegel, B. (2004). *Pervasive Developmental Disorders Screening Test* (2nd ed.). San Antonio, TX: Psychological Corporation.

Simpson, R. L. (2005). *Autism spectrum disorders: Interventions and treatments for children and youth.* Thousand Oaks, CA: Corwin Press.

Simpson, R. L., & Myles, B. S. (1993). Successful integration of children and youth with autism in mainstreamed settings. *Focus on Autistic Behavior, 7,* 1–12.

Skinner, B. F. (1938). *The behavior of organisms: An experimental analysis.* New York: Appleton-Century-Crofts.

Smith, V., Mirenda, P., & Zaidman-Zait, A. (2007). Predictors of expressive vocabulary growth in children with autism. *Journal of Speech-Language Hearing Research, 50,* 149–160.

South, M., Williams, B. J., McMahon, W. M., Owely, T., Filipek, P. A., & Shernoff, E. (2002). Utility of the Gilliam Autism Rating Scale in research and clinical populations. *Journal of Autism and Developmental Disorders, 32,* 593–599.

Sparks, B. F., Friedman, S. D., Shaw, D. W., Aylward, E. H., Echelard, D., Artru, A. A., et al. (2002). Brain structural abnormalities in young children with autism spectrum disorder. *Neurology, 59,* 184–192.

Stahmer, A. (1995). Teaching symbolic play skills to children with autism using pivotal response training. *Journal of Autism and Developmental Disorders, 25,* 123–141.

Stahmer, A. (1999). Using pivotal response training to facilitate appropriate play in children with autistic-spectrum disorders. *Child Language Teaching and Therapy, 15* (1), 29–40.

Stahmer, A. C. (2007). The basic structure of community early intervention programs for children with autism: Provider descriptions. *Journal of Autism and Developmental Disorders, 37*(7), 1344–1354.

Stone, W. L., Coonrod, E. E., Turner, L. M., & Pozdol, S. L. (2004). Psychometric properties of the STAT for early autism screening. *Journal of Autism and Developmental Disorders, 34,* 691–701.

Stone, W. L., & Ousley, O. Y. (1997). *Screening tool for autism in two-year-olds.* Nashville, TN: Vanderbilt University.

Sussman, F. (1999). *More than words: Helping parents promote communication and social skills in children with autism spectrum disorders.* Toronto. Ontario: A Hanen Centre Publication.

Taylor, B. A., & Harris, S. L. (1995). Teaching children with autism to seek information: Acquisition of novel information and generalization of responding. *Journal of Applied Behavior Analysis, 28,* 3–14.

Taylor, B., Miller, E., Lingham, R., Andrews, N., Simmons, A., & Stowe, J. (2002). Measles, mumps, and rubella vaccination and bowel problems or developmental regression in children with autism: Population study. *British Medical Journal, 324,* 393–396.

Teal, M. B., & Wiebe, M. J. (1986). A validity analysis of selected instruments used to assess autism. *Journal of Autism and Developmental Disorders, 16,* 485–494.

Tincani, M., Crozier, S., & Alazett, S. (2006). The picture exchange communication system: Effects on demanding and speech development for school-aged children with autism. *Journal of Autism and Developmental Disorders, 37,* 1803–1814.

Toth, K., Munson, J., Meltzoff, A. N., & Dawson, G. (2006). Early predictors of communication development in young children with autism spectrum disorder: Joint attention, imitation, and toy play. *Journal of Autism and Developmental Disorders, 36,* 993–1005.

Tsai, L. Y. (2005). Recent neurobiological research in autism. In D. Zager (Ed.), *Autism spectrum disorders: Identification, education, and treatment* (3rd ed., pp. 47–87). NJ: Erlbaum.

Turner, L. M., Stone, W. L., Pozdol, S. L., & Coonrod, E. E. (2006). Follow-up of children with autism spectrum disorders from age 2 to 9. *Autism, 10,* 243–265.

United States Department of Education, 24th Annual Report to Congress of the Implementation of the Individuals with Disabilities Education Act (2002).

United States Department of Health and Human Services (1999). *Mental health: A report of the surgeon general.* Rockville, MD: Author.

van Kleek, A. (1994). Potential cultural bias in training parents as conversational partners with their children who have delays in language development. *American Journal of Speech-Language Pathology, 3,* 67–78.

Verstraeten, T., Davis, R. L., DeStefano, F., Lieu, T. A., Rhodes, P. H., Black, S. B., Shinefield, H., & Chen, R. T. (2003). Safety of thimerosal-containing vaccines: A two-phased study of a computerized health maintenance organization data base. *Pediatrics, 112,* 1039–1048.

Volkmar, F. R., & Klin, A. (2005). Issues in classification of autism and related conditions. In F. Volkmar, R. Paul, A. Klin, & D. Cohen (Eds.). *Handbook on autism and pervasive developmental disorders* (3rd ed., Vol. 1, pp. 5–41). Hoboken, NJ: Wiley.

Watson, L. R., & Flippin, M. (2008). Language outcomes for young children with autism spectrum disorders. *The ASHA Leader, 13*(7), 8–12.

Wetherby, A., & Prizant, B. (2003). *Communication and Symbolic Behavior Scales— Developmental Profiles.* Baltimore: MD: Brookes.

Wetherby, A. M., Prizant, B. M., & Hutchinson, T. (1998). Communicative, social-affective, and symbolic profiles of young children with autism and pervasive developmental disorder. *American Journal of Speech-Language Pathology, 7,* 79–91.

Wetherby, A. M., Prizant, B. M., & Schuler, A. L. (2000). Understanding the nature of communication and language impairments. In A. M. Wetherby & B. M. Prizant (Eds.), *Autism spectrum disorders: A transactional developmental perspective* (pp. 109–142). Baltimore, MD: Brookes.

Wetherby, A. M., Woods, J., Allen, L., Cleary, J., Dickinson, H., & Lord, C. (2004). Early indicators of autism spectrum disorders in the second year of life. *Journal of Autism and Developmental Disorders, 34,* 473–493.

Wiig, E., & Secord, W. (1989). *Test of Language Competence-expanded edition.* San Antonio, TX: Harcourt Assessment.

Wilder, L. K., Dyches, T. T., Obiakor, F. E. & Anzelone, B. (2004). Multicultural perspectives on teaching students with autism. *Focus on Autism and Other Developmental Disabilities, 19,* 105–113.

Wolfensberger, W. (1972). *The principle of normalization in human services.* Toronto: National Institute on Mental Retardation.

Woods, J. J., & Wetherby, A. M. (2003). Early identification of and intervention for infants and toddlers who are at risk for autism spectrum disorder. *Language, Speech, and Hearing Services in the Schools, 34,* 180–193.

World Health Organization. (2005). *International statistical classification of diseases and health related problems-ICD-10* (2nd ed.). Geneva, Switzerland: Author.

Yoder, P., & Stone, W. L. (2006a). A randomized comparison of the effect of two prelinguistic communication interventions on the acquisition of spoken communication in preschoolers with ASD. *Journal of Speech, Language, and Hearing Research, 49,* 698–711.

Yoder, P., & Stone, W. L. (2006b). Randomized comparison of two communication interventions for preschoolers with autism spectrum disorders. *Journal of Counseling and Clinical Psychology. 74*(5), 426–435.

CHAPTER 18

Health-Impaired

MOLLY L. NOZYCE
AND ROY GRANT

E VERY CHILD'S DEVELOPMENTAL course is intimately related to his or her
health and medical condition as well as interactions with the environment. These factors together contribute to the child's cognitive and
social outcomes and eventual academic and life success. To understand how
and why children develop the way they do, their development must be
viewed in a context that includes any genetic, neurobiological, or medical
condition that may affect them. When assessments are done, the evaluation
of a child's strengths and weaknesses and choice of intervention techniques
best suited to the child's developmental profile must take these conditions
into account.

It is estimated that up to 15% of infants are at risk for developmental delays,
primarily due to their birth weight and gestational age (Widerstrom &
Nichol, 1997). About one child in five with any type of medical impairment
will need developmental intervention including special education services
(Msall et al., 2003). This chapter will examine the most common medical
conditions associated with infant and early childhood developmental delays
and the role of the Early Intervention (EI) program in obtaining therapeutic
services for these infants and children. Over time, EI has become the principle
provider of developmental assessment and intervention for infants and
toddlers birth to 36 months of age. As EI programs are typically outside of
medical systems of care, psychologists and other practitioners often encounter
infants and young children with complex medical conditions. The most
common medical conditions observed in EI programs will be reviewed, highlighting information that is relevant to the developmental assessment of
medically involved infants and young children. Perhaps the most important
point to be made in serving this population is that clinicians who perform
developmental evaluations and provide intervention services need to coordinate their work with the child's medical providers in a *medical home*

model. The medical home model was developed to describe best practices in providing care to children with special care needs. The key elements of this model are that the care delivered is comprehensive, coordinated, compassionate, family centered, and culturally relevant (Cooley & McAllister, 2004).

THE EARLY INTERVENTION PROGRAM

The right to a free, appropriate public education was guaranteed to children with special needs 3–21 years of age in 1975 through federal legislation. This right was subsequently expanded to include infants and toddlers within the Individuals with Disabilities Education Act ([IDEA]; reauthorized 2004). Part C of IDEA is the legislative basis for the Early Intervention Program (EI).

Under IDEA, pediatricians and other medical professionals who care for infants and toddlers are considered *primary referral sources* required to promptly refer children suspected of a developmental delay to their local EI program. If parents accept the referral, EI provides a multidisciplinary evaluation to determine eligibility for developmental intervention services. The evaluation must cover five developmental domains: adaptive, motor, cognitive, communication, and social-emotional.

While this program structure facilitates access to care, it has also led to developmental intervention frequently being fragmented from health care. This may be a significant problem for infants and toddlers who are *medically involved*, that is, who have a primary medical diagnosis with which developmental delay is associated (Grant, 2005). A small subgroup of children with special health care needs is considered to be *medically fragile*. This term generally refers to infants and children who need special assistance, often including assistive technology, in activities of daily living (e.g., eating, breathing; Buescher, Whitmire, Brunssen, & Kluttz-Hile, 2006).

PREMATURITY AND LOW BIRTH WEIGHT

The most commonly occurring medical condition associated with infant and early childhood developmental delay is prematurity/low birth weight. The Centers for Disease Control and Prevention (CDC) reports that in 2005, 12.7% of U.S. births were premature (< 37 weeks gestation), representing more than 525,000 infants. Only 3.6% of births (~150,000) were less than 34 weeks gestation. The Institute of Medicine of the National Academies (2007) reports that the highest rate of prematurity occurred among African-Americans (17.8% in 2003).

Prematurity is associated with low birth weight (LBW), which the World Health Organization defines as $\leq 2,500$ grams. Low birth weight is additionally classified as *very low birth weight* (VLBW), from 1,001 to 1,500 grams, and *extremely low birth weight* (ELBW), ≤ 1,000 grams. Neonates weighing between 501 and 1,500 grams (representing virtually all viable ELBW and VLBW neonates) comprise less than 2% of live births. Low birth weight is a major risk factor for infant death; however, there has been recent improvement in the survival rate of LBW neonates especially among those weighing 800 grams or less. This increased survival, attributable to new techniques and technologies in neonatal intensive care units (NICUs), is associated with increased incidence of central nervous system (CNS) anomalies and developmental disabilities associated with such low weight births. These include mental retardation, cerebral palsy, sensorineural hearing loss, blindness, and epilepsy (Aylward, 2005; Godenberg & Culhane, 2007).

Gestational age refers to the number of weeks that the neonate was in utero prior to birth. It is calculated relative to the date of the mother's last menstrual period. *Small for gestational age* (SGA) refers to neonates who are smaller than typical based on their gestational age and includes those with *intrauterine growth retardation* (IUGR). Risk of an SGA birth is associated with maternal chronic hypertension and maternal age (teenage or over 36 years old; Catov, Nohr, Olsen, & Nexx, 2008). Babies born SGA are at higher risk of congenital heart defects and other medical problems associated with extreme prematurity (Bardin, Zelkowitz, & Papageorgiou, 1997; Malik et al., 2007).

Premature birth, especially 32 weeks gestation or fewer, is associated with a variety of neonatal morbidities. These include *bronchopulmonary dysplasia* (BPD, also referred to as chronic lung disease), *intraventricular hemorrhage* (IVH, a bleed inside or around the ventricles, which is graded from 1 to 4 based on severity), sepsis (an inflammatory state caused by infection), and *retinopathy of prematurity* (ROP, caused by abnormal growth of blood vessels in the retina which may bleed causing retinal scarring and sometimes retinal detachment). Premature infants generally require more intensive pediatric care than do full-term infants (Wade et al., 2008).

Wang and colleagues (2006) published recommendations of an expert panel for neurodevelopmental follow-up of VLBW children. These include pediatric follow-up in high-risk infant clinics if available and education of primary care providers in the special needs of the population; ophthalmology exams to rule out ROP; hearing screening in addition to any newborn screening that may have taken place; formal developmental assessments before 15 months of age and again around 24 months of age; timely provision of physical therapy if indicated; psychoeducational testing for ELBW infants at least by preschool age; and psychosocial family assessment with referral for any needed services.

These recommendations reflect the extensive evidence that premature infants are at high risk of developmental and learning problems. One study of developmental outcomes of premature infants (< 30 weeks' gestation) found that at 5.5 years of age, 61% had a delay or disability, with 44% having delays in multiple domains. Multiple disabilities were associated with lower birth weight, BPD, and neurodevelopmental delay at 24 months of age (van Baar, van Wassenaer, Briet, Dekker, & Kok, 2005). These results are similar to a large population-based study ($N = 170,874$), which found a strong association between lower birth weight and developmental delays established through multidisciplinary evaluation or relevant medical diagnosis (genetic, metabolic, neurologic, and attachment disorders) during the first 3 years of life. Seventy percent of infants born at 450–749 grams had developmental delays or disabilities, as did 56% with birth weight between 750 and 999 grams. The disability rate fell to 36% for infants with birth weight between 1,000 and 1,499 grams (Thompson et al., 2003), for whom number of days on oxygen and IVH were predictors of poor neurologic and/or cognitive outcomes (Piecuch, Leonard, & Cooper, 1998). For moderately low birth weight babies (1,500–2,499 grams), psychosocial factors such as maternal education had a greater impact on developmental outcomes than did birth weight (Boardman, Powers, Padilla, & Hummer, 2002).

Signs of atypical motor development are the most prominent developmental finding among premature infants during the first year of life. These may be transient in nature but are more likely to persist and involve delayed acquisition of motor milestones if characterized by *hypotonia* (weak or floppy muscle tone; Fetters, 1996).

Although birth weight has been found to have a significant impact on an infant's development, gestational age is also critical. Even babies born between 34 and 36 weeks gestation have been found to be at higher risk for mortality and morbidity including respiratory distress, apnea, feeding difficulties, and hearing loss. These neonates are physiologically immature and do not adapt as readily to their environment as do full-term babies (Engle, Tomashek, Wallman, & Committee on Fetus and Newborn, 2007; Raju, 2007).

Prematurity continues to impact a child's development well into the school-age years. Children born prematurely are at higher risk for both learning and behavior problems than those born full term. In particular, specific learning disabilities and attention deficit hyperactivity disorder (ADHD) are seen significantly more often in preemies than in children born at full term (Larroque et al., 2008; Shum, Neulinger, I'Callaghan, & Mohay, 2008)

CORRECTION FOR PREMATURITY

When assessing premature or other medically involved infants, it is important to fully describe qualitative issues such as muscle tone anomalies and their impact on functionality. For the purpose of scoring a formal assessment instrument administered to a premature infant or toddler, it is often suggested that a *corrected* or *adjusted* age be used as the basis for scoring.

Corrected age is derived by subtracting the number of months premature from the child's chronological age in months. For example, a toddler born at 28 weeks gestation and chronological age 18 months at the time of evaluation would be considered to be 15 months old for the purpose of scoring a standardized test (18 months minus 3 months to correct for prematurity).

Correction, if done, usually continues through chronological age 24 months. Correction for prematurity, however, does not take into account qualitative differences in motor and other functioning between very premature infants and typically developing full-term infants. A typically developing infant is capable of picking up a block deftly and would be scored as passing that item on a standardized test. A child with issues related to muscle tone and/or other neurological problems may also be able to pick up a block, but might not do so deftly and with age-appropriate coordination. Physical and/or occupational therapy may be clinically indicated for this child even though the developmental milestone has minimally been met. The evaluation report should reflect the fact that the milestone was met and also describe the specific issues that were observed to negatively affect functionality (e.g., muscle tone anomalies, poorly coordinated movements, tremulousness, etc.). This constitutes the use of *informed clinical opinion* to supplement standardized test scores in determining eligibility for EI services (Aylward, 1997).

Standardized developmental assessments for infants are very motor loaded with many test items requiring use of fine or gross motor skills. Although important, motor skills are only one component of development. By focusing on motor milestones the evaluator may overestimate the premature infant's overall developmental abilities. It is also important to assess the infant's ability to achieve homeostasis, which relates to how well the infant can regulate state and adapt to the environment. Premature infants have particular difficulty with these tasks due to physical immaturities, especially in the central nervous and gastrointestinal systems. This causes difficulties in their ability to integrate and process stimuli and manage transitions. These issues may subsequently lead to long-term difficulties in development. Focusing on these qualitative issues is particularly important when developmental assessment is done for a program in which eligibility for intervention is based on degree of developmental delay, such as EI. Correction for prematurity without examining the underlying precursors to development may prevent needed interventions from being provided (Wilson & Cradock, 2004).

MOTOR DELAY AND CEREBRAL PALSY

Infant motor impairments may be classified into one of four disorders: static, progressive, spinal cord/peripheral nerve disorders, and anatomical structural defects. Static central nervous system (CNS) disorders are caused either by anomalous fetal development or a postnatal insult such as infection or trauma. Progressive diseases of the brain or nerves are associated with motor dysfunction and include muscular dystrophy, spinal muscular atrophy, and certain tumors. Spinal cord/peripheral nerve disorders include spina bifida, a congenital malformation affecting neural tube closure that is generally not fully resolved surgically. Anatomical structural defects and deformities include orthopedic impairments like clubfoot and more serious disorders like childhood arthritis (Blasco, 1995).

Motor delays are also associated with medical impairments, including congenital organ anomalies. Infants with serious cardiac conditions such as *tetralogy of Fallot* (characterized by multiple defects including a hole between the ventricles and heart muscle anomalies) may require extensive rehabilitation services for motor delays that are in part associated with their relative immobility while hospitalized. Regardless of the medical condition, social-emotional delays may occur in these children as a result of possible disruptions to the parent-child relationship. This may be due to heightened parental anxiety in reaction to the nature and urgency of their child's medical needs and to periods of separation while the child is hospitalized, possibly for months at a time (Weinberg, Kern, Weiss, & Ross, 2001). Cardiac surgery during the first year of life is significantly associated with lower scores on neurodevelopmental testing and abnormalities on neurological examination (Dittrich et al., 2003).

Cerebral palsy (CP) is a disorder of muscle control or coordination resulting from malfunctioning of or damage to the brain. CP affects a child's motor abilities, and may also affect communication, cognition, and/or adaptive behavior skills. The prevalence of CP has been estimated at 2 cases per 1,000 live births, about evenly distributed between premature and full-term infants. The risk of CP increases with decreasing gestational age and is highest among extreme preterm infants (less than 27 weeks gestation), where prevalence may be as high as 19%. The incidence of CP has increased as the survival rate of extremely preterm, ELBW infants has improved (Allen, 2008; Himpens, Van den Broeck, Oostra, Calders, & Vanhaesebrouck, 2008).

Perinatal asphyxia or hypoxia (a period immediately after birth during which there was insufficient oxygen to the brain), SGA birth, inflammation of the placenta, infections, and multiple birth status are risk factors for CP. Up to 10% of cases of CP have a postnatal cause such as traumatic brain injury, meningitis, encephalitis, and stroke. Among premature and LBW infants, the need for assisted ventilation is a significant risk factor. Mental retardation is diagnosed in more than half of individuals with CP (Graziani et al., 1992; Nelson, 1996).

Common motor problems that characterize CP are spasticity (increased resistance to muscle stretch), which affects 65% of children with CP, and ataxia (poor coordination of voluntary movements), which affects about 10% of children with CP. Involuntary stereotypical movements (dyskinesia) is noted in 19% of children with CP. These neurological deficits may impair gross and fine motor functioning, including walking and later writing, as well as adaptive functioning (e.g., self-feeding, swallowing). Cerebral palsy is classified based on the specific nature of movement, muscle tone anomalies, and limbs that are involved. In addition, children with CP may have visual impairment due to cranial nerve deficits that affect eye movements (Palmer & Hoon, 1995).

Because of the dynamic nature of infant growth and development, diagnosis of CP prior to 1 year of age may not be appropriate. Through chronological age 7 months, apparent neurological abnormalities among preterm infants are common and often resolve by 12 months of age. A typical example is transient dystonia, which is characterized by increased extensor muscle tone and persistent primitive reflexes. Monitoring high-risk neonates (e.g., through enrollment in NICU follow-up clinics) allows for ongoing developmental monitoring and accurate diagnosis of up to 90% of cases of CP by 24 months of age (O'Shea, 2002).

While there is no single specific neurological deficit predictive of a later diagnosis of CP, there are specific signs that may be observed early and, if observed, should lead to continued monitoring with diagnostic assessment by 24 months of age. While scopes of practice for the professions vary among the states, CP is typically a diagnosis made by a physician. Primary care pediatricians may make the diagnosis, but, especially for former premature infants, evaluation by a developmental pediatrician, psychiatrist, or neurologist is recommended. Signs that warrant further diagnostic assessment include neck hyperextension and shoulder retraction, abnormal trunk muscle tone, abnormal extremity (arm and leg) muscle tone, asymmetrical movement, tremulousness, fisting (inability to keep hands open), inability to bear weight on forearms in a prone position, and difficulty balancing the head while in a sitting position. Standardized tests of motor development such as the Movement Assessment of Infants (MAI), the Alberta Infant Motor Scale (AIMS), and the Test of Infant Motor Performance (TIMP) may be useful in the early identification of infants who should be referred to rule out CP (Harris, 1991; Spittle, Doyle, & Boyd, 2008).

Before beginning physical or occupational therapy, the EI service provider requires a medical prescription specifying the frequency (number of sessions per week) and duration (number of minutes per session) of therapy. The American Academy of Pediatrics (AAP, 1999) recommends that pediatricians asked to write therapy prescriptions specify the cause of developmental delay, if known, including any underlying medical diagnosis. If the infant has special medical needs, AAP considers the pediatrician to be responsible for specifying any adverse reactions that may be associated with movement and/or specific therapeutic interventions, and for recommending precautions to ensure that the child is safely handled. Infants with motor delays and/or tonal anomalies require ongoing surveillance and periodic developmental reassessment to ensure that any emerging cognitive and/or communication delays are identified, and that any other intervention services newly found to be appropriate are also provided (New York State Department of Health [NYSDOH] Early Intervention, n.d.).

The NYSDOH Early Intervention Program convened an expert panel to review the evidence for efficacy of motor therapy interventions. Their findings are included in the NYSDOH Clinical Practice Guideline for Motor Disorders. The panel's recommendations emphasize the need to involve parents in establishing treatment goals; the integration of activities that promote cognitive growth in the delivery of therapies to remediate motor deficits; the use of techniques that lend themselves to the development of skills useful in multiple environments; interventions to provide the child with alternative strategies to facilitate motor function while preventing compensatory strategies that may impede developmental progress; prevention of problems secondary to atypical postures; and assurance that parents have the information they need to understand and manage their infant's needs at home. In early infancy, they recommend therapists focus on activities including tactile exploration of the infant's own body; orientation to midline; symmetrical rolling; managing transitions (prone to supine, horizontal to vertical when developmentally appropriate); and play activities to strengthen abdomen, neck, hip, and trunk (NYSDOH Clinical Practice Guideline, n.d.).

DYSPHAGIA (FEEDING DISORDERS)

Feeding disorders are pervasive among developmentally delayed infants. The cause is often hypotonia accompanied by weak muscles around the mouth, leading to feeding, chewing, and swallowing disorders. More serious feeding disorders are associated with poor health and nutrition status (American Thoracic Society Documents, 2003; Fung et al., 2002; Schwarz, 2003).

The epidemiology of feeding disorders is not well known, with data collection hindered by inconsistent definitions and diagnostic criteria (Lefton-Greif & Arvedson, 2007). There are two distinct types of dysphagia—oropharyngeal and esophageal. *Oropharygeal dysphagia* is characterized by difficulty initiating swallow once food is in the mouth and is associated with conditions including muscle inflammation or abnormality and neuromuscular diseases like myasthenia gravis. *Esophageal dysphagia* manifests immediately after attempting to swallow food and may involve greater difficulty swallowing liquids. The child may regurgitate liquids through the nose, choke, cough, drool, and so on.

Esophageal dysphagia for both solids and liquids is associated with neuro-muscular disorders.

Medical tests, such as videofluoroscopic or barium swallowing studies for oropharyngeal dysphagia and manometry (measurement of pressure in the lower esophagus) for esophageal dysphagia help identify the cause of these conditions. Treatment planning should follow identification of the specific cause of the feeding disorder (Alper & Studt, 2007).

Because services to infants and young children with disabilities are increasingly provided through IDEA programs, the location for delivery of feeding therapies has shifted from medical settings to home, community, and school settings. This shift in service delivery models has brought with it several challenges. These include the need for evidence-based treatments and the necessity to balance feeding therapies with other aspects of the child's health (nutrition, hydration, pulmonary health). It is essential that parents be accurately informed of the effects and possible unintended side effects of any treatment and provided information regarding the credentials and skill level of the therapist working with the child. Clinicians must work within their scope of practice, training and expertise. When EI services for feeding are authorized, it must be specified that the professional—whether a speech–language pathologist, occupational therapist or nurse—be specifically trained in feeding therapy (Arvedson & Lefton-Greif, 2007).

One study of the needs of parents of children receiving feeding therapy revealed that more training for speech–language pathologists is necessary in providing interventions for dysphagia. Other areas that may need improvement are clinicians' ability to instruct parents in interventions that they can do with their children to improve feeding/swallowing abilities, and coordination of these interventions with the child's medical providers (Stoner, Bailey, Angell, Robbins, & Polewski, 2006).

SEIZURE DISORDER

According to the CDC, a seizure may be characterized as abnormal electrical activity in the brain that causes involuntary changes in body movement or function, sensation, awareness, or behavior. Epilepsy is a disorder defined by recurrent seizures. While an estimated 5% of children will have at least one seizure before the age of 20, only one-fourth of them will meet criteria for a diagnosis of epilepsy. The lifetime prevalence of epilepsy (ever having been diagnosed with epilepsy) in the United States is 3% from infancy through age 80 (CDC, 2008; MacAllister & Schaeffer, 2007). Estimates of the current prevalence of childhood epilepsy (defined as having had a seizure within the past 5 years or having a seizure disorder controlled by medication, for children through age 15) range from 4 to 9 per 1,000. About one-third of children with epilepsy have a functional developmental disability such as mental retardation or cerebral palsy (Murphy, Trevathan, & Yeargin-Allsopp, 1995).

Seizures occur in up to 3.5% of newborns, with the highest incidence occurring among VLBW and ELBWs. Often, these neonatal seizures are brief and the signs subtle so they may be missed by even trained observers. Some neonatal seizure activity can only be identified if the newborn is monitored on an electroencephalograph (EEG). Generally, neonatal seizures are indicative of some level of brain injury. They often cease in a short period of time (within a few days to a few weeks). Protracted neonatal seizures are suggestive of possible inborn metabolic disorder (Nordille & De Vivo, 2002; Tharp, 2002).

Childhood epilepsy is classified into a number of defined syndromes and conditions. *West syndrome* (infantile spasms) begins during the first year of life, typically at 4–6 months of age. Infantile spasms may be *symptomatic* (with a clear cause, such as microcephaly or cerebral atrophy), *cryptogenic* (symptomatic of another neurological disorder but with no identified etiology to the seizures), or *idiopathic* (no identified cause to the seizures and no identified neurological disorder). There are three markers associated with this diagnosis: spasms, psychomotor deterioration, and a specific EEG finding (hypsarrhythmia, a very disorganized brain wave pattern). Infantile spasms are generally controlled with corticosteroids or other medication (e.g., benzodiazepines). *Severe myoclonic epilepsy,* which begins in infancy, is not well controlled with medication and is associated with developmental delay. *Lennox–Gastaut syndome* (LGS) is rare (1–2 new cases per 100,000 children) and characterized by different types of seizure activity and in most cases mental retardation.

Petit mal seizures are brief in duration. They have more recently been called *absence seizures* and when considered a syndrome (childhood absence epilepsy) are sometimes referred to as pyknolepsy. Accounting for up to 11% of all seizure disorders (adult and child), absence seizures are typically well controlled with medication. *Partial seizures* may be simple or complex and also may be of primary (genetic or congenital) or secondary (acquired) etiology. In partial seizures, the child retains consciousness throughout the duration of seizure activity. *Benign epilepsy* (also called benign Rolandic epilepsy) is the most common childhood epilepsy seizure disorder. It is characterized by primary partial seizures. Typical age of onset is in middle childhood, 8–10 years, although it may be diagnosed in children as young as 3 years old. In controlled developmental testing, children with benign epilepsy did as well as a comparison sample of children without epilepsy in most areas but showed deficits in verbal fluency, verbal memory, and planning. They were reported to be distractible with shorter attention spans, impulsivity, and sometimes mood swings. In rare instances, partial seizures are diagnosed as

Kojenikow's syndrome, in which seizure activity lasts for days or longer. This may be due to tumors, traumatic brain injury, or other underlying causes.

Rasmussen's syndrome also may begin in early childhood; its etiology unknown and it is associated with progressive cognitive impairment. *Landau–Kleffner syndrome* is rare and is characterized by loss of speech–language abilities and in most cases seizures. With treatment, language functioning may be recovered, especially in children who had stronger baseline language skills. Grand mal seizures are now referred to as *generalized tonic-clonic seizures* (GTC) and typically do not manifest until later in childhood (after age 10; MacAllister & Schaffer, 2007; Morton & Pellock, 2000). Seizure activity that lasts more than 30 minutes is referred to as *status epilepticus* and, when it occurs, should be viewed as a medical emergency (Kuntz, 1996).

Seizures occur among children with a variety of developmental disabilities including mental retardation, with greater severity of retardation associated with increased frequency of seizures (Richardson, Koller, & Katz, 1980). Seizures during infancy are associated with a higher risk of a later diagnosis of autism spectrum disorders (ASD; Saemundsen, Ludvigsson, Hilmarsdottir, & Rarnsson, 2007). About one-fourth of children diagnosed with epilepsy have a learning disability; most often, these seizures are idiopathic (Beghi, Cornaggia, Frigeni, & Beghi, 2007).

GENETIC SYNDROMES

Genes are the medium by which traits are inherited from generation to generation. Every human cell (except the ovum and sperm) contains 46 chromosomes (23 pairs, one each from the mother and father). The 23rd pair determines the child's sex. When there is a mutation or other chemical abnormality in a single gene or gene pair, the result is a genetic disorder. These include a wide range of genetic syndromes and birth defects (Nichickel & Widerstrom, 1997).

Down syndrome, the most commonly occurring genetic syndrome, is generally identified shortly after birth. Recognizable characteristics include hypotonia, *open mouth posture* with the mouth open and tongue protruding, and craniofacial abnormalities affecting the nose (small, with low bridge), eyes (speckling of the iris), ears (small, with small or absent lobes), short neck, wide gap between the fingers and toes, and other characteristic physical features. Most cases of Down syndrome result from trisomy 21, which means that each cell in the body has three copies of the chromosome 21 instead of the usual two copies. As is the case with many syndromes, Down syndrome is associated with mental retardation as well as a range of medical problems, including congenital heart defects, hearing loss, sleep apnea, hip abnormalities, visual impairment, and digestive problems (Jones, 2006).

About one of five children with Down syndrome has an orthopedic problem, especially affecting the upper cervical spine (Mik, Ghove, Scher, Widmann, & Green, 2008).

Hypotonia is likely to be the most common problem noted in infant assessment. Based on achievement of motor milestones for age, these babies may appear to have only minor developmental delays and therefore not require or be eligible (based on purely quantitative eligibility determination) for therapeutic interventions. This is a serious misconception. Therapeutic interventions should be initiated as soon as possible to avoid more serious impairments later in life due to poor muscle tone and possible vision and hearing impairments. An essential premise of early intervention is that beginning cognitive and communication intervention as soon as possible will ameliorate the degree of later delay. Early intervention has the additional advantage of sensitizing parents to their child's developmental needs, reducing the likelihood of social-emotional problems (Mahoney, Perales, Wiggers, & Herman, 2006).

Fragile X syndrome is characterized by trinucleotide repeat expansion in the FMR 1 (fragile X mental retardation 1) gene that is on the X chromosome. It is considered to be the most common inherited cause of mental retardation (with Down syndrome being considered the most common chromosomal cause of mental retardation). Because of its genetic profile Fragile X syndrome is seen more often in males than females. Its prevalence had been estimated at 1 case per 1,000 males but this later was considered to be an overestimate. A meta-analysis of prevalence studies found a more accurate estimate to be 1 case in ~4,000 males, or 0.026% of the male population. This rate refers to the full Fragile X genetic mutation (Becket, Yu, & Long, n.d.; Turner, Webb, & Robinson, 1996).

There are characteristic cardiovascular abnormalities associated with Fragile X syndrome, specifically mitral valve prolapse and aortic root dilation. These are generally not manifested until later in childhood or adolescence and are not likely to be observed in young children with Fragile X syndrome. It is therefore important to monitor the cardiovascular health of young children diagnosed with Fragile X syndrome over time (Crabbe, Bensky, Hornstein, & Schwartz, 1993).

The specific genetic mutation associated with mental retardation in Fragile X syndrome is also associated with behaviors similar to those observed in children diagnosed with autism. These behavioral features are resistant to change. The prevalence of psychiatric disorders among children with Fragile X syndrome is estimated to be 10 times that of the general population, with rates of major mental illness ranging from 17% to 22% depending on the child's age (Sabaratnam, Murthy, Wijeratne, Buckingham, & Payne, 2003). When a standardized autism screening tool (i.e., Childhood Autism Rating

Scale [CARS]; Schopler, Reichler, & Renner, 1986) was used among boys as young as 24 months with Fragile X syndrome, their profile could not readily be distinguished from that of children with autism. The more severely developmentally delayed boys with Fragile X syndrome scored higher on the CARS (i.e., showed more autistic-like symptoms that were of greater severity; Bailey et al., 1998). The relationship between the genetic anomalies in Fragile X syndrome and autism are not yet fully understood and require further multi-disciplinary research.

Other genetic syndromes in which a higher than typical prevalence of autism has been found include Down syndrome; *Angelman syndrome* (with a prevalence of 1 per 12,000 and characteristics including developmental delay, mental retardation, speech–language impairment, atypical gait, and socially inappropriate laughing and excitability); and *Prader–Willi syndrome* (prevalence, 1 per 29,500 and characterized by hypotonia, delayed development, and mental retardation). *Sotos syndrome* is characterized by congenital macrocephaly and dysmorphic facial features including a prominent forehead with the appearance of a receding hairline. Young children with Sotos syndrome present multiple developmental delays, and in some cases autism has also been diagnosed. Prevalence estimates of Sotos syndrome vary widely, from 1 per 10,000 to 1 per 50,000. *Turner's syndrome* is more common, with a range of prevalence estimates from 1 per 2,000 to 1 per 5,000, and affects females. Recognizable features of Turner's syndrome include short stature; atypical hands and feet; and dysmorphic facial features affecting the ears, mouth and teeth, and hairline. *Williams syndrome* is very rare, with from 2 to 5 cases per 100,000 population. In addition to facial dysmorphism, Williams syndrome is characterized by cardiovascular anomalies and an atypical developmental pattern with visual–spatial cognitive deficits and well developed verbal communication (Zafeirou, Ververi, & Vargiami, 2007).

Early identification of genetic syndromes has multiple advantages including allowing for early developmental assessment and intervention as well as early assessment and treatment planning for medical conditions such as organ anomalies and perceptual impairments. In performing infant developmental assessments, in addition to assessing motor, adaptive, cognitive, communication, and social-emotional development, it is recommended that the clinician look for facial dysmorphic features affecting the eyes, nose, mouth, and ears. Pediatric examinations for infants and young children with delayed development should include regular measurement of head circumference to identify macro- or microcephaly. The many recognizable patterns of malformation observed in genetic syndromes are described and photographically illustrated in the standard reference work on the subject by Jones (2006).

PRENATAL EXPOSURE TO LICIT AND ILLICIT SUBSTANCES

The specific teratogenic effect of maternal alcohol use on the fetus was termed *fetal alcohol syndrome* (FAS) in 1973 by Jones and Smith. The pattern of altered growth and dysmorphic features may be recognized in early infancy (Jones & Smith, 1973). These are most noticeable in the eyes (epicanthal folds), nose (short, flattened, and with a low bridge), and mouth (thin upper lip). Since 1978, *fetal alcohol effect* (FAE) has referred to growth and developmental problems associated with confirmed maternal alcohol use during pregnancy that does not meet diagnostic criteria for FAS. The clinical utility of this term has been questioned, and the phrases *alcohol-related birth defects* (ARBDs) and *alcohol-related neurodevelopmental disorder* (ARND) have been suggested as more descriptive alternatives where clinically appropriate. The estimated incidence of FAS is ~1.4 per 1,000 live births; however, this may underestimate actual incidence because alcohol exposure is often not well identified or documented. Higher incidence estimates based on smaller studies or studies done with specific populations range up to 3.9 per 1,000 (Sampson et al., 1997).

The diagnostic category *fetal alcohol spectrum disorder* (FASD) is used as a framework to capture the range of impact of in-utero exposure on the fetus. Included in FASD are FAS, ARBD, ARND, and *partial fetal alcohol syndrome* (PFAS), which is characterized by at least two characteristic facial anomalies and at least one other abnormality (growth retardation, microcephaly, or other structural brain anomaly, otherwise unexplained developmental and behavioral deficits; Manning & Hoyne, 2007).

Fetal alcohol syndrome is associated with heavy and consistent maternal alcohol consumption during pregnancy, not with casual and occasional social drinking. Not all fetuses with heavy in-utero alcohol exposure experience any degree of damage. Estimates of the probability of fetal damage range very widely, from 1% to 50%, indicating a lack of understanding of the mechanisms of risk and resilience that are involved. Neurodevelopmental deficits associated with FAS affect memory, attention, motor development, visual–spatial functioning, speech–language development, and cognition including planning and verbal reasoning. FAS is considered to be a common underlying cause of mental retardation (Niccols, 2007).

Cognitive deficits are manifested in infancy. By 12 months of age, infants with FAS have lower mean Mental Development Index (MDI) scores on the Bayley Scales of Infant Development than do nonexposed infants (Testa, Quigley, & Das Eiden, 2003). It is estimated that 40% of children diagnosed with FAS also meet diagnostic criteria for ADHD. About 25% will have a learning disability, and 30% a speech–language disorder. Up to 10% will also have epilepsy (Burd, Cotsonas-Hassler, Martsolf, & Kerbeshian, 2003).

Neurological differences between alcohol-exposed infants and those with no prenatal exposures begin to manifest by 7 months of age, which facilitates early identification and referral for early intervention services (Van Der Leeden et al., 2001). A brief FAS screening tool intended for use in preschool and school settings has been developed (The FAS Screen) and has excellent reported specificity (94.1%) and sensitivity (100%; Burd et al., 1999). This 32-item screening instrument takes 8 to 10 minutes to complete and has been well accepted in community settings (Poitra et al., 2003).

As is the case in all syndromes with craniofacial anomalies, children with FAS are at increased risk of hearing loss because of malformation of the ear. Recurrent otitis media (ear infections) may occur and, especially without timely and appropriate medical treatment, may be associated with conductive hearing loss. Frequent episodes of otitis media in FAS are often related to recurrent respiratory infections secondary to compromised immune system, eustachian tube dysfunction, and/or cleft palate (Church & Gerkin, 1988).

Developmental outcomes for children with FAS may be negatively affected by environmental restrictions as are often observed when maternal alcohol abuse continues. Other potential risk factors include maternal depression, disruptions of the caregiver environment (e.g., multiple extended family or foster care placements), and maltreatment. Children prenatally exposed to alcohol are especially vulnerable to the impact of these and other environmental stressors associated with suboptimal developmental outcomes (Coggins, Timler, & Olswang, 2007). Conversely, the developmental impact of FAS may be ameliorated by providing a supportive, stimulating environment and early intervention for developmental delays. A comprehensive review of FASD for the EI provider was published by Olson, Jirikowic, Kartin, and Astley (2007).

The developmental impact of prenatal exposure to cocaine may also be mediated by the care environment. Unlike FAS, prenatal cocaine exposure is not associated with characteristic dysmorphic features or congenital anomalies. Its impact may best be understood as a risk factor for developmental delays, especially speech–language and cognitive functioning, rather than an independent cause of these problems (Cone-Wesson, 2005).

Early development is negatively impacted by in-utero exposure to cocaine. Multiple studies have shown that exposed infants do less well on formal measures of motor development such as the motor cluster of the Brazelton Neonatal Behavioral Assessment Scale (BNBAS), the MAI, and the AIMS. These deficits may continue through age 24 months (Arendt, Angelopoulos, Salvator, & Singer, 1999). The development of early cognitive skills such as attention and auditory comprehension may also be affected, with cocaine-exposed toddlers sometimes being reported as having a lower mean MDI on the Bayley Scales of Infant Development (Singer et al., 2001). Developmental outcomes are also affected by birth weight (Frank et al., 2006).

Follow-up studies of cocaine-exposed children have found that the risk of minor cognitive deficits persists into early adolescence (Bennett, Bendersky, & Lewis, 2008). While children who were prenatally exposed to cocaine have been found to be more likely to receive special education services than children who were not exposed, the most significant predictor was low child IQ score, which is independently associated with risk of compromised academic achievement (Levine et al., 2008).

These findings suggest that children who were prenatally exposed to cocaine should be viewed as being at risk and monitored for developmental status throughout early childhood, with referrals made for intervention services as soon as clinically warranted. This is a different impression of the impact of prenatal cocaine exposure than was suggested by the earlier studies, which were accompanied by media-fueled hysteria about *crack babies* who would be permanently damaged and present an enormous and long-lasting financial drain on society (Zuckerman & Frank, 1992). Analysis of these early studies revealed the many complexities involved in inferring a causal connection between prenatal cocaine exposure and developmental outcomes. This reflects the degree to which developmental outcomes are multidetermined, with multiple confounding variables likely to be present in the environment of drug-exposed infants and young children. These include psychosocial stressors which are independently associated with developmental risk including the level of parenting skill, domestic violence, nutrition status, medical conditions, housing quality, maternal depression, continued maternal substance abuse, and lack of toys and other age appropriate language and cognitive stimulation. Many early studies seeking to describe the teratogenic impact of cocaine failed to adequately control for these confounding variables; some were also flawed by small sample size and other methodological defects (Neuspeil, 1994).

PERINATAL HIV

Developmental delays and neurologic complications have been identified in children who are infected with HIV since the earliest descriptions of the disease. HIV infects a variety of cell types in the brain causing a range of problems. Specific expressive and receptive language impairments and psychomotor delays have been documented over time and are associated with the direct or indirect CNS effect of HIV. In addition, HIV-infected children frequently exhibit behaviors such as impulsivity, hyperactivity, and difficulties attending and focusing. Academic difficulties are a direct result of these developmental and behavioral problems.

Several etiologies have been proposed for these difficulties; however, brain damage secondary to HIV infection is considered one of the principal determinants. Through neuroimaging techniques, there is now ample evidence of HIV involvement in the neurologic functioning of the frontal cortex, basal ganglia, and connecting structures in the CNS. Nevertheless, studying the factors associated with developmental and behavioral problems in HIV-infected children is complicated due to the impact of environmental factors which may include prenatal drug exposure, family dysfunction, and poverty (Jeremy et al., 2005; Nozyce et al., 2006).

In the United States, the most frequent cause of HIV infection in children is maternal–child transmission (*vertical transmission*) by which the disease is transmitted by an HIV-positive mother to the fetus during pregnancy or delivery. A child can also become infected through maternal breast milk during the first few months of life. Not all women who have HIV will transmit it to their children. Before the availability of medications to treat HIV, up to 30% of children born to HIV-infected women became infected. However, a group of drugs called antiretrovirals works well in stopping HIV transmission. Appropriate use of these medications reduces vertical transmission to less than 2%. Screening pregnant women for HIV and providing antiretroviral medication if they are infected has dramatically reduced the number of children born with HIV. In 1991, an estimated 1,650 babies were born with perinatal HIV. This was reduced to an estimated range from 144–236 a decade later (CDC, 2006). The evidence for prenatal HIV screening has been summarized for the U.S. Preventive Services Task Force (Chou, Smits, Hoyt Huffman, Fu, & Korthuis, 2005).

Most children with AIDS are currently entering adolescence and adulthood. Many of them continue to be followed developmentally through National Institutes of Health (NIH) funded programs. Since HIV impacts the adult brain differently than it does the developing brains of children, these ongoing evaluations will provide important information regarding brain development and later cognitive and behavioral functioning of children born with HIV.

HEARING LOSS AND VISUAL IMPAIRMENT

HEARING LOSS

The incidence of congenital severe sensorineural hearing loss is approximately 1 to 2 cases per 1,000 live births. Most states have universal newborn hearing screening programs in place, and many link these to their EI program (Widen, Bull, & Folsom, 2003). However, because up to 30% of cases of hearing loss may be acquired postnatally, and even mild unilateral hearing loss may affect development and school performance (Schlesinger, 1995), newborn screening is not adequate to ensure early detection (Polinski, 2003).

Premature infants and those with IUGR are at elevated risk of hearing loss. Preemies with BPD have an elevated risk of progressive hearing loss beginning in infancy. Congenital infections including congenital cytomegalovirus (CMV), meningitis, and rubella are associated with elevated risk for sensorineural hearing loss. Other medically related risk factors for hearing loss include treatment with ototoxic drugs (including some antibiotics as well as chemotherapy agents), hypoxia and prolonged oxygen treatment, and seizures. As described earlier, genetic syndromes with craniofacial anomalies (such as FAS and Down syndrome) also pose a heightened risk of hearing loss.

The American Speech–Language–Hearing Association (2004) recommends that all children with developmental delays have a hearing test. Hearing screening is rarely done in routine pediatric care for infants and young children. Primary care pediatricians typically begin to include hearing screening in well examinations when the child turns 3 years of age. At that time objective hearing screening, for example otoacoustic emission (OAE) or auditory brain stem response (ABR) technology, is less likely to be used than less accurate subjective methods (e.g., *pure tone screening* by which tones of different frequencies are delivered through headphones to the child who has to perform some volitional action such as pointing to the ear or raising a hand to indicate that the tone was heard; Eiserman et al., 2008; Wall, Senicz, Evans, Woolley, & Hardin, 2006). The accuracy of pure tone screening is influenced by the degree of ambient environmental noise and the child's ability to follow the directions for response to the auditory stimulus.

Audiology referrals were often included as part of developmental assessments when they were done in medical or diagnostic and treatment clinical settings. This was facilitated by the location of the necessary audiology personnel and equipment in hospitals and other therapeutic settings. With the advent of EI and splitting of developmental from medical care, we have seen an increase in children receiving speech-language intervention without their hearing status being known. Data from the New York City EI program showed a dramatic lag between participants authorized for speech–language therapy (74%) and those who had a hearing test through EI (4.5%; Goodwin, 2002). The EI eligibility assessment for medically involved infants and toddlers should include objective audiological testing. Periodic retesting is indicated if the initial test was negative.

Early identification of hearing loss is especially important because there is a strong body of evidence that early intervention to correct this condition leads to dramatically improved developmental outcomes. This is in part attributable to cochlear implantation, by which a device is surgically implanted with external and internal components that electrically stimulate functioning auditory nerves in the inner ear (cochlea) to provide the sensation of hearing. Hearing aids, which may also effectively provide dramatic improvement of hearing ability, amplify sounds. With cochlear implantation, sounds are transmitted by the external components (microphone, processor, and transmitter) to a receiver implanted just below the skin of the skull and then to electrodes that have been implanted in the cochlea. Cochlear implantation can be done with infants as young as 6 months (Valencia, Rimell, Friedman, Oblander, & Helmbrech, 2008).

Infants who receive cochlear implants before their first birthday develop preverbal communication behavior in a manner similar to hearing infants (Tait, De Raeve, & Nikolopoulos, 2007). Early cochlear implantation is associated with improved progress towards speech intelligibility and conversational speech production for young children with severe and profound hearing loss. These outcomes are better than were obtained with early use of hearing aids (Flipsen, 2008). Nonetheless, extremely impressive developmental outcomes—in terms of speech–language, cognitive, and social-emotional functioning—are well documented for early identification and intervention with hearing aids supplemented by speech–language therapy (Winter & Eisenberg, 1999; Yoshinaga-Itano, 2003).

Many of the early social and speech–language signs associated with autism spectrum disorder (ASD) also may be seen in infants and toddlers with significant hearing loss (Tas et al., 2007). It is strongly recommended that hearing loss be ruled out when young children are assessed for ASD.

VISUAL IMPAIRMENT

A visual impairment occurs when any part of the optical system is defective, diseased, or malfunctions. Visual impairment due to defect is usually present at birth (congenital). These defects include absence of an iris, absence of the eyes themselves, dislocation of the lens, or holes in the retina. There are also hereditary conditions such as albinism. Diseases can be prenatal, postnatal, or adventitious (acquired later in life). A visual impairment can also occur when the CNS is damaged, since the brain not only governs and coordinates the optical system but also interprets and processes the visual stimuli sent to it by the eyes. *Cortical visual impairment* (CVI) is the most common cause of permanent visual impairment in children (Hoon, 1996).

Including visual assessment in the infant developmental evaluation is essential because vision screening of preverbal children is not routinely done in pediatric primary care. The AAP recommends that visual acuity and binocular screening be done starting at 36 months of age; however, in a random national sample of pediatricians, only 37% reported compliance with that recommendation and about 20% did not begin screening until age 5 years (Wall et al., 2002).

The risk of visual impairment is elevated for premature, LBW babies due to *retinopathy of prematurity* (ROP). The potential impact of ROP ranges from nearsightedness to blindness. An estimated 90% of infants born at < 750 grams develop some degree of ROP, which often spontaneously corrects itself. All preemies with a prior diagnosis of ROP should have their vision tested as part of the EI evaluation and monitored over time by an ophthalmologist (McNab & Blackman, 1998). For VLBW infants, problems with visual–motor integration and fine motor functioning may be present (Gabbard, Goncalves, & Santos, 2001). An occupational therapy evaluation should be part of the multidisciplinary evaluation determining EI eligibility for children born prematurely at whatever age they are referred.

Early signs of visual impairment may be identified through careful observation of the infant. These include atypical response of the pupil to light, difficulty visually tracking an object, inability to focus on an object, abnormal positioning of the head to observe close objects, and difficulty recognizing familiar faces or objects (Hanson & Hanline, 1996; Scheiner, 1995). Guidelines for vision screening by nonmedically trained personnel have been developed for infants and toddlers suspected of developmental delay. The protocol includes visual inspection of the eyes and eyelids, papillary response to light, alternate cover test, corneal light reflex test, sustained fixation on an object, tracking, convergence, visual acuity, and observation for compensatory behaviors such as squinting. Minimal special equipment is needed for these screening activities (e.g., use of a penlight; Colorado Education Department, 2005).

MEDICALLY INVOLVED INFANTS IN THE EARLY INTERVENTION PROGRAM

Nationally, 2.4% of the age-eligible population is served in EI programs for developmental delays (www.IDEAdata.org, 1995–2005). Data from the Early Childhood Longitudinal Study (Rosenberg, Zhang, & Robins, 2008), however, suggests that far more infants and toddlers need developmental intervention and are not identified or referred. Reasons for this disparity include inconsistent use of developmental screening tools in pediatric primary care (King & Glascoe, 2003). There is evidence that EI referral patterns of primary care pediatricians are influenced by whether or not there is a medical condition associated with the developmental delay, with diagnosed infants and toddlers more likely to be referred (Silverstein, Sand, Glascoe, Gupta, & Tonniges, 2006).

Eligibility for EI services may be determined through multidisciplinary developmental assessment establishing a degree of delay consistent with the state's eligibility requirements or by diagnosis of a physical or mental condition associated with a high probability of resulting in developmental delay (IDEA, 2004; NYSDOH, 2005; North Carolina Department of Health and Human Services, 2006). Medically involved infants such as we have discussed are *automatically* eligible for EI intervention services based on their medical diagnosis. The purpose of the developmental assessment is to inform their intervention plan (*individualized family service plan* [IFSP]). The standards for prematurity and low birth weight and for hearing loss (severity, whether unilateral or bilateral) to establish eligibility by diagnosis vary among the states. In many states, the medical diagnosis of *extreme prematurity* (birth weight $\leq 1,000$ grams and/or 26 weeks gestation or fewer) establishes EI eligibility by diagnosis (Grant, 2005; Hebbeler et al., 2007b).

States also have the option to determine the disability threshold to find infants and toddlers eligible for EI eligibility because of developmental delay. States also decide whether to include in EI infants and toddlers at risk of developmental delay because of biomedical and/or psychosocial factors (e.g., children with high lead levels, children born to mentally retarded or mentally ill parents, homeless children, children in foster care). These decisions—eligibility threshold and whether to include at-risk children—influence the size and cost of the state's EI program. While counties administer their EI programs directly, eligibility criteria may only be changed at the state level.

The most common eligibility threshold based on formal testing and informed clinical opinion is a delay of at least 25% in two or more developmental domains or at least 33% in one developmental domain. States with more restrictive eligibility criteria require up to a 50% delay in one domain. Milder developmental delay (15%) is accepted for eligibility in a small number of states. In all cases, level of delay may be established in terms of standard deviations below the mean on a norm-referenced test. Most states do not include at-risk children for EI services but rather have a tracking system to facilitate timely EI referrals for high-risk infants (Shackelford, 2004). Formal tests used in EI must have adequate psychometric properties, but states may not require or forbid the use of specific standardized instruments.

The high representation of infants and toddlers with complex medical needs in EI has been documented with diverse data sources including the National Early Intervention Longitudinal Study (NEILS), which used parent report (Hebbeler et al., 2007a); statewide review of birth certificate data against EI referrals in Massachusetts (Clements, Barfield, Kotelchuck, Lee, & Wilber, 2006); and a study of infants and toddlers referred by their pediatricians for EI evaluation at a New York City tertiary care hospital.

In the New York City study, which used EI assessment data and medical chart review in a tertiary care hospital setting, it was found that 81% of referred children under 19 months of age were medically involved (defined as LBW/premature, neurologically impaired, diagnosed with a genetic syndrome or congenital organ anomaly, or infectious disease such as meningitis). About half of the LBW babies were born at $< 1,000$ grams and < 26 weeks gestation (Grant, Nozyce, Gordon, Garwood, & Kucera, 2003).

These findings demonstrate the importance of integrating developmental services in EI with the child's health care. This is underlined by the difficulty these children and families may have accessing care elsewhere. A state-by-state review of Medicaid coverage for the principal services provided by EI (physical, occupational, and speech–language therapies) shows that Medicaid covers all three services in only 15 states. If Medicaid is provided through a managed care plan, there may be a limit to the number of allowable visits for therapies, further restricting access to services through the health care system (Cooley & McAllister, 2004). Even with health insurance, each year about 10% of children with special health care needs do not receive at least one medically necessary service. Children with severe disabilities are at highest risk of missing needed interventions (Dusing, Skinner, & Mayer, 2004). The developmental assessment should include parent interview to ensure that medical services appropriate to the child's level of need are in place, and referrals should be made if needed.

PARENT SUPPORT SERVICES

Many psychological stressors are associated with the birth and parenting of a premature, medically involved infant. A longitudinal prospective study of mothers of VLBW infants found that they had more symptoms of anxiety, depression, and obsessive-compulsive disorders at 1 month postpartum than did mothers of full-term infants. Their degree of psychological distress increased with the infant's high-risk status. At 2 years postpartum, mothers of high-risk VLBW infants continued to show higher rates of symptoms consistent with moderate depressive disorder. Higher measured signs of depression were significantly associated with lower infant developmental scores through 36 months of age (Singer et al., 1999).

A qualitative study of mothers of infants born at < 33 weeks gestation found that at 1 year postpartum, the mothers reported problems with fatigue, depression, anxiety, and physical symptoms (Garel, Dardennes, & Blondel, 2006). Using a standardized inventory of current depressive symptoms, investigators found that 63% of mothers of premature NICU graduates presented symptoms consistent with maternal depression for the first 6 months postpartum. Continuing signs of depression were most prevalent among single mothers and mothers of infants with ongoing medical risk factors (Miles, Holditch-Davis, Schwartz, & Scher, 2007). Premature birth and medical and developmental risk are associated with heightened levels of maternal stress and trauma. This in turn may affect mother–child interactions and negatively impact the baby's early development (Muller-Nix et al., 2004).

The EI program is intended to provide family-centered care. Access to parent support services, however, is variable, especially since the overwhelming majority of EI therapies are provided in home and community, rather than agency-based settings. The role of the service coordinator assigned to all EI families is different from that of a case manager in a medical or developmental disability setting, and may be restricted to providing only counseling around participation in the EI program (NYSDOH, n.d.). While the EI program is likely to be the default provider, if not the provider of choice, for infant–toddler physical, occupational, and speech–language therapy, it may not be an adequate source of needed parent support services.

THE EFFICACY OF EARLY INTERVENTION SERVICES

The neurobiological basis for developmental intervention during infancy and early childhood is the extreme plasticity of the human brain during the first 3 years of life. This period is characterized by the rapid and, to an extent, selective formation of synapses in the brain (communication links among nerve cells), which, while strongly determined genetically, is partially influenced by environmental factors (DiPietro, 2000). There is emerging objective evidence (brain scans, EEG) that brain function and structure may be positively influenced by early intervention services for high-risk infants. This is reflected, for example, in a statistically significant increase in Bayley Scales of Infant Development scores, both MDI and Performance Development Index (PDI), in premature infants re-tested at 9 months of age. Outcomes for the intervention group were compared with those for matched controls (Als et al., 2004).

This kind of controlled outcome study is essential to establishing the efficacy of EI services. Without intervention, there will be developmental progress for all but the most severely impaired infants. For example, studies show that most VLBW infants demonstrate improved speech–language and cognitive functioning over time, with a decline being noted only for those who experienced significant IVH and CNS injury (Ment et al., 2003). Making the case that developmental progress is attributable to developmental intervention services rather than maturation alone is a challenge even in high-risk populations.

A summary of evidence for the efficacy of early intervention services for various developmental and underlying medical conditions is found in

Guralnick (1997). Common to the studies cited and summarized are the conclusions that no single intervention approach should be adopted in all cases; it is incumbent upon clinicians to appropriately assess the individual child and develop an intervention strategy accordingly. Involving parents and providing social supports enhance therapeutic outcomes. It must be noted, however, that the studies included generally preceded the operational phase (which began in 1994–1995) of the Early Intervention Program. The same applies to the still valuable review of early intervention outcome studies by Majnemer (1998).

The National Early Intervention Longitudinal Study (NEILS) sought to address issues in EI such as the demographics of the children and families served, the specific services infants and toddlers receive, and outcomes (which were ascertained by parent interview and review of EI records; IDEA, 2004). Findings from a NEILS telephone survey to determine EI outcomes focused on parent self-report of competency to care for their child with special needs, ability to advocate for themselves and their child, and access to support services (Bailey, Hebbeler, Spiker, Scarborough, Mallik, & Nelson, 2005).

Because EI programs do not use the same assessment methods, often do not use norm-referenced or other objectively scored assessment instruments, and do not routinely do formal re-testing to determine developmental outcomes (often relying on subjective assessment of progress relative to IFSP goals), review of EI records such as done in the NEILS longitudinal study will describe how EI programs function and whom they serve but not provide the richness of data potentially available from multisite outcome studies. Only objective baseline and follow-up assessments of developmental functioning will provide the evidence needed to establish EI program efficacy. Such data are essential to make the case that these very costly state and county programs should continue to be funded at their current levels, or even expanded. Medically involved infants are especially vulnerable to problems arising from the current paucity of efficacy studies. Efforts at the state level to control EI spending have often involved attempts to shift costs back to the health care system or deny EI services for developmental problems secondary to diagnosed medical conditions (Grant, 2005).

RECOMMENDATIONS FOR PRACTICE

Increasingly, the medium through which infant and toddler developmental assessments are delivered has shifted away from health care to home and community settings. This makes it essential that psychologists and other developmental professionals become knowledgeable about the common medical conditions that affect this population.

The following are recommendations that will facilitate optimal evidence-based care for medically involved infants and toddlers with developmental delays:

1. Care for medically involved infants must be integrated and coordinated. This includes case conferencing among the multiple developmental specialists involved in providing developmental services and the coordination of developmental services with medical care.

2. When assessing infants, qualitative (how the child interacts with the environment) as well as quantitative (test score) data should be used to accurately communicate the infant's developmental level. It is the responsibility of evaluators to record and report developmental findings in accordance with eligibility requirements of publicly funded entitlement programs such as the Early Intervention Program.

3. When assessing infants, underlying precursors for developmental delays (e.g., muscle tone and state regulation) should also be evaluated.

4. When testing premature infants, reliance on standardized test scores alone, especially if correcting for prematurity, may lead to overestimation of overall developmental level. It is recommended that qualitative aspects of the child's functioning be described and considered in evaluation reports and eligibility determination in program like EI.

5. Hearing and vision testing should be included in the assessment of medically involved infants.

6. Fully involving parents in planning intervention strategies and, to the extent feasible, involving parents in exercises and activities at home to reinforce therapeutic goals, is highly recommended.

7. Evaluators and therapists should ensure that parents understand the nature of the child's medical and developmental condition, and provide information and explanations in language that the parents understand.

8. Clinical outcomes should be tracked in a methodical and objective manner against goals, and changes in intervention strategy should be made if warranted based on these outcomes.

9. Psychologists should initiate and participate in multisite, multidisciplinary longitudinal studies of the clinical efficacy and potential savings associated with EI services. Attention should be paid to the number, frequency, and duration of EI services provided, the setting (home, day care, special preschool), and degree of parent involvement as they influence outcomes.

10. There are many different ways to conceptualize ethical issues affecting infants with disabilities. Sometimes these focus on life and death decisions, or ways to manage children with extremely severe developmental

disabilities such as static encephalopathy. We emphasize several ethical principles that are essential to good practice:

a. Parents should be accurately informed about their child's diagnosis, prognosis, and treatment options. False reassurance is neither helpful nor recommended.

b. Parents should know the scope of practice of the evaluators and therapists who are working with their infant.

c. It is incumbent upon these professionals to work within both their scope of practice and specific training and expertise. Referrals should be made when an infant's needs fall outside of those areas.

IMPLICATIONS FOR TRAINING

The degree to which infants and toddlers with special health care needs are seen in developmental settings for evaluation and intervention, including in the Early Intervention Program, may present a unique set of difficulties for professionals. This is particularly apparent when these children require evaluations that assess their cognitive and developmental functioning. Professionals evaluating children with serious underlying medical conditions should have an understanding of the impact of that condition on developmental functioning. Examples are the effect that recurrent seizures have on the developing brain or the neurodevelopmental impact of grade 3 or 4 intraventricular hemorrhages on extremely premature infants. Additionally, children with medical conditions may require special handling. They may be particularly sensitive to movement, may tire easily, and sometimes require special positioning. Understanding these issues not only affects the quality of evaluation and intervention but ensures the infant's comfort in these settings.

Evaluating infants, whether or not they are medically involved, requires expertise in the proper use of test instruments and an understanding of infant development. Some test instruments available for the birth to three population are different in administration and scoring than assessments for preschool and school age children. The use of tests without the requisite knowledge and experience can lead to inappropriate diagnoses and interventions.

Assessing an infant requires the evaluator to examine *why* an infant is not able to perform a task. Thus, evaluators must be familiar with issues related to muscle tone and reflexes. They must also observe how the child interacts with people and with objects in the environment. The infant's overall quality of response must also be taken into account. Whether the infant is comfortable, tired, hungry, or sleepy may affect performance. The mother's state of mind and mood may have an impact on the infant's functioning.

How the infant performs a task is also of extreme importance. For example, one infant might be able to pick up a block deftly and quickly, while another infant of the same age might struggle to do so because of an inability to manage fine motor skills. Although both infants would be scored as having passed this item on the test, they clearly manifest significant differences in functioning.

Professionals involved with the evaluation of children with medical conditions or with infants should receive special training that will allow them to understand the special needs of this population. This training must include a theoretical framework on infant and early child development, a basic understanding of medical conditions seen in infants and young children, and training in evaluating underlying precursors to development such as state regulation and muscle tone. Frequently professional programs and associations do not sufficiently emphasize the unique aspects of infancy and early childhood in general, and issues of medically fragile children in particular. Addressing these issues directly in graduate education, including through appropriate internship and externship opportunities, will help develop a cadre of professionals with the training and experience to appropriately diagnose and plan intervention strategies for these high risk infants and young children.

REFERENCES

Allen, M. C. (2008). Neurodevelopmental outcomes of preterm infants. *Current Opinion in Neurology, 21,* 123–128.

Alper, B. S., & Studt, L. (2007, March). Dysphagia. *The Clinical Advisor,* 138–139.

Als, H., Duffy, F. H., McAnulty, G. B., Rivkin, M. J., Vajapeyam, S., Mulkern, R. V., et al. (2004). Early experience alters brain function and structure. *Pediatrics, 113,* 846–857.

American Academy of Pediatrics, Committee on Children with Disabilities (1999). The pediatrician's role in development and implementation of an individual education plan (IEP) and/or and individual family service plan (IFSP). *Pediatrics, 104,* 124–127.

American Speech–Language Hearing Association. (2004). *Guidelines for the audiologic assessment of children from birth to 5 years of age.* Retrieved September 30, 2007, from www.asha.org/NR/rdonlyres/0BB7C840-27D2-4DC6-861B1709ADD78BAF/0/v2GLAudAssessChild.pdf.

American Thoracic Society Documents (2003). Statements on the care of the child with chronic lung disease of infancy and childhood. *American Journal of Respiratory and Critical Care Medicine, 168,* 356–396.

Arendt, R., Angelopoulos, J., Salvator, A., & Singer, L. (1999). Motor development of cocaine-exposed children at age two years. *Pediatrics, 103*, 86–92.

Arvedson, J. C., & Lefton-Greif, M. A. (2007). Ethical and legal challenges in feeding and swallowing intervention for infants and children. *Seminars in Speech and Language, 28*, 232–238.

Aylward, G. P. (1997). *Infant and child neuropsychology.* New York: Plenum Press.

Aylward, G. P. (2005). Neurodevelopmental outcomes of infants born prematurely. *Journal of Developmental and Behavioral Pediatrics, 26*, 427–440.

Bailey, D. B., Hebbeler, K., Spiker, D., Scarborough, A., Mallik, S., & Nelson, L. (2005). Thirty-six month outcomes for families of children who have disabilities and participated in early intervention. *Pediatrics, 116*, 1346–1352.

Bailey, D. B., Mesibov, G. B., Hatton, D. D., Clark, R. D., Roberts, J. E., & Mayhew, L. (1998). Autistic behavior in young boys with fragile X syndrome. *Journal of Autism and Developmental Disorders, 28*, 499–508.

Bardin, C., Zelkowitz, P., & Papageorgiou, A. (1997). Outcome for small-for-gestational age and appropriate-for-gestational age infants born before 27 weeks gestation. *Pediatrics, 100*, e4–e8.

Becket, L., Yu, Q., & Long, A. N. (n.d.). *The impact of fragile X: Prevalence, numbers affected, and economic impact.* A white paper prepared for the National Fragile X Foundation. Retrieved August 14, 2008, from www.fragilex.org/PrevalenceWhite PaperAdaptedforFQ.pdf.

Beghi, M., Cornaggia, C. M., Frigeni, B., & Beghi, E. (2007). Learning disorders in epilepsy. *Epilepsia, 47*(2), 14–18.

Bennett, D. S., Bendersky, M., & Lewis, M. (2008). Children's cognitive ability from 4 to 9 years old as a function of prenatal cocaine exposure, environmental risk, and maternal verbal intelligence. *Developmental Psychology, 44*, 919–928.

Blasco, P. A. (1995). Motor delays. In S. Parker & B. Zuckerman (Eds.), *Behavioral and developmental pediatrics: A handbook for primary care* (pp. 211–215). Boston: Little, Brown, & Co.

Boardman, J. D., Powers, D. A., Padilla, Y. C., & Hummer, R. A. (2002). Low birth weight, social factors, and developmental outcomes among children in the United States. *Demography, 39*, 353–368.

Buescher, P. A., Whitmire, J. T., Brunssen, S., & Kluttz-Hile, C. E. (2006). Children who are medically fragile in North Carolina: Using Medicaid data to estimate prevalence and medical care costs in 2004. *Maternal and Child Health Journal, 10*, 461–466.

Burd, L., Cotsonas-Hassler, T. M., Martsolf, J. T., & Kerbeshian, J. (2003). Recognition and management of fetal alcohol syndrome. *Neurotoxicology and Teratology, 25*, 681–688.

Burd, L., Cox, C., Poitra, B., Wentz, T., Ebertowski, M., Martsolf, J. T., et al. (1999). The FAS Screen: A rapid screening tool for fetal alcohol syndrome. *Addiction Biology, 4*, 329–336.

Catov, J. M., Nohr, E. A., Olsen, J., & Nexx, R. B. (2008). Chronic hypertension related to risk for preterm and term small for gestational age births. *Obstetrics and Gynecology, 112*, 290–296.

Centers for Disease Control and Prevention. (2005). *National vital statistics report. Births: Final data for 2005.* Retrieved August 14, 2008, from www.cdc.gov/nchs/data/nvsr/nvsr56/nvsr56_06.pdf.

Centers for Disease Control and Prevention (2006, June 2). Achievements in public health: Reduction in perinatal transmission of HIV in the United States, 1985–2005. *Morbidity and Mortality Weekly, 55,* 592–2997.

Centers for Disease Control and Prevention. (2008). *Epilepsy: One of the nation's most common disabling neurological conditions.* Retrieved June 13, 2008, from www.cdc.gov/epilepsy/.

Chou, R., Smits, A. K., Hoyt Huffman, L., Fu, R., & Korthuis, P. T. (2005). Prenatal screening for HIV: A review of the evidence for the U.S. preventive services task force. *Annals of Internal Medicine, 143,* 38–54.

Church, M. W., & Gerkin, K. P. (1988). Hearing disorders in children with fetal alcohol syndrome: Findings from case reports. *Pediatrics, 82,* 147–154.

Clements, K. M., Barfield, W. D., Kotelchuck, M., Lee, K. G., & Wilber, N. (2006). Birth characteristics associated with early intervention referral, evaluation for eligibility, and program eligibility in the first year of life. *Maternal and Child Health Journal, 10,* 433–441.

Coggins, T. E., Timler, G. R., & Olswang, L. B. (2007). A state of double jeopardy: Impact of prenatal alcohol exposure with adverse environments on the social communicative abilities of school-age children with fetal alcohol spectrum disorder. *Language, Speech, and Hearing Services in the Schools, 38,* 117–127.

Colorado Education Department. (2005, January). *Visual screening guidelines: Children birth to five years. Developed for the use of child find personnel.* Retrieved May 28, 2008, from http://www.cde.state.co.us/early/downloads/early_vision_manual.pdf.

Cone-Wesson, B. (2005). Prenatal alcohol and cocaine exposure: Influences on cognition, speech, language, and hearing. *Journal of Communication Disorders, 38,* 279–302.

Cooley, W. C., & McAllister, J. W. (2004). Building medical homes: Improvement in primary care for children with special health care needs. *Pediatrics, 113,* 1499–1506.

Crabbe, L. S., Bensky, A. S., Hornstein, L., & Schwartz, D. C. (1993). Cardiovascular anomalies in children with fragile X syndrome. *Pediatrics, 91,* 714–715.

DiPietro, J. A. (2000). Baby and the brain: Advances in child development. *Annual Review of Public Health, 21,* 455–471.

Dittrich, H., Buhrer, C., Grimmer, I., Dittrich, S., Abdul-Khaliq, H., & Lange, P. E. (2003). Neurodevelopment at 1 year of age in infants with congenital heart disease. *Heart, 89,* 436–441.

Dusing, S. C., Skinner, A. C., & Mayer, M. L. (2004). Unmet need for therapy services, assistive devices and related services: Data from the National Survey of Children with Special Health Care Needs. *Ambulatory Pediatrics, 4,* 448–454.

Eiserman, W. D., Harel, D. M., Shisler, L., Buhrmann, J., White, K. R., & Foust, T. (2008). Using otoacoustic emissions to screen for hearing loss in early childhood settings. *International Journal of Pediatric Otorhinolaryngology, 72,* 475–482.

Engle, W. A., Tomashek, K. M., Wallman, C., & Committee on Fetus and Newborn. (2007). Late-preterm infants: A population at risk. Guidance for the clinician in rendering care. *Pediatrics, 120,* 1390–1401.

Fetters, L. (1996). Motor development. In M. J. Hanson (Ed.), *Atypical infant development* (pp. 403–451). Austin, TX: Pro-Ed, Inc.

Flipsen Jr., P. (2008). Intelligibility of spontaneous conversational speech produced by children with cochlear implants: A review. *International Journal of Pediatric Otorhinolaryngology, 72,* 559–564.

Frank, D. A., Jacobs, R. R., Beeghly, M., Augustyn, M., Bellinger, D., Cabral, H., et al. (2006). Levels of prenatal cocaine exposure and scores on the Bayley Scales of Infant Development: Modifying effects of caregiver, early intervention, and birth weight. *Pediatrics, 110,* 1143–1152.

Fung, E. B., Samson-Fang, L., Stallings, V. A., Conway, M., Liptak, G., Henderson, R. C., et al. (2002). Feeding dysfunction is associated with poor growth and health status in children with cerebral palsy. *Journal of the American Dietetic Association, 102,* 361–370.

Gabbard, C., Goncalves, V. M., & Santos, D. C. C. (2001). Visual–motor integration problems in low birth weight infants. *Journal of Clinical Psychology in Medical Settings, 8,* 199–204.

Garel, M., Dardennes, M., & Blondel, B. (2006). Mothers' psychological distress 1 year after very preterm birth. Results of the epipage qualitative study. *Child: Care, Health, and Development, 33,* 137–143.

Godenberg, R. L., & Culhane, J. F. (2007). Low birth weight in the United States. *American Journal of Clinical Nutrition, 85*(Suppl.), 584S–590S.

Goodwin, H. (2002). Data gathered in support of ''Why every child who has an early intervention plan should have a hearing test.'' New York City Department of Mental Health, Early Intervention Program. No longer available (September 20, 2007).

Grant, R. (2005). State strategies to contain costs in the early intervention program: Policy and evidence. *Topics in Early Childhood Special Education, 25,* 243–250.

Grant, R., Nozyce, M., Gordon, A. H., Garwood, J., & Kucera, E. (2003, November). *Developmental and medical status of infants and toddlers referred to the Early Intervention program.* Paper presented at the 131st Annual Meeting of the American Public Health Association, San Francisco, CA.

Graziani, L. J., Mitchell, D. G., Kornhauser, M., Pidcock, F. S., Merton, D. A., Stanley, L., et al. (1992). Neurodevelopment of preterm infants: Neonatal neuro-sonographic and serum bilirubin studies. *Pediatrics, 89,* 229–234.

Guralnick, M. J. (Ed.). (1997). *The effectiveness of early intervention.* Seattle, WA: Brookes.

Hanson, M. J., & Hanline, M. F. (1996). Behavioral competencies and outcomes: The effects of disabilities. Visual development. In M. J. Hanson (Ed.), *Atypical infant development* (2nd ed., pp. 151–152). Austin, TX: Pro-Ed.

Harris, S. R. (1991). Movement analysis—an aid to early diagnosis of cerebral palsy. *Physical Therapy, 71,* 215–221.

Hebbeler, K., Spiker, D., Bailey, D., Scarborough, A., Mallik, S., Simeonsson, R., et al. (2007a, February). *Early intervention for infants and toddlers with disabilities and their families: Participants, services, and outcomes. Final report of the National Early Intervention Longitudinal Study (NEILS)*. Retrieved September 17, 2007, from SRI International web site: www.sri.com/neils/pdfs/NEILS_Report_02_07_Final2.pdf.

Hebbeler, K., Spiker, D., Bailey, D., Scarborough, A., Mallik, S., Simeonsson, R., et al. (2007b, January). *Early intervention for infants and toddlers with disabilities and their families: Participants, services, and outcomes.* Retrieved December 3, 2007, from SRI International web site: http://www.sri.com/neils/pdfs/NEILS_Report_02_07_Final2.pdf.

Himpens, E., Van den Broeck, C., Oostra, A., Calders, P., & Vanhaesebrouck, P. (2008). Prevalence, type, distribution, and severity of cerebral palsy in relation to gestational age: A meta-analytic review. *Developmental Medicine and Child Neurology, 50,* 334–340.

Hoon, A. H. (1996). Visual impairment in children. In A. J. Capute & P. J. Accardo (Eds.), *Developmental disabilities in infancy and childhood: Vol. 2. The spectrum of developmental disabilities* (2nd ed., pp. 461–477). Baltimore, MD: Brookes.

Individuals with Disabilities Education Act, Pub. L. No. 108–446, Sec 632 [5][A][ii] (December 2004). Retrieved September 15, 2007, from www.copyright.gov/legislation/pl1108-446.pdf.

Individuals with Disabilities Education Act (IDEA) Data, Data Accountability Center (n.d.). Retrieved September 15, 2007, from www.IDEAdata.org.

Institute of Medicine of the National Academies. (2007). *Preterm birth: Causes, consequences, and prevention.* [Brochure].Washington, DC: Author.

Jeremy, R. J., Kim, S., Nozyce, M., Nachman, S., McIntosh, K., Pelton, S. I., et al. (2005). Neuropsychological functioning and viral load in stable antiretroviral therapy-experienced HIV-infected children. *Pediatrics, 115,* 380–387.

Jones, K. L. (2006). *Smith's recognizable patterns of human malformation* (6th ed.). Philadelphia, PA: Elsevier Saunders.

Jones, K. L., & Smith, D. W. (1973). Recognition of the fetal alcohol syndrome in early infancy. *The Lancet, 2*(7836), 999–1001.

King, T. M., & Glascoe, F. P. (2003). Developmental surveillance of infants and young children in pediatric primary care. *Current Opinions in Pediatrics, 15,* 624–629.

Kuntz, K. R. (1996). Seizures. In L. A. Kutz, P. W. Dowrick, S. E. Levy, & M. L. Batshaw (Eds.), *Handbook of developmental disabilities: Resources for interdisciplinary care* (pp. 397–400). Gaithersburg, MD: Aspen.

Larroque, B., Ancel, P. Y., Marchand, L., Andre, M., Arnaud, C., Pierrat, V., et al. (2008). Neurodevelopmental disabilities and special care of 5-year-old children born before 33 weeks of gestation (the EPIPAGE study): A longitudinal cohort study. *Lancet, 371,* 813–820.

Lefton-Greif, M. A., & Arvedson, J. C. (2007). Pediatric feeding and swallowing disorders: State of health, population trends, and application of the international classification of functioning, disability, and health. *Seminars in Speech and Language, 28,* 161–165.

Levine, T. P., Liu, J., Das, A., Lester, B., Lagasse, L., Shankaran, S., et al. (2008). Effects of prenatal cocaine exposure on special education in school-aged children. *Pediatrics, 122,* e83–e91.

MacAllister, W. S., & Schaeffer, S. G. (2007). Neuropsychological deficits in childhood epilepsy syndromes. *Neuropsychology Review, 17,* 427–444.

Mahoney, G., Perales, F., Wiggers, B., & Herman, B. (2006). Responsive teaching: Early intervention for children with Down syndrome and other disabilities. *Down Syndrome Research and Practice, 11,* 18–28.

Majnemer, A. (1998). Benefits of early intervention for children with developmental disabilities. *Seminars in Pediatric Neurology, 5,* 62–69.

Malik, S., Cleves, M. A., Zhao, W., Correa, A., Hobbs, C. A., & the National Birth Defects Prevention Study. (2007). Association between congenital heart defects and small for gestational age. *Pediatrics, 119,* e976–e982.

Manning, M. A., & Hoyne, H. E. (2007). Fetal alcohol spectrum disorders: A practical clinical approach to diagnosis. *Neuroscience and Biobehavioral Reviews, 31,* 230–238.

McNab, T. C., & Blackman, J. A. (1998). Medical complications of critically ill newborn: A review for early intervention professionals. *TECSE, 18,* 197–205.

Ment, L. R., Vohr, B., Allan, W., Katz, K. H., Schneider, K. C., Westerveld, M., et al. (2003). Change in cognitive function over time in very low-birth-weight infants. *Journal of the American Medical Association, 289,* 705–711.

Mik, G., Ghove, P. A., Scher, D. M., Widmann, R. F., & Green, D. W. (2008). Down syndrome: Orthopedic issues. *Current Opinion in Pediatrics, 20,* 30–36.

Miles, M. S., Holditch-Davis, D., Schwartz, T. A., & Scher, M. (2007). Depressive symptoms in mothers of prematurely born infants. *Journal of Developmental and Behavioral Pediatrics, 28,* 36–44.

Morton, L. D., & Pellock, J. M. (2000). Overview of childhood epilepsy and epileptic syndromes and advances in therapy. *Current Pharmaceutical Design, 6,* 879–900.

Msall, M. E., Avery, R. C., Tremond, M. R., Lima, J. C., Rogers, M. L., & Hogan, D. P. (2003). Functional disability and school activity limitations in 41,300 school-age children: Relationship to medical conditions. *Pediatrics, 111,* 548–553.

Muller-Nix, C., Forcada-Guex, M., Pierrehumbert, B., Jaunin, L., Borghini, A., & Ansermet, F. (2004). Prematurity, maternal stress, and mother-child interactions. *Early Human Development, 79,* 145–158.

Murphy, C. C., Trevathan, E., & Yeargin-Allsopp, M. (1995). Prevalence of epilepsy and epileptic seizures in 10-year-old children: Results from the metropolitan Atlanta developmental disabilities study. *Epilepsia, 36,* 866–872.

Nelson, K. B. (1996). Epidemiology and etiology of cerebral palsy. In A. J. Capute & P. J. Accardo (Eds.), *Developmental disabilities in infancy and childhood: Vol. 2. The spectrum of developmental disabilities* (2nd ed., pp. 73–79). Baltimore, MD: Brookes.

Neuspeil, D. R. (1994). Behavior in cocaine-exposed infants and children: Association versus causality. *Drug and Alcohol Dependence, 36,* 101–107.

New York State Department of Health, Bureau of Early Intervention (2005, July). *Standards and procedures for evaluations, evaluation reimbursement, and eligibility requirements and determinations under the early intervention program.* Retrieved September 13, 2007, from http://www.health.state.ny.us/community/infants_

children/early_intervention/memoranda/2005-02/docs/memorandum_2005-02 .pdf

Niccols, A. (2007). Fetal alcohol syndrome and the developing socio-emotional brain. *Brain and Cognition, 65*, 135–142.

Nichickel, R. E., & Widerstrom, A. H. (1997). Developmental disorders in infancy. In A. H. Widerstrom, B. A. Mowder, & S. R. Sandall, (Eds.), *Infant development and risk: An introduction* (2nd ed., pp. 89–121). Baltimore, MD: Brookes.

Nordille Jr., D. R., & De Vivo, D. C. (2002). Classification of infantile seizures: Implications for identification and treatment of inborn errors of metabolism. *Journal of Child Neurology, 17*(Suppl. 2), 3S3–3S8.

North Carolina Department of Health and Human Services Infant Toddler Program. (2006). *New Eligibility Definition for the NC Infant Toddler Program.* Retrieved September 13, 2007, from www.ncei.org/ei/pdf/EligibilityDefn.pdf.

Nozyce, M. L., Lee, S. S., Wiznia, A., Nachman, S., Mofenson, L. M., Smith, M. E., et al. (2006). A behavioral and cognitive profile of clinically stable HIV-infected children. *Pediatrics, 117*, 763–770.

NYSDOH (n.d.). *Early intervention clinical practice guideline. Report of the Recommendations. Motor disorders. Assessment and intervention for young children (Age 0-3 years).* Retrieved December 3, 2007, from www.health.state.ny.us/community/infants_ children/early_intervention/docs/guidelines_motor_disorders_assessment_and_ intervention.pdf.

Olson, H. C., Jirikowic, T., Kartin, D., & Astley, S. (2007). Responding to the challenge of early intervention for fetal alcohol spectrum disorders. *Infants and Young Children, 20*, 172–189.

O'Shea, T. M. (2002). Cerebral palsy in very preterm infants: New epidemiological insights. *Mental Retardation and Developmental Disabilities, 8*, 135–145.

Palmer, F. B., & Hoon, A. H. (1995). Cerebral Palsy. In S. Parker & B. Zuckerman (Eds.), *Behavioral and developmental pediatrics: A handbook for primary care* (pp. 88– 94). Boston: Little, Brown & Co.

Piecuch, R. E., Leonard, C. H., & Cooper, B. A. (1998). Infants with birth weight 1,000– 1,499 grams born in three time periods: Has outcome changed over time? *Clinical Pediatrics, 37*, 537–546.

Poitra, B. A., Marion, S., Dionne, M., Wilkie, E., Dauphinais, P., Wilkie-Pipion, M., et al. (2003). A school-based screening program for fetal alcohol syndrome. *Neurotoxicology and Teratology, 25*, 725–729.

Polinski, C. (2003). Hearing outcomes in the neonatal intensive care unit graduate. *Newborn and Infant Nursing Reviews, 3*, 99–103.

Raju, T. N. K. (2007). Commentary. Late preterm births: Challenges and opportunities. *Pediatrics, 121*, 402–403.

Richardson, S. A., Koller, H., & Katz, M. (1980). Seizures and epilepsy in a mentally retarded population over the first 22 years of life. *Applied Research in Mental Retardation, 1*, 123–138.

Rosenberg, S. A., Zhang, D., & Robins, C. C. (2008). Prevalence of developmental delays and participation in early intervention services for young children. *Pediatrics, 121*, e1503–e1509.

Sabaratnam, M., Murthy, N. V., Wijeratne, A., Buckingham, A., & Payne, S. (2003). Autistic-like behaviour profile and psychiatric morbidity in fragile X syndrome. *European Child & Adolescent Psychiatry, 12*, 172–177.

Saemundsen, E., Ludvigsson, P., Hilmarsdottir, I., & Rarnsson, V. (2007). Autism spectrum disorders in children with seizure during the first year of life—a population-based study. *Epilepsia, 48*, 1724–1730.

Sampson, P. D., Streissguth, A. P., Bookstein, F. L., Little, R. E., Clarren, S. K., Dehaene, P., et al. (1997). Incidence of fetal alcohol syndrome and prevalence of alcohol-related neurodevelopmental disorder. *Teratology, 56*, 317–326.

Scheiner, A. P. (1995). Blindness. In B. Zuckerman (Ed.), *Behavioral and developmental pediatrics: A handbook for primary care* (pp. 81–85). Boston: Little, Brown & Co.

Schlesinger, H. S. (1995). Hearing loss. In S. Parker & B. Zuckerman (Eds.), *Behavioral and developmental pediatrics: A handbook for primary care* (pp. 174–179). Boston: Little, Brown & Co.

Schopler, E., Reichler, R. J., & Renner, B. R. (1986). *The Childhood Autism Rating Scale (CARS) for diagnostic screening and classification of Autism.* New York: Irvington.

Schwarz, S. M. (2003). Feeding disorders in children with developmental disabilities. *Infants and Young Children, 16*, 317–330.

Shackleford, J. (2004, February). *State and jurisdictional definitions for infants and toddlers with disabilities under IDEA.* NECTAC notes issue no. 14. Retrieved August 18, 2008, from www.nectac.org/~pdfs/pubs/nnotes21.pdf.

Shum, D., Neulinger, K., I'Callaghan, M., & Mohay, H. (2008). Attentional problems in children born very preterm or with low birth weight at 7–9 years. *Archives of Clinical Neuropsychology, 23*, 103–112.

Silverstein, M., Sand, N., Glascoe, F. P., Gupta, V. B., & Tonniges, T. P. (2006). Pediatrician practices regarding referral to early intervention services: Is an established diagnosis important? *Ambulatory Pediatrics, 6*, 105–109.

Singer, L. T., Arendt, R., Minnes, S., Salvator, A., Siegel, A. C., & Lewis, B. A. (2001). Developing language skills of cocaine-exposed infants. *Pediatrics, 107*, 1057–1064.

Singer, L. T., Salvator, A., Guo, S., Collin, M., Lilien, L., & Baley, J. (1999). Maternal psychological distress and parenting stress after the birth of a very-low-birth-weight infant. *Journal of the American Medical Association, 281*, 799–805.

Spittle, A. J., Doyle, L. W., & Boyd, R. N. (2008). A systematic review of the clinimetric properties of neuromotor assessments for preterm infants during the first year of life. *Developmental Medicine and Child Neurology, 59*, 254–266.

Stoner, J. B., Bailey, R. L., Angell, M. E., Robbins, J., & Polewski, K. (2006). Perspectives of parents/guardians of children with feeding/swallowing problems. *Journal of Developmental and Physical Disabilities, 18*, 333–353.

Tait, M., De Raeve, L., & Nikolopoulos, T. P. (2007). Deaf children with cochlear implants before the age of 1 year: Comparison of preverbal communication with normally hearing children. *International Journal of Pediatric Otorhinolaryngology, 71*, 1605–1611.

Tas, A., Yagiz, R., Tas, M., Esme, M., Uzun, C., & Karasaligoglu, A. R. (2007). Evaluation of hearing children with autism by using TEOAE and ABR. *Autism, 11*, 73–79.

Testa, M., Quigley, B. M., & Das Eiden, R. (2003). The effects of prenatal alcohol exposure on infant mental development: A meta-analytic review. *Alcohol & Alcoholism*, *38*(4), 295–304.

Tharp, B. R. (2002). Neonatal seizures and syndromes. *Epilepsia*, *43*(Suppl. 3) 2–10.

Thompson, J. R., Carter, R. L., Edwards, A. R., Roth, J., Ariet, M., Ross, N. L., et al. (2003). A population based study of the effects of birth weight on early developmental delay or disability in children. *American Journal of Perinatology*, *20*, 321–332.

Turner, G., Webb, T., & Robinson, H. (1996). Prevalence of Fragile X syndrome. *American Journal of Medical Genetics*, *64*, 196–197.

Valencia, D. M., Rimell, F. L., Friedman, B. J., Oblander, M. R., & Helmbrech, J. (2008). Cochlear implantation in infants less than 12 months of age. *International Journal of Pediatric Otorhinolaryngology*, *72*, 767–773.

van Baar, A. L., van Wassenaer, A. G., Briet, J. M., Dekker, F. W., & Kok, J. H. (2005). Very preterm birth is associated with disabilities in multiple developmental domains. *Journal of Pediatric Psychology*, *30*, 247–255.

Van Der Leeden, M., Van Dongen, K., Kleinhout, M., Phaff, J., De Groot, C. J., De Groot, L., et al. (2001). Infants exposed to alcohol prenatally: Outcome at 3 and 7 months of age. *Annals of Tropical Paediatrics*, *21*, 127.

Wade, K. C., Lorch, S. A., Bakewell-Sachs, S., Medoff-Cooper, B., Silber, J. H., & Escobar, G. J. (2008). Pediatric care for preterm infants after NICU discharge: High number of office visits and prescription medications. *Journal of Perinatology*, *28*, 696–701.

Wall, T. C., Marsh-Tootle, W., Evans, H., Fargason Jr., C. A., Ashworth, C. S., & Hardin, J. M. (2002). Compliance with vision-screening guidelines among a national sample of pediatricians. *Pediatrics*, *2*, 449–455.

Wall, T. C., Senicz, E., Evans, H. H., Woolley, A., & Hardin, J. M. (2006). Hearing screening practices among a national sample of primary care pediatricians. *Clinical Pediatrics*, *45*, 559–566.

Wang, C. J., McGlynn, E. A., Brook, R. H., Leonard, C. H., Piecuch, R. E., Hsueh, S. I., et al. (2006). Quality-of-care indicators for the neurodevelopmental follow-up of very low birth weight children: Results of an expert panel process. *Pediatrics*, *117*, 2080–2091.

Weinberg, S., Kern, J., Weiss, K., & Ross, G. (2001). Developmental screening of children diagnosed with congenital heart defects. *Clinical Pediatrics*, *40*, 497–501.

Widen, J. E., Bull, R. W., & Folsom, R. C. (2003). Newborn hearing screening: What it means for providers of early intervention services. *Infants and Young Children*, *16*, 249–257.

Widerstrom, A. H., & Nichol, R. E. (1997). Determinants of risk in infancy. In A. H. Wilderstrom, B. A. Mowder, & S. R. Sandall (Eds.), *Infant development and risk: An introduction* (2nd ed., pp. 61–87). Baltimore, MD: Brookes.

Wilson, S., & Cradock, M. M. (2004). Review: Accounting for prematurity in developmental assessment and the use of age-adjusted scores. *Journal of Pediatric Psychology*, *29*(8), 641–649.

Winter, M., & Eisenberg, L. (1999). Amplification for infants: Selection and verification. *The Otolaryngolic Clinics of North America, 32*, 1051–1065.

Yoshinaga-Itano, C. (2003). Early intervention after universal neonatal hearing screening: Impact on outcomes. *Mental Retardation and Developmental Disabilities Research Reviews, 9*, 252–266.

Zafeirou, D. I., Ververi, A., & Vargiami, E. (2007). Childhood autism and associated comorbidities. *Brain and Development, 29*, 257–272.

Zuckerman, B., & Frank, D. A. (1992). "Crack kids": Not broken. *Pediatrics, 89*, 337–339.

PART IV

INFANT AND EARLY CHILDHOOD CONTEMPORARY ISSUES

CHAPTER 19

Psychopharmacology

LAURA M. ANDERSON
and LEADELLE PHELPS

T HERE IS A strong movement in both psychology and medicine toward identifying practices that result in positive outcomes. The American Psychological Association (APA, 2006) refers to such an approach as *evidence-based practice*. Interest in evaluating treatment procedures has been piqued by poor or ambiguous outcomes, the lack of application from research findings to actual practices, and external demands for accountability (Traughber & D'Amato, 2005). Never have these concerns been more evident than in the prescription of psychotropic medications for young children. In spite of a striking paucity of controlled research studies, the number of preschoolers receiving psychotropic medications is increasing at an alarming rate (American Academy of Child and Adolescent Psychiatry [AACAP], 2004; Gleason et al., 2007; Kaplan, 2008; Luby, 2007).

For example, in a seven-state Medicaid study, Zito and colleagues (2007) found that 2.3% of 274,518 preschoolers received one or more psychoactive medications in 1 year alone. The prevalence rates were as follows: (1) 0.96% for those age 2 years, (2) 2.08% at age 3, and (3) 3.99% at age 4. This study additionally revealed an approximate doubling of prescriptions in a 6-year period (Zito et al., 2007). Although the use of stimulant medication, the most common treatment, did not increase, there was a significant proliferation noted in atypical antipsychotic and antidepressant prescriptions. Other studies have documented that the majority of psychoactive medications prescribed to preschoolers are psychostimulants (DeBar, Lynch, Powell, & Gale, 2003; Gleason et al., 2007; Luby, Stalets, & Belden, 2007). Using a health maintenance organization (HMO) sample, DeBar and colleagues found that 16% of preschoolers who presented with behavioral problems received psychopharmacological treatment, most frequently psychostimulant medication. Luby and colleagues (2007) concurred, reporting 12% of preschoolers in a community sample having received medication for at least 1 month.

In higher risk populations (e.g., medically complex attention deficit/hyperactivity disorder [ADHD], preschoolers in psychiatric hospitals), higher rates of psychotropic drug prescription are reported, generally 50–79%, with more frequent use of multiple medications (Pathak et al., 2004). In spite of these relatively high prevalence rates, there is not an ample research base in this area. Hence, evidence-based practice should reflect the familiar dictum: "First do no harm." Yet medications with no or few efficacy studies on young children will likely continue to be prescribed (American Academy of Pediatrics [AAP] Committee on Drugs, 2002).

CURRENT STATUS OF PRESCHOOL PSYCHOPHARMACOLOGY

ETHICAL CONSIDERATIONS

The Food and Drug Administration (FDA) has approved only four psychotropic medications for children under the age of 6: the dextroamphetamines (Dexedrine, Adderall) for the treatment of ADHD, and chlorpromazine (Thorazine), haloperidol (Haldol), and risperidone (Risperdal) for the reduction of combativeness and perseverative behaviors common in children with developmental disorders or severe oppositional defiant disorder (Anderson et al., 2007; Gleason et al., 2007). Yet off-label (use of a medication to treat a disorder for which there is not FDA approval) prescriptions of psychotropic medication for preschoolers have become a widespread practice (AAP Committee on Drugs, 2002). Although the FDA has provided incentives to increase the development and testing of medications for the pediatric population, psychotropic research trials on children under age 6 have been very limited (Balakrishnan, Grieve, Tordoff, & Norris, 2006; Greenhill et al., 2003; McDougle & Krystal, 2007). Indeed, ethics is called to mind when considering the lack of safety and efficacy data combined with the vulnerable developmental status of children under age 6. In particular, four ethical principles are relevant when considering prescribing or evaluating the effectiveness of psychoactive prescriptions for preschool children: (1) respect for autonomy, (2) justice, (3) beneficence, and (4) nonmaleficence (Spetie & Arnold, 2007).

Respecting *autonomy*, whether in research or practice, requires the professional to (1) ensure that the participant or patient understands and consents to treatment, (2) respect a patient's wish for confidentiality, (3) educate patients or participants about autonomy limits, and (4) adjust applications of this principle to the person's developmental stage (Spetie & Arnold, 2007). Needless to say, the preschooler being treated or evaluated for psychopharmacological intervention complicates the criteria of autonomous treatment. The preschooler's developmental level and cognition makes the preschooler more prone to "egocentric, magical, animistic, alogical, and pre-operational thinking" (Spetie & Arnold, 2007, p. 18). Typical preschool thought (i.e., apart from the psychiatric population) does not allow a child to evaluate overarching concepts such as (1) risk/benefit ratio, (2) perspective-taking regarding another's potential hidden agenda or priorities, or (3) assessment of the value of incentives offered (Gleason et al., 2007). The parental role is critical in considering a preschooler's autonomy, as the parent may be distressed over recent child symptoms and/or motivated by external incentives. It is incumbent upon the provider to assess the parental capacity of operating in their child's best interests.

Within preschool psychopharmacology, the concept of *justice* has been paradoxical, given the vulnerable status of preschoolers and children. Historically, to protect young children (and, essentially, preserve justice), there was an increased reluctance to include them in drug trials that might include risk. Thus, as previously mentioned, they have been the most neglected age group in drug studies (Spetie & Arnold, 2007). *Justice* can be maintained when well-planned preschool psychopharmacological research (i.e., including justifiable, noncoercive, fair incentives for participants) is balanced with the principles of *beneficence and nonmaleficence* (Gleason et al., 2007; Greenhill et al., 2003). In their comprehensive review regarding ethical principles as applied to preschool psychopharmacology, Spetie and Arnold recommended (1) comprehensive risk assessments, (2) the utilization of placebo-controlled trials to assess treatment efficacy, (3) noncoercive reimbursement such as insurance against harm resulting from research, and (4) nonpharmacological screening phase treatments.

NEURODEVELOPMENTAL PROCESSES

The developmental trajectory of a child under age 6 deserves special attention. During a child's earliest years, the developing brain and its neural circuitry demonstrate great plasticity and rearrangement (Shonkoff & Phillips, 2000). Animal and neonatal studies (Gleason et al., 2007) have demonstrated long-term effects on synaptic sensitivity and neurotransmitter receptor activity following early exposure to psychoactive agents. However, neither studies with child participants nor long-term studies regarding safety and efficacy (i.e., to determine appropriate dosage and metabolism of different agents) have been conducted (Gleason et al.; Luby, 2007; Wilens, Faraone, Biederman, & Gunawardene, 2003).

Considering the unique developmental processes taking place within the preschool brain, it is inappropriate to extrapolate results from psychotropic drug studies of older children (Spetie & Arnold, 2007). This is especially true given that drug indications for *older children* are often extrapolated from studies of adults (Abrams, Flood, & Phelps, 2006). Thus, preschoolers are once again doubly vulnerable, as their brains are functioning within a different developmental context than older children. This *dual extrapolation* highlights the urgent need for more work in areas of pharmacokinetics, safety, efficacy, and effectiveness. Both short-term and longitudinal data are needed in order to facilitate the implementation of sound, evidence-based practice in preschool psychopharmacology.

Psychotherapeutic or Nonpharmacological Treatments

When a preschooler is displaying seemingly atypical or maladaptive symptomatology, the first line of defense is generally the child's pediatrician. Of course, pediatricians are trained per their medical specialty. It is possible that the trends in medication prescriptions have something to do with practitioner availability. If a pediatrician does not have an adequate mental health practitioner to refer the child, the pediatrician's scope of practice may limit them to psychopharmacological interventions.

Promising evidence is emerging for decreasing externalizing behavior problems (Shernoff & Kratochwill, 2007; Sonuga-Barke, Daley, Thompson, Laver-Bradbury, & Weeks, 2001; Webster-Stratton, Reid, & Hammond, 2004) and ameliorating child stress reactions (Choate, Pincus, & Eyberg, 2005; Lieberman, Van Horn, & Ippen, 2005). Intervention effectiveness studies for preschool posttraumatic stress disorder (PTSD) and mania-like symptoms are also under way, though the gold standard randomized controlled trial has not yet been published (Gleason et al., 2007). Very recently, models of preschool mental health consultation have emerged in order to meet the needs of this population while addressing the issue of practitioner availability/utilization (Perry, Dunne, & McFadden, 2008; Williford & Shelton, 2008).

In general, risk/benefit assessments suggest that, whenever possible, nonpharmacological interventions should be considered before children under 6 are administered medications with undocumented efficacy and safety. The context of psychosocial treatment *as a first step* underscores the need for child psychologists who maintain current knowledge of their field. Although there may not be a solid evidence base for preschool psychopharmacology, there is an emerging evidence-base for needs-based problem solving in this area.

Assessment and Diagnostics

Assessment   It is recommended that preschool assessments take place within the context of a multidisciplinary team—with multiple informants, across multiple settings, and at multiple points in time (DelCarmen-Wiggins & Carter, 2004; Phelps, Brown, & Power, 2002). Comprehensive developmental, medical, and family histories are also critical. Ideally, structured, standardized, and validated instruments can enhance the information obtained in a comprehensive assessment (Gleason et al., 2007). Furthermore, culturally competent assessment teams should assess the acceptability/feasibility of an intervention and the family's readiness for change when introducing a new psychotropic drug to the family routine (Phelps et al., 2002). Finally, assessment should become an ongoing feedback loop, with medication monitoring and cross-ecological symptom evaluation taking place regularly to facilitate data-driven decision making.

Feasibility is paradoxically called to mind in the aforementioned paragraph when considering the current context of (most) primary care settings. Is a physician generally prepared, able, and willing to conduct a medication evaluation over multiple sessions within the context of a multidisciplinary team? It is neither practical nor feasible to carry out a proper preschool psychopharmacological assessment in the context of today's health care system. As Gleason and colleagues (2007) indicated, though, it would facilitate optimal decision making: "For a primary care prescriber, multiple appointments, collection of collateral information from other caregivers, and consultation with the child's mental health specialist to provide the foundation for treatment decisions while allowing a primary care provider to practice within the scope of his or her knowledge" (p. 1534).

Diagnosis   Reliable and valid diagnostic criteria (e.g., from the *Diagnostic and Statistical Manual of Mental Disorders,* 4th edition, Text Revision [DSM-IV-TR], APA, 2000) typically drive psychological and psychiatric service provision in children and adults. For very young children, however, the treatment of psychological problems not meeting clear-cut criteria has been symptom-based, to date. Although amelioration of these symptoms can be clinically significant, the *symptomatic* use of psychotropics in preschoolers has an even less stable evidence base than the use of psychotropics for preschoolers based on clear-cut diagnostic criteria (Spetie & Arnold, 2007).

Establishing clear-cut criteria is, however, more problematic in very young children than in older children and adults (DelCarmen-Wiggins & Carter, 2004). There is, relatively speaking, only limited understanding of normal versus abnormal behavior at this age, making standardized diagnoses more difficult. Is a child developmentally atypical or pathological? Will a child "grow out of it" or adjust to a situation or stressor? Developmental phenomena such as hyperactivity, imaginary friends, separation anxiety, impulsivity, and negativism can substantially blur the usual boundaries of psychopathology at this age (Gleason et al., 2007; Spetie & Arnold, 2007). The development of new, validated, clinical rating scales for preschool psychopathology and psychopharmacology could facilitate the process of intervening with preschool psychopathology.

Gleason and colleagues (2007) reported two diagnostically sensitive nosologies for addressing concerns about the *DSM-IV*'s lack of attention to preschoolers: the *Diagnostic Crieria: 0-3R* (Zero to Three Diagnostic Classification Task Force, 2005) and the *Research Diagnostic Criteria: Preschool Age* (AACAP Task Force, 2003). Both nosologies are evidence-informed, developmentally sensitive modifications of DSM-IV criteria, intended to increase the reliability and validity of preschool psychopathological assessment and diagnosis. The more recent DC:0-3R also addresses specific clinical manifestations of mental health problems in infants and toddlers with a special emphasis on attachment to caregivers (Gleason et al., 2007).

In summary, much more work on systematic assessment and diagnosis in children under age 6 must be done before methodologically sound effectiveness research can be conducted in this area. Reliable, valid assessment measures are needed, while research on developmental psychopathology is necessary to examine the clinical validity of psychiatric symptoms in young children. Medication assessments cannot be piecemeal or haphazard, regardless of the current sociomedical climate. Clinical trials in preschoolers must use thorough and sensitive measures that can detect adverse effects of medications on physiological functioning as well as multiple domains of development. Instruments cannot always be extrapolated from older children: they must be revised or *devised* to be developmentally appropriate. Finally, efficacy, safety, and feasibility evaluation must be ongoing, standardized, and ethically sound. Needless to say, there is work to be done before we can safely *study* the effectiveness of, much less safely *administer*, psychotropic medication in preschool children.

THE STATE OF THE EVIDENCE BASE: PSYCHOACTIVE MEDICATIONS IN PRESCHOOLERS

As stated earlier, there is not yet a broad evidence base guiding the use of psychotropic medications for children under age 6 (AACAP, 2004). Although there has been one multisite, randomized, placebo-controlled trial – the *Preschoolers with Attention-Deficit/Hyperactivity Disorder Treatment Study* (PATS; Greenhill et al., 2006; Riddle, 2007), the majority of data have come from case studies, retrospective chart reviews, open label studies, and extrapolations from work with older populations (Gleason et al., 2007; Luby, 2007). The PATS was designed to assess the efficacy and safety of short-term methylphenidate (MPH) in 3- to 5-year-olds with ADHD (Kollins et al., 2006; Riddle, 2007; Wigal et al., 2006). The design of PATS was complex and included eight phases: (1) enrollment/screening; (2) uncontrolled parent training (10 weeks); (3) baseline assessment; (4) one-week, open-label, safety lead-in; (5) 5-week, random sequence, double-blind, crossover titration; (6) 10-month, open-label maintenance; and (7) 5-week, placebo-substitution discontinuation (Riddle, 2007). A special issue in the *Journal of Child and Adolescent Psychopharmacology* (2007) summarized the latest findings.

Overall, the PATS results suggest that MPH is an effective short-term and long-term (i.e., up to 10 months) treatment. The best mean daily dose for preschoolers (i.e., 14 mg/day) was found to be considerably lower than in older children; however, with longer-term treatment, higher total doses were needed (e.g., about 20 mg/day). Side effects (e.g., irritability, sleeplessness, dry mouth) were generally tolerable and were less invasive than the ADHD symptomatology (Wigal et al., 2006). However, decreases in height and weight growth during long-term treatment were significant among treatment groups (Swanson et al., 2006). Nonetheless, significant functional improvement emerged in global functioning and social skills during long-term treatment (Abikoff et al., 2007; Riddle, 2007).

Interestingly, the PATS data also gave unique information about ADHD in preschoolers. Anxiety disorders, communication disorders, and oppositional defiant disorders were found to be the most common comorbidities, and those children with multiple comorbidities were the most likely to be medication resistant (Ghuman et al., 2007; Riddle, 2007; Vitiello et al., 2007). Parent and teacher ratings did not always agree, consistent with other findings (Hardy et al., 2007; Lien, Carlson, Hunter-Oehmke, & Knapp, 2007; Michelson et al., 2004; Murray et al., 2007). Furthermore, DSM criteria did not match preschoolers' symptom sets for ADHD: that is, a two-factor model (e.g., inattention and impulsivity/hyperactivity) fit the data only after several symptoms were removed, suggesting that criteria should be modified for preschoolers (Murray et al.; Posner et al., 2007; Riddle, 2007).

Finally, the PATS data revealed important information regarding the use of blood versus buccal (i.e., cheek swab) genotyping in studies of ADHD in preschoolers. Swanson and colleagues (2006) examined the impact of the source of DNA (from blood versus buccal cells) on genotyping success rate and allele percentages for candidate genes investigated in the PATS. Compared to methods available in 2004 (see McGough et al., 2006), the genotyping success rate was significantly higher for DNA from blood cells (91%) versus buccal cells (54%). Furthermore, allele proportion was found to vary by source of cell for some polymorphisms. As Riddle (2007) so aptly summarized, Swanson and colleagues have called to mind a methodological issue in pediatric pharmacogenetics: "How does the investigator balance the advantage of obtaining buccal cells (more children will likely participate) versus the disadvantage (lower genotyping success rate and altered allele frequencies)?" (Riddle, p. 545, based on Swanson et al.).

Proven pharmacological interventions for other childhood disorders beyond ADHD are sorely needed. Luby (2007) pointed out how sharply this *lack* of data stands out despite the advances that have been made in other areas of early intervention. Early identification, recognition, prevention, and treatment of disorders in so many areas of development have been emphasized, yet studies within psychopharmacology are sorely absent. An entire special issue of the *Journal of Child and Adolescent Psychopharmacology* (2007) emphasized the dearth of controlled data for psychopharmacological treatment of preschoolers as of 2007. As Luby indicated in her guest editorial, this is an area truly in its infancy and in urgent need of more evidence.

CLOSING THE GAP: THE PRESCHOOL PSYCHOPHARMACOLOGY WORKING GROUP (PPWG)

To address concerns about the growing use of medication in preschoolers, despite a lack of sound empirical evidence, the Preschool Psychopharmacology Working Group (PPWG) of the American Academy of Child and Adolescent Psychiatry (AACAP) developed algorithms to treat preschoolers based on extensive literature reviews, expert consensus, and combined clinical experiences (Gleason et al., 2007). The primary goal of the PPWG was to review the current state of evidence for clinicians and to develop a set of standardized, evidence-informed guidelines to guide practitioners (Gleason et al.; Kaplan, 2008).

Specific algorithms were developed for the treatment of preschoolers with (1) ADHD; (2) disruptive behavior disorders; (3) major depressive disorder; (4) bipolar disorder; (5) anxiety disorders, such as separation anxiety disorder, selective mutism, and specific phobia; (6) PTSD; (7) obsessive–compulsive disorder (OCD); (8) pervasive developmental disorders; and (9) primary sleep disorders (Gleason et al., 2007; Kaplan, 2008).

The treatment algorithms share five common factors. First, given the developmental significance and importance of assessment and diagnosis in any clinical practice, they are included in each algorithm to emphasize the fact that these processes can be even more complex in children under age 6 (DelCarmen-Wiggins & Carter, 2004). Reassessment of diagnosis and clinical conceptualization is recommended at each treatment initiation point in order to acknowledge young children's rapid development (Gleason et al., 2007).

Second, psychotherapeutic treatment steps are included as a critical component of each algorithm. For some diagnoses, the weight of evidence supporting psychosocial interventions is stronger than for medication, making it an empirically driven recommendation (Gleason et al., 2007). Third, each step is marked with the level of evidence supporting that particular step, allowing the clinician to consider the body of literature and apply it to the particular individual's unique situation or context.

Fourth, each algorithm includes recommendations for a discontinuation trial after successful psychopharmacological treatment in order to recognize the importance of reassessing the need for medication in rapidly developing preschoolers (Gleason et al., 2007). Fifth and finally, the PPWG recognizes that patients may arrive at the end of a treatment algorithm with continued distress or impairment. If this occurs, clinical consultation is recommended, ideally with a colleague who has expertise in early childhood psychiatry (Gleason et al.; Kaplan, 2008).

Although each algorithm addresses an individual diagnosis, the PPWG offers a number of universal guidelines in order to facilitate careful, thoughtful clinical practice. The universal guidelines are as follows:

1. Avoid medication when therapy is likely to produce results.
2. An adequate trial of psychotherapy precedes consideration of medication and psychotherapy continues if and when medication is used.
3. Medication should be considered in the context of a clinical diagnosis and substantial functional impairment.
4. A system should be developed to track symptoms and impairment before initiating treatment.
5. Parent referral or treatment for psychopathology may maximize their ability to participate in treatment as well as family mental health.
6. Informed consent includes explicit information about FDA approval status and level of evidence supporting psychopharmacological recommendations.
7. The *N of 1* trial approach should be considered when initiating medication.
8. Medication discontinuation trials should reduce unnecessary medication treatment.
9. The use of medications to treat side effects from other medications is not recommended (Gleason et al., 2007; Kaplan, 2008).

Gleason and colleagues (2007) of the PPWG indicated that the applications of the algorithms may reduce the number of preschoolers who are prescribed psychiatric drugs. By publishing the algorithms, the PPWG seeks to encourage future research and alert practitioners to the current state of the evidence base (Kaplan, 2008).

PRESCHOOL PSYCHOPHARMACOLOGY: CONCLUDING REMARKS & FUTURE IMPLICATIONS

The field of preschool psychopharmacology simply needs more evidence. Although it is not "simple," per se, practitioners can begin collecting data with as many patients/clients as possible. In the meantime, more multivariate, birth-cohort studies are needed (Egger & Angold, 2006; Gleason et al., 2007; Luby, 2007). Examination of efficacy, safety, feasibility, and acceptability across different cohorts at different points in time is essential.

We must examine health disparities within the realities of today's system. For example, perhaps a Latino or African American family is referred to her/ his pediatrician first because of cultural sensitivity to psychotherapy. Perhaps that person may have considered a psychosocial intervention if he or she had received a culture-friendly evaluation from a multidisciplinary treatment team (DuPaul, Perez, Kuo, Stein, & Sedberry, 2007). Or, conversely, what if a child from a particular culture is plagued with a serious psychopathological disturbance? What if her or his parent or guardian is resistant to medication because of a lack of understanding or availability of culturally sensitive practitioners? Science and practice can merge to address process and outcome variables.

In terms of practice recommendations, the PPWG has made many within their algorithms, and all practitioners are encouraged to visit the AACAP web site (www.aacap.org) in order to learn more. Comprehensive assessment, diagnostic, and treatment planning and evidence-informed practice are essential. Medication and symptom logs with parents can assist with data-driven decision making.

Sometimes practitioner availability is the biggest hurdle for preschool families. Massachusetts is one state that has begun multiple efforts to help pediatricians through the Massachusetts Child Psychiatry Access Project (MCPAP) and the Children's Behavioral Health Initiative of the Executive Office of Health and Human Services and MassHealth (Kaplan, 2008). The state's Medicaid and children's health insurance plans reside under MassHealth.

MCPAP consists of six mental health teams, including therapists and child psychiatrists, working beneath the supervision of child psychiatry divisions of academic medical centers across the state. Each team's objective is to enroll all of the pediatric primary care practices in its geographic area. Then, once enrolled, primary care physicians have access to several services for their patients, regardless of insurance status. These services include informal telephone consultation, timely psychiatric diagnostic evaluations, and interim counseling. The MCPAP is especially focused on primary care providers who need assistance with children less than 5 years of age (Kaplan, 2008).

As of December 31, 2007, MassHealth also began requiring providers to use standardized behavioral health screening as part of the Early Periodic Screening, Diagnosis, and Treatment project. Resources for referring those with positive screen results are also provided (Kaplan, 2008). Although this is just a first step, it is an example of one state's attempt to respond to the need for more standardized practice in preschool mental health and psychopharmacology.

The practice of preschool psychopharmacology is in its infancy: there is no doubt that more evidence is needed for the development of confident, empirically driven, scientist practitioners. Again, though, insufficient evidence cannot preclude helping preschoolers and their families who are receiving scripts for psychoactive medications. Preschool psychopharmacology may be an area where it becomes a psychologist's ethical duty to advocate for more research while also sharing the state of the evidence base with families and practitioners. Collaborating within the medical climate of billable hours and managed care is neither easy nor enjoyable in all circumstances. If the scientist–practitioner is to act in the best interests of the preschool child, however, he or she will become an ambassador of coordinating (1) comprehensive, (2) evidence-informed, and (3) developmentally sensitive psychopharmacological evaluation and monitoring for our youngest, most vulnerable citizens.

REFERENCES

AACAP Task Force on Research Diagnostic Criteria: Infancy Preschool Age. (2003). Research diagnostic criteria for infants and preschool children: The process and empirical support. *Journal of the American Academy of Child and Adolescent Psychiatry, 42,* 1504–1512.

Abikoff, H. B., Vitiello, B., Riddle, M. A., Cunningham, C., Greenhill, L. L., & Swanson, J. M. (2007). Methylphenidate effects on functional outcomes in the Preschoolers with ADHD Treatment Study (PATS). *Journal of Child and Adolescent Psychopharmacology, 17,* 581–592.

Abrams, L. M., Flood, J., & Phelps, L. (2006). Psychopharmacology in the schools. *Psychology in the Schools, 41,* 493–502.

American Academy of Child and Adolescent Psychiatry [AACAP]. (2004). 2004N-0330-*Joint Meeting of the Psychopharmacologic Drugs Advisory Committee and the Pediatric Advisory Committee.* Retrieved January 15, 2005, from www.aacap.org/Announcements/AACAP_Comment.htm.

American Academy of Pediatrics [AAP] Committee on Drugs. (2002). Uses of drugs not described in the package insert (off-label uses). *Pediatrics, 110,* 181–182.

American Psychiatric Association (2000). *Diagnostic and Statistical Manual of Mental Disorders* (4th ed., Text Revision). Washington, DC: Author.

American Psychological Association Presidential Task Force on Evidence-based Practice. (2006). Evidence-based practice in psychology. *American Psychologist, 61,* 271–285.

Anderson, G. M., Scahill, L., McCracken, J. T., McDougle, C. J., Aman, M. G., & Tierney, E. (2007). Effects of short- and long-term risperidone treatment on prolactin levels in children with autism. *Biological Psychiatry, 61,* 545–550.

Balakrishnan, K., Grieve, J., Tordoff, J., & Norris, P. (2006). Pediatric licensing status and the availability of suitable formulations for new medical entities approved in the United States between 1998 and 2002. *Journal of Clinical Psychopharmacology, 46,* 1038–1043.

Choate, M. L., Pincus, D. B., & Eyberg, S. M. (2005). Parent-child interaction therapy for treatment of separation anxiety disorder in young children: A pilot study. *Cognitive Behavior Therapy, 12,* 136–145.

Debar, L. L., Lynch, F., Powell, J., & Gale, J. (2003). Use of psychotropic agents in preschool children: Associated symptoms, diagnoses, and health care services in a health maintenance organization. *Archives of Pediatric & Adolescent Medicine, 157,* 150–157.

DelCarmen-Wiggins, R., & Carter, A. (Eds.). (2004). *Handbook of infant, toddler, and preschool mental health assessment.* New York: Oxford University Press.

DuPaul, G. J., Perez, V. H., Kuo, A., Stein, M.T., & Sedberry, D. (2007). Juan: A 9-year-old Latino boy with ADHD. *Journal of Developmental and Behavioral Pediatrics, 28,* 53–57.

Egger, H. L., & Angold, A. (2006). Common emotional and behavioral disorders in preschool children: Presentation, nosology, and epidemiology. *Journal of Child Psychology and Psychiatry, 47,* 313–337.

Ghuman, J. K., Riddle, M. A., Vitiello, B., Greenhill, L. L., Chuang, S. Z., & Wigal, S. B. (2007). Comorbidity moderates response to methylphenidate in the Preschoolers with Attention-Deficit/Hyperactivity Disorder Treatment Study (PATS). *Journal of Child and Adolescent Psychopharmacology, 17,* 563–579.

Gleason, M. M., Egger, H. L., Emslie, J. E., Greenhill, L. L., Kowatch, R. A., & Lieberman, A. F. (2007). Psychopharmacological treatment for very young children: Contexts and guidelines. *Journal of the American Academy of Child and Adolescent Psychiatry, 46,* 1532–1572.

Greenhill, L. L., Kollins, S., Abikoff, H., McCracken, J., Riddle, M., & Swanson, J. (2006). Efficacy and safety of immediate-release methylphenidate treatment for preschoolers with ADHD. *Journal of the American Academy of Child & Adolescent Psychiatry, 45,* 1284–1293.

Greenhill, L. L., Jensen, P. S., Abikoff, H., Blumer, J. L., Deveaugh-Geiss, J., & Fisher, C. (2003). Developing strategies for psychopharmacological studies in preschool children. *Journal of the American Academy of Child & Adolescent Psychiatry, 42,* 406–414.

Hardy, K. K., Kollins, S. H., Murray, D. W., Riddle, M. A., Greenhill, L. L., & Cunningham, C. (2007). Factor structure of parent- and teacher-rated attention deficit/hyperactivity disorder symptoms in the Preschoolers with Attention-Deficit/Hyperactivity Disorder Treatment Study (PATS). *Journal of Child and Adolescent Psychopharmacology, 17,* 621–633.

Kaplan, A. (2008). Psychiatric medication guidelines set for preschoolers. *Psychiatric Times, 25,* 1–2.

Kollins, S., Greenhill, L., Swanson, J., Wigal, S., Abikoff, H., & McCracken, J. (2006). Rationale, design, and methodology of the pre-school ADHD treatment study (PATS). *Journal of the American Academy of Child and Adolescent Psychiatry, 45,* 1275–1283.

Lieberman, A. F., Van Horn, P., & Ippen, C. G. (2005). Toward evidence-treatment: Child–parent psychotherapy with preschoolers exposed to marital violence. *Journal of the American Academy of Child & Adolescent Psychiatry, 44,* 1241–1248.

Lien, M. T., Carlson, J. S., Hunter-Oehmke, S., & Knapp, K. A. (2007). A pilot investigation of teachers' perceptions of psychotropic drug use in schools. *Journal of Attention Disorders, 11,* 172–177.

Luby, J. L. (2007). Guest editorial: Psychopharmacology of psychiatric disorders in the preschool period. *Journal of Child and Adolescent Psychopharmacology, 17,* 149–151.

Luby, J. L., Stalets, M., & Belden, A. (2007). Psychotropic prescriptions in a sample including both healthy and mood and disruptive disordered preschoolers: Relationships to diagnosis, impairment, prescriber type, and assessment methods. *Journal of Child & Adolescent Psychopharmacology, 17,* 205–215.

McDougle, C. J., & Krystal, J. H. (2007). Pediatric psychopharmacology: Mood, anxiety, and disruptive behavior/pervasive developmental disorders. *Psychopharmacology, 191,* 1–3.

McGough, J., McCracken, J., Swanson, J., Riddle, M., Kollins, S., & Greenhill, L. (2006). Pharmacogenetics of methylphenidate response in preschoolers with ADHD. *Journal of the American Academy of Child & Adolescent Psychiatry, 45,* 1314–1322.

Michelson, D., Buitelaar, J. K., Danckaerts, M., Gilberg, S., Spencer, T. J., & Zuddas, A. (2004). Relapse prevention in pediatric patients with ADHD treated with atomoxetine: A randomized, double-blind, placebo-controlled study. *Journal of the American Academy of Child and Adolescent Psychiatry, 43,* 806–904.

Murray, D., Kollins, S. H., Hardy, K. K., Abikoff, H. B., Swanson, J. M., & Cunningham, C. (2007). Parent versus teacher ratings of attention-deficit/hyperactivity disorder symptoms in the Preschoolers with Attention-Deficit/Hyperactivity Disorder Treatment Study (PATS). *Journal of Child and Adolescent Psychopharmacology, 17,* 605–619.

Pathak, S., Arszman, S. P., Daniehan, A., John, E. S., Smirnov, A., & Kowatch, R. A. (2004). Psychotropic utilization and psychiatric presentation of hospitalized very young children. *Journal of Child and Adolescent Psychopharmacology, 4,* 433–442.

Perry, D. F., Dunne, M. C., & McFadden, L. (2008). Reducing the risk for preschool expulsion: Mental health consultation for young children with challenging behaviors. *Journal of Child and Family Studies, 17,* 44–54.

Phelps, L., Brown, R. T., & Power, T. J. (2002). *Pediatric psychopharmacology: Combining medical and psychosocial interventions.* Washington, DC: American Psychological Association.

Posner, K., Melvin, G. A., Murray, D. W., Gugga, S. S., Fisher, P., & Skrobala, A. M. (2007). Clinical presentation of attention-deficit/hyperactivity disorder in preschool children: The Preschool Attention-Deficit/Hyperactivity Disorder Treatment Study (PATS). *Journal of Child and Adolescent Psychopharmacology, 17,* 547–562.

Riddle, M. A. (2007). New findings from the Preschoolers with Attention-Deficit/Hyperactivity Disorder Treatment Study (PATS). *Journal of Child and Adolescent Psychopharmacology, 17,* 543–546.

Shernoff, E. S., & Kratochwill, T. R. (2007). Transporting an evidence-based classroom management program for preschoolers with disruptive behavior problems to a school: An analysis of implementation, outcomes, and contextual variables. *School Psychology Quarterly, 22,* 449–472.

Shonkoff, J. P., & Phillips, D. A. (2000). *From neurons to neighborhoods: The science of early childhood development: Committee on integrating the science of early childhood development, Institute of Medicine.* Washington, DC: National Academy Press.

Sonuga-Barke, E. J. S., Daley, D., Thompson, M., Laver-Bradbury, C., & Weeks, A. (2001). Parent-based therapies for preschool attention-deficit/hyperactivity disorder: A randomized, controlled trial with a community sample. *Journal of the American Academy of Child and Adolescent Psychiatry, 40*, 402–408.

Spetie, L., & Arnold, E. L. (2007). Ethical issues in child psychopharmacology research and practice: Emphasis on preschoolers. *Psychopharmalogia* (Berlin), *191*, 15–26.

Swanson, J., Greenhill, L., Wigal, T., Kollins, S., Stehli, A., & Davies, M. (2006). Stimulant-related reductions of growth rates in the PATS. *Journal of the American Academy of Child and Adolescent Psychiatry, 45*, 1304–1313.

Traughber, M. C., & D'Amato, R. C. (2005). Integrating evidence-based neuropsychological services into school settings: Issues and challenges for the future. In R. C. D'Amato, E. Fletcher-Janzen, & C. R. Reynolds (Eds.), *Handbook of School Neuropsychology* (pp. 827–757). Hoboken, NJ: Wiley.

Vitiello, B., Abikoff, H. B., Chuang, S. Z., Kollins, S. H., McCracken, J. T., & Riddle, M. A. (2007). Effectiveness of methylphenidate in the 10-month continuation phase of the Preschoolers with ADHD Treatment Study (PATS). *Journal of Child and Adolescent Psychopharmacology, 17*, 593–604.

Webster-Stratton, C., Reid, M. J., & Hammond, M. (2004). Treating children with early-onset conduct problems: Intervention outcomes for parent, child, and teacher training. *Journal of Clinical Child and Adolescent Psychology, 33*, 105–124.

Wigal, T., Greenhill, L., Chuang, S., McGough, J., Vitiello, B., & Skrobala, A. (2006). Safety and tolerability of methylphenidate in preschool children with ADHD. *Journal of the American Academy of Child and Adolescent Psychiatry, 45*, 1294–1303.

Wilens, T. E., Faraone, S. V., Biederman, J., & Gunawardene, S. (2003). Does stimulant therapy of attention-deficit/hyperactivity disorder beget later substance abuse? A meta-analytic review of the literature. *Pediatrics, 111*, 179–185.

Williford, A. P., & Shelton, T. L. (2008). Using mental health consultation to decrease disruptive behaviors in preschoolers: Adapting an empirically-supported intervention. *Journal of Child Psychology and Psychiatry, 49*, 191–200.

Zero to Three Diagnostic Classification Task Force (2005). *Diagnostic Classification of Mental Health and Development Disorders of Infancy and Early Childhood: DC:0–3R.* Washington, DC: Zero to Three Press.

Zito, J. M., Safer, D. J., Valluri, S., Gardner, J. F., Korelitz, J. J., & Mattison, D. R. (2007). Psychotherapeutic medication prevalence in Medicaid-insured preschoolers. *Journal of Child and Adolescent Psychopharmacology, 17*, 195–203.

CHAPTER 20

Trauma

ANASTASIA E. YASIK

ALTHOUGH MANY TRAUMAS and crises are encountered throughout life, how the event is processed is dependent on age and developmental stage. Young children are particularly vulnerable since they lack sophisticated coping resources and, further, are dependent on others (e.g., caregivers, parents) for security. This chapter reviews the types and prevalence of traumatic events, as well as young children's myriad stress reactions. Further, current diagnostic classification systems are presented in conjunction with evidence-based assessment measures and interventions for trauma-exposed children and their families. Multicultural, training, and ethical issues are also presented.

TYPES OF TRAUMAS EXPERIENCED

Regrettably, infants, toddlers, and young children are exposed to traumatic events in the United States and throughout the world on a daily basis. The types of traumas that occur in early childhood are similar to those that might be experienced by older children, adolescents, and adults. For example, young children may be exposed to motor vehicle accidents (MVAs), community and school violence (e.g., physical assaults, shootings, seeing someone killed), complex trauma (i.e., exposure to multiple or chronic stressors), domestic violence, medical trauma (e.g., invasive procedures), natural disasters, physical abuse/neglect, refugee and war zone trauma, sexual abuse, terrorism, and/or traumatic grief (i.e., death of a loved one via a traumatic event) (National Child Traumatic Stress Network, 2008).

FREQUENCY OF TRAUMATIC EVENTS IN EARLY CHILDHOOD

The U.S. Department of Health and Human Services (DHHS, 2008) recently published *Child Maltreatment 2006* which presents statistical data, collected by the National Child Abuse and Neglect Data System (NCANDS), on cases of child abuse and neglect known to the U.S. Child Protective Services (CPS). According to this report, during 2006 approximately 905,000 children were found to be victims of child abuse or neglect. Of this number, 64.1% suffered neglect, 16% were physically abused, 8.8% were sexually abused, 6.6% were emotionally or psychologically maltreated, and 2.2% were medically neglected. Furthermore, 15.1% of victims experienced other types of maltreatment (e.g., abandonment, threat of harm).

When examined by age of the child victim, it is apparent that the youngest children are those who suffer the highest rates of victimization. Nearly three-quarters of child victims (72.2%) ages birth to 1 year and 1–3 years of age (72.9%) were neglected compared to the 55.0% neglect rate of victims 16 and older. In contrast, child victims younger than 7 years of age were less likely to experience sexual abuse (0.4–8.2%) and/or physical abuse (10.8–15.3%) relative to children 12 and older (physical abuse 20.1–22%; sexual abuse 16.1–16.5%). Perpetrators of maltreatment were most often mothers acting alone (39.9%), followed by fathers acting alone (17.6%), mother and father acting together (17.8%), unknown perpetrators (7.6%), mother and other acting together (6.0%), other relative (4.9%), and other individuals (e.g., daycare worker, friend, neighbor, other professional) accounting for the remaining 8.2% (DHHS, 2008).

With respect to accident related traumas a host of events (e.g., bicycle accidents, dog bites, fires, MVAs) have been investigated and suggest high degrees of traumatic exposure in the early years of life. For example, the 2005 MVA injury rate for children younger than 5 years was 276 per 100,000 and increased to 380 per 100,000 between the ages of 5–9 years. Nearly 52 per 100,000 children between the ages of 0–9 years accounted for pedestrian-related injuries in 2005 (National Highway Traffic Safety Administration, 2008). Bicycling accidents were more frequent occurring in 288 per 100,000 children aged 0–9 years during 2006. Playground-related injuries resulting in emergency room visits are most common for children ages 5–9 (Phelan, Khoury, Kalkwarf, & Lanphear, 2001). Furthermore, the risk for dog bites is greatest among children 0 to 9, with 200 per 100,000 being bitten by a dog. Children under 4 are at greater risk for fire-related injuries (Centers for Disease Control and Prevention [CDC], 1998). Given the degree of exposure to traumatic events, early childhood psychologists need to understand the reactions infants, toddlers, and children may have to such traumatic events.

STRESS REACTIONS IN CHILDREN

Numerous studies have examined children exposed to accidents, criminal victimization (e.g., sexual abuse, sexual assault), natural disasters, and war-related stressors (e.g., Gabbay, Oatis, Silva, & Hirsch, 2004; Saigh, Yasik, Sack, & Koplewicz, 1999). Research suggests that children who are maltreated evidence a host of problems such as learning difficulties, affect regulation difficulties, behavioral difficulties, and increased risk for substance abuse (Chaffin, Kelleher, & Hollenberg, 1996; Giaconia et al., 1995). Whether or not a child develops posttraumatic stress disorder (PTSD) subsequent to a traumatic event can increase the likelihood of negative long-term consequences as research shows that children who develop PTSD are more likely to evidence academic impairment (Saigh, Mroueh, & Bremner, 1997), cognitive difficulties (Yasik, Saigh, Oberfield, & Halamandaris, 2007), internalizing and externalizing difficulties (Saigh, Yasik, Oberfield, Halamandaris, & McHugh, 2002).

However, the majority of studies in the literature have focused on school-age populations. Dyregrov and Yule (2006) note that few longitudinal studies have been conducted on the natural course of stress reactions in children, especially preschool populations. Furthermore, the great majority of the child trauma studies have utilized diagnostic criteria established for adults which may not be appropriate for early childhood populations. This section provides an overview of studies addressing traumatic stress reactions in children younger than 7 years of age.

WAR-RELATED STRESS

The first longitudinal study of stress reactions in preschoolers was conducted by Laor et al. (1997) who studied Israeli preschoolers (aged 3–5 years) and their mothers exposed to Scud missile attacks during the Gulf War. Comparisons were made between families displaced from their homes due to damage sustained during the war, families not displaced as their homes remained intact, and those from an area not directly hit by missiles. Results indicated that 7.8% of preschoolers evidenced sufficient symptoms of PTSD to warrant a diagnosis. Furthermore, displaced children, as well as their mothers, evidenced significantly more PTSD symptoms than those in the other two groups.

More recently, Sadeh, Hen-Gal, and Tikotzky (2008) reported on the effects of war-related stressors (i.e., Israel-Lebanon War of 2006) on 74 preschool children (2–7 years). Most of the children were reported to have experienced 3 or 4 war-related experiences (e.g., casualty in the family, environmental damage, hearing explosions, living in war shelters). Eighty-four percent of children presented with at least one symptom at a severe level and 55% had three or more symptoms at a severe level. Approximately 80% of children evidenced separation fears. Furthermore, 60% were reported to be nervous, agitated, or aggressive; have anxiety and fears due to their war experiences; and have strong reactions to noise. Excessive crying and nightmares were present in approximately 50% of children. None of the stress reactions were significantly associated with age, gender, or family composition at the camp. However, higher exposure level was correlated significantly with measures of stress reactions.

DISASTER-RELATED STRESS

Scheeringa and Zeanah (2008) reported on the after effects of Hurricane Katrina on 70 preschool children (aged 3–6 years) and their caregivers who resided in New Orleans. While 65.8% of participants were evacuated from the city, the remaining 34.2% were trapped in the city. The group that remained in the city evidenced significantly more symptoms of PTSD ($M = 6.1$) than the evacuated group ($M = 5.1$). Similarly, the group that remained evidenced significantly more symptoms ($M = 2.2$) of separation anxiety disorder (SAD) than the group that was evacuated ($M = 1.5$).

Vila et al. (2001) assessed children (aged 4–13 years) and their parents 6–7 months following an industrial accident in which the ground caved in due to former iron mining activity. Three groups were established: those who had been evacuated from their homes (*disaster*), families from nonevacuated regions (*threatened*), and families from an area not in danger of ground collapse (*control*). Approximately 70% of the disaster group included children aged 0–7 years, while the other groups only included children 8 and older. Children in the disaster group, in contrast to the threatened and control groups, were found to have significantly more behavioral problems as per parent report. A trend toward significance was noted for the Conners' Parent Rating Scale (CPRS), with children 4–7 years having higher scores than children 8 and older. Symptoms of PTSD among children younger than 7 were not examined in this study due to a lack of appropriate assessment instruments for self-report of symptoms.

CRIMINAL VICTIMIZATION

With regard to criminal victimization studies, Levendosky, Huth-Bocks, Semel, and Shapiro (2002) reported on the effects of witnessing domestic violence in a sample of 39 preschoolers (aged 3–5 years). All of the mothers reported that their children had been "intensely upset" by witnessing the event(s). With regard to symptom presentation, 77% of children were reported to talk about the violent event, 44% became upset when something reminded him or her about the event, 41% demonstrated an exaggerated startle response, 36% developed a fear of separation from their primary caregiver since the event, 23% engaged in traumatic play, and 21% had an increase in frightening dreams since the event. Reexperiencing symptoms were significantly correlated with increased externalizing behaviors, with 29% of the sample having clinically significant scores on the Child Behavior Checklist (CBCL; Achenbach, 1991). Despite this high degree of symptomatology, only one child (3%) met diagnostic criteria for PTSD according to the *Diagnostic and Statistical Manual of Mental Disorders*, 4th edition, Text Revision (DSM-IV-TR; APA, 2000).

Scheeringa, Zeanah, Myers, and Putnam (2005) explored the posttraumatic reactions of 62 children (20 months to 6 years) 1, 2, and 3 years after exposure to different traumatic events (i.e., invasive medical procedures, MVA, other accidents, witnessed domestic violence). One year after their traumatic experiences, 66.7% had reexperiencing symptoms, 38.7% had avoidance and numbing symptoms, and 45.2% had symptoms of increased arousal. Based on modified PTSD criteria (explained in more detail below), 25.8% of children had PTSD at year 1, 23.4% at year 2, and 22.9% at year 3. Those children who were diagnosed with PTSD at time 1 continued to have significantly more symptoms than those children without a diagnosis of PTSD at time 1. Symptoms persisted for 2 years, despite children receiving community-based interventions. As the amount of children who demonstrated impaired functioning at times 2 (48.9%) and 3 (74.3%) exceeds the percent of children diagnosed with PTSD at these time points, clinicians should not only address diagnostic issues but also consider symptom presentation and functional impairment when conducting assessments.

CURRENT DIAGNOSTIC CLASSIFICATIONS

The diagnostic category of posttraumatic stress disorder (PTSD) was first introduced into the diagnostic nomenclature with the publication of the *Diagnostic and Statistical Manual of Mental Disorders*, 3rd edition (DSM-III; APA, 1980). However, the idea that PTSD may present differently in children was not considered until the DSM-III-R (APA, 1987). Currently, two diagnostic classification systems are utilized in the United States for classifying stress reactions in infants, toddlers, and young children. These classification systems are the DSM–IV-TR (APA, 2000) and the *Diagnostic Classification of Mental Health and Developmental Disorders of Infancy and Early Childhood–Revised* (DC:0-3R; Zero to Three, 2005).

DIAGNOSTIC AND STATISTICAL MANUAL OF MENTAL DISORDERS

The DSM-IV-TR describes PTSD as the development of characteristic symptoms following exposure to "an extreme traumatic stressor involving direct personal experience of an event that involves actual or threatened death or serious injury, or other threat to one's physical integrity, or witnessing an event" (APA, 2000, p. 463). In order to diagnosis PTSD via DSM-IV-TR criteria the person must also present with situational reactivity described as "intense fear, helplessness, or horror" to the event. The three symptom areas for PTSD in the DSM-IV-TR (and the required number of symptoms per symptom area) include: reexperiencing of the traumatic event (1), avoidance of and/or numbing related to traumatic reminders (3), and increased arousal (2). With respect to diagnosing PTSD in children the DSM-IV-TR presents three diagnostic notes for reexperiencing symptoms. Specifically, "Young children usually do not have the sense that they are reliving the past; rather, the reliving of the trauma may occur through repetitive play" (APA, 2000, p. 466). Also, "In younger children, distressing dreams of the event may, within several weeks, change into generalized nightmares of monsters, of rescuing others, or of threat to self or others" (APA, 2000, p. 466). Despite the thorough process that went into developing these criteria, early childhood professionals need to be cognizant of the fact that the DSM-IV field trials for PTSD did not include children below the age of 15 years (Kilpatrick et al., 1998). Thus the applicability of these criteria for children younger than 15 has not been firmly established and has been called into question for very young children.

In a series of studies, Scheeringa and colleagues (Scheeringa, Zeanah, Drell, & Larrieu, 1995; Scheeringa, Peebles, Cook, & Zeanah, 2001; Scheeringa, Zeanah, Myers, & Putnam, 2003) examined the validity of the DSM-IV diagnostic criteria for use with preschool children. Specifically, Scheeringa et al. (2003) examined 62 children aged 20 months to 6 years who had been exposed to abuse, injuries, MVAs, or witnessed traumas and 63 healthy, nontraumatized children. Based on the *Posttraumatic Stress Disorder Semi-Structured Interview and Observation Record for Infants and Young Children* (Sheeringa & Zeanah, 1994), none of the traumatized children met the DSM-IV diagnostic criteria for PTSD. However, 68% of traumatized children evidenced at least one reexperiencing symptom and 45% evidenced two or more increased arousal symptoms. In contrast, only 2% of traumatized children evidenced three or more DSM-IV avoidance and numbing symptoms, while 11% of traumatized children evidenced two or more avoidance and numbing symptoms and 39% evidenced one or more symptoms. Thus, Scheeringa et al. (1995, 2003) proposed that only one avoidance and numbing symptom be required for diagnosing PTSD in young children, compared to the three-symptom requirement of the DSM-IV.

In order to explore the utility of the DSM-IV criteria for diagnosing PTSD and the alternative criteria proposed by Scheeringa et al. (1995, 2003), Ohmi et al. (2002) assessed child symptoms via maternal report among a sample of preschool children ($N = 32$; aged 32–73 months) following a petroleum gas leak explosion in a nursery school in Japan. Six months after the explosion no child met DSM-IV criteria for PTSD; however, 25% of children had PTSD based on the alternative criteria, providing further support for the lack of sensitivity of the DSM-IV in diagnosing traumatic stress reactions in infants and toddlers. Therefore, clinicians should consider the age-appropriateness of the diagnostic criteria utilized.

DIAGNOSTIC CLASSIFICATION: 0-3 REVISED

In an attempt to develop a diagnostic nomenclature appropriate for very young children, the Diagnostic Classification: 0-3 (DC:0-3; Zero to Three, 1994) utilized task forces comprised of clinicians and researchers who gathered information from infant and child mental health programs throughout the United States, Canada, and Europe to establish diagnostic criteria for a variety of disorders evidenced at this early age (e.g., anxiety disorders of infancy and early childhood, disorders of affect, mood disorders, traumatic stress disorder). Initial diagnostic formulations were developed from behavioral case descriptions and recurring patterns of behavioral problems. Discussion regarding the information gathered ensued with the development of diagnostic categories based on expert consensus.

The DC:0-3 introduced *traumatic stress disorder* to the nomenclature and with the DC:0-3R, the term posttraumatic stress disorder (PTSD) was utilized. According to the hierarchical structure of the DC:0-3R, a diagnosis of PTSD should be consider as a primary diagnosis if the child has experienced a significant stressor or traumatic event. In contrast to the DSM-IV-TR, the requirement of situational reactivity is not included in the DC:0-3R. The DSM-IV-TR and DC:0-3R also differ in the minimum number of symptoms per symptom cluster needed to establish a diagnosis. In contrast to the DSM-IV-TR, the DC:0-3R criteria require only one symptom per symptom cluster (APA, 2000; Zero to Three, 2005).

Furthermore, the DC:0-3R describes symptoms in more developmentally appropriate terminology than the DSM-IV. Reexperiencing symptoms include: post-traumatic play, recurrent recollections of the traumatic event (e.g., statements or questions about the event), repeated nightmares, distress upon exposure to traumatic reminders, and flashbacks or dissociation objectively noted by observers. The second symptom area includes the following aspects of numbing: increased social withdrawal, restricted range of affect, and a decrease or constriction of play. Increased arousal is evidenced by night terrors, difficulty going to sleep, difficulty staying asleep, hypervigilance, and startle response (Zero to Three, 2005).

While the DC:0-3 included the loss of developmental skills as well as development of new symptoms (e.g., aggressive behaviors, behavioral difficulties) as part of the diagnostic criteria for traumatic stress disorder, the DC:0-3R did not include these criteria. The work of Sheeringa et al. (1995, 2003) speaks to this criterion. Sheeringa et al. (2003) found that 79% of traumatized children presented with new symptoms not present before the trauma. This was the most frequent symptom area and was not considered useful in differentiating children with and without PTSD. As such, the inclusion of new symptoms in diagnosing traumatic stress disorder was called into question. With regard to the inclusion of loss of previously acquired developmental skills, 21% of traumatized children lost two or more such symptoms and 52% had the loss of one or more developmental skills. Based on this information, it was similarly proposed that there was insufficient evidence for the inclusion of loss of developmental skills as a diagnostic criterion, resulting in the current DC:0-3R criteria for PTSD.

ADDITIONAL DIAGNOSTIC CLASSIFICATIONS

The hierarchical structure of the DC:0-3R next considers if the child has experienced the loss of a primary caregiver. According to the DC:0-3R, Prolonged Bereavement/Grief Reaction includes a change in the child's functioning, subsequent to such a loss, resulting in at least three symptoms (e.g., cries, calls, searches for absent caregiver; refuses comfort; withdraws; disrupted sleep; developmental regression) present for at least 2 weeks (Zero to Three, 2005). Along these same lines, the term *traumatic grief* has been utilized to describe "a condition in which a child or adolescent has lost a loved one in circumstances that are objectively or subjectively traumatic and in which trauma symptoms impinge on the child's ability to negotiate the normal grieving process" (Cohen & Mannarino, 2004, p. 819).

Taken from a different perspective, the Interdisciplinary Council on Developmental and Learning Disorders established the *Diagnostic Manual for Infants and Young Children* (ICDL-DMIC, 2005). This model takes a multi-dimensional, developmental approach to diagnosis based on the Developmental, Individual-Difference, Relationship-Based (DIR; Greenspan, 2006; Greenspan & Wieder, 2004) model that focuses on developmental capacities, individual processing differences, and relationships between child and caregiver. Within the ICDL-DMIC one of the seven axes included is "Stress" (Axis VII), which is intended to recognize stressors which may impact the child's emotional functioning and age-appropriate development. An emphasis is placed on clinical judgement to determine if the child's functioning and mental health are impacted by an identified stressor (Greenspan & Wieder, 2008). However, the ICDL-DMIC does not establish a diagnosis of PTSD.

Van der Kolk (2005) discussed the reactions of children who have been exposed to child abuse and domestic violence. The distinction was drawn between exposure to single incident stressors that would be more likely to lead to PTSD and those more chronic stressors that might lead to PTSD and a host of other difficulties. Van der Kolk referred to this as *complex trauma*, which is defined as "the experience of multiple, chronic and prolonged, developmentally adverse traumatic events, most often of an interpersonal nature (e.g., sexual or physical abuse, war, community violence) and early-life onset" (2005, p. 402). Van der Kolk and colleagues (Cook et al., 2005; Van der Kolk, 2005) proposed that children exposed to complex trauma would evidence impairment in 7 domains: attachment (e.g., distrust, interpersonal difficulties, social isolation), biology (e.g., somatization), affect regulation (e.g., difficulty communicating needs, emotional self-regulation difficulties), dissociation (e.g., derealization, depersonalization), behavioral control (e.g., aggression, impulse control problems, oppositionality), cognition (e.g., attentional difficulties, learning difficulties), and self-concept (e.g., guilt, low self-esteem).

COMORBIDITY

Complicating the issue of diagnosis in infants and toddlers is the frequency with which hyperactive behaviors are present in this age group. Young children are frequently referred for disorders of impulse control (e.g., attention deficit hyperactivity disorder [ADHD]) that result in overactivity which parents and caregivers find difficulty to manage. These most prominent symptoms, however, may be masking important underlying etiological factors (i.e., a traumatic event). Furthermore, this inaccurate emphasis on externalizing problems may impede the identification and implementation of an appropriate intervention (e.g., trauma focused intervention).

Thomas and Guskin (2001) explored the relationship between the DSM-III-R/IV and the DC:0-3 diagnoses among a sample of 82 children aged 18–47 months who had presented to an early childhood psychiatry clinic due to disruptive behaviors. According to DSM criteria, 68.3% of the sample was diagnosed with an emotional disorder (e.g., anxiety disorder not otherwise specified [NOS], mood disorder NOS, separation anxiety disorder [SAD]) or behavioral disorder (i.e., ADHD, disruptive behavior disorder NOS, oppositional defiant disorder [ODD]). Of the 34.1% of children with a behavioral disorder, 7.1% were diagnosed with traumatic stress disorder via DC:0-3. Traumatic stress disorder was also diagnosed in 3.7% of children with a DSM diagnosis of emotional disorder and 3.7% of those with a DSM diagnosis of adjustment disorder. In the overall sample, 13.4% of children had PTSD according to the DSM, and 23.2% were diagnosed with traumatic stress disorder via DC:0-3 criteria. All of the children diagnosed with PTSD were also identified by the DC:0-3 criteria as having traumatic stress disorder.

Along these same lines, Scheeringa et al. (2003) reported that 63% of preschoolers with PTSD had SAD, 38% had ADHD, and 75% had ODD based on DSM-IV diagnostic criteria. Similarly, those preschoolers with PTSD had significantly higher CBCL total, internalizing, and externalizing problem behaviors relative to traumatized preschoolers without PTSD and healthy controls. Similarly, children exposed to Hurricane Katrina (Scheeringa & Zeanah, 2008) presented with a number of conditions including PTSD. Specifically, 33.8% had ODD, 21.4% had major depression, 25% had ADHD, and 14.7% had SAD. Children with PTSD may present with a host of behavioral and affective symptoms that may often divert attention from the possible etiological traumatic event.

RISK FACTORS

Early childhood professionals should consider factors beyond the traumatic event that may increase the risk of a young child developing PTSD. Many variables have been explored as risk factors for the development of PTSD in children. Some of these factors include, but are not limited to, age, developmental stage, gender, intensity of the traumatic event, proximity to the event, personality characteristics of the child, and parental psychopathology (Rojas & Papagallo, 2004; Saigh et al., 1999). Unfortunately, much of the research exploring these risk factors has not included infants and toddlers. Given this particularly vulnerable developmental stage, how parents respond to a traumatic event can be a critical factor in how the child responds.

Laor et al. (1997) reported that among Israeli preschoolers maternal avoidance symptoms were the only significant predictor of children's symptoms at 30 months. Among the 3-year-olds in the displaced group, maternal intrusive and avoidant symptoms were significantly correlated with the child's post-traumatic symptoms. At age 4, only maternal intrusive symptoms correlated with child symptoms. In contrast, among 5-year-olds there was a non-significant relationship between maternal and child symptoms. In light of this information, Laor et al. concluded that older children were less dependent on maternal reactions than younger children. Similarly, Vila et al. (2001) noted a decrease in behavioral difficulties among traumatized youth with increased age.

Similarly, Almqvist and Broberg (1999) examined risk and protective factors among 50 Iranian refugee preschoolers (aged 4–8 years) and reported that maternal mental health difficulties were significant predictors of children's mental health problems (e.g., PTSD). More recently, Scheeringa and Zeanah (2008) reported that following Hurricane Katrina 35.6% of parents who participated in their study meet DSM-IV-TR criteria for PTSD. Furthermore, children's symptoms (i.e., PTSD, MDD, ODD, SAD) were significantly correlated with the parent or caregiver's symptoms of PTSD and MDD. Interestingly, children's ADHD symptoms were not significantly correlated with parental or caregiver symptoms.

Clearly, these studies suggest a connection between parent and child reactions to traumas. In 2001, Scheeringa and Zeanah analyzed the results of 17 studies (only 4 included preschool age children) that examined both parent and child reactions subsequent to a traumatic event. With the exception of one study, parent maladaptive functioning was associated with less adaptive functioning in the child. Based on this review, Scheeringa and Zeanah proposed the concept of *Relational PTSD* to describe "the co-occurrence of posttraumatic symptomatology in an adult caregiver and a young child when the symptomatology of one partner, usually the adult, exacerbates the symptomatology of the other" (p. 809). Scheeringa and Zeanah introduced the following three patterns of interaction that may be evident in parent–child relationships following a traumatic event: Withdrawn/Unresponsive/Unavailable Pattern (i.e., the parent's symptoms limit the parents availability to the child), Overprotective/Constricting Pattern (i.e., resulting from overwhelming fear that the child will be traumatized again), and Reenacting/Endangering/Frightening Pattern (i.e., the parent is preoccupied with discussing the trauma to the extent that the child is retraumatized).

These studies emphasize the importance of evaluating the reaction of all family members exposed to traumatic events. Given parental psychological difficulties, parents' availability may be impaired and thus impede the healing process for young children. Due to their own avoidance symptoms, parents may avoid discussing the event with their child. Parents may also avoid discussions of the event to protect their children from further traumatization. Conversely, children may avoid discussing the event with their parents as they recognize this discussion is upsetting to the parent. Similarly, children may model their own parent's reactions, whether they be adaptive or maladaptive (Dyregrov & Yule, 2006; Scheeringa & Zeanah, 2001). Parental participation is essential to the treatment of stress reactions in children. Early childhood professionals need to maintain a family perspective, considering factors that might influence participation (i.e., parental reactions to traumatic events) in the therapeutic process.

ASSESSMENT

To date a number of instruments have been developed to assess for exposure to stressful life events, PTSD symptoms, and related symptoms in children. In general, these assessment measures can be divided into structured or semi-structured interviews, self-report measures, and parent/caregiver report measures that attempt to identify exposure to traumatic events and or stressors as well as identify the presence of PTSD symptoms. Some of these measures also incorporate items that assess for associated features frequently found in young children exposed to stressors. In addition to these measures, which may focus on posttraumatic stress-related symptoms, a number of instruments are useful for evaluating general psychopathology (e.g., depression, attention difficulties, externalizing behaviors, dissociation, bereavement, anger) that may be evident in those exposed to single incident as well as more chronic stressors. This section provides an overview of measures that may be appropriate for young children.

AGE-APPROPRIATENESS

The majority of measures available to diagnosis PTSD in children are intended for children with at least a minimum age of 6 years. Only two measures reported by the National Center for PTSD (2008) are appropriate for children younger than 6 years of age (i.e., Traumatic Events Screening Inventory [ages 4 +]; TESI, Ford & Rogers, 1997; Trauma Symptom Checklist for Young Children [ages 3–12]; TSCYC, Briere, 2005). A review of the literature also identifies additional measures with a developing evidence base that might prove useful with early childhood populations.

ASSESSING TRAUMA EXPOSURE

Stover and Berkowitz (2005) reviewed the assessment literature and identified four measures that may be used to assess violence exposure among preschool populations. These measures are the Trauma Exposure Symptom Inventory–Parent Report (TESI-PR; Ford et al., 2000) for 3- to 18-year-olds, TESI-PR-Revised (Ghosh-Ippen et al., 2002) for 0- to 6-year-olds, Violence Exposure Scale for Children–Preschool Version (VEX-PV; Fox & Leavitt, 1995) for 4- to 10-year-olds, and Violence Exposure Scale for Children-Revised Parent Report (VEX-PRR, Fox & Leavitt, 1995) for 4- to 6-year-olds. These measures assess for a wide range of traumatic exposures (e.g., abuse, accidents, community violence, terrorism). Unfortunately, very minimal evidence for the psychometric rigor of these instruments is available (Stover & Berkowitz, 2005).

STRUCTURED INTERVIEWS

There are several structured interviews based on the DSM-IV criteria for PTSD that are appropriate for children that also include an initial section to determine exposure to a traumatic event. These measures include: Dimensions of Stressful Events (DOSE; Fletcher, 1996a), Traumatic Events Screening Inventory (TESI; Parent and Child Forms available; Ford & Rogers, 1997; Ippen et al., 2002), Childhood PTSD Interview (Parent and Child Forms available; Fletcher, 1996b), Children's PTSD Inventory (CPTSDI; Saigh et al., 2000); Children's Impact of Traumatic Events Scale-Revised (CITES-2; Wolfe, Gentile, Michienzi, Sas, & Wolfe, 1991), and Clinician Administered PTSD Scale for Children and Adolescents (CAPS-CA; Nader et al., 1996). The UCLA PTSD Index for DSM-IV (UPID; Pynoos, Rodriguez, Steinberg, Stuber, & Frederick, 1998) is an interview appropriate for children ages 6–17 and provides a tentative diagnosis of PTSD (from doubtful to very severe).

Some of these measures are downward extensions of their adult counterparts. For example, the CAPS-CA is based on the Clinician-Administered PTSD Scale for adults. Several of these measures (i.e., CPTSDI, CITES-2, CAPS-CA) have a proven track record with use in research and clinical settings as well as psychometric data to support their reliability and validity (Ohan, Myers, & Collett, 2002). However, with the exception of the TESI, they are intended for children 6 years of age and older.

Scheeringa and Zeanah (1994) developed the Postraumatic Stress Disorder Semi-Structured Interview and Observation Record to combine parent report and direct observation of the child (12 months to 6 years) to formulate a diagnosis. The scale permits the clinician to consider DSM-IV as well as DC:0-3 criteria. Although promising, this instrument has limited psychometric evidence (Scheeringa, Peebles, Cook, & Zeanah, 2001; Scheeringa, Zeanah, Myers, & Putnam, 2003) at this time and requires a high level of clinical skill to administer and interpret appropriately (Stover & Berkowitz, 2005).

SELF-REPORT AND PARENT-REPORT MEASURES

Other measures that assess PTSD symptoms (i.e., are not diagnostic) include: Child PTSD Symptom Scale (CPSS; Foa, Johnson, Feeny, & Treadwell, 2001), Trauma Symptom Checklist for Children (TSCC; Briere, 1996), and TSCYC. The CPSS is a self-report measure adapted from the Posttraumatic Diagnostic Scale (PTDS; Foa, Cashman, Jaycox, & Perry, 1997) for adults. The CPSS is appropriate for ages 8 to 18 and has a developing evidence base to support its use (Foa, Johnson, Feeny, & Treadwell, 2001). The TSCC is a self-report measure for children (8–16 years) with 6 clinical scales (i.e., anger, anxiety, depression, dissociation, posttraumatic stress, and sexual concerns) and has an alternate version that excludes items related to sexual concerns. The TSCYC is a caretaker-report for children ages 3–12. The TSCYC has three separate PTSD scales (i.e., arousal, avoidance, intrusion) along with 5 other clinical scales (i.e., anger/aggression, anxiety, depression, dissociation, sexual concerns). Evidence for the psychometric properties of the TSCC and TSCYC is presented by Briere (1996, 2005).

BROADBAND STRUCTURED INTERVIEWS

Given the possible range of reactions to traumatic events (Dyregrov & Yule, 2006, NCPTSD, 2008, Scheeringa et al., 2003), comprehensive structured interviews that focus on a broader range of problems (e.g., depression, anxiety) as well as PTSD should be considered. The Anxiety and Depression Interview for Children (ADIS-C; Silverman & Albano, 1996) is an example of such an instrument as well as the Diagnostic Interview for Children and Adolescents (DICA-IV; Reich, Welner, & Herjanic, 2000) and the Children's Interview for Psychiatric Syndromes (ChIPS; Weller, Weller, Teare, & Fristad, 1999). These instruments contain a PTSD module for children as young as 6 years. Furthermore, structured interviews for children typically have parallel parent and child versions so that information from both sources can be obtained.

In an attempt to reach those younger than age 6, Egger and Angold (2004) have developed an interview (i.e., Preschool Age Psychiatric Assessment [PAPA]) for parents of children ages 2–5. The PAPA is a downward extension of the Children and Adolescent Psychiatric Assessment (CAPA, 9–18 years) and considers both the DSM-IV and DC:0-3 diagnostic criteria. The PAPA has several modules including: Depression, Life Events, PTSD, Parental Psychopathology, and others. The PAPA has an emerging evidence base for its utility as a measure of traumatic stress reactions in the preschool age population (Egger et al., 2006).

GENERAL SYMPTOM CHECKLISTS

As noted previously, children may respond to trauma in many different ways, with some experiencing more internalizing difficulties and others more externalizing difficulties. With this in mind, early childhood psychologists should consider general symptom checklists as part of their assessment of children exposed to traumatic events. One of the most frequently utilized measures is the Child Behavior Checklist (CBCL; Achenbach & Rescorla, 2000) which is appropriate for children ages 1½–18 years. Evidence demonstrates an association between PTSD and clinically elevated scores on the CBCL among older children (7 and up; Saigh et al., 2001). For many years there has been debate regarding the utility of developing a PTSD scale from items on the CBCL (Dehon & Scheeringa, 2006; Levendosky et al., 2002; Ruggiero & McLeer, 2000; Slim et al., 2005; Wolfe, Gentile, & Wolfe, 1989). However, as the CBCL was not intended to be a measure of PTSD specifically, it is recommended that the CBCL serve as a complement to the diagnostic measures already discussed above. The CBCL is easy to administer, available in many languages, has a strong psychometric history, and covers a broad range of symptoms (e.g., depression, anxiety, attention problems, aggression). Other measures that would be appropriate for the preschool population include the Behavior Assessment System for Children (BASC-2; Reynolds & Kamphaus, 2004) and the Social Skills Rating Scale (SSRS; Gresham & Elliot, 2007). Measures specific to social-emotional functioning in early childhood populations would also be beneficial (see Chapter 13).

ASSESSMENT OF PARENT FUNCTIONING

Although not the focus of this chapter, it is imperative, given the growing evidence base supporting a connection between parent and child reactions to trauma (Laor et al., 1997; Scheeringa & Zeanah, 2008), to determine parents' reactions to stressful events. Thus adult measures should be included to assess symptoms of PTSD (e.g., Clinician Administered PTSD Scale, Blake et al., 1995; Structured Clinical Interview for DSM-IV PTSD Module (First, Spitzer, Gibbon, & Williams, 2002), and other related conditions (e.g., Beck Depression Inventory, Beck, Steer, & Brown, 1996; Beck Anxiety Inventory, Beck & Steer, 1990; Symptom Checklist–90 Revised, Derogatis, 1986; Parenting Stress Index, Abidin, 1995). In addition, early childhood practitioners should consider current family functioning and parenting skills in the assessment battery (see Chapters 7 and 8).

INTERVENTIONS

When prevention efforts (see Chapter 21) are not effective in preventing exposure to traumatic events, it is essential that an intervention be conducted as soon as possible (Dyregrov, 2001). The National Center for PTSD (2008) provides an extensive list of the available treatments for children and adolescents, appropriate age ranges (few are for preschool age or younger), and information regarding the interventions' evidence base. This section reviews those interventions with a well-established evidence base as well as other interventions that have been developed for very young children (e.g., under age 8 years). Furthermore, the current state of evidence and practice for psychopharmacological interventions is considered.

COGNITIVE BEHAVIORAL INTERVENTIONS

Trauma Focused-CBT (TF-CBT; Cohen, Mannarino & Deblinger, 2006) integrates CBT principles with principles from attachment, family, and psychodynamic theories. The goals of treatment include reducing symptoms of PTSD, depression, anxiety, and other trauma-related symptoms (e.g., behavioral difficulties, guilt, shame). In addition, TF-CBT attempts to improve children's adaptive functioning and family functioning. It is appropriate for children ranging in age from 3 to 18, is brief (12–16 sessions), and has been used in urban, suburban, and rural settings. It has been used to treat traumatic grief reactions and PTSD subsequent to a variety of traumatic events. Furthermore, TF-CBT has been utilized with families from various cultural groups (e.g., Latino, African-American, Asian) and has been adapted for several other countries (e.g., Pakistan, Russia, Thailand).

The components of TF-CBT include: affect identification and regulation, cognitive coping, conjoint parent-child sessions, enhancing safety and future development, *in vivo* desensitization, psychoeducation, parent training, relaxation training, trauma narration, and cognitive processing (Cohen et al., 2006). Based on a number of randomized clinical trials that included both preschoolers as well as school-age children (Cohen, Deblinger, Mannarino, & Steer, 2004; Cohen & Mannarino, 1996, 1997, 1998; Cohen, Mannarino, & Knudsen, 2005; Deblinger, Lippmann, & Steer, 1996; Deblinger, Mannarino, Cohen, & Steer, 2006; Deblinger, Stauffer, & Steer, 2001; King et al., 2000), there is evidence that TF-CBT is effective in reducing child symptoms, reducing parental symptoms (e.g., anger, depression, anxiety), and reducing the use of harsh discipline. Training information is available online[1] and involves one to two days of skills-based training along with other supplemental activities (e.g., readings, online training course).

Scheeringa et al. (2007) provided further evidence for the applicability of CBT for preschool children with two case presentations. The first case involved a 4 year, 6 month old who had been involved in a MVA and the second was a 3 year, 7 month old exposed to Hurricane Katrina. In contrast to TF-CBT, this intervention focused specifically on the child. For both cases, reduction in PTSD symptoms was evident at post-treatment. Another CBT intervention developed for children as young as 2 years old is the Assessment-Based Treatment for Traumatized Children: Trauma Assessment Pathway (TAP; Taylor, Gilbert, Mann, & Ryan, 2005). However, at this time there is limited research evidence to support its use (Kolko, 1996a, 1996b).

Other CBT interventions for children have been developed to incorporate cultural aspects into treatment protocols. For example, Culturally Modified Trauma-Focused Treatment (CM-TFT, deArellano & Danielson, 2005) was

---

1. www.musc.edu/tfcbt.

developed for use with Latino children (ages 4–18) and their families. Honoring Children–Mending the Circle (ages 3–7) and Honoring Children–Respectful Ways (ages 3–18; Subia BigFoot, 2007) were developed for use with American Indian and Alaskan Native children. Currently, there are no published studies to support the use of CM-TFT, HC-MC, and HC-RW.

PARENT-CHILD INTERACTION THERAPY

Parent-Child Interaction Therapy (PCIT) has been utilized with children (ages 4–12) who have experienced physical abuse and focuses on improving the parent-child relationship. To enhance the parent-child relationship parents are taught and coached on five relationship-building skills (i.e., praise, reflection, imitation, description, enthusiasm). In addition, parents are coached on how to utilize positive discipline strategies. PCIT is highly structured, involves live-coached sessions, and is relatively brief (12–20 sessions). There is a growing evidence base that PCIT is associated with reduction in repeat incidents of physical abuse and with improved parent–child interactions (Chaffin et al., 2004; Hood & Eyberg, 2003). McDiarmid and Bagner (2005) have proposed techniques for adapting PCIT for use with children with developmental disabilities. PCIT has also been used with Spanish speaking populations (Borrego, Anhalt, Terao, Vargas, & Urquiza, 2006) and adaptations for use with Mexican American families have appeared in the literature (McCabe, Yeh, Garland, & Lau, 2005). Training is extensive involving 40 hours of direct supervision followed by 4 to 6 months of consultation with trainers.[2]

CHILD–PARENT PSYCHOTHERAPY

Child-Parent Psychotherapy (CPP; Lieberman & Van Horn, 2005) is based on attachment theory while incorporating aspects from other theoretical backgrounds (e.g., cognitive behavioral, developmental, psychodynamic, trauma). The focus of CPP is the impact of trauma on the parent-child relationship among young children (0–6 years) who have been exposed to domestic violence and/or maltreatment (e.g., neglect, sexual abuse, physical abuse). CPP has been conducted in both English and Spanish and has been utilized with several cultural groups (e.g., Asian, Latino, Native American). In addition to focusing on the parent-child relationship, CPP also addresses normalizing trauma reactions, safety and security concerns, and improving the child's functioning (e.g., affect regulation, adaptive behaviors). In contrast to TF-CBT and PCIT, CPP can last up to 50 sessions (one hour per week for

---

2. Training information can be obtained at www.cincinattichildrens.org/TTTC.

12 months). As with PCIT, there is a growing evidence base that CPP is associated with improvements in child symptoms (e.g., behavior problems, traumatic stress symptoms), maternal symptoms (e.g., avoidance), and parent-child relations (Cicchetti, Rogosch, & Toth, 2006; Lieberman, Van Horn & Ghosh-Ippen, 2005; Toth, Maughan, Manly, Spagnola, & Cicchetti, 2002).

Other Psychotherapeutic Interventions

The Attachment, Self-Regulation, and Competency (ARC) intervention is an intervention geared towards children (ages 5–17) who have experienced complex or chronic traumas. As implied in the name, ARC attempts to establish secure attachments, enhance self-regulatory abilities, and improve competencies (Kinniburgh, Blaustein, Spinazzola, & van der Kolk, 2005). However, the evidence base for this intervention is not currently available but data should be forthcoming as several investigators are evaluating the efficacy of ARC.

Psychopharmacological Interventions

The evidence base for pharmacological interventions significantly lags behind that of psychotherapeutic interventions (e.g., CBT) for trauma reactions in infants, toddlers, and children. Of course, there are numerous developmental and ethical concerns that need to be addressed when considering pharmacological interventions in early childhood (see Chapter 19). To date, the only evidence for the effectiveness of pharmacological interventions for PTSD in young children comes from small-scale studies.

Harmon and Riggs (1996) reported on the use of clonidine to treat seven children (ages 3–6 years) who developed PTSD subsequent to sexual and/or physical abuse. Five of the seven children demonstrated moderate improvement in a number of symptom areas (e.g., affect regulation, generalized anxiety, hyperarousal, hypervigilance, impulsivity, insomnia, nightmares, oppositionality). Risperidone has also been utilized to alleviate acute stress reactions in three preschool-age children who had experienced serious burns as a result of physical abuse (Meighen, Hines, & Lagges, 2007).

Despite the fact that there are no randomized controlled trials of medications used to treat PTSD in children, a significant portion of clinicians (89%) surveyed by the Preschool Psychopharmacology Working Group (PPWG) reported using medication for preschool children with PTSD. In contrast, the PPWG recommends that evidence-based interventions (e.g., TF-CBT, PCIT) be implemented for a minimum of 12 weeks (6 months for CPP) prior to considering pharmacological interventions. If these are not effective, a course of play therapy is recommended before considering pharmacological interventions. However, the PPWG concluded that they could not recommend the use of psychopharmacological intervention for PTSD in preschoolers (Gleason et al., 2007).

CONCLUSIONS & FUTURE DIRECTIONS

The applicability of the DSM-IV-TR diagnostic criteria for PTSD is insufficient for use with young children, especially infants and toddlers. Based on much of the work by Scheeringa et al. (1995, 2001, 2003), it appears that the DSM-IV criteria set symptom thresholds and the requirement of situational reactivity that are insensitive to the presentation of traumatic stress reactions in young children. Instead, early childhood practitioners should consider the DC:0-3R diagnostic criteria for younger children as evidence suggests these criteria have greater sensitivity for infants and toddlers comparable to the DSM-IV system. However, early childhood professionals should be aware that children between the ages of 4 and 14 have not been included in development of either the DSM-IV-TR or DC:0-3R classification systems. Further complicating the issue is the extent of comorbid conditions associated with PTSD in early childhood (Scheeringa & Zeanah, 2008). Clearly, further investigation into the presentation of traumatic reactions in infants and toddlers is necessary.

Given the lack of sensitivity in the diagnostic nomenclature to stress reactions in early childhood populations, it is not surprising to note that there are few empirically validated assessment measures of PTSD in this population. While there are measures available for older children, this raises an ethical dilemma as the APA (2002) Ethical Guidelines indicate that "Psychologists use assessment instruments whose validity and reliability have been established for use with members of the population tested" (Principle 9.02). Clinicians should use their training in psychometric theory to evaluate the adequacy of measures for their intended use with an early childhood population. Furthermore, until psychometrically sound instruments become available early childhood practitioners need to inform their clients of the strengths and limitations of the assessment results and interpretations.

In addition to diagnostic assessments, early childhood practitioners must consider the context of the traumatic experience and the involvement and reactions of parents. Given that parental psychopathology is denoted as a risk factor for posttraumatic reactions in children (Laor et al., 1997; Scheeringa & Zeanah, 2008), it is incumbent upon early childhood practitioners to conduct a comprehensive evaluation. This may pose some difficulty for early childhood practitioners whose training may not include evaluation of adult psychopathology. In accord with the APA Ethical Principles clinicians may consult with other professionals demonstrating appropriate expertise or may themselves obtain appropriate training.

While the use of psychopharmacological interventions is not supported for PTSD in early childhood populations, there is a growing evidence base for the use of CBT techniques in treating young children with PTSD. Ethically, early childhood psychologists must base the choice of intervention "upon established scientific and professional knowledge of the discipline" (Principle 2.04; APA, 2002). As such, clinicians who have not been trained in utilizing CBT techniques should either obtain such training or refer to a clinician with such expertise.

In conclusion, much work is needed with regard to understanding early childhood reactions to traumatic events. Diagnostic and assessment issues will continue to be of concern until early childhood populations are consider in the diagnostic nomenclature. A growing evidence base supports the inclusion of caregivers and parents throughout the assessment and intervention process. The continued use and evaluation of CBT techniques is essential, along with the evaluation of alternative intervention possibilities that might serve to address cultural and diversity issues.

REFERENCES

Abidin, R. (1995). *Parenting Stress Index* (3rd ed.) Odessa, FL: Psychological Assessment Resources.

Achenbach, T. M. (1991). *Manual for the Child Behavior Checklist/4-18 and 1991 Profile.* Burlington: University of Vermont, Department of Psychiatry.

Achenbach, T. M., & Rescorla, L. (2000). *Child Behavior Checklist for Ages 1½–5.* Burlington: University of Vermont, Department of Psychiatry.

Almqvist, K., & Broberg, A. G. (1999). Mental health and social adjustment in young refugee children 3½ years after their arrival in Sweden. *Journal of the American Academy of Child and Adolescent Psychiatry, 38,* 723–730.

American Psychiatric Association. (1980). *Diagnostic and Statistical Manual of Mental Disorders* (3rd ed.) Washington, DC: Author.

American Psychiatric Association. (1987). *Diagnostic and Statistical Manual of Mental Disorders* (3rd ed., Revised). Washington, DC: Author.

American Psychiatric Association. (2000). *Diagnostic and Statistical Manual of Mental Disorders* (4th ed., Text Revision). Washington, DC: Author.

American Psychological Association. (2002). Ethical principles of psychologists and code of conduct. *American Psychologist, 57,* 1060–1073.

Beck, A. T., & Steer, R. A. (1990). *Beck Anxiety Inventory.* New York: Psychological Corporation.

Beck, A. T., Steer, R. A., & Brown, G. K. (1996). *Beck Depression Inventory* (2nd ed.). New York: Psychological Corporation.

Blake, D. D., Weathers, F. W., Nagy, L. M., Kaloupek, D. G., Gusman, F. D., Charney, D. S., et al. (1995). The development of a clinician-administered PTSD scale. *Journal of Traumatic Stress, 8,* 75–90.

Borrego, J., Anhalt, K., Terao, S. Y., Vargas, E. C., & Urquiza, A. J. (2006). Parent-Child Interaction Therapy with a Spanish speaking family. *Cognitive and Behavioral Practice, 13,* 121–133.

Briere, J. (1996). *Trauma Symptom Checklist for Children: Professional manual.* Odessa, FL: Psychological Assessment Resources.

Briere, J. (2005). *Trauma Symptom Checklist for Young Children: Professional manual.* Odessa, FL: Psychological Assessment Resources.

Centers for Disease Control and Prevention. (1998). *National Center for Health Statistics. National vital statistics system.* Hyattsville, MD: U.S. Department of Health and Human Services, CDC, National Center for Health Statistics.

Chaffin, M., Kelleher, K., & Hollenberg, J. (1996). Onset of physical abuse and neglect: Psychiatric, substance abuse, and social risk factors from prospective community data. *Child Abuse & Neglect, 20,* 191–203.

Chaffin, M., Silovsky, J. F., Funderburk, B., Valle, L. A., Brestan, E. V., Balachova, T., et al. (2004). Parent-Child Interaction Therapy with physically abusive parents: Efficacy for reducing future abuse reports. *Journal of Consulting and Clinical Psychology, 72,* 500–510.

Cicchetti, D., Rogosch, F. A., & Toth, S. L. (2006). Fostering secure attachment in infants in maltreating families through preventive interventions. *Development and Psychopathology, 18,* 623–650.

Cohen, J. A., Deblinger, E., Mannarino, A. P., & Steer, R. A. (2004). A multi-site, randomized controlled trial for sexually abused children with PTSD symptoms. *Journal of the American Academy of Child and Adolescent Psychiatry, 43,* 393–402.

Cohen, J. A., & Mannarino, A. P. (1996). A treatment outcome study for sexually abused preschool children: Initial findings. *Journal of the American Academy of Child and Adolescent Psychiatry, 35,* 42–50.

Cohen, J. A., & Mannarino, A. P. (1997). A treatment study for sexually abused preschool children: Outcome during a one-year follow-up. *Journal of the American Academy of Child and Adolescent Psychiatry, 36,* 1228–1235.

Cohen, J. A., & Mannarino, A. P. (1998). Interventions for sexually abused children: Initial treatment outcome findings. *Child Maltreatment, 3,* 17–26.

Cohen, J. A., & Mannarino, A. P. (2004). Treatment of childhood traumatic grief. *Journal of Clinical Child and Adolescent Psychology, 33,* 819–831.

Cohen, J. A., Mannarino, A. P., & Deblinger, E. (2006). *Treating trauma and traumatic grief in children and adolescents.* New York: Guilford Press.

Cohen, J. A., Mannarino, A. P., & Knudsen, K. (2005). Treating sexually abused children: One year follow-up of a randomized controlled trial. *Child Abuse & Neglect, 29,* 135–145.

Cook, A., Spinazzola, J., Ford, J., Lanktree, C., Blaustein, M., Cloitre, M., et al. (2005). Complex trauma in children and adolescents. *Psychiatric Annals, 35,* 390–398.

deArellano, M. A., & Danielson, C. K. (2005). *Culturally-modified trauma focused treatment.* Unpublished manuscript, Medical University of South Carolina.

Deblinger, E., Lippmann, J., & Steer, R. (1996). Sexually abused children suffering posttraumatic stress symptoms: Initial treatment outcome findings. *Child Maltreatment, 1*, 310–321.

Deblinger, E., Mannarino, A., Cohen, J., & Steer, R. (2006). A follow-up study of a multisite, randomized, controlled trial for children with sexual abuse-related PTSD symptoms. *Journal of the American Academy of Child and Adolescent Psychiatry, 45*, 1474–1484.

Deblinger, E., Stauffer, L. B., & Steer, R. A. (2001). Comparative efficacies of supportive and cognitive behavioral group therapies for young children who have been sexually abused and their non-offending mothers. *Child Maltreatment, 6*, 332–343.

Dehon, C., & Sheeringa, M. S. (2006). Screening for preschool posttraumatic stress disorder with the Child Behavior Checklist. *Journal of Pediatric Psychology, 31*, 431–435.

Derogatis, L. R. (1986). *Manual for the Symptom Checklist 90 Revised (SCL-90R).* Baltimore: Author.

Dyregrov, A. (2001). Early intervention—a family perspective. *Advances in Mind-Body Medicine, 17*, 168–174.

Dyregrov, A., & Yule, W. (2006). A review of PTSD in children. *Child and Adolescent Mental Health, 11*, 176–184.

Egger, H. L., & Angold, A. (2004). The Preschool Age Psychiatric Assessment (PAPA): A structured parent interview for diagnosing psychiatric disorders in preschool children. In R. DelCarmen-Wiggens & A. Carter (Eds.), *The handbook of infant, toddler, and preschool mental health assessment* (pp. 223–246). New York: Oxford University Press.

Egger, H. L., Erkanli, A., Keeler, G., Potts, E., Walter, B. K., & Angold, A. (2006). Test-retest reliability of the Preschool Age Psychiatric Assessment (PAPA). *Journal of the American Academy of Child and Adolescent Psychiatry, 45*, 538–549.

First, M. B., Spitzer, R. L., Gibbon, M., & Williams, J. (2002). *Structured Clinical Interview for DSM-IV-TR Axis I Disorder Version, Non-patient Edition (SCID-I/NP).* New York: Biometrics Research, New York State Psychiatric Institute.

Fletcher, K. (1996a). Psychometric review of Dimensions of Stressful Events (DOSE) Ratings Scale. In B. H. Stamm (Ed.), *Measurement of stress, trauma, and adaptation* (pp. 144–151). Lutherville, MD: Sidran Press.

Fletcher, K. (1996b). Psychometric review of the Childhood PTSD Interview. In B. H. Stamm (Ed.), *Measurement of stress, trauma, and adaptation* (pp. 87–89). Lutherville, MD: Sidran Press.

Foa, E. B., Cashman, L., Jaycox, L., & Perry, K. (1997). The validation of a self-report measure of posttraumatic stress disorder: The Posttraumatic Diagnostic Scale. *Psychological Assessment, 9*, 445–451.

Foa, E. B., Johnson, K. M., Feeny, N. C., & Treadwell, K. R. H. (2001). The Child PTSD Symptom Scale: A preliminary examination of its psychometric properties. *Journal of Clinical Child Psychology, 30*, 376–384.

Ford, J., & Rogers, K. (1997). *Traumatic Events Screening Inventory.* White River Junction, VT: National Center for PTSD.

Ford, J. D., Racusin, R., Ellis, C. G., Daviss, W. B., Reiser, J., Fleisher, A., et al. (2000). Child maltreatment, other trauma exposure, and posttraumatic symptomatology among children with oppositional defiant and attention deficit hyperactivity disorders. *Child Maltreatment, 5,* 205–218.

Fox, N. A., & Leavitt, L. A. (1995). *The Violence Exposure Scale for Children-VEX (Preschool Version).* College Park, MD: Department of Human Development, University of Maryland.

Gabbay, V., Oatis, M. D., Silva, R. R., & Hirsch, G. S. (2004). Epidemiological aspects of PTSD in children and adolescents. In R. R. Silva (Ed.), *Posttraumatic stress disorders in children and adolescents: Handbook* (pp. 1–17). New York: Norton.

Ghosh-Ippen, C., Ford, J., Rascusin, R., Acker, M., Bosquet, K., Rogers, C., et al. (2002). *Trauma Events Screening Inventory-Parent Report Revised.* San Francisco: The Child Trauma Research Project of the Early Trauma Network and The National Center for PTSD Dartmouth Child Trauma Research Group.

Giaconia, R. M., Reinherz, H. Z., Silverman, A. B., Pakiz, B., Frost, A. K., & Cohen, E. (1995). Traumas and posttraumatic stress disorder in a community population of older adolescents. *Journal of the American Academy of Child and Adolescent Psychiatry, 34,* 1369–1380.

Gleason, M. M., Egger, H. L., Emslie, J. E., Greenhill, L. L., Kowatch, R. A., & Lieberman, A. F. (2007). Psychopharmacological treatment for very young children: Contexts and guidelines. *Journal of the American Academy of Child and Adolescent Psychiatry, 46,* 1532–1572.

Greenspan, S. I. (2006). *Engaging autism: Using the floortime approach to help related, communicate, and think.* Cambridge, MA: Da Capo Press.

Greenspan, S. I., & Wieder, S. (2004). Developmental pathways to mental health: The DIR model for comprehensive approaches to assessment and intervention. In K. M. Finello (Ed.), *The handbook of training and practice in infant and preschool mental health* (pp. 377–401). San Francisco: Wiley.

Greenspan, S. I., & Wieder, S. (2008). The Interdisciplinary Council on Developmental and Learning Disorders Diagnostic Manual for Infants and Young Children: An overview. *Journal of Canadian Academy of Child and Adolescent Psychiatry, 17,* 76–89.

Gresham, F. M., & Elliott, S. N. (2007). *Social Skills Rating System.* Minneapolis, MN: Pearson Education.

Harmon, R. J., & Riggs, P. D. (1996). Clonidine for posttraumatic stress disorder in preschool children. *Journal of the American Academy of Child and Adolescent Psychiatry, 35,* 1247–1249.

Hood, K. K., & Eyberg, S. M. (2003). Outcomes of Parent-Child Interaction Therapy: Mothers' reports of maintenance three to six years after treatment. *Journal of Clinical Child and Adolescent Psychology, 32,* 419–429.

Interdisciplinary Council on Developmental and Learning Disorders (IDCL). (2005). *Diagnostic manual for infancy and early childhood: Mental health, developmental, regulatory-sensory processing, language and learning disorders–IDCL-DMIC.* Bethesda, MD: Author.

Ippen, C. G., Ford, J., Racusin, R., Acker, M., Bosquet, M., Rogers, K., et al. (2002). *Traumatic Events Screening Inventory-Parent Report Revised*. White River Junction, VT: National Center for PTSD.

Kilpatrick, D. G., Resnick, H. S., Freedy, J. R., Pelcovitz, D., Resick, P., Roth, S., & van der Kolk, B. (1998). Posttraumatic stress disorder field trial: Evaluation of the PTSD construct: Criteria A through E. In T. Widiger, J. Frances, H. A. Pincus, R. Ross, M. First, W. Davis, & M. Kline (Eds.), *DSM-IV Sourcebook* (Vol. 4). Washington, DC: American Psychiatric Publishing.

King, N., Tonge, B. J., Mullen, P., Myerson, N., Heyne, D., Rollings, S., et al. (2000). Treating sexually abused children with post-traumatic stress symptoms: A randomized clinical trial. *Journal of the American Academy of Child and Adolescent Psychiatry, 59*, 1347–1355.

Kinniburgh, K., Blaustein, M., Spinazzola, J., & van der Kolk, B. (2005). Attachment, self-regulation and competency. *Psychiatric Annals, 35*, 424–430.

Kolko, D. J. (1996a). Clinical monitoring of treatment course in child physical abuse: Psychometric characteristics and treatment comparisons. *Child Abuse & Neglect, 20*, 23–43.

Kolko, D. J. (1996b). Individual cognitive-behavioral treatment and family therapy for physically abused children and their offending parents: A comparison of clinical outcomes. *Child Maltreatment, 1*, 322–342.

Laor, N., Wolmer, L., Mayes, L. C., Gershon, A., Weizman, R., & Cohen, D. J. (1997). Israeli preschool children under scuds: A 30-month follow-up. *Journal of the American Academy of Child and Adolescent Psychiatry, 36*, 349–356.

Levendosky, A. A., Huth-Bocks, A. C., Semel, M. A., & Shapiro, D. L. (2002). Trauma symptoms in preschool-age children exposed to domestic violence. *Journal of Interpersonal Violence, 17*, 150–164.

Lieberman, A. F., & Van Horn, P. (2005). *"Don't hit my mommy!" A manual for Child-Parent Psychotherapy with young witnesses of family violence*. Washington, DC: Zero to Three Press.

Lieberman, A. F., Van Horn, P., & Ghosh-Ippen, C. (2005). Toward evidence-based treatment: Child-Parent Psychotherapy with preschoolers exposed to marital violence. *Journal of the American Academy of Child and Adolescent Psychiatry, 44*, 1241–1248.

McCabe, K. M., Yeh, M., Garland, A. F., & Lau, A. (2005). The GANA Program: A tailoring approach to adapting Parent Child Interaction Therapy for Mexican Americans. *Education & Treatment of Children, 28*, 111–129.

McDiarmid, M. D., & Bagner, D. M. (2005). Parent-Child Interaction Therapy for children with disruptive behavior and developmental disabilities. *Education & Treatment of Children, 28*, 130–142.

Meighen, K. G., Hines, L. A. & Lagges, A. M. (2007). Risperidone treatment of preschool children with thermal burns and acute stress disorder. *Journal of Child and Adolescent Psychopharmacology, 17*, 223–232.

Nader, K., Kriegler, J. A., Blake, D. D., Pynoos, R. S., Newman, E., & Weathers, F. W. (1996). *Clinician Administer PTSD Scale, Child and Adolescent Version*. White River Junction, VT: National Center for PTSD.

National Center for Posttraumatic Stress Disorder. (2008). *Assessment: Child measures of trauma and PTSD*. Retrieved July 30, 2008, from www.ncptsd.va.gov/ncmain/assessment/childmeasjsp.

National Child Traumatic Stress Network. (2008). *Empirically supported treatments and promising practices*. Retrieved July 30, 2008, from www.nctsnet.org/nccts/nav.do?pid=ctr_top_trmnt_prom.

National Highway Traffic Safety Administration (NHTSA). (2008). *Traffic safety facts 2005: A compilation of motor vehicle crash data from the fatality analysis reporting system and the general estimates system*. Washington, DC: National Center for Statistics and Analysis.

Ohan, J. L., Myers, K., & Collett, B. R. (2002). Ten-year review of rating scales. IV: Scales assessing trauma and its effects. *Journal of the American Academy of Child and Adolescent Psychiatry, 41*, 1401–1422.

Ohmi, H., Kojima, S., Awai, Y., Kamata, S., Sasaki, K., Tanaka, Y., Mochizuki, Y., Hirooka, K., & Hata, A. (2002). Post-traumatic stress disorder in pre-school aged children after a gas explosion. *European Journal of Pediatrics, 161*, 643–648.

Phelan, K. J., Khoury, J., Kalkwarf, H. J., & Lanphear, B. P. (2001). Trends and patterns of playground injuries in United States children and adolescents. *Ambulatory Pediatrics, 1*, 227–233.

Pynoos, R., Rodriguez, N., Steinberg, A., Stuber, M., & Frederick, C. (1998). *UCLA PTSD Index for DSM-IV*. UCL Trauma Psychiatry Service: Los Angeles, CA.

Reich, W., Welner, Z., & Herjanic, B. (2000). *Diagnostic Interview for Children and Adolescents-IV*. North Tonawanda, NY: Multi-Health Systems.

Reynolds, C. R., & Kamphaus, R. W. (2004). *Behavior Assessment System for Children, Second Edition (BASC-2)*. Bloomington, MN: Pearson Assessments.

Rojas, V. M., & Papagallo, M. (2004). Risk factors for PTSD in children and adolescents. In R. R. Silva (ed.), *Posttraumatic stress disorder in children and adolescents, handbook* (pp. 38–59). New York: Norton.

Ruggiero, K. J., & McLeer, S. V. (2000). PTSD Scale of the Child Behavior Checklist: Concurrent and discriminant validity with non-clinic-referred sexually abused children. *Journal of Traumatic Stress, 13*, 287–299.

Sadeh, A., Hen-Gal, S., & Tikotzky, L. (2008). Young children's reactions to war-related stress: A survey and assessment of an innovative intervention. *Pediatrics, 121*, 46–53.

Saigh, P. A., Mroueh, M., & Bremner, J. D. (1997). Scholastic impairments among traumatized adolescents. *Behaviour Research and Therapy, 35*, 429–436.

Saigh, P. A., Yasik, A. E., Oberfield, R. A., Green, B. L., Halamandaris, P. V., Rubenstein, H., et al. (2000). The Children's PTSD Inventory: Development and reliability. *Journal of Traumatic Stress, 30*, 369–380.

Saigh, P. A., Yasik, A. E., Oberfield, R. A., Halamandaris, P. V., & McHugh, M. (2002). An analysis of the internalizing and externalizing behaviors of traumatized urban youth with and without PTSD. *Journal of Abnormal Psychology, 3*, 462–470.

Saigh, P. A., Yasik, A. E., Sack, W. H., & Koplewicz, H. S. (1999). Child-adolescent posttraumatic stress disorder: Prevalence, risk factors and comorbidity. In

P. A. Saigh & J. D. Bremner (eds.), *Posttraumatic stress disorder: A comprehensive textbook* (pp. 18–43). Boston: Allyn & Bacon.

Scheeringa, M. S., Peebles, C. D., Cook, C. A., & Zeanah, C. H. (2001). Toward establishing procedural, criterion, and discriminant validity for PTSD in early childhood. *Journal of the American Academy of Child and Adolescent Psychiatry, 40,* 52–60.

Scheeringa, M. S., Salloum, A., Arnberger, R. A., Weems, C. F., Amaya-Jackson, L., & Cohen, J. A. (2007). Feasibility and effectiveness of cognitive-behavioral therapy for posttraumatic stress disorder in preschool children: Two case reports. *Journal of Traumatic Stress, 20,* 631–636.

Scheeringa, M. S., & Zeanah, C. H. (1994). *Posttraumatic Stress Disorder Semi-Structured Interview and Observational Record for Infants and Young Children.* New Orleans: Tulane University.

Scheeringa, M. S., & Zeanah, C. H. (2001). A relationship perspective on PTSD in infancy. *Journal of Traumatic Stress, 14,* 799–815.

Scheeringa, M. S., & Zeanah, C. H. (2008). Reconsideration of harm's way: Onsets and comorbidity patterns of disorders in preschool children and their caregivers following Hurricane Katrina. *Journal of Clinical Child & Adolescent Psychology, 37,* 508–518.

Scheeringa, M. S., Zeanah, C. H., Drell, M. J., & Larrieu, J. A. (1995). Two approaches to the diagnosis of posttraumatic stress disorder in infancy and early childhood. *Journal of the American Academy of Child and Adolescent Psychiatry, 34,* 191–200.

Scheeringa, M. S., Zeanah, C. H., Myers, L., & Putnam, F. W. (2003). New findings on alternative criteria for PTSD in preschool children. *Journal of the American Academy of Child and Adolescent Psychiatry, 42,* 561–570.

Scheeringa, M. S., Zeanah, C. H., Myers, L., & Putnam, F. W. (2005). Predictive validity in a prospective follow-up of PTSD in preschool children. *Journal of the American Academy of Child and Adolescent Psychiatry, 44,* 899–906.

Silverman, W. K., & Albano, A. M. (1996). *ADIS: Anxiety Disorders Interview Schedule for DSM-IV: Child version.* San Antonio, TX: Psychological Corporation.

Slim, L., Friedrich, W. N., Davies, W. H., Trentham, B., Lengua, L., & Pithers, W. (2005). The Child Behavior Checklist as an indicator of posttraumatic stress disorder and dissociation in normative, psychiatric, and sexually abused children. *Journal of Traumatic Stress, 18,* 697–705.

Stover, C. S., & Berkowitz, S. (2005). Assessing violence exposure and trauma symptoms in young children: A critical review of measures. *Journal of Traumatic Stress, 18,* 708–717.

Subia BigFoot, D. (2007, April). *Honoring children: Implementation of four evidence based treatments in Indian country.* Presented at the 25th Annual Conference on Child Abuse and Neglect, Oklahoma City, OK.

Taylor, N., Gilbert, A., Mann, G., & Ryan, B. E. (2005). *Assessment-based treatment for traumatized children: A trauma assessment pathway.* San Diego, CA: Chadwick Center for Children & Families.

Thomas, J. M., & Guskin, K. A. (2001). Disruptive behavior in young children: What does it mean? *Journal of the American Academy of Child and Adolescent Psychiatry, 40,* 44–51.

Toth, S. L., Maughan, A., Manly, J. T., Spagnola, M., & Cicchetti, D. (2002). The relative efficacy of two interventions in altering maltreated preschool children's representational models: Implications for attachment theory. *Developmental Psychopathology, 14*, 877–908.

U.S. Department of Health and Human Services, Administration for Children, Youth, and Families. (2008). *Child maltreatment 2006*. Washington, DC: U.S. Government Printing Office.

Van der Kolk, B. A. (2005). Developmental trauma disorder. *Psychiatric Annals, 35*, 401–408.

Vila, G., Witkowski, P., Tondini, M. C., Perez-Diaz, F., Mouren-Simeoni, M. C., & Jouvent, R. (2001). A study of posttraumatic disorders in children who experienced an industrial disaster in the Briey region. *European Child and Adolescent Psychiatry, 10*, 10–18.

Weller, E. B., Weller, R. A., Teare, M., & Fristad, M. A. (1999). *Children's Interview for Psychiatric Syndromes (ChIPS)*. Washington, DC: American Psychiatric Press.

Wolfe, V. V., Gentile, C., Michienzi, T., Sas, L., & Wolfe, D. A. (1991). The Children's Impact of Traumatic Events Scale: A measure of post-sexual abuse PTSD symptoms. *Behavioral Assessment, 13*, 359–383.

Wolfe, V. V., Gentile, C., & Wolfe, D. A. (1989). The impact of sexual abuse on children: A PTSD formulation. *Behavior Therapy, 20*, 215–228.

Yasik, A. E., Saigh, P. A., Oberfield, R. A., & Halamandaris, P. V. (2007). Posttraumatic stress disorder: Memory and learning performance in children and adolescents. *Biological Psychiatry, 61*, 382–388.

Zero to Three. (1994). *Diagnostic Classification of Mental Health and Developmental Disorders of Infancy and Early Childhood*. Washington, DC: Author.

Zero to Three. (2005). *Diagnostic Classification of Mental Health and Developmental Disorders of Infancy and Early Childhood* (rev. ed.). Washington, DC: Author.

CHAPTER 21

Violence Prevention

MICHELLE GUTTMAN

T HE SERIOUSNESS OF violence in young children's lives is clearly evident, with infants as young as 1 year showing adjustment difficulties related to observed violence (Levendosky, Leahy, Bogat, Davidson, & von Eye, 2006; McDonald, Jouriles, Briggs-Gowan, Rosenfield, & Carter, 2007). For example, McDonald et al. find that mere exposure to family violence increases infant risk for adjustment difficulties. Aggressive behaviors can be identified by age 3, including intentions to harm (Loeber, Keenan, & Zhang, 1997) and, in addition, exposure to domestic violence at age 4 is related to children's aggressive behavior at age 6 (Litrownik, Newton, Hunter, English, & Everson, 2003).

Beyond early exposure to violence, there are numerous contributory factors to youth violence. Feder, Levant, and Dean (2007) maintain that the availability of weapons, family factors (e.g., aggressive interaction styles, harsh discipline), learning problems, teasing and bullying, and violence-infused media (e.g., music videos, video games) all play a role. For example, they cite statistics that access to weapons is widespread, with nearly 40% of all households holding at least one gun (Garbarino, 1999). Further, although violent crime has dropped nationwide, youth gun violence is a significant issue (Fingerhut & Christoffel, 2002).

Even a decade ago, the Children's Defense Fund (1997) reported that every day 10 children are murdered, 16 die from guns, 316 are arrested for crimes of violence, and 8,042 are victims of reported abuse or neglect. More recently, Fingerhut and Christoffel (2002) find that firearms are involved in killing or injuring more than 20,000 children under the age of 20 annually. Although deaths associated with school violence are rare, the U.S. Secret Service determined that most shooters are white males, from two-parent families, who act alone, with a plan, and generally are socially isolated, perhaps bullied by peers (Vossekuil, Fein, Reddy, Borum, & Modzeleski, 2002). DeVoe, Peter, Noonan, Snyder, and Baum (2005) point out that although school violence is more than troubling, data reveals a decrease, since the early 1990s, in school-based assaults, homicides, thefts, and other violent crimes.

Nonetheless, teasing and bullying is widespread (Garbarino, 1999), with Cleary (2000) reporting approximately one-third of New York State high school students feeling they had been bullied. Bullying often is considered aggression and abuse (Craig & Pepler, 2007). Indeed, researchers find that 10–20% of kindergarten- and elementary–age children are teased, threatened, or attacked frequently by their peers (Batsche & Knoff, 1994; Leff, Kupersmidt, Patterson & Power, 1999). Craig and Pepler (2007) consider bullying as peer abuse which takes different forms developmentally. Two characteristics seem consistently involved, power assertion (e.g., aggression, coercion) and repetition.

Due to the presence of aggression in early childhood, violence prevention and intervention are a pressing issue for those working with young children and their families. The purpose of this chapter is to discuss violence prevention in relation to young children, their families, and caregivers. An exploration of the developmental considerations and deleterious effects related to violence exposure is presented. A review of theoretical perspectives on aggression is followed by a discussion of early childhood violence prevention programs. Multicultural/diversity concerns, ethical issues and training issues are discussed to highlight current issues pertinent to developing violence prevention programs.

EFFECTS OF VIOLENCE ON YOUNG CHILDREN

Watching the news, reading newspapers, viewing video games, listening to music, and observing children in school as well as in their home environment, the presence of violence in young children's lives is apparent. Children are witnessing violence at alarmingly high rates. According to the results of studies on community violence, especially in lower income urban areas, more than 33% of children report being the direct victim of violence (Boney-McCoy & Finkelhor, 1995) and over 75% of children report having been exposed to community violence (Hill & Jones, 1997). In the home setting, although incidence rates are unclear, Levendosky et al. (2006) found that infants exposed to angry verbal conflict are at risk across all adjustment problem areas (e.g., atypical/maladaptive behavior, externalizing problems).

What children observe early in life shapes not only how they perceive their environment, but also how they respond to conflicts that arise in various situations (DaSilva, Sterne, & Anderson, 2000). Early researchers, such as Bandura (1973), recognized that when children observe violence, there is an increased likelihood of responding in aggressive ways; in addition, exposure to violence increases the chances of children developing further problems as they mature (Huesmann, 1988). Specifically, Huesmann, Eron, Lefkowitz and Walder (1984) found that early displays of aggression are highly correlated with later aggressive behavior. More recently, McDonald et al. (2007) found that exposure to violence toward a family member, as well as angry adult conflicts, increase adjustment problem risk. Thus, witnessing violence toward a family member, even as young as 1 to 3 years of age, puts young children at risk for social-emotional difficulties.

The negative impact of exposure to violence begins early in life. Violence has significant effects on the psychological and physical abilities of young children to thrive and may result in devastating effects on children's functioning at home, school, and in peer relationships. For example, Yates, Dodds, Sroufe, and Egeland (2003) determine that preschool-age children witnessing inter-parent physical violence, compared to youngsters who do not, tend to exhibit greater adjustment difficulties in middle childhood and adolescence.

Even before a child is born, violence can have a profound effect. Studies show that battered pregnant women often deliver low-birth-weight babies who are at increased risk for exhibiting developmental problems (Prothrow-Stith & Quaday, 1995). Further, exposure to domestic violence during pregnancy seems to negatively affect women's caregiving representations, resulting in poor parenting practices once children are born (Theran, Levendosky, Bogat, & Huth-Bocks, 2005). Thus, ineffective parenting in conjunction with exposure to violence adversely affect young children.

From a developmental perspective, even in the earliest phases of infant and toddler development, associations are found between exposure to violence and the presence of externalizing, internalizing, and post-traumatic symptoms (El-Sheikh, Cummings, Kouros, Elmore-Staton, & Buckhalt, 2008; Marks, Glaser, Glass, & Horne, 2001). Infants exposed to violence show irritability, sleep disturbances, and a fear of being alone (Osofsky, 1995a, 1995b). In addition, infants who live in homes where domestic violence is present exhibit trauma symptoms and have more reactions of distress to conflict compared to infants in homes without domestic violence (Bogat, DeJonghe, Levendosky, von Eye, & Davidson, 2006; DeJonghe, Bogat, Levendosky, von Eye, & Davidson, 2005). School age children have a better understanding of the intentions behind violence and may blame themselves. At this age, children also experience increased anxiety, sleep disturbances, difficulty paying attention and concentrating, poor school performance, and social adjustment difficulties (Berkowitz, 2003b; Osofsky, 1995b). Young children may experience regression in achievement of developmental milestones, such as in toileting and language (Osofsky, 1995b).

A decade ago, Edelson (1999) reviewed the literature focusing on the behavioral, emotional, and cognitive problems of children who witness domestic violence. Studies using the Child Behavior Checklist show that these children exhibited aggressive and antisocial behavior as well as fearful and inhibited behavior. More specifically, children in this study who witnessed such violence exhibit higher levels of anxiety, depression, trauma symptoms, and temperament problems compared to those who were not exposed to violence. More recently, Kitzmann, Gaylord, Holt, and Kenny (2003) examined 118 studies on the psychosocial outcomes of children exposed to interparental violence. They find that violence exposed children show physical and verbal aggression in response to conflict. These children also tend to exhibit negative affect as well as negative cognitions. Furthermore, Litrownik et al. (2003) found that exposure to domestic violence at the age of 4 years old is positively related to displays of aggression at 6 years old.

In addition to domestic violence, exposure to marital aggression (verbal and psychological) is associated with negative implications for young children (El-Sheikh et al., 2008). Although witnessing aggression against the mother is more upsetting to children than when it is toward the father, research demonstrates that children are also distressed when paternal aggression is present (El-Sheikh et al., 2008; Goeke-Morey, Cummings, Harold, & Shelton, 2003). Children who are exposed to marital aggression against either parent are at an increased risk for overall health problems, including acute and chronic medical issues, reduced physical growth, fatigue, digestive problems, abdominal pains, and headaches (El-Sheikh et al., 2008; El-Sheikh, Harger, & Whitson, 2001; Stiles, 2002).

Guerra, Huesmann, and Spindler (2003) examined how exposure to or witnessing violence in the community affects young children. These researchers conducted a 6-year longitudinal study (i.e., from first to sixth grade) to examine the effects of witnessing community violence on aggressive cognitions and behavior of children living in urban neighborhoods. Results indicate that aggressive behavior shows high continuity across all grades and years. In addition, aggressive fantasy and normative beliefs about aggression show high year-to-year continuity (i.e., aggressive beliefs get stronger) that increase with age (Guerra et al., 2003).

Using an extensive community sample, McDonald et al. (2007) studied the relationships among infant–toddler social-emotional functioning, adult anxiety and depression, socio-demographic variables (e.g., parent education, single versus dual-parent household), and exposure to angry adult conflict and violence. Their results suggest young children exposed to angry verbal conflict are at elevated risk across all adjustment problem areas. In contrast, young children in the violence groups seem at higher risk specifically in terms of atypical/maladaptive behavior. Indeed, their results imply angry verbal conflict is related to young children's adjustment problems independent from witnessing violence against a family member. Although McDonald et al. (2007) establish these relationships, they are unclear what processes are responsible for the additional risk associated with exposure to violence.

There is a growing body of evidence that bullying and being bullied is associated with adverse outcomes for both the bullies and victims (Carney, 2000; Craig & Pepler, 2007; Merrell, Gueldner, Ross, & Isava, 2008; Pelligrini, 2001; Rodkin & Hodges, 2003). Bullying can be exhibited through physical aggression, relational aggression, verbal harassment, or intimidation. For children who perpetrate bullying and for those who are victims of bullying, there are specific descriptive characteristics for each group. Bullies tend to have poorer academic skills in comparison to their peers, lack empathy, and have cognitive distortions related to perceived threats in their environments (Merrell et al., 2008). In addition, Merrell et al. found that children who are bullies tend to come from home environments where parental modeling takes the form of coercive and aggressive problem solving with a lack of consistent and effective discipline. Bullies are also at a high risk for long-term adverse outcomes, including antisocial behavior and substance use (Craig & Pepler, 2007). Victims of bullying are described as physically smaller/weaker than the bully and are often anxious, depressed, fearful, and insecure, having poor self-esteem (Merrell et al.). These children are also at risk for more severe anxiety, depression, and somatic complaints (Rigby, 2003).

In addition to the negative effects of witnessing or being exposed to violence, there are serious repercussions on children's development when they are disciplined with corporal punishment. Straus (2001, p. 4) defined corporal punishment as "the use of physical force with the intention of causing a child pain but not injury, for the purposes of correction or control of the child's behavior." Corporal punishment is not associated with any positive outcomes beyond immediate compliance to parents' requests or directives (Gershoff, 2002; Mulvaney & Mebert, 2007). Research shows that corporal punishment toward children has many harmful consequences that affect present and long-term development. Specifically, the negative consequences include increasing children's aggressive behavior and their likelihood of being delinquent (Gershoff, 2002). These children are also at risk for poor psychological and cognitive functioning as well as internalizing problems, including depression and lower self-esteem (Mulvaney & Mebert, 2007). In a longitudinal study that examined the impact of parental corporal punishment on children's behavior, researchers found that corporal punishment was associated with increased internalizing behavior during toddlerhood as well as increased externalizing behavior problems in toddlerhood and at first grade (Mulvaney & Mebert, 2007).

These studies on exposure to violence or directly experiencing aggression (e.g., physical punishment) point to the importance of preventive interventions. Prevention efforts may influence young children's emerging cognitive perceptions related to aggression and play a crucial role in preventing the harmful effects of exposure to violence.

THEORETICAL PERSPECTIVES ON AGGRESSION

One of the most recognized early theories of aggression is Bandura's social learning theory. This theory postulates that children learn aggressive behavior the same way they learn other kinds of behavior, namely, through observation and imitation (Bandura, 1973). Children internalize the behavior they frequently witness in role models (e.g., parents, peers, media characters) and incorporate these actions into their own behavioral repertoire. According to Bandura, children acquire entire repertoires of novel aggressive behavior from observing aggressive models and retain these response patterns over extended periods of time. Another important aspect of this process is the consequence that follows aggressive behavior. If followed by rewarding consequences, the likelihood of imitating the behavior and believing that this is the favorable way to act increases. Therefore, observing violence, along with the perception of positive consequences for the individual, can lead to imitation of aggressive behavior and the cognitive incorporation of proviolence attitudes and beliefs.

Huesmann (1988, 1998) added an information-processing perspective to Bandura's social learning theory, leading to the social–cognitive observational learning theory. In this theory, three cognitive structures are involved: schemas about a hostile world, scripts for social problem solving that rely on aggression, and normative beliefs that aggression is acceptable. Through repeated real-time or media observations of violence (e.g., people in their lives, the media), children develop biased world schemas for attributing hostility to the world and others around them (Huesmann, 1988). Such attributions increase children's likelihood of behaving aggressively.

In addition, observation of violence leads to the acquisition of aggressive social scripts that are easily retrieved from memory and become established in children's behavioral repertoires. Therefore, based on exposure to violence, children develop normative beliefs about the acceptability of aggression and increase their likelihood of using aggressive behavior to solve interpersonal conflicts. Huesmann (1998) argues that children repeatedly exposed to violence habituate to aggression and do not experience violence as aversive. Therefore, acceptance of violence as a response makes it likely that violence exposed children will plan or think about carrying out aggressive acts.

Other early theories on the development of aggression build on Bandura's and Huesmann's theories and focus on cognitive factors, parenting behaviors, and the home environment. Perry and Bussey (1984) postulate that aggressive children frequently come from home environments with parents who are rejecting, lacking in warmth, using discipline strategies based on power, and are permissive or indifferent toward their child's display of aggressive behavior. Patterson, Debaryshe, and Ramsey (1989) developed the coercive family interaction model to explain the development of aggression. Similar to Bandura's theory, this theory uses a social learning perspective and postulates that children learn aggression as a result of imitation and the rewards they receive for acting aggressively. Patterson et al. (1989) theorize that parents of aggressive children often reinforce such behavior through approval or attention. These parents also model aggression through their parenting style, which includes frequent commands placed on the children combined with harsh, inconsistent physical punishment.

Cognitive factors also assist in explaining the development of aggressive behavior in children. Perry, Perry, and Rasmussen (1986) focus on two types of social cognitions that include perceptions of self-efficacy and expectations about response outcomes. In this model, aggressive children are more likely to find it easier to engage in aggressive behavior and more difficult to inhibit their aggressive impulses. In addition, these children have the cognitive distortion that positive outcomes will result from their aggressive behavior. Dodge and Crick (1990) developed a cognitive model of aggression that involves five steps. These include encoding of social cues, interpretation of social cues, response search, response evaluation, and response enactment. These researchers reported that effective processing at each of these steps will result in competent skills in the specific situation but deficient processing can possibly result in aggressive behavior. In regard to children's perceptions of others' behavior, this model postulates that aggressive children are more likely to interpret ambiguous behavior by others as deliberately antagonistic (Dodge & Crick, 1990).

The more current theoretical perspectives on the origins of aggression highlight an evolutionary view, cognitive neoassociations, and catharsis. The evolutionary theory of aggressive behavior focuses on the first 3 years of life and posits that aggression first appears toward the end of the first year and peaks in children between the ages of 2 and 3 years old (Tremblay, Hartup, & Archer, 2005). In this theory, aggression is viewed as a normative feature of early childhood (Ostrov, Ries, Stauffacher, Godleski, & Mullins, 2008) with young children focusing on learning how not to use aggression rather than being taught to be aggressive through their environments (Tremblay et al.). The evolutionary perspective stresses that aggression is adaptive and that individuals learn how to control aggressive tendencies in the course of development (Tremblay et al.).

The cognitive neoassociation theory posits that aggressive thoughts are linked together in memory and form an associative network (Berkowitz, 2003a; Bushman, 2002). According to this theory, when an aggressive thought is activated, this activation expands to the network links and further primes associated aggressive thoughts, emotional reactions and behavior. Therefore, aggressive thoughts produce negative affect which automatically stimulate thoughts, memories, physiological responses, and motor reactions linked with both fight and flight tendencies (Bushman, 2002).

Although noted throughout the history of research on aggression (e.g., Aristotle, Freud), catharsis has regained popularity as well as controversy. Current research has begun to view catharsis as a contributor to aggression rather than as an effective release for aggressive behavior (Bushman, 2002; DiGiuseppe & Tafrate, 2003; Drewes, 2008). The catharsis theory states that when an individual releases their anger and aggressive feelings, either by acting aggressively toward inanimate objects or by viewing aggression, they can obtain a positive psychological state (Drewes, 2008). Contrary to this view, researchers demonstrate that behaving aggressively increases, not lessens, aggressive behavior even though it may lead to a short term reduction in physiological arousal (Bushman, 2002; DiGiuseppe & Tafrate, 2003; Drewes, 2008). Bushman (2002) studied the effects of catharsis and discovered that such venting increases angry feelings and aggressive behaviors. In actuality, venting represents practicing how to behave aggressively and this could further enhance the presence of aggressive thoughts, feelings, and behaviors.

Children's exposure to media violence (e.g., movies, music, television shows, movies, video games) is another possible contributor to the development of aggression. Research in this area confirms that the more violent programs a child watches, the more aggressive the child becomes and this occurs for all ages, with both boys and girls, across all socioeconomic groups (Anderson, Berkowitz, Donnerstein, Huesman, Johnson, Linz, et al., 2003; Anderson & Bushman, 2001). Huesmann, Moise-Titus, Podolski, and Eron (2003) indicate that children's television viewing between ages 6 and 9, their identification with aggressive same-sex television characters, and their perceptions that television violence is realistic are significantly correlated with adult aggression for both males and females.

Thus, there are both short-term and long-term consequences to children's exposure to media violence. Specifically, short-term exposure increases the likelihood of physically and verbally aggressive behavior, aggressive thoughts, and aggressive emotions. Media violence produces long-term effects consisting of the acquisition of lasting aggressive scripts and aggression supporting beliefs about social behavior (Anderson et al., 2003).

With regard to violent video games, the studies reviewed provide support for a connection between playing violent games and the increased likelihood of engaging in aggression (Anderson et al., 2003). Since children are active participants in these games and not just observers, as they are when watching television, the active participation may place them at an increased risk for becoming aggressive. Research has also shown that violent video games may be more harmful than violent television and movies because they are inter-active and engrossing, and require the player to identify with the aggressor (Anderson & Dill, 2000).

EARLY VIOLENCE PREVENTION PROGRAMS

There is strong evidence (Leff, Power, Massy, Costigan, & Nabors, 2001; Warman & Cohen, 2000) that many severely antisocial youth exhibit a "life course" development of aggression, where childhood acts of aggression pro-gress from being mild (e.g., bullying, teasing) to more serious (e.g., physical fighting) to extreme (e.g., assault, robbery, rape). To illustrate, an estimated 30% of 6th to 10th graders in the United States were either a bully, a target of bullying, or both (Nansel, Overpeck, Pilla, Ruan, Simons-Morton, & Scheidt, 2001). In a representative national survey conducted in 2003, U.S. adults reported approximately 1.56 million incidents of victimization by perpetra-tors estimated to be age 12–20 years (Pastore, 2005). Furthermore, in a 2005 nationally representative sample of youth in grades 9–12, 13.6% reported being in a physical fight on school property in the 12 months preceding the survey, 18.2% of male students and 8.8% of female students reported being in a physical fight on school property, 6.0% did not go to school on one or more days in the 30 days preceding the survey because they felt unsafe at school or on their way to or from school, 6.5% reported carrying a weapon (gun, knife, or club) on school property on one or more days, and 7.9% reported being threatened or injured with a weapon on school property one or more times in the 12 months preceding the survey (Center for Disease Control and Prevention [CDC], 2006). These statistics highlight the trajectory of how incidents of violence perpetrated by or against youth progress from milder acts of bullying to more serious and violent acts of aggression.

A review of these grim statistics points to the importance of focusing preventive interventions on violence during early childhood, especially since violent behavior occurs along a developmental continuum of behavioral severity. Since there is strong evidence that children learn through observa-tion, early intervention programs usually focus on parents as well as those who work with families and young children. Most developers of such programs focus on interventions that begin early in life to help children develop higher order thinking skills, empathy, impulse control, anger man-agement, peaceful conflict resolution, and assertive communication (Leff, Power, Manz, Costigan, & Nabors, 2001).

There are a number of early violence prevention programs that have been evaluated in regard to their success at reducing the effects of violence on young children. These programs include the Adults and Children Together

(ACT) Against Violence Prevention Program, bullying prevention programs, Childreach, the Fast Track Project, First Step to Success, the Incredible Years, Peacebuilders, and Second Step: A Violence Prevention Curriculum.

ADULTS AND CHILDREN TOGETHER (ACT) AGAINST VIOLENCE PREVENTION PROGRAM

The Adults and Children Together (ACT) Against Violence Prevention Program began in December 2000 and was developed by the American Psychological Association (APA) and the National Association for the Education of Young Children (NAEYC) along with the assistance from experts on child development and violence prevention (DaSilva et al., 2000). The ACT Program is based on research demonstrating that the early years (i.e., ages 0–8) constitute a critical time when children are learning basic skills that have a long-lasting impact on their lives. The goal of ACT is to disseminate research-based knowledge on violence prevention to those who work with young children to help use alternatives to violence for solving the problems they encounter (DaSilva et al., 2000). The ACT Program was developed to do the following: offer early violence prevention knowledge and skills to professionals and other adults in young children's lives; provide a program built on knowledge gained from research-based violence prevention information focusing on young children; and to encourage collaboration among community organizations to address early violence prevention (DaSilva et al., 2000). The ACT Program is a social–cognitive intervention based on the following assumptions:

- Children learn by observing and imitating adults and others.
- Violence results in part from an individual's lack of problem-solving and social skills needed to deal with conflicts.
- Adults can learn to model and teach skills that will help children deal with their social relationships in a non-aggressive way.

The ACT Program consists of four modules addressing important skills for early violence prevention: anger management, social problem solving, discipline, and media violence. Unlike many other violence prevention programs, ACT focuses solely on adults and is designed to help adults learn how to teach and model positive ways for young children to deal with anger and resolve conflicts.

In an evaluation on the ACT Program's effectiveness, Guttman, Mowder, and Yasik (2006) surveyed early childhood professionals before and after receiving the ACT Training. The researchers found that this program significantly increased participants' knowledge regarding violence related to early childhood in all four modules of the ACT Program. This study provided preliminary evidence for the ACT Program as a successful early childhood violence prevention program.

Bullying Prevention Programs

Bullying is a major concern in the schools and bullying interventions programs are becoming widespread for elementary school aged children. Cornell (2006) stressed that programs that have been successful for reducing school violence include conflict resolution training, peer mediation, mentoring, supervised after-school recreational programs, family-focused programs, and family therapy. One such program is the School Wide Positive Behavioral Support. This program takes a comprehensive and proactive approach toward school violence and has been shown to reduce behavior problems and increase feelings of safety for children in school (Meltzer, Biglan, Rusby, & Sprague, 2001; Sprague & Horner, 2006).

The WITS Program is another school bullying intervention program for children in the first and second grades and includes teacher delivered peer victimization prevention (Leadbetter, Hoglund, & Woods, 2003). In an evaluation of this program, students receiving this program exhibited significant decreases in relational aggression (Leadbetter et al., 2003). Orpinas, Horn, and Staniszeski (2003) evaluated a schoolwide anti-bullying intervention for children in grades K–5 and reported that children in grades K–2 who received the intervention showed significant decreases in aggression and victimization, whereas those in grades 3–5 showed significant decreases in victimization. Although school bullying interventions produce modest positive outcomes, they are more likely to affect knowledge, attitudes, and self-perceptions rather than bullying behavior (Merrell et al., 2008).

Childreach

Childreach was created in 1995 at the request of the early childhood education community in Cincinnati. More specifically, there were concerns related to the number of children in early childhood centers exhibiting severe, aggressive behavior (Goodwin, Pacey, & Grace, 2003). Childreach is an early identification, short-term intervention program for children under the age of 6 and was designed to address hostility and aggression in preschool and child care settings. This program includes consultation with staff and parents, intervention for the child and family, staff training, parent training, and referral liaison services. Specifically, when a child is referred for Childreach services by a parent, teacher or child care worker, a Childreach worker obtains parent permission and conducts a thorough observation of the child in the setting where the behavior is displayed. The Childreach worker consults with all individuals involved in the child's daily routines, including parents, teachers, and child care staff to gain an understanding of the child in various settings. The Childreach worker then develops a behavioral intervention for the home and classroom, and supports the adults who work with this child. In addition, therapy for the parents, staff training, and parent/staff education are provided if necessary (Goodwin et al., 2003).

Since the program's beginning, Childreach has served more than 500 children. Evaluation of Childreach found that children in the program demonstrated significant improvements in all areas of behavior (e.g., hostility, peer relations, productivity, withdrawal) except in the area of dependency (Goodwin et al., 2003). In addition, preschool teachers and child care staff report high levels of satisfaction with the Childreach program. Overall, the data demonstrate that Childreach is an effective secondary prevention program for decreasing violent and aggressive behavior in preschoolers.

FAST TRACK PROJECT

The Fast Track Project was initiated in 1990 to evaluate the feasibility and effectiveness of a comprehensive, long-term prevention program targeting young children at risk for conduct disorders (Conduct Problems Prevention Research Group, 2002). The Fast Track Project identifies at-risk children as early as kindergarten and involves both children and their parents. The program consists of social skills and anger-control training, academic tutoring, parent training, and home visiting. In the school setting, these children participated in a classroom program, called PATHS (Promoting Alternative Thinking Strategies). PATHS focuses on self-control, emotional awareness and understanding, peer-related social skills, and social problem solving to increase social competence. The parent program addresses discipline strategies, promotes parental involvement in the child's schooling, and reinforces consistent monitoring of the child's activities (Conduct Problems Prevention Research Group, 2002). In addition to individual work for the child and for the parents, group meetings and home visits are conducted with children and parents together to work on skills learned and to improve parent-child relations.

The Conduct Problems Prevention Research Group (2002) evaluated the effectiveness of the program, which began when children were in first grade and after the children had completed third grade. The research group found that 37% of the high-risk intervention group were no longer seen by their teachers as having serious conduct problems in contrast with 27% of the controls. Parent ratings provide further support for prevention of conduct problems at home. The research group emphasized the importance of these outcomes because the children were initially screened as being in the top 10%

of high-risk students. Parenting behavior and children's social cognitive skills that had previously emerged as outcomes at the end of the first year of the program continued to show positive effects of the intervention. Teachers report the greatest difference in Fast Track Project children occurs from the end of grade 1 to the end of grade 3, noting lower rates of child aggressive, disobedient, and disruptive behaviors.

FIRST STEP TO SUCCESS

The First Step to Success Program is an intensive classroom and home-based early identification and intervention program designed to prevent kindergarten children from developing antisocial and aggressive behavior (Walker, Severson, Feil, Stiller, & Golly, 1998). This program focuses on children who enter school with early signs of aggression. There are three components to this program, which takes approximately 12 weeks to complete. The first component consists of a comprehensive screening to identify high-risk kindergarten students. The second component includes a classroom-based intervention designed to reduce these students' aggressive behaviors and increase their prosocial skills. In the final component, a home-based intervention is used to strengthen parenting skills and improve home–school communication (Walker et al., 1998).

An evaluation of the First Step to Success Program finds decreases in aggressive behavior as reported by teachers and increases in teacher ratings of prosocial behavior (Golly, Stiller, & Walker, 1998; Walker et al., 1998). Due to the results of this evaluation, the researchers stress the importance of intervening at the point of school entry in order to divert at-risk children from aggressive behavior patterns.

THE INCREDIBLE YEARS

The Incredible Years is a research-based curriculum for reducing children's aggression and behavior problems and increasing their social and emotional competence at home and at school (Taylor, Schmidt, Pepler, & Hodgins, 1998). There are separate programs for parents, teachers, child care providers, and children ages 3–8 years. In the parent-training component, there is an emphasis on nonviolent discipline strategies and teaching children problem solving skills, anger management, and social skills. For teachers, there is training on the importance of praise, assistance in decreasing inappropriate behavior in the classroom, and strategies to promote children's social and emotional competence in school. For children, there is empathy training, learning rules, problem solving, anger management, how to make friends, and how to be successful in school. Taylor et al. (1998) reported that home, laboratory, and classroom observations show that The Incredible Years' parent, teacher, and child programs are effective in reducing aggressive behaviors in children and these results are sustained in 2- and 3-year follow-up studies.

PEACEBUILDERS

PeaceBuilders is a universal (i.e., schoolwide), elementary school–based (grades K–5) violence prevention program that aims to change the school climate by teaching students, staff, and parents rules and activities to improve social competence and reduce aggressive behavior in children (Flannery et al., 2003). In PeaceBuilders, the program is purposely woven into the school's everyday routine rather than in a time- or subject-limited process. In addition to the classroom curriculum, PeaceBuilders involves the entire school, both out of and in the classroom, together with parents and the community. The program focuses on conditions that provoke aggressive behavior with the following of simple positive behavioral rules, such as "praise people" and "right wrongs," encouraged and rewarded. In addition, this program specifically rewards prosocial behavior and provides strategies to assist in decreasing the accidental reinforcement of negative behavior by teachers and peers (Flannery et al., 2003).

Flannery et al. found that participation in the PeaceBuilders program improves students' social competence. In addition, declines in teacher-reported aggressive behavior were found, especially for children in the program for 2 years. These results highlight the importance of intervening early in children's lives to help direct them toward a positive developmental course that can be maintained over time. Beyond asserting the importance of intervention, Flannery et al. also stress the importance of early preventive interventions, especially strategies focusing on increasing positive skills as well as those targeting a reduction in aggressive behavior in young children.

SECOND STEP: A VIOLENCE PREVENTION CURRICULUM

Second Step is a social and emotional skills curriculum for preschool through middle school children that aims to teach children to change attitudes and behaviors that contribute to violence (Grossman et al., 1997). This is accomplished by having teachers focus on developing children's emotional understanding, empathy, impulse control, problem solving, and anger management skills through 30 specific lessons tailored to the age of the children (Grossman et al., 1997). In addition to the teacher training, there is a companion program that teaches parents to practice and reinforce pro-social behaviors at home. Recently, a preschool through fifth grade supplemental manual in Spanish and a family guide to assist parents in practicing Second Step strategies at home have been created (Frey, Hirschstein, & Guzzo, 2000).

Grossman et al. (1997) evaluated whether Second Step results in a reduction in aggressive behavior and an increase in pro-social behavior among elementary school children. This study utilized a randomized treatment control design and the participants included 790 second- and third-grade students. Results show that physical aggression decreases and prosocial behavior increases among students who are in the Second Step program.

EFFECTIVENESS OF SCHOOL-BASED VIOLENCE PREVENTION PROGRAMS

During 2004 to 2006, the Task Force on Community Preventive Services from the CDC conducted a systematic review of published scientific evidence concerning the effectiveness of universal school-based programs. The CDC (2007) defined "universal" as programs administered to all children in classrooms regardless of individual risk, not only to those who already have manifested violent or aggressive behavior or risk factors for these behaviors. Specifically, this review assessed universal school-based programs and their success in reducing or preventing violent and aggressive behavior among children and adolescents as well as in increasing emotional self-awareness, emotional control, self-esteem, positive social skills, social problem solving, conflict resolution, and team work. The results of this review provide strong evidence that universal school-based programs decrease rates of violence and aggressive behavior among school-aged children. Program effects were demonstrated at all grade levels. On the basis of this strong evidence of the effectiveness of these programs, the Task Force recommends the use of universal school-based programs to prevent or reduce violent behavior (CDC, 2007).

MULTICULTURAL/DIVERSITY CONCERNS

Multicultural and diversity issues are crucial areas to consider in the development and implementation of violence prevention programs. Issues of diversity, which can include ethnicity, sexual orientation, gender, age, socioeconomic status, culture, religion and language, cannot be overlooked due to the influence they have on children and their families. Although researchers highlight the significance of cultural factors that can either strengthen or weaken the likelihood of an aggressive response, violence prevention programs have unfortunately either overlooked, oversimplified, or underrated the importance of cultural factors (Hudley & Taylor, 2006; Le & Stockdale, 2008; Wright & Zimmerman, 2006).

Violence prevention programs implemented in school settings may raise specific issues of engagement and acceptance from minority families. The research on parental involvement in schools often shows a pattern of minimal participation rather than active involvement among minority families (Harry, Allen, & McLaughlin, 1995). Likely, minority families' minimal participation may be attributable to feelings of intimidation. That is, schools may lack cultural sensitivity and acceptance, resulting in parental reluctance to participate in schools' violence prevention initiatives.

Schools and other settings providing violence prevention programs need to empower culturally and linguistically diverse parents and families to participate in efforts to curb childhood violence. A number of strategies are available to involve families from diverse backgrounds in violence prevention programs. First, parents, families, and caregivers should be included as policy makers through school-based or community-based parent advisory committees (Hyman & Perrone, 1998). Second, parents and families can be encouraged to provide support to other families with children who are exhibiting violent and aggressive behaviors. Third, especially important for school-based programs, parents and families who are intimidated by schools can participate in interactive small groups that may facilitate the sharing of information (Hyman & Perrone, 1998). Once a comfort level is reached that permits openness from the participants in the program, parents/caregivers may need encouragement to share their diverse experiences (e.g., how their backgrounds influence child rearing, attitudes regarding discipline) and receive feedback and recommendations from other participants and program leaders.

Effective violence prevention programs address specific cultural concerns (e.g., cultural beliefs, norms, values) in preventative and remedial rather than negatively critical ways. This issue is especially important when discipline strategies are taught in a violence prevention program. The program developers need to be cognizant of the vast range of cultural beliefs on discipline toward children and present culturally sensitive strategies helpful to diverse families. Overall, the development of violence prevention programs for children incorporates multicultural and diversity issues in order to be effective.

ETHICAL ISSUES

Ethical issues are another area of focus in developing and implementing early childhood violence prevention programs. One major area pertains to the confidentiality of information discussed during the programs. According to the American Psychological Association's Ethical Principles of Psychologists and Code of Conduct (2002), psychologists have a primary obligation to protect confidential information, take precautions to ensure protection of confidential information and recognize the limits of confidentiality. Based on this ethical standard, the leaders of the violence prevention program are bound by confidentiality.

A conflict with confidentiality might occur if the issue of child abuse or neglect arises. The topic of mandated reporting needs presentation at the beginning of the group to stress the limits of confidentiality. Group leaders may need to talk privately to a parent/caregiver regarding information they have shared in the program that may be putting the child in danger. Overall, leaders may have to take further action, such as reporting child abuse or neglect, to ensure the safety of the child but this should be accomplished privately and not in front of the group.

Although the participants in the program may have a moral obligation to maintain confidentiality throughout involvement in the training program, they are not bound by the ethical standards. Therefore, the issue of confidentiality needs discussion at the onset of the program to openly present the potential problems and encourage sensitivity to participant privacy. Thus, program leaders encourage the participants to be respectful of each other and not discuss shared personal information outside of the training program.

For early childhood violence prevention programs to be successful, participants need to feel they are in a safe environment during the program. In addition to confidentiality of information within the program setting, leaders also ensure that information and participant identity is not revealed in other settings or to individuals unrelated to the training program. If any information is used in other contexts (e.g., supervision, training), all identifiable information is removed or disguised unless permission from the participant is obtained.

Another ethical issue pertains to professional competence in the area of treatment being provided. In relation to violence prevention programs, this means that the program leaders should have appropriate education, training, and experience in providing the program. They need to present their qualifications accurately and recognize any limits of their skills. For example, leader training is required so that someone does not read straight from a training manual with no other knowledge of violence prevention or childhood development. A final ethical issue relates to accurate presentations of the materials used to advertise the program. Specifically, all print and electronic advertisements should present accurate information about the program, including an accurate description of the program objectives, the audience for which the program is intended, information about the presenters' credentials, information on fees, and should not include guarantees as to the program's effectiveness or success (APA, 2002).

TRAINING ISSUES

Training issues related to childhood violence prevention programs are a final area for consideration. Specifically, early violence intervention and prevention needs to focus on parents and caregivers since they typically are the most salient individuals in preventing poor outcomes for children. These programs need to supply parents with developmentally framed psychoeducational information (Berkowitz, 2003b). In addition, training programs need to be developmentally appropriate. For example, if the program focuses on very young children, the information presented should be appropriate to early childhood development, cognitive level of the children, and age-appropriate discipline strategies.

Training for the early childhood service provider at the very least involves knowledge in areas such as child development, family dynamics, and social–cultural issues and evidence-based practice. Evidence-based practice requires that practitioners employ the most current, research-supported materials to address violence prevention. Beyond knowledge base, violence prevention development and implementation necessitates cultural sensitivity and strong interpersonal skills. Finally, training in program evaluation is critical since practitioners are in a position to not only deliver but also evaluate program strengths and weaknesses. Program evaluation supports improvement in violence prevention activities and builds the evidence base for these important activities.

CONCLUSION

This chapter has provided a discussion of the impact of violence in the lives of young children as well as a review of specific early childhood violence prevention programs. An awareness of the impact of violence on young children is crucial for early childhood professionals, teachers, parents, and caregivers. In the violence prevention literature, there are a number of programs that focus on young children and/or the adults in these children's lives. Early childhood professionals, community leaders, parents, family members, and caregivers need to take the lead in reducing the violence that children experience, hear about, and see in the media and in their environments. There is now clear evidence that appropriate violence prevention programs, providing useful information for professionals and families, can help accomplish the goal of reducing the impact of violence in the lives of children.

REFERENCES

American Psychological Association. (2002). *Ethical standards of psychologists.* Washington, DC: Author.

Anderson, C. A., Berkowitz, L., Donnerstein, E., Huesmann, L. R., Johnson, J. D., Linz, D., et al. (2003). The influence of media violence on youth. *Psychological Science in the Public Interest, 4*(3), 81–110.

Anderson, C. A., & Bushman, B. J. (2001). Effects of violent video games on aggressive behavior, aggressive cognition, aggressive affect, physiological arousal, and pro-social behavior: A meta-analytic review of the scientific literature. *Psychological Science, 12,* 353–359.

Anderson, C. A., & Dill, K. E. (2000). Video games and aggressive thoughts, feelings and behavior in the laboratory and in life. *Journal of Personality and Social Psychology, 78*(4), 772–790.

Bandura, A. (1973). *Aggression: A social learning analysis.* Englewood Cliffs, NJ: Prentice Hall.

Batsche, G. M., & Knoff, H. M. (1994). Bullies and their victims: Understanding a pervasive problem in the schools. *School Psychology Review, 23,* 165–174.

Berkowitz, S. J. (2003a). Affect, aggression and antisocial behavior. In R. J. Davidson, K. Scherer, & H. H. Goldstein (Eds.), *Handbook of affective sciences* (pp. 804–823). New York: Oxford University Press.

Berkowitz, S. J. (2003b). Children exposed to community violence: The rationale for early intervention. *Clinical Child and Family Psychology Review, 6*(4), 293–302.

Bogat, G. A., DeJonghe, E., Levendosky, A. A., von Eye, A., & Davidson, W. S. (2006). Trauma symptoms in infants who witness violence towards their mothers. *Child Abuse and Neglect: The International Journal, 30,* 109–125.

Boney-McCoy, S., & Finkelhor, D. (1995). Psychosocial sequelae of violent victimization in a national youth sample. *Journal of Consulting and Clinical Psychology, 63*(5), 726–736.

Bushman, B. J. (2002). Does venting anger feed or extinguish the flame? Catharsis, rumination, distraction, anger and aggressive responding. *Personality and Social Psychology Bulletin, 28,* 724–731.

Carney, J. V. (2000). Bullied to death: Perceptions of peer abuse and suicidal behavior during adolescence. *School Psychology International, 21,* 213–223.

Centers for Disease Control and Prevention. (2006). Youth risk behavioral surveillance – United States. *Morbidity and Mortality Weekly Report, 55* (No. SS-5).

Centers for Disease Control and Prevention. (2007). The effectiveness of universal school-based programs for the prevention of violent and aggressive behavior. *Morbidity and Mortality Weekly Report, 56* (No. RR-7).

Children's Defense Fund. (1997). *Every day in America.* CDF REPORTS, 18(2), 15. Washington, DC: Author.

Cleary, S. D. (2000). Adolescent victimization and associated suicidal and violent behaviors. *Adolescence, 35,* 671–682.

Conduct Problems Prevention Research Group. (2002). Fast Track prevention trial: Evaluation through third grade. *Journal of Abnormal Child Psychology, 30,* 1–52.

Cornell, D. G. (2006). *School violence: Fears versus facts*. Mahwah, NJ: Erlbaum.

Craig, W. M., & Pepler, D. J. (2007). Understanding bullying: From research to practice. *Canadian Psychology, 48*(2), 86–93.

DaSilva, J., Sterne, M. L., & Anderson, M. P. (2000). *ACT Against Violence Training Program manual*. Washington, DC: American Psychological Association and National Association for the Education of Young Children.

DeJonghe, E., Bogat, G. A., Levendosky, A. A., von Eye, A., & Davidson, W. S. (2005). Infant exposure to domestic violence predicts heightened sensitivity to adult verbal conflict. *Infant Mental Health Journal, 26,* 268–281.

DeVoe, J. F., Peter, K., Noonan, M., Snyder, T. D., & Baum, K. (2005). *Indicators of school crime and safety: 2005* (NCES 2006–001/NCJ 210697). U.S. Departments of Education and Justice. Washington, DC: U.S. Government Printing Office.

DiGiuseppe, R., & Tafrate, R. C. (2003). Anger treatment for adults: A meta-analytic review. *Clinical Psychology: Science and Practice, 10,* 70–84.

Dodge, K. A., & Crick, N. R. (1990). Social information processing bases of aggressive behavior in children. *Personality and Social Psychology Bulletin, 16,* 8–22.

Drewes, A. A. (2008). Bobo revisited: What the research says. *International Journal of Play Therapy, 17*(1), 52–65.

Edelson, J. L. (1999). Children's witnessing of adult domestic violence. *Journal of Interpersonal Violence, 14*(8), 839–870.

El-Sheikh, M., Cummings, E. M., Kouros, C. D., Elmore-Staton, L., & Buckhalt, J. (2008). Marital, psychological and physical aggression and children's mental and physical health: Direct, mediated, and moderated effects. *Journal of Consulting and Clinical Psychology, 76*(1), 138–148.

El-Sheikh, M., Harger, J., & Whitson, S. (2001). Exposure to parental conflict and children's adjustment and physical health: The moderating role of vagal tone. *Child Development, 72,* 1617–1636.

Feder, J., Levant, R. F., & Dean, J. (2007). Boys and violence: A gender-informed analysis. *Professional Psychology: Research and Practice, 38*(4), 385–391.

Fingerhut, L. A., & Christoffel, K. K. (2002). Firearm-related death and injury among children and adolescent. *Future of Children, 12*(2), 25–37.

Flannery, D. J., Vazsonyi, A. T., Liau, A. K., Guo, S., Powell, K. E., Atha, H., et al. (2003). Initial behavior outcomes for the PeaceBuilders universal school-based violence prevention program. *Developmental Psychology, 39*(2), 292–308.

Frey, K. S., Hirschstein, M. K., & Guzzo, B. A. (2000). Second Step: Preventing aggression by promoting social competence. *Journal of Emotional and Behavioral Disorders, 8,* 102–112.

Garbarino, J. (1999). *Lost boys: Why our sons turn violent and how we can save them*. New York: Free Press.

Gershoff, E. T. (2002). Corporal punishment by parents and associated child behaviors and experiences: A meta-analytic and theoretical review. *Psychological Bulletin, 128*(4), 539–579.

Goeke-Morey, M. C., Cummings, E. M., Harold, G. T., & Shelton, K. H. (2003). Categories and continua of destructive and constructive marital conflict tactics from the perspective of U.S. and Welsh children. *Journal of Family Psychology, 17*, 327–338.

Golly, A. M., Stiller, B., & Walker, H. M. (1998). First Step to Success: Replication and social validation of an early intervention program. *Journal of Emotional and Behavioral Disorders, 6*, 243–250.

Goodwin, T., Pacey, K., & Grace, M. (2003). Childreach: Violence prevention in preschool settings. *Journal of Child and Adolescent Psychiatric Nursing, 16*(2), 52–60.

Grossman, D. C., Neckerman, H. J., Koepsell, T. D., Liu, P., Asher, K. N., Beland, K., et al. (1997). Effectiveness of a violence prevention curriculum among children in elementary school. *Journal of the American Medical Association, 277*(20), 1605–1611.

Guerra, N. G., Huesmann, L. R., & Spindler, A. (2003). Community violence exposure, social cognition, and aggression among urban elementary school children. *Child Development, 74*(5), 1561–1576.

Guttman, M., Mowder, B. A., & Yasik, A. (2006). The ACT Against Violence Training Program: A preliminary investigation of knowledge gained by early childhood professionals. *Professional Psychology: Research and Practice, 37*(6), 717–723.

Harry, B., Allen, N., & McLaughlin, M. (1995). Communication versus compliance: African American parents' involvement in special education. *Exceptional Children, 61*, 364–377.

Hill, H. M., & Jones, L. P. (1997). Children's and parents' perceptions of children's exposure to violence in urban neighborhoods. *Journal of the National Medical Association, 89*(4), 270–276.

Hudley, C., & Taylor, A. (2006). What is cultural competence and how can it be incorporated into preventive interventions? In N. G. Guerra & E. Phillip-Smith (Eds.), *Preventing youth violence in a multicultural society* (pp. 249–269). Washington, DC: American Psychological Association.

Huesmann, L. R. (1988). An information processing model for the development of aggression. *Aggressive Behavior, 14*, 13–24.

Huesmann, L. R. (1998). The role of social information processing and cognitive schema in the acquisition and maintenance of habitual aggressive behavior. In R. E. Geen & E. Donnerstein (Eds.), *Human aggression: Theories, research, and implications for policy* (pp. 73–109). New York: Academic Press.

Huesmann, L. R., Eron, L. D., Lefkowitz, M. M., & Walder, L. O. (1984). Stability of aggression over time and generations. *Developmental Psychology, 20*, 1120–1134.

Huesmann, L. R., Moise-Titus, J., Podolski, C., & Eron, L. D. (2003). Longitudinal relations between children's exposure to TV violence and their aggressive and violence behavior in young adulthood: 1977–1992. *Developmental Psychology, 39*(2), 201–221.

Hyman, L. A., & Perrone, D. C. (1998). The other side of school violence: Educator policies and practices that may contribute to student misbehavior. *Journal of School Psychology, 36*(1), 7–27.

Kitzmann, K. M., Gaylord, N. K., Holt, A. R., & Kenny, E. D. (2003). Child witnesses to domestic violence: A meta-analytic review. *Journal of Consulting and Clinical Psychology, 71*(2), 339–352.

Le, T. N., & Stockdale, G. (2008). Acculturative dissonance, ethnic identity, and youth violence. *Cultural Diversity and Ethnic Minority Psychology, 14*(1), 1–9.

Leadbetter, B., Hoglund, W., & Woods, T. (2003). Changing contexts? The effects of a primary prevention program on classroom levels of peer-relational and physical victimization. *Journal of Community Psychology, 31*, 397–418.

Leff, S. S., Kupersmidt, J. B., Patterson, C., & Power, T. J. (1999). Factors influencing teacher predictions of peer bullying and victimization. *School Psychology Review, 28*, 505–517.

Leff, S. S., Power, T. J., Manz, P. H., Costigan, T. E., & Nabors, L. A. (2001). School-based aggression prevention programs for young children: Current status and implications for violence prevention. *School Psychology Review, 30*(3), 344–362.

Lerner, R. (1992). Bonding is the key. *Adolescent Counselor, 13*, 17.

Levendosky, A. A., Leahy, K. L., Bogat, G. A., Davidson, W. S., & von Eye, A. (2006). Domestic violence, maternal parenting, maternal mental health, and infant externalizing behavior. *Journal of Family Psychology, 20*(4), 544–552.

Litrownik, A. J., Newton, R., Hunter, W. M., English, D., & Everson, M. D. (2003). Exposure to family violence in young at-risk children: A longitudinal look at the effects of victimization and witnessed physical and psychological aggression. *Journal of Family Violence, 18*, 59–73.

Loeber, R., Keenan, K., & Zhang, Q. (1997). Boys' experimentation and persistence in developmental pathways toward serious delinquency. *Journal of Child and Family Studies, 6*, 321–357.

Marks, C. R., Glaser, B. A., Glass, J. B., & Horne, A. M. (2001). Effects of witnessing severe marital discord on children's social competence and behavioral problems. *Family Journal, 9*(2), 94–101.

McDonald, R., Jouriles, E. N., Briggs-Gowan, M. J., Rosenfield, D., & Carter, A. S. (2007). Violence toward a family member, angry adult conflict, and child adjustment difficulties: Relations in families with 1- to 3-year-old children. *Journal of Family Psychology, 21*(2), 176–184.

Meltzer, C. W., Biglan, A., Rusby, J. C., & Sprague, J. R. (2001). Evaluation of a comprehensive behavior management program to improve school-wide positive behavior support. *Education and Treatment of Children, 24*, 448–479.

Merrell, K. W., Gueldner, B. A., Ross, S. W., & Isava, D. M. (2008). How effective are school bullying intervention programs? A meta-analysis of intervention research. *School Psychology Quarterly, 23*(1), 26–42.

Mulvaney, M. K., & Mebert, C. J. (2007). Parental corporal punishment predicts behavior problems in early childhood. *Journal of Family Psychology, 21*(3), 389–397.

Nansel, T. R., Overpeck, M., Pilla, R. S., Ruan, W. J., Simons-Morton, B., & Scheidt, P. (2001). Bullying behaviors among US youth: Prevalence and association with psychosocial adjustment. *Journal of the American Medical Association, 285*(16), 2094.

Osofsky, J. D. (1995a). Children who witness domestic violence: The invisible victims. *Social Policy Report: The Society for Research in Child Development, 9*(3), 1–16.

Osofsky, J. D. (1995b). The effect of exposure to violence on young children. *American Psychologist, 50*(9), 782–788.

Ostrov, J. M., Ries, E. E., Stauffacher, K., Godleski, S. A., & Mullins, A. D. (2008). Relational aggression, physical aggression and deception during early childhood: A multimethod, multi-informant short-term longitudinal study. *Journal of Clinical Child and Adolescent Psychology, 37*(3), 664–675.

Pastore, A. L. (2005). *Sourcebook of Criminal Justice Statistics 2003.* Washington, DC: U.S. Department of Justice, Bureau of Justice Statistics, U.S. Government Printing Office.

Patterson, G. R., Debaryshe, B. D., & Ramsey, E. (1989). A developmental perspective on antisocial behavior. *American Psychologist, 44,* 329–335.

Pelligrini, A. (2001). The roles of dominance and bullying in the development of early heterosexual relationships. *Journal of Emotional Abuse, 2,* 63–73.

Perry, D. G. & Bussey, K. (1984). *Social Development.* Englewood Cliffs, NJ: Prentice Hall.

Perry, D. G., Perry, L. C., & Rasmussen, P. (1986). Cognitive social learning mediators of aggression. *Child Development, 57,* 700–711.

Prothrow-Stith, D., & Quaday, S. (1995). *Hidden causalities: The relationship between violence and learning.* Washington, DC: National Health & Education Consortium and National Consortium for African American Children.

Rigby, K. (2003). Consequences of bullying in schools. *Canadian Journal of Psychiatry, 48,* 583–590.

Rodkin, P. C., & Hodges, V. E. (2003). Bullies and victims in the peer ecology: Four questions for psychologists and school professionals. *School Psychology Review, 32,* 384–400.

Sprague, J. R., & Horner, R. H. (2006). Schoolwide positive behavioral supports. In S. R. Jimerson & M. J. Furlong (Eds.), *Handbook of school violence and school safety: From research to practice* (pp. 413–427). Mahwah, NJ: Erlbaum.

Stiles, M. M. (2002). Witnessing domestic violence: The effects on children. *American Family Physician, 66,* 2052–2066.

Straus, M. A. (2001). *Beating the devil out of them: Corporal punishment in American families* (2nd ed.). Edison, NJ: Transaction.

Taylor, T. K., Schmidt, F., Pepler, D., & Hodgins, H. (1998). A comparison of eclectic treatment with Webster-Stratton's Parents and Children Series in a children's mental health center: A randomized controlled trial. *Behavior Therapy, 29,* 221–240.

Theran, S. A., Levendosky, A. A., Bogat, G. A., & Huth-Bocks, A. C. (2005). Stability and change in mothers' internal representations of their infants over time. *Attachment and Human Development, 7,* 1–16.

Tremblay, R. E., Hartup, W. W., & Archer, J. (Eds.). (2005). *Developmental origins of aggression.* New York: Guilford Press.

Vossekuil, B., Fein, R.A., Reddy, M., Borum, R., & Modzeleski, W. (2002). *The final report and findings of the Safe School Initiative: Implications for the prevention of school attacks in the United States.* Washington, DC: U.S. Secret Service and U.S. Department of Education.

Walker, H. M., Severson, H. H., Feil, E. G., Stiller, B., & Golly, A. (1998). First Step to Success: Intervening at the point of school entry to prevent antisocial behavior patterns. *Psychology in the Schools, 35*(3), 259–269.

Warman, D. M., & Cohen, R. (2000). Stability of aggressive behaviors and children's peer relationships. *Aggressive Behavior*, *26*, 277–290.

Wright, J. C., & Zimmerman, M. A. (2006). Culturally sensitive interventions to prevent youth violence. In N. G. Guerra & E. Phillip-Smith (Eds.), *Preventing youth violence in a multicultural society* (pp. 221–247). Washington, DC: American Psychological Association.

Yates, T. M., Dodds, M. F., Sroufe, L. A., & Egeland, B. (2003). Exposure to partner violence and child behavior problems: A prospective study controlling for child physical abuse and neglect, child cognitive ability, socioeconomic status, and life stress. *Developmental Psychopathology*, *15*, 199–218.

CHAPTER 22

Child Care and Early Education

MARY DEBEY

INCREASINGLY, INFANTS, TODDLERS, and preschool-age children spend a large amount of time outside of the home (U.S. Department of Education, 2006). In order to work most effectively with young children and their families, it is important for mental health professionals to understand and appreciate the environments where young children spend so much of their time. Since the quality of such environments is crucial for healthy growth and development, an understanding of the variables that define quality along with the variety of early childhood education options from which families may choose is essential.

Early childhood education refers to all education and child care programs that serve young children from birth through age 8 (National Association for the Education of Young Children [NAEYC], 2008). As adults quickly learn when a young child surprisingly mimics a word intended only for adults to hear, children learn in all environments. Young children do not distinguish learning from playtime, so for young children all environments are learning environments. Therefore, whether a child is in child care for long hours each day or in a preschool a few hours a week, the quality of the experience is critical (Barnett, 2002; Gilliam & Zigler, 2004; Shonkoff & Phillips, 2000; Stoney, Mitchell, & Warner, 2006).

Many young children are in some type of center-based early childhood program prior to kindergarten. The U.S. Department of Education (2006) estimated that 43% of 3-year-olds and 69% of 4-year-olds were enrolled in a center-based early childhood program in 2005. Outside of the home, pre-kindergarten children are found in care by relatives and family friends, family and center-based child care, public and private preschools such as Head Start, and Early Head Start, and early childhood special education programs. Unlike elementary and secondary education, which guarantees a free public education, parents with prekindergarten children are primarily responsible for finding and financing their child's education and care.

The goal of early childhood care and education is to provide safe language-rich environments where infants, toddlers, and young children explore their world; deeply connect with materials, other children and adults; and develop healthy bodies and minds (NAEYC, 2008). This chapter surveys options for early childhood education and child care and addresses assessment of quality for programs serving young children.

PROGRAMS FOR CHILDREN FROM LOW-INCOME FAMILIES

PROJECT HEAD START—THE ONGOING NATIONAL PROGRAM

In 1964, as part of the Great Society programs, the federal government launched Project Head Start designed to help break the cycle of poverty through comprehensive preschool programs for children from low-income families. Federally funded by the Department of Health and Human Services and locally administered by community-based, nonprofit organizations, and school systems, Head Start serves 3- and 4-year-olds and requires that 10% of the children in a program be eligible for special education services (Head Start Basics, 2008). Thus, Head Start mandates classroom integration of typically and atypically developing children. A Head Start program may use a center-based model in which the children come to a center, a home-based model in which a *home visitor* works with caregivers and the child in the home, or provide a combination of the two models (U.S. Department of Health and Human Services, 2008).

Both home-based and center-based approaches offer four major components, including education, health, parent involvement, and social services (U.S. Department of Health and Human Services, 2008). The education component is designed to meet the developmental needs of each child through a variety of learning experiences which foster physical, intellectual, language, social, and emotional growth. The health component emphasizes early identification and prevention of health problems through a comprehensive program, including immunizations, medical, dental, mental health, and nutritional services. Parent involvement, a major factor in the success of Head Start (Castro, Bryant, Peisner-Feinberg, & Skinner, 2004), includes parent education, volunteering in the classroom, and involvement on committees and policy councils. The social services component tailors a program for each family after their needs are determined by the family, in collaboration with a family worker or home visitor. Social services may include community outreach, job referrals, emergency assistance, and crisis intervention.

Head Start has shown gains in children's cognitive, health, and social development. Studies show positive long-term effects on grade repetition, special education, and high school graduation rates (Barnett, 2002) and Head Start graduates are significantly more likely to complete high school and attend college than siblings who did not attend Head Start (Garces, Thomas, & Currie, 2002).

EARLY HEAD START

Based on the success and popularity of Head Start, Early Head Start projects were piloted in 1994 to provide services to low-income families with children under age 3 and pregnant women (Pelosi, 2007). Early Head Start focuses on helping families promote their child's physical, emotional, intellectual, and social development through home-based programs primarily. Coordinating with local Head Start programs to ensure a continuity of services through the prekindergarten years, Early Head Start programs provide parenting education, family support services (e.g., linking families to services in the community, setting family goals, and crisis intervention), comprehensive health and mental health services (e.g., prevention and early identification of health problems through the monitoring of physical evaluations and inoculation records, dental screenings, and vision and hearing testing), and nutrition education (Administration for Children and Families, 2008). By promoting parenting that supports learning within a child's first three years, at age 3 children who attended Early Head Start performed significantly better on measures of cognitive, language, and social-emotional developmental skills and were more engaged with parents during play than those who did not participate (U.S. Department of Health and Human Services, 2002).

PROGRAMS SERVING YOUNG CHILDREN WITH SPECIAL NEEDS

The original Individuals with Disabilities Education Act (IDEA, 1975), guaranteed that all disabled children (ages 0–21 years) receive a free and appropriate public education within the least restrictive environment (LRE). LREs in early childhood include settings where young children spend their time, such as in the home, preschools, play groups, and child care (Council for Exceptional Children, Division for Early Childhood, 1996). Young children's active participation in LREs should be guided by a developmentally and individually appropriate curriculum (Division of Early Childhood, 2008). Although, originally enacted by Congress in 1975, IDEA was amended several times and in 2004 the legislation became the Individuals with Disabilities Education Improvement Act (IDEIA). IDEIA provides guidelines for states and school districts providing special education and related services for school-age as well as young children.

Inclusive Programs

In the spirit of fostering Least Restrictive Environments, IDEIA (2004) promotes the creation of inclusive classrooms. These are classrooms in early childhood settings serving both typically developing children and children with a disability. The Council for Exceptional Children, Division for Early Childhood (1996) describes inclusion as a value that supports the participation of all children in natural settings both in the home and in programs for young children. Due to the wide variety of children and family needs, early childhood inclusion programs take several different forms (Guralnick, 2001; Schwartz, Sandall, Odom, Horn, & Beckman 2002), such as early childhood special education programs with a distribution of children with and without disabilities, and child care centers and preschools where a single child with special needs may have the assistance of a paraprofessional, an itinerant teacher or therapist. Inclusion benefits the social development of all children regardless of disability (Holahan & Costenbader, 2000; Odom, Vitztum, Wolery, Lieber, Sandall, & Hanson, 2004), and children with disabilities who are in inclusion programs generally do well socially (e.g., making friends) (Buysse, Goldman, & Skinner, 2002). Collaboration among parents, teachers, and specialists is the key in the creation of high-quality inclusion programs (Hunt, Soto, Maier, Liboiron, & Bae, 2004; Odom, Schwartz, & ECRII Investigators, 2002).

Early Intervention

The programs that offer services for infants and toddlers (0–2 years) with special needs are known as *Early Intervention Programs* (Sandall, McClean, & Smith, 2000). Part C of IDEIA (2004) requires states participating in this federally funded program to serve infants and toddlers with a diagnosed physical or mental health condition associated with or without a high probability of a developmental delay due to environmental and/or biological risk factors. Each state is provided with financial assistance from the federal government to provide comprehensive services to intervene at the early stages of the disability. Infants or toddlers with a disability in one or more of the following developmental areas may qualify: physical, cognitive, adaptive, communicative, and social and/or emotional.

An early intervention service coordinator has the initial contact with the family and together they create an Individualized Family Service Plan (IFSP) during the first visit. The IFSP describes the child, the family, the assessments, anticipated outcomes, services needed, transition support, and a plan for review. The service coordinator assists and enables families to access services and oversees procedural safeguards such as parental notification of meetings, parental consent, and confidentiality. A network of professionals may offer services including screening, assessment, family training, counseling, education, speech and language, occupational and physical therapy, psychological, audiology, vision, social work, and transportation. Bailey et al. (2006) posit five outcomes to assess the effectiveness of early intervention services including ensuring that: families understand their child's strengths and special needs; families know their rights and can advocate effectively; families can help their child develop and learn; families have support systems; and families are able to gain access to services.

Early Childhood Special Education

Early childhood special education programs provide a variety of educational services to children age 3 until they reach kindergarten. IDEIA Part B (2004) requires states to offer Early Childhood Special Education services if states receive federal funds. The process of enrolling a young child begins with an initial screening and if deemed appropriate, a full evaluation by qualified professionals (e.g., psychologists, educators, speech and language pathologists). If a child is determined eligible, an Individualized Education Program (IEP) is written and agreed on by both a team of professionals and parents. The IEP is a legally binding document that describes the educational and therapeutic needs and objectives for the child, and specifies the program designed to meet each child's unique needs (Sandall et al., 2000).

Research regarding early childhood special education has shown that providing quality services to young children with special needs can ameliorate and sometimes prevent developmental problems, reduce retention in later grades, lower educational costs, and improve relationships between parents and children (New York City Early Childhood Professional Development Institute, 2008).

STATE FUNDED EARLY CHILDHOOD EDUCATION

Universal Prekindergarten

Based on research linking early childhood education and future school success (Schweinhart, 2004), an increasing number of states are offering Universal Prekindergarten (UPK) programs (NAEYC, 2006). Using already existing early childhood programs or space in public schools, UPK strives to provide high-quality early childhood education to all children the year prior to entering kindergarten. In 2006, 45 states offered some type of state-funded prekindergarten program, many of them modeled after the comprehensive Head Start model (NAEYC). Children attending Universal Prekindergarten have shown increased school readiness in language, literacy, and mathematical development (Barnett, Lamy, & Jung, 2005).

BILINGUAL AND DUAL-LANGUAGE PROGRAMS

Bilingual programs in early childhood education strive to be additive (i.e., a second language is added to the first) instead of subtractive (i.e., the child's first language is replaced by the second language). Until recently, early childhood bilingual education in the United States was aimed at teaching English to non-English-speaking children. Within this model, parents of non-English-speaking children are often concerned that their children may lose their first language and be deprived of the social advantages gained from using their mother tongue if educated in English-only classrooms (Gibson, 1998). When children do not understand the home language, communication with family is limited and the complex set of values, beliefs, wisdom, and understanding that provide the foundation for their children's learning and development may be impeded (Gibson). A strong foundation in the child's home language is important to school readiness (Im, Osborn, Sánchez, & Thorp, 2007) and language and literacy development in the home language supports the development of language and literacy in English (Paez & Rinaldi, 2006).

There is growing evidence that learning a second language while maintaining the first is beneficial. Children who speak more than one language show greater mental flexibility, which is helpful in figuring out math concepts and word problems (Zebsko & Antunez, 2000). Thus, many English-only-speaking parents wanting their child to be better prepared for the global environment increasingly seek out programs in which their child can learn a second language (DeBey & Bombard, 2007). To meet the needs of parents wanting second languages for their children while maintaining the home language and parents of English-only children seeking out second language instruction, early childhood programs and school districts have increasingly added *dual language programs*. In a dual language program, two languages are incorporated into a language-rich classroom.

In early childhood education the languages are not taught as separate subjects, but each language is integrated into both free choice and teacher-directed activities throughout the entire day. In an ideal program there is a 50–50 mix of children speaking each language resulting in a large number of peers fluent in each language (Curtain & Dahlberg, 2003). Some programs alternate the languages on a daily basis, while in early elementary schools the languages are often subject specific (e.g., math may be in Spanish and science taught in English). In programs serving younger children with more than one teacher in the room, each teacher may continue to speak in a given language throughout the day and children hear and use each language depending on the teacher with whom they are interacting (DeBey & Bombard, 2007). Espinosa (2008) found that all young children are capable of learning two languages and that becoming bilingual has long-term cognitive, academic, social, cultural, and economic benefits.

CHILD CARE

Child care defines early childhood programs that have longer hours than preschools and assume the custodial aspects of care such as feeding, nap time, diapering, toilet training, and other tasks that are part of the daily care of young children. Out-of-home child care is a necessity for many families, since in the United States 53.8% of mothers who work outside the home place their infants in child care (U.S. Department of Labor, Bureau of Labor Statistics, 2005). Balancing work and parenting is challenging for all income groups, and particularly problematic, since the United States is one of the few industrialized countries that does not offer paid parental leave following the birth of a baby (Center on the Developing Child at Harvard University, 2007).

WHO CARES FOR YOUNG CHILDREN IN NEED OF CHILD CARE

Socioeconomic status (SES) is a predictor of the type of child care arrangement a family chooses. Preschool-age children whose parents are more educated and more affluent are more likely to participate in center-based care arrangements than be in the care of relatives (Huston, Chang, & Gennetian, 2002; Capizzano & Adams, 2004). Regardless of SES, the majority of children 0–4 are cared for during the workday by someone other than their parents (Federal Interagency Forum on Child and Family Statistics, 2008). Table 22.1 details the child care settings for children ages 0–4 with employed mothers.

Table 22.1
Primary Child Care Arrangements for Children Ages 0–4
with Employed Mothers

Setting	Percentage
Mother	3.2%
Father	17.5%
Grandparents	18.6%
Other relative	6.2%
Center-based	24.3%
Other nonrelative	17.2%
Other	13.0%

Source: Federal Interagency Forum on Child and Family Statistics (ChildStats.gov, 2008). *Child care: Primary child care arrangements for children ages 0–4 with employed mothers by selected characteristics, selected years 1985–2002.* ChildStats.gov.

Kith and Kin   Kith and Kin refers to child care that is provided by family members. Parents often depend on family members to care for children before they enter kindergarten. When mothers work outside the home, 21% of the children under age 5 are cared for by the father and mother, utilizing split shifts, or stay-at-home fathers (Federal Interagency Forum on Child and Family Statistics, 2008). Looking outside of the nuclear family, a grandparent cares for the young child about 18% of the time, and a relative other than a grandparent 6% of the time. Apart from the trust associated with family, the benefits of a family member's caring for a young child are often financial and flexibility in drop off, pick up, and sick care (Paulsell, Mekos, Del Grosso, Rowand, & Banghart, 2006).

Center-Based and Family Child Care   Center-based child care programs are used by one-quarter of all children under the age of 5 with employed mothers (Federal Interagency Forum on Child and Family Statistics, 2008). Center-based settings vary from large centers serving several hundred children to small programs with a few classrooms. Center-based child care is sponsored by non-profit and for-profit organizations (Wilson & Tweedie, 2008) including community organizations, hospitals, colleges, religious groups, corporations, and private individuals.

On-site child care refers to programs in settings where a parent is employed. Employers who typically provide on-site child care often include the high-tech and health care industries, and other worksites that need 24-hour workers, such as airline reservation companies (Connelly, DeGraff, & Willis, 2004). These researchers found that on-site child care is not only affordable, but in many cases it is profitable and that a majority of workers are willing to contribute to the cost of employer-sponsored day care whether or not they used this benefit.

Due to the shortage of affordable center care, family child care is increasing throughout the United States (Morrissey, 2007). A small family child care home is defined by the Children's Foundation (2001) as providers who are compensated for child care in their homes and care for usually up to six children. A large family child care home is defined as an arrangement in which seven to twelve children are cared for by a compensated caregiver (The Children's Foundation). In a study of family child care, the U.S. Department of Health and Human Services (2000) found no difference in the physical, social-emotional, or cognitive development of children in quality family child care than those in center-based programs.

FINDING CHILD CARE

Looking for child care outside of the family, parents often rely on friends to help select a caregiver. A friend who is satisfied with a child care arrangement is a strong indicator that a parent will also choose this option. There is an added feeling of security when parents know that a friend is also around the center or family child care home. Parents talk about the comfort of having "another pair of eyes" (Meyers & Jordan, 2006). As a child moves from infancy through the early childhood years, parental preferences for child care changes. Parents of infants and toddlers are much more likely to use informal home-based child care arrangements than parents of preschoolers who prefer center-based options (Capizzano, Adams, & Sonestein, 2000).

Searching for child care, parents consider the cost, convenience, and the quality of the program (Hofferth, Brayfield, Deich, & Holcomb, 1991). Convenience represents variables that make child care workable for parents including the location and hours of operation. Nationally, there are not enough child care openings to meet the growing need for affordable child care, so finding care can take a considerable amount of time (Paulsell, Nogales, & Cohen, 2003). The shortage is greatest in infant and toddler rooms (Kreader, Ferguson, & Lawrence, 2005) where directors report parents who call to place their baby on a long waiting list sometimes before conception. Due to the intensity of care needed for infants and toddlers, the cost of providing quality care is high.

THE EFFECT OF EARLY EDUCATION AND CHILD CARE ON YOUNG CHILDREN

The short- and long-term effects of child care on the health and development of young children is a concern for parents and educators. Although the separation from a primary caregiver affects each child differently, research shows that there are both positive aspects of group care and areas of concern. Child care does not affect all groups of children equally. For example, Loeb, Bridges, Bassok, Fuller, and Rumberger (2007) found in a study of 14,000 kindergartners that while center-based day care programs modestly benefited middle-class children in early language and mathematics learning, youngsters from low-income families experienced a double gain. The researchers found that cognitive skills in pre-reading and math were strongest when children entered a center-based program from age 2 to 3. A study by The National Institute of Child Health and Human Development (2006) found that:

- Children who are cared for exclusively by their mothers do not develop differently across domains than those who were also cared for by others.
- Parent and family characteristics were more strongly linked to overall child development than were child care features.

- Regardless of the family characteristics, quality, quantity, and type of care were modestly linked to the children's development.
- Children in higher quality child care had somewhat better language and cognitive development during the first 4½ years of life, and were somewhat more cooperative than those who experienced lower quality care during the first three years of life.
- Children with more hours in child care displayed somewhat more behavior problems in child care and in kindergarten classrooms than those with fewer hours.
- Children in child care centers showed somewhat higher levels of behavior problems in child care and in kindergarten classrooms than children who were in other nonmaternal child care arrangements.

QUALITY AND EARLY CHILDHOOD EDUCATION AND CARE

The quality of an early childhood program matters (Barnett, 2002; Gilliam & Zigler, 2004; Shonkoff & Phillips, 2000; Stoney et al., 2006). In early childhood education and care, quality is divided into structural and process variables. Both types of variables, measurement of these variables, and the benefits of quality care and education are discussed below.

STRUCTURAL VARIABLES

Structural quality describes variables in early childhood programs such as teacher–child ratio, group size, teacher education, and health and safety standards. Each variable is objective and easily measured. Individual states are responsible for maintaining the quality of child care and early education centers, and most states have developed structural regulations. Structural variables do not address what actually occurs in the program, but do consider difficult-to-measure variables such as curriculum delivery, social-emotional climate, and support for peer interactions. When structural variables are optimal, adults can pay closer attention to each child's development and well being (Helburn & Howes, 1996).

Adult-to-Child Ratio   The adult-to-child ratio relates to the amount of time adults have to attend to each child. A higher number of adults to children allows adults to observe more carefully, which is a key component of quality programs, and permits babies to be held more often, crying children to be comforted more quickly, and more concepts and language presented as children play and go through the routines of the day (Phillipsen, Burchinal, Howes, & Cryer, 1997). As the child moves from infancy to kindergarten, the number of children an adult can care for increases. Although few states specifically define an ideal teacher-child ratio, the majority of states do regulate it. In 2005, the majority of the states required a 4:1 ratio for infants and a 10:1 ratio for 4-year-olds (National Child Care Information Center, 2005).

Group Size The National Institute of Child Health and Human Development (NICHD) Study of Early Child Care (1996) found that group size, regardless of the adult to child ratio, is associated with quality early childhood education programs. The majority of states limit the average group size for infants to eight, while the average group size for 3- and 4-year-olds is 18. When the group size exceeds these numbers, the noise level is higher and there is a greater likelihood that some children will receive less than optimal care. In larger groups, adults spend less time in conversation with children, are less responsive and socially engaging, and more restrictive (Vandell, & Wolfe, 2000).

Teacher Education The level of education and specialized training of the adults caring for children are highly correlated with the quality of a program (NICHD Early Child Care Research Network, 1996; Phillipsen et al., 1997). Caregivers who have more formal education provide care that is more stimulating and supportive. Highly educated and specially trained caregivers are also more likely to organize materials and activities into more age-appropriate environments for children (NICHD Early Child Care Research Network). The National Association for the Education of Young Children provides education standards for early childhood teacher preparation programs which include promoting child development and learning; building family and community relationships; observing, documenting and assessing to support young children and families; teaching and learning; and becoming a professional (Hyson, 2003).

Caregiver education and training have been shown to be the best indicators predicting overall quality of a child care home. Caregivers having more education and training are less detached from the children and provide high quality care (Kwon, 2007). Unfortunately, finding and keeping highly educated teachers, necessary to maintain program quality, is difficult given that teachers in child care earn far less than their counterparts in public schools. The low salary and longer hours have resulted in a national child care teacher turnover average of 30% a year, creating problems in stability and quality of early childhood programs (Whitebook & Sakai, 2000).

Health and Safety Variables Health and safety variables refer to the physical space and sanitary practices in the program (Vandell & Wolfe, 2000). Space regulations, such as the number of square feet per child for play, napping, and readily accessible bathroom facilities allow the adults to provide better care.

For example, accessible bathroom facilities allow for greater hygienic practices such as hand washing by staff and children (Niffenegger, 1997; St. Sauver, Khurana, Kao, & Foxman, 1998), which is associated with fewer respiratory illnesses and other infectious diseases.

PROCESS VARIABLES

Process variables refer to how children experience an early childhood program including their interactions with materials, other children, and adults. For example, the room arrangement, schedule, and materials are carefully thought out to meet the changing needs of the children. The adults in high quality programs guide and respond to children in a sensitive and positive manner and children are actively engaged in socially appropriate play that promotes optimal physical, social, and cognitive development (Vandell & Wolfe, 2000).

MEASURING QUALITY

In 1985 the NAEYC developed a voluntary accreditation system designed to improve the quality of early childhood programs by assessing both the structural and process variables. The NAEYC Program Accreditation assesses early childhood programs using standards in the following areas: building relationships among staff, children and families; implementing a curriculum that addresses physical, social, emotional, language, and cognitive development; teaching using developmentally, culturally, and linguistically appropriate and effective approaches; ongoing systematic, formal, and informal assessment of child progress; the promotion of nutrition and health; qualified teachers; knowing and sharing information with families, and assessing and linking with community resources; developing and sustaining a safe physical environment; and the implementation of policies and systems that support stable staff and strong personnel, fiscal, and program management. Together, the 10 standards provide a framework for measuring the quality of an early childhood program.

In addition to the accreditation process, there are several instruments that measure early childhood program quality. The Early Childhood Environment Rating Scale, Revised (ECERS-R) is the most widely used evaluation instrument in early childhood group settings (Harms, Cryer & Clifford, 2004). ECERS-R (Harms et al.) is composed of 37 items that evaluate seven aspects of center-based care for preschool children including: personal care routines, furnishings, language reasoning experiences, motor activities, creative activities, social development, and staff needs. The Family Child Care Environment Rating Scale-Revised (Harms, Cryer, & Clifford, 2007) is similar to the

ECERS-R but is sensitive to the uniqueness of home care. The Infant/Toddler Environment Rating Scale–Revised (Harms, Cryer, & Clifford, 2006) examines space and furnishings, personal care routines, listening and talking, activities, interaction, program structure, and parents and staff.

BENEFITS OF QUALITY EARLY CHILDHOOD EDUCATION

Providing high-quality early childhood education for children from low-income families more than pays for itself. Although providing quality early childhood education requires an investment, when outcomes for low-income children are considered, the programs return $4 to $7 in benefits for every $1 invested (Barnett & Masse, 2007; Schweinhart, Montie, Xiang, Barnett, Belfield, & Nores, 2005). Savings include fewer students in special education programs, lower rates of crime and delinquency, and higher incomes after children reach adulthood. To achieve such results the programs need to be of high quality (Barnett & Masse, 2007; Foster & Vazquez, 2002). The benefit of high-quality early childhood education for children from low-income families is proving to be very long term. From 1962 to 1967, the Perry Preschool Project in Ypsilanti Michigan randomly divided 3- and 4-year-old children from low-income families into two groups, one receiving a high-quality preschool program and the comparison group receiving no program (High/Scope Preschool Study, 2008). Schweinhart et al., (2005) found in a follow-up of the Perry Preschool Project that at age 40, those who participated in the project were more likely to hold a job, earn over $20,000, and less likely to be arrested or involved in drug and violent crime.

There is growing evidence that investing in on-site child care is good for business. The National Report on Work & Family (American Business Collaboration for Quality Dependent Care, 2000) reported from a survey of 1,500 employees at companies participating in the American Business Collaboration that nearly two-thirds believe their productivity has improved as a result of the child care programs supported by their employers. According to the survey, 40% of the respondents felt less stressed by family responsibilities, 35% were better able to concentrate on work, and 30% left work less often to deal with family situations.

Code of Ethical Conduct and Statement of Commitment Working with young children involves making difficult decisions that sometimes have moral and ethical implications (NAEYC, 2005). The NAEYC established a Code of Ethical Conduct and Statement of Commitment to help those working with young children and their families. The Code sets forth a framework of professional relationships one strives for with children, families, colleagues, the community and society. The Code (NAEYC) is based on core values that are deeply rooted in the history of early childhood education including a commitment to:

- Appreciate childhood as a unique and valuable stage of the human life cycle.
- Base our work on knowledge of how children develop and learn.
- Appreciate and support the bond between the child and family.
- Recognize that children are best understood and supported in the context of family, culture, community, and society.
- Respect the dignity, worth, and uniqueness of each individual (child, family member, and colleague) and to respect diversity in children, families, and colleagues.
- Recognize that children and adults achieve their full potential in the context of relationships that are based on trust and respect.

DEVELOPMENTALLY APPROPRIATE PRACTICES

The Developmentally Appropriate Practices (Copple & Bredekamp, 2009) provide empirically-based principles and practices that help guide early childhood programs for all children and families. As the population of children in the United States becomes more diverse, early childhood educators are encouraged to become more culturally and linguistically sensitive and to provide more inclusive practices based on the principles of developmentally appropriate practice. By respecting and valuing the home culture and language, teachers can promote and encourage the active involvement and support of all families (Copple & Bredderkamp). The principles include:

- Domains of children's development—physical, social, emotional, and cognitive—are closely related. Development in one domain influences and is influenced by development in other domains.
- Development occurs in a relatively orderly sequence, with later abilities, skills, and knowledge building on those already acquired.
- Development proceeds at varying rates from child to child as well as unevenly within different areas of each child's functioning.
- Early experiences have both cumulative and delayed effects on individual children's development; optimal periods exist for certain types of development and learning.
- Development proceeds in predictable directions toward greater complexity, organization, and internalization.
- Children are active learners, drawing on direct physical and social experience as well as culturally transmitted knowledge to construct their own understandings of the world around them.

- Development and learning result from interaction of biological maturation and the environment, which includes both the physical and social worlds that children live in.
- Play is an important vehicle for children's social, emotional, and cognitive development, as well as a reflection of their development.
- Development advances when children have opportunities to practice newly acquired skills as well as when they experience a challenge just beyond the level of their present mastery.
- Children demonstrate different modes of knowing and learning and different ways of representing what they know.
- Children develop and learn best in the context of a community where they are safe and valued, their physical needs are met, and they feel psychologically secure (Copple & Bredekamp, 2009, pp. 5–9).

RESPONDING TO LINGUISTICALLY AND CULTURAL DIVERSITY

Increasingly, young children in early childhood programs need to negotiate and adapt to a culturally diverse sets of rules, values, expectations, and behaviors which are sometimes made more difficult due to not understanding or speaking English. The challenge for early childhood programs is to assist children and families in making this transition and to offer a program that is culturally and linguistically sensitive to a diverse population (NAEYC, 1995). To do this, early childhood educators need to "accept the legitimacy of children's home language, respect (hold in high regard) and value (esteem, appreciate) the home culture, and promote and encourage the active involvement and support of all families, including extended and nontraditional family units" (NAEYC, p. 2).

PROGRAMS AND CURRICULA MODELS IN EARLY EDUCATION

Since the early 1900s, philosophers, physicians, and educators have developed program models to provide for the education and care of young children. Although many of the models such as Montessori and Waldorf were developed for children from low-income families, today they are used across socioeconomic groupings. Curriculum models reflect differences in program values and inform the role of the teacher, the focus of the curriculum, the classroom structure, and assessment (Goffin & Wilson, 2001). Although there is little evidence that one program model produces better outcomes, the outcomes do reflect the goals of the program (Goffin & Wilson).

There is growing concern within the early childhood community that the national emphasis on academic performance has led to programs that are more teacher-directed and didactic with little time for play (Elkind, 2008). Unstructured play is essential for helping children reach important social, emotional, and cognitive developmental milestones (Webb, 2007). Although play may look differently in early childhood classrooms, a Montessori teacher encourages play with materials and a Waldorf teacher creates environments for imaginative play, most consider play important for physical, cognitive, and social-emotional development.

SPECIFIC CURRICULUM APPROACHES

The following early childhood program models are used throughout the United States and internationally. They are the Bank Street Approach, Creative Classroom, High/Scope, Montessori, Reggio Emilia, Waldorf Education, and Applied Behavioral Analysis.

The Bank Street Approach   Founded in 1916 in New York City, the Bank Street approach focuses on child-centered education. Also called the *Developmental-Interaction Approach*, in Bank Street inspired programs, teachers carefully set up classroom environments optimal for children's learning and development. Guiding the teacher's work are the following principles: (1) development generally moves from the simple to more complex, (2) development does not happen on a fixed trajectory, (3) developmental progress includes both stability and instability, and (4) development progresses from the more physical to conceptual and symbolic. In addition, the program promotes a sense of self, constructed from experiences that involve conflicts (Nager & Shapiro, 2000).

The Creative Curriculum   The Creative Curriculum is a program that assists teachers in setting up high-quality environments in the classroom. This includes deciding on the materials, the room arrangement and the schedule. The Creative Curriculum also defines the teacher's role in the design and implementation of activities and the assessment of children's development and learning experiences. The Creative Curriculum includes a developmental assessment that assists teachers in recording a child's development three times a year (Dodge, Colker, & Heroman, 2002). Widely used by Head Start Programs throughout the United States, the curriculum is divided into three developmental areas: infants and toddlers, preschool (3–5 years), and the primary grades (K–2).

High/Scope The High/Scope Approach is based on child development principles and active learning. The components of active learning in the High/Scope model emphasize the manipulation of materials, free choice time, the encouragement of language, and support from the adults. Children plan, carry out, and reflect upon their work in a process called *Plan, Do, Review*. There are separate curriculum systems for infant and toddler care and education, preschool education, early literacy, movement and music, elementary education, and youth programs. The curriculum consists of teaching practices, defined curriculum content areas, assessment tools, and a training model (Hohmann, Weikart, & Epstein, 2008).

Montessori   Dr. Montessori founded the Casa dei Bambini in Rome, Italy, in 1907 for a group of children who were spending most of their time on the streets. Montessori education emphasizes learning through the five senses. Children in Montessori classes learn at their own individual pace and according to their own choice of activities from carefully designed materials and activities. In Montessori classrooms, children are free to make choices and engage in purposeful activities with the guidance of a Montessori-trained adult (Stephenson, 2006).

Reggio Emilia   The Reggio Emilia approach to early childhood education began in the municipal infant–toddler centers and preschools in northern Italy. The philosophy is built on community-constructed values, child development principles, and a belief that children construct knowledge through active exploration in well-designed classrooms. Inspired by Dewey, Piaget, Vygotsky, Gardner, and Bruner, the Reggio approach includes an emergent curriculum developed around the interests of children with in-depth projects lasting from a week to the school year. Each project includes representational development of ideas and concepts using drama, art, print, puppetry, and music. Further, collaboration in large and small groups to strengthen interpersonal skills and observation and documentation of both the children's and teacher's growth are mainstays of the program (Edwards, Gandini, & Forman, 1998).

Waldorf Education   Waldorf education is committed to the development of the whole child including the physical, cognitive, social, and spiritual domains. The Waldorf early childhood classroom is unique in the use of color, light, and materials. Stressing a close relationship to nature, children use stones, pine cones, shells, and other artifacts from nature instead of the plastic toys found in many early childhood classrooms. Founded in 1919 by Rudolf Steiner, the program is based on the belief that children develop in a unique manner and that rushing development is harmful. Through the use of carefully selected stories and free play, both in the classroom and out of doors, young children are encouraged to engage in fantasy, imaginative play, and imitation (Petrash, 2002).

Applied Behavioral Analysis and Didactic Approaches   In early childhood education, behavioral programs are most often used in intervention programs for children with special needs. Behaviorism focuses on decreasing negative behaviors (punishment) and increasing positive behaviors (reinforcement). Although most teachers use behavioral techniques, such as taking away a ball that has just been thrown indoors in order to decrease throwing things indoors, in behavioral-based approaches such as Applied Behavioral Analysis (ABA) behavioral techniques are at the core of the program (Sulzer-Azaroff & Mayer, 1991).

The most common method of ABA is the discrete trial technique that is a three-part teaching technique. In the discrete trial method a child is provided with a stimulus along with the desired response. The child is rewarded for repeating the desired response and incorrect responses are ignored. As the child demonstrates more correct responses the cues for correct responses are withdrawn until he or she responds independently. A particular trial may be repeated several times in succession over many days.

Didactic approaches focus on teacher directed activities and carefully prescribed lessons and work sheets. Children in didactic-centered programs often do well on short-term assessments but do not keep up with peers in the later school years (Schweinhart & Weikart, 1997).

NATIONAL ORGANIZATIONS SUPPORTING THE EDUCATION AND CARE OF YOUNG CHILDREN

NATIONAL ASSOCIATION FOR THE EDUCATION OF YOUNG CHILDREN

The National Association for the Education of Young Children is the leading organization for early childhood educators in the United States. Dedicated to improving the well-being of all young children, NAEYC strives to support and improve the quality of educational and developmental services for all children from birth through age 8. The three major goals of NAEYC are to improve professional practice and working conditions in early childhood education, support early childhood programs by working to achieve a high-quality system of early childhood education, and build an inclusive organization of groups and individuals who are committed to promoting excellence in early childhood education for all young children (National Association for the Education of Young Children, 2008).

NAEYC developed and sponsors the voluntary Accreditation of Programs for Young Children, the Accreditation of Associate Degree Programs, and the Accreditation of Baccalaureate and Graduate Degree Programs. The NAEYC Accreditation Standards are recognized by the National Council for the Accreditation of Teacher Education (NCATE).

COUNCIL FOR EXCEPTIONAL CHILDREN—DIVISION OF EARLY CHILDHOOD

The Division for Early Childhood (DEC) is a division of the Council for Exceptional Children (CEC), which is dedicated to enriching the lives and improving the services for young children with special needs and their families. The DEC promotes parent–professional collaboration in the planning, design, and implementation of early childhood intervention services; advocates for policy, planning, and best practice in prevention and intervention; and supports those who work with or on behalf of infants and young children with special needs and their families. The DEC has developed the Early Childhood Special Education Standards recognized by the National Council for the Accreditation of Teacher Education (Division for Early Childhood, 2008).

THE NATIONAL ASSOCIATION OF CHILD CARE RESOURCE & REFERRAL AGENCIES

The National Association of Child Care Resource & Referral Agencies promotes child care in the United States by providing assistance to over 800 state and local Child Care Resource & Referral agencies. The local agencies help families find high-quality affordable child care and provide training, resources, and best practices standards to local child care providers. The group promotes national policies and partnerships that facilitate universal access to high-quality child care. Further, they collect, analyze, and report current child care data and research as well as offer child care and parenting information and resources to families (National Association of Child Care Resource & Referral Agencies, 2008).

ZERO TO THREE

Zero to Three is a multidisciplinary organization with a mission to inform, educate, and support the adults who influence the lives of infants and toddlers. The organization translates research into practical information through the publication of the *Zero to Three* journal. The organization also administers the Early Head Start National Resource Center, which trains professionals through the National Training Institutes, influences policies through the Zero to Three Policy Center, and increases parental and public awareness (Zero to Three, 2008).

SUMMARY

Since many young children require care outside the home, it is important that mental health professionals are aware of the various options in early education and care in order to guide parents in their choices. Educational and care opportunities for young children include a myriad of options including child care, Head Start, preschool, early childhood special education programs and Universal Prekindergarten as well as many types of programs adhering to various curricula models. In addition, the quality of an early childhood program, for which there are defined and measurable variables, is crucial for the optimal development of young children. Research consistently demonstrates that quality programs are beneficial and cost effective, especially for children growing up in low-income families. Therefore, mental health professionals need to understand and appreciate the unique features of early childhood settings so they can assist parents in making informed decisions.

REFERENCES

Administration for Children and Families. (2008). *Early Head Start information folder*. Retrieved on September 11, 2008 from www.headstartinfo.org/infocenter/ehs_tkit3.htm.

American Business Collaboration for Quality Dependent Care. (2000). *The national report on work & family*. Cambridge: Abt Associates.

Aronson, S. & Shope, T. (2005). Improving the health and safety of children in non-parental early education and child care. *Pediatrics in Review, 26*, 86–95.

Bailey, D. B., Bruder, M. B., Hebbeler, K., Carta, J., Defosset, M., Greenwood, C., et al. (2006). Recommended outcomes for families of young children with disabilities. *Journal of Early Intervention*. Washington DC: DEC.

Barnett, W. S. (2002). The Battle over Head Start: What the research shows. Presentation at a Science and Public Policy Briefing sponsored by the Federation of Behavioral, Psychological, and Cognitive Sciences.

Barnett, W.S., Lamy, C., & Jung, K. (2005). The Effects of State Pre-kindergarten on Young Children's School Readiness in Five States. The National Institute for Early Education Research, Rutgers University. Retrieved August 12, 2008 from www.strategiesforchildren.org/eea/6research_summaries/05_PreKreadiness5States.pdf.

Barnett, W. S., & Masse, L. N. (2007). Comparative benefit-cost of the Abecedarian program and its policy implications. *Education of Economics Review, 26*, 113–125.

Buysse, V., Goldman, B. D., & Skinner, M. (2002). Setting effects on friendship formation among young children with and without disabilities. *Exceptional Children, 68*, 503–517.

Capizzano, J., & Adams, G., (2004). *Children in low-income families are less likely to be in center-based child care*. Washington, DC: Urban Institute.

Capizzano, J., Adams, G. & Sonestein, F. (2000). *Child care arrangements for children under five: Variation across states* (New Federalism: National Survey of America's Families, Series B, No. B-7). Washington, DC: Urban Institute.

Castro, D. C., Bryant, D. M., Peisner-Feinberg, E. S., & Skinner, M. L. (2004). Parent involvement in Head Start programs: The role of parent, teacher, and classroom characteristics. *Early Childhood Research Quarterly, 19*, 413–430.

Center on the Developing Child at Harvard University. (2007). A science-based framework for early childhood policy using evidence to improve outcomes in learning, behavior, and health for vulnerable children. Retrieved on September 11, 2008 from www.developingchild.harvard.edu.

The Children's Foundation. (2001). *The 2001 child care center licensing study*. Washington, DC: Children's Foundation.

Connelly, R., DeGraff, D., & Willis, R. (2004). *Kids at work: The value of employer-sponsored on-site child care centers*. Kalamazoo, MI: Upjohn Institute for Employment Research.

Copple, C., & Bredekamp, S. (2009). *Developmentally appropriate practice in early childhood programs serving children from birth through age eight* (3rd ed.). Washington, DC: NAEYC.

Copple, C. E., Cline, M. G., & Smith, A. N. (1987). *Path to the future: Long-term effects of Head Start in the Philadelphia School District*. U.S. Department of Health and Human Services: Washington, DC.

The Council for Exceptional Children, Division for Early Childhood (1996). *Inclusion.* A position paper. Retrieved on August 18, 2008, from www.dec-sped.org/pdf/positionpapers/PositionStatement_Inclusion.pdf.

Curtain, H., & Dahlberg, C. (2003). *Languages and children—making the match. New languages for young learners*, Grades K–8. Columbus, OH: Allyn & Bacon.

DeBey, M., & Bombard, D. (2007). Expanding children's boundaries: An approach to second language learning and cultural understanding. *Young Children Journal*, 62(2). 88–93.

Division for Early Childhood. (2008). *About us.* Retrieved on September 12, 2008 from www.dec-sped.org/aboutdec.html.

Dodge, D. T., Colker, L. J., & Heroman, C. (2002). *The creative curriculum for preschool*. Washington, DC: Teaching Strategies.

The Education for All Handicapped Children Act Amendments of 1986 Part H. PL 99–457, 98th Cong. (1986).

Edwards, C. P., Gandini, L. & Forman, G. E. (Eds.). (1998). *The hundred languages of children: The Reggio Emilia approach—advanced reflections*. Greenwich, CT: Ablex.

Elkind, D. (2008). Can we play? *Greater Good Magazine: The Science of a Meaningful Life IV*(4). Retrieved on September 12, 2008 from http://greatergood.berkeley.edu/greatergood/2008spring/Elkind344.html.

Espinosa, L. (2008). Challenging common myths about young English language learners. *Foundation for child development policy brief: Advancing PreK-3*. New York: FCD.

Federal Interagency Forum on Child and Family Statistics. (2008). *Child care: Primary child care arrangements for children ages 0–4 with employed mothers by selected characteristics, selected years 1985–2002.* Retrieved August 18, 2008 from www.childstats.gov/americaschildren/tables/pop8b.asp.

Foster, E. M., & Vazquez, A. (2002). Costs and benefits: Investments and returns. In C. J. Groark, Mehaffie, K. E., McCall, R. B., & Greensburg, M. T. (Eds.), *From science to policy: Research issues, programs and policies in early care and education*. Universities Children's Policy Collaborative.

Galinsky, E., Howes, C., Kontos, S., & Shinn, M. (1994). *The study of children in family child care and relative care: Highlights of findings*. New York: Families and Work Institute.

Garces, E., Thomas, D., & Currie, J. (2002). Longer-term effects of Head Start. *American Economic Review*, 92, 999–1012.

Garrett, P., Lubeck, S., & Wenk, D. (1990). Childbirth and maternal employment: Data from a National Longitudinal Survey. In Hyde, J. S. & Essex, M. J. (Eds.), *Parental leave and child care: Setting a research agenda*. Philadelphia, PA: Temple University Press.

Gibson, M. A. (1998). Promoting academic success among immigrant students: Is acculturation the issue? *Educational Policy*, 12, 615–633.

Gilliam, W., & Zigler, E. (2004). *State Efforts to Evaluate the Effects of Prekindergarten: 1977 to 2003*. New Haven: Yale University Child Study Center. Retrieved August 18, 2008, from http://nieer.org/resources/research/StateEfforts.pdf.

Ginsberg, M. (2001). *Computers and young children: Early years are learning years*. Washington, DC: NAEYC.

Goffin, S. G., & Wilson, C. (2001). *Curriculum models and early childhood education: Appraising the relationship* (2nd ed.). Upper Saddle River, NJ: Merrill/Prentice Hall.

Gormley, W. T., Gayer, T., Phillips, D., & Dawson, B. (2005). The effects of Universal Pre-K on cognitive development. *Developmental Psychology*, 41(6), 872–884.

Guralnick, M. J. (2001). A framework for change in early childhood inclusion. In M. J. Guralnick (Ed.). *Early childhood inclusion: Focus on change*. Baltimore: Brookes.

Harms, T., Cryer, D., &, Clifford, R. M. (2006). *Infant/toddler environment rating scale* (Rev. ed). New York: Teachers College Press.

Harms, T., Cryer, D., & Clifford, R.M. (2007). *Family child care environmental rating scale* (Rev. ed.). New York: Teachers College Press.

Harms, T., & Clifford, R. M. & Cryer, D. (2004). *Early childhood environment rating scale* (Rev. ed.). New York: Teachers College Press.

Head Start Basics. *Issue Background*. Retrieved on September 11, 2008, from www.nhsa.org/download/advocacy/fact/08FactSheetHSBasics.pdf.

Helburn, S., & Howes, C. (1996). Child care cost and quality. *The Future of Children: Financing Child Care*, 6 (2). Retrieved August 11, 2008, from www.futureofchildren.org/usr_doc/vol6no2ART4.pdf.

High/Scope Educational Research Foundation. *High/Scope Perry Preschool Study*. Retrieved August 18, 2008, from www.highscope.org/Content.asp?ContentId=219.

Hofferth, S. L., Brayfield, A., Deich, S., & Holcomb, P. (1991). *National child care survey, 1990*. Washington, DC: Urban Institute.

Hohmann, M., Weikart, D. P., & Epstein, A. S., (2008). *Educating young children: Active learning practice for preschool and child care programs*. Ypsilanti, MI: High/Scope Press.

Holahan, A., & Costenbader, V. (2000). A comparison of developmental gains for preschool children with disabilities in inclusive and self-contained classrooms. *Topics in Early Childhood Special Education*, 20, 224–235.

Hunt, P., Soto, G., Maier, J., Liboiron, N., & Bae, S. (2004). Collaborative teaming to support preschoolers with severe disabilities who are placed in general education early childhood programs. *Topics in Early Childhood Special Education, 24*, 123–142.

Huston, A. C., Chang, Y. E., & Gennetian, L. (2002). Family and individual predictors of child care use by low-income income families in different policy contexts. *Early Childhood Research Quarterly, 17*, 441–469.

Hyson, M. (Ed.). (2003). *Preparing Early Childhood Professionals: NAEYC's Standards for Programs.* Washington DC: NAEYC.

Im, J., Osborn, C., Sánchez, S., & Thorp, E. (2007). *Cradling literacy: Building teachers' skills to nurture early language and literacy birth to five.* Washington, DC: Zero to Three Policy Center.

Individuals with Disabilities Education Improvement Act of 2004. (2004). PL 108–446, 108th Congress.

Individuals with Disabilities Education Act. (1997). PL 101–476, 94th Congress.

Kreader, L., Ferguson, D., & Lawrence, S. (2005). *Infant and toddler child care quality.* (Research to Polity Connections No, 2). New York: National Center for Children in Poverty, Columbia University Mailman School of Public Health.

Kwon, K. (2007). What is more important for quality in family child care homes, caregiver education or adult-child ratio? A policy brief from research conducted by Burchinal, M., Howes, C., & Kontos, S. (2006). Infant Toddler Specialists of Indiana Network. Retrieved July 7, 2008, from www.researchconnections.org/location/ccrca6872.

Loeb, S., Bridges, M., Bassok, D., Fuller, B., & Rumberger, R. W. (2007). How much is too much? The influence of preschool centers on children's social and cognitive development. *Economics of Education Review, 26*(1), 52–66.

Meyers, M. K., & Jordan, L. P. (2006). Choice and accommodation in parental child care decisions. *Community Development: Journal of the Community Development Society, 37*(2), 53–70.

Morrissey, T., & Banghart, P. (2007). Family child care in the United States. *Child care & early education: Research connections.* New York: Columbia University.

Murray, J., & Murray, A. D. (2008). Television in infancy and early childhood: Uses & effects. *Encyclopedia of infant and early childhood development.* San Antonio, TX: Mind Science Foundation.

Nager, N., & Shapiro, E. K. (Eds.). (2000). *Revisiting a progressive pedagogy: The developmental-interaction approach.* Albany, NY: State University of New York Press.

National Association of Child Care Resource & Referral Agencies. (2008). *About NACRRA.* Retrieved on September 12, 2008, from www.naccrra.org/about/.

National Association for the Education of Young Children. (2008). *About NAEYC.* Retrieved September 12, 2008, from www.naeyc.org/about/.

National Association for the Education of Young Children. (2006). *Quick facts: State pre-kindergarten programs.* Retrieved July 7, 2008, from www.naeyc.org/.

National Association for the Education of Young Children. (2005). *Code of ethical conduct and statement of commitment.* Retrieved on August 18, 2008, from www.naeyc.org/about/positions/PSETH05.asp.

National Association for the Education of Young Children. (1995). *Responding to cultural and linguistic diversity: Recommendation for dfective early childhood education.* NAEYC Position Paper. Retrieved July 12, 2008, from www.naeyc.org/about/positions/pdf/PSDIV98.PDF.

National Child Care Information Center. (2005). *Child:staff ratios and maximum group size requirements.* Retrieved on July 7, 2008, from www.nara.affiniscape.com/displaycommon.cfm?an=1&subarticlenbr=104.

National Institute of Child Health and Human Development Early Child Care Research Network. (1996). Characteristics of infant child care: Factors contributing to positive care giving. *Early Childhood Research Quarterly, 11,* 269–306.

National Institute of Child Health and Human Development. (2006). *The NICHD study of early child care and youth development: Findings for children up to age 4½.* Washington, DC: U.S. Department of Health and Human Services.

New York City Early Childhood Professional Development Institute. (2008). *Why is early childhood special education important?* Retrieved August 18, 2008, from www.earlychildhoodnyc.org/about/specialed.cfm.

Niffenegger, J. P. (1997). Proper hand washing promotes wellness in child care. *Journal of Pediatric Health Care, 11,* 26–31.

Odom, S. L., Schwartz, I. S., & ECRII Investigators. (2002). So what do we know from all this? Synthesis points of research on preschool inclusion. In S. L. Odom (Ed.), *Widening the circle: Including children with disabilities in preschool programs* (pp. 154–174). New York: Teachers College Press.

Odom, S. L., Vitztum, J., Wolery, R., Lieber, J., Sandall, S., & Hanson, M. (2004). Preschool inclusion in the United States: A review of research from an ecological system perspective. *Journal of Research in Special Educational Needs, 4,* 17–49.

Paez, M., & Rinaldi. C. (2006). Predicting English word reading skills for Spanish-speaking students in first grade. *Topics in Language Disorders, 26*(4), 338–350.

Paulsell, D., Mekos, D., Del Grosso, P., Rowand, C., & Banghart, P. (2006). Strategies for supporting quality in kith and kin child care: Findings from the Early Head Start Enhanced Home Visiting Pilot Evaluation; Final Report. Washington, DC: Mathematica Policy Research.

Paulsell, D., Nogales, R., & Cohen, J. (2003). Quality child care for infants and toddlers: Case studies of three community strategies. Washington, DC: Zero to Three Policy Center.

Pelosi, N. (2007). Pelosi: Head Start is one of America's most popular investments because it is one of our most effective. San Francisco 8th District. Retrieved August 11, 2008, from www.house.gov/pelosi/press/releases/Dec07/HeadStart2.html.

Petrash, J. (2002). *Understanding Waldorf education: Teaching from the inside out.* Beltsville, MD: Gryphon.

Peyton, V., Jacobs, A., O'Brien, M., & Roy, C. (2001). Reasons for choosing child care: Associations with family factors, quality, and satisfaction. *Early Childhood Research Quarterly, 16,* 191–208.

Phillipsen, L. C., Burchinal, M. R., Howes, C. & Cryer, D. (1997). The prediction of process quality from structural features of child care. *Early Childhood Research Quarterly, 12,* 281–303.

Pungello, E. P., & Kurtz-Costes, B. (1999). Why and how working women choose child care: A review with a focus on infancy. *Developmental Review, 19*, 31–96.

Sandall, S., McClean, M., & Smith, B. (2000). *DEC recommended practices in early intervention/early childhood special education*. Arlington, VA: Council for Exceptional Children.

Schwartz, I., Sandall, S., Odom, S., Horn, E., & Beckman, P. (2002). I know it when I see it: In search of a common definition of inclusion. In S. Odom (Ed.), *Widening the circle: Including children with disabilities in preschool programs*. New York: Teachers College Press.

Schweinhart, L. J. (2004). *The High/Scope Perry Preschool Study through age 40: Summary, conclusions, and frequently asked questions*. Ypsilanti, MI: High/Scope Press.

Schweinhart, L. J., Montie, J., Xiang, Z., Barnett, W. S., Belfield, C. R., & Nores, M. (2005). *Lifetime effects: The High/Scope Perry Preschool study through age 40* (Monographs of the High/Scope Education Research Foundation, 14). Ypsilanti, MI: High/Scope.

Schweinhart, L. J., & Weikart, D. P. (1997). The High/Scope preschool curriculum comparison study through age 23. *Early Childhood Research Quarterly, 12*, 117–143.

Shonkoff, J., & Phillips, D. (2000). *From neurons to neighborhoods: The science of early child development*. Washington, DC: National Academies Press.

St. Sauver, J., Khurana, M., Kao, A., & Foxman, B. (1998). Hygienic practices and acute respiratory illness in family and group day care homes. *Public Health Reports, 111*, 544–551.

Stephenson, S. (2006). *Child of the world: Montessori for Ages 3–12+*. Arcata, CA: Olaf.

Stoney, L., Mitchell, A., & Warner, M. (2006). Smarter reform: Moving beyond single-program solutions to an early care and education system. *Community Development: Journal of the community development society, 37*(2), 102–115.

Sulzer-Azaroff, B., & Mayer, R. (1991). *Behavior analysis for lasting change*. Fort Worth, TX: Holt, Reinhart & Winston.

U.S. Department of Education, NCES. The Condition of Education in 2006, Indicator 2: Enrollment in Early Childhood Education Programs. Retrieved July 12, 2008, from http://nces.ed.gov/programs/coe/2006/pdf/02_2006.pdf.

U.S. Department of Health and Human Services. Administration for Children and Families. Office of Head Start. (2000). *Evaluation of Head Start family child care demonstration: Final Report*.

U.S. Department of Health and Human Services. Administration for Children and Families. Office of Head Start. (2002). *Early Head Start research. Making a difference in the lives of infants, toddlers and their families: The impacts of Early Head Start: Final Technical Report*.

U.S. Department of Health and Human Services. Administration for Children and Families. Office of Head Start. (2008). *About Head Start*. Retrieved July 7, 2008, from http://eclkc.ohs.acf.hhs.gov/hslc/About%20Head%20Start.

U.S. Department of Labor, Bureau of Labor Statistics. (2005). Employment Characteristics of Families in 2005. *Employment Characteristics of Families Summary*. Retrieved July 7, 2008, from www.bls.gov/news.release/famee.nr0.htm.

Vandell, D.L. & Wolfe, B. (2000). *Child care quality: Does it matter and does it need to be improved?* Madison, WI: University of Wisconsin: Institute for Research on Poverty, Special Report No. 78.

Webb, S. (2007). Educating children in the new millennium: Child's play. *Education Week*, October 10.

Whitebook, M., & Sakai, L. (2000). *Turnover begets turnover: An examination of job and occupational instability among child care center staff.* Berkley, CA: Center for Study of Child Care Employment.

Wilson, E., & Tweedie, P. (2008). *Selecting quality child care.* National Network for Child Care. Retrieved on September 5, 2008, from www.nncc.org.

Zebsko, N., & Antunez, B. (2000). If your child learns in two languages. *A parents' guide for improving educational opportunities for children acquiring English as a second language.* Washington, DC: National Clearinghouse for Bilingual Education.

Zero to Three. (2008). *About us: Fact sheet.* Retrieved on September 12, 2008, from www.zerotothree.org/site/PageServer?pagename=ter_abt_factsheet.

CHAPTER 23

Response to Intervention

PAUL C. MCCABE

ASSESSMENT IN EARLY childhood has taken on an increased sense of urgency and importance within the past decade, in part due to a parallel trend of the rising importance of high-stakes testing in the school years. The high-stakes testing movement for school-age children has heightened focus on early childhood as the period when precursor skills to literacy, numeracy, and other developmental skills emerge and are practiced. Although scholars have cautioned against the use of high-stakes testing in early childhood (e.g., Bagnato & Ho, 2006), the proponents argue that the better prepared preschoolers are to learn academic skills, the more successful their learning will be, and the better they will perform on standardized tests later in grade school.

Relatedly, research in the past decade has focused on alternative procedures for identifying children at risk for learning delays or disabilities (LD). Predominant models of LD identification were rooted in the medical model, and therefore emphasized a pathology or deviance approach versus a developmental focus. Response to Intervention (RTI) is a framework that emphasizes developmental tasks versus deviance, and therefore is well suited for early childhood (McCabe, 2006; VanDerHeyden & Synder, 2006). RTI is an approach that utilizes the general education curriculum, is implemented by teachers, and seeks to identify children at risk for learning delays to receive more targeted intervention.

This chapter presents RTI as an alternative approach to the traditional assessment methods of early childhood and one that is advantageous in preparing young children for school success (measured, among other ways, by high-stakes testing). The advantages of RTI are reviewed, as well as challenges specific to implementation in early childhood settings. Research on RTI and the predictive validity of early developmental indicators and developmental markers in predicting later school achievement is presented, including the appropriateness of RTI with disabled and diverse populations.

TRADITIONAL ASSESSMENT IN EARLY CHILDHOOD

Early childhood practice is often derived from downward extension of practices designed for older children or even adults. This is in contrast to recommended practices for early childhood that focus on development, including normal variation in development from one child to another and across ages (National Association for the Education of Young Children, 1997). An example is the use of procedures where cognitive and achievement measures used with older children to identify learning delays and/or disabilities are extended downward for use in early childhood. Learning disability has traditionally been defined as a significant impairment in one or more areas of achievement skill (e.g., reading, writing, math), and is measured by obtaining cognitive and achievement test scores. A child whose achievement test score in a particular skill domain is significantly lower than his or her cognitive test scores (considered to be an overall measure of ability) is judged to have a learning disability. This approach, also known as the deviance model, implies that the tests used to measure cognition and achievement are reliable and valid, and that what they are measuring, ability and achievement, can be accurately used to measure a learning disability. However, a number of scholars have argued that these tests do not reliably differentiate between children with and without learning disabilities, and that a discrepancy of ability and achievement is meaningless without direct application to the curriculum and intervention (Fuchs, Mock, Morgan, & Young, 2003; Ysseldyke, 2005).

Another important distinction of the deviance model is that it relies on a *wait-and-fail* approach where children will not meet criteria for a learning disability unless their achievement scores are sufficiently discrepant from their ability. In many cases, students must perform poorly for years and continue to fall behind their peers until the deviance scores have reached a significant threshold that would qualify the child as learning disabled (Fuchs et al., 2003). At this point, the child has missed out on years of intervention and support.

There are parallels between the deviance approach and the medical model, in which an individual is not diagnosed with a medical disorder until he or she has met predetermined criteria or reached a quantitative threshold of deviance from healthy counterparts. The service delivery and resource allocation in the medical model is designed such that services are provided for those individuals who meet this *sickness* threshold. Medical insurers may refuse treatment to individuals who fail to meet the diagnostic threshold, yet these individuals are at risk for disease that could be prevented with early intervention and prevention. Likewise, in education the resources have traditionally been allocated to provide more intensive instruction and intervention (e.g., special education services) to only those students meeting diagnostic criteria for an educational classification. This classification has been based on a deviance score approach. As a result, those students at risk for learning delays, but not yet significantly deviant in their performance, have been underserved and preventable learning gaps have widened.

The developmental perspective is increasingly being considered in how young children explore, learn, and acquire skills that will help them succeed academically, socially, and physically. The neurodevelopment of young children is plastic, resilient, and accommodating, indicating that interventions designed to correct mislearned behaviors and developmental errors or teach new skills are best taught early, and in a naturalistic, developmental context (Blair, 2002; National Research Council and Institute of Medicine, 2000; Semrud-Clikeman, 2005). The importance of assessing learning delays and developmental lags early was highlighted by a statement from the National Joint Committee on Learning Disabilities (2006), who recommended screening, identification of risk and protective factors, systematic observation, and the possibility of a comprehensive examination in early childhood to identify those children who may need more intensive intervention.

Furthermore, some scholars have argued that assessment practices in early childhood must be rooted in authentic, experientially-based practices (Bredekamp & Copple, 1997; NAEYC, 1997; Neisworth & Bagnato, 2004). They argue that most conventional, norm-referenced tests have not been developed specifically for toddlers and preschoolers, and lack a developmentally appropriate evidence base supporting their use in intervention. Assessments geared for this age must be based on authentic experiences including the typical routine of the child, and assess the competencies and practices that the child is expected to master (Bagnato, 2005; Neisworth & Bagnato, 2004). The RTI framework is a better fit for authentic assessment as it relies less on comprehensive, standardized assessments and instead measures children's progress on developmental markers and growth indicators.

RESPONSE TO INTERVENTION IN EARLY CHILDHOOD

What Is RTI?

Response to Intervention is a framework for monitoring all children's progress and identifying those who are not responding to the general curriculum so they can receive a more intensive, individualized intervention. Unlike the traditional assessment or medical model approach, which targets only those children suspected of delays or disabilities, RTI requires that all children participate in the ongoing screening and monitoring. Thus, RTI is a universal screening procedure, yet one that is continuous, quick, easy to administer, and easily integrated into the typical classroom environment.

RTI is also systematic and data based (Brown-Chidsey & Steege, 2005). It also includes steps for follow-up when children are identified as at risk in the benchmark skill that is assessed. Data is collected from the benchmark assessments that provide information regarding the children's response to instruction, and data is also used to determine if certain children require more intensive instruction.

RTI is typically conceptualized as a multitiered framework, and scholars have debated whether three or four tiers provide the best fit for the problem-solving model (Johnson, Mellard, & Byrd, 2005; Marston, 2005). Figure 23.1 presents a schematic representation of a three-tiered RTI framework. At Tier 1, all children are provided an empirically valid and high quality instruction that is linked with benchmark goals and local, state, or national standards of development. Children are assessed with benchmark assessments that are reliable and predictive of desired developmental outcomes. For example, young children may be tested with an expressive vocabulary benchmark, since vocabulary development is associated with later reading and language abilities. Children who score below a specified cutoff or criterion are identified as being at risk in that skill, and targeted for more intensive and supplemental instruction at Tier 2. Criteria for cutoff levels are determined by the RTI coordinator or psychologist. They are typically based on normative data or local norms (if available) and indicate that children scoring below a certain percentile (e.g., 20th percentile) are likely to require more intensive instruction, and children below an even lower criterion (e.g., 5th

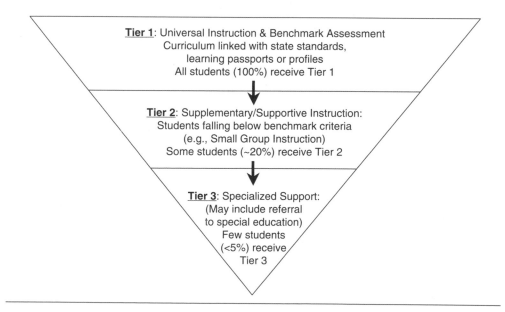

Figure 23.1   RTI 3-Tiered Model of Instruction (McCabe, 2006).

or 10th percentile) may be classified as having a severe delay (Shinn, 2007). However, it is important to point out that much of what we know about criterion or cut-off scores has been derived from research on achievement benchmarks in grade school, and are not specific to developmental milestones in early childhood. Additional research is needed to establish valid cutoff scores for developmental benchmarks that reflect the rapid growth and highly variable development in early childhood and yet are predictive of important outcomes (VanDerHeyden & Snyder, 2006).

Benchmark assessments continue and those children in Tier 2 may be given more frequent assessments to measure their response to supplemental intervention. Those children who continue to fail to respond to the instruction may be given an alternative empirically validated instruction, or moved to Tier 3 for more intensive intervention and more frequent monitoring. Children at Tier 3 who fail to respond may then be referred for a comprehensive evaluation to determine if other psychological, neurological, developmental, and/or sociocultural factors are impeding learning. Qualification for special education services may result from the comprehensive evaluation. Throughout the tiered model, problem-solving and data-based decision making are employed by the teacher, school personnel, and family to decide the best possible intervention strategy for the child (Brown-Chidsey & Steege, 2005).

One of the strengths of the RTI framework with the emphasis on data-based decision making is the ease of employing a problem-solving strategy within the framework. Deno's (2005) five-step problem-solving model fits well within the RTI framework and can guide multidisciplinary teams through the appropriate steps to identify empirically valid instruction for all students. The steps include (1) problem identification, (2) problem definition, (3) development of intervention plans, (4) implementation of the intervention plan, and (5) evaluation of the proposed solution. Teams that utilize the problem-solving approach can systematically review and refine intervention delivery through data-based decision making. Because there may be many potential solutions to remedy a given problem, the problem-solving approach provides a more systematic and data-driven process to obtain the desired outcome (Fuchs et al., 2003). This approach meets the some of the technical adequacy standards defined by the U.S. Office of Special Education Programs National Center on Student Progress (2005), which include specification of rates of improvement, benchmarks, sensitivity to increments in learning, reliability, validity, and usefulness in curriculum and goal planning (Hagans-Murillo, 2005).

Alternatively, another approach to intervention within the RTI framework is using a standard protocol. Instead of using individually tailored interventions *vis-a-vis* the problem-solving approach, standard protocol involves providing the same intervention to a small group of children who exhibit similar delays. At the end of the intervention, children are categorized as *responders* or *nonresponders* to the intervention (Fuchs et al., 2003; Hagans-Murillo, 2005). The idea is that nonresponders likely have underlying skill deficits that prevent them from responding to the empirically valid instruction that was effective with others with similar delays. The assumption is that nonresponding children have an underlying disability that is not due to a lack of quality instruction. This approach requires additional research to draw a link between nonresponding and disability, but an advantage is that schools with less resources could target more children with the same intervention (Hagans-Murillo).

While the RTI framework utilizing a problem-solving or standard protocol approach appears promising and components of the model are well established, research regarding best practices of implementation and standardization is lacking (Coleman, Buysse, & Neitzel, 2006; Griffiths, VanDerHeyden, Parson, & Burns, 2006). Some researchers have questioned whether RTI has sufficient empirical support to reliably identify children with complex learning delays or disabilities through the use of narrowly focused, brief assessments (Kavale, 2005). There is also the issue of variable teacher instruction, so it may be difficult to ascertain if children fail to respond due to poor or erratic teaching and not the intervention itself (Gerber, 2005). Further research is needed on the duration and intensity of interventions, types of intervention strategies, method of intervention delivery, technologically sound monitoring tools, and appropriate decision points and benchmark assessments used to determine whether an intervention has or has not been effective (Coleman et al., 2006; Griffiths et al., 2006). Further, most of the extant research on RTI has focused on grade school children, due to the greater focus on instruction at these ages, as well as compulsory education laws that make it feasible to employ a universal procedure like RTI. It is less clear how RTI can be extended to early childhood, which has a greater developmental focus and universal participation is unavailable in most states (McCabe, 2006). Additional research is also needed on what it means to deliver empirically valid instruction in early childhood, given that early childhood curriculum is exploratory, multisensory, and experiential, and can be vastly different from the rote training and practiced exercises used in targeted interventions with older children.

RTI in Early Childhood

Despite the limitations in the research on *best practices* with regard to RTI implementation, the logic of applying RTI to early childhood is evident. Precursor skills to reading, writing, math, and spelling abilities are learned during early childhood. Preschool children with delays or deficits in identified skills are more likely to evidence later reading and achievement difficulties, suggesting that early identification and targeted remediation of these skills can help to ameliorate the achievement gap (Al Otaiba & Fuchs, 2002). VanDerHeyden and Snyder (2006) argue that the application of RTI to early childhood will result in improving child outcomes through enhancing problem-solving efforts, and lead to increased research on early childhood development, precursors to later academic skills, and data that reflect whether additional interventions are effective in accelerating children's development.

Research is increasing that links delays and at-risk conditions in early childhood to later learning and behavioral problems. This research base, while not complete, has nevertheless provided the groundwork on which RTI decision points can be made. For example, evidence is mounting that preschool children with poor phonological awareness are at significant risk for reading difficulties (Deno, 2005), and a review of studies indicates that poor phonological awareness predicts reading disabilities in students who are unresponsive to intervention (Al Otaiba & Fuchs, 2002). Vocabulary development is also predictive of later reading and language abilities and can be easily targeted in preschool (Neuman & Roskos, 2005). Young children with difficulties engaging in rapid auditory processing are at greater risk for language-based learning disability (Choudhury, Leppanen, Leevers, & Benasich, 2007). In the area of mathematics, children with poor number knowledge and ability to count sequentially with one-to-one correspondence are at risk for math learning disabilities (Griffin, 2007). Furthermore, young children with a family history of developmental delays and/or genetic disorders, living in poverty and exposed to other social stressors, suffering chronic health problems, and those experiencing social and behavioral maladjustment are at risk for later learning difficulties. Interventions that target these skill delays as well as related environmental and biological factors are most likely to produce desired gains.

The preliminary evidence from recent studies examining RTI procedures in preschool appears to confirm its utility. VanDerHeyden, Snyder, Broussard, and Ramsdell (2008) examined the RTI framework in early literacy intervention with at-risk preschoolers (enrolled in Head Start or a rural preschool program). Measures of alliteration and rhyming were used to monitor progress, and DIBELS (Dynamic Indicators of Basic Early Literacy Skills) measures, Letter Naming Fluency (LNF), and Initial Sound Fluency (INF) were used as the outcome measures. Additional screening was conducted with the Brigance Preschool Screen (Brigance, 1985). Following a month interval with weekly benchmark assessments, rhyming, and alliteration levels, slopes, and level/slope values were predictive of later INF and LNF levels, slopes, and level/slope values. Interventions that targeted rhyming and alliteration skills, both individual and classwide, produced meaningful change to the growth slope. However, neither method emerged as the instructional method of choice in terms of overall gains. Interestingly, when the classes were analyzed according to high versus low performers (i.e., upper 25% and lowest 25%), it was found that the low performers increased scores in alliteration and rhyming in both individual and classwide instruction conditions, while the high performers showed little growth in either condition. This means that the majority of change in the growth slopes was attributed to the lowest performers, thus supporting RTI as a decision-making framework to target at-risk learners (VanDerHeyden et al.).

A similar intervention model, EMERGE, was implemented in Head Start classrooms to promote the development of early literacy and language skills (Gettinger & Stoiber, 2008). The program includes evidenced-based practices, a tiered RTI hierarchy, professional development, family involvement, and progress monitoring of the children. Tier 2 instruction was provided as small-group instruction by classroom teachers, and Tier 3 intervention was provided as individual tutoring by undergraduate and graduate students several times weekly. Preliminary evidence indicated higher performance in the EMERGE classrooms across multiple indicators of early literacy and language development than control classrooms who did not participate in EMERGE.

The evidence is growing in support of high-quality, comprehensive instruction and intervention for young children who are at risk for learning and developmental delays. Early Head Start programs targeting low-income families with infants and toddlers have led to higher scores on cognitive and language measures at age 3 than matched controls. In addition, Early Head Start children scored higher in emotional engagement with the parent, had greater sustained attention in play and lower levels of aggression. Parents of children in Early Head Start were more emotionally supportive, provided more language and literacy exposure, and were less likely to use corporal punishment (Love et al., 2005). Similar results of enhanced maturational progress of children at developmental risk were found in a community-based initiative utilizing authentic assessment and program evaluation (Bagnato, Suen, Brickley, Smith-Jones, & Dettore, 2002). Results from these and similar studies support the use of comprehensive monitoring and authentic assessment practices in early childhood that lead to significant gains in learning and development. However, despite their efficacy, comprehensive programs like Early Head Start are expensive and complex to manage, requiring significant support at the federal, state, and local level.

Legislative and Funding Support for RTI in Early Childhood

The most recent reauthorization of the Individuals with Disabilities Education Improvement Act (IDEIA; 2004) reinforced the need for problem-solving, team-based approaches to addressing the needs of children with disabilities. This included a focus on early intervention, preliteracy development, language development, and enhancement of preacademic skills, all of which are neatly addressed in an early childhood RTI framework (Barnett, VanDer-Heyden, & Witt, 2007). RTI can be used to help determine the educational needs and specialized services of young children given the cumulative data and intervention history generated through instructional trials (Barnett et al., 2007). Provisions were made in IDEIA to provide up to 15% of funding for students who have not been identified as needing special education services but need additional academic and behavioral support.

However, funding through IDEIA is likely insufficient to cover the costs of implementing RTI on a wide-scale basis, particularly in the early childhood years. In addition, the discontinuous service delivery between birth and age 5 makes it much more difficult to implement a universal and longitudinal RTI framework. Children ages birth to 3 years who are in need of specialized services are served through the state Early Intervention program, while children ages 3–5 years are served by the local education agency (LEA) of the state's department of education. A child receiving services from an early age may have to transition from Early Intervention to the preschool system, and again from the preschool system to the school-aged special education system. Every transition point has the potential to multiply the difficulties in providing seamless, comprehensive, data-based intervention and monitoring.

Furthermore, while there are several federally funded initiatives to provide comprehensive instruction to young children (e.g., Early Head Start, Head Start, Good Start Grow Smart, Child Care and Development Fund) these initiatives are not universal and tend to focus on at-risk populations, such as low-income families. In addition, state quality standards and benchmark indicators for early childhood vary considerably (Neuman & Roskos, 2005). Just over 20% of 3- and 4- year-olds in the United States are enrolled in a state pre-K program, or just over one million children (Barnett, Hustedt, Friedman, Boyd, & Ainsworth, 2007). While this represents substantial growth in pre-K programs nationally, with 30 of the 38 states with pre-K programs increasing enrollment, it nonetheless indicates that most 3- and 4- year-olds are not enrolled in a state-funded universal preschool program. This means that the implementation of RTI, which requires universal participation and ongoing monitoring, is only realistically occurring in a piecemeal fashion, and learning outcomes and benchmark assessments may or may not be specifically linked to the state standards. While RTI has great promise as an assessment and monitoring framework for young children, its efficacy will be best determined with widescale implementation.

The RTI framework can only be as good as how well it demonstrates predictive validity for desired outcomes. RTI borrows much from the field of curriculum-based measurement (CBM) and curriculum-based assessment (CBA), which have over 20 years of empirical support. Research demonstrates that assessing children using authentic curricular materials has predictive validity and can be meaningfully and readily applied to the curriculum. Briefly, CBA is associated with a mastery hierarchy, where children are taught successive skills, assessed for mastery of those skills, and new skills are introduced that build on the hierarchy when the previous skill reaches mastery criterion (VanDerHeyden, 2005). Conversely, CBM is associated with general outcome measurement model, in which assessment occurs over a longer period of time and is conducted to measure if the intended outcome behavior is reached. In other words, CBA measures the behavior or skill that is being targeted, while CBM measures the behavior or skill that is ultimately desired (VanDerHeyden). For example, in targeting math counting skills as a desired outcome, the CBA approach might first target oral counting with one-to-one correspondence, and when this skill has reached the desired criterion, then begin teaching number identification and recognition. Conversely, the CBM approach would assess the child repeatedly on an outcome measure of counting skills regardless of the subskill being taught. This is an important distinction because with CBM, the assessment focuses on whether or not an intervention is helping move the child toward mastery of desired final behavior, whereas CBA is focused on developing subskills of the final behavior and those subskills may or may not be predictive of whether the child masters the final behavior (VanDerHeyden). This has relevance in terms of applying RTI to early childhood, where evaluators might be interested in developing certain subskills in children and assessing those skills through CBA (e.g., sorting blocks by shape), or instead be focusing on a outcome behavior which would be monitored through CBM (e.g., visual–spatial ability, such as measured by the capacity to match and sort objects by shape, size, color, or other dimension).

Outcome measures reflecting desired developmental behaviors in early childhood and CBM assessments to measure progress toward those behaviors have been developed. General Outcome Measurement (GOM) reflects a relatively new approach to assessment where the same outcome measurement is given repeatedly to assess the child's progress toward that outcome (Deno, 1997). This contrasts with criterion-referenced tests used in traditional assessment where the child is assessed on a set of skills within certain domains of behaviors that are matched for the child's developmental age (Carta et al., 2002). The GOM method of assessment is more closely aligned with the CBM model of assessing children's progress toward a desired outcome.

In 1996, the Office of Special Education Programs funded the Early Childhood Research Institute on Measuring Growth and Development, a collaborative of researchers from Kansas, Oregon, and Minnesota to develop an assessment system to monitor young children's progress toward desired developmental outcomes (McConnell et al., 1998; Synder, Wixson, Talapatra, & Roach, 2008). The collaborative created Individualized Growth and Developmental Indicators (IGDIs), reflecting children's behavior and skills across a variety of developmental domains. IGDIs are linked to GOMs that have been determined as developmentally important in early childhood, including communication, problem solving, and social competence. IDGIs are available for infants and toddlers ages birth to 3 (in the areas of communication, movement, cognition and problem solving, social competence, and parent-child interactions) at www.igdi.ku.edu/index.htm, and for preschool ages 3–5 (in early literacy and language) at http://ggg.umn.edu/. Additional IGDIs are currently being developed.

Research on the predictive validity and technical adequacy of IGDIs is preliminary but initial results appear promising. Outcome studies examining IGDI assessments and general outcomes have been published in the areas of early literacy (Missall & McConnell, 2004; Missall et al., 2007; VanDerHeyden et al., 2008), math (Floyd, Hojnoski, & Key, 2006; Key, 2007; VanDerHeyden, Broussard, & Cooley, 2006), expressive language (Luze et al., 2001), cognitive development and problem solving (Greenwood, Walker, Carta, & Higgins, 2006), social skills (Carta, Greenwood, Luze, Cline, & Kuntz, 2004), and movement (Greenwood, Luze, Cline, Kuntz, & Leitschuh, 2002). These studies have supported IGDIs use for tracking skills over time as well as predicting general outcome measures.

Several studies using IGDI assessments with children vulnerable for language difficulties have yielded results supporting their use. The Picture Naming IGDI was demonstrated to be sensitive to language growth with young children with autism spectrum disorders, and predicted language ability between 39 and 69 months of age (Cadigan & Missall, 2007). Picture Naming IGDI was also used with preschoolers categorized as English language learners (ELL) and successfully distinguished ELL children from native English speakers, as well as differences between ELLs' first and second language, and predicted growth of first and second language skills over time (Nitsiou, 2006). Additional IGDI assessments that are culturally fair and valid for linguistically diverse children are needed, particularly those intended to measure language acquisition over time, or language delay and/or impairment. For example, Picture Naming IGDI has been adapted for use with

Spanish-speaking children using the same picture stimuli as the English version and has demonstrated adequate reliability and validity. However, Rhyming and Alliteration IGDIs require the creation of new assessment stimuli as each new language has unique rhyming and alliteration rules.

IGDI assessment is showing promise as GOMs that use common materials found in natural environments of children, adequately track progress over time, are inexpensive and easy to administer, and predict desired skills and outcomes (Wackerle, 2007). The assessments are designed to be easily incorporated into the curriculum. Training will help teachers learn more about the RTI framework and how benchmark screening can inform their teaching. However, IGDI assessments do not require an extensive background in assessment to become familiarized with the administration and scoring procedures, making them ideal for early childhood educators whose training in assessment may vary considerably. Studies on IGDIs measuring their efficacy with typical, disabled, and culturally diverse populations are needed, as well as additional reliability and validity data. This is particularly important if IGDI data will be used in the future as a component of evaluations, interventions, and planning decisions.

FUTURE DIRECTIONS AND CHALLENGES

McCabe (2006, p. 173) argued that several important prerequisites need to occur before RTI can be implemented and evaluated on a widescale basis in early childhood. These includes:

- Universalizing preschool for ages 3–5.
- Linking empirically valid interventions with quality standards.
- Coordinating and funding partnerships between school and community-based early childhood programs.
- Improving opportunities for teacher training and professional development.
- Improving funding for high-quality research on empirically validated practices and identifying developmental indicators and benchmarks that predict desired outcomes.

As an example of the above, the disparity in educational opportunity in preschool or child care settings for children birth to age 5 is staggering, as well as the quality of care in those settings. Many child care settings offer what are essentially baby-sitting services, while others may offer an enriched, developmentally appropriate curriculum. Most preschools, by definition, offer an early childhood curriculum; however, the quality of the curriculum varies widely and may or may not be linked to state standards. The terms *child care* and *child education* should not be conceptualized as separate entities, as both are necessary conditions for optimal development (Bowman, Donovan, & Burns, 2000). Children cannot learn unless they are cared for within a physically supportive and warm environment, and quality care involves stimulation that enriches all facets of development such as cognition, language, motor, socialization, and emotional development (Bowman et al., 2000). Federal and state licensing entities should mandate standards of early childhood education and care similar to those of school-age children. Accrediting organizations such as the National Association for the Education of Young Children (NAEYC; 1998, 2008) already have recommended practices and learning standards that could be easily adopted by states. In fact, in 2007 there were 44 states with early learning standards, and the remaining states were in the process of developing them (NAEYC, 2008). Early childhood environments that offer a high-quality curriculum, that is developmentally appropriate and responsive to children and families' unique needs will be ideally suited for an RTI framework.

STAFF TRAINING AND POLICY

In addition, teachers and staff who work with the early childhood population need adequate training in assessment and intervention with all learners, but particularly those who exhibit delays. Training requirements for child care and preschool staff vary widely from state to state and between settings (e.g., family day care, center-based day care, preschool center, Montessori, Head Start). Entry-level requirements range from high school diploma to postgraduate degree, and states may or may not have minimal training requirements to work as a child care worker. Many early childhood teachers are inadequately prepared to conduct assessments and monitor progress of their students beyond informal observation (Bowman et al., 2000).

RTI requires a basic knowledge of developmental trajectory, growth slopes, benchmark assessments, and outcome measurement. Psychologists and educators who implement RTI need to be thoroughly trained in the procedures and assessment methodology, and for many this will be their first experience with large-scale assessment. Threats to the fidelity of RTI implementation can occur due to inadequate staff training in assessment and intervention (Burns, Jacobs, & Wagner, 2008). In addition, teachers need to be observed to evaluate treatment integrity, but teachers may raise concerns regarding how the observations and data will be used to judge their teaching efficacy. A psychologist or a specially trained teacher may be best suited for the role of training and evaluation of treatment integrity, rather than a principal or administrator. Specific policies should be created regarding how RTI fidelity data are used, and any personnel actions that may arise from the data (Burns et al., 2008).

Relatedly, RTI requires the implementation of high-quality, empirically valid instruction and intervention. This can be accomplished only to the degree that teachers and administrators are prepared to evaluate and adopt curricula meeting those high standards. For example, the aforementioned EMERGE model included a component that focused on professional development. This was achieved through 3-hour professional development training sessions held monthly that focused on Tier 1 instruction, using assessment data to alter instruction or plan Tier 2 intervention, and design literacy-rich environments (Gettinger & Stoiber, 2008). A second component of training was on-site literacy coaching and planning with the objective to model strategies, work with teachers and children, provide scaffolded support for teachers, and monitor implementation integrity (Gettinger & Stoiber). It is unclear what level of training is required by teachers to effectively conduct screening, monitor progress, alter and implement appropriate interventions, and use technology to analyze data and make decisions on the data (Fuchs & Fuchs, 2006). Additional research is needed to determine the minimal level of training required by staff to implement RTI procedures and maintain implementation integrity.

In addition to training and professional development, RTI requires a commitment by an agency, district, or state to be widely implemented (Barnett, VanDerHeyden, et al., 2007). Coordination is needed among public, private, religious, and other civic organizations that host early childhood education centers. Coordination is also needed between LEAs and departments of health to organize a more seamless intervention and transition from Early Intervention to preschool to grade school. Local education agencies are likely to be the most appropriate coordinator of RTI services given current funding streams, availability of personnel who could assist in training, implementation, and monitoring, and the LEA's obligation to provide special education services to all children in the catchment area.

ETHICAL ISSUES

Burns et al. (2008) discuss ethical and legal issues associated with implementing RTI in schools. Although their discussion is not specifically directed to early childhood, the issues addressed are applicable. First, there is the issue of parent involvement, including when it is necessary to obtain parental consent. Tiers 1 and 2 involve general instruction and small group instruction that occur under the purview of the general education teacher, and as such do not require parental consent according to IDEIA 2004 (Burns et al., 2008; IDEIA, 2004). However, the multidisciplinary team may require additional information obtained through a review of student records or teacher consultation, at which point it is ethically responsible to notify the family. Furthermore, when the activity of the psychologist and/or team involve more intensive questioning, screening, and assessment for the child and his/her family beyond what is expected with ordinary classroom practices, parental consent should be obtained (Burns et al.).

However, the situation may arise where parents request an individual evaluation for their child during the RTI process. In accordance with IDEIA 2004, an evaluation would need to be conducted within 60 days of the request. If the request occurs during the RTI implementation when the school has already begun more intensive instruction, and it is decided that an individual evaluation is not immediately required, the school must notify the parents in writing (Burns et al.).

It is important that further research is conducted on the validity of RTI procedures and data used to assist in special education eligibility determinations, and whether RTI meets the ethical and legal standards for assessment practices (Burns et al., 2008). Ethical assessments must be multifaceted, comprehensive, fair, useful, and valid (Jacob & Hartshorne, 2007). While RTI is showing promise as a fair, useful, and valid assessment, it is unclear how it can be considered multifaceted and comprehensive when it is applied to measure discrete academic skills (Burns et al., 2008). Among the biggest challenges in using RTI as an assessment procedure is the reliance on quality classroom instruction. Additional research is needed to determine what types of data, methods of quality instruction, and problem-solving steps are needed to make valid decisions for academic interventions.

SUMMARY

All children ages 3 years and older should be invited to attend a high-quality early childhood educational experience *without* cost to the family. More states are moving toward universal pre-K coverage, but this should be extended down to age 3 as well. In doing so, all children could have an opportunity to receive a developmentally appropriate educational experience that helps to augment cognitive, communicative, social, emotional, and physical development. If all children are regularly assessed and monitored for developmental indicators, it would be easier to identify those children who are non-responders to instruction and may benefit from more intensive services. Many children could even catch up with their peers before beginning kindergarten. Such a systematic, widescale, data-based problem-solving approach would be a significant improvement over the piecemeal approach to early childhood education and intervention presently occurring in most states.

The RTI problem-solving framework has the potential to significantly improve educational delivery to the early childhood population through a coordinated, data-based intervention model. Current educational practices and interventions in early childhood vary widely and often favor those children in wealthier communities that can afford a team-based problem-solving and intervention approach. However, research has demonstrated that a comprehensive, data-based assessment and monitoring approach can improve outcomes for all children. And children who are the neediest due to developmental, genetic, or economic disadvantage have the most to gain from a comprehensive service model.

Research is needed on the optimal strategies for implementing RTI in early childhood; the validity of GOMs in predicting desired outcomes later in grade school; and identification of high-quality instruction and intervention that is developmentally focused for early childhood. Research is also needed examining the RTI framework with different populations of disabled youngsters, as well as culturally and linguistically diverse populations. If early intervention through RTI procedures can be demonstrated to ameliorate delays and reduce the number of special education referrals later in childhood (as the preliminary evidence is suggesting), it is a compelling message to policy makers, educators, and parents that investment in early childhood education and intervention is worthwhile and should be prioritized.

REFERENCES

Al Otaiba, S., & Fuchs, D. (2002). Characteristics of children who are unresponsive to early literacy intervention: A review of the literature. *Remedial and Special Education*, 23(5), 300–316.

Bagnato, S. J. (2005). The authentic alternative for assessment in early intervention: An emerging evidence-based practice. *Journal of Early Intervention*, 28, 17–22.

Bagnato, S. J., & Ho, H. Y. (2006). High-stakes testing with preschool children: Violation of professional standards for evidence-based practice in early childhood intervention. *KEDI Journal of Educational Policy*, 3, 23–43.

Bagnato, S. J., Suen, H. K., Brickley, D., Smith-Jones, J., & Dettore, E. (2002). Child developmental impact of Pittsburgh's Early Childhood Initiative (ECI) in high-risk communities: First-phase authentic evaluation research. *Early Childhood Research Quarterly*, 17, 559–580.

Barnett, D. W., VanDerHeyden, A. M., & Witt, J. C. (2007). Achieving science-based practice through response to intervention: What it might look like in preschools. *Journal of Educational and Psychological Consultation*, 17, 31–54.

Barnett, W. S., Hustedt, J. T., Friedman, A. H., Boyd, J. S., & Ainsworth, P. (2007). *The State of Preschool 2007: State Preschool Yearbook*. New Brunswick, NJ: The National Institute for Early Education Research. Retrieved from http://nieer.org/year book/pdf/yearbook.pdf.

Blair, C. (2002). School readiness: Integrating cognition and emotion in a neuro-biological conceptualization of children's functioning at school entry. *American Psychologist, 57*(2), 111–127.

Bowman, B., Donovan, S., & Burns, M. S. (2000). *Eager to learn: Educating our preschoolers*. Washington, D.C.: National Academies Press.

Bredekamp, S., & Copple, C. (1997). *Developmentally appropriate practice—Revised*. Washington, DC: National Association for the Education of Young Children.

Brigance, A. N. (1985). *Brigance Screens-II*. Billerica, MA: Curriculum Associates.

Brown-Chidsey, R., & Steege, M. W. (2005) *Response to Intervention: Principles and strategies for effective practice*. New York: Guilford Press.

Burns, M. K., Jacobs, S., & Wagner, A. R. (2008). Ethical and legal issues associated with using response-to-intervention to assess learning disabilities. *Journal of School Psychology, 46*, 263–279.

Cadigan, K., & Missall, K. N. (2007). Measuring expressive language growth in young children with autism spectrum disorders. *Topics in Early Childhood Special Education, 27*, 110–118.

Carta, J. J., Greenwood, C. R., Luze, G. J., Cline, G., & Kuntz, S. (2004). Developing a general outcome measure of growth in social skills for infants and toddlers. *Journal of Early Intervention, 26*, 91–114.

Carta, J. J., Greenwood, C. R., Walker, D., Kaminski, R., Good, R., McConnell, S. R., et al. (2002). Individual Growth and Development Indicators (IGDIs): Assessment that guides intervention for young children. In M. Ostrosky & E. Horn (Eds.), *Assessment: Gathering meaningful information. Young Exceptional Children Monograph Series #4*, 15–28.

Choudhury, N., Leppanen, P. H., Leevers, H. J., & Benasich, A. A. (2007). Infant information processing and family history of specific language impairment: Converging evidence for RAP deficits from two paradigms. *Developmental Science, 10*, 213–236.

Coleman, M. R., Buysse, V., & Neitzel, J. (2006). *Recognition and response: An early intervening system for young children at-risk for learning disabilities*. Chapel Hill: The University of North Carolina at Chapel Hill, FPG Child Development Institute.

Deno, S. (1997). Whither thou goest . . . perspectives on progress monitoring. In J. W. Lloyd, E. J. Kameenui, & D. Chard (Eds.), *Issues in educating students with disabilities* (pp. 77–99). Mahwah, NJ: Erlbaum.

Deno, S. L. (2005). Problem-solving assessment. In R. Brown-Chidsey (Ed.), *Assessment for intervention: A problem-solving approach*. (pp. 10–40). New York: Guilford Press.

Floyd, R. G., Hojnoski, R., & Key, J. (2006). Preliminary evidence of the technical adequacy of the Preschool Numeracy Indicators. *School Psychology Review, 35*, 627–644.

Fuchs, L. S., & Fuchs, D. (2006). A framework for building capacity for responsiveness to intervention. *School Psychology Review, 35*, 621–626.

Fuchs, D., Mock, D., Morgan, P. L., & Young, C. L. (2003). Responsiveness-to-Intervention: Definitions, evidence, and implications for the learning disabilities construct. *Learning Disabilities Research & Practice, 18*(3), 157–171.

Gerber, M. M. (2005). Teachers are still the test: Limitations of response to instruction strategies for identifying children with learning disabilities. *Journal of Learning Disabilities, 38*(6), 516–524.

Gettinger, M., & Stoiber, K. (2008). Applying a response-to-intervention model for early literacy development in low-income children. *Topics in Early Childhood Special Education, 27*, 198–213.

Greenwood, C. R., Luze, G. J., Cline, G., Kuntz, S., & Leitschuh, C. (2002). Developing a general outcome measure of growth in movement for infants and toddlers. *Topics in Early Childhood Special Education, 22*, 143–157.

Greenwood, C. R., Walker, D., Carta, J. J., & Higgins, S. K. (2006). Developing a general outcome measure of growth in the cognitive abilities of children 1 to 4 years old: The Early Problem-Solving Indicator. *School Psychology Review, 35*, 535–551.

Griffin, S. (2007). Early intervention for children at risk of developing mathematical learning difficulties. In D. B. Berch & M. M. Mazzocco (2007). *Why is math so hard for some children? The nature and origins of mathematical learning difficulties and disabilities.* (pp. 373–395). Baltimore, MD: Brookes.

Griffiths, A-J., VanDerHeyden, A. M., Parson, L. B., & Burns, M. K. (2006). Practical applications of response-to-intervention research. *Assessment for Effective Intervention, 32*, 50–57.

Hagans-Murillo, K. (2005). Using a response-to-intervention approach in preschool to promote literacy. *The California School Psychologist, 10*, 45–54.

Individuals with Disabilities Education Improvement Act. (2004). *Individuals with Disabilities Education Improvement Act of 2004*, Public Law No. 108–1446.

Jacob, S., & Hartshorne, T. S. (2007). *Ethics and law for school psychologists.* Hoboken, NJ: Wiley.

Johnson, E., Mellard, D. F., & Byrd, S. E. (2005). Alternative models of learning disabilities identification: Considerations and initial conclusions. *Journal of Learning Disabilities, 38*(6), 569–572.

Kavale, K. A. (2005). Identifying specific learning disability: Is responsiveness to intervention the answer? *Journal of Learning Disabilities, 38*(6), 553–562.

Key, J. M. (2007). Effects of a teacher-delivered mathematics intervention on the mathematical skills of preschoolers of low socioeconomic status in head start settings. *Dissertation Abstracts International, 68*(8-A), 3272.

Love, J. M., Kisker, E. E., Ross, C., Raikes, H., Constantine, J., Boller, K., et al. (2005). The effectiveness of Early Head Start for 3-year-old children and their parents: Lessons for policy and programs. *Developmental Psychology, 41*, 885–901.

Luze, G. J., Linebarger, D. L., Greenwood, C. R., Carta, J. J., Walker, D., Leitschuh, C., et al. (2001). Developing a general outcome measure of growth in the expressive communication of infants and toddlers. *School Psychology Review, 30*, 383–406.

Marston, D. (2005). Tiers of intervention in responsiveness to intervention: Prevention outcomes and learning disabilities identification patterns. *Journal of Learning Disabilities, 38*, 539–544.

McCabe, P. C. (2006). Responsiveness to intervention (RTI) in early childhood: Challenges and practical guidelines. *Journal of Early Childhood and Infant Psychology, 2*, 157–180.

McConnell, S. R., McEvoy, M., Carta, J., Greenwood, C., Kaminski, R., Good, R., et al. (1998). *Research and development on individual growth indicators for children birth to age eight.* (Technical Report 4).

Missall, K. N., & McConnell, S. R. (2004). Early literacy development: Skill growth and relations between classroom variables for preschool children. *Journal of Early Intervention, 29*, 1–21.

Missall, K. N., Reschly, A., Betts, J., McConnell, S. R., Heistad, D., Pickart, M., et al. (2007). Examination of the predictive validity of preschool early literacy skills. *School Psychology Review, 36*, 433–452.

NAEYC. (1997). *Developmentally appropriate practice in early childhood programs serving children from birth through age 8: A position statement of the National Association for the Education of Young Children.* Washington, DC: NAEYC.

NAEYC. (2008). *Developmentally appropriate practice in early childhood programs serving children from birth through age 8: A DRAFT position statement of the National Association for the Education of Young Children.* Washington, DC: NAEYC. Retrieved from www.naeyc.org/about/positions/pdf/draftdap0208.pdf.

National Center on Student Progress Monitoring. (2005). *Review of progress monitoring tools.* Washington, DC: Author.

National Joint Committee on Learning Disabilities. (2006). *Learning disabilities and young children: Identification and intervention.* Available from www.ldonline.org.

National Research Council and Institute of Medicine. (2000). *From neurons to neighborhoods: The science of early childhood development.* Committee on Integrating the Science of Early Childhood Development. Jack P. Shonkoff and Deborah A. Phillips (Eds.), Board on Children, Youth, and Families, Commission on Behavioral and Social Sciences and Education. Washington, DC: National Academy Press.

Neisworth, J. T., & Bagnato, S. J. (2004). The mismeasure of young children: The authentic assessment alternative. *Infants and Young Children, 17*, 198–212.

Neuman, S. B., & Roskos, K. (2005). The state of state pre-kindergarten standards. *Early Childhood Research Quarterly, 20*, 125–145.

Nitsiou, C. (2006). Tracking the status of language development in language-minority kindergarteners. *Early Child Development and Care, 176*, 817–833.

Semrud-Clikeman, M. (2005). Neuropsychological aspects for evaluating learning disabilities. *Journal of Learning Disabilities, 38*(6), 563–568.

Shinn, M. R. (2007). Identifying students at risk, monitoring performance, and determining eligibility within response to intervention: Research on educational need and benefit from academic intervention. *School Psychology Review, 36*, 601–617.

Snyder, P. A., Wixson, C. S., Talapatra, D., & Roach, A. T. (2008). Instruction-focused strategies to support response-to-intervention frameworks. *Assessment in Early Childhood, 34*, 25–35.

VanDerHeyden, A. M. (2005). Intervention-driven assessment practices in early childhood/early intervention: Measuring what is possible rather than what is present. *Journal of Early Intervention, 28,* 28–33.

VanDerHeyden, A. M., Broussard, C., & Cooley, A. (2006). Further development of measures of early math performance for preschoolers. *Journal of School Psychology, 44,* 533–553.

VanDerHeyden, A. M., & Snyder, P. (2006). Integrating frameworks from early childhood intervention and school psychology to accelerate growth for all young children. *School Psychology Review, 35,* 519–534.

VanDerHeyden, A. M., Snyder, P., Broussard, C., & Ramsdell, K. (2008). Measuring response to early literacy intervention with preschoolers at risk. *Topics in Early Childhood Special Education, 27,* 232–249.

Wackerle, A. K. (2007). Test review: Selection of general growth outcomes for children between birth and eight. *Assessment for Effective Intervention, 33,* 51–54.

Ysseldyke, J. E. (2005). Assessment and decision making for students with learning disabilities: What if this is as good as it gets? *Learning Disability Quarterly, 28,* 125–128.

CHAPTER 24

R.I.C.H. Applications

THOMAS J. KEHLE,
MELISSA A. BRAY, and
SARAH E. GRIGERICK

Bowlby's (1982) ethological theory of attachment provides an explanation and interpretation of how children later perceive themselves within social contexts. It is the relationship with the caregiver that teaches the young child that support can be achieved from outside sources. This then leads to a secure attachment that forms and lends itself to independent exploring and seeking of social contacts. Simply stated, attachment is defined as a universal emotional bond established between a child and parent/caregiver during the first two years of life (Ainsworth, 1989). Specifically, the mother must physically respond (i.e., pick up infant, protect from danger, feed, change diaper, rock to sleep) to her infant's needs (i.e., infant cries, infant laughs, infant looking, infant cling or touch). This emotional trusting relationship forms the bond for a secure attachment.

The parent's sensitivity and receptiveness to the infant or the quality of their attachments is assumed to be crucial in fostering the child's physical and psychological development and influential in life outcomes. Further, according to Bowlby (1982), quality attachments predispose the child to develop trust in others that facilitates formation and maintenance of friendships.

Ainsworth and Bell (1970) originally provided the empirical support for Bowlby's theory of attachment. They employed the strange situation procedure to do so. They classified infants into four different attachment styles: (1) securely attached (infant used mother as a base to explore from), (2) anxious–avoidant (infant could not use mom as a base and generally avoided her at reunion), (3) anxious-ambivalent/resistant (could not use mom as base and rejected her at reunion), and (4) disorganized/disoriented

---

This chapter is an extension of a previous article by Kehle, Bray, and Grigerick (2007).

(no pattern evident). When a secure attachment is not developed, lifelong problems may ensue. Such mental health problems include poor self-esteem, depression, trust issues, anxiety, oppositional and antisocial behaviors (Kennedy & Kennedy, 2007).

Most likely, children's first friendship, in the form of a secure attachment, is with the primary caretaker and subsequently influences the quality of later friendship formations as defined as enjoyment of each other's company (Kehle, Bray, & Grigerick, 2007). Throughout the life span, friendships are fundamental to psychological and physical health (Kehle et al.; Uchino, Cacioppo, & Kiecolt-Glaser, 1996). Conversely, the lack of friendships is indicative of not only poor mental health and arrested development of social skills (Elicker, Englund, & Sroufe, 1992), but also abridged physical functioning (e.g., asthmatic symptoms, rheumatoid arthritis, hypertension) (Luszcz & Giles, 2002; Seeman, 2000). This is particularly true if individuals have no friendships outside of their immediate family (Kehle & Bray, 2004). Consistent with Bowlby (1982), secure attachment relationships are also associated with an increased sense of security that promotes independence, exploration, and social contact seeking (Ainsworth & Bell, 1970; Kehle et al., 2007).

MacDonald and Leary's (2005) social pain theory complements attachment theory by suggesting social acceptance for physical survival evolved into sensitivity to social exclusion, experienced as *pain affect*. Social pain is a brief, quickly abated signal that redirects the child with secure attachments away from social isolation to social inclusion. Theoretically, individuals respond to social and physical threats similarly with a *flight-or-fight* panic response. The instantaneous aggressive reaction is functional with respect to responding to physical threats, but dysfunctional with respect to responding to social exclusion threats. Children who expect and experience social exclusion are susceptible to increased feelings of physical pain (e.g., headaches; stomachaches; nausea) (MacDonald, Kingsbury, & Shaw, 2005).

The relationship between secure attachments and peer acceptance is robust. Szewczyk-Sokolwski, Bost, and Wainwright (2005) found that secure attachments, based on preschool peer perceptions, predicted approximately 50% of the variance in peer acceptance. Kindergarten-age children with secure attachments engage peers in play more frequently, are more likely to form friendships (Kerns & Barth, 1995; Youngblade & Belsky, 1992), and are more apt to be perceived by their teachers as more socially and academically competent (Pianta, Longmaid, & Ferguson, 1999; Wentzel, 1991) than those without secure attachments.

Conversely, insecure attachment styles before age 2 predict dysfunctional behavior in preschool. Insecure attachments are inversely related to attention to task, classroom participation, and academic performance (Granot & Mayseless, 2001; Jacobsen & Hoffman, 1997). Barclay (1966), in an early study, found approximately 60% of children lacking peer acceptance also had poor teacher ratings, and at age 16 dropped out of school. Further, children with poor peer acceptance were not only at risk for dropping out of school, but also for later maladjustment including aggression, depression, anxiety, school-related violence, and criminality (Blankemeyer, Flannery, & Vazsonyi, 2002; Hamre & Pianta, 2001; Parker, 1987; Shafii & Shafii, 2003).

According to Kehle et al. (2007), and consistent with both attachment and social pain theories, the quality of parent-child attachment is probably influenced by both heritable and environmental factors. Therefore, infants may have a predisposition toward a level of attachment quality that in turn is maintained by the consequences of environmental selection. That is to say, the behaviors associated with attachment disorders are maintained by the principles of operant conditioning, or selection by consequences (Kehle & Bray, 2004b; Skinner, 1974). Consequently, and similar to natural selection, the environmental explanation or functional relationship between the child's environment and attachment disorders are difficult to discern (Kehle & Bray, 2004b; Skinner, 1971).

Thus, early attachment security appears fundamental and is related to (1) independence and exploration (Ainsworth & Bell, 1970), (2) friendship formation (Kerns & Barth, 1995; Youngblade & Belsky, 1992), (3) academic and occupational competence (Pianta et al., 1999; Kehle & Bray, 2004a), and (4) physical health (MacDonald et al., 2005). Outlining a theory of psychological wellness, Kehle and his colleagues (Kehle, 1989; 1999; Kehle & Barclay, 1979; Kehle & Bray, 2004a; Kehle, Bray, Chafouleas, & McLoughlin, 2002; Kehle, Clark, & Jenson, 1993; Kehle, Bray, & Grigerick, 2007) suggested that perhaps the best definition of psychological health or happiness is what primary caregivers want for their children (see Kehle & Bray, 2004a, for a complete description). For example, mothers, regardless of ethnicity and socioeconomic status, want their children to grow up and have essentially the same four things: resources, intimacy, competence, and health (RICH); in fact, their aspirations are correlates of secure attachments (Kehle & Bray, 2004a).

The RICH characteristics strongly suggest life without fear. In other words, mothers essentially want their children to go through life happy, or without anxiety. These characteristics are apparent across the life span from infancy through adulthood (Kehle & Bray, 2004a). The terms associated with the acronym RICH are described as follows:

> *Resources*. From childhood through adulthood, the appropriate allocation of resources is perhaps best defined as having control over how individuals spend their time. This results in a feeling of independence, which is synonymous with a sense of individual freedom. In other words, there is little or no bifurcation between one's public and private life (in adulthood), or a sense of not working. An analogous concept relative to childhood would be employing play as a learning tool. The child is not aware that he or she is actually engaged in schoolwork but the child is indeed learning.
>
> *Intimacy*. Intimacy is defined as the initiation and maintenance of friendship. Further it is characterized by learning from, and enjoyment of a friend's company. Across the life span, one primary characteristic is

apparent: Individuals without friends are at risk for less than their optimal academic performance, health-related issues, and overall poor social functioning (Kennedy & Kennedy, 2007).

Competence. The sense of competence is the consequence of being competent relative to some social or personal standard. Competence is attributed to one's own abilities and is situation or task specific. A child who demonstrates a competent accomplishment, which is confirmed by either themselves or others, experiences an increase in his self-confidence in that specific area (Kehle & Bray, 2004a). This specific occurrence also promotes an overall enhancement of subjective well-being (Kehle & Bray, 2004a).

Health. The individual is aware of practices that are conducive to physical health and also has an allegiance to these practices (Kehle et al., 2007). For example, a child with asthma that controls his or her lung functioning to the extent asthmatic symptoms are attenuated concomitantly experiences reductions in anxiety, depression, and an overall increase in happiness or subjective well-being (Bray, Kehle, Grigerick, Loftus, & Nicholson, 2008; Bray et al., 2006).

As previously stated, cross-culturally, and regardless of ethnicity and socioeconomic status, mothers theoretically want their children to have these RICH characteristics (Kehle et al., 1993). These characteristics permeate effective child rearing and undoubtedly are correlates of secure attachments (Kehle et al., 1993).

Although not substantiated by evidence-based research, according to Kehle et al. (2007), attachment quality and the subsequent ability to initiate and maintain friendships (i.e., intimacy) is highly interrelated with the other three RICH attributes (i.e., resources, competence, health). As a result, collectively they may be considered reflective of psychological health and assumed synonymous with happiness and the absence of anxiety and fear. Kehle et al. essentially relied on Bertrand Russell's (1930) definition of happiness in developing the RICH characteristics, maintaining that each characteristic is integral to the three others. Each RICH aspect is relatively obtainable by all individuals, although there are developmental variations. Young children who develop secure attachments appear to have an *élan vital* or vital manner about them that is inconsistent with anxiety (Kehle et al., 1993). They are happier and well-adjusted individuals (Kehle et al.). Improvement or detriment of any one of the characteristics would seemingly lead to an improvement or detriment in the remaining three. For example, if a child is under excessive adult control or a diminishment in fostering the child's independence, there will also be a diminishment in all of the remaining RICH characteristics.

The four RICH characteristics also encompass all valid reinforcers (e.g., verbal praise) and promote movement toward any of the four characteristics. Any valid reinforcer is one that promotes an increase in the child's sense of independence, ability to initiate and maintain friendships, and physical health. As parents are well aware, life is a series of decisions. Teaching their children to make decisions that promote movement toward the RICH characteristics is tantamount to teaching them to be happy. The four characteristics seem adequate since they seem able to define a psychologically healthy or happy person (Kehle et al., 2007).

To claim that the four characteristics are the same construct, that is, happiness is evident in that each one is defined by the remaining three. As applied to young children, for example, a child who is capable of initiating and maintaining friendships is also defined as someone who has a feeling of competence.

A literature review conducted by the current authors revealed that correlational data underpins most assumptions about the relationship between insecure attachments and negative life outcomes. As Kehle et al. (2007) indicated, "There is a dearth of empirically-based literature that clearly establishes the efficacy of interventions designed to promote healthy, or attenuate insecure, attachments" (p. 53). However, assessment strategies and interventions based on RICH theory can address at any point during the life span the detrimental effects of insecure attachments.

ASSESSMENT STRATEGIES

According to Boris et al. (2004), "there are neither established diagnostic measures nor a clinical gold standard for assessment of attachment disorders" (p. 570). However, typical assessment strategies involve both a semistructured interview of the caregiver, as well as an observational assessment of caregiver-child interactions (e.g., the Strange Situation Procedure, [SSP]) (Ainsworth, Blehar, Waters, & Wall, 1978). However, the SSP may not be a valid diagnostic index since there are several artificial components, particularly including an analog setting (Clarke-Stewart, Goossens, & Allhusen, 2001). Due to SSP drawbacks, the California Attachment Procedure (CAP) was developed (Clarke-Stewart et al.). The CAP assesses mother–child attachment but excludes the component of mother–child separation. Furthermore, toddlers are not likely to be in the secure classification category (Clarke-Stewart et al.).

While the SSP and its variants are dependent on the artificial environment of the laboratory, the Attachment Q-Sort (AQS) allows for assessment in the natural home setting. The 100-item AQS was developed by Waters and Deane (1985) and subsequently in 1995, Waters modified the AQS methodology so that the Q-set encompassed 90 items. The Q-set is appropriate for ages 1–5. In the original AQS the behaviors were ranked from most descriptive to least descriptive of the child under observation and sorted into piles that then can be compared to the behavioral profile of a prototypically secure child (Waters & Deane, 1985). The AQS appears valid as a measure of attachment security since there is both convergent validity with the SSP and predictive validity with parental sensitivity measures (Van IJzendoorn, Vereijken, Bakermans-Kranenburg, & Riksen-Walraven, 2004).

The Disturbances of Attachment Interview (DAI) was developed by Smyke and Zeanah (1999). The DAI is a semistructured interview with caregivers that assesses 12 items related to attachment such as who does the child seek when distressed, how do they respond when comfort is offered, and reaction to unfamiliar faces. The interview has relatively good test–retest reliability. However, evidence of DAI diagnostic utility needs further confirmation for lack of evidence supporting predictive validity (Smyke, Dumitrescu, & Zeanah, 2002).

Generally, the above stated indices have questionable validity, particularly regarding diagnostic considerations as well as the design of evidence-based treatments. As a result, there have been further attempts to refine attachment disorder criteria relative to the development of specific assessment techniques (Boris et al., 2004). For example, projective procedures have been developed to assess the child's internal working model of attachment through doll play or other narrative procedures (O'Connor & Zeanah, 2003). Currently, attachment assessment needs more study to determine which combination of assessment techniques provide the most valid diagnosis of attachment-related disorders and result in the design of evidence-based intervention approaches.

Regardless of the psychometric difficulties with assessment, the identified long-term outcomes of insecure attachments include inadequate emotional expression, dependence (Ainsworth & Bell, 1970), depression, poor peer relationships, difficulty initiating and maintaining friendships, lack of social skills (Kerns & Barth, 1995; Youngblade & Belsky, 1992), lack of empathy, aggressiveness, dysfunctional social behavior, academic, occupational (Pianta et al., 1999; Kehle & Bray, 2004a), and physical health problems (MacDonald & Leary, 2005). Thus, insecure attachment is related to a myriad of maladjusted behaviors that are amenable to treatment (Kennedy & Kennedy, 2007).

The efficaciousness of behaviorally-based treatments for these dysfunctional behaviors is not at all dependent on identification of the cause. Therefore, diagnosing whether an attachment disorder existed in infancy does not appear particularly necessary in the design of treatments for children and adolescents. However, diagnosing an attachment disorder during infancy may be beneficial in addressing the caregiver–infant relationship, and perhaps attenuating later negative outcomes.

With respect to the RICH theory, the assessment of the degree of attachment security is sometimes considered, although it is most always assumed that insecure attachment was experienced in infancy if subsequent disabling anxiety is noted (Kehle & Bray, 2004a). Anxiety has been shown to be inversely related to psychological health or happiness as defined by the RICH theory (Bray et al., 2006; Kehle et al., 1993). Therefore, the assessment of anxiety in young children is recommended and afforded by any of several psychometrically sound indices such as the State-Trait Anxiety Inventory for Children (Speilberger, 1973) or the Revised Children's Manifest Anxiety Scale (Reynolds & Richmond, 1985). In addition to the use of anxiety indices, indices that measure social relationships within specific settings such as the classroom to determine the degree of peer acceptance and teacher support yield data that are related to levels of anxiety and facilitate the design of prescriptive interventions (Barclay & Kehle, 1979). In summary, sociometric indices, assessment of interpersonal relations, social skills ratings, the Behavior Assessment System for Children (Reynolds & Kamphaus, 1992), and the Child Behavior Checklist (Achenbach, 1991a) along with the Teacher version (Achenbach, 1991b), and Youth and Self-Report forms (Achenbach, 1991c) are all excellent indices to determine the level of peer acceptance, and social functioning in young children.

CHILD-ORIENTED INTERVENTION APPROACHES

There are few evidence-based interventions to address attachment disorders. However, one recent example is Marvin, Cooper, Hoffman and Powell's (2002) Circle of Security intervention. It is a visually-based technique based on attachment theory and supported by neurological research. Program objectives include teaching caregivers to observe their interactions with their child in order to respond more appropriately to the child's needs. Clinician, parent, and child engage in reflective dialogue to promote exploration and attachment seeking. Further, Circle of Security interventions attempt to remediate defensive mechanisms.

Another intervention approach that is focused on the child, while remaining fundamentally grounded in the relational bond between parent and infant, is called Watch, Wait, and Wonder (Cohen et al., 1999). The program is a form of psychotherapeutic intervention where the mother–infant dyad is designed to remediate problems in infancy and early childhood. Briefly described, Watch, Wait, and Wonder usually occurs with the caregiver and child on the floor. It necessitates the caregiver interacting in response to the child's cues. The caregiver functions therapeutically to gain awareness and understanding of possible attachment needs. Subsequently, the caregiver and therapist reflect on the session. The therapist primarily encourages the caregiver to discuss any insight on attachment issues with their child.

However, after a review of the literature, there has been limited success with these treatments as defined as moving from insecure to secure attachment categories. For example, Cohen et al.'s (1999) results indicated that 21%

of a sample of 67 infants and toddlers moved to secure attachment categories. Furthermore, very little is currently known about which interventions work best for specific attachment categorizations, and few follow-up studies have been completed that would allow an appraisal of enduring effects.

Attachment disorders as indicated by the relative lack of ability in initiating and maintaining friendship later on in childhood and adolescence have been addressed by other treatment programs. An intervention that appears to be gaining empirical support is the Resilient Peer Treatment (RPT), developed by Fantuzzo et al. (1996), which attempts to form friendships by pairing the socially withdrawn child with a nonwithdrawn peer and having them simulate positive play within the general classroom setting. RPT is based on a developmental–ecological model. Outcome variables that have been successfully addressed with RPT include more positive communication with peers, and a decrease in solitary play.

Similarly, the use of video self-modeling with children with attachment disorders may be efficacious. The children repeatedly view edited videotapes of themselves engaged in exemplary social interactions in settings that were historically problematic for them. The following case example of a 9-year-old student illustrates this procedure. The following case was taken from Kehle, Madaus, and Baratta (1998) of a child placed in a self-contained classroom for children with serious emotional disturbance.

On the basis of parental report, Jane's symptoms in infancy included considerable colic and failure to thrive as evidenced by her difficulty in gaining weight. These early possible symptoms of attachment disorder were greatly exacerbated at age 4 when it was likely that she was molested in a public beach restroom. At this point, Jane exhibited symptoms of attachment disorder, selective mutism, and diurnal enuresis. Jane started preschool at age 4. Her personal manner abruptly changed when she got into the family car to be driven to preschool. She became depressed, upset, sullen, and mute. Preschool teacher reports indicated Jane was completely mute and exhibited depressed behaviors. "She would lower her head, clench her fists, and appear quite frightened. Jane would stand motionless in the doorway of the classroom until a staff member would assist her. Her movements throughout the half-day of the preschool were characterized by tiny, hardly measurable steps and labored breathing" (Kehle et al., 1998, p. 251). Jane refused to speak to teachers or her classmates. The staff thought that this unusual behavior was some form of extreme separation anxiety; however, after 6 months of attending preschool, Jane's mutism and depression did not abate. Jane's enuresis was not noticed during her half-day preschool program.

In kindergarten, the teacher reported that Jane remained totally mute, depressed, detached, and unresponsive. Further, she refused to use the school's bathroom. However, probably because the kindergarten program was also half-day, Jane waited until she returned home to urinate. This changed when Jane started the first grade—she would urinate in her clothing once or twice a day. Almost immediately, and with cooperation of the parents, Jane started to wear diapers, and after urination she was escorted to the nurse's office to change into a fresh diaper and a dry set of clothing.

Jane's attachment disorders, selective mutism, depression, and enuresis resulted in her total isolation. Nevertheless, Jane's academic competence was considerably above average (Kehle et al., 1998). In the second grade, Jane was placed in a self-contained classroom for children with serious emotional disturbance. Her special education teacher described Jane as a very scared and nervous young girl. "Her typical daily manner would be to very slowly walk into the classroom with her head held low, hang up her coat and knapsack, without taking out her class homework assignments, and stand there, near the coat rack, motionless" (Kehle et al., p. 251).

In the home environment, Jane did not discuss her school-related problems with her parents. Her behavior, for the most part, was relatively normal in the home with one very disturbing exception. Jane would not use the bathroom alone during bowel movements. She required her mother to be in the bathroom with her and for the mother to place her hands over Jane's ears.

Diagnostically, Jane exhibited symptoms associated with both attachment disorder and selective mutism. Cognitively, she performed quite well on intelligence tests with full-scale scores of approximately 124. There was a discrepancy between her performance on standardized academic achievement tests that were commensurate with her cognitive ability, and her poor to failing teacher grades. Her grades were primarily the consequence of not complying with teacher requests for completion of homework and class assignments (Kehle et al., 1998). On standardized checklists, Jane was perceived as a child that was both withdrawn and possessed thought problems.

The self-modeling video intervention, augmented with self-reinforcement and fading, was employed, where on five occasions over a period of 5 weeks Jane viewed a 7-minute edited video depicting exemplar social behavior, such as responding to teacher questions within the content of the social interaction of the classroom. In reality, segments of a video of her appropriate responses to questions asked by her father within her classroom after school were edited into a video depicting the teacher asking the same questions. Therefore, the edited intervention video depicted exemplary responses to the teacher's questions when in reality she was responding to her father's questions (see Kehle et al., 1998, for a complete description of the intervention). During the fifth week of intervention, Jane's verbal communication with the teachers and classmates increased to a level that was indistinguishable from her classmates. Her enuresis and refusal to use the school's bathroom was eliminated at the same time by having her escorted to an empty school bathroom by another child her age. A 1-year followup revealed normal social behavior, and above average to superior grades (mostly A's) in a general education class. The symptoms of attachment disorder including depression, inhibition, unresponsiveness, detachment, oppositional, and defiant behavior were no longer present.

Edited video self-modeling interventions are very efficacious. There are hundreds of experimental studies using the intervention to effectively address behaviors that are very resistant to intervention including children with autism spectrum disorders (Bellini & Akullian, 2007).

CULTURAL CONTEXTS

There is a paucity of research on attachment behaviors conducted in non-English-speaking cultures. Therefore, the literature on attachment is at a disadvantage in validating assessment methods and treatment approaches across diverse populations. Nevertheless, a few recent studies have made strides to remedy this problem, looking at the relevance of applying European standards of secure attachment behavior to caregiver–child dyads in Africa, Japan, and Latino cultures.

A study of mothers and children in the Black township of Alexandra located in Johannesburg, South Africa, compared attachment categorizations based on scores derived from two assessment methods: the observation-based Attachment Q-Sort (AQS) and the Working Model of the Child Interview, a semi-structured interview (Minde, Minde, & Vogel, 2006). They found that agreement between the AQS and interview ratings for securely attached children was only 29% (compared to 71% for insecurely attached children) when culture was not taken into account, suggesting that mothers in South African culture reflect on and describe their attachment bonds with their children in fundamentally different ways than do European and Anglo mothers.

Posada et al. (1995) conducted a cross-cultural study that involved data collection in seven countries in an attempt to identify ideal secured-base behaviors. They concluded that the there was more convergence with Anglo norms than divergence. Nevertheless, certain specific behaviors did illicit preference differences among mothers. For example, Asian mothers valued their children's willingness to interact with adults more than European mothers. Further, South American mothers appeared to value their children's return to base or *safe haven* behavior more than mothers from other countries.

Carlson and Harwood (2003) compared ratings of physical control, emotional expression, and maternal sensitivity in Puerto Rican and Anglo parent-child dyads with attachment classifications based on the SSP. Results indicated that Puerto Rican mothers were more physically controlling with their children than Anglo mothers. Physical control, a trait in European cultures thought to be hindering to children's independence, tends to lead to insecure attachment classifications. In fact, Puerto Rican children who experienced the highest rates of physical control were also the most likely to be securely attached at 12 months. The opposite was seen among Anglo mother–child dyads, where high use of parental control was predictive of insecure avoidant attachment, in concert with cultural expectations.

Researchers looked to the Japanese concept of *amae*, or mother–child interdependence, in teasing out the similarities and differences in attachment beliefs in both Japanese and American cultures (Rothbaum, Kakinuma, Nagaoka, & Azuma, 2007). After interviewing mothers from both countries, differences emerged in the types of behaviors thought to be both desirable and indicative of a securely attached child. Japanese mothers tended to associate their children's obliging or adaptive behaviors with attachment security while American mothers valued a wider range of positive attributes, including independent exploration and self-aggrandizement, as being closely tied to secure attachment classifications.

While these studies represent an important first step in understanding differences in attachment representations across cultures, these above findings need to be incorporated into current assessment techniques and intervention strategies and validated among multicultural populations.

TRAINING RECOMMENDATIONS

To be considered adequately trained in the area of attachment disorders curricula that address developmental psychology is a must. Knowledge about child development from infancy through young adulthood is highly recommended. Attachment disorders which begin in infancy are manifested in many and complex ways across the lifespan. Therefore, a broad under-standing of development facilitates the comprehension of how to incorporate assessment and subsequent treatment of attachment disorders. Familiarity with Bowlby and Ainsworth's seminal works provide groundwork for under-standing this important area. From there, courses in motivation, learning, special education, child psychopathology/social-emotional issues, and cognition would provide the student with excellent bases for practice (Cyr & van IJzendoorn, 2007). Ultimately, practical and internship experiences are recommended to provide the student with ample opportunities to practice their assessment and treatment skills.

ETHICAL CONSIDERATIONS

The American Psychological Association's code of ethics and conduct (APA, 2002) applies to attachment disorders. It states that the psychologist's primary responsibility is to their client, adequate training is necessary, confidentiality maintained, and parent permission for direct service is obtained. Therefore, when it comes to infants and young children with attachment disorders psychologists must target their efforts on the young individual. Specifically, the psychologist must have adequate training in assessment and treatment of attachment disorders in order to engage in service delivery with these individuals with such issues. Also, since many of the assessment indices and treatment programs are experimental in nature, it may in some cases appear unethical to suggest such practices when the outcomes are unknown. In these instances, it is left up to the psychologist's experience and judgment as to what is recommended. When employing an indirect consultative model the psychologist again has the responsibility of the client even in this model where the client is not treated directly. Therefore, if there is a conflict with another member of the consultation team, the psychologist has an ethical obligation to the client. A good example of this is Gerald Caplan's (1990) case study of an infant whom he felt was not securely attached and bonded to the mother after birth. He felt the infant should not be sent home and should remain in the hospital. The team did not agree, and ultimately the infant went home with medical equipment to monitor breathing. The child died at the home and Dr. Caplan felt deeply responsible in some ways. He recommended, in accord with APA ethics, going above the team members and when necessary stating that he would resign in these matters which may be life threatening. In addition, at all times client confidentiality must be maintained and parent permission is required for direct service. It is important to note that when providing services through an indirect model like consultation, that written notes taken by the psychologist are open for parent/guardian review. The APA code of ethics must guide practice.

SUMMARY

The negative life outcomes associated with insecure attachment can be ameliorated across the life span. Attachment may be defined in the context of social acceptance, secure attachment or the later ability to initiate and maintain friendships. These are all components of psychological health or happiness and as such should be seriously addressed in the preparation of health service providers. Therefore, curricula in psychology and education programs should include training in the design and implementation of treatments to address attachment disorders, particularly with the promotion of friendship formation.

REFERENCES

Achenbach, T. M. (1991a). *Manual for the Child Behavior Checklist and 1991 profile.* Burlington, VT: Associates in Psychiatry.

Achenbach, T. M. (1991b). *Manual for the teacher report form and 1991 profile*. Burlington, VT: Associates in Psychiatry.

Achenbach, T. M. (1991c). *Manual for the youth self-report and 1991 profile*. Burlington, VT: Associates in Psychiatry.

Ainsworth, M. (1989). Attachments beyond infancy. *American Psychologist, 44*, 709–716.

Ainsworth, M. D. S., & Bell, S. (1970). Attachment, exploration, and separation: Illustrated by the behavior of one-year-olds in a strange situation, *Child Development, 41*, 49–67.

Ainsworth, M. D. S., Blehar, M. C., Waters, E., & Wall, S. (1978). *Patterns of attachment: A psychological study of the strange situation*. Hillsdale, NJ: Erlbaum.

American Psychological Association. (2002). Ethical principles of psychologists and code of conduct. View the 2002 Code online at www.apa.org/ethics/code2002.html.

Barclay, J. R. (1966). Sociometric choices and teacher ratings as predictors of school dropout. *Journal of School Psychology, 4*, 40–44.

Barclay, J. R., & Kehle, T. J. (1979). The impact of handicapped students on other students in the classroom. *Journal of Research and Development in Education, 12*, 80–92.

Bellini, S., & Akullian (2007). A meta-analysis of video modeling and video self-modeling interventions for children and adolescents with autism spectrum disorders. *Exceptional Children, 73*, 261–284.

Blankemeyer, M., Flannery, D. J., & Vazsonyi, A. T. (2002). The role of aggression and social competence in children's perceptions of the child-teacher relationship. *Psychology in the Schools, 39*(3), 293–304.

Boris, N. W., Hinshaw-Fuselier, S., Smyke, A. T., Scheeringa, M., Heller, S., & Zeanah, C. H. (2004). Comparing criteria for attachment disorders: Establishing reliability and validity in high-risk samples. *Journal of the American Academy of Child and Adolescent Psychiatry, 43*(5), 568–577.

Bowlby, J. (1982). *Attachment and loss: Vol. 1. Attachment* (2nd ed.). New York: Basic Books.

Bray, M. A., Kehle, T. J., Grigerick, S. E., Loftus, & Nicholson, H. (2008). Children with asthma: Assessment and treatment in school settings. *Psychology in the Schools, 45*, 63–73.

Bray, M. A., Kehle, T. J., Theodore, L. A., Alric, J. M., Peck, H. L., Margiano, S. G., et al. (2006). Written emotional expression as an intervention for asthma: A replication. *Journal of Applied School Psychology, 22*, 141–165.

Caplan, G. (1990). *Mental health consultation—Digitally Remastered 1990 interview with Gerald Caplan* (Item #2002-5). In this interview, taped originally on August 13, 1990, child and family psychiatrist Gerald Caplan is interviewed by William Erchul. This digitally remastered video features a discussion of Caplan's groundbreaking ideas regarding mental health consultation, prevention, and community mental health. American Psychological Association, Division 16: Washington, DC.

Carlson, V. J., & Harwood, R. L. (2003). Attachment, culture, and the caregiving system: The cultural patterning of everyday experiences among Anglo and Puerto Rican mother-infant pairs. *Infant Mental Health Journal, 24*(1), 53–73.

Clarke-Stewart, K. A., Goossens, F. A., & Allhusen, V. D. (2001). Measuring infant-mother attachment: Is the strange situation enough? *Social Development, 10*(2), 143–169.

Cohen, N. J., Muir, E., Lojkasek, M., Muir, R., Parker, C. J., Barwick, M., & Brown, M. (1999). Watch, Wait, and Wonder: Testing the effectiveness of a new approach to mother-infant psychotherapy. *Infant Mental Health Journal, 20*(4), 429–451.

Cyr, C., & van IJzendoorn, M. H. (2007). Commentary: Attachment in the Schools: Toward attachment-based curricula. *Journal of Early Childhood and Infant Psychology, 3*, 95–118.

Elicker, J., Englund, M., & Sroufe, L. A. (1992). Predicting peer competence and peer relationships in childhood from early parent-child relationships. In R. Parke & G. W. Ladd (Eds.), *Family and Peer Relationships: Modes of Linkage* (pp. 77–106). Hillsdale, NJ: Lawrence Erlbaum.

Fantuzzo, J., Sutton-Smith, B., Atkins, M., Stevenson, H., Coolahan, K., Weiss, A., et al. (1996). Peer-mediated treatment of socially withdrawn maltreated preschool children: Cultivating natural community resources. *Journal of Consulting and Clinical Psychology, 64*, 1377–1386.

Granot, D., & Mayseless, O. (2001). Attachment security and adjustment to school in middle childhood. *International Journal of Behavioral Development, 25*(6), 530–541.

Hamre, B. K., & Pianta, R. C. (2001). Early teacher-child relationships and the trajectory of children's school outcomes through the eighth grade. *Child Development, 72*(2), 625–638.

Jacobsen, T., & Hofmann, V. (1997). Children's attachment representations: Longitudinal relations to school behavior and academic competency in middle childhood and adolescence. *Developmental Psychology, 33*(4), 703–710.

Kehle, T. J. (1989, March). *Maximizing the effectiveness of interventions: The RICH model.* Paper presented at the National Association of School Psychologists, Boston.

Kehle, T. J. (1999, August). *RICH-based interventions.* Invited address at the annual meeting of the American Psychological Association, Boston, MA.

Kehle, T. J., & Barclay, J. R. (1979). Social and behavioral characteristics of mentally handicapped students. *Journal of Research and Development in Education, 12*, 45–56.

Kehle, T. J., & Bray, M. A. (2004a). R.I.C.H. theory: The promotion of happiness. *Psychology in the Schools, 41*, 43–49.

Kehle, T. J., & Bray, M. A. (2004b). Current perspectives on school-based behavioral interventions: Science and reality of the classroom. *School Psychology Review, 33*, 417–420.

Kehle, T. J., Bray, M. A., Chafouleas, S. M., & McLoughlin, C. S. (2002). Promoting intellectual growth in adulthood. *School Psychology International, 23*(2), 233–241.

Kehle, T. J., Bray, M. A., & Grigerick, S. E. (2007). Infant and child attachment as it relates to school based outcomes. *Journal of Early Childhood and Infant Psychology, 3*, 65–78.

Kehle, T. J., Clark, E., & Jenson, W. R. (1993). The development of testing as applied to school psychology. *Journal of School Psychology, 31*, 143–161.

Kehle, T. J., Madaus, M. R., & Baratta, V. S. (1998). Augmented self-modeling as a treatment for children with selective mutism. *Journal of School Psychology, 36*, 247–260.

Kennedy, J. H., & Kennedy, C. E. (2007). Applications of attachment theory in school psychology. *Journal of Early Childhood and Infant Psychology, 3*, 7–25.

Kerns, K. A., & Barth, J. M. (1995). Attachment and play: Convergence across components of parent-child relationships and their relations to peer competence. *Journal of Social and Personal Relationships, 12*(2), 243–260.

Luszcz, M. A., & Giles, L. (2002). Benefits of close social relationships for health and longevity of older adults. *Internal Journal of Behavioural Development: Newsletter, 41*, 15–17.

MacDonald, G., Kingsbury, R., & Shaw, S. (2005). Adding insult to injury: Social pain theory and response to social exclusion. In K. D. Williams, J. P. Forgas, & W. von Hippel (Eds.), *The social outcast: Ostracism, social exclusion, rejection, & bullying* (pp. 77–90). New York: Psychology Press.

MacDonald, G., & Leary, M. R. (2005). Why does social exclusion hurt? The relationship between social and physical pain. *Psychological Bulletin, 131*(2), 202–223.

Marvin, R. S., Cooper, G., Hoffman, K. T., & Powell, B. (2002). The Circle of Security project: Attachment-based intervention with caregiver-pre-school child dyads. *Attachment and Human Development, 4*(1), 107–124.

Minde, K., Minde, R., & Vogel, W. (2006). Culturally sensitive assessment of attachment in children aged 18–40 months in a South African township. *Infant Mental Health Journal, 27*(6), 544–558.

O'Connor, T. G., & Zeanah, C. H. (2003). Attachment disorders: Assessment strategies and treatment approaches. *Attachment & Human Development, 5*(3), 223–244.

Parker, J. G. (1987). Peer relations and later personal adjustment: Are low-accepted children at risk? *Psychological Bulletin, 102*, 357–389.

Pianta, R. C., Longmaid, K., & Ferguson, J. E. (1999). Attachment-based classifications of children's family drawings: Psychometric properties and relations with children's adjustment in kindergarten. *Journal of Clinical Child Psychology, 28*(2), 244–255.

Posada, G., Gao, Y., Wu, F., Posada, R., Tascon, M., Schoelmerich, A., et al. (1995). The secure-base phenomenon across cultures: Children's behavior, mothers' preferences, and experts' concepts. *Monographs of the Society for Research in Child Development, 60*(2–3), 27–48.

Reynolds, C. R., & Richmond, B. O. (1985). *Revised Children's Manifest Anxiety Scale.* Los Angeles Western American Guidance.

Reynolds, C. R., & Kamphaus, R. W. (1992). *Behavior Assessment System for Children.* Circle Pines, MN: American Guidance.

Rothbaum, F., Kakinuma, M., Nagaoka, R., & Azuma, H. (2007). Attachment and amae: Parent-child closeness in the United States and Japan. *Journal of Cross-Cultural Psychology, 38*(4), 465–486.

Russell, B. (1930). *The conquest of happiness.* New York: Norton.

Seeman, T. E. (2000). Health promoting effects of friends and family on health outcomes in older adults. *American Journal of Health Promotions, 14*, 362–370.

Shafii, M., & Shafii, S. L. (2003). School violence, depression, & suicide. *Journal of Applied Psychoanalytic Studies, 5*(2), 155–169.

Skinner, B. F. (1971). *Beyond freedom and dignity.* New York: Knopf.

Smyke, A. T., Dumitrescu, A., & Zeanah, C. H. (2002). Attachment disturbances in young children I: The continuum of caretaking casualty. *Journal of the American Academy of Child and Adolescent Psychiatry, 41*, 972–989.

Smyke, A. T., & Zeanah, C. H. (1999). Disturbances of attachment interview. *Journal of the American Academy of Child and Adolescent Psychiatry, 38*, 982.

Speilberger, C. D. (1973). *State-Trait Anxiety Inventory for Children*. Palo Alto, CA: Consulting Psychologists Press.

Szewczyk-Sokolowski, M., Bost, K. K., & Wainwright, A. B. (2005). Attachment, temperament, and preschool children's peer acceptance. *Social Development, 14*(3), 379–397.

Uchino, B. N., Cacioppo, J. T., & Kiecolt-Glaser, J. K. (1996). The relationship between social support and physiological processes: A review with emphasis on underlying mechanisms and implications for health. *Psychological Bulletin, 119*, 488–553.

Van IJzendoorn, M. H., Vereijken, C. M. J. L., Bakermans-Kranenburg, M. J., & Riksen-Walraven, J. M. (2004). Assessing attachment security with the Attachment Q Sort: Meta analytic evidence for the validity of the observer AQS. *Child Development, 75*(4), 1188–1213.

Waters, E. (1995). The attachment Q-set. In E. Waters, B. E. Baughn, G. Posada, and K. Kondo-Ikemura (Eds.), Care giving, cultural, and cognitive perspective on secure-based behavior and working model: New growing point of attachment theory and research. *Monographs of the Society for Research in Child Development, 60*, 234–236.

Waters, E., & Deane, K. E. (1985). Defining and assessing individual differences in attachment relationships: Q-methodology and the organization of behavior in infancy and early childhood. *Monographs of the Society for Research in Child Development, 50*(1–2), 41–65.

Wentzel, K. R. (1991). Social competence at school: Relation between social responsibility and academic achievement. *Review of Educational Research, 61*(1), 1–24.

Youngblade, L. M., & Belsky, J. (1992). Parent-child antecedents of 5-year-olds' close friendships: A longitudinal analysis. *Developmental Psychology, 28*(4), 700–713.

CHAPTER 25

Current Status and Future Directions

BARBARA A. MOWDER,
FLORENCE RUBINSON,
and ANASTASIA E. YASIK

T HE OVERARCHING THEME throughout this book is reliance on science and research. Indeed, an overview of the chapters reveals a wide range of evidence-based early childhood professional practice. The knowledge base is broad and, depending on the area (e.g., self-regulation), complex and substantial. The specific information base necessary for early childhood practice includes, for example, a solid understanding of research methodology and applying research to practice. Beyond an inherent embracing of research is a related commitment to continuing professional development as well as participation in the development and dissemination of current research and study.

This final chapter reviews the characteristics of evidence-based practice and outlines the relationship of evidence-base to early childhood services. What makes early childhood practice distinct within psychological service provision is discussed in terms of defining characteristics (i.e., distinct developmental issues; the importance of parents and families; essential multicultural and diversity factors; working with other early childhood professional groups; models of practice, prevention, and treatment). The chapter concludes with a synopsis of training implications, ethical issues, and the current state of infant and early childhood psychology.

EVIDENCE-BASED EARLY CHILDHOOD PRACTICE

The Evidence-Based Practice (EBP) Task Force for the American Psychological Association (APA, 2005), reports that evidence-based practice involves "the integration of the best available research with clinical expertise in the context of patient characteristics, culture, and preferences'' (p. 5). Thus, EBP includes not only research but also clinical knowledge and consideration for individual differences in clients (and in the case of early childhood and infant psychology, their parents). The EBP Task Force differentiates evidence-based practice (a broader more inclusive term) from empirically supported treatments (ESTs; the evaluation of the effectiveness of a specific intervention). Therefore, ESTs are but one aspect of an evidence base. The EBP Task Force indicates that several sources of evidence (e.g., clinical observation, qualitative research, systematic case studies, single case experimental designs, public health and ethnographic research, process-outcome studies, effectiveness research, randomized clinical trials, meta-analyses) are acceptable in determining effective psychological practice (APA, 2005). Whereas many of the chapters in this text provide support for current practice (e.g., consultation, play therapy), there remain numerous areas within infant and early childhood psychology (e.g., ADHD, autism, PDD, psychopharmacology) in dire need of future research, both empirically supported as well as other sources of evidence.

As assessment and intervention are inexorably linked, the continued pursuit of reliable and valid measures for young children, from diverse backgrounds and with a variety of presenting problems, is paramount. These issues were articulated in Chapters 4 and 5 of the text. For example, training in tests and measurement, especially test construction, evaluation, and standards (e.g., *Standards for Educational and Psychological Testing*, 1999) is essential, in addition to knowledge of major test instruments and observation techniques. Many of the current diagnostic and or screening devices discussed in this text are based on classification systems with, in some cases, limited empirical support for the validity of diagnosis for young children.

Also clear is the substantial lack of evidence for the assessment of young children from multicultural/bilingual and diverse backgrounds. Without psychometrically sound measures, the evidence-base for interventions is questionable, since assessment data gathered is utilized to track children's progress and document responses to intervention. The evidence-base for assessment techniques varies, with some measures being downward extensions of measures intended for older children and other measures developed specifically for infants, toddlers, and young children.

The use and meaning of early childhood assessment requires careful consideration of many issues. Assessment of infants, toddlers, and young children requires a multimethod, multisource, and multisetting approach (Meisels & Atkins-Burnett, 2006; Merrell, 2008). Valid assessment of young children is influenced by children's uneven development across developmental areas, difficulty establishing rapport, as well as the technical inadequacies of standardized instruments used to evaluate young children

(Bracken, Keith, & Walker, 1998; Nagle, 2000). Bagnato and Simeonsson (2007) endorse the use of a clinical perspective for observations needed to capture complex neurodevelopmental issues and the relational lives of young children.

To be effective, psychologists utilize their strong theoretical and scientific training in conjunction with clinical expertise to determine which assessments and interventions have the evidence-base to support usage based on individual client characteristics (e.g., developmental status, cultural differences). Numerous authors throughout the text discuss the need to consider not only if but for whom treatment is effective. Studies identifying relevant processes as well as outcomes are essential to determine what is effective for different behaviors or symptoms within and across individual clients and families. In the future, research may determine what interventions, or intervention components, enhance effectiveness and how interventions may be adapted for different client considerations (e.g., child's age, cultural considerations, family environment). In the end, knowing what works, for whom, when, why, and how are key questions to keep in mind and pursue.

EARLY CHILDHOOD PRACTICE

Broadly, from this book and related early childhood materials, there are a number of defining characteristics of early childhood practice. These characteristics, salient in professional practice with young children and their families, contribute to the unique aspects of early childhood practice. The defining characteristics clarify the need for specific knowledge, training, and sensitivity in this psychological service specialty area. Thus, early childhood practice is exemplified by a focus on a distinct developmental period (i.e., infancy and early childhood), parents and families, multicultural and diversity contexts, working with other early childhood professionals (e.g., early childhood educators, early childhood special educators, speech and language therapists), appropriate models of practice (e.g., ethics), and distinctive prevention and treatment services.

Distinct Developmental Period

The practice of early childhood psychology requires a recognition that infancy and early childhood are distinct developmental periods in which young children differ appreciably from older children, adolescents, and adults in terms of, for example, cognitive skills, language and communication, self-regulation, and social-emotional functioning. The early childhood professional needs a firm foundation in the appreciation of developmental theories applicable to a range of areas of development to incorporate an understanding of developmentally typical versus atypical into clinical practice. Many of the chapters throughout this text embrace this perspective and utilize developmental knowledge in a clinically sensitive manner.

Parents and Families

Working with young children, practitioners recognize the fundamental relationship between parents/primary caregivers and infants, toddlers, and young children. The importance of this primary relationship is evident throughout the book in discussions of typical and atypical development, internalizing and externalizing symptoms, assessment and intervention, practice, and early care and education. Indeed, at no time in their development are children more dependent on their caregivers or more connected to their families than during early childhood (Donahue, Falk, & Provet, 2000). Beyond individual young children, parents and families also need significant professional attention. Historically, parent and family issues were either overlooked or set aside, primarily due to the early reliance on the medical model of service provision.

This omission poses a major problem in service provision since children, as well as service providers, depend on parents and child caregivers. That is, children need protection and rearing, and service providers depend on parents/caregivers to be involved, including, for instance, accepting and implementing treatment recommendations. Increasingly, meeting the needs of parents and families is in and of itself recognized as important; however, clinical materials (e.g., assessment measures) and related treatments (e.g., parent education programs) have lagged behind other early childhood service provision areas.

Mowder and Shamah in Chapter 7, "Parent Assessment and Intervention," point out that the primary caregivers in complex family situations (e.g., blended families, gay- and lesbian-headed families, grandparents as primary caregivers) are not always easy to discern, since there is no common definition of parent. This point is vitally important in practice with young children and their families since without a clear definition of parent, practitioners rely on their own interpretations, ideas often tied to cultural values about parenting and families which may result in significant miscommunications (Lamm, Keller, Yovsi, & Chaudhary, 2008; Mowder, Harvey, Moy, & Pedro, 1995).

More specifically, the parent or primary caregiver is essential in the assessment process, since in many ways they are experts on their children. Young children neither seek out mental health services nor are they reliable informants with the ability to describe, for instance, referral issues or troubling behaviors. Therefore, practitioners rely on significant adults in children's lives for information regarding children's cognitive, social-emotional, adaptive, behavioral, and academic functioning. Evangelista in Chapter 1, "Infant and Early Childhood Psychology," makes the point that parents' concerns and their goals for their children represent significant priorities in assessment of young children. Although practitioners also glean data from sources other than parents and families (e.g., observations of young children, standardized tests), parents and families have beneficial perspectives, insights, and historical knowledge.

Many of the interventions described in this book call for parent involvement. For example, Rubinson in Chapter 9, "Consultation," presents successful child and parent outcomes involving consultation, especially conjoint consultation involving collaboration between parents and educators. Although parent participation in assessment and intervention does not guarantee successful outcomes for young children, parent involvement and the perspective of parents as collaborators in problem solving strengthens the possibility of positive outcomes (Seligman & Darling, 2007).

In the end, best practice in infant and early childhood psychology involves the inclusion of parents or other caregivers during the assessment and intervention processes. Based on the evidence reviewed in this text, the inclusion of parents is generally believed to enhance treatment outcomes. Parent functioning is often integral to young children's functioning and, therefore, continued investigation of how best to incorporate parents and other caregivers into the intervention process to enhance child and parent outcomes is essential.

MULTICULTURAL AND DIVERSITY COMPETENCE

Associated with the critical importance of parents and families, each author throughout the book recognizes the integral roles multiculturalism and diversity play in the provision of psychological services. As families in the United States become increasingly diverse, there is a growing need for mental health professionals to increase their knowledge base and develop skills to address the ever-increasing likelihood of serving young children and families with cultural and linguistic backgrounds different from their own. These cross-cultural experiences require practitioners to have among their repertoire of skills, cultural competence.

Cultural competence requires understanding and appreciating a wide-ranging variety of beliefs, attitudes, and values, held by varied groups. These beliefs influence child-rearing practices, communication patterns, and perspectives on child development, parenting, disabilities, and mental health treatment. Cultural competence requires attention to not only ethnic culture, but also gender, race, language, religion, and sexual identity. For example, culture, gender, and race influence relationships within families, between families and practitioners, and between families and the institutions with whom they interact. Practitioners' successful attempts to address cultural diversity often yields culturally relevant outcomes that caregivers and families likely will incorporate in their lives (Ramey & Ramey, 1998).

Complete cultural competence remains a major challenge and not an established reality (APA, 2003). Understanding the uniqueness of cultural groups, especially for families with mixed cultural influences, is complex with a multitude of variables that require practitioner attention. For example, the acculturation process is critical to understanding the family's level of adaptation to U.S. culture (Lieber, Chin, Kazuo, & Mink, 2001). Acculturation involves numerous processes (e.g., assimilation, integration, separation) moderated by varying reactions to individual stress (Berry, 1997). Minority children and families often bear the stresses associated with exposure to poverty, bias, social and institutional oppression, and environmental risks (Lopez & Rogers, 2007).

Bi/multilingualism is a particularly important factor for practitioners to understand when working with young children and their families. Although researchers appreciate the mechanics of second language acquisition, the associated cognitive and social-emotional factors are not well understood. Assessment of culturally and linguistically diverse children continues to challenge mental health practitioners in their efforts to conduct fair and nonbiased evaluations (Rhodes, Ochoa, & Ortiz, 2005; Thordardottir, Rothenberg, Rivard, & Naves, 2006). In addition, although consultation between early childhood practitioners and families is fundamental, diversity issues interject their own set of challenges (e.g., perceptual differences regarding mental health services). Therefore, understanding the influence culture and diversity have on young children and their families represents a high priority for future research.

Working with Other Professionals

Although this book does not delineate the relevant professionals involved in early childhood practice, noting the importance of other professionals is essential. Indeed, young children and their families often require complex service integration (see, for example, Chapter 2) involving close cooperation and coordination among professionals and parents. Therefore, early childhood psychologists recognize other professionals' competence and professional perspectives (e.g., specific ethical guidelines), integrating services for children and families as appropriate.

Models of Early Childhood Practice

Traditional models of psychological service (e.g., medical model) often are inappropriate to the needs of young children and their families. More specifically, the medical model usually focuses on discerning the individual's intrinsic or specific difficulties or deficiencies. In other words, important contextual issues (e.g., parenting perspectives, cultural beliefs) often are overlooked. In a related sense, traditional classification systems (utilized to varying degrees of success with older children, adolescents, and adults), fail to recognize the importance of parents, families, and the multicultural, diverse context in which children develop.

In terms of evidence-based practice, the categorical systems used in the diagnosis of mental health disorders in young children present some challenges for practitioners. Authors throughout this book refer to the *Diagnostic and Statistical Manual*, 4th edition, Text Revision (DSM-IV-TR; American Psychiatric Association, 2000) as the primary framework used to identify mental health and developmental disorders in early childhood. However, the DSM-IV-TR has been criticized for being based largely on research with older children, reflecting a lack of developmental sensitivity, and for excluding the influence of primary caregivers and family functioning (Jensen & Hoagwood, 1997). Terjesen and Kuraski in their chapter on attention deficit hyperactivity disorders point out that in young children with ADHD, the DSM-IV criteria may also describe typical early childhood behaviors such as squirming in a seat or being easily distracted. These behaviors are typical in early childhood and may not necessarily reflect a clinical disorder. Similarly, Yasik in Chapter 20 reviewed research evidence that calls into question the utility of the DSM-IV-TR criteria in diagnosing PTSD in young chidren. Nevertheless, many practitioners continue to rely on the DSM-IV in their work with young children and their families.

In response to these and other concerns, Zero to Three: National Center for Clinical Infant Programs, published an alternative to the DSM-IV-TR, the *Diagnostic Classification of Mental Health and Developmental Disorders of Infancy and Early Childhood, Revised* (DC:0-3R; Zero to Three, 2005). DC:0-3R adjusts diagnoses so they become developmentally appropriate for young children and present early childhood behavior within the context of family. Although the DC:0-3R framework reflects research with young children, more so than the DSM-IV-TR with its focus on adult and childhood disorders, more research is needed to demonstrate the utility of DC:0-3R as a uniform set of mental health diagnosis for young children (Brassard & Boehm, 2007; Evangelista & McLellan, 2004).

Classification systems do not necessarily capture young children's difficulties. Both systems commonly used to diagnose or classify young children are problematic in various ways, which raises questions regarding whether young children need to meet a set of specific criteria before services are made available. For example, Costa and Romer Witten (Chapter 16) suggest that the subtypes of PDD are merely a convenient shorthand for clinicians and that children's symptom profiles are of utmost importance in designing appropriate interventions. Certainly, in the absence of evidence-based criteria for diagnosing young children, such diagnoses are of limited value. In this regard, the important question is when to intervene, since intervention early in a young child's life is likely to be more significant than later intervention.

PREVENTION AND TREATMENT

Many factors unique to practice in early childhood (e.g., working with families) call into question traditional approaches to practice (e.g., focusing exclusively on the child, failing to appreciate the family, multicultural factors, and the diverse contexts in which children develop). These issues are inherent for assessment and intervention services and bring with them training implications for established and developing professional practitioners.

The efficacy of prevention and early intervention is well established in the mental health professions. Drewes (Chapter 10, ''Play Therapy'') and Chinitz (Chapter 13, ''Social-Emotional Issues'') put forth the idea that the early years are vulnerable times that can be significantly influenced by social, familial, environmental, physiological, and genetic factors. Guttman in Chapter 21, ''Violence Prevention,'' presents a strong case for the inclusion of violence prevention programs in early childhood practice. A recurring theme throughout the book involves inclusion of parents, families, and educators in practitioners' work with young children. Indeed, Guttman cites successful violence prevention programs that depend on the actions of significant adults in young children's lives.

Further, DeBey in Chapter 22, ''Child Care and Early Education,'' points to the importance and preventive aspects of quality early care and education. The Response to Intervention (RTI) problem-solving framework, as described by McCabe in Chapter 23, also has the potential to significantly improve educational delivery to the early childhood population through a coordinated, data-based model for young children attending general education preschools and child care centers. Thus, young children could have an opportunity to receive a developmentally appropriate early educational experience that enhances cognitive, communicative, social, emotional, and physical development. Consultation is gaining prominence as an adjunct and even alternative to traditional practice with young children (Gilliam & Shahar, 2006; Green, Everhart, Gordon, & Gettman, 2006). Rubinson in Chapter 9, ''Consultation,'' points to the capacity of parents, families, and educators to change and improve environments for young children. Although these areas of practice currently enjoy a modest evidence-base, greater efforts are necessary to increase the evidence-base as well as relate the evidence-base to practice.

Treatment issues specific to young children require practitioner and researcher attention. For example, there is no doubt that the practice of psychopharmacological interventions for young children is increasing without sufficient evidence. Anderson and Phelps in Chapter 19, "Psychopharmacology," posit that early childhood needs to develop confident, empirically driven, scientist practitioners who have an ethical duty to advocate for more research into psychopharmacology use with young children, while also sharing the state of the evidence-base with families and practitioners.

EARLY CHILDHOOD TRAINING

There are no curricular guidelines for training in early childhood psychology as there are for early childhood educators and early childhood special educators (see Chapter 1). However, there are obvious, distinct knowledge areas involved, such as a thorough grounding in human development (e.g., prenatal, life span), with related preparation in typically and atypically developing individuals. In addition, understanding parent roles and family functioning with a thorough, comprehensive understanding of multicultural and diversity issues are key. In early childhood practice, psychologists also rely on and appreciate all of the various professional practice areas (e.g., early childhood special education) serving young children and their families. Ethical considerations abound in early childhood practice and early childhood psychologists not only recognize other professional practice areas, but understand other early childhood fields (e.g., early childhood special education, nursing, speech-language) have their own practice guidelines, standards not necessarily consistent with those of psychologists (e.g., *APA Ethical Principles of Psychologists and Code Of Conduct*, 2002).

ETHICAL ISSUES

Ethical issues require special attention in early childhood and infant psychology, given the particularly vulnerable populations with whom practitioners work. In contrast to clinical work with adults, the early childhood practitioner has to contend with the issue of "who is the client?" Is the client the child, the parent, or the dyad? Professionals have debated the issue of client in their work with children for many years; however, the issue becomes more complex when young children are involved since they cannot advocate for themselves.

Psychologists need to follow established ethical standards for respecting the confidentiality of private information, yet they need to work with other agencies, with educators, and with parents to develop procedures that allow for joint planning when collaborative approaches will benefit the child. This issue becomes particularly complicated when the practitioner has to consider differing attitudes and objectives within families and between families and other agents involved with the young child. In addition, the families and other professionals with whom practitioners work are often not bound by considerations of confidentiality and may have differing standards of conduct. Thus, confidentiality is an issue that should be clarified early on in relationships with families and other professionals.

When working with parents, the practitioner must also consider their own area of expertise (e.g., child psychology versus adult psychopathology) and consider the need for consultation with professionals experienced in working with adults. Furthermore, as early childhood and infant psychology continues to grow and gather a stronger evidence-base, practitioners are ethically obligated to engage in continued education (APA, 2002; APA, 2005).

SUMMARY

A clear and consistent theme throughout this text has been the need for future research to inform practice in infant and early childhood psychology. Although some areas have an extensive evidence-base, considerably more areas are in need of developmentally sensitive research. For example, many of the authors review and critique the developmental appropriateness of the available diagnostic systems and assessment instruments. In many areas, little is known about the effectiveness of interventions and for those interventions demonstrated to be effective, little is known as to why they are efficacious. Compounding the issue is a general lack of information regarding cultural differences and issues of diversity relevant to assessment and intervention. Clearly, although infant and early childhood psychology has demonstrated an expansion of research and services over the years, much more research is needed with regard to many areas.

From a training and ethical stance, greater articulation of the issues noted throughout the text are needed. Most authors for this text provide training and ethical considerations for their respective topic areas. However, currently there are no specific training or ethical guidelines to inform the early childhood professional or those seeking to become practitioners serving young children and their families. Training and ethical standards specific to early childhood psychology are essential for the continued growth of infant and early childhood psychology as a unique discipline. Further, policy implications that are sensitive to the developmental aspects of service provision with young children and their families are critical. Early childhood psychology is an emerging practice area with substantial evidence-base for practice. At the same time, there is tremendous opportunity and need for further research.

REFERENCES

AERA, APA, & NCME. (1999). *Standards for educational and psychological testing.* Washington, DC: Author.

American Psychiatric Association. (2000). *Diagnostic and statistical manual of mental disorders* (4th ed., text revision). Washington, DC: Author.

American Psychological Association. (2002). *Ethical principles of psychologists and code of conduct.* Washington, DC: Author.

American Psychological Association. (2003). Guidelines on multicultural education, training, research, practice, and organizational change for psychologists. *American Psychologist, 58,* 377–402.

American Psychological Association. (2005). *Report of the 2005 Presidential Task Force on Evidence-Based Practice.* Washington, DC: Author.

Bagnato, S. J., & Simeonsson, R. J. (2007). *Authentic assessment for early childhood intervention: Best practices.* New York: Guilford Press.

Berry, J. W. (1997). Immigration, acculturation, and adaptation. *Applied Psychology: An International Review, 46,* 5–68.

Bracken, B. A., Keith, L. K., & Walker, K. C. (1998). Assessment of preschool behavior and social-emotional functioning: A review of thirteen third-party instruments. *Journal of Psychoeducational Assessment, 16,* 153–169.

Brassard, M. R., & Boehm, A. E. (2007). *Preschool assessment: Principles and practices.* New York: Guilford Press.

Donahue, P. J., Falk, B., & Provet, A. G. (2000). *Mental health consultation in early childhood.* Baltimore, MD: Brookes.

Evangelista, N., & McLellan, M. J. (2004). The Zero to Three diagnostic system: A framework for considering emotional and behavioral problems in young children. *School Psychology Review, 33,* 159–173.

Gilliam, W. S., & Shahar, G. (2006). Pre-kindergarten expulsion and suspension: Rates and predictors in one state. *Infants and Young Children, 19,* 228–245.

Green, B. L., Everhart, M. C., Gordon, L., & Gettman, G. M. (2006). Characteristics of effective mental health consultation in early childhood settings: Multilevel analysis of a national survey. *Topics in Early Childhood Special Education, 26*(3), 142–152.

Jensen, P. S., & Hoagwood, K. (1997). The book of names: DSM-IV in context. *Development and Psychopathology, 9,* 231–249.

Lamm, B., Keller, H., Yovsi, R. D., & Chaudhary, N. (2008). Grandmaternal and maternal ethnotheories about early child care. *Journal of Family Psychology, 22,* 80–88.

Lieber, E., Chin, D., Kazuo, N., & Mink, I. T. (2001). Holding on and letting go: Identity and acculturation among Chinese immigrants. *Cultural Diversity and Ethnic Minority Psychology, 7*(3), 247–261.

Lopez, E. C., & Rogers, M. R. (2007). Multicultural competencies and training in school psychology: Issues, approaches, and future directions. In G. B. Esquivel, E. C. Lopez, & S. Nahari (Eds.), *Handbook of multicultural school psychology: An interdisciplinary perspective* (pp. 47–70). Mahwah, NJ: Erlbaum.

Meisels, S. J., & Atkins-Burnett, S. (2006). Evaluating early childhood assessments: A differential analysis. In K. McCartney & D. Phillips (Eds.), *Blackwell handbook of early childhood development* (pp. 533–549). Malden, MA: Blackwell.

Merrell, K. W. (2008). *Behavioral, social, and emotional assessment of children and adolescents* (3rd ed.). Mahway, NJ: Erlbaum.

Mowder, B., Harvey, V. S., Moy, L., & Pedro, M. (1995). Parent role characteristics: Parent views and their implications for school psychologists. *Psychology in the Schools, 32,* 27–37.

Nagle, R. J. (2000). Issues in preschool assessment. In B. A. Bracken (Ed.), *The psychoeducational assessment of preschool children* (3rd ed., pp. 19–32). Needham Heights, MA: Allyn & Bacon.

Ramey, C. T., & Ramey, S. L. (1998). Early intervention and early experience. *American Psychologist, 53,* 109–120.

Rhodes, R. L., Ochoa, S. H., & Ortiz, S. O. (2005). *Assessing culturally and linguistically diverse students: A practical guide.* New York: Guilford Press.

Seligman, M., & Darling, R. B. (2007). *Ordinary families, special children: A systems approach to childhood disability* (3rd ed.) New York: Guilford Press.

Thordardottir, E., Rothenberg, A., Rivard, M., & Naves, R. (2006). Bilingual assessment: Can overall proficiency be estimated from separate measurement of two languages? *Journal of Multilingual Communication Disorders, 4,* 1–21.

Zero to Three, (2005). *Diagnostic classification of mental health and developmental disorders of infancy and early childhood* (Rev. ed., DC:0–3R). Washington, DC: Zero to Three Press.

Author Index

Subject Index

assessments of, 183–184
self-regulatory, 322–323, 327–328
Learning theory, in interventions for PDD, 479
LEAs, *see* Local education agencies
Least restrictive environment (LRE), 643
Legislation. *See also specific laws*
and cultural/ethnic sensitivity, 78, 82–83
regarding scope of early childhood services, 45
related to ASD, 505
support for RTI framework, 674–675
Leiter International Performance Scale-Revised, 175
Lennox-Gastaut syndrome (LGS), 546
LEP, *see* Limited English proficient
LGS, *see* Lennox-Gastaut syndrome
Life theme, 490
Limited English proficient (LEP), 81
Lines of difference, 99
Linguistic diversity, 9–10. *See also* Multiculturalism
Linguistic sensitivity, 516–517
Linguistic subsystems, 131
Literacy skills, 28
Local education agencies (LEAs), 675, 680
Logic model, for program design, 12
Loss-grief cycle, in parents, 59
Low birth weight, 167
and health impairment, 538–541
visual impairment with, 556
Low-income families, 642–643. *See also* Poverty
early education for children from, 642–643, 653
Early Head Start for, 395, 674
mental health disorders in, 386
LRE, *see* Least restrictive environment

M

MacArthur–Bates Communicative Development
Inventories, 512–513
MacArthur Communicative Developmental Inventories, 175
MacArthur Story Stem Battery (MSSB), 392
MAI, *see* Movement Assessment of Infants
Major depressive disorder, 582–583
Maladaptive behaviors:
in emotional self-regulation, 320
learned from poor models, 325
and level of acculturation, 79
Maladaptive communicative strategies, assessment of, 512
Mandated reporting, 633
Marital aggression, effects of, 620
Marschak Interaction Method (MIM), 295
Massachusetts Child Psychiatry Access Project (MCPAP), 584
Massachusetts Executive Office of Health and Human Services, 584
MassHealth, 584
Maternal and Child Health Bureau, 399
Maternal Sensitive Behavior, 96
Math learning disabilities, 673
M-CHAT, *see* Modified Checklist for Autism in Toddlers
McMaster Family Assessment Device (FAD), 243
McMaster Model of Family Functioning (MMFF), 243
MCPAP, *see* Massachusetts Child Psychiatry Access Project
Means-ends behavior, in infants, 322
Mechanistic models of development, 476, 477, 479
Medial prefrontal cortex, 178
Media violence, development of aggression and, 624
Medicaid, 558

Medicaid Bureau, 399
Medical histories, in neurodevelopmental assessments, 173
Medical home model, for care of health-impaired infants and children, 537–538
Medically fragile children, 538
Medically involved children, 538
Medical model, 14–16, 708–709
and learning disabilities, 668
in treatment of ASD, 514–515
Medical professionals, as EI service providers, 49
Medical services, access to, 32
Memory:
declarative, 182
and learning, 183
neurodevelopmental assessment of, 176, 180–184
nondeclarative, 181
working, 181
Mental health:
assessments of, 57–58
influence of significant adults on, 261
Mental health consultation, 5–6
client-centered, 263
consultee-centered, 263–264
in home visiting programs, 27
for prekindergarten teachers, 261
program-centered, 264
research on, 272
for social-emotional disorders, 400
for traumatic events, 7
Mental health disorders:
in children from foster care settings, 384
in children under 5 years of age, 386
family management therapy for, 247
Mental Health in Early Intervention
(Foley and Hochman), ix
Mental health models:
of consultation, 262–264
for early childhood services, 16–21
Mental health services:
access to, 32
as EI services, 63
Mentalization, model of, 103–104
Mental retardation, 132, 194
and Down syndrome, 547
and Fragile X syndrome, 548
and seizure disorders, 547
Metaphors, in comparative analysis, 474
Methylphenidate (MPH), 368, 580–581
Mexican American families, PCIT for, 428, 605
MFT, *see* Multiple-family therapy groups
Miami Court Team Program, 402
Miami Dade County Juvenile Court, 402
Michigan Association for Infant Mental Health, 404
Microcoding, in observations of families, 244
Miller Assessment for Preschoolers, 361
Miller method, 478
MIM, *see* Marschak Interaction Method
Mindfulness practices, for anxiety, 334
Minding the Baby program, 102
Minority families, acceptance of violence prevention programs by, 632
Mirror neuron system, 473, 487
Misbehavior, 492
Mixed receptive-expressive language disorders, 187
MMFF, *see* McMaster Model of Family Functioning
MMR vaccine, 503–504